ANALYZING THE THIRD WORLD

ANALYZING THE THIRD WORLD

Essays from *COMPARATIVE POLITICS*

Edited by Norman W. Provizer

G.K.HALL &CO.
70 LINCOLN STREET, BOSTON, MASS.

SCHENKMAN PUBLISHING COMPANY
Cambridge, Mass.

48911

Copyright © 1978 by Schenkman Publishing Company, Inc.

Library of Congress Cataloging in Publication Data
Main entry under title:
Analyzing the Third World.

   Includes bibliographical references.
   1. Underdeveloped areas — Politics and government —
Addresses, essays, lectures.   2. Comparative government —
Addresses, essays, lectures.   I. Provizer, Norman W.
II. Comparative politics.
JF60.A49   1978b   320.9'172'4   78-16951
ISBN 0-87073-943-3 pbk.
ISBN 0-8161-8250-7 cl.—G.K. Hall & Co.

This book is dedicated to
my partner/wife Rosalyn
my parents Samuel and Sybil Provizer
and my aunts Ida, Marcia, and the late Ann Sanitsky

CONTRIBUTORS

The list of persons who, in some way, contributed to this volume would rival the technical credits for *Star Wars* (the movie).

A special thanks, however, must be extended to: Patricia Hughes White and Margaret Bayldon, who, as Managing Editors of *Comparative Politics*, participated in this project from its very inception; Helen Kryka, Juanel Votaw, and Glenzetta Walker, who typed order out of chaos; Alfred Schenkman, who kept the faith; and to the twenty co-authors of this book, who made it all possible.

Needless to say, all errors of fact and vision are solely the responsiblity of the editor.

Norman W. Provizer, a native of Chelsea, Massachusetts, is currently an Assistant Professor of Political Science at the Louisiana State University, Shreveport. He received his A.B. from Lafayette College and his Ph.D. from the University of Pennsylvania; he has held research grants from the Anspach Institute of International Affairs and Diplomacy at the University of Pennsylvania, from the National Endowment for the Humanities, and from the LSU Foundation. His articles have appeared in a number of journals, including *Comparative Politics* and the *Journal of African Studies*.

Roy C. Macridis is Professor of Politics, Brandeis University. He is the author of the seminal work *The Study of Comparative Government*, as well as of numerous other books in the area of comparative politics. (Vol. I, No. 1, October 1968).

Samuel P. Huntington is the Frank G. Thomson Professor of Government at Harvard University. His writings cover a variety of fields within political science, and he is the author of the widely used *Political Order in Changing Societies*. (Vol. III, No. 3, April 1971).

Kenneth Sherrill is an Associate Professor of Political Science, Hunter College of The City University of New York. (Vol. I, No. 2, January 1969).

---

* The conclusion of each contributor sketch gives the reference to the issue of *Comparative Politics* in which the author's article originally appeared.

Rupert Emerson is Professor of Government, Harvard University, and the author of *From Empire to Nation*. (Vol. I, No. 3, April 1969).

Rene Lemarchand is Professor of Political Science at the University of Florida. He has written numerous articles on African politics, and is the author of *Political Awakening in the Congo* and *Rwanda and Burundi*. (Vol. IV, No. 2, January 1972).

Keith Legg is an Associate Professor of Political Science, University of Florida, and the author of books on southern Europe and international politics. (Vol. IV, No. 2, January 1972).

John R. Mathiason is a Social Affairs Officer in the Department of Economic and Social Affairs, United Nations Secretariat. (Vol. IV, No. 3, April 1972).

John D. Powell is an Associate Professor of Political Science, Tufts University, and the author of *Political Mobilization of Venezuelan Peasants*. (Vol. IV, No. 3, April 1972).

Myron Weiner is Professor of Political Science at the Massachusetts Institute of Technology. He has written extensively on Indian politics, including *Party-Building in a New Nation, The Politics of Scarcity,* and *Party Politics in India*. (Vol. VIII, No. 2, January 1976 with postscript).

John O. Field is a Lecturer in Political Science, The Massachusetts Institute of Technology, and co-director, with Professor Weiner, of the Indian Election Data Project at MIT's Center for International Studies. (Vol. VIII, No. 2, January 1976 with postscripts).

Joungwon Alexander Kim is associated with a Wall Street law firm, and is author of *Divided Korea: The Politics of Development*. He was formerly a Research Fellow in East Asian Legal Studies at Harvard Law School. (Vol. V, No. 2, January 1973).

Norman W. Provizer is an Assistant Professor of Political Science at the Louisiana State University, Shreveport. (Vol. IX, No. 3, April 1977).

Michael C. Hudson is the Executive Director of the Center for Contemporary Arab Studies, Georgetown University, and the author of *The Precarious Republic: Political Modernization in Lebanon*. (Vol. I, No. 2, January 1969 with postscript).

Amos Perlmutter is Professor of Political Science at American University. Among his published works are *Egypt: The Praetorian State* and *The Military and Politics in Modern Times*. (Vol. I, No. 3, April 1969).

Henry Bienen is Professor of Politics and International Affairs, Princeton University. He has written books on both Tanzania and Kenya, and is the editor and co-author of *The Military Intervenes* and *The Military and Modernization*. (Vol. VI, No. 4, July 1974).

R. D. McKinlay is a Lecturer in Politics, University of Lancaster, Fylde College. (Vol. VIII, No. 1, October 1975).

A. S. Cohan is a Lecturer in Politics, University of Lancaster, Fylde College, and the author of *Theories of Revolution*. (Vol. VIII, No. 1, October 1975).

Lewis Edinger is Professor of Government at Columbia University, and has written a number of volumes on political leadership. (Vol. VII, No. 2, January 1975).

Paul Dettman is affiliated with the Political Science department at Kent State University. (Vol. VI, No. 2, January 1974).

John Kautsky is Professor of Political Science, Washington University. His works include *Political Change in Underdeveloped Countries, Communism and the Politics of Development,* and *The Political Consequences of Modernization.* (Vol. I, No. 4, July 1969).

Baldev Raj Nayar is Professor of Political Science at McGill University. He has written several books on India, including *The Modernization Imperative and Indian Planning, Minority Politics in the Punjab,* and *National Communication and Language Policy in India.* (Vol. VI, No. 3, April 1974).

CONTENTS

INTRODUCTION AND OVERVIEW

The Idea of the Third World

In recent years, the phrase "the Third World" has become part and parcel of common parlance in the United States. Fueled by the politics of energy and the growing concern over a number of scarce resources, interest in the Third World has expanded beyond the walls of academia into the arena of everyday life.

Whether or not the dire prophecies of an earth depleted, overpopulated, and saturated with pollutants are accurate, it takes but little imagination to see that the future will, in no small way, be shaped by events occurring in *le Tiers Monde*. In a world ever contracting, *les damnés de la terre* (the wretched of the earth[1]) will not be without a voice; the global "silent majority," despite protestations to the contrary, will and should be heard.

Yet the usage of a phrase, even if it be ubiquitous, does not preclude the existence of multiple meanings. The fact that words are expressed does not necessarily signal that there is a single, common definition accepted by all. So it is with "the Third World."

Emerging with the era of decolonization and the rise in East-West tensions that followed the conclusion of World War II, the Third World represented those nations, new and old alike, which rested between the First World of the industrial West and the Second World of the Communist "bloc." In this sense, Third World countries were distinguishable from the states most intimately involved in the system of East-West conflict. From the perspective of bipolarity, Third World nations were the uncommitted of the world's regions.

The view of the Third World as the nonaligned retains a certain validity in the current context of global affairs, but time and the flow of events have directed us to a somewhat different perspective on the nature of the Third World. Given that one of the earliest and most symbolically important of Third World meetings, the 1955 Bandung Conference, "was a gathering not of uncommitted but of Afro-Asian states regionally defined and including Asian members of SEATO as well as the Communist states of China and North Vietnam,"[2] such a changing perspective is neither surprising nor lacking in past roots.

As the number of Third World states dramatically increased, the primary locus of concern shifted from a fear of being destroyed in the battle between "two elephants"[3] to anxiety over a hydra-like "developed" world standing in the way of a redress of global imbalances. Cutting across the horizontal line of East-West conflict, the vertical division of the world into a "developed" North and an "underdeveloped" South has grown in importance.

This almost Manichaean vision of the global order was based on the perception of several interrelated dualities which dominate the hearts as well as the minds of both leaders and led within the Third World.[4] From this perspective, the earth is a place of rich and poor; of masters and servants; of colonizers and colonized; of strong and weak; of urban and rural; and of white and non-white. We thus moved toward the congruence of the idea of the Third World with that class of countries labeled less developed, and states such as Yugoslavia no longer remained at the center of gravity.

"We are the Underdeveloped," sings the Third World.[5] Our past, present, and future separate us from them and provide the commonalities which bind us together despite our diversity. As such, the Third World connotes "a self-defined and self-conscious association of nation-states,"[6] whose membership is closely, but not exclusively, linked to a range of empirical socio-economic referents (of which per capita Gross National Product is a prime example), and whose members have and continue to struggle for liberation from "colonial" rule and for development and modernity.[7]

Needless to say, caution must be exercised in the use of the terms *development* and *modernity* in order to avoid the excesses of the unilinear evolutionary syndrome. To state that the Third World countries share a common passion to develop and to enter the "modern" world does not mean that they must or will be carbon copies of what has come before; nor does it necessarily posit a mythology of stasis and final end-states in the organization of human affairs. This passion to develop, to modernize, is not without its ambiguities and contradictions; the question of the appropriate level of technology and the issue of perpetual underdevelopment as satellites, if Third World nations are incorporated into the global "capitalist" system, are indeed very real.[8] Nonetheless, the existence of such debated problem areas does not extirpate the desire of the Third World to improve its political and material position *vis à vis* the "developed" nations.

Specifics may be in doubt, but the generality remains valid. And whether it be for good or for ill, the countries of the Third World thus see themselves not only as the "underdeveloped," but also as the "developing." "The winds of change" are blowing; while their exact direction is not always known, their reality is certain.

Importantly, this view of the Third World from a global perspective is intimately interwoven with the dynamics of *intrasystem* politics; to speak of development in splendid isolation is not enough. The Third World's shared search for a future, at the least, implies a degree of internal transformation and multidimensional discontinuities which is related to the theme of nationalism and the vexatious processes of state and nation-building.[9] In short, the Third World's vision of its future is inextricably linked to the forging of nations and the establishment of viable state frameworks. It is on these most difficult of tasks that this volume focuses.

Our approach is to present essays from *Comparative Politics* which analyze the Third World in terms of commonally shared intra-state dynamics. The first section of the volume, "Comparative Politics, Modernity, and Change," provides a review of and a basic foundation in the concepts most widely utilized in the study of countries associated with *le Tiers Monde*. The second section, "Politics and the Social Order," examines the interrelationships of individuals, society, and politics from what is, primarily, a behavioral perspective. The middle section, "The Organization of Politics," deals more directly with the structure of Third World political systems, and it is followed by a section on "Politics and the Men on Horseback" which considers the critical role played by the military in these systems. The final section, "Leadership and Public Policy," looks at those who hold "the royal spear" in the states of the Third World and probes the policies sounded by their "drums of rule."[10]

Throughout the volume, attention is drawn to the internal attitudinal, behavioral, and organizational problems and transitions which characterize countries of the Third World. Given the multi-dimensionality of the discontinuities of change (i.e., the psycho-cultural dimension, the socio-cultural dimension, the ecological-economic dimension, and the political-ideological dimension) and the plethora of components existent within each dimension, numerous conceptual, as well as methodological difficulties are inevitable. Such difficulties, while noted in the appropriate sections of the volume, will not be resolved with any false sense of finality in the pages of this collection. Analyzing the Third World is too involved and complex for self-righteous and often self-serving answers in black and white. Simplifications are valid within their sphere and are useful as tools or means of understanding, but they are not in themselves ends.

With this warning about oversimplification firmly implanted, we turn to a consideration of three broad issue areas that are related to the preceding discussion. The first of these is related to the idea that while the focus of this volume is on the Third World, the world outside is not ignored. It is true that many of our perceptions of the internal dynamics of Third World states have been warped by a Western-centric form of determinism, yet significant distortion also develops when we embark on a "neo-parochial concentration"[11] on the distinctiveness of these states. Joseph Gusfield, for example, has pointed out that:

> [T]o be 'modern' appears in many new nations as an aspiration toward which certain groups seek to move society. 'Modern' becomes a perceived state of things functioning as a criterion against which to judge specific actions and a program of actions to guide policy.[12]

Thus there is within the states of the Third World a kind of "teleological insight" at work, through which the future of "developing" states is seen in part from the perspective of the experiential patterns of the *"developed" states*.[13] The past may well be a questionable guide for the future, but it is not without substantial import when the vision of the future is rooted in the images of the past.

Clearly, this is not a call for the return to crude determinism; the use of "teleological insight" is one of ". . . *choice* among possibilities, not a fixed and self-evident set of propositions."[14] Rather, it is merely a recognition that the selection of forms implies a range of limits and imperatives. It is this recognition which provides the comparative rationale for the inclusion of a number of essays in this volume, including those by Sherrill, Kautsky, and McKinlay and Cohan.

The second issue area that draws our attention centers on the convergence of national and international systems, on what has been termed "linkage politics." The Third World, as already noted, is defined both by the factors of global hierarchy and conditions and problems of internal order. Intrasystem dynamics provide the focal point for this volume, but it is obvious that no neat boundary exists between the internal and external dimensions of politics. Third World states are affected by and react to numerous sequences of behavior that originate in the "developed" world.[15]

Irving Louis Horowitz, following the path of Andre Gunder Frank, has, in this vein, argued that:

> Too rarely is it appreciated that underdeveloped conditions may be the consequence of the developed sectors. *Underdeveloped,* in contrast to simply *undeveloped,* economies are in the condition they are in large measure because of the intervention and interference of fully developed nations.[16]

Debates abound on various aspects of this issue and though it is unlikely that the states of the Third World will truly insulate themselves for development, the questions raised over the impact of external penetration must be kept in mind as we examine internal dynamics.

This brings us to the last and, in many ways, the most conspicuous of the issue areas to be discussed. Here our inquiry revolves around the proposition that the Third World is not a monolithic whole but is rather a generic category which contains several differentiated "species." It is not too difficult a task to discern the variegated nature of the Third World, related to distinctions in size (physical and population); power potential; infra-structure formation (political, as well as economic and social); the degree, kind and saliency of cleavages; political-ideological orientations; governing styles; and wealth and resource richness.

In fact, disparities along the lines of wealth and resource richness within the Third World have led to a growing usage of the phrase "the Fourth World" as a label for the poorest of the poor, the least developed of the less developed "still essentially trapped by poverty."[17] While such disparities are clearly evident, as is the power inequality between a "nuclear" India or a rapidly arming Iran and a Rwanda or a Gambia, the commonalities that we have previously noted remain.

By referring to the Third World as a generic category, cognizance is given both to the common threads that run across Third World states and to the distinctive groupings existent within the category. The Third World is a "genus" with shared characteristics defined in perceptual and organizational terms (e.g., the "Group of 77" in the United Nations[18]); and within that "genus" a number of distinguishable "species" of states are subsumed. The experience of Latin American nations may be, in some ways, at variance with that of Afro-Asian states, yet the threads which bind them together allow us to speak of their common membership in the Third World. Similarly, Communist or Marxist states are not necessarily excluded from the Third World category because of certain "species" characteristics. Briefly stated, there is unity in the diversity which allows us to speak of the Third World from an isomorphic perspective; there is diversity in the unity which makes it imperative that we recognize idiosyncratic and "species" variations.

Even this view does not eliminate all of the difficulties linked to the fuzzy boundaries of the Third World. Though it takes little perspicacity to see that Japan does not fall into the Third World category, what of China? In many ways, it can be argued that China is within the category of the Third World. Yet, given the recognition of the "Middle Kingdom" as a key pole in a multipolar global order, that country is dealt with only tangentially. Consideration of the boundaries of the Third World also includes the question of South Africa and other settler-states. Here the core of the settler-state is not a part of the Third World, however the state itself and its majority population is often perceived in Third World terms.

Taking all of these issues into account, it is tempting to reason that the Third World is merely a residual category, a "rag-bag" of remnants lacking any coherence. But it is not. "Despite protests from many purists . . . this is a world that is beset by common problems . . . subject to similar patterns of dominance and manipulation."[19] There exists, as we have noted, common characteristics and a shared set of "political presuppositions" which includes the passion to pursue that illusive and ill-defined goal of modernization.[20]

To some, the Third World is represented by the proposition: "Unless they stand together, they are likely to fall together."[21] Yet, even more importantly, the states of the Third World are bound together by "the cruel choice,"[22] the shared dilemma emanating from transition and transformation.

Denis Goulet has stated that:

> Development processes are both cruel and necessary. They are necessary because all societies must come to terms with new aspirations and irresistible social forces. Yet the choices they face are cruel because on balance, it is far from certain that achieving development's benefits makes men happier or freer.[23]

With this thought in mind, we turn to our analysis of the Third World, the states of Africa, Asia, the Middle East, and Latin America which rank last in a world of win, place and show.[24]

NOTES

1. The Third World is from the French *le Tiers Monde*. Irving Louis Horowitz, in *Three Worlds of Development* (New York: Oxford University Press, 1966), p. 5, notes that Frantz Fanon's "book on Algeria [*Les Damnes de la terre*] is probably the first to use [*le Tiers Monde*] as a colloquial expression for the newly emergent nations."

2. Laurence Martin, "Introduction: The Emergence of the New States," in

Martin (ed.), *Neutralism and Nonalignment* (New York: Frederick Praeger, 1963), p. xiv. The Bandung Conference was attended by some 29 nations, at the Colombo Conference held in August 1976, some 85 states were represented; for a brief overview see William Borders, "Nonaligned Nations Have Come a Long Way Since Bandung," *The New York Times*, August 22, 1976, p. E-3.

3. From the African proverb: "When two elephants fight, it is the grass that suffers." See Cecil Crabb, Jr., *The Elephants and the Grass: A Study of Nonalignment* (New York: Frederick Praeger, 1965).

4. For a different viewpoint, see Kwame Nkrumah, "The Myth of the 'Third World'" in Nkrumah, *Revolutionary Path* (New York: International Publishers, 1973), pp. 435–438. There Nkrumah argues that: "Today then, the 'Third World' is neither a practical political concept nor a reality" (p. 438).

5. "A few years ago a new song was heard during the carnival at Rio de Janeiro. Its refrain began with the words, 'We are the Underdeveloped!' It was a very cheerful song, with a touch of irony, perhaps of definance." From Peter Berger, *Pyramids of Sacrifice* (Garden City: Doubleday, 1976), p. 7.

6. Horowitz, *Three Worlds of Development*, Second Edition. (New York: Oxford University Press, 1972), p. 17.

7. See Alex Inkeles and David Smith, *Becoming Modern* (Cambridge: Harvard University Press, 1974), p. 3.

8. On the lower level technology issue, see E. F. Schumacher, "Industrialization through 'Intermediate Technology,'" in Ronald Robinson (ed.), *Developing the Third World: The Experience of the Nineteen Sixties* (Cambridge: Cambridge University Press, 1971). On the question of "perpetual underdevelopment," see Andre Gunder Frank, "The Sociology of Development and the Underdevelopment of Sociology," in Frank, *Latin America: Underdevelopment or Revolution?* (New York: Monthly Review Press, 1969).

9. Nationalism is connected to both the attitudinal-behavioral formation of a national identity (i.e., nation-building) and the structural construction of a state organization (i.e., state-building).

10. Quotes are from "The Spear, Bead and Bean Story," in Taban Io Liyong, *Eating Chiefs: Lwo Culture from Lolwe to Malkal* (London: Heineman, 1970), p. 3.

11. Richard Rose, "Modern Nations and the Study of Political Development," in Stein Rokkan (ed.), *Comparative Research across Cultures and Nations* (The Hague: Mouton, 1968), p. 121. In this regard, see the latest volume in the studies in Political Development series sponsored by the Committee on Comparative Politics of the Social Science Research Council — Charles Tilly (ed.), *The Formation of National States in Western Europe* (Princeton: Princeton University Press, 1975).

12. Joseph Gusfield "Tradition and Modernity: Misplaced Polarities in the Study of Social Change," in Jason Finkle and Richard Gable (eds.), *Political Development and Social Change*, Second Edition (New York: John Wiley, 1971), p. 22.

13. *Ibid.* The phrase "teleological insight" is from Robert Scalapino, "Ideology and Modernization — The Japanese Case," in David Apter (ed.), *Ideology and Discontent* (New York: The Free Press, 1964), p. 106. There Scalapino states that:

Teleological insight is the capacity or, more accurately, the *assumed* capacity — to discern the future of one's own society by projecting it in accordance with conditions and trends in the 'advanced' world. The impact of teleological insight upon creativity, political-social interrelation, and timing in the ideological development of the 'emergent' world can scarcely be exaggerated.

From this perspective, the very acceptance of the nation or territorial-state framework by the Third World is of enormous significance.

14. Gusfield, "Tradition and Modernity," p. 22, emphasis added.

15. See James Rosenau, "The Concept of Linkage," in Rosenau (ed.), *Linkage Politics*, (New York: The Free Press, 1969), p. 45, for his sequence of behaviour and response definition of linkage.

16. Irving Louis Horowitz, "The Search for a Development Ideal: Models and Their Utopian Implications," in Wilard Beling and George Totten (eds.), *Developing Nations: Quest for a Model* (New York: Van Nostrand Reinhold, 1970), p. 92. Also see Andre Gunder Frank, *Capitalism and Underdevelopment in Latin America* (New York: Monthly Review Press, 1967).

17. Here too we face a situation in which there is no single accepted definition. Quotation is from Helen Low and James Howe, "Focus on the Fourth World," in Howe, (ed.), *The U. S. and World Development: Agenda for Action 1975* (New York: Praeger, 1975), p. 35. Their basic distinction for the Fourth World is:

By early 1970's a sizable group of developing countries had achieved sustained economic growth at an annual rate above 6 per cent. At the same time, however, it became apparent that other developing countries were not participating in the general trend, and that these nations in effect constituted a 'Fourth World' still esentially trapped by poverty.

A *Time* survey article (December 22, 1975), on the other hand, divided the less developed countries (the LDCs) into a Third, a Fourth, and a Fifth World and noted that the Fifth World is "perhaps doomed to remain on a permanent dole" (p. 35). Adding further complications is the fact that the Fourth World is also used in another sense, that is to refer to "victims of group oppression;" see, for example, Ben Whitaker (ed.), *The Fourth World: Victims of Group Oppression* (New York: Schocken Books, 1973).

18. The Group of 77 name continues to be utilized although the "membership" has now risen to more than 110 states.

19. Ranji Kothari, *Footsteps into the Future* (New York: The Free Press, 1975), p. 30.

20. See S. E. Finer, *Comparative Government* (Harmondsworth, England: Penguin Books, 1974), p. 98.

21. Kothari, *Footsteps into the Future*, p. 30.

22. This is the title of Denis Goulet's work, *The Cruel Choice: A New Concept in the Theory of Development* (New York: Atheneum, 1971).

23. *Ibid*, p. 326.

24. Consider Gavin Kennedy's comment in *The Military in the Third World* (New York: Charles Scribner's Sons, 1974), p. 2:

Other terminology, such as 'backward' countries, 'underdeveloped countries,' 'developing countries,' 'less developed countries' and so on, has implications which can produce objections to its use in all circumstance. 'Third World' is relatively neutral in this respect — though still suggests a rank ordering.

Also note Robert Packenham's comment, in *Liberal America and the Third World*, (Princeton: Princeton University Press, 1973), p. 3, that the Third World:

> Refers to all the underdeveloped countries of Asia, Africa, and Latin America, not just to those which are neutral in the Cold war. 'Underdeveloped' is a term of convenience, not a judgement about the quality of all aspects of life in Third World countries. It is a synonym for 'Third World' and one that is commonly used even among people from those countries.

Lastly, Wolf, in *United States Policy and the Third World* (Boston: Little Brown, 1967), pp. vii–viii, makes the point that the usage of the label "the Third World," rather than "underdeveloped," moves us from a predominantly economic perspective to one in which political, social, and military factors are more clearly brought into focus.

COMPARATIVE POLITICS
MODERNITY AND CHANGE

Introduction

The origins of the comparative study of politics are as ancient as the study of politics itself. Yet, by the mid-1950s, the face of comparative politics began to undergo a critical transformation.[1] While the reasons for this transformation were complex, and not without antecedents, it is difficult to deny the important, stimulus role played by the changing context and concerns linked to the emerging states of the Third World. The watchwords of the time were to become development, modernization, and change.

One of the earliest and foremost critics of the "traditional approach" to comparative government was Roy Macridis. In a slim volume published in 1955, Macridis characterized the "traditional approach" as being "essentially parochial, monographic, descriptive, bound to the West and particularly to Western Europe, excessively formalistic and legalistic, and insensitive to theory-building and theory-testing." Simply stated, the study of comparative government was too narrow in its geographical and conceptual range, as well as in the scope of its analysis.

It is thus appropriate that the opening essay in this section is Macridis' "Comparative Politics and the Study of Government." Writing years after his seminal book first appeared, Macridis evaluates the shifting orientations in comparative politics, especially relative to the impact of behavioralism. Importantly, Macridis, though recognizing the positive impact of the behavioral revolution, points to its unfortunate tendency to neglect "the study of governmental structures and forms" and the importance of the state variable.[2] Here his discussion revolves around the fallacies of "imputism" and the concommitant disappearance of choice and politics from the liturgy of "political" analysis.

In short then, Macridis reminds us that while the utilization of psychological, socio-cultural, and economic perspectives in analyzing Third World politics has merit, such perspectives should not preclude the study of governmental institutions and political elites. This viewpoint is one which will draw our attention throughout the volume.

While Macridis provides us with a point of departure, the second article in this section reviews the major strands of intellectual thought used in analyzing the Third World. In "The Change to Change: Modernization, Development, and Politics," Samuel Huntington notes that:

> Not until the mid-1950s did a renaissance in the study of comparative politics get under way. That renaissance began with a concern with modernization and the comparison of modern and traditional political systems. It evolved in the early 1960s into a preoccupation with the concept of political development, approached by way of systems theory, statistical analysis, and comparative history. In the late 1960s, the focus on political development in turn yielded to broader efforts to generate more general theories of political change.

Huntington fills out this sequence by first examining the general theory of modernization, its intellectual history, and the characteristics widely assigned to the process. Following this overview, Huntington discusses modernization revisionism—an approach which called into question the zero-sum perspective so often taken toward the "Great Dichotomy."

He then explores the concept of political development/modernization and the major paths followed in examining the political development/modernization question. Here special attention is paid to the theoretical work of Almond and Powell, the synthesis produced by Pye, and Huntington's own dissent which emphasized the distinction between political development and political modernization.

This valuable resume of the conceptual and methodological orientations which affect our perceptions of the Third World concludes by concentrating on the growing "concern for the formulation of more general theories of political change"—a formulation which recognizes that "a political system can be thought of as an aggregate of components [e.g., culture, structure, groups, leadership, and policies] all changing, some at rapid rates, some at slower ones"—and thus investigates the questions: "What types of change in one component tend to be related to similar changes or the absence of change in other components?" and "What are the consequences of different combinations of componential changes for the system as a whole?"

With these perspectives in mind, we turn in the third essay in this section back to the issue of modernity and modernization. For despite the numerous difficulties found in these terms it is nonetheless rather apparent that they cannot be ignored within the current context of the Third World. While caution must be employed, Lerner's parable of the grocer and the chief in Balgat, Turkey retains its power and significance.[3]

If the goal of Third World societies is to create a modern state and if a modern state requires "participating citizens . . . who exercise their rights and perform their duties as members of a community larger than that of the kinship network and the immediate geographical locality," then there is "no more relevant and challenging task . . . than to explain the processes whereby people move from being traditional to becoming modern personalities."[4]

This task is one of enormous complexity and one surrounded by vexatious problems. In "The Attitudes of Modernity," Kenneth Sherrill aims "to distill and operationalize some of the significant aspects of theories of political modernization." Interestingly, this attitudinal analysis takes place "within the context of the study of American politics," and is based on the proposition that an examination of "the way in which the United States has developed and maintained these characteristics of modernity" may allow us to make "certain prescriptive remarks about strategies to follow in the modernization process."

After looking at a number of hypotheses about "the politically modern man" (ranging from "the politically modern man identifies with the national political community" to "the politically modern man is characterized by a general faith in the government"), Sherrill concludes that good reason exists, based on data gathered in the U.S., to accept most of these hypothetical statements as being "accurate descriptions of the political orientations of modern men and to believe that these attitudes form a syndrome, or latent ideology, of modernity."[5] Clearly, such conclusions are not without importance for our analysis of the Third World.

This brings us to the final essay in this section, Rupert Emerson's "The Problem of Identity, Self-hood, and Image in the New Nations." While Emerson concentrates on the situation in Africa, the basic principles explored in the article are applicable to much of the Third World. For, in many ways, the search for national-identity lies at the core of our overall concern with development, modernization, and change.

To a considerable extent, nationalism in the Third World was born in reaction to colonialism. John Kautsky, for example, has argued that:

> In the absence of a common language, culture, religion, or race, what is it, then, that provides the focus for the unity among politically conscious elements from all strata of the population that is characteristic of nationalist movements in underdeveloped countries as of European nationalist movements? Speaking of underdeveloped countries in general, there would seem to be no positive factor at all, but rather the dislike of a common enemy, the colonial power.[6]

Yet, over time, negative feelings are no substitute for positive impulses, especially where the idea of nation and the territoriality of the state are not coterminous.

Herein lies the crux of the problem; self-determination was paramount, but who was to constitute the self? Relative to this question, Emerson notes that broad acceptance was given to "three basic propositions: [1] that all colonial peoples want to get out from under colonialism as speedily as possible, [2] that each colonial territory as established by the imperial powers constitutes a nation whose aspirations to become an independent state have unchallengeable validity, and [3] that the political independence and territorial integrity of the states thus created must be safeguarded against attack from within or without."

The first proposition presents us with little difficulty, for who could deny the existence of a wave of anticolonialism, a wave now rushing against the few remaining bastions of "colonial" rule? The second and third propositions however, while widely accepted, raise more serious questions. The maintenance of states with severe internal fragmentation along the lines of "cultural sub-nationalism"[7] can be both a challenging and costly affair. The Nigerian Civil War, mentioned by Emerson, which raged from 1967 through 1970 and which witnessed the "creation" and the "death" of Biafra was but one grim reminder of this fact. "The enduring challenge of diversity" linked to "the politics of cultural pluralism"[8] within the Third World will not soon fade into oblivion.

In this respect, Emerson points out that: "To a greater degree than was expected . . . the effect of independence and modernization in some cases has not been mobilization into the national community but . . . a strengthening of the more parochial tribal affiliation." Like the state, ethnicity has not withered away, but, rather, has ofttimes undergone a renaissance in newly politicized contexts.[9]

We are thus led to two final considerations. The first of these is that we must never discount the appearance of the "uninvited guest", who embodies the unanticipated consequences of actions. The second of these is that human beings are multi-leveled creatures, who can simultaneously hold views which seem to be contradictory. Sub-nationalism, state-nationalism, and supra-nationalism (e.g., Pan-Africanism, Pan-Arabism) can all exist within the "world view" of single individuals and group clusters. While there are those who have difficulty in grasping this point, it is, nonetheless, a necessary first step in analyzing the Third World.

NOTES

1. See David Apter and Charles Andrain, "Comparative Government: Developing New Nations," in Apter, *Political Change* (London: Frank Cass, 1973); Roy Macridis, *The Study of Comparative Government* (New York: Random House, 1955); and Robert Holt and John Richardson, Jr., "Competing Paradigms in Comparative Politics," in Holt and John Turner (eds.), *The Methodology of Comparative Research* (New York: The Free Press, 1970).

2. Also note Jorgen Rasmussen's, " 'Once You've Made a Revolution, Everything's the Same': Comparative Politics," in George Graham, Jr. and George Carey (eds.), *The Post-Behavioral Era* (New York: David McKay, 1972).

3. Daniel Lerner, *The Passing of Traditional Society* (New York: The Free Press, 1964), pp. 19-42; also see S. N. Eisenstadt, "Post-Traditional Societies and the Continuity and Reconstruction of Tradition," *Daedalus*, Vol. CII, No. 1 (Winter 1973).

4. Alex Inkeles and David Smith, *Becoming Modern* (Cambridge: Harvard University Press, 1974), pp. 4 and 5.

5. See *Ibid*, pp. 293–295, for a discussion of "a general modernity syndrome."

6. John Kautsky, "The Politics of Underdevelopment and Industrialization," in Kautsky (ed.), *Political Change in Underdeveloped Countries* (New York: John Wiley, 1962), p. 38.

7. This phrase is from Victor Olorunsola (ed.), *The Politics of Cultural Sub-Nationalism in Africa* (Garden City: Doubleday, 1972).

8. See Crawford Young, *The Politics of Cultural Pluralism* (Madison: The University of Wisconsin Press, 1976), Chapter 1.

9. On the importance of the "politicization of ethnicity," see Joan Vincent, "Anthropology and Political Development," in Colin Leys (ed.), *Politics and Change in Developing Countries* (Cambridge: Cambridge University Press, 1969), p. 52; Burton Benedict, "Pluralism and Stratification," in Leonard Plotincov and Arthur Tuden (eds.), *Essays in Comparative Social Stratification* (Pittsburgh: University of Pittsburgh Press, 1970), p. 40; and Benedict, *Mauritius: Problems of a Plural Society* (London: Pall Mall Press, 1965), pp. 43–67.

Comparative Politics
and the Study of Government

The Search for Focus

Roy C. Macridis

Years ago, it seems now decades ago, I outlined in a little book some of the most widespread dissatisfactions with what was at the time the study of comparative government—the way it was taught, the kinds of preoccupations and research it inspired, and more generally its place in the discipline.[1] I concluded, not unjustifiably it seems to me in retrospect, that the traditional approach was essentially parochial, monographic, descriptive, bound to the West and particularly to Western Europe, excessively formalistic and legalistic, and insensitive to theory-building and theory-testing. I suggested at the time a crude conceptual outline in terms of which individual systems could be studied and compared. It comprised the following three categories: interests and interest configuration, ideology, and governmental structures. The first corresponded to what are generally referred to today as the "input" factors. I defined interest in a broad sense. It encompassed primarily manifested and articulated interests rather than "latent" interests. My definition had, therefore, a concrete and direct relevance to the political process. Ideology was a loose term I gave to all the relevant political attitudes as they manifest themselves and as they have crystallized in various political systems over a period of time. I think it corresponds to what some call today the political culture. Finally, by "government" I understood the structures through which public officials, selected in one manner or another, make decisions. I viewed a political system in terms of its capacity to translate interests and aspirations into policy and to resolve conflicts[2] by transforming both interests and aspirations into decisions that are widely accepted. In this view, stability and consensus correlate directly with performance and responsiveness.

I did not go beyond this crude formulation. Perhaps I lacked the appropriate theoretical sophistication. But I also felt, and continue to feel, that given the state of our discipline, an attempt to develop a well-knit and broad-gauge theoretical scheme was, and remains, not only premature but downright unproductive. I felt, and continue to feel, that the major task of comparative politics was, and remains, that of raising political questions,

[1] *The Study of Comparative Government* (New York, 1955). For a discussion of the evolution and later state of the field, see Harry Eckstein and David E. Apter, eds. *Comparative Politics: A Reader* (New York, 1963), particularly the excellent general introduction by Harry Eckstein. See also, Roy C. Macridis and Bernard E. Brown, eds. *Comparative Politics: Notes and Readings*, 3rd ed. (Homewood, 1968).

[2] The term "authoritative allocation of values," suggested by David Easton to define a political system, is misleading unless the words convey only what the author understands. There are many "values" that are not "authoritatively allocated" in a social system.

illuminating through parallel studies aspects of political behavior and decision-making, providing us gradually with a body of experience and data and sharpening our evaluation of governmental structures and policies. Only in the long run could hypotheses be developed and tested, and only then could a scientific outlook in the proper sense of the term be discerned at least as a distant promise. Finally, I pointed out that one of the major functions of the study of comparative government was to broaden the horizons of the students of American politics and help them shed their parochialism. I argued the obvious: that the study of foreign governmental forms, policies, and political predicaments helps us step out of our system and look at it from outside. Plato's allegory of the cave may be used to illustrate the plight of the scholars of American politics who have consistently and persistently failed to take this obvious advice.[3]

Much has happened since my little book appeared and the study of comparative politics—rather than of comparative governments—has been greatly modified. Many of my suggestions have now become part of the field—not, of course, because I made them, but because many factors have converged to fashion a new outlook and a new approach. The "behavioral revolution" or the "successful protest" to which Robert Dahl wrote an elegant epitaph came down upon us with a crash.[4] It is my purpose here not to judge this revolution as a whole,[5] but rather to evaluate some of its most serious contributions—not all of them beneficial—to the study of comparative politics.

I

Behavioralism provided, to begin with, a salutary emphasis upon political factors other than the governmental forms. Although their discovery was not entirely original, it opened up the study of what we may call the contextual factors within which political structures and forms develop and political roles flourish. Borrowing in great part from sociology and anthropology, behavioralism put a stress upon careful definitions of the empirical problems to be investigated and upon the formulation of hypotheses and their testing. It sharpened the tools of our analysis by introducing new techniques—surveys, interviewing, the compilation of aggregate data—in an effort to provide correlations between various socioeconomic and psychological factors and political behavior. Weighing, measuring, and correlating are among the most positive aspects of the behavioral revolution in politics. When applied to a political scene, American or foreign, of which the observers had adequate knowledge, the emphasis was most beneficial.[6]

[3] Students of American political institutions, after paying tribute to the "genius," the "pragmatism," and the "consensual nature" of the polity, are now beginning to ask questions they should have raised long ago.

[4] Robert A. Dahl, "The Behavioral Approach in Political Science: Epitaph for a Monument to a Successful Protest," *American Political Science Review*, LV (December 1961), 763-772.

[5] See Heinz Eulau, *The Behavioral Persuasion in Politics* (New York, 1963); and Eulau, ed. *Political Behavior in America: New Directions* (New York, 1966).

[6] For instance, Angus Campbell, Philip E. Converse, Warren E. Miller, and Donald E. Stokes, *The American Voter* (New York, 1960). Also, E. Deutsch, D. Lindon, and P. Weill, *Les Familles politiques aujourd'hui en France* (Paris, 1966).

The students were picking dark or shadowy areas and throwing light upon them. Their findings, or at least their observations, added to the picture we had and helped us refine it. The findings, in other words, made sense and produced new data about the system being studied because we already had a great deal of information about the system.

Where the behavioral revolution went wrong was at its two extremes— in its efforts to build "grand theory" or "system theory," at the one extreme, and in its study of what may well be called political trivia, at the other. In between the two lay a fertile field for study and exploration. But it is to the extremes that most of the work was directed, generally with disappointing results. This will become abundantly clear, I hope, when I discuss the following points that exemplify the state of the discipline today: its failure to establish criteria of relevance and its gross neglect of the study of governmental structures and forms.

II

The search for relevance and the criteria of relevance has bedeviled political thought and inquiry. It is an issue that cannot be easily resolved. Society as an overall system, i.e., a set of interrelations, roles, and structures, consists of a number of subsystems for which no hard and fast boundaries can be drawn. In a sense, all that is social is also political, firmly rooted in history. What is social can be broken down analytically into subsystems, but again, the lower we move in identifying subsystems, the harder it becomes to set boundaries. The "web" is there.

Conceivably then every manifestation, every attitude or relationship, every motivation or idea in society has a relevance to politics. It may engender aspirations; it may shape interests; it may evoke demands; it may call for decisions; it may lead to conflicts about values and interests which necessitate arbitration. Child-rearing, the school curriculum, modes of entertainment, sex relations, to say nothing of economic interests and activities, are all *potentially* related to politics. Yet what is potential is not actual in empirical terms. In most cases and for most of the time, the great host of social, economic, and interpersonal relations has no actual relevance to politics and therefore to the discipline. Yet each and all *may* at a given time and place, and under a set of conditions that is impossible to foresee, assume a political relevance, only to subside again into an apolitical stance.

The dilemma is obvious. Should we study everything that is *potentially* political?[7] Should we narrow our definition and, if so, how? Behavioralism provides the worst possible answer—study everything. It postulates that every aspect of political behavior relates to every aspect of social behavior. Hence we may finish by studying manifestations and attitudes and relationships that have no discernible political relevance.

To be sure, there are no *a priori* grounds on the strength of which one can discard this holistic approach. The element of potentiality is ever present, and our inability to develop any rules about the intricate phenomenon that

---

[7] The pitfalls are obvious in David Truman's *The Governmental Process* (New York, 1951). For a criticism of the latent-group theory, see my "Interest Groups in Comparative Analysis," *Journal of Politics*, XXIII (February 1961), 25-45.

accounts for the actualization of what is potential makes it impossible to condemn potentiality as a criterion of relevance. Only two closely related grounds for its rejection can be suggested. The first is what Professor La-Palombara has called the rule of parsimony,[8] and the second is what I call the concern with focus. Parsimony suggests the choice of those categories and concepts on the basis of which we are as sure as we can be that what we are studying is politically relevant. Concern with focus simply suggests the most direct way to get at politically relevant phenomena.

Relevance and focus: a set of priorities   First and above all, I think it is our obligation to study all those organized manifestations, attitudes, and movements that press directly for state action or oppose state action. No matter what terms we use—decision-making, authoritative allocation of values, regulation, adjudication, enforcement—we are concerned with the same old thing, the state. What is it asked to do? And what is it that people in a community do not want to see it do? To deny this pervasive empirical phenomenon, in the name of a given theory, is to deny our art or, for those who prefer, our science. The demand for state action or the demand that a given action cease is the very guts of politics. No science of politics—or for that matter, no science—can be built upon concepts and theories that disregard or avoid empirical phenomena. Why do the French farmers throw their peaches in the river and their beets on the highway? Why do the American students leave their comfortable homes to demonstrate in the streets? Why have American workers patterned their political demands in one way, but French workers in another? Obviously, to control, to influence, or to oppose state action.

Thus, my second priority also relates to what I have called the state, resurrecting what may appear to many graduate students to be an ancient term. I mean by it, of course, what we have always understood the term to mean, stripped of all its metaphysical trimmings. It means all the structures and organizations that make decisions and resolve conflicts with the expectation that their decisions will be obeyed: the civil service, the legislature, the executive, the judiciary, the host of public or semipublic corporations and organizations that are called upon to resolve differences and to make decisions. I include also the agencies whose function is to study facts, to deliberate about them, to identify areas of conflict, and to suggest policy decisions. The most relevant issue here is not the one that David Easton discusses, or rather suggests, i.e., a theory of likely problems and predicaments —especially when the theory is pitched at a very high level of generalization.[9] I think that what is instead important is to study the preparedness of the state to discern predicaments or problems. Potential problems can be theorized about. The actual political phenomenon, however, is the existing machinery through which problems are perceived—the agencies, the research, the flow of information, the manner in which individual values and constituency considerations enter into the minds of the men and women

[8] Joseph LaPalombara, "Macrotheories and Microapplications in Comparative Politics: A Widening Chasm," in this issue of *Comparative Politics*.
[9] *A Systems Analysis of Political Life* (New York, 1955), esp. Chs. 4, 14. and 15.

who work for the state—and finally includes that happy or fatal moment when the state copes with, ignores, or is simply unable to perceive the problem. The state can also, while perceiving the problem, either alleviate the predicament or suggest solutions utterly unrelated to it. It was not only the Queen of France who showed a gross lack of discernment when she suggested that they eat cakes. In what is reputed to be the most enlightened and modern political system, the President and the Congress acted in the best tradition of Marie Antoinette by declaring, "Let them have open housing. . . ."

It is this second priority—the study of the state and all state agencies; their organization and performance; the scope of their decision-making; the attitudes of the men and women who perform within their structures the roles of informing, studying, consulting, and deciding; and the major constituencies they serve—that has been so sadly neglected in the last decade or so. Few are the studies that focus on the state as an agency of deliberation, problem identification, and problem-solving. Few are the studies of the institutions of the state in the modern developed systems.[10] This is no accident at all. After the state was ostracized from the vocabulary of politics, we found it far more fashionable to study the systems in which there was no state, i.e., the so-called developing, emerging, or new systems.[11] The result was to eschew the urgent and nagging empirical situations in the modern and highly industrialized societies where our fate is to be decided —in order to study political phenomena and especially political development in the societies where there was no state. No wonder Professor Huntington began to despair of studying the process of development in any terms other than "institutionalization," i.e., the building of institutions with authority and legitimacy, such as the state and the party.[12]

My third priority is the study of political attitudes—the "civic culture," as Professor Almond puts it, or what Professor Beer calls "the structure of norms and beliefs,"[13] and what others have very loosely called ideology. But whatever name we give to them, the phenomena to be studied must point directly to the beliefs, norms, and orientations *about* the state (authority, scope of action, legitimacy, sense of participation, and involvement). If we are to remain strictly within the confines of relevance we must narrow our scope to those manifestations and attitudes that directly link the personal, economic, or psychological phenomena with the political. The linkage between "micro" and "macro" so well developed by Professor Almond in his *Civic Culture* in order to identify meaningful political orientations needs to be carried a step forward. This can be done only when we reintroduce the state and its agencies and link them directly to political orientations.

---

[10] See, however, among others, Kenneth Waltz, *Foreign Policy and Democratic Politics* (Boston, 1967); Andrew Shonfield, *Modern Capitalism* (London, 1965); Richard F. Fenno, *The President's Cabinet* (Cambridge, Mass., 1959).

[11] The emphasis was given by the SSRC Committee on Comparative Politics, whose contributions to the field, however, can receive only the highest possible praise.

[12] Samuel P. Huntington, "Political Development and Political Decay," *World Politics*, XVII (April 1965), 386-430.

[13] Gabriel A. Almond and Sidney Verba, *The Civic Culture* (Boston, 1965); Samuel H. Beer and Adam B. Ulam, eds. *Patterns of Government*, 2nd ed. (New York, 1962), Introduction by Samuel H. Beer.

Unless we take this step, we shall remain at the "micro" level. We shall not link attitudes to structures and forms, to decisions and policies. The specifics about governmental decisions and performance will elude us.

Finally, my fourth priority—which in a real sense is no priority at all— relates to the study of what may be called the infrastructure of the political world: attitudes and ideas; social, economic, and cultural institutions; norms and values that are prevalent in any given society, national or international. There is no reason why we shouldn't study child-rearing, the patterns of socialization, the degree of concentration of economic power, the identification of personality types and traits, family life patterns, small groups and private associations, religious attitudes, and so on. All of these, as I indicated, may have a relevance to politics. In a number of cases—and they are the ones that count—the relevance is only too clear. It suggests itself by the very nature of the empirical phenomenon we are studying. It links a given organized political manifestation with a contextual factor that may explain it. It would be difficult to understand the role of the French military up until the Dreyfus case without knowing something about the education they received in Jesuit schools. But in this case we study education because we begin with the army as a political force operating within the government and the state. We go deeper into contextual factors in order to find an explanation of a manifest political phenomenon.

What I am trying to suggest by these priorities, then, is primarily a change of focus. My concern is simply to pinpoint what is political. We begin with the political; we catch it, so to speak, in its most visible, open, and raw manifestation; we begin with the top of the iceberg before we go deep to search for its submerged base. We focus on the state and its agencies, on its types of action or inaction, and on all those organized manifestations that call for action or inaction on its part. We study the forms of decision-making and analyze and evaluate its substance. We explore its impact upon groups, interests, and power elites within the system; we study in turn their reactions to state actions and their counterdemands as they are manifested through various media from political parties down to voting.

The fallacy of inputism   Two terms that have gained wide currency in the last decade are "input" and "output." The system converts demands into decisions. Through the feedback mechanism, output factors influence the input side. Emphasis is placed upon the input factors, but the state is given a degree of autonomy and independence, and through a process that is by no means clear, it can influence supports and demands.[14] The difficulty comes with the selection of the input factors, i.e., with the same problem of relevance that we have discussed. Do we study again all societal manifestations on the assumption that they all make inputs? Do we consider attitudinal data, aggregate data, hard and soft data ranging from the number of hospital beds to child-father relations? Where and in what manner do we define the subject matter for study, and what is our cutoff point? Political scientists are often like thirsty men who go looking for water in a contextual Sahara when more often than not it is right there fresh from the

[14] David Easton, "An Approach to the Analysis of Political Systems," *World Politics,* IX (April 1957), 383-400.

spring—or at least from a well-chlorinated reservoir. Their search in the contextual wasteland brings only further difficulties upon them, for there is no theory, no conceptual scheme that links—in any form that is testable —the amassed socioeconomic and psychological data with the political. In fact, emphasis upon the input factors very often not only neglects the political but sometimes explicitly avoids it.

I am inclined to define what I call "inputism" as the study of society by political scientists without a political focus and very often without a political question. The job is enticingly easy. All that is needed is a questionnaire, interviewers, a pool of respondents, the *UN Statistical Yearbook,* and a counter-sorter or, even better, a computer. I wish to reemphasize the phrase "without a political focus and very often without a political question." When the empirical political situation and the empirical political phenomenon we are investigating make it necessary—as often happens—to study the socioeconomic or psychological factors on the input side, then such study is focused and relevant, for the input factors are analyzed to "explain" the situation we are investigating. We hypothesize that the attitude of the French military with regard to a series of political decisions or with regard to the process of decision-making was, among other things, shaped by the education they received at the Jesuit schools. The linkage between the two, I believe, can be made. It will not fully explain the attitude of the military. But I think it may provide one of the first steps leading to explanation. We start with the concrete political problem. Inputism would reverse the priorities, advocating the study of the socialization of the elite groups in the French educational system, with the unwarranted expectation that such study would clarify "politics" in general and help us explain political behavior. What behavior? With regard to what problem? At what time?

Inputism tends to lead to three fallacies: that of determinism, that of scientism, and that of superficiality. All three fallacies are related.

According to determinism, it is the input factors that shape political action. The political phenomenon is almost invariably reduced either to a number of nonpolitical determinants, in which case we have a multiple kind of reductionism, or to one factor, in which case we have a single-factor reductionism. In either case, the state can play virtually no independent problem-solving or attitude-forming role. It is only through a process of feedback—not clearly understood and not easily demonstrated—that governmental action may influence the determinants that then in turn will act upon the governmental decision-making process. Politics constantly remains a dependent variable. It is, to use Bentley's expression, the parallelogram of interest action and interaction, that is, the parallelogram of all socioeconomic and psychological determinants that will shape the decision-making machinery and will determine its output. The famous "black box," as the graduate students have come to know the government, is at its best a filter mechanism through which interests express themselves and at its worst a simple transmission mechanism. The role of the state is reduced to the narrow confines of an organization that channels, reflects, and expresses commands and instructions that come from "elsewhere." The hint to political scientists is obvious: study everything *but* the machinery of the state and its organizational structures; study the "elsewhere."

Scientism constitutes the effort to measure as accurately as possible the weight, scope, and persistence of the input factors, on the purely gratuitous assumption that they are or can be linked causally to political phenomena. The assumption is gratuitous because we have failed as yet to establish any such causal links and because it is doubtful that we ever will. The assumption is confounded when the political phenomena with which the input factors are to be linked are not clearly stated. Sometimes system theory suggests the broadest possible relationship among "concepts," rather than variables—consensus, stability, performance; sometimes it offers a very narrow-gauge hypothesis linking some political manifestation to one non-political variable (for example, voting with income or race). The first attempt obviously bogs down into analytical exercise rather than empirical testing, while the second one will never attain the level of testability on the basis of which higher-level propositions can be made. Even when system theory establishes clear-cut concepts linked to empirical phenomena from which testable propositions can emerge, it is impossible to move back from the propositions to the concepts and to the overall theory through a series of verifiable tests that exclude all alternative propositions, concepts, and theories. Scientism therefore leads us from hyperfactualism to hyper-theorizing—the latter becoming progressively an exercise (often brilliant) in intellectual virtuosity. It lacks, however, the only thing that really counts—empirical relevance.

Since no theory as yet offered has shown its worth in causally linking determinants with political phenomena, our efforts very often end with the superficial juxtaposition of a given determinant with a given political phenomenon—that is to say, with correlations. Since no adequate theory has been offered, however, and since we therefore have no explanation, correlational findings are a somewhat more sophisticated version of the "sun spot" theory. Martin Lipset's book *Political Man* is an illustration of this.[15] At the end of this excellent study, the reader is not sure whether open democratic societies are affluent because they are open and democratic or whether it is the other way round.

III

Determinism, scientism, and correlational studies that have a distinct trait of superficiality typify the state of a discipline that has consistently eschewed the hard and persistent empirical phenomena that ought to concern it in the name of theory-building and theory-testing. Structures and processes and the manifestly political institutions through which decisions are made have been relegated to the level of epiphenomena. The examination and evaluation of policies have been handed over to the journalists and politicians, and the formulation of a judgment *in the name of knowledge* is considered incompatible with the canons of a self-imposed scientific objectivity. It is these trends that account for the state of the discipline as a whole, and they affect particularly the study of comparative politics, or the comparative study of politics. The state of the discipline can be summed up in one phrase: the gradual disappearance of the political. To repeat, if gov-

15 Seymour Martin Lipset, *Political Man* (New York, 1960).

ernment is viewed as the reflection of the parallelogram of socioeconomic and psychological and other determinants, the prescription for political science becomes a proscription of the study of government.

Yet the behavioral revolution has also had, as I have noted, beneficial effects. We shall never return exclusively to normative speculation, and we shall never be satisfied with judgments about political phenomena without the benefit of careful measurement. We shall continue to distinguish sharply between "facts" and "values," and we shall subject our postulates to a critical examination, demanding always clarity of definitions and terms. Where the propositions about behavior can be tested, we shall test them under all the canons of controlled inquiry that the social sciences have developed. We shall continue to seek to build theory, i.e., a set of interrelated and interconnected propositions, each of which has direct empirical meaning and relevance, and we shall continue to develop narrow hypotheses that can be tested, i.e., invariably falsified. We shall use the many tools of empirical inquiry available to us—survey opinion data, attitudinal data, aggregate data—and in both the construction of our research and our search for the explanation of political phenomena, we shall feel free to borrow, when the occasion demands, from the theoretical sophistication of many disciplines—sociology, anthropology, economics, and psychology—and, of course, to use the empirical data that history provides. But the time has come to qualify and reconsider our quest for a *science* of politics in the full sense of the term. But in the last analysis this may be a contradiction in terms. There can be no science where the element of human will and purpose predominates. Politics is a problem-solving mechanism; its study must deal with it and not with the laws surrounding behavior. The ultimate irony is that even if laws could be discovered, then our discipline would be primarily concerned with an effort to explain why they are not obeyed—why the laws are really non-laws. Natural sciences began by addressing themselves to empirical phenomena in order to understand them, explain them, and control them. The ultimate goal of the natural sciences has been to control nature. The higher the level of generalization that subsumes a number of measurable relationships, the higher the potentiality of control. It is the other way around with politics. The study of politics explicitly divorces knowledge from action and understanding from control. The laws that we constantly seek will tell us little about our political problems and what to do about them. Our concern becomes scholastic.[16]

I therefore suggest that we reconcile ourselves to the fact that while we can have an understanding of some political phenomena, a history of politics and political movements, an understanding of the functioning of governmental forms and structures, a concern and indeed a focus on major concepts such as power, decision-making, interest, organization, control, political norms and beliefs, obedience, equality, development, consensus, performance, and the like, we do not and cannot have a science of politics. We can have, at most, an art. Second, and this is the sign of the art, we may manage to arrive at some inductive generalizations based upon fragmentary empirical evidence. An inductive generalization is at best a statement about

[16] Barrington Moore, Jr. "The New Scholasticism and the Study of Politics," *World Politics*, VI (October 1953), 122-138.

behavior. It can be derived from identical action and interaction under generally similar conditions over a long period of time in as many different contexts as possible. The behavior is not explained, but the weight of evidence allows us to anticipate and often predict it. A series of solidly supported inductive generalizations may in the last analysis be the most fruitful way to move gradually to a scientific approach, as it provides us with a rudimentary form of behavioral patterns. Our knowledge of politics is then at most an understanding of our accumulated experience. It is in this area that comparative politics has an important role to play. By carefully identifying a given behavior or structure or movement and by attempting to study it in as many settings as possible and over as long a period of time as possible, we can provide generalizations backed by evidence.

If we view our discipline as an art and if we limit its goals to inductive generalizations about politics, i.e., a well-ordered and catalogued table or listing of accumulated experience, then two or three imperatives for research emerge, providing focus and satisfying the need for parsimony. First, we must study the practitioners of the art, the political leaders who hold office and, more generally, the governing elites that aspire to or possess political power. Second, we must study the structures and organizations and mechanisms through which the elites gain political power and exercise it, that is the parties and other political associations. Third, we must be concerned with the governmental institutions through which demands are channeled or, just as often, by which they are generated. These imperatives do not exhaust our immediate task, but give us a starting point.

In studying the governmental elites and the institutions through which they gain and exercise power, we ought to consider the art of government as a problem-solving and goal-oriented activity. This kind of activity characterizes any art. The task of government is to identify problems (or to anticipate them) and provide for solutions. Our study then is constantly to ask ourselves, How well is the art performed? Who within the government listens, who foresees, who advises and suggests policy? What are the skills of the practitioners, and what are their objective capabilities? Finally, what is the impact of a decision upon the problem or the predicament it was designed to alleviate or to remove? The practitioner is not strictly bound by determinants. Communal life suggests and often sets goals of performance and achievement that become more than normative goals. They become in a way the "operative goals" that give direction to political action. The governing elite plays an independent role in seeking out the goals and in implementing them. Shonfield in his book on planning refers to the French planning as the result of an "elitist conspiracy."[17] More often than not decision-making is an elitist conspiracy whose study and assessment would be far more rewarding than the survey and elaboration of all the input factors or the nonpolitical determinants.

But in the last analysis government is an act of will that can shuffle and reshuffle many of the determinants. Government involves choice, and the parameters are often wider than we are inclined to think. Any government will begin by surveying the conditions that appear to indicate the limits of freedom and choice; a government must always ask "what it has." But any

[17] *Modern Capitalism.*

government must also be in a position to assess what it wills. To say this is not to return to metaphysical speculation about the "will" of the state or the government. It is simply to reintroduce as integral parts of our discipline the state's performance and choices and the institutions through which they are implemented.

IV

The central focus of politics, therefore, and of the study of comparative politics is, in my opinion, the governmental institutions and political elites, their role, their levels of performance and nonperformance. Stating this in such blunt terms appears to be utterly naïve. Shall we return then to the descriptive study of governmental institutions? Far from it. What I am suggesting is a starting point and a focus of investigation. Any such investigation, we know today, will inevitably lead us, as it should, far and wide in search of the contextual factors (rather than determinants) within the framework of which a government operates and to which its action, its performance, and its policies may often be attributed. We shall have to probe the infrastructure, but without losing sight of either our focus or the relevant question we began our investigation with.

I can think, in the manner of Machiavelli and Montesquieu and Tocqueville, of a number of relevant questions, all of which we tend to evade either because they are "difficult" or because they are not amenable to "scientific inquiry" or because they involve "value judgments": What accounts for a well organized civil service? What is the impact of large-scale organizations —parties, bureaucracy, and so on—upon the citizen? Under what conditions does public opinion exercise its influence on the government? What accounts for political instability? Is an executive who is responsible to the people more restrained than one responsible to the legislature? How and under what conditions does representation degenerate into an expression of particular interests? Under what conditions do the young people maintain political attitudes different from those of their fathers, and at what point do they revolt? Why does a ruling class become amenable to reform? Under what conditions do ruling groups become responsive to popular demands?

I can multiply these questions, but I think these illustrate my point. None of them can lead to hard hypotheses and proof (or disproof). Some cannot be easily answered. But this is not too important unless we are to accept that only those questions that can lead to testing in the rigorous, and therefore impossible, meaning of the term have the freedom of the market. In fact, the questions I suggest lead to a comparative survey, both historical and contemporaneous, of some of the most crucial political phenomena: responsiveness, performance, change, development, and a host of others. Such a survey will inevitably produce inductive generalizations, perhaps in the manner of Machiavelli, but with far more sophisticated tools and greater access to data than was ever the case before. It will inevitably help us to qualify our questions and to reformulate them as hypotheses that will suggest other qualifications—new variables, if you wish—and lead to further investigation—testing if you wish—and the reformulation of the questions —the gradual development of theory, if you like.

Through the study of governmental institutions and political elites, we shall be concerned with fundamental problems of politics. The first symptoms and indicators of all pervasive political phenomena—revolution, authority and stability, legitimacy, participation—are registered in the composition, organization, and performance of the government. I suggest that we begin with these and broaden our horizon as our study goes on. The policies pursued, their consistency, their congruence with the existing social and economic problems, the governors' awareness of such problems—all constitute good indicators of stability or instability.

My second suggestion, therefore, for the study of comparative politics is to concentrate on the policies pursued by various governments in differing political systems—to highlight the conditions of performance or non-performance, as the case may be. Here one of the cardinal tasks of political science is not to study all the integrative factors, as has been the case, but to identify problems that may lead to conflict—not when conflict erupts, but when the society is at the threshold, so to speak, of a conflict situation. The study of the impact of the decisions made by the government can provide us with an excellent laboratory for comparative analysis. *Conflict-policies-decisions-consequences,* this is the heart of the political life. If the political scientists and particularly the students of comparative politics were to concentrate on these central manifestations, they would liberate themselves from the shackles that bind them today, according to which the "determinants" come first and the political questions second. Problems and questions about economic planning, the decay of the representative institutions fashioned in the nineteenth century, the impact of the expanding population upon individual freedoms or of "bigness" upon the individual citizen as a participant member of the body politic, the handling of the new instruments of violence and the growth of the power and status of those who command them, the military, these are the basic problems that affect us. To evade them in the name of science is to abandon our vocation to understand, to explain, to point to dangers, and to draw from our accumulated experience both suggestions and warnings.

Last, we must be prepared in the light of the experience we have studied and accumulated to move forward and offer policies. In doing so we do not enter the forbidden territory of "political action" nor, as it is so naïvely argued so often, do we simply leave our scientific hat in the office to don the activist hat. We do not move from "fact" to "value"—to repeat the facile distinction made by Max Weber, as if the dichotomy between the two did not involve a value judgment. We remain at the level of problem identification and problem-solving, and we *suggest* remedies to the policy-makers. The more detached our suggestions, the better based upon political experience (in the broad sense), the more plausible they are likely to be. And if we evaluate the same problem differently and suggest different solutions and reach different conclusions, this is only an indication, provided all canons of objectivity and reasoning are respected, that ours is an art. The body of accumulated experience must still be refined and studied if we are to gain an understanding that we can all share alike.

The Change to Change

Modernization, Development, and Politics

Samuel P. Huntington*

I. Political Science and Political Change

Change is a problem for social science. Sociologists, for instance, have regularly bemoaned their lack of knowledge concerning social change. In 1951 Talcott Parsons flatly stated, in italics, that *"a general theory of the processes of change in social systems is not possible in the present state of knowledge."* Thirteen years later Don Martindale could see little improvement. Sociology, he argued, could account for structure but not for change: *"its theory of social change,"* said he, also in italics (!), *"is the weakest branch of sociological theory."* Other sociologists have expressed similar views.[1] Yet, as opposed to political scientists, the sociologists are relatively well off. Compared with past neglect of the theory of political change in political science, sociology is rich with works on the theory of social change. These more generalized treatments are supplemented by the extensive literature on group dynamics, planned change, organizational change, and the nature of innovation. Until very recently, in contrast, political theory in general has not attempted to deal directly with the problems of change. "Over the last seventy-five years," David Easton wrote in 1953, "political research has confined itself largely to the study of given conditions to the neglect of political change."[2]

* This essay was written while I was a Fellow of the Center for Advanced Study in the Behavioral Sciences in Palo Alto. It will subsequently appear in a volume edited by Daniel Bell, *Theories of Social Change,* copyright by The Russell Sage Foundation. I am indebted to Ronald D. Brunner and Raymond F. Hopkins for helpful comments.

[1] Talcott Parsons, *The Social System* (Glencoe, 1951), p. 486; Don Martindale, "Introduction," in George K. Zollschan and Walter Hirsch, eds. *Explorations in Social Change* (Boston, 1964), p. xii; Alvin Boskoff, "Functional Analysis as a Source of a Theoretical Repertory and Research Tasks in the Study of Social Change," ibid., p. 213; Robin Williams, *American Society* (New York, 1960), p. 568. By 1969, however, Williams felt a little more optimistic about the prospects for a breakthrough in the sociological study of change. See Robin Williams, *Sociology and Social Change in the United States* (St. Louis, Washington University Social Science Institute, Studies in Comparative International Development, vol. 4, no. 7, 1968–69).

[2] David Easton, *The Political System* (New York, 1953), p. 42.

Why did this happen? Several factors would seem to play a role. While the roots of political science go back to Aristotle (whose central concern was "to consider things in the process of their growth"), modern political science is a product of the late nineteenth and early twentieth centuries. It came into being in the stable political systems of Western Europe and North America, where radical change could be viewed as a temporary deviation in, or extraordinary malfunctioning of, the political system. In Parson's terminology, political scientists might study change *in* a system (such as the fluctuations in power of political parties or of Congress and president), but they did not concern themselves with change *of* the system.[3] Political scientists neglected change because they focused their primary attention on states where change did not seem to be much of a problem.

Reinforcing this tendency was the antihistorical temper of the more avant garde movements in political science. Born of history out of law, political science could establish itself as a discipline only by establishing its independence from its parents. Consequently, political scientists de-emphasized their ties with history and emphasized the similarities between their discipline and other social sciences. Political science evolved with the aid of periodic infusions of ideas, concepts, and methods from psychology (Harold Lasswell in the 1930s), social psychology (David Truman and the group approach of the late 1940s), sociology (structural-functionalism of the 1950s), and economics (equilibrium, input-output, game theory, in the 1960s). The behavioral stress on survey data, interviewing, and participant-observation reinforced the rejection of history.

Political scientists attempt to explain political phenomena. They view politics as a dependent variable, and they naturally look for the explanations of politics in other social processes and institutions. This tendency was reinforced by the Marxian and Freudian intellectual atmosphere of the 1930s and 1940s. Political scientists were themselves concerned with the social, psychological, and economic roots of political behavior. Consequently, social change, personality change, and economic change were, in their view, more fundamental than political change. If one could understand and explain the former, one could easily account for the latter.

Finally, political change tended to be ignored because comparative politics tended to be ignored. With rare exceptions, such as the work of Carl Friedrich and a few others, political scientists did not attempt systematic comparative analyses of similar processes or functions in different political systems or general comparisons of political systems as systems. In book titles and course titles, comparative government meant foreign

[3] Talcott Parsons, *The Social System* (Glencoe, 1951), pp. 480 ff.

government. The study of political change is, however, intimately linked to the study of comparative politics. The study of change involves the comparison of similarities and differences through time; comparative politics involves the analysis of similarities and differences through space. In addition, the comparison of two political systems which exist simultaneously but which differ significantly in their major characteristics inevitably raises the questions: Is one system likely to evolve into a pattern similar to that of the other? Are the two systems related to each other in an evolutionary sense? Thus, the analysis of political change is not likely to progress unless the study of comparative politics is also booming.

Not until the mid-1950s did a renaissance in the study of comparative politics get under way. That renaissance began with a concern with modernization and the comparison of modern and traditional political systems. It evolved in the early 1960s into a preoccupation with the concept of political development, approached by way of systems theory, statistical analysis, and comparative history. In the late 1960s, the focus on political development in turn yielded to broader efforts to generate more general theories of political change.

II. The Context of Modernization

General theory of modernization   The new developments in comparative politics in the 1950s involved extension of the geographical scope of concern from Western Europe and related areas to the non-Western "developing" countries. It was no longer true that political scientists ignored change. Indeed, they seemed almost overwhelmed with the immensity of the changes taking place in the modernizing societies of Asia, Africa, and Latin America. The theory of modernization was embraced by political scientists, and comparative politics was looked at in the context of modernization. The concepts of modernity and tradition bid fair to replace many of the other typologies which had been dear to the hearts of political analysts: democracy, oligarchy, and dictatorship; liberalism and conservatism; totalitarianism and constitutionalism; socialism, communism, and capitalism; nationalism and internationalism. Obviously, these categories were still used. But by the late 1960s, for every discussion among political scientists in which the categories "constitutional" and "totalitarian" were employed, there must have been ten others in which the categories "modern" and "traditional" were used.

These categories were, of course, the latest manifestation of a Great Dichotomy between more primitive and more advanced societies which has been a common feature of Western social thought for the past one hundred years. Their post-World War II incarnation dates from the elaboration by Parsons and Edward Shils of their pattern variables in the early 1950s and the subsequent extension of these from "choices" confronting an "actor" to characteristics of social systems undertaken by Frank Sutton in his 1955 paper on "Social Theory and Comparative Politics."[4] Sutton's summary of modern and traditional societies (or, in his terms, "industrial" and "agricultural" societies) encompasses most of the generally accepted distinguishing characteristics of these two types:

Agricultural Society	Modern Industrial Society
1. Predominance of ascriptive, particularistic, diffuse patterns	1. Predominance of universalistic, specific, and achievement norms
2. Stable local groups and limited spatial mobility	2. High degree of social mobility (in a general—not necessarily "vertical"—sense)
3. Relatively simple and stable "occupational" differentiation	3. Well-developed occupational system, insulated from other social structures
4. A "deferential" stratification system of diffuse impact	4. "Egalitarian" class system based on generalized patterns of occupational achievement
	5. Prevalence of "associations," i.e., functionally specific, nonascriptive structures

The essential difference between modern and traditional society, most theorists of modernization contend, lies in the greater control which modern man has over his natural and social environment. This control, in turn, is based on the expansion of scientific and technological knowledge. To a sociologist such as Marion Levy, for instance, a society is "more or less modernized to the extent that its members use inanimate sources of power and/or use tools to multiply the effects of their efforts."[5] Cyril Black, an historian, argues that modern society results from adaptation of "historically evolved institutions . . . to the rapidly changing functions that reflect the unprecedented increase in man's knowledge, permitting control over his environment, that accompanied the scientific revolution."[6] Among political scientists, Dankwart A. Rustow holds that modernization involves a "rapidly widening control over nature through closer cooperation among men."[7] To virtually all theorists, these dif-

[4] Frank X. Sutton, "Social Theory and Comparative Politics," in Harry Eckstein and David Apter, eds. *Comparative Politics: A Reader* (New York, 1963), pp. 67 ff.

[5] Marion Levy, *Modernization and the Structure of Societies* (Princeton, 1966), I:11.

[6] Cyril E. Black, *The Dynamics of Modernization* (New York, 1966), p. 7.

[7] Dankwart A. Rustow, *A World of Nations* (Washington, 1967), p. 3.

ferences in the extent of man's control over his environment reflect differences in his fundamental attitudes toward and expectations from his environment. The contrast between modern man and traditional man is the source of the contrast between modern society and traditional society. Traditional man is passive and acquiescent; he expects continuity in nature and society and does not believe in the capacity of man to change or to control either. Modern man, in contrast, believes in both the possibility and the desirability of change, and has confidence in the ability of man to control change so as to accomplish his purposes.

At the intellectual level, modern society is characterized by the tremendous accumulation of knowledge about man's environment and by the diffusion of this knowledge through society by means of literacy, mass communications, and education. In contrast to traditional society, modern society also involves much better health, longer life expectancy, and higher rates of occupational and geographical mobility. It is predominantly urban rather than rural. Socially, the family and other primary groups having diffuse roles are supplanted or supplemented in modern society by consciously organized secondary associations having more specific functions. Economically, there is a diversification of activity as a few simple occupations give way to many complex ones; the level of occupational skill and the ratio of capital to labor are much higher than in traditional society. Agriculture declines in importance compared to commercial, industrial, and other nonagricultural activities, and commercial agriculture replaces subsistence agriculture. The geographical scope of economic activity is far greater in modern society than in traditional society, and there is a centralization of such activity at the national level, with the emergence of a national market, national sources of capital, and other national economic institutions.

The differences between a modern polity and a traditional one flow from these more general characteristics of modern and traditional societies. Political scientists have attempted various formulations of these differences. Perhaps the most succinct yet complete checklist is that furnished by Robert E. Ward and Rustow.[8] A modern polity, they argue, has the following characteristics which a traditional polity presumably lacks:

1. A highly differentiated and functionally specific system of governmental organization;
2. A high degree of integration within this governmental structure;
3. The prevalence of rational and secular procedures for the making of political decisions;

[8] Dankwart A. Rustow and Robert E. Ward, "Introduction," in Ward and Rustow, eds. *Political Modernization in Japan and Turkey* (Princeton, 1964), pp. 6–7.

4. The large volume, wide range, and high efficacy of its political and administrative decisions;
5. A widespread and effective sense of popular identification with the history, territory, and national identity of the state;
6. Widespread popular interest and involvement in the political system, though not necessarily in the decision-making aspects thereof;
7. The allocation of political roles by achievement rather than ascription; and
8. Judicial and regulatory techniques based upon a predominantly secular and impersonal system of law.

More generally, a modern polity, in contrast to a traditional polity, is characterized by rationalized authority, differentiated structure, mass participation, and a consequent capability to accomplish a broad range of goals.[9]

The bridge across the Great Dichotomy between modern and traditional societies is the Grand Process of Modernization. The broad outlines and characteristics of this process are also generally agreed upon by scholars. Most writers on modernization implicitly or explicitly assign nine characteristics to the modernization process.

1. Modernization is a *revolutionary* process. This follows directly from the contrasts between modern and traditional society. The one differs fundamentally from the other, and the change from tradition to modernity consequently involves a radical and total change in patterns of human life. The shift from tradition to modernity, as Cyril Black says, is comparable to the changes from prehuman to human existence and from primitive to civilized societies. The changes in the eighteenth century, Reinhard Bendix echoes, were "comparable in magnitude only to the transformation of nomadic peoples into settled agriculturalists some 10,000 years earlier."[10]

2. Modernization is a *complex* process. It cannot be easily reduced to a single factor or to a single dimension. It involves changes in virtually all areas of human thought and behavior. At a minimum, its components include: industrialization, urbanization, social mobilization, differentiation, secularization, media expansion, increasing literacy and education, expansion of political participation.

3. Modernization is a *systemic* process. Changes in one factor are related to and affect changes in the other factors. Modernization, as Daniel Lerner has expressed it in an oft-quoted phrase, is "a process

[9] See Samuel P. Huntington, *Political Order in Changing Societies* (New Haven, 1968), pp. 32–37.

[10] Black, *Modernization,* pp. 1–5; Reinhard Bendix, "Tradition and Modernity Reconsidered," *Comparative Studies in Society and History,* IX (April 1967), 292–93.

with some distinctive *quality* of its own, which would explain why modernity is felt as a *consistent whole* among people who live by its rules." The various elements of modernization have been highly associated together "because, in some historic sense, they *had to* go together."[11]

4. Modernization is a *global* process. Modernization originated in fifteenth and sixteenth century Europe, but it has now become a worldwide phenomenon. This is brought about primarily through the diffusion of modern ideas and techniques from the European center, but also in part through the endogeneous development of non-Western societies. In any event, all societies were at one time traditional; all societies are now either modern or in the process of becoming modern.

5. Modernization is a *lengthy* process. The totality of the changes which modernization involves can only be worked out through time. Consequently, while modernization is revolutionary in the extent of the changes it brings about in traditional society, it is evolutionary in the amount of time required to bring about those changes. Western societies required several centuries to modernize. The contemporary modernizing societies will do it in less time. Rates of modernization are, in this sense, accelerating, but the time required to move from tradition to modernity will still be measured in generations.

6. Modernization is a *phased* process. It is possible to distinguish different levels or phases of modernization through which all societies will move. Societies obviously begin in the traditional stage and end in the modern stage. The intervening transitional phase, however, can also be broken down into subphases. Societies consequently can be compared and ranked in terms of the extent to which they have moved down the road from tradition to modernity. While the leadership in the process and the more detailed patterns of modernization will differ from one society to another, all societies will move through essentially the same stages.

7. Modernization is a *homogenizing* process. Many different types of traditional societies exist; indeed, traditional societies, some argue, have little in common except their lack of modernity. Modern societies, on the other hand, share basic similarities. Modernization produces tendencies toward convergence among societies. Modernization involves movement "toward an interdependence among politically organized societies and toward an ultimate integration of societies." The "universal imperatives of modern ideas and institutions" may lead to a stage "at which the various societies are so homogeneous as to be capable of forming a world state. . . ."[12]

[11] Daniel Lerner, *The Passing of Traditional Society* (Glencoe, 1958), p. 438.

[12] Black, *Dynamics of Modernization*, pp. 155, 174.

8. Modernization is an *irreversible* process. While there may be temporary breakdowns and occasional reversals in elements of the modernizing process, modernization as a whole is an essentially secular trend. A society which has reached certain levels of urbanization, literacy, industrialization in one decade will not decline to substantially lower levels in the next decade. The rates of change will vary significantly from one society to another, but the direction of change will not.

9. Modernization is a *progressive* process. The traumas of modernization are many and profound, but in the long run modernization is not only inevitable, it is also desirable. The costs and the pains of the period of transition, particularly its early phases, are great, but the achievement of a modern social, political, and economic order is worth them. Modernization in the long run enhances human well-being, culturally and materially.

Modernization in intellectual history　This theory of modernization, as it emerged in the 1950s, contrasted sharply with the theories of historical evolution and social change which prevailed in Western thought during the 1920s and 1930s. The social theory of these decades was overwhelmingly pessimistic in its view of the future of man and society. Two schools of pessimism can be distinguished. One, typified by writers such as Oswald Spengler, Vilfredo Pareto, Pitirim Sorokin, and Arnold Toynbee, focused on the patterns of evolution of particular civilizations or cultures. They attempted to generalize sequences of the origins, growth, maturity, and decline of these great human societies. Theirs were, in essence, cyclical theories of history. The lesson applied to contemporary Western civilization was that it was at, or had passed, its zenith and that it was beginning the process of degeneration. The other strand of pessimism focused more exclusively on Western society. Its proponents tended to argue that Western society had earlier been integrated and conducive to human self-fulfillment. At some point in the past, however, a fundamental change had set in and Western history had begun a downward course. The breakup of human community, the attenuation of religious values, the drift into alienation and anomie, the terrifying emergence of a mass society: these were the products of secularization, industrialization, urbanization, and democratization. The processes which the 1950s viewed benevolently as modernization, the 1930s viewed with alarm as disintegration. Some authors dated the fall from grace with the Reformation; others, with the Renaissance, the industrial revolution, or the French Revolution. At some point, however, Western history went off the track, and a special process started. It began with the rejection of religion and the breakup of community and led consistently and irreversibly down the steep hill to mass politics, world wars, the purge trials, and Dachau. In some versions of this essentially conservative

Weltanschauung, modern liberalism became only a "soft" version of the fundamental misconceptions which underlay communism and fascism. "In almost every instance," as Reinhold Niebuhr said, "the communist evil is rooted in miscalculations which are shared by modern liberal culture. . . ." "If you will not have God (and He is a jealous God)," agreed T. S. Eliot, "you should pay your respects to Hitler or Stalin."[13]

Other thinkers stressed the decline of religion less and the disintegrative effects of industrialization and democratization more. Some, like Karl Mannheim and Hannah Arendt, warned of the totalitarian tendencies toward mass society.[14] Those who were reluctant to trace the downward turn of the West back to the sixteenth or even the eighteenth century saw World War I as the turning point. At about that time, Lasswell argued, the trend of history was reversed "*from* progress toward a world commonwealth of free men, *toward* a world order in which the garrison-prison state reintroduces caste-bound social systems." In similar vein, Walter Lippmann started in 1938 to develop his argument that 1917 was the truly revolutionary year in which governments began to crack under the strains of war and upheaval and Western society began moving toward paralysis, chaos, and totalitarianism.[15] The secular pessimism of the interwar years reflected the perceived catastrophes and chaos of Western society brought about by the processes of industrialization, urbanization, and the like. The modernizing optimism of the 1950s and 1960s reflected the perceived social, economic, and political successes of Western society brought on by those same processes.

The modernization theory of the 1950s and 1960s thus contrasts starkly with the secular pessimism of the 1920s and 1930s. Its most striking resemblance is, instead, to the evolutionary optimism of a half century earlier. The social theory of the late twentieth century more closely resembles that of the late nineteenth century than it does that of the early twentieth century. Victorian styles of thought, like Victorian styles in furniture, suddenly acquired a new respectability in the late 1950s. The Great Dichotomy of tradition and modernity had itself, of course, received its most influential original formulations in Sir Henry Maine's 1861 distinctions between status and contract, in Ferdinand Tonnies' contrast between *gemeinschaft* and *gesellschaft* in 1887, and in Max

[13] Reinhold Niebuhr, *Christian Realism and Political Problems* (New York, 1953), p. 5; T. S. Eliot, *The Idea of a Christian Society* (New York, 1940), p. 64.

[14] Karl Mannheim, *Man and Society in the Age of Reconstruction* (London, 1940); Hannah Arendt, *The Origins of Totalitarianism* (New York, 1951).

[15] Harold D. Lasswell, "The Universal Peril: Perpetual Crisis and the Garrison-Prison State," in Lyman Bryson, Louis Finkelstein, and R. M. MacIver, eds. *Perspectives on a Troubled Decade: Science, Philosophy, and Religion, 1939–1949* (New York, 1950), p. 323; and Walter Lippmann, *The Public Philosophy* (Boston, 1955), pp. 3–8.

Weber's discussion of traditional and rational sources of authority.[16] Similarly, many of the characteristics and consequences which the post-World War II theorists ascribed to the Grand Process of Modernization will be found in the writings of nineteenth-century writers such as Herbert Spencer and Karl Marx. In both cases, human society is seen as moving in response to essentially economic causes through an identifiable sequence of ever more beneficent phases.

The nineteenth-century theories of progress were discredited by world wars, economic collapse, political chaos, and totalitarianism in the first part of the twentieth century. Neither Social Darwinism nor Marxism provided an accurate key to the future. The question remains whether twentieth century theories of progress will be any more successful. Twentieth century social scientists have been as confident of modernization in the Third World as nineteenth century Marxists were of revolution in the First World. The latter were predicting the future by the extension of the past; the former are predicting the future by the transfer of the past. The failure of the one suggests caution as to the possibilities for success of the other.

The optimism of the Social Darwinists and Marxists of the late nineteenth century was rooted in the contemplation of the progress which Western society was making at that time and consequently looked forward to the future bliss of Spencer's industrial society or Marx's socialist commonwealth. It was an optimism of future progress. The optimism of the twentieth century theorists of modernization, on the other hand, is essentially an optimism of retroactive progress. Satisfaction about the present leads to an optimism about the past and about its relevance to other societies. The modernization theory of the 1950s and 1960s had little or nothing to say about the future of modern societies; the advanced countries of the West, it was assumed, had "arrived"; their past was of interest not for what it would show about their future but for what it showed about the future of those other societies which still struggled through the transition between tradition and modernity. The extraordinary acceptance of modernization theory in both Western and non-Western societies in the 1950s derived in part from the fact that it justified complacency in one and hope in the other. The theory of modernization thus rationalized change abroad and the status quo at home. It left blank the future of modernity. Modernization theory combined an

---

[16] Sir Henry Maine, *Ancient Law: Its Connection with the Early History of Society and Its Relation to Modern Ideas* (London, 1861); Ferdinand Tonnies, *Gemeinschaft und Gesellschaft* (Leipzig, 1887); Max Weber, *Wirtschaft und Gesellschaft,* Part I (Tübingen, 1922).

extraordinary faith in the efficacy of modernity's past with no image of the potentialities of modernity's future.[17]

Modernization revisionism   Modernization theory, like any social theory, thus suffered from a limited perspective deriving from its particular temporal and social origins. In addition, however, there were some logical and inherent weaknesses in the theory itself. In the later 1960s a small-scale corrective reaction set in which tended to pinpoint some of the difficulties of mainstream modernization theory. Among the theorists associated with modernization revisionism were Joseph Gusfield, Milton Singer, Reinhard Bendix, Lloyd and Suzanne Rudolph, S. N. Eisenstadt, and F. C. Heesterman.[18] Perhaps significantly, the empirical work of many of these scholars focused on India, the twentieth century's most complex traditional society. The criticisms which these analysts made of the traditional theory of modernization focused on: (a) the meaning and usefulness of the concepts of modernity and tradition; (b) the relationship between modernity and tradition; and (c) the ambiguities in the concept of modernization itself.

In the first place, as many modernization theorists themselves pointed out, modernity and tradition are essentially asymmetrical concepts. The

[17] The late 1960s saw the emergence of "postmodern" theorizing, the leading scholars of which, however, had not been primarily involved in the analysis of the transition from tradition to modernity. These theories arose out of concern with the impact of technology on modern rather than traditional society. See Daniel Bell, "Notes on the Post-Industrial Society," *The Public Interest*, VI (Winter 1967), 24–35, and VII (Spring 1967), 102–18, and Zbigniew Brzezinski, *Between Two Ages: America's Role in the Technetronic Era* (New York, 1970). Both Brzezinski and Bell would probably assign many of the nine characteristics of modernization mentioned above to the transition from modernity to what follows. Both stand generally in the optimistic stream and in that sense share more with the modernization theorists than they do with the early twentieth century pessimists. More than the modernization theorists, however, both have been criticized by other writers who view with alarm the prospect of a postindustrial or technetronic society. Political scientists have yet to probe very deeply the political implications of this new historical transition.

[18] See Joseph R. Gusfield, "Tradition and Modernity: Misplaced Polarities in the Study of Social Change," *American Journal of Sociology*, LXXII (January 1966), 351–62; Reinhard Bendix, "Tradition and Modernity Reconsidered," *Comparative Studies in Society and History*, IX (April 1967), 293–346; Lloyd and Suzanne Rudolph, *The Modernity of Tradition* (Chicago, 1967); S. N. Eisenstadt, "Breakdowns of Modernization," *Economic Development and Cultural Change*, XII (July 1964), 345–67, and "Tradition, Change, and Modernity," Eliezer Kaplan School of Economic and Social Sciences, Hebrew University; J. C. Heesterman, "Tradition in Modern India," *Bijdragen Tot de Taal-, Land- en Volkenkunde*, Deel 119 (1963), 237–53; Milton Singer, ed. *Traditional India: Structure and Change* (Philadelphia, 1959); Rajni Kothari, "Tradition and Modernity Revisited," *Government and Opposition*, III (Summer 1968), 273–93; C. S. Whitaker, Jr., *The Politics of Tradition: Continuity and Change in Northern Nigeria, 1946–1966* (Princeton, 1970).

modern ideal is set forth, and then everything which is not modern is labeled traditional. Modernity, as Rustow said, "can be affirmatively defined," while "tradition remains largely a residual concept."[19] Dichotomies which combine "positive" concepts and residual ones, however, are highly dangerous analytically. In point of fact, they are not properly dichotomies at all. They encourage the tendency to assume that the residual concept has all the coherence and precision of the positively defined concept. They obfuscate the diversity which may exist in the residual phenomenon and the fact that the differences between one manifestation of the residual concept and another manifestation of the same concept may be as great as or greater than the differences between either of the residual manifestations and the more precisely defined other pole of the polarity. This is a problem common to many dichotomies; the concept "civil-military relations," for instance, suffers from a similar disability and one which has had a serious impact upon the understanding of the relationship between the military and the multifarious nonmilitary groups in society, whose differences among themselves often exceed their differences from the military.[20] Tradition is likewise simply too heterogeneous to be of much use as an analytical concept. The characteristics which are ascribed to traditional societies are the opposites of those ascribed to modern societies. Given the variety among nonmodern societies, however, obviously the "fit" of any particular society to the traditional ideal type will be haphazard and inexact at best. Pigmy tribes, Tokugawa Japan, medieval Europe, the Hindu village are all traditional. Aside from that label, however, it is difficult to see what else they have in common. Traditional societies are diverse in values and heterogeneous in structures.[21] In addition, the concept of a tradition as essentially changeless came under attack. Traditional societies, it was argued, are not static. "The view that tradition and innovation are necessarily in conflict has begun to seem overly abstract and unreal."[22]

The concept of modernity also suffers some ambiguities. These stem from the tendency to identify modernity with virtue. All good things are modern, and modernity consequently becomes a mélange of incompatible virtues. In particular, there is a failure to distinguish between what is modern and what is Western. The one thing which modernization

[19] Rustow, *World of Nations,* p. 12.

[20] See Samuel P. Huntington, "Civilian Control of the Military: A Theoretical Statement," in Heinz Eulau, Samuel J. Eldersveld, and Morris Janowitz, eds. *Political Behavior: A Reader in Theory and Research* (Glencoe, 1956), 380–85 and "Civil-Military Relations," *International Encyclopedia of the Social Sciences* (New York, 1968), II: 487.

[21] See, especially, Singer, ed. *Traditional India,* pp. x–xvii and Heesterman, "Tradition in Modern India," pp. 242–43.

[22] Gusfield, "Misplaced Polarities," p. 352.

theory has not produced is a model of Western society—meaning late twentieth century Western European and North American society—which could be compared with, or even contrasted with, the model of modern society. Implicitly, the two are assumed to be virtually identical. Modern society has been Western society writ abstractly and polysyllabically. But to a nonmodern, non-Western society, the processes of modernization and Westernization may appear to be very different indeed. This difficulty has been glossed over because the modern, non-Western box in the four-way breakdown of modern-nonmodern and Western-non-Western societies has, at least until the present, been empty. Presumably, however, Japan is either in or about to enter that box, and it is consequently not surprising that a Japanese scholar should take the lead in raising squarely the issue of how much of modernity is Western and how much of Western society is modern.[23] How do two modern societies, one of which is non-Western, resemble each other as compared to two Western societies, one of which is nonmodern? (It should also be noted that non-Western is, like nonmodern, a residual concept: the differences between two non-Western societies may well be greater than the differences between any one non-Western society and a Western society.)

Other questions have developed about the relations between tradition and modernity. The simpler theories of modernization implied a zero-sum relation between the two: the rise of modernity in society was accompanied by the fading of tradition. In many ways, however, modernity supplements but does not supplant tradition. Modern practices, beliefs, institutions are simply added to traditional ones. It is false to believe that tradition and modernity "are mutually exclusive."[24] Modern society is not simply modern; it is modern *and* traditional. The attitudes and behavior patterns may in some cases be fused; in others, they may comfortably coexist, one alongside the other, despite the apparent incongruity of it all. In addition, one can go further and argue not only that coexistence is possible but that modernization itself may strengthen tradition. It may give new life to important elements of the preexisting culture, such as religion. "Modern developments," as Heesterman has said, "more often than not go to strengthen tradition and give it a new dimension. To take a well-known example: modern means of mass communications, such as radio and film, give an unprecedented spread to traditional culture (broadcasting of Sanskrit mantras or of classical Indian music, films on mythological and devotional themes)." Tribal and other ascriptive

[23] See Hideo Kishimoto, "Modernization versus Westernization in the East," *Cahiers d'Histoire Mondiale,* VII (1963), 871–74, and also Heesterman, "Tradition in Modern India," 238.

[24] Bendix, "Tradition and Modernity," p. 326, and also Whitaker, *Politics of Tradition,* pp. 3–15.

"traditional" identities may be invigorated in a way which would never have happened in "traditional" society. Conversely, traditional attitudes and behavior may also help modernization: the extended family may become the entrepreneurial unit responsible for economic growth; the caste may be the group facilitating the operation of political democracy. "Traditional symbols and leadership forms can be vital parts of the value bases supporting modernizing frameworks."[25]

For all the ambiguities involved in the concepts of modernity and tradition, their rough outlines nonetheless appear possessed of comparative conceptual clarity when compared with the fuzziness which goes with the concept of modernization. In general, the writings on modernization were much more successful in delineating the characteristics of modern and traditional societies than they were in depicting the process by which movement occurs from one state to the other. They focused more on the direction of change, from "this" to "that," than on the scope, timing, methods, and rate of change. For this reason, they were more theories of "comparative statics" than they were theories of change.[26] The dichotomic developmental theories, moreover, were often ambiguous as to whether the phases which they posited were actual stages in historical evolution or whether they were Weberian ideal-types. As ideal-types, they were abstract models which could be used to analyze societies at any point in time. As historical concepts, however, the traditional category was presumably losing relevance and the modern category was gaining it. Inevitably, also, the dual character of the concepts undermined the conceptual dichotomy. Obviously all actual societies combine elements of both the traditional and modern ideal-types. Consequently, all actual societies are transitional or mixed. Viewed in terms of static ideal-types, this analysis presented no problems. One could still use the traditional and modern models to identify and relate the traditional and modern characteristics of any particular society. Viewed as a theory of history or change, however, the addition of a transitional category tended to exclude the traditional and modern stages from the historical process. Traditional society (like the state of nature) could only have existed as a hypothetical starting point in the distant past. A truly modern society would only exist if and when traditional remnants disappear in the distant future. Traditionalism and modernity thus cease to be stages in the historical process and become the beginning and

[25] Gusfield, "Misplaced Polarities," p. 352; Heesterman, "Tradition in Modern India," p. 243; Lloyd I. and Suzanne Hoeber Rudolph, "The Political Role of India's Caste Associations," *Pacific Affairs*, XXXIII (March 1960), 5–22.

[26] See Wilbert Moore, "Social Change and Comparative Studies," *International Social Science Journal*, XV (1963), 523; J. A. Ponsioen, *The Analysis of Social Change Reconsidered* (The Hague, 1962), pp. 23–25.

ending points of history. But if all real societies are transitional societies, a theory is needed which will explain the forms and processes of change at work in transitional societies. This is just what the dichotomic theory failed to provide.

Beyond this, each of the assumptions which underlay the original, simple image of modernization could also be called into question. Contrary to the view that modernization is revolutionary, it could be argued that the differences between traditional and modern societies are really not that great. Not only do modern societies incorporate many traditional elements, but traditional societies often have many universalistic, achievement oriented, bureaucratic characteristics which are normally thought of as modern.[27] The cultural, psychological, and behavioral continuities existing within a society through both its traditional and modern phases may be significantly greater than the dissimilarities between these phases. Similarly, the claim that modernization is a complex process could be challenged by the argument that modernization involves fundamental changes in only one dimension and that changes in other dimensions are only consequences of changes in that fundamental dimension. This was, of course, Marx's argument.

Contrary to Lerner's view of the systemic qualities of modernization, it can be argued that the various elements of the modernization process are historically discrete and that, while they have their roots in common causes, progress along one dimension has no necessary relationship to progress along another. Such a view is, indeed, implied by rejection of the mutually exclusive nature of modernity and tradition. If these concepts, moreover, are thought of simply as ideal types, and "If we are to avoid mistaking ideal types for accurate descriptions, we must take care to treat the clusters of attributes as *hypothetically,* not as actually, correlated." In addition, as Bendix went on to argue, a distinction ought to be maintained between modernization and modernity. "Many attributes of modernization, like widespread literacy or modern medicine, have appeared, or have been adopted, in isolation from other attributes of a modern society. Hence, modernization in some sphere of life *may* occur without resulting in 'modernity.' "[28] By extension, this argument also challenges the assumption that modernization is a global process. Modernization may be simply a peculiarity of Western culture; whatever changes are taking place in African and Asian cultures could be of a fundamentally different character and have very different results from those changes which occurred in Western societies.

[27] Bendix, "Tradition and Modernity," pp. 313–14; Gusfield, "Misplaced Polarities," pp. 352–53.

[28] Bendix, pp. 315, 329; Eisenstadt, "Tradition, Change, and Modernity," pp. 27–28.

The early assumptions about the timing and duration of modernization were also brought under criticism. The latecomers, it could be argued, can modernize rapidly through revolutionary means and by borrowing the experience and technology of the early modernizers. The entire process can thus be telescoped, and the assumption that there is a well-defined progression of phases—preconditions, takeoff, drive to maturity, and the like—through which all societies must move is likely to be invalid. Contrary to the common idea that modernization produces homogenization or convergence, it could be said that it may reinforce the distinctive characteristics of each society and thus broaden the differences between societies rather than narrow them. To the contrary of the idea that modernization is irreversible, it could be argued that it is a cyclical process with major ups and downs over time or that a turning point in the process will eventually be reached where the "upward" secular trend of modernization will be replaced by a sustained "downward" trend of disintegration or primitivization. Finally, contrary to the view that modernization is a progressive process, it may be argued, as earlier twentieth century thinkers asserted, that modernization destroys the more intimate communities in which alone man can realize his full personality; it sacrifices human, personal, and spiritual values to achieve mass production and mass society. This type of argument against change was very popular at times in the past. The relative absence of such a traditional, romantic opposition to modernization among theorists in modern societies and politicians in modernizing societies was some evidence of the extent to which the fever of modernization gripped the intellectually and politically conscious world of the 1950s. Nonetheless, by the late 1960s some opposition to and criticism of modernization along these lines were beginning to appear among intellectuals in many developing societies.

III. The Concept of Political Development

Definitions of the concept Sharing the concern of other social scientists with the Great Dichotomy of modernity and tradition and the Grand Process of Modernization, political scientists in the 1960s began to pursue more actively their interests in what was variously called political modernization or political development. Their starting point was the concepts of tradition and modernity; eventually this essentially comparative and static focus gave way to a more dynamic and developmentally oriented set of concerns. This shift can be clearly seen in the work of the Social Science Research Council (SSRC) Committee on Comparative Politics and particularly of Gabriel Almond, its chairman and intellectual leader during the 1950s and early 1960s.

The volume which undoubtedly played the major role in first focusing the attention of political scientists on developmental problems was *The Politics of the Developing Areas,* edited by Almond and James S. Coleman and published in 1960 under the sponsorship of the Comparative Politics Committee and the Princeton Center for International Studies. The bulk of the book consisted of descriptions and analyses in terms of a common format of politics in five developing areas. The principal intellectual impact of the book, however, came from the introduction by Almond and, to a lesser degree, the conclusion by Coleman. This impact was very largely the result of their application to the politics of non-Western countries of a general concept of the political system. Almond used this framework to distinguish between "developed" and "underdeveloped" or "developing" political systems. Developed political systems are characteristic of modern societies and underdeveloped ones of traditional societies. Almond's concepts of "traditionality" and of "modernity" or, as he seemed to prefer, "rationality," are described in Parsonian terms derived from the central stream of sociological analysis. Almond's distinctive contribution in this respect, however, was the insistence that all political systems are culturally mixed, combining elements of modernity and tradition. "All political systems—the developed Western ones as well as the less-developed non-Western ones—are transitional systems. . . ." He was appropriately critical of some sociological theorists for promoting "an unfortunate theoretical polarization" in not recognizing this "dualistic" quality of political systems.[29]

The Politics of the Developing Areas is a work in comparative politics, not one in political development. This volume presents a behavioral and systems approach for the analysis of comparative politics; it does not present a concept or theory of political development. The phrase "political development" is, indeed, notably absent from its vocabulary. It is concerned with the analysis of the political systems of societies which are presumed to be developing (or modernizing) and the comparison of those systems with the political systems presumed to exist in modern societies. Its key categories are system, role, culture, structure, function, socialization. With the possible exception of socialization, no one of these refers to a dynamic process. They are categories essential to the comparative analysis of political systems; they are not oriented to the change and development of political systems. Almond posited a number of functions which must be performed in any political system and then compared systems in terms of the structures which perform those functions. "What we have done," he said, "is to separate political function from political structure." Almond also argued that, "We need dualistic models *rather*

[29] Gabriel Almond, "Introduction: A Functional Approach to Comparative Politics," in Almond and James S. Coleman, eds. *The Politics of the Developing Areas* (Princeton, 1960), pp. 23–24.

than monistic ones, and developmental *as well as* equilibrium models if we are to understand differences precisely and grapple effectively with the processes of political change."[30] In this book, Almond and his associates presented the elements of a dualistic model of the political system, but they did not attempt to present a "developmental model" which would contribute to the understanding of "the processes of political change."

For Almond that task came six years later with another major theoretical work coauthored with C. Bingham Powell, Jr. Unlike the earlier volume, this book was concerned with political dynamics and focused explicitly on political development as a subject and as a concept. Almond recognized the limitations of his earlier work in relation to the problems of political change. That earlier framework, he said, "was suitable mainly for the analysis of political systems in a given cross section of time. It did not permit us to explore developmental patterns, to explain how political systems change and why they change."[31] The earlier set of political functions (now called "conversion functions") was now supplemented by categories which described more fully the demands and supports which operate on the "input" side of the political system and by categories which described the "output" capabilities of the political system in relation to its environments (extractive, regulative, distributive, symbolic, and responsive).

Political development, Almond and Powell argued, is the response of the political system to changes in its societal or international environments and, in particular, the response of the system to the challenges of state building, nation building, participation, and distribution. Political development itself was thought of primarily in terms of political modernization. The three criteria of political development were held to be: structural differentiation, subsystem autonomy, and cultural secularization. Almond thus came face to face with the problem which was gripping many other political scientists at that time: What is political development?

The answers to this question were more numerous than the answerers. Almost every scholar or group of scholars concerned with the politics of the developing areas had to come up with at least one formulation. Even to attempt to itemize them all here would be a tiresome and not particularly useful task. Fortunately, however, in 1965 Lucian W. Pye compiled a fairly comprehensive listing of ten meanings which had been attributed to the concept of political development:

[30] Ibid., p. 25.

[31] Gabriel A. Almond and G. Bingham Powell, Jr., *Comparative Politics: A Developmental Approach* (Boston, 1966), p. 13.

1. the political prerequisite of economic development;
2. the politics typical of industrial societies;
3. political modernization;
4. the operation of a nation-state;
5. administrative and legal development;
6. mass mobilization and participation;
7. the building of democracy;
8. stability and orderly change;
9. mobilization and power;
10. one aspect of a multidimensional process of social change.

In a noble effort at synthesis, Pye attempted to summarize the most prevalent common themes on political development as involving movement
toward: increasing *equality* among individuals in relation to the political
system; increasing *capacity* of the political system in relation to its environments; and increasing *differentiation* of institutions and structures
within the political system. These three dimensions, he argued, are to be
found "lying at the heart of the development process."[32] In a similar vein,
another effort to generalize about definitions of political development
found four oft-recurring concepts: rationalization, national integration,
democratization, and mobilization or participation.[33]

This "quest for political development," in John Montgomery's phrase,[34]
necessarily led political scientists to grapple with three more general issues. First, what was the relationship between political development and
political modernization? The tendency was to think of political development as virtually identical with political modernization. Political development was one element of the modernization syndrome. Political scientists might disagree as to what types of change constituted political
development, but whatever they did choose was almost invariably thought
of as a part of the more general process of modernization. The principal
dissent from this point of view came in 1965 from Samuel P. Huntington,
who argued that it was highly desirable to distinguish between political
development and modernization. The identification of the two, he said,
limited too drastically the applicability of the concept of political development "in both time and space." It became restricted to a particular
phase of historical evolution, and hence it was impossible to talk about
the "political development" of the Greek city-state or of the Roman
Empire. In addition, political development as political modernization
made the former a rather confusing complex concept, tended to reduce

[32] Lucian W. Pye, *Aspects of Political Development* (Boston, 1966), pp. 31–48.

[33] Samuel P. Huntington, "Political Development and Political Decay," *World
Politics*, XVII (April 1965), 387–88.

[34] John D. Montgomery, "The Quest for Political Development," *Comparative
Politics*, I (January 1969), 285–95.

its empirical relevance, and made it difficult if not impossible to conceive of its reversibility, i.e., to talk about political decay.[35]

A second issue which political scientists had to deal with in their definitional efforts was whether political development was a unitary or a complex concept. Since so many people had so many ideas as to what constituted political development, the prevalent tendency was to think of it as a complex concept. This tendency was explained or, perhaps, rationalized by Pye on the grounds that the "multi-function character of politics . . . means that no single scale can be used for measuring the degree of political development."[36] Hence, most scholars used several dimensions: Pye himself, as indicated above, suggested three; Almond also had three; Ward and Rustow, eight; Emerson, five; Eisenstadt, four.[37] This all seems very reasonable, since political development clearly would appear to be a complex process. Yet, obviously also, this approach can lead to difficulties. What are the relationships among the component elements of political development? Thus, although Pye argued that equality, capacity, and differentiation constitute the development syndrome, he also had to admit that these do not "necessarily fit easily together." On the contrary, "historically the tendency has usually been that there are acute tensions between the demands for equality, the requirements for capacity, and the processes of greater differentiation." In a similar vein, Almond argued that "there is a tendency" for role differentiation, subsystem autonomy, and secularization "to vary together," but that the relation between each pair of these three variables "is not a necessary and invariant one."[38] Almond, indeed, presented a two-way matrix with secularization and differentiation on one axis and subsystem autonomy on the other. He found some type of political system to occupy each of the nine boxes in his matrix. The question thus necessarily arises: What does political development mean if it can mean everything? On the other hand, if political development is defined as a unitary concept, the tendency is either to define it narrowly—as Huntington, for instance, did in identifying it exclusively with institutionalization—and thus to rob it of many of the con-

[35] Huntington, "Political Development and Political Decay," pp. 389–93.

[36] Lucian W. Pye, "Introduction," in Pye, ed. *Communications and Political Development* (Princeton, 1963), p. 16.

[37] See Pye, *Aspects*, pp. 45–48; Almond and Powell, *Comparative Politics*, pp. 299 ff.; Ward and Rustow, *Japan and Turkey*, pp. 6–7; Rupert Emerson, *Political Modernization: The Single-Party System* (Denver, 1963), pp. 7–8; S. N. Eisenstadt, "Bureaucracy and Political Development," in Joseph LaPalombara, ed. *Bureaucracy and Political Development* (Princeton, 1963), p. 99.

[38] Pye, *Aspects*, p. 47; Almond and Powell, *Comparative Politics*, p. 306. For an intriguing analysis of some of these problems, see Fred W. Riggs, "The Dialectics of Developmental Conflict," *Comparative Political Studies*, I (July 1968), 197 ff.

notations and the richness usually associated with it, or to define it very generally, as for instance Alfred Diamant did, which in effect masks a complex concept under a unitary label.[39]

A third problem in the definitional quest concerned the extent to which political development was a descriptive concept or a teleological one. If it was the former, it presumably referred either to a single process or to a group of processes which could be defined, in terms of their inherent characteristics, as processes. If it was a teleological concept, on the other hand, it was conceived as movement toward a particular goal. It was defined not in terms of its content but in terms of its direction. As in the more general case of modernization, the goals of political development were, of course, valued positively. The definition of political development in terms of goals would not have created difficulties if there were clear-cut criteria and reasonably accurate indices (e.g., the political equivalent of per capita Gross National Product) to measure progress toward those goals. In the absence of these, however, there was a strong tendency to assume that, because both scholarly analyst and, presumably, the political actors he was analyzing, wanted political development, it was therefore occurring. The result was that "Almost anything that happens in the 'developing' countries—coups, ethnic struggles, revolutionary wars—becomes part of the process of development, however contradictory or retrogressive this may appear on the surface."[40]

These definitional problems raised very real questions about the usefulness of political development as a concept. Referring to Pye's list of ten definitions, Rustow argued that this "is obviously at least nine too many."[41] In truth, however, one should go one step further. If there are ten definitions of political development, there are ten too many, and the concept is, in all likelihood, superfluous and dysfunctional. In the social sciences, concepts are useful if they perform an aggregating function, that is, if they provide an umbrella for a number of subconcepts which do share something in common. Modernization is, in this sense, an umbrella concept. Or, concepts are useful because they perform a distinguishing function, that is, because they help to separate out two or more forms of something which would otherwise be thought of as undifferentiated. In this sense, manifest functions and latent functions are distinguishing concepts.

[39] Alfred Diamant, "The Nature of Political Development," in Jason L. Finkle and Richard W. Gable, eds. *Political Development and Social Change* (New York, 1966), p. 92.

[40] Huntington, "Political Development and Political Decay," p. 390.

[41] Dankwart A. Rustow, "Change as the Theme of Political Science" (Paper delivered at International Political Science Association Round Table, Torino, September 1969), pp. 1–2.

Political development in general is of dubious usefulness in either of these ways. To the extent that political development is thought of as an umbrella concept encompassing a multiplicity of different processes, as in the Almond and Pye cases discussed earlier, these processes often turn out to have little in common except the label which is attached to them. No one has yet been able to say of the various elements subsumed under the label political development what Lerner, at a different level, was able to say about the broader processes subsumed under the label modernization: that they went together because "in some historical sense, they *had* to go together." Instead, it is clear that the elements included in most complex definitions of political development do not have to go together and, in fact, often do not. In addition, if political development involves differentiation, subsystem autonomy, and secularization, as Almond suggests, do not the really interesting and important questions concern the relations among these three, as Almond himself implies in his conclusion? The use of the term political development may thus foster a misleading sense of coherence and compatibility among other processes and obscure crucial questions from discussion. To the extent, on the other hand, that political development is identified with a single, specific process, e.g., political institutionalization, its redundancy is all the more obvious. What is to be gained analytically by calling something which has a good name by a second name? As either an aggregating concept or a distinguishing concept, in short, political development is superfluous.

The principal function that political development has in fact performed for political scientists is neither to aggregate nor to distinguish, but rather to legitimate. It has served as a way for political scientists to say, in effect: "Hey, here are some things I consider valuable and desirable goals and important subjects to study." Such would indeed appear to be the principal function for the discipline served by the debates over the meaning of political development. This aspect of the use of the concept has perhaps been particularly marked in the arguments over the relation of democratization to political development and the perennial uneasiness faced by political scientists when they consider the issue: Is the Soviet Union politically developed? The concept of political development thus serves in effect as a signal of scholarly preferences rather than as a tool for analytical purposes.[42]

[42] Some people may say that people in glass houses should not throw stones on the grounds that I did, after all, argue that political development should be defined as political institutionalization in my 1965 article on "Political Development and Political Decay." My answer would be: true enough. But I do not mind performing a useful function by throwing stones and thus encouraging others to move out of their glass houses, once I have moved out of mine. In my 1968 book, *Political Order in Changing Societies,* which otherwise builds extensively on the 1965 article, the concept of political development was quietly dropped. I focus instead

The popularity of the concept of political development among political scientists stems perhaps from the feeling that they should have a political equivalent to economic development. In this respect, political science finds itself in a familiar ambiguous methodological position between its two neighboring disciplines. In terms of the scope of its subject matter, political science is narrower than sociology but broader than economics. In terms of the agreement within the discipline on goals, political scientists have more shared values than sociologists, but fewer than economists. Sociology is comprehensive in scope; economics is focused in its goals; political science is not quite one or the other. The eclecticism and diffuseness of sociological theory are excused by the extent of its subject. The narrowness and parochialism of economics are excused by the precision and elegance of its theory.

In this situation, it is quite natural for political scientists to borrow concepts from sociologists and to imitate concepts of economists. The sociological concept of modernization is, quite properly, extended and applied to political analysis. The concept of political development is created in the image of economic development. In terms of choosing its models, one might generalize, a discipline will usually tend to copy the more structured and "scientific" of its neighboring disciplines. This leads to difficulties comparable to those normally associated with the phrase "misplaced concreteness." Economists, it will be said, do differ over what they mean by economic development and how one measures it. These differences, however, shrink to insignificance in comparison with the difficulties which political scientists have with the term political development. If, on the other hand, political scientists had modeled themselves on the sociologists and talked about political change in imitation of social change rather than political development in imitation of economic development, they might have avoided many of the definitional and teleological problems in which they found themselves.

Approaches to political development   Many of the things that are often labeled studies in political development are not such in any strict sense. The study of political development is not the study of politics in societies at some given level of development. If this were the case, there would be few if any studies of politics which were not studies in political development, since those polities which are usually assumed to be developed are also presumably still developing. Yet not infrequently studies in the politics of less developed societies are treated as if they were studies in

---

on what I conceive to be the critical relationship between political participation and political institutionalization without worrying about the issue of which should be labeled "political development."

political development. Tunisia, it is said, is a developing society; therefore, its polity is developing polity; therefore, a study in Tunisian politics is a study in political development. The fallacy here is to look at the subject of the study rather than at the concepts with which that subject is studied. Depending on the concepts which were used and hence the questions which were asked, for instance, a study of John F. Kennedy's presidency might be a study in the uses of power, the institutionalization of an office, legislative-executive relations, consensus-building, the psychology of leadership, the role of intellectuals in politics. Or it could, conceivably, be a study in political development or political change. Exactly the same possibilities would exist for a study of Habib Bourguiba's presidency. There is nothing in the latter which makes it inherently more "developmental" than the former. Precisely the same is true for the innumerable studies of the role of the military, bureaucracy, and political parties in developing societies. More likely than not, these are simply studies of particular institutions in particular types of societies rather than studies in change or development. Depending upon the conceptual framework with which these subjects were approached, they could just as easily be studies in civil-military relations, organizational behavior, and political behavior, as studies in political development. They are the latter only if the categories employed are formulated in terms of change.

It could, of course, be argued that change is so pervasive that it is virtually synonymous with politics itself and that hence it cannot be studied as a separate subject. The rejoinder is that, to be sure, politics is change, but politics is also ideas, values, institutions, groups, power, structures, conflict, communication, influence, interaction, law, and organization. Politics can be studied, and has been studied, in terms of each of these concepts. Each sheds a different light on the subject, illuminates different areas, suggests different relationships and generalizations. Why not also analyze politics in terms of change or development?

In fact during the 1950s and 1960s a variety of scholars did just that. Many different approaches were employed. Without making any claim to inclusiveness or to systematic rigor, it is perhaps useful to focus on three of these approaches: system-function, social process, and comparative history.

System-function   In the analysis of political development, a close relation existed between systems theory, in the strict sense, and structural-functional theory. It is, indeed, impossible to apply a functional approach without employing some concept of the political system. The varieties of theory encompassed in this general category are reflected in the names: Talcott Parsons, Marion Levy, David Easton, Gabriel Almond, David Apter, Leonard Binder, Fred Riggs. The principal contribution of these scholars has been to develop a set of concepts and categories, central to which are those of "system" and "function," for the analysis and comparison of types of political systems. Among their other key concepts are: structure, legitimacy, input and output, feedback, environment, equilibrium. These concepts and the theories associated with them provide an overall model of the political system and the basis for distinguishing types of political systems in terms of the structures which perform the functions which must be performed in all political systems.

The advantages of the system-function approach clearly rest in the generality of the concepts which it deploys on the plains of analysis. One problem of the approach for the study of political change is the defect of this great virtue. It is primarily a conceptual framework. This framework does not necessarily in and of itself generate testable hypotheses or what are often referred to as "middle level generalizations." Scholars using the framework may come up with such hypotheses or generalizations, but it is an open question whether the conceptual framework is not more of a hindrance than a help in this respect. The approach itself provides little incentive for scholars to dig into empirical data. Indeed, the tendency is in just the opposite direction. The theory becomes an end in itself. It is striking how few facts there are not only in general works, such as Levy's two volumes, but even in case studies attempting to apply the system-function approach to a specific society, such as Binder's study of Iran.[43]

A more fundamental problem is that this approach does not inherently focus on the problem of change. It is possible to employ the concept of "system" in a dynamic context, focusing on lags, leads, and feedback. In actuality, however, much of the theorizing on political development which started from a systems approach did not primarily employ these dynamic elements in that approach. The stress was on the elaboration of models of different types of political systems, not different types of change from one system to another. In his two-volume opus, *Modernization and the Structure of Societies,* Levy, for instance, is overwhelmingly concerned with the second element in his two-component title. The bulk of his work is devoted to discussing the characteristics of societies in general and then distinguishing between those of "relatively modernized societies" and of "relatively nonmodernized societies." The question of modernization and its political components gets short shrift in the first and last chapters of this 800-page work. As we noted earlier, Almond himself saw somewhat comparable limitations in the framework which he used in *The Politics of Developing Areas.* The much more elaborate and change-oriented

---

[43] See Levy, *Modernization and the Structure of Societies,* and Leonard Binder, *Iran: Political Development in a Changing Society* (Berkeley and Los Angeles, 1962).

scheme which he and Powell present in *Comparative Politics: A Developmental Approach* does not entirely escape from this difficulty. Among those works in the system-function tradition directly concerned with political development, David Apter's *The Politics of Modernization* has probably been most successful in bringing to the fore dynamic concerns with the rate, forms, and sources of change. Yet to the extent that he has done this, it has in large part flowed from his independent concerns with normative questions and ideologies, which are derived from sources other than the system-function framework which he also employs. The structural-functional approach, as Kalman Silvert has pointed out, was initially employed by social scientists interested in studying either very primitive societies (the anthropologists) or very complex societies (Parsons). It is an approach peculiarly limited in what it can contribute to the understanding of societies undergoing fundamental change. It is, moreover, rather ironic that political scientists should have seized upon this approach in order to study political change at the same time that the approach was coming under serious criticism within sociology because of its insensitivity to, and limited usefulness in, the study of change.

As has often been pointed out, a related difficulty in attempting to deal with change in this intellectual context is the extent to which the concept "equilibrium" also tends to be implicitly or explicitly linked to the system-function approach. The equilibrium concept presupposes the existence of a system composed of two or more functionally related variables. Changes in one variable produce changes in others. The concept, as Easton has pointed out, is closely linked with the ideas of multiple causation and pluralism. In addition, however, equilibrium also means that the variables in the system tend to maintain "a particular pattern of interaction."[44] In its pure form the theory conceives of equilibrium as a state of rest. In all forms it presupposes tendencies toward the restoration of an original condition or a theoretically defined condition of equilibrium.

Equilibrium theory has obvious limitations as a framework for exploring political change. As one sociologist observed, the theory "does not attend to intrinsic sources of change, does not predict changes that have persistent directionality (but only those that restore balance if that is disturbed), and thus does not readily handle past changes that clearly affect the current state of the system."[45] In effect, change is viewed as an extraneous abnormality. It is held to be the result of strain or tension, which gives rise to compensating movements that tend to reduce the strain or tension and thus restore the original state. Change is "unnatural"; stability or rest is "natural." Some thinkers have attempted to reconcile equi-

[44] Easton, *Political System,* pp. 266–67, 272 ff.; Harold Lasswell and Abraham Kaplan, *Power and Society* (New Haven, 1950), p. xiv.

[45] Moore, "Social Change and Comparative Studies," pp. 524–25.

librium and change through the concept of moving equilibrium. By itself, however, this concept is inadequate to account for change. If the equilibrium remains the same but is itself moving as a whole, the concept does not explain the cause or direction of its movement. If the equilibrium is itself changing, then moving equilibrium really means multiple equilibria, and again some theory is necessary to explain the succession of one equilibrium by another.

Social process   The social-process approach to political development starts not with concepts of the social system and the political system but rather with a focus on social processes—such as industrialization, urbanization, commercialization, literacy expansion, occupational mobility—which are presumed to be part of modernization and to have implications for political change. The emphasis is on the process, not the system. The approach is more behaviorally and empirically oriented than the system-function approach, and it typically leads to the accumulation of substantial amounts of data, often quantitative in nature (surveys or aggregate ecological data), about these social processes which it then tries to relate to political changes. While the scholar working with the system-function approach typically attempts to impute functions, the scholar employing the social-process approach attempts to correlate processes. He may attempt to move beyond correlation to causation and to shed light on the latter through various techniques of causal or path analysis.

The scholars most prominently associated with this type of approach to political development and related questions in the 1950s and 1960s included Daniel Lerner, Karl Deutsch, Raymond Tanter, Hayward Alker, Phillips Cutright, and Michael Hudson. The two most important early works, which stimulated much of what followed, were Lerner's *The Passing of Traditional Society* (1958) and Deutsch's 1961 article, "Social Mobilization and Political Development."[46] The system-function scholar begins with a concept of the political system, then differentiates different types or models of political systems, and finally attempts to spell out the consequences and implications of these distinctions. His approach typically is concerned with linking a pattern of action to the system as a whole, i.e., identifying its function within the system, while the social-process scholar is concerned with relating one pattern of action to another pattern of action.

The great virtue of the social-process approach is its effort to establish

[46] Karl W. Deutsch, "Social Mobilization and Political Development," *American Political Science Review*, LV (September 1961), 493–514. For a suggestive effort to relate Almond, Huntington, and SSRC Comparative Politics Committee theories of political development to the available quantitative data, see Raymond F. Hopkins, "Aggregate Data and the Study of Political Development," *Journal of Politics*, XXXI (February 1969), 71–94.

relationships between variables and particularly between changes in one set of variables and changes in another. In this respect, it does focus directly on change. Its limitations in dealing with change are threefold. First, more often than not, the variables which have been used concern levels of development rather than rates of development. Since it is empirically oriented, the variables employed are shaped by the availability of data. Data on levels of literacy in different societies at the same time (i.e., now) are easier to come by than data on levels of literacy in the same society over time. The latter, however, are necessary for longitudinal analysis and the use of rates of change in literacy. While cross-sectional analyses may be useful and appropriate in studying some types of relationships, they are also frequently inferior to longitudinal analyses in studying other types of relationships. The difficulty of getting data on the changes in variables over time in most modernizing societies in Asia, Africa, and even Latin America has consequently led many social-process analysts back to the study of Western European and North American societies. Here is a clear case where knowledge of political change or political development is advanced by studying developed rather than developing societies. A related difficulty is the extent to which the social-process approach has been applied primarily to the comparison of national societies, which are often units too large and complex to be useful for comparative generalization for many purposes.

A second problem in the social-process approach concerns the links between the usually social, economic, and demographic independent variable and the political dependent ones. The problem here is the general methodological one of the causal relationship between an economic or social change (which is in some sense "objective") to political changes which are normally the result of conscious human effort and will. If the problem is, for instance, to explain voting participation in elections or the frequency of coups, how meaningful is it to correlate these phenomena with rates of economic growth, fluctuations in price levels, or literacy levels? The relation between the "macro" socioeconomic changes and "macro" political changes has to be mediated through "micro" changes in the attitudes, values, and behavior of individuals. The explanation of the latter is the weak link in the causal chain which is assumed to exist in most social-process analysis. To date, the most prevalent and effective means of dealing with this problem has been the various forms of the "relative deprivation" and "frustration-aggression" hypotheses utilized to relate socioeconomic changes to political instability.[47] Finally, at the dependent end of the causal chain, social process analysts often have trou-

[47] Ibid.; James C. Davies, "Toward a Theory of Revolution," *American Sociological Review*, XXVII (February 1962), 5 ff.; Ivo K. and Rosalind L. Feierabend, "Aggressive Behaviors within Polities, 1948–1962: A Cross-National Study," *Journal of Conflict Resolution*, X (September 1966), 253–54; Ted Gurr, *Why Men Rebel* (Princeton, 1970).

ble in defining political variables, identifying indices for measuring those variables, and securing the data required for the index.

One more general criticism which can be raised about the social-process approach concerns the extent to which it makes politics dependent upon economic and social forces. That the latter are a major influence on politics is obvious, and this influence is perhaps particularly important in societies at middle levels of social-economic modernization. In its pure form, which, to be fair, most of its practitioners rarely use, the social-process approach would leave little room for social structure and even less for political culture, political institutions, and political leadership. One of the great problems of the social-process approach to political change has been to overcome this initial deficiency and to find ways for assigning independent roles to cultural, institutional, and leadership factors.

Comparative history   A third approach to political development is somewhat more diverse and eclectic then the two just considered. Its practitioners share enough in common, however, to be loosely grouped together. They start neither with a theoretical model nor with a focus on the relationship between two or more variables, but rather with a comparison of the evolution of two or more societies. What "the system" is to the system-functions man and "process" is to the social-process man, "society" is to the comparative-history man. He is, however, interested not just in the history of one society but rather in the comparison of two or more societies. The system-functions man conceptualizes; the social-process man correlates; the comparative history man, naturally, compares. Among social scientists concerned with political development who would fit primarily into this school are Cyril Black, S. N. Eisenstadt, Dankwart Rustow, Seymour Martin Lipset, Barrington Moore, Jr., Reinhard Bendix, and, in some measure, Lucian W. Pye and the members of the SSRC Committee on Comparative Politics.

The work of these people tends to be highly empirical but not highly quantitative. They are, indeed, concerned with precisely those factors with which the social-process analysts have difficulty: institutions, culture, and leadership. Their approach is to categorize patterns of political development either by general stages or phases through which all societies must pass or by distinctive channels through which different societies may pass, or by some combination of these "vertical" and "horizontal" types of categories. Moore, for instance, distinguishes three patterns of modernization, under bourgeois (England, United States), aristocratic (Germany, Japan), and peasant (Russia, China) auspices. While he admits there may conceivably be a fourth way (India?), he is very dubious that this possibility will materialize. Consequently, every modernizing society will presumably have to find its way to modernity by way of liberal capitalism, reactionary fascism, or revolutionary communism. Cyril Black, on the other hand, starts by identifying four phases of modernization through which all societies pass: the initial challenge to modernity; the consolidation of modernizing leadership; economic and social transformation from a rural, agrarian to an urban, industrial society; and the integration of society, involving the fundamental reordering of social structure. He then specifies five criteria for distinguishing among societies in terms of how they have evolved through these phases and proceeds to classify all contemporary societies into "seven patterns of political modernization" on the basis of these criteria. He thus combines vertical and horizontal categories into a truly all-encompassing scheme of comparative history, and he very appropriately subtitles his book, "A Study in Comparative History."[48]

In a slightly different vein, Dankwart Rustow and the SSRC Committee on Comparative Politics have attempted to identify the types of problems which confront modernizing societies and to compare the evolution of these societies in terms of the sequences with which they have dealt with these problems. Rustow argues that there are three key requirements of political modernization: "identity is essential to the nation, authority to the state, equality to modernity; the three together form the political basis of the modern nation-state."[49] The critical differences among societies concern the extent to which they had to deal with these problems simultaneously or sequentially, and, if the latter, the order in which these problems were dealt with. On the basis of comparative analysis, Rustow suggests that the identity-authority-equality sequence leads to the most successful and least traumatic modernization. In a somewhat similar spirit and parallel endeavor, the SSRC Committee identified five crises which societies would have to deal with in the process of political modernization: identity, legitimacy, penetration, participation, and distribution. A rough equivalence presumably exists between these two efforts as well as that of Almond:

Almond—*Challenges*	Rustow—*Requirements*	CCP—*Crises*
nation-building	identity	identity
state-building	authority	legitimacy, penetration
participation, distribution	equality	participation, distribution

[48] Barrington Moore, Jr., *Social Origins of Dictatorship and Democracy* (Boston, 1966); Cyril E. Black, *The Dynamics of Modernization: A Study in Comparative History* (New York, 1966).

[49] Rustow, *World of Nations*, p. 36. For a thoughtful discussion of sequences in political development, see Eric A. Nordlinger, "Political Development: Time Sequences and Rates of Change," *World Politics*, XX (April 1968), 494–520.

Interestingly, the SSRC Committee originally had a sixth crisis, integration, which concerned the "problems of relating popular politics to governmental performance. . . ."[50] This, however, turned out to be a rather nebulous and slippery crisis to handle; eventually it was dropped from the scheme.

The great virtue of the comparative-history approach is that it starts by looking at the actual evolutions of societies, attempts to classify those evolutions into patterns, and then attempts to generate hypotheses about what factors are responsible for the differences in patterns. It starts, in short, with the "real" stuff of history, at the opposite end of the methodological scale from the system-function approach with its abstract model of the system. Nor does it, like the social-process approach, assume that certain variables, such as urbanization and instability, can be lifted out and generalized about independently of their context. This approach thus clearly lacks generality. In effect, it comes back to a focus on the historically discrete phenomenon of modernization, and it deals with particular phases in the evolution of particular societies. Like most "developmental" analyses, its concepts are "less generalized than those of equilibrium analysis."[51] In comparison to the system-function man with his conceptual complexity and the social-process man with his high-powered quantitative analyses, the comparative-history fellow often seems like a rather pedestrian, traditional plodder, whose findings lack theoretical and scientific precision. On the other hand, he is, unlike his competitors, usually able to communicate those findings to readers who will not read jargon and cannot read numbers.

Each of these three approaches has obviously contributed much to the study of political development. At the same time each has the defect of its virtues. From the viewpoint of a theory of political change, the system-function approach is weak in change, the social-process approach is weak in politics, and the comparative history approach is weak in theory. By building upon and combining the strengths of all three approaches, however, it may be possible to overcome the deficiencies of each.

IV. Theories of Political Change
The study of modernization and political development thus generated concern for the formulation of more general theories of political change. In the late 1960s the analysis of political change became in itself a direct focus of political science work, quite apart from any relations it might have had with the social-economic-cultural processes of modernization

[50] See Pye, *Aspects*, pp. 62–67.
[51] Lasswell and Kaplan, *Power and Society*, p. xv.

or the teleological preoccupations which underlay much of the work on political development. In the course of a decade the work of political scientists moved from a generalized focus on the political system to the comparative analysis of modern and traditional political systems, to a more concrete concern with the discrete historical process of modernization, to an elaboration of related concepts of political development, and then back to a higher level of abstraction oriented toward general theories of political change. The transition from the static theory to dynamic theory, in short, was made by way of the historical phenomenon of modernization.

These new theories of political change were distinguishable from earlier approaches because of several characteristics. First, the theoretical frameworks could be utilized for the study of political changes in societies at any level of development. Second, these frameworks were either unrelated to the process of modernization or, at best, indirectly related to that process. Third, the variables and relationships which were central to the theories were primarily political in character. Fourth, the frameworks were sufficiently flexible to encompass sources of change and patterns of change in both the domestic and the international environments of the political system. Fifth, in general the theories were relatively more complex than earlier theories of political modernization and political development: they encompassed more variables and looked at the more extensive relationships among those variables.

One transitional approach was presented by Huntington in his 1968 volume on *Political Order in Changing Societies*. In this volume, the central focus of political change is held to be the relationship between political participation and political institutionalization. The relationship between these determines the stability of the political system. The fundamental source of expansion of political participation is the nonpolitical socioeconomic processes identified with modernization. The impact of modernization on political stability is mediated through the interaction between social mobilization and economic development, social frustration and nonpolitical mobility opportunities, and political participation and political institutionalization. Huntington expresses these relationships in a series of equations:[52]

(1) $\dfrac{\text{Social mobilization}}{\text{Economic development}} = \text{Social frustration}$

(2) $\dfrac{\text{Social frustration}}{\text{Mobility opportunities}} = \text{Political participation}$

(3) $\dfrac{\text{Political participation}}{\text{Political institutionalization}} = \text{Political instability}$

[52] Huntington, *Political Order*, p. 55.

Starting with a central concern of the social-process approach to modernization, i.e., the relationship between socioeconomic changes (urbanization, industrialization), on the one hand, and the political participation, political instability, and violence, on the other, this approach thus attempts to introduce into the analysis elements of social (mobility opportunities) and political (political institutionalization) structure.

Huntington is concerned with the relationship between political participation and political institutionalization. The source of the former is ultimately in the processes of modernization. What about the sources of the latter? Here he is less explicit. Implicitly, however, he suggests that there are two principal sources. One is the political structure of the traditional society. Some traditional political systems are more highly institutionalized than others (i.e., more adaptable, complex, coherent, and autonomous); these presumably will be better able to survive modernization and accommodate broadened patterns of participation. In addition, Huntington suggests that at particular phases in the process of modernization certain types of political leadership (aristocratic, military, revolutionary) and certain types of conflict may also produce institutionalization.

The relationship between political institutionalization and political participation, however, is clearly one that can be abstracted from a concern with modernization. The latter may be one major historical source of changes in participation, but it need not be the only one. The problem of balancing participation and institutionalization, moreover, is one which occurs in societies at all levels of development. The disruptions involving Negroes and students in the United States during the late 1960s could be profitably analyzed from this framework. In central cities and in universities, existing structures were challenged to provide new channels through which these groups, in the cliché of the times, could "participate in the decisions which affect them."

This theoretical approach, originally focused on the relationship between two political variables, could be extended to include more or different ones. One of the striking characteristics of much of the work on political development was the predominance of concern with the *direction* of change over the concern with the *objects* of change. This, of course, reflected the origins of political development research in the study of the transition from traditional to modern society. The first step in analyzing political change, however, is simply, as William Mitchell put it, to identify "the objects that are susceptible to changes."[53] It is to identify what are or may be the components of a political system and then to establish what, if any, relations exist in the changes among them. Such an approach focuses on *componential change*.

[53] William C. Mitchell, *The American Polity* (New York, 1962), pp. 369–70.

A political system can be thought of as an aggregate of components, all changing, some at rapid rates, some at slower ones. The questions to be investigated then become: What types of change in one component tend to be related to similar changes or the absence of change in other components? What are the consequences of different combinations of componential changes for the system as a whole? The study of political change can be said to involve: (1) focusing on what seem to be the major components of the political system; (2) determining the rate, scope, and direction of change in these components; and (3) analyzing the relations between changes in one component and changes in other components. The political system can be defined in a variety of ways and conceived of as having various components, as, for instance, the following five:

(a) culture, that is, the values, attitudes, orientations, myths, and beliefs relevant to politics and dominant in the society;

(b) structure, that is, the formal organizations through which the society makes authoritative decisions, such as political parties, legislatures, executives, and bureaucracies;

(c) groups, that is, the social and economic formations, formal and informal, which participate in politics and make demands on the political structures;

(d) leadership, that is, the individuals in political institutions and groups who exercise more influence than others on the allocation of values;

(e) policies, that is, the patterns of governmental activity which are consciously designed to affect the distribution of benefits and penalties within the society.

The study of political change can fruitfully start with the analysis of changes in these five components and the relations between change in one component and change in another. How is change in the dominant values in a system related to change in its structures? What is the relation between mobilization of new groups into politics and institutional evolution? How is turnover in leadership related to changes in policy? The starting assumption would be that, in any political system, all five components are always changing, but that the rate, scope, and direction of change in the components vary greatly within a system and between systems. In some instances, the rate of change of a component may approach zero. The absence of change is simply one extreme rate of change, a rate rarely if ever approximated in practice. Each component, moreover, is itself an aggregate of various elements. The political culture, for instance, may include many subcultures; the political structures may represent a variety of institutions and procedures. Political change may be analyzed both in terms of changes among components and in terms of changes among the elements of each component.

Components and elements are the objects of change. But it is still necessary to indicate what types of changes in these are significant to the study of *political* change. One type of change which is obviously relevant is change in the power of a component or element. Indeed, some might argue that changes in power are the only changes with which political analysis should be concerned. But to focus on power alone is to take the meaning out of politics. Political analysis is concerned with the power of ideologies, institutions, groups, leaders, and policies. But it is also concerned with the content of these components and with the interrelation between changes in content and changes in power. "Power" here may have the usual meaning assigned to it in political analysis.[54] The "content," on the other hand, has to be defined somewhat differently for each component. The content of a political culture is the substance of the ideas, values, attitudes, and expectations dominant in the society. The content of the political institutions of the society, on the other hand, consists of the patterns of interaction which characterize them and the interests and values associated with them. The content of political groups refers to their interests and purposes and the substance of the claims which they make on the political system. The content of the leadership refers to the social-economic-psychological characteristics of the leaders and the goals which they attempt to realize. And the content of policies, of course, involves the substance of the policies, their prescriptions of benefits and penalties.

The analysis of political change may in the first instance be directed to simple changes in the power of components and elements of the political system. More important, however, is the relation between changes in the power of individual components and elements and changes in their content. If political analysis were limited to changes in power, it could never come to grips with their causes and consequences. The recurring problems of politics involve the trade offs of power and content. To what extent do changes in the power of a political ideology (measured by

[54] Major contributions to the analysis of power by contemporary social scientists include: Lasswell and Kaplan, *Power and Society*, pp. 74 ff.; Herbert Simon, "Notes on the Observation and Measurement of Political Power," *Journal of Politics*, XV (November 1953), 500–16; James G. March, "An Introduction to the Theory and Measurement of Influence," *American Political Science Review*, XLIX (June 1955), 431–51; Robert A. Dahl, "The Concept of Power," *Behavioral Science*, II (July 1957), 201–15; Carl J. Friedrich, *Man and His Government* (New York, 1963), pp. 159–79; Talcott Parsons, "On the Concept of Influence," *Public Opinion Quarterly*, XXVI (Spring 1963).

the number of people who adhere to it and the intensity of their adherence) involve changes in the substance of the ideology? Under what circumstances do rapid changes in the power of political leaders require changes in their purposes and goals (the "moderating" effects of power) and under what circumstances may the power of leaders be enhanced without significant changes in their purposes? History suggests, for instance, that professional military officers can acquire political power in liberal, socialist, or totalitarian societies only at the expense of abandoning or modifying the conservative military values.[55] In most systems, the enhancement of the power of an ideology, institution, group, leader, or policy is bought at the price of some modification of its content. But this is by no means an invariable rule, and a variety of propositions will be necessary to specify the trade offs between power and content for different components in different situations. One important distinction among political systems may indeed be the prices which must be paid in content for significant increases in the power of elements. Presumably the more highly institutionalized a political system is, the higher the price it exacts for power.

Political change may thus be analyzed at three levels. The rate, scope, and direction of change in one component may be compared with the rate, scope, and direction of change in other components. Such comparisons can shed light on the patterns of stability and instability in a political system and on the extent to which change in one component depends upon or is related to change or the absence of change in other components. The culture and institutions of a political system, for instance, may be thought of as more fundamental to the system than its groups, leaders, and policies. Consequently, stability might be defined as a particular set of relationships in which all components are changing gradually, but with the rates of change in culture and institutions slower than those in other components. Political stagnation, in turn, could be defined as a situation in which there is little or no change in the political culture and institutions but rapid changes in leadership and policies. Political instability may be a situation in which culture and institutions change more rapidly than leaders and policies, while political revolution involves simultaneous rapid change in all five components of the system.

As a second level of analysis, changes in the power and content of one element of one component of the system may be compared with changes in the power and content of other elements of the same component. This would involve, for instance, analysis of the rise and fall of ideologies and beliefs, of institutions and groups, and leaders and policies, and the changes in the content of these elements associated with their

[55] See Samuel P. Huntington, *The Soldier and the State* (Cambridge, 1957), pp. 80–97 and *passim*.

changing power relationships. Finally, at the most specific level of analysis, attention might be focused upon the relation between changes in power and changes in content for any one element, in an effort to identify the equations defining the price of power in terms of purposes, interests, and values.

A relatively simple set of assumptions and categories like this could be a starting point either for the comparative analysis of the more general problems of change found in many societies or for the analysis in depth of the change patterns of one particular society. It could furnish a way of bringing together the contributions which studies of attitudes, institutions, participation, groups, elites, and policies could make to the understanding of political change.

A somewhat different approach, suggested separately by both Gabriel Almond and Dankwart Rustow, focused on *crisis change* and also provided a general framework for analyzing political dynamics. Earlier theories of comparative politics and development, Almond argued, could be classified in terms of two dimensions.[56] To what extent did they involve an equilibrium or developmental models? To what extent were they predicated upon determinacy or choice? Reviewing many of the writers on these problems, Almond came up with the following classification:

Approaches to Comparative Politics

	Equilibrium	Developmental
Determinacy	I Parsons Easton	III Deutsch Moore Lipset
Choice	II Downs Dahl Riker	IV Harsanyi Leiserson

He then went on to argue that each of these approaches has its appropriate place in the analysis of political change. Change from one state to another can be thought of as going through five phases. In the first phase, an antecedent equilibrium can be assumed to exist, and for the analysis of this phase Type I and Type II theories are most appropriate. Change can be assumed to begin with the impact on the equilibrium of exogenous variables from the nonpolitical domestic environment or from the international environment of the political system. These Phase 2 developments produce changes in the structure of polit-

[56] Gabriel A. Almond, "Determinacy-Choice, Stability-Change: Some Thoughts on a Contemporary Polemic in Political Theory," (Center for Advanced Study in the Behavioral Sciences, Stanford University, August 1969).

ical demand and in the distribution of political resources, and can be most appropriately analyzed by Type III theories. In the next phase, political factors—the changing structure of political demand and distribution of political resources—become the independent variables. Political leadership manipulates these variables so as to produce new political coalitions and policy outcomes. For this purpose, Type IV "coalition theory and leadership skill and personality theory" are most useful. In the next or fourth phase, these policy outcomes and political coalitions produce cultural and structural changes. The relations in this phase require analysis by all four types of theories. Finally, a new "consequent equilibrium" emerges in Phase 5, which again can be studied in terms of Type I and Type II theories.

In formulating this theoretical framework, Almond once again played a leading and a representative role in changing thinking on comparative politics. Unlike his earlier formulations, this framework was precisely designed to deal with the problem of change and it was also clearly independent of any particular historical context. It was not tied in with modernizaton. It was instead a general framework for the analysis of political change which could be applied to a primitive stateless tribe, a classical Greek city-state, or to a modern nation-state. It encompassed both political and nonpolitical variables and recognized that each could play both dependent and independent roles. Perhaps most significantly, it effectively incorporated leadership and choice into a model of political change. All in all, it neatly synthesized several conflicting approaches to development and change in such a way as to capitalize on the particular strengths of each. The model was especially relevant to the analysis of intense changes of limited duration. Hence, it is not surprising that Almond and his associates applied it to the study of clearly delimitable historical crises, such as the Reform Act of 1832, the creation of the Third Republic, the Meiji Restoration, the Bolshevik Revolution, and the Cárdenas reforms of the 1930s.[57]

In a parallel endeavor, Rustow came up with a somewhat similar model.[58] Political change, he suggested, is the product of dissatisfaction with the existing situation. This dissatisfaction produces political action;

[57] For an initial application of the Almond model, see Wayne A. Cornelius, Jr., "Crisis, Coalition-Building, and Political Entrepreneurship in the Mexican Revolution: The Politics of Social Reform under Lázaro Cárdenas," (Project on Historical Crises and Political Development, Department of Political Science, Stanford University, July 1969).

[58] Dankwart A. Rustow, "Change as the Theme of Political Science," pp. 6–8. See also his "Communism and Change," in Chalmers Johnson, ed. *Change in Communist Systems* (Stanford, 1970), pp. 343–58, and "Transitions to Democracy: Toward a Dynamic Model," *Comparative Politics,* II (April 1970), 337–63.

political action, indeed, is *always* the result of dissatisfaction. This action either succeeds or fails. If it succeeds, the organization, movement, or other group responsible for the success either develops new goals or it withers and dies. If its effort for change fails, either the group responsible for the effort dissolves or it continues to pursue its old objective with decreasing expectation of ever achieving it. In addition, Rustow argues, the forces involved in the creation of a government or the conquest of power by a group or individual are very different from those which sustain the government or keep the individual or group in power over the long haul. A theory of political change has to account for and to systematize these differences. Thus Rustow, like Almond, puts a primary emphasis on the choices which have to be made by political leadership.

A third approach to the analysis of political change was developed by Ronald D. Brunner and Garry D. Brewer.[59] In their study of the political aspects of modernization, they developed a model of a *complex change* involving twenty-two variables and twenty parameters. Ten of the variables and eight of the parameters were disaggregated in terms of rural and urban sectors; three variables and three parameters constituted the demographic subsystem, nine variables and six parameters the economic subsystem, and ten variables and eleven parameters the political subsystem. The relations among these variables and parameters were expressed in twelve equations derived from general theories of modernization and from analysis of the evolution of Turkey and the Philippines from the 1940s to the 1960s. Their model included variables which could be directly influenced by governmental action and others not subject to such influence. Using the model it is possible to calculate the probable effects on support for the governments (measured by the proportion of the population voting for the government party) and on the standard of living (measured by per capita consumption) of governmental policy changes—such as birth control programs producing a 5 percent decrease in the rate of natural increase of population, increases or decreases of 5 percent in urban tax rates, and changes in the relative preference accorded the urban and rural sectors in governmental expenditures. Alternatively, one policy parameter—such as governmental preference for urban and rural sectors—can be intensively analyzed to demonstrate how various degrees of change within it might affect dependent variables such as government support and standard of living.

The Brunner-Brewer approach opened up new horizons in political analysis. Theoretically, it provided a highly simplified but highly precise

[59] Ronald D. Brunner and Garry D. Brewer, *Organized Complexity: Empirical Theories of Political Development* (New York, 1971).

model of a political system encompassing a significant number of demographic, economic, and political variables, the relations among which could be expressed by equations. Practically, it pointed scientific inquiry in a direction which could ultimately provide policymakers with a means of analyzing the probable consequences of policy choices for outcomes directly relevant to their purposes. In effect, this model building introduced into political science the type of complex analysis of relations among variables which has long prevailed in economics. On the other hand, the Brunner-Brewer approach was limited by its initial theoretical assumptions and the relevance of those assumptions to the actual political systems to which the model was oriented. The twelve-equation model furnished a reasonably good guide to the interaction of the variables and parameters in Turkey and the Philippines during the 1950s and 1960s. Its relevance to the future was based on the assumption that the structure of the model and the magnitude of the parameters did not vary over time. The model provided ways of testing the consequences of major changes in governmental policy or major changes in other variables brought about by other means. It did not provide means for predicting major changes of the system unless or until these changes were reflected in significant changes in some variables in the model. Thus, the model could not predict a military coup bringing to power a radical, nationalist junta of officers. Once such a junta came to power the model might be able to predict some of the consequences of new policies they introduced. Its ability to do this would depend upon the continued existence of the relationships among variables which had existed in the past. The first goals of the revolutionary junta might be to change those relationships. Thus, the usefulness of the Brunner-Brewer approach was limited by the degree of discontinuity in the political system.

These various theories of componential change, crisis change, and complex change all tended, in one way or another, to liberate political analysis from the static assumptions which had limited it in one earlier phase and from the teleological concerns with modernization and development which had preoccupied it in a later phase. They indicated increasing parallelism between the study of political change and the study of social change. Most important, they were the very modest and first steps toward the formulation of general theories of political dynamics, the initial response to Rustow's challenge: "Aside from the refinement of evolutionary models and the more sophisticated use of historical data, is it not time to introduce some notion of change into our very conception of politics itself?"[60]

[60] Dankwart A. Rustow, "Modernization and Comparative Politics: Prospects in Research and Theory," *Comparative Politics*, I (October 1968), 51.

The Attitudes of Modernity

Kenneth S. Sherrill*

The aim of this article is to distill and operationalize some of the significant aspects of theories of political modernization within the context of the study of American politics. These fields of study are applicable to one another in two areas. First, operating under the assumption that the United States is a modern nation, we might isolate those salient features of American politics that are absent from political systems that are, by common consent, not yet modern systems. We might then study the way in which the United States has developed and maintained these characteristics of modernity, and we might then make certain prescriptive remarks about strategies to be followed in the modernization process. This is a highly ethnocentric approach to the study of modernization, but this type of ethnocentrism, which is explicit and conscious, may be less wrong than the latent ethnocentrism that pervades much of the work in the field of political modernization.[1]

The assumption that the United States is modern permits another approach to the analysis of the problems of political modernization. Were we to derive a description of a modern polity from the areas of consensus in the political development literature, we might then test the accuracy with which the description is mirrored in American politics. If parts (or all) of the descriptions were inaccurate pictures of the United States, we might then reject them as descriptions of a generalized modern political system.

The second area in which the study of political modernization is applicable to the study of American politics is a more explicitly normative one. Instead of testing the accuracy of a description of "the modern" by seeing whether or not it is an accurate description of the United States, we might test the proposition that the United States is modern by comparing it with our model of modernity. If we believe that modernity is a desirable state of being, then we might argue for certain changes in the nature of American politics.

Thus, it becomes clear that the way in which we go about defining modernity determines the types of questions we ask and, hence, the types of conclusions we reach about modernity. Furthermore, the way in which

* I would like to thank Robert L. Hardgrave, Timothy M. Hennessey, and Nancy A. Shilling for their comments on earlier versions of this manuscript. Of course, all blame for error is mine.

[1] Leading sources of the "anti-ethnocentric" critique are Fred R. von der Mehden, *Politics of the Developing Nations* (Englewood Cliffs, 1964), p. 3; Fred W. Riggs, *Administration in the Developing Countries: The Theory of Prismatic Society* (Boston, 1964), p. 35; Ann Ruth Willner, "The Underdeveloped Study of Political Development," *World Politics*, XVI (April 1964), 471; Robert A. Packenham, "Political Development Doctrines in the American Foreign Aid Program," ibid., XVIII (January 1966), 194-195; J. Roland Pennock, "Political Development, Political Systems, and Political Goods," ibid. (April 1966), 415-434; Gabriel A. Almond and James S. Coleman, eds. *The Politics of the Developing Areas* (Princeton, 1960), Introduction, p. 3; Lucian W. Pye, *Aspects of Political Development* (Boston, 1966), p. 34.

we define the modern will raise ethical issues concerning competing end states. Many definitions of modernity have been offered in the past decade, and the editors of a recent anthology were forced to write: "In this volume . . . we have not tried to adhere to a rigid definition of political development. . . . The authors of the papers in this volume thus tend to reflect the view that there is, in a generic sense, a phenomenon of political development and modernization."[2]

If political scientists continue to operate on the assumption that our major dependent variable exists in nothing more precise than a generic sense, we may end up exacerbating the problems that have piqued our curiosity. Without engaging in a lengthy review of definitions of political development or modernization, let me suggest that we develop a parsimonious scheme for arraying these definitions in terms of two basic dimensions.

First, definitions of political modernity tend to deal with one or both of two classes of phenomena. Phenomena in the first class are structural. They include such things as literacy rates or the existence of a rational bureaucracy and a party system within the framework of institutional stability and efficiency. Phenomena in the second class are attitudinal. We are here concerned with the orientations of the mass public as well as of the elite toward their role in politics, toward themselves, and toward their fellow men.

The second dimension that serves to distinguish conceptions of the modern is the way in which the concept is given a formal definition. The traditional approach had been to assign "ideal type" definitions to those characteristics that serve to distinguish the modern societies from the traditional ones. Max Weber writes, "The construction of a purely rational course of action in such cases serves the sociologist as a type ('ideal type') which has the merit of clear understandability and the lack of ambiguity."[3] This kind of definition introduces a large normative element. An actor's efforts can be evaluated in terms of how well he conforms to the ideal pattern of action. Similarly we should be able to evaluate a nation in terms of how well it conforms to our ideal pattern of political modernity.

Although compliance with an ideal pattern may be possible in an ideal world, political scientists frequently find insurmountable barriers existing in the real world. This has led to an alternative approach to defining our major variable. Writing in the context of democratic theory, Robert A. Dahl sets forth "the descriptive method." This "is to consider as a single class of phenomena all those nation states and social organizations that are commonly called democratic by political scientists, and by examining the members of this class to discover, first, the distinguishing characteristics they have in common, and second, the necessary and sufficient conditions for social organizations possessing these characteristics."[4]

The descriptive approach will lead us to the observation that not all people in a modern society conform to the ideal type of the modern citizen. Are we then to reject the ideal-type model as being unrealistic or undesir-

[2] Lucian W. Pye and Sidney Verba, eds. *Political Culture and Political Development* (Princeton, 1965), pp. 12-13.
[3] *The Theory of Social and Economic Organization,* ed. and trans. Talcott Parsons (New York, 1964), p. 92.
[4] *A Preface to Democratic Theory* (Chicago, 1956), p. 63.

able? Or, worse, are we to confuse the two approaches and declare that the real is the ideal? If we were to fall into either of these methodological traps we would lose our criteria for evaluating modern societies. The ultimate absurdity would be to ask, How much does a nation measure up to itself?

We may now codify our classificatory scheme for definitions of the modern. First, we ask if the definition is concerned with one or both of our major classes—structural and attitudinal. If it is concerned with only one of them, which one is it, and what are the implications of concentration on only one of them? Second, is the definition of each variable ideal-type or descriptive?

Max Weber, for example, is concerned with both the structural and attitudinal dimensions, and he provides ideal-type definitions of both sets.[5] Lucian Pye utilizes an ideal-type definition of the structural characteristics of a modern political system and gives its attitudinal dimension a descriptive definition.[6] Almond and Verba emphasize the attitudinal components of the civic culture, but provide descriptive definitions of both major dimensions.[7] Peter Snow measures political development exclusively in terms of the emergence of a rational institutional framework for politics.[8] Leonard Doob, at the other extreme, focuses on the attitudinal changes that come with becoming more civilized.[9] This article will be concerned almost exclusively with the attitudinal dimension, and the political attitudes of modern men will be defined in terms of ideal types.

The purpose of developing this classificatory scheme is not to argue that one type of definition is more or less valid than another, but rather to demonstrate the range of variation in our concerns and to enable us to begin to distinguish the consequences for research and policy of these differing types of definitions. Certainly David Apter's use of ideal types results in conclusions markedly different from those of Almond and Verba. While many have challenged Almond and Verba's work as having a marked conservative bias,[10] this charge can scarcely be leveled at Apter, who writes: ". . . How can the West serve as the model for a highly industrialized society if it . . . ignores many of its obligations in the fields of civil rights, poverty, education, and foreign affairs? . . . The future of democratic society will depend on its ability to find new and effective ways to secure personal identity through liberty and solidarity through knowledge. This has always been the basis of the democratic ideal. These are the ultimate standards by which we evaluate both ourselves and others."[11]

The descriptive approach reveals that no society is purely modern and

[5] Pages 328-331 ff.

[6] Pye, ed. *Communications and Political Development* (Princeton, 1963), p. 18.

[7] Gabriel A. Almond and Sidney Verba, *The Civic Culture* (Princeton, 1963), pp. 31 ff.

[8] "A Scalogram Analysis of Political Development," *American Behavioral Scientist*, IX (March 1966), 33-36.

[9] *Becoming More Civilized: A Psychological Exploration* (New Haven, 1960).

[10] See, for example, Peter Bachrach, *The Theory of Democratic Elitism: A Critique* (Boston, 1960); Christian Bay, "Politics and Pseudopolitics: A Critical Evaluation," *American Political Science Review*, LIX (March 1965), 39-51; Lewis Lipsitz, "If, as Verba Says, the State Functions as a Religion, What Are We To Do Then To Save Our Souls?" ibid., LXII (June 1968), 527-535; and Kenneth S. Sherrill, "Political Modernization as an Attitudinal Syndrome," a paper presented at the Annual Meeting, American Political Science Association, September 1966.

[11] *The Politics of Modernization* (Chicago, 1965), p. 463.

that all societies combine the modern and the traditional. Changes in the mixture of components frequently occur; what is modern to one generation will appear traditional to their children. Sidney Verba notes that "what seem today to be fundamental sets of beliefs may be quickly set aside."[12]

This should make us recognize that confounding the real with the ideal is a most dangerous procedure when studying modernization. The study of political modernization is inevitably filled with normative issues. To put the matter bluntly, there is general agreement that being modern is a good thing. Fred Riggs writes, "To be modern is to be up-to-date, contemporary. Normatively speaking, it is 'better' to be modern than out of date. Hence, 'modernization' conveys the notion of moving toward a preferred condition."[13] A descriptive model inevitably places its imprimatur on the nations on which the model is based, just as Almond and Verba place theirs on the United States and the United Kingdom.

The remainder of this article will be devoted to outlining the political attitudes of modern men in a democratic political system. It will be specifically concerned with those attitudes believed to be supportive of a democratic system. It will not contend that only democracies are modern, but rather than democracy is the type of modern system we prefer and toward which we are interested in developing. It focuses on the attitudes of modern men rather than on structural variables, recognizing that both sets of variables are significant and probably highly interrelated. There is ample justification for emphasizing the attitudinal component. As one scholar has put it, "The land, not the people, is the constant factor."[14] Almond and Verba concur: "What is to be learned about democracy is a matter of affect and feeling. . . ."[15]

We generally assume that there are certain types of attitudes that can be used to distinguish among individual societies, as well as among larger classes of societies, such as the modern and the traditional or the democratic and the authoritarian. In describing a society, we generally assume that all of its members share these central attitudes. We invariably find that a society is characterized by a distribution of attitudes that can be described in terms of its mode (or a number of its modes) and the degree of dispersion about the mode.[16]

Modern people share a peculiar world view. Their political attitudes are integrated into a more general set of orientations toward the outside world

[12] "Conclusion: Comparative Political Culture," in Pye and Verba, p. 521.

[13] P. 38.

[14] Hermann Weilenmann, "The Interlocking of Nation and Personality Structure," in Karl W. Deutsch and William Foltz, eds. *Nation-building* (New York, 1963), pp. 33-55, at p. 49.

[15] P. 5. For other support of this position, see Everett E. Hagen, *On the Theory of Social Change* (Homewood, 1962), p. 86; Daniel Lerner "Introduction [to Attitude Research in Modernizing Areas]," *Public Opinion Quarterly*, XXII (Fall 1958), 217-222, at 217; Kurt W. Back, "The Change-prone Person in Puerto Rico," ibid., 330-340, at 330; Doob, p. 5.

[16] This approach has been widely used in recent years. See, for example, Almond and Verba, pp. 12-36; V. O. Key, Jr. *Public Opinion and American Democracy* (New York, 1961), pp. 27-93; Alex Inkeles and Daniel Levinson, "National Character: The Study of Modal Personality and Social-cultural Systems," in Gardner Lindsey, ed. *Handbook of Social Psychology*, Vol. II (Cambridge, Mass., 1954); and Robert E. Lane and David V. Sears, *Public Opinion* (Englewood Cliffs, 1964), pp. 83-113.

and toward their role in it to form a latent political ideology[17] unlike a forensic ideology such as that described by the authors of *The American Voter*,[18]
which is the base of political debate within a society. A latent political
ideology characterizes the beliefs of society as a whole.

We shall now turn to an exposition of what many political scientists believe to be the component of this latent ideology. A summary of the political
modernization literature reveals great consensus about these attitudinal
components.

*As an initial disclaimer, it should be emphasized that we are engaged in
a review of the literature for the purpose of developing a consensus list of
hypotheses that might then be subjected to verification in the current state
of American politics. The fact that we state a hypothesis in no way means
that we necessarily agree with it or are unwilling to reject it when faced
with the weight of evidence.* Whenever possible, each of these hypotheses
will be followed by some recently collected survey data that should serve
as a preliminary check on the validity of the statement.

1. *The politically modern man identifies with the national political
community.*

At the simplest level, this means that an individual thinks of himself as
an American or an Englishman or whatever, rather than as a member of
some group competing with the nation for his loyalties. Such a group might
include a familial, geographic, or economic organization. The hypothesis
that a person in a modern society identifies with the nation does not demand
that his other identifications cease to exist, but rather that national identity
take precedence over these other loyalties, should they come into conflict.
Perhaps no other hypothesis can find such widespread support in the national development literature. Before a nation can count on being able to
mobilize its citizenry to meet any crisis, it must be sure that the nation, and
not some other group, has first claim on the commitments of that citizenry.[19]

17 Robert E. Lane, *Political Ideology* (New York, 1962), p. 3. This notion of latent
ideology has much in common with Gabriel Almond's original conception of political
culture: "Every political system is embedded in a particular pattern of orientations
toward political action. I have found it useful to refer to this as *political culture*." Almond, "Comparative Political Systems," *Journal of Politics*, XVIII (August 1956), 391-
409, at 396. Philip E. Converse introduces a similar concept in "The Nature of Belief
Systems in Mass Publics," in David Apter, ed. *Ideology and Discontent* (New York, 1964),
pp. 206-261.
18 Angus Campbell et al. *The American Voter* (New York, 1960), pp. 192-193.
19 Lucian Pye is most frequently associated with the concept of national identity in
recent years. See his *Politics, Personality, and Nation-building: Burma's Search for
Identity* (New Haven, 1962), pp. 4-6. Pye is by no means alone in this position. Other
major sources are Sidney Verba, in Pye and Verba, pp. 529-532; Rupert Emerson, *From
Empire to Nation* (Boston, 1962), pp. 102 ff.; Richard Butwell, "Individual and Collective
Identity and Nation-building," *World Politics*, XV (April 1963), 488-494; Max F. Millikan
and Donald L. M. Blackmer, eds. *The Emerging Nations* (Boston, 1961), p. 76; Robert E.
Lane, "The Tense Citizen and the Casual Patriot: Role Confusion in American Politics,"
Journal of Politics, XXVII (November 1965), 735-760; Lane, *Political Ideology*, pp. 111 ff.;
Samuel P. Huntington, "Political Development and Political Decay," *World Politics*, XVII
(April 1965), 386-430, at 387; James S. Coleman, "Conclusion: The Political Systems of
Developing Areas," in Almond and Coleman, p. 532; Daniel Lerner, "A Note on National-
ism and Political Identity," *Public Opinion Quarterly*, XX (Spring 1956), 289-292; Leonard
Doob, "South Tyrol: An Introduction to the Psychological Syndrome of Nationalism,"
ibid., XXVI (Summer 1962), 172-184. On the relationship between primary groups and
national identity in the United States, see Morton Grodzins, *The Loyal and the Disloyal*
(Chicago, 1956).

This hypothesis has obvious intuitive appeal. We know that one of the major problems faced by new nations is the transfer of loyalties from "the parochialism and internationalism of many traditional cultures to a pre-occupation with the supra-local but less than worldwide units of the territorial, and eventually, the national state."[20] We might suspect that social or political mobilization occurs whenever a political system is faced with a major crisis, whether it be political modernization, war, or famine. At these times, the sense of identification with the natonal political community should be heightened. When politics is not salient to the individual, as may be the case in an age of peace and prosperity when the national community is not faced with major challenges, we might expect outward manifestations of the sense of national identity to dwindle. In fact, national identity may prove to be little more than fealty to the most efficient problem-solving agency around.

In a world dominated by functionally specific and contractual relationships, there may be a revival of the crisis of national identity that the new nations face. And, just as Pye finds in the case of political elites in Burma,[21] the modern man whose loyalties are contractually determined will face a crisis of personal identity. Political identity, like social identity, helps a man to describe or define himself through the use of attributes derived from those of the group. These attributes give him cues as to which values, traits, opinions, and ways of acting are appropriate for him to adopt. In the absence of appropriate identifications or reference groups, people frequently cannot decide among the alternatives they may face. Anxiety is the cost of being free of the irrational components of identity—be they national identifications or other sorts of social identifications. One way of avoiding this anxiety is simply to withdraw from the problems causing the anxieties. In this case, withdrawal would be from politics. If large numbers of a country's population were to withdraw from the political world, the nation would once again face the problems of political mobilization. It should therefore be obvious that a modern political structure demands a citizenry that identifies with it.[22]

At this point, we may introduce some interesting data. In the course of their five-nation study, Almond and Verba asked their respondents whether or not they agreed with the statement, "The individual owes first loyalty to the state and only secondarily to his personal welfare." When the responses are related to generally agreed-upon levels of modernization, we have a most surprising distribution.

While agreement with the statement is not the ideal measure of the sense of national identity, the findings reported in Table 1 do raise some questions about the relationship between national identity and political modernization. Perhaps it is impossible to measure the sense of national identity ex-

20 Karl W. Deutsch, "Social Mobilization and Political Development," *American Political Science Review,* LV (September 1961), 493-514, at 500.

21 *Politics, Personality, and Nation-building,* pp. 255-266.

22 In addition to Pye, *Politics, Personality, and Nation-building,* see Lane, *Political Ideology,* p. 389; Erik Erikson, "The Problem of Ego Identity," *Journal of the American Psychoanalytic Association,* IV (1956); Campbell et al., pp. 120-145; Theodore M. Newcomb, "Attitude Development as a Function of Reference Groups: The Bennington Study," in Eleanor Maccoby et al., eds. *Readings in Social Psychology,* 3d ed. (New York, 1958), pp. 265-275.

Table 1. Loyalty to State v. Personal Welfare *(by nation)*

	Agree	Disagree	Don't Know/ Other	No Answer	Total
Mexico	91.9%	4.8%	3.3%	....	100%
Italy	48.1	32.7	19.2	....	100
Germany	40.6	44.7	14.7	....	100
United Kingdom	37.8	54.8	7.4	....	100
United States	25.0	68.3	6.6	0.1%	100

Source: Inter-University Consortium for Political Research, *Codebook for the Five-Nation Study.* The number of cases for each country is about a thousand. The United States survey was made in March 1960; the others, in June and July 1959.

cept in times of crisis or political mobilization. Thus, as long as politics remains quiescent in nations such as the United States, we cannot actually know what the level of national identity is. We can only hope that it can be mobilized in times of crisis, and then hope for some quick-witted social scientist to measure it before the events making for the political community's salience ebb away.[23]

At this point, it becomes necessary to add further confusion to the issue. It is generally assumed that in modern political systems the nation does not compete with primary and secondary groups for the loyalty of the individual. Rather, an individual's other loyalties tend to be supportive of his national identification. However, the functionally specific and contractual nature of modern societies means that the modern man can distinguish between personal and political relationships.[24] This proposition is so basic as to be worthy of testing in and of itself:

1a. *The politically modern man can distinguish between personal and political relationships.*

There are two basic reasons why this proposition is necessary. First, it is a guaranty of honesty and equality in politics. As long as authoritative decisions reflect friendship or kinship patterns instead of rational applications of specific criteria, politics does not meet the expectations of a modern society.

The second reason for the maintenance of the distinction between personal and political relationships is that this distinction lowers the intensity of political involvement and therefore facilitates the processes of change. When, as in traditional societies, political relationships are largely determined by social and political relationships, "the political struggle tends to

[23] An analogous argument is made by Sidney Verba in his very interesting article "The Kennedy Assassination and the Nature of Political Commitment," in Bradley S. Greenberg and E. B. Parker, eds. *The Kennedy Assassination and the American Public* (Stanford, 1965), pp. 348-360.

[24] Karl W. Deutsch, "Integration and the Social System," in Philip E. Jacob and James V. Toscano, *The Integration of Political Communities* (Philadelphia, 1964), p. 202; Pye, *Politics, Personality, and Nation-building,* pp. 16-17; Millikan and Blackmer, p. 19; Verba, in Pye and Verba, p. 549; Doob, pp. 34, 187; David C. McClelland, *The Achieving Society* (Princeton, 1961), p. 173; Bert F. Hoselitz, *Sociological Aspects of Economic Growth* (New York, 1959), p. 33.

revolve around issues of prestige, influence and personalities, and not around questions of alternative courses of policy action. . . . Any change in political identification generally requires a change in one's social and personal relationships."[25] In the modern society, on the other hand, it is assumed that such considerations are not made. Political disagreement is tolerated because the people expect distinctions to be drawn between institutions such as politics, the family, religion, and economics. This is a consequence not only of expecting functional specificity, but also of becoming increasingly skillful in abstracting from the immediate situation to a more general case.[26]

As was the case with the more general problem of national identification, this is a particularly difficult concept to measure. If Pye's hypothesis is correct, modern repondents will justify their political preferences in terms of some sort of forensic ideology, in terms of positions on certain issues that the respondents deem to be significant, in terms of economic motivation, or in terms of a Downsian loyalty to one or the other of the political parties. *They will not justify their political choices on the basis that one of the alternatives is better for, or traditionally allied with, an ethnic, religious, geographic, or kinship unit.*

The data presented in Table 2 provide no support for this hypothesis. Overwhelmingly, Americans use both personal and political criteria when evaluating candidates for the Presidency. Furthermore, the ability to distinguish between the personal and the political in evaluating political objects is not significantly correlated with any of the other attitudes we shall identify with modernity. If we have any faith in our measures, we must reject this hypothesis.

Table 2. Respondents' Bases for Evaluating Candidates

	All Candidates		Johnson		Goldwater	
	N	%	N	%	N	%
Personal only	199	12.7	351	24.3	361	25.9
Personal and political	1,214	77.4	805	55.7	698	50.1
Political only	155	9.9	290	20.1	333	23.9
Total	1,568	100.0	1,446	100.1	1,392	99.9

Source: Inter-University Consortium for Political Research, 1964 Election Study, conducted by the Survey Research Center, University of Michigan.

Let us move on to a second major hypothesis:

2. *The politically modern man has a strong ego.*

This hypothesis is obviously related to the problems of identity discussed earlier, but merits independent consideration because of the implications

25 Pye, *Politics, Personality, and Nation-building,* pp. 16-17.
26 Doob, pp. 34, 87. In a content analysis of children's stories, McClelland finds (p. 173) that in rapidly developing societies, contractual relationships and material and impersonal cooperation pressures are more frequent than in less rapidly developing societies, and that the opposite is true for traditional institutional interaction pressure.

for democratic theory that have been drawn from it. A strong ego may be described as the ability to order one's life in a rational manner, to control one's environment, and to control one's own impulse life. Men who have strong egos tend to generalize their ability to control themselves and their environment to a general feeling of self-confidence. This includes both the willingness to take an active part in politics and the belief that such participation can be worthwhile.

Men with weak egos tend to perceive the world as a Hobbesian jungle in which all would give way to their impulses were it not for the restraining force exercised by those few who are capable of mastering themselves and their environment. Thus, the weak ego provides support for totalitarian regimes—whether they be in the modern world or in traditional societies.[27] Lane writes, "Only the strong egos can support a free society, can bear the burden of choice, can accept the responsibility for internal control in the absence of social control," and therefore can accept self-government.[28] Lasswell concludes that "failure to develop democratic character is a function of interpersonal relations in which low estimates of the self are permitted to develop."[29]

Men with strong egos must play a special role in the process of modernization. Modernization is dependent on the existence of a number of innovating personalities, people who are able to cope with ambiguity and who are able to leave the comfortable world of tradition behind them and forge new forms with confidence and, perhaps, a feeling that it is their duty to achieve the new society and win converts for it.[30]

I have devised two quasi-scales to measure aspects of ego strength. The first measures the belief that the respondent can master the environment; the second measures his confidence in interpersonal relations.[31] Marginal distributions of these scales are presented in Table 3.

[27] The major exponent of this position has been Harold D. Lasswell. See his *Power and Personality* (New York, 1948), pp. 162 ff., and his "Democratic Character," in *The Political Writings of Harold D. Lasswell* (New York, 1951), pp. 465-525, esp. pp. 480 ff. Lasswell traces this idea back to Aristotle and Plato (ibid., p. 468). See also Lane, *Political Ideology*, pp. 43 ff.; Morris Rosenberg, "Self-Esteem and Concern With Public Affairs," *Public Opinion Quarterly*, XXVI (Summer 1962), 201-211.

[28] *Political Ideology*, p. 54.

[29] "Democratic Character," p. 521.

[30] Everett Hagen, in *On the Theory of Social Change*, pp. 92 ff., develops this idea to a much greater extent. See also Kurt Back, "The Change-prone Person."

[31] The questions in these and subsequent scales are not included for lack of space. I will make the data for these scales available upon request. Utilizing the system of trichotomizing variables demonstrated by Allen L. Edwards, *Techniques of Attitude Scale Construction* (New York, 1956), pp. 184-197, the CR (coefficient of reproducibility) for the first scale is .849 (minimum marginal reproducibility = .620), and for the second scale it is .829 (MMR = .607). The normal CR of .900 for Guttman scales refers to dichotomized variables rather than the trichotomizations used here, which save information.

The data used for these scales, which were provided by the Inter-University Consortium for Political Research, are from the 1964 Election Study conducted by the University of Michigan. I would like to thank the ICPR, the University of Michigan Survey Research Center, and the Department of Political Science at the University of North Carolina for making these data available. I would also like to thank Mr. Neil Ludlam of the UNC Computation Center and Mr. Peter B. Harkins of the UNC Department of Political Science for their invaluable aid with some of the massive computational aspects of the larger project from which this article is drawn. They are, of course, in no way responsible for the quality of the analysis of the data.

Table 3. Levels of Ego Strength

Score*	Mastery Scale		Interpersonal Confidence Scale	
6 (high)	457	31.4%	199	13.1%
5	59	4.1	20	1.3
4	405	28.0	376	26.7
3	67	4.6	156	10.6
2	266	18.4	390	26.9
1	54	3.8	44	3.0
0 (most fatalistic)	140	9.7	263	18.4
No answer	2	.1	2	.1
Total	1,450	100.1	1,450	100.1

*Scores were obtained as follows: 2 for each response indicating a strong ego, 0 for a response indicating a weak ego, and 1 for a response such as "It depends."
Source: ICPR, 1964 SRC Election Study.

We can then claim tentative confirmation for the position that Americans, as politically modern men, are characterized by something akin to ego strength. However, we must note that our respondents are much more sure of their ability to make plans and to master their environment than they are of their ability to hold their own in political discussions. Furthermore, many Americans fall toward the lower extremes of the distribution, indicating once again that there is room for further political modernization among the American people. A full 41.7 percent of the people who are highest in interpersonal confidence are also highest in the mastery of environment, while 14.8 percent of those who are lowest on the former scale are also lowest on the latter. If the politically modern man can be characterized by a latent political ideology, we should expect the component attitudes to be highly intercorrelated.

3. *The politically modern man is opinionated.*

The notion that the politically modern man has, and expresses, political opinions should follow directly from the first two hypotheses. Having no opinion may well be a consequence of not having an appropriate reference group in a given area.[32] Not having political opinions can therefore follow from the absence of national identity. The willingness to express opinions also indicates a strong ego—an image of the self as worthy of expressing opinions and an image of society as respecting this worthiness.[33]

People living in traditional societies lack the skills needed to have political opinions, just as they lack the other psychic prerequisites for being opinionated. When faced with an issue that has never before confronted them in their everyday life, they lack the knowledge needed to make a decision, even if they feel worthy of expressing opinions. Traditional man

[32] Eugene Hartley, "The Social Psychology of Opinion Formation," *Public Opinion Quarterly*, XIV, No. 4 (1950), 673.
[33] Lane, *Political Ideology*, p. 387.

believes that his opinions are undesired or irrelevant. Daniel Lerner finds that "persons who are urban, literate, participant, and empathic *differ* from persons who lack any of these attributes"—and they differ on a significant personal trait distinctive of the modern style. Such a trait is "having opinions" on public matter. Traditional man has habitually regarded public matters as none of his business. For the modern man in a participant society, on the contrary, such matters are fraught with interest and importance. A public opinion grows out of the expectation that many people will have views on public issues; it is sustained by the reciprocal view that what people think about such issues will make a difference in their solution.[34]

We can make two major inferences from this. First, the way of life in traditional society prevents the development of political opinions among a wide sector of the population, people who either believe that it is not right for them to hold opinions or are incapable of holding or expressing opinions because they lack the skills—or the motivation to obtain the skills —involved in being opinionated. Second, when only a few people are involved in the exchange of political ideas, they can monopolize the political process. Oligarchic rule becomes inevitable when the mass of the people cannot express their ideas about the major issues the country is facing. If democracy is a system of government responsive to the will of the people being ruled, democratic government is only possible in systems in which the people have opinions, that is, in modern systems. (This should not be interpreted to mean that all modern systems are democratic systems. No single variable is a sufficient cause of democratic government. The point is that having an opinionated public is a necessary condition of democracy. If having opinions serves to distinguish modern people from traditional, then being modern is a prerequisite to being truly democratic.)

We have devised a simple measure of opinionatedness by counting the total number of political opinions that a respondent can voice if he answers every question he is asked in a survey. (Unless otherwise noted, all data are drawn from the 1964 Survey Research Center Election Study. See footnote 31.) We then subtract from that number the total number of times that a respondent was unwilling or unable to voice a political opinion. We then divide the maximum number of possible opinions by the remainder. The quotient is our index of opinionatedness, which equals unity if the respondent expresses the maximum number of opinions and equals zero if he expresses no opinions. That is,

$$\text{Opinionatedness} = \frac{\text{Maximum N of Opinions} - \text{N of Unexpressed Opinions}}{\text{Maximum N of Opinions}}$$

Our findings in this area are most gratifying and are presented in Table 4.

The idea that the modern political man has opinions is related to a fourth hypothesis, essentially stating that he has the wherewithal to have opinions, and that this trait is significant in and of itself.

4. *The politically modern man is empathic.*

The major conclusion to emerge from Daniel Lerner's study of modernization in the Middle East is that empathy is "the inner mechanism which

[34] Daniel Lerner, *Passing of Traditional Society*, pp. 70-71, 99.

Table 4. Opinionatedness Scores

Opinionatedness Range	N	Percent of Total Sample
.10–.19 (lowest)	1	0.1
.20–.29	2	0.2
.30–.39	2	0.2
.40–.49	11	0.7
.50–.59	26	1.7
.60–.69	165	10.5
.70–.79	875	55.5
.80–.89 (highest)	489	31.1
Total	1,571	100.0

enables newly mobile persons to *operate efficiently* in a changing world. Empathy . . . is the capacity to see oneself in the other fellow's situation."[35] When people lack empathy, they can deal only with known people in known situations. They cannot engage in political debate because they cannot imagine the conditions that would give rise to debate; they cannot imagine the psychologically or geographically distant people with whom they might engage in such debate. There is no need for the shared symbols, national ideologies, or national identities that would facilitate these debates. Indeed, all of these characteristics cannot develop until major segments of the population achieve empathy, the ability to imagine other situations and to imagine oneself living in them.

Empathy involves two psychological mechanisms. The first, projection, endows the object with characteristics of the self. This establishes a common ground between the individual and distant objects, such as the nation or another citizen in another town. The second mechanism, introjection, attributes to the self desirable aspects of the object. The modernizing man is thus motivated to change his life to be like the desirable life he sees others living.[36]

Lerner measured empathy by asking people what they would do if they were to hold the job of some other person, such as a newspaper editor or a national leader.[37] Analogous questions were asked in the 1964 SRC Election Study:

> "What would you say are the most important problems the government should take care of when the new President and Congress take office in January?"

> "Are there any problems that the government in Washington has gotten into that you think it should stay out of?"

We assume responses to these questions to be similar to responses to the question, "What would you do if you were running the government?"

[35] *Passing of Traditional Society*, pp. 49-50.
[36] Ibid., pp. 49 ff.
[37] Ibid., pp. 96-100.

Once again, we find support for the hypothesis. Respondents in the SRC Study were asked to name up to six issues: three that the government should take care of and three that it should avoid. We find that 86.4 percent of the sample could name at least one issue that they considered important, and the modal respondent named three issues. The distribution is presented in Table 5.

Table 5. Empathy Scores

Issues Named	N	%
0	214	13.6
1	259	16.5
2	331	21.1
3	402	25.6
4	216	13.7
5	103	6.5
6	46	2.9
Total	1,571	99.9

Marginal distributions, however, do not tell the entire story. We find that our measure of empathy is strongly related to other measures of politically modernity, such as feelings of political efficacy and political involvement, thus supporting Lerner's emphasis on the importance of empathy.

Furthermore, there is a strong relationship betwen race and income and the ability to name issues, i.e., to be politically empathic. The average white respondent can name 2.5 issues; the average Negro respondent can name 1.5 issues. (Difference in means test is significant beyond the .0005 level.) When family income falls below $3,000 a year, a respondent has great difficulty naming more than two issues; respondents with family incomes of over $15,000 a year average 3.2 issues. We now have more evidence in support of the argument for a "syndrome" of being modern, together with preliminary evidence that the characteristics of being politically modern are not randomly distributed throughout the population. *Rather than having slack resources, Negroes and poor people are cumulatively disadvantaged. If people are not aware of major issues, they cannot mobilize to protect their interests.* (It is interesting in this context that only 57.5 percent of the Negro respondents could name an issue *other* than race relations—and this is about as salient as an issue can get—and 29.6 percent could name no issue at all. Only 11.6 percent of the whites were unable to name even one.) Obviously, the people who are most empathic are at an advantage. These people are the well-to-do and the white.

In order to imagine other people in other places, a person has to be exposed to information. There are two basic sources of information: interpersonal communication, which is a universal phenomenon, and the mass media, which are more characteristic of the modern world than of traditional societies. We must therefore state two corollaries to the hypothesis that the politically modern man is empathic:

4a. The politically modern man is highly exposed to the mass media. As a consequence:

4b. The politically modern man is well informed.

The mass media expose people to a vast, and vicarious, universe that would otherwise be beyond the experience of the average man. Furthermore, the media provide enough homogeneity in this exposure to permit discussion about this world of vicarious experiences. In the absence of mass communication, public opinion becomes segmented. National politics becomes difficult, and central mobilization to meet national crises is frustrated.

The media perform a "status conferral" function: by attributing to persons, events, and ideas the quality of being legitimate centers of attention,[38] the media in the new nations can legitimize new norms and focus public attention on the goals of modernization by seeming to be a voice of authority.[39] Thus the media can, in the hands of skilled leaders, develop a sense of political identity among the villagers, propel new leaders to prominence, and endow ideas with the blessings of the nation and the leaders as well as of the media.

The use of the mass media as a source of prestige suggestion facilities a switch from a particularistic world view to a more universalistic one. The traditional man learns to respect and value the opinions of a "generalized other," or public opinion. Respecting the views of other people lays the foundation for a system in which public opinion, rather than traditional leaders and institutions, determines the goals to be pursued and the rules of the game. This, it is argued, gives the system greater flexibility in responding to changed situations and in formulating new demands. It also provides the basis for "market morality" in which the same price buys the same quantity of material of the same quality for all prospective consumers. What holds for economics should also hold in the political realm: in the "market place of ideas, market morality implies equality and popular sovereignty."[40]

Thus, media exposure has two major consequences for the modernization process. First, it gives people information and teaches them "to have opinions on matters which are, strictly speaking, none of [their] business."[41] Second, it encourages "other-directedness," which means that "the link between the past of the individual and any subsequent behavior is attenuated if not altogether obliterated."[42]

[38] Robert K. Merton and Paul F. Lazarsfeld, "Mass Communication, Popular Taste, and Organized Social Action," in Bernard Rosenberg and D. M. White, eds. *Mass Culture* (Glencoe, 1957), pp. 461-462.

[39] McClelland, *Achieving Society*, p. 193. This position is widely held. See Lerner, *Passing of Traditional Society*, pp. 64-68; Millikan and Blackmer, p. 20; Wilbur Schramm, "Communication Development in the Development Process," in Pye, *Communications and Political Development*, pp. 30-57, esp. pp. 38-53. In general, see this Pye volume and Schramm's *Mass Media and National Development* (Stanford, 1964), passim.

[40] McClelland, pp. 193-195. See also Lane and Sears, pp. 84-93; Everett M. Rogers, "Mass Media Exposure and Modernization Among Colombian Peasants," *Public Opinion Quarterly*, XXIX (Winter 1965), 614-625.

[41] Lerner, "Introduction," 221.

[42] Lasswell, "Democratic Character," p. 487. The more positive value placed on other-directedness may come as a slight surprise to readers of David Riesman's *The Lonely Crowd* (New Haven, 1950).

Little need be said about the importance of information to the politically modern man. In order to participate in politics, people must have at least rudimentary information about what is going on. They must come to believe they comprehend the workings of society and must have some knowledge about the alternatives to traditional life if they are to bring about change. Almond and Verba argue that "democratic competence is closely related to having valid information about political issues and processes and to the ability to use information in the analysis of issues and the devising of alternative strategies."[43]

The first part of this hypothesis receives ready confirmation. Over 95 percent of the 1964 SRC sample reported following the election campaign in one or more of the mass media (with over half naming television as being the most important, and about a fifth choosing the newspapers). Slightly over half reported attending to three or four of the media.

A simple information test can be constructed from the 1964 Election Study. The respondents were asked to identify the home states and religions of Goldwater and Johnson, the party controlling Congress, the local candidates for Congress, and the political party controlling Cuba and China. Although these questions were not difficult, Table 6 shows a reasonable range in information scores.

Table 6. Information Scores

Score	N	%
0	21	1.5
1	31	2.2
2	68	4.7
3	86	6.0
4	102	7.1
5	107	7.4
6	147	10.2
7	205	14.2
8	203	14.1
9	240	16.7
10	231	16.0
Total	1,441*	100.1

*Nine not ascertained; 121 not reinterviewed.

We have been arguing that empathy supports the process of modernization partly because it generates faith in a generalized other, partly because it is related to realizing the possibility of bringing about desired changes. These two characteristics are combined in the fifth hypothesis:

[43] P. 95. Many authors stress the importance of information to modernization. See Schramm, *Mass Media*, p. 246; Doob, *Becoming Civilized*, p. 29; and McClelland, p. 399. Y. B. Damle uses information levels as his operational measure of modernization in "Communication on Modern Ideas and Knowledge in Indian Villages," *Public Opinion Quarterly*, XX (Spring 1956), 257-270.

5. *The politically modern man is basically optimistic.*

The politically modern man holds an optimistic attitude toward his own potentialities and toward the characteristics of his fellow men. He is concerned with the need to achieve, and he is characterized by faith in people. In his pathbreaking book *The Achieving Society*, David McClelland finds that the achievement motive (n Achievement), or concern with the need to achieve, is highly correlated with subsequent economic growth, but largely unrelated to previous levels of development. Thus, he concludes, the stress placed on achievement in children's readers, folk tales, and popular literature probably represents national aspirations, or the tendency of the public at large to think about achievement for the next generation. In fact, motivational change precedes economic change by thirty to fifty years.[44]

There is general agreement that the modern man is more sanguine about the future than the traditional man is. Kurt Back measures "modernism" by asking his respondents to compare the present generation of youth to previous generations. He finds that optimistic responses are related to self-confidence, belief in the future, faith in people, belief in the worth of education and of personal effort, and creativity and ambition.[45] Everett E. Hagen contends that innovative personalities are characterized by strong concerns with the needs to achieve, to be autonomous, and to have warm interpersonal relationships (when the need to be dependent on others is low).[46] Robert E. Ward believes that a modern society is characterized by the ability to control and influence its circumstances and by optimism about the possible use of this potential.[47] In general, optimism is taken to be supportive of participation in political dialogue. The authors of *The American Voter* write: "Persons with a relatively pessimistic outlook tend to be persons who feel *ineffective* in their own political activity, they experience a *lack of competence* in guiding their own lives, and they *attempt to avoid conflict* or disagreement in their relationships with other people."[48] Attempts to measure levels of optimism have not been highly successful. However, optimism is no doubt implied by the corollary trust in mankind.

5a. *The politically modern man is characterized by a general faith in people.*

Trust in the motivations and capabilities of one's fellow citizens is related to identification with them (and hence to feelings of national identity), to the image of the self, to willingness to engage in collective activities with others, and to the belief that self-government is both desirable and possible. A general consequence of faith in man is the emergence of empathic feelings characteristic of modern men. McClelland finds that "in societies which

---

[44] P. 138. For other evidence in support of the argument presented thus far, see pp. 67 ff.

[45] "The Change-prone Person."

[46] "How Economic Growth Begins," *Public Opinion Quarterly*, XXII (Fall 1958), 375-390, at 377.

[47] "Political Modernization and Political Culture in Japan," *World Politics*, XV (July 1963), 569-596, at 570.

[48] Campbell et al., p. 396. They also find (p. 397) that in the United States, Northerners are more optimistic than Southerners, and that optimistic Southerners participate more than do pessimistic Southerners.

develop rapidly economically *the force which holds society together has shifted from tradition, particularly impersonal tradition, to public opinion, which helps define changing and functionally specific interpersonal relationships.*"[49]

Once again, we find a close association between the attitudes associated with modernization and those associated with a democratic political outlook. Harold Lasswell contends that the maintenance of an open, rather than a closed, ego is "the outstanding characteristic of democratic character," that the democratic view of other people is warm, inclusive, and expanding, rather than frigid, exclusive, and constricting, as is the view of the closed ego.[50] Lasswell's conclusion that deep confidence in man's benevolent potentialities supports democratic politics is supported by Morris Rosenberg's investigations of the political consequences of misanthropy, which reveal that believing that people are not trustworthy, sympathetic, and cooperative is related to believing that the authorities do not care about the average man, that participation in politics is therefore fruitless, and that democracy is not feasible.[51]

We have constructed a trichotomized faith-in-man scale, scored in the same manner as the ego-strength measures reported earlier.[52] The marginal distributions are as follows:

Table 7. Levels of Faith in People

Faith in People	N	%
6 (high)	551	38.0
5	43	3.0
4	284	19.6
3	24	1.7
2	211	14.6
1	22	1.5
0	313	21.6
No answer	2	0.1
Total	1,450	100.1

Source: ICPR, 1964 SRC Election Study.

[49] P. 192. Once again, taking the United States as a model of modernity, we might generalize from Florence Kluckhohn's discussion of the American "core culture" (which includes the belief that man is capable of "rational mastery over nature" and that human nature is "evil, but perfectable") to the position that modern man is characterized by optimistic attitudes toward other men. "Dominant and Substitute Profiles of Cultural Orientations," *Social Forces*, XXVIII (1950), 376-393, at 382.

[50] "Democratic Character," p. 495. This position is very similar to the one adopted by Lane in *Political Ideology*, pp. 405-406. Lane cites G. M. Gilbert, *The Psychology of Dictatorship* (New York, 1950), pp. 278-280, in support of the position that the "constricted empathy" of the Germans enabled them to endure their oppression of others without feeling much guilt. Thus, empathic feelings and faith in man may be much more characteristic of open systems than they are of modern systems—or else Germany is simply a deviant case.

[51] Morris Rosenberg, "Misanthropy and Political Ideology," *American Sociological Review*, XXI (December 1956), 690-695.

[52] See fn. 31. CR = .844; MMR = .581.

We can again report some preliminary data supportive of the notion of a syndrome of politically modern attitudes. We see that many Americans score high on faith in people, but that there is also a sizable concentration at the lower extreme of the distribution. Of the respondents who fall lowest on the faith-in-people scale, 18.9 percent also score lowest on our measure of empathy, while only 9.6 percent of those who are highest on faith in people do. At the other extreme, 45.5 percent of the most empathic are also among the most trusting, while only 22.7 percent of those least empathic score high on faith in people.

Our sixth hypothesis is directly related to the notion that modern men trust one another:

> 6. *The politically modern man is concerned with the need to affiliate with others.*

The affiliative motive (n Affiliation) is concern with "establishing, maintaining, or restoring a positive affective relationship with another person. This relationship is most adequately described by the word 'friendship.' "[53] As was the case with n Achievement, n Affiliation is positively related to subsequent development. However, it also bears a significant relationship to the type of political system that develops. High n Affiliation, when found with low n Power (concern with the means of influencing a person), is associated with all the democratic societies in McClelland's sample. With one possible exception, all of the "police states" in the sample—including pre-Franco Spain, pre-Hitler Germany, and prerevolutionary Russia—were high on n Power and low on n Affiliation scores. McClelland interprets this motivational pattern to be a psychological prerequisite for political authoritarianism and ruthlessness.[54] Strong affiliative needs may reflect concern and sensitivity for the opinions and behavior of others.

This motive, when combined with a strong and open ego, is reflected in the willingness to join organizations. Membership in voluntary organizations provides training in civic norms as well as a link between primary groups and the government. The data in Table 8 indicate that over 40 percent of Americans do not belong to such organizations. Organizational membership is not the best indicator of n Affiliation, but it is closely related to our seventh hypothesis:

> 7. *The politically modern man is participant.*

Strictly speaking, participation should be treated as the behavioral manifestation of the attitudes of modernity rather than as an attitude. However, modern men are so often typified as being participant that it makes more sense to discuss the behavior itself. Almond and Verba write that the "new

---

[53] McClelland, p. 160.

[54] Ibid., pp. 169-170. Furthermore, when n Affiliation is high, high n Power does not lead to authoritarianism. McClelland cites the United States in 1950 as an example of such a society (p. 170). One of the problems with content analysis is that it works with arbitrarily determined boundaries. We therefore have difficulty in making inferences from the characteristics of the aggregate to those of the individual. We can only wonder about the motivational patterns of McCarthyites.

Table 8. Membership in Voluntary Organizations

Number of Organizations	N	%
0	412	42.6
1	242	25.0
2	136	14.0
3	89	9.2
4 or more	89	9.2
Total	968*	100.0

*Two not ascertained.
Source: Five-Nation Study.

world political culture" will be "a political culture of participation."[55] We would be hard pressed to find anyone to dispute this position.

The authors who relate increased political participation to modernization generally take one or more of three main positions. The first position, typified by Daniel Lerner, essentially defines modernization as being increasing participation: "Modernization, in our view, is a secular trend unilateral in direction—from traditional to participant lifeways."[56] To the degree that a society has nonparticipant members, we are told, the society has not completely modernized. The problem with this approach, as with the other two, is that we are usually not told *how much* people have to participate before they can be considered participants, or in *which activities* they must participate in order to be modern. For example, we might consider voting to be participation in politics, but in dichotomizing between the participants and nonparticipants, are we to draw the line at voting, partaking in political demonstrations, being active in a political movement, or listening to and talking about political information? The second aspect of this problem reflects the fact that modernization is an aspect of more than just the political sector of life. Participation in the mass media is undoubtedly typical of the modern man; but what about media exposure when its role as a source of new demands is only a latent function? When a sample of Burmese moviegoers was asked to name the memorable products of Western culture to which they had been exposed, responses included *Rock, Baby, Rock, Blackboard Jungle,* and *Son of Robin Hood.*[57] Undoubtedly, the empathic personalities in the theater discovered new potential lifeways from this sort

---

[55] P. 4. Among those emphasizing the importance of participation in modernization, see Frederick W. Frey, "Political Development, Power, and Communications in Turkey," in Pye, *Communications and Political Development,* p. 301; Lasswell, "Democratic Character," pp. 473 ff.; Lerner, "Introduction," 220; Lerner, *Passing of Traditional Society,* p. 50; Millikan and Blackmer, pp. 41-42; Deutsch, "Social Mobilization," 500; Edward Shils, *Political Development in the New States* (The Hague, 1962), p. 16, cited in Willner, "The Underdeveloped Study," 471; Huntington, "Political Development and Political Decay," 388; Herbert Hyman, "Mass Media and Political Socialization," in Pye, *Communications and Political Development,* p. 132; Lasswell, "The Policy Sciences of Development," *World Politics,* XVII (January 1965), 290; S. N. Eisenstadt, "Modernization and the Conditions of Sustained Growth," *World Politics,* XVI (July 1964), 576-594, at 590; Karl W. Deutsch, *Nationalism and Social Communication,* 2d ed. (Cambridge, Mass., 1966), p. 81.

[56] *Passing of Traditional Society,* p. 68.

[57] Hyman, "Mass Media," p. 128.

of media exposure, but shall we call this an indicator of political modernization?

The second widely held position about increased participation deals with the existence of opportunities for participation, rather than with the actual levels of participation. Here, we are primarily concerned with the existence of an open system and with public resources for participation. Actual levels of participation reflect the interests and motivations of the population rather than structural barriers to participation or enforced, ritualistic participation.[58]

The final position held by those associating participation with modernization is that participation is an effective indicator of something else that the author values, such as responsibility and practicality,[59] satisfaction with the system,[60] or identification with society.[61] It is assumed by these authors either that participation usually does not reflect the opposite of these values or that activity on such a basis is not genuine participation.

If we look at absolute levels of political participation in the United States, we find a now-familiar pattern of a large number of people voting, but only a few participating in politics beyond the level of voting. Table 9 reports the levels of participation in the 1964 Presidential election, based on the now-standard political participation scale.[62]

Table 9. Levels of Participation in the 1964 Election

Level	N	%
Nonvoter	266	18.4
Voter	700	48.3
Participant in campaign	425	29.3
Club member	59	4.0
Total	1,450	100.0

Source: ICPR, SRC Election Study.

At least at the level of voting, this hypothesis is confirmed. However, our results are more striking if we look at higher levels of participation. The second most widespread means of participation reported was talking to other people and trying to show them why they should vote for one of the candidates or parties. Almost a third of the sample participated in this manner, and their mean score on our measure of empathy was 3.1. The score for the people who did not so participate was 2.2.

As it is, we know that political participation is related to political interest, political involvement, intensity of party identification, the sense of citizen duty (which may be analogous to the sense of national identity), and the

[58] See Millikan and Blackmer, pp. 41-42.
[59] Verba, in Pye and Verba, pp. 557-558.
[60] Almond and Verba, p. 247.
[61] Lane, *Political Life* (New York, 1959), p. 344.
[62] See D. R. Matthews and J. W. Prothro, *Negroes and the New Southern Politics* (New York, 1967). The CR for Table 9 is .986.

sense of political efficacy, all of which are regularly attributed to the politically modern man.[63]

As for the first six hypotheses, this article argues that political participation reflects the remaining three sets of attitudes: that the politically modern man is interested in politics, that he thinks his participation can have some meaningful consequences, and that he trusts the government to be honest, fair, and rational.

> 8. *The politically modern man is concerned with, but not obsessed or excessively worried by, political events.*

Unlike our earlier hypotheses, which simply indicated that the development of a certain attitude toward politics indicated becoming politically modern, this hypothesis involves both upper and lower thresholds. It should be obvious that a person who is simply not interested in politics is not politically modern. The proposition that too much emotional investment in politics also indicates an immature set of political attitudes is as fascinating as it is unclear.

Once again, we encounter a position holding that modern politics is democratic politics. When no one is interested in politics, when politics seems to be irrelevant to the lives men lead, men are unwilling to take part in political activities. The lack of minimal popular involvement in politics enables traditional elites to control the system. At the opposite extreme, if everyone placed great personal importance on every political issue, the only issues that could be resolved without endangering the continued existence of the system would be those on which there was agreement verging on unanimity (and if there is an absence of serious disagreement, we are stretching a point to call these matters "issues"). Thus the only decisions that could be made would be decisions that maintained the status quo. We can now understand the need for both upper and lower thresholds of political involvement if a system is to modernize. However, knowing that thresholds of political involvement must exist does not tell us where these thresholds should be in a modern political system. Certainly, modern systems are capable of working with much higher levels of involvement than premodern systems. It is more significant to know which issues arouse high levels of emotional involvement than it is to know the absolute levels of involvement. Obviously, we are not very worried when citizens of a modern nation are willing to risk their lives to defend a constitutional democracy against a Hitler or a Stalin, and we are concerned when people take to the streets demanding food.

In fact, we seem to find that as nations modernize, levels of political involvement rise, as does the incidence of disagreement about politics. The product of a parochial world in which man and nature are viewed as one in being, tied to fate, is a tradition-bound consensus. This consensus is broken down by geographic mobility and exposure to new ideas through the mass media. The emergence of disagreement marks a major advance on the road to being modern. But what must also emerge is a tolerance for this disagreement. The American political culture has been characterized as one

---

[63] Campbell et al., pp. 96-107.

that "accepts politics and partisanship, and believes them to be good," while a traditional culture believes that "consensus, whether found or made, is the most desirable context for the conduct of politics."[64] If modernization brings about diversity, then it also increases the probability of disagreement based on differing perspectves. As S. N. Eisenstadt argues, ". . . The more differentiated and variegated the structure, the higher the extent and intensity of . . . conflicts; the very process of modernization necessarily creates a high level of conflicts."[65] A central characteristic of being modern is not only to have opinions, but also to be able to cope with conflicts, to develop a procedural consensus so that substantive conflicts can be resolved.

Willingness to develop procedural consensus recognizes that the individual has some stake in the maintenance of a civil society, that he places a positive value on more than one sort of political output. As Lasswell writes, the democratic character is "multi-valued, rather than single-valued, and disposed to share rather than to hoard or monopolize."[66]

The measurement of the intensity of political affect is understandably complex.[67] Necessarily, however, our attention is directed to the intensity of conflict between groups of men who identify with opposing political parties, and a necessary corollary to Hypothesis 8 is:

> 8a. *The politically modern man is partisan, but his partisanship is an "open partisanship."*

The exact meaning of "open partisanship" is, at best, obscure. Almond and Verba describe it as being a form of political life that is open enough for people to feel free to express their political opinions, and in which suppression is not required to provide safety from extreme intensity.[68] In their conception, it is not the modern, participant orientations that lead to open partisanship, but rather the nonparticipant modes that temper conflict. The contradictory characteristics of their data pose a number of problems for their hypothesis.

In all five of the countries they studied, "interparty antagonism appears to be significantly reduced by education,"[69] and the educated are the most participant. Meanwhile, they find that in all five countries increased education is positively related to reporting feeling "angry" during political campaigns.[70]

It might be possible to recast Almond and Verba's notion to mean that political cleavages are not exacerbated by social cleavage. Lucian Pye seems to believe that such is the case in traditional societies. He writes that in these societies, "the indigenous basis for political parties is usually regional,

64 Susanne Hoeber Rudolph, "Consensus and Conflict in Indian Politics," *World Politics*, XIII (April 1961), 385-399, at 385, 389.

65 "Modernization and the Conditions of Sustained Growth," p. 584.

66 "Democratic Character," pp. 497-498.

67 See Kenneth S. Sherrill, "Political Modernization and the United States," unpubl. diss., University of North Carolina, 1967, pp. 129-131, for a discussion of the measurement and distribution of political concern.

68 *Civic Culture*, p. 123.

69 Ibid., p. 132.

70 Ibid., pp. 151-152.

ethnic, or religious groupings, all of which stress considerations not usually emphasized in Western, secular politics."[71]

The most useful formulation of the concept of open partisanship will be one that looks at specifically political disagreement and mistrust, realizing that the possibility of such disagreement may be intensified by regional, religious, ethnic, or racial conflict. On the other hand, political conflict may intersect these other lines of social cleavage, perhaps making one type of cleavage less significant than the other or reducing the intensities of both through the moderating effects of multiple loyalties. Open partisanship is measured through party members' views of members of opposition parties. As patterns of cleavage vary from country to country, open partisanship will be manifested in various ways. But we must question the position that open partisanship can be guaranteed by the existence of a segment of the population which lacks sufficient commitment to politics to be participant. In fact, the presence of such a segment may well indicate that there is not open partisanship and that it is easier to withdraw from politics than to engage in the intense battles of such a system.

Respondents in the 1964 Election Study were asked, "Do you think that there are any important differences between what the Democrats and Republicans stand for? (If yes,) what are they?" Excluding the 49.5 percent of the respondents who could see no difference, we can consider open partisans to be those people who did not in any way indicate that the other party was dangerous or threatening to any group with which the respondent identified. The "closed partisan" was the person who responded that the opposition party was bad for people like himself or dangerous to the well-being of the country as a whole. The closed partisans (who tended to be Democrats) were outnumbered by the open partisans in a three-to-one ratio. The relevant data are in Table 10.

Table 10.   Patterns of Partisanship

Type*	N	%
Apartisan	638	49.5
Closed partisan	158	12.2
Open partisan	493	38.2
Total	1,289	99.9

*Independents excluded.

Our ninth hypothesis states that willingness to participate in politics is a function of the degree to which a person thinks he can participate effectively.

9. *The politically modern man feels that he can influence authoritative decisions.*

This feeling is variously described as a sense of political efficacy or as a

[71] *Politics, Personality, and Nation-building*, p. 17. This position is probably highly inaccurate. See Robert A. Dahl, ed. *Political Oppositions in Western Democracies* (New Haven, 1966), passim.

sense of subjective civic competence. We will refer to it as the sense of political efficacy, and we will take this belief to mean that the individual thinks that his political activity is likely to result in an outcome he desires (which might not have occurred had he not been active). The feeling of political efficacy has both rational and nonrational components. On one hand, it reflects the individual's ego strength. Without regard to any objective circumstances, a person may have enough self-esteem to believe that he can be politically effective, or he may be so insecure as to believe that he cannot be effective. A person may be so caught up in the democratic myth as to believe that all citizens are potentially influential, or he may be so alienated as to believe that he could not influence the system, in spite of both his great personal qualities and the democratic myth. On the other hand, the feeling of political efficacy may reflect a rational evaluation of the degree to which the system is an open one and of the influence that a person may have, given his political resources and alternative strategies. The feeling of political efficacy reflects the individual's image of himself and of the system.[72]

Given what we have said about the strength of the politically modern man's ego and the presumably open nature of modern political systems, we should expect the modern man to feel efficacious. Almond and Verba find that the sense of civic competence increases with education in all five countries they studied, and that the sense of the ability to participate effectively increases the degree to which the system is viewed as being legitimate. Daniel Lerner finds that in all the Middle Eastern nations investigated in his study, the sense of effectiveness increases as the scale moves from the least to the most modern countries.[73]

Utilizing the Survey Research Center's political-efficacy index, we find that more respondents score low than high on the index. With a maximum score of 5, the average score was 2.9. The marginal distribution is in Table 11.

Table 11. Efficacy Scores

Efficacy Scores	N	%.
1 (low)	240	15.3
2	357	22.7
3	427	27.2
4	374	23.8
5 (high)	164	10.4
No answer	9	0.6
Total	1,571	100.0

Source: 1964 SRC Election Study.

While some may contend that the questions were too rigorous to be an accurate measure of efficacy feelings, we cannot help but notice that over two-thirds of the respondents felt that politics and government sometimes

[72] This position is developed at some length in Lane, *Political Life*, pp. 149 ff. See also Key, *Public Opinion*, pp. 192-195.
[73] Lerner, *Passing of Traditional Society*, p. 100.

were too complicated for "a person like me" to understand what's going on. Over a third felt that public officials don't "care much what people like me think." That these people are among the less politically modern Americans is indicated by the fact that those scoring 3 or more on the measure of empathy also scored above the mean on the efficacy index.

10. *The politically modern man is characterized by a general faith in the government.*

This final proposition is in certain ways a logical prerequisite of the sense of political efficacy, but it is also a consequence of all that has gone before. Faith in government does not imply a blind belief that the government will do nothing but the right things, but rather implies that the modern man believes that the government will go about *deciding* what to do in the right way. This distinction underlies the distinction between a society in which a traditional institutional structure is blindly followed and one in which men view the output of the system as a reflection of the open competition of participant citizens who have legitimate disagreements about what the government ought to do. Faith in government is the belief that the government is honest, rational, and fair. Almond and Verba see it as "the sense of trust in the political elite—the belief that they are not alien and extractive forces, but part of the same political community. . . . [This] makes citizens willing to turn power over to them."[74] As a nation modernizes it must go through a crisis of legitimacy, in which a decision is reached about the proper nature and responsibilities of the government. Until this crisis is weathered, the process of modernization is hindered by a peculiar admixture of diffuse distrust of generalized—and distant—other and an uncritical and childlike trust in all forms of authority.[75]

As was noted in our discussion of faith in people, there is a strong relationship between this attitude and the belief that the authorities care about the average man. Similarly, faith in the government could be related to the development of a sense of national identity, to optimism, other-directedness, media exposure, participation, involvement, and efficacy feelings.

We have devised two measures of faith in government from our data. The first is a trichotomized scale,[76] which measures general faith in the electoral process and the power of electoral control over governmental decisions; the second is a weighted index of faith in the holders of public office. Table 12 provides the relevant marginals.

For one reason or another, Americans have more faith in the potency of electoral control than they have in the qualities of public officeholders. Perhaps people who question the competence of public officials (e.g., who think that some of them are "a little crooked," or "waste the taxpayers' money," or cannot always be trusted to do "what is right") believe that the only thing that prevents total chaos is a system of regular elections with political parties. Nevertheless, there is some association between faith in the electoral processes and faith in government. A quarter of the respondents ranking lowest in faith in elections also rank lowest in faith in government; about

Table 12. Faith in Elections and Government

Faith in Elections		
Score	N	%
0 (low)	78	5.4
1	78	5.4
2	130	8.9
3	232	16.0
4	304	21.0
5	275	19.0
6 (high)	351	24.2
Total	1,448	99.9

Faith in Government		
Score	N	%
0 (low)	94	6.5
1	71	4.9
2	137	9.4
3	106	7.3
4	147	10.1
5	224	15.4
6	151	10.4
7	273	18.8
8	151	10.4
9	66	4.6
10 (high)	22	1.5
Don't know/no answer	8	0.6
Total″	1,450	99.9

Source: 1964 SRC Election Study.

twice as many respondents as we would expect by chance who are highest in faith in government are also highest in faith in elections.

There is also some evidence that belief in electoral control is related to our measure of empathy. More than half of the respondents who rank lowest on the faith-in-elections scale cannot name more than one issue that the new government should take care of. Once again, we have some evidence that the political attitudes attributed to modern men are systematically interrelated in a syndrome, or latent ideology, of being modern.

Summary and Conclusions

We have argued that the politically modern man is characterized by a latent ideology or syndrome of orientations toward the political world. These orientations have been described as follows:

1. The politically modern man identifies with the national political community.

1*a*. The politically modern man can distinguish between personal and political relationships.

2. The politically modern man has a strong ego.

3. The politically modern man is opinionated.

4. The politically modern man is empathic.

4*a*. The politically modern man is highly exposed to the mass media. As a consequence:

4*b*. The politically modern man is well informed.

5. The politically modern man is basically optimistic.

5*a*. The politically modern man is characterized by a general faith in people.

6. The politically modern man is concerned with the need to affiliate with others.

7. The politically modern man is participant.

8. The politically modern man is concerned with, but not obsessed or excessively worried by, political events.

8*a*. The politically modern man is partisan, but his partisanship is an "open partisanship."

9. The politically modern man feels as if he can influence authoritative decisions.

10. The politically modern man is characterized by a general faith in the government.

On the basis of some preliminary analysis of data recently gathered in the United States, we have found good reason to accept most of those statements as accurate descriptions of the political orientations of modern men and to believe that these attitudes form a syndrome, or latent ideology, of modernity. We have also found that many Americans have consistently low scores on these measures, and that these low scores are most widespread among Negroes and people whose family income is under $3,000 a year. This raises the possibility that structural changes in American society will be reflected in a different distribution of those attitudes. If the United States ever solves the problems of racism and poverty, the current mixture of orientations toward the political system may undergo fundamental changes. Maintaining the current mixture of orientations, which some scholars uncritically accept, may require maintaining racial oppression and poverty. By focusing on the concept of political modernization, we have suggested that conclusions based on cross-sectional surveys are not necessarily immutable.

The Problem of Identity, Selfhood, and Image in the New Nations

The Situation in Africa

Rupert Emerson*

Thirty-nine states with more to come, and far more than thirty-nine peoples —all in search of an identity in Africa.[1]

The continent in the last seven or eight decades has undergone such revolutionary turns of fortune, almost wholly thrust upon it from outside, that it would be an utter miracle if the processes of change and adaptation were not still in full swing, with little more than question marks available as to the outcome in a variety of important spheres. Even though it is possible to say that much traditional life still goes on in rural Africa and that even in the urban centers more of the old survives than the outsider can be aware of, fundamental transformations are under way throughout the continent. The point of no return has long since been reached. To cite a single statistic: in 1955 the entire continent contained only five independent states, and even at the beginning of 1960 only five more colonies had joined the ranks of the free.

The sharp massive jolt of colonialism was followed at a speed which almost no one expected by the global wave of anticolonialism. Freedom came in some instances to peoples who had barely demonstrated an active interest in independence and in many instances to peoples ill-prepared for it in terms of achieving an equal place in the highly complex contemporary world. The result inevitably has been that for many Africans both their sense of identity and their image of the society in which they live are uncertain and unstable. It may well be that they are endowed, for good or ill, with a wider and more open choice of identities than has in any normal circumstance been available to other peoples; but then the circumstances of Africa are far from normal.

Self-Determination

For the Third World and its partisans, self-determination has become the bright and shining sword of our day, freeing peoples from the bondage of empire. Yet the sword must be recognized as double-sided—sharp and cutting on one side of its blade but blunt and unserviceable on the other.

* This article was prepared for delivery at the Annual Meeting of The American Political Science Association, Washington, D.C., September 1968. I am much indebted to the Center for International Affairs, Harvard University, for research support and aid in its preparation.
[1] This article deals not with all thirty-nine African states but primarily with those that make up independent black Africa.

Two intimately interrelated questions habitually appear as soon as the issue of self-determination is posed: Who constitutes the self to be determined, and by what means and by whom is the determination to be undertaken? The range of possibilities under both headings is large, and the choices made may drastically affect the outcome. At the extremes, self-determination may either encompass the whole of an assumed macro-"national" territory, giving no heed to minorities which may have quite different alignments in mind, or it may operate at the level of small and separable local entities such as villages and urban precincts, always considering that the end result must be a reasonably coherent territory or territories. The means range from the assumption, not left open to question or empirical testing, that the populace of the entire territory wants what its leaders say it wants, to provision for a plebiscite that will pose whatever questions seem in order in the given situation—the fate of the whole territory as a single indivisible block, its division among adjoining territories, or the secession of a piece or pieces of it either as independent states or as parts of neighboring states whose people may be ethnically related.

Whatever political theory may say about a properly democratic society, the trend since World War I has been to eliminate the plebiscite and either to take for granted the "national" allegiance and commitment of all the people involved or to assume that they have been adequately consulted in a general election which, directly or indirectly, raised the question of self-determination as one of the issues confronting the electorate. The disfavor with which plebiscites tend to be viewed derives not only from the disorders and political tensions which they are likely to arouse, but also from the conviction of nationalist leaders that no consultation of the people is necessary or even appropriate. To consult the people is to cast doubt upon the valid claim of the leaders to represent the general will and, in a different vein, to invite dissident groups to spread subversive and probably tribalist doctrines that are inspired, so it may be charged, by the neocolonialists.

In the recent political evolution of Africa in the era of decolonization, a simple formula has been worked out to apply in all but a few special cases, notably those involving trust territories of the United Nations. This formula consists of three basic propositions: (1) that all colonial peoples want to get out from under colonialism as speedily as possible, (2) that each colonial territory as established by the imperial powers constitutes a nation whose aspirations to become an independent state have unchallengeable validity, and (3) that the political independence and territorial integrity of the states thus created must be safeguarded against attack from within or without.

The first of these propositions has a sufficient ring of authenticity to make dubious any serious critical examination, although the footnotes that might appropriately be added are by no means without interest. Certainly it is beyond argument that in the main colonial peoples have repudiated colonialism and welcomed independence; but it is more open to question how deeply the African masses had internalized the demand for *Uhuru* or Freedom Now by the time the colonial regime had withdrawn. The answer is perhaps to be found less in the existence of an all-embracing positive demand for freedom than in the readiness of the masses to follow their own nationalist leadership when it overtly clashed with the expatriate colonial authorities. In a number of the African colonies, and most strikingly in the case of several of the French territories, even this readiness was not effectively tested, since independence was granted far less because of a successful local mobilization of nationalist forces than because of a general withdrawal from colonial overlordship.[2]

Among those Africans who opposed independence or sought to have its coming delayed, three major categories can be distinguished. The category presumably of least consequence was composed of the few who had made a profitable peace with colonialism. Often displayed by the colonial regime as representatives of the people—under British auspices, for example, Africans were named as unofficial members of Legislative Councils—they were almost swept into the discard as the rising nationalist forces took over. The two other categories, far more important both in numbers and in political weight, consisted of tribes or other ethnic groups which felt themselves seriously disadvantaged by the coming of independence at the time and under the circumstances which were proposed. One of these was made up of the smaller peoples, or those less favored politically, such as the Ashanti and the people of the Northern Territories in Ghana and a number of the tribes in Kenya and Congo (Kinshasa). The other, not wholly distinguishable from the first, comprised peoples who found that they had fallen behind in the process of modernization and were therefore less able than their rivals to hold their own in the management of a modern society. Here the most striking example is that of the Northern Region of Nigeria where the Muslim emirates, imbued with a deep sense of their own superiority, found themselves no match for the southerners, particularly the Ibos, who had beaten them to a mastery of the ways and skills of the modern world. Although a different order of issues was involved, we might also mention the determined resistance to an independence in Kenya and Southern Rhodesia that implied the subjection of the African majority to the white settler minority: here continued control by the Colonial Office seemed obviously preferable to domination by the local Europeans.

The second of the three propositions composing the African or, more broadly, the anticolonial formula for self-determination requires no considerable commentary here, both because it is a familiar theme and because several phases of it are considered elsewhere in this article. The heart of the matter is that, whatever the shortcomings of the colonial boundaries that were laid down in the scramble for Africa, and however little the people they enclosed constituted nations in any real sense, if Africans were to seek the political kingdom, the only instruments readily at hand were the existing colonial regimes which could be taken over substantially intact; indeed, in the first round, by far the easiest answer was that Africans should replace Europeans in the top management of the colonies turned

2 John A. Ballard asserts that prior to the forcing of the independence issue by the Mali Federation in December 1959, the four colonies that made up French Equatorial Africa had presented no request for independence, and even after that event their leaders gave no clear indication that independence was either necessary or desirable; but as other countries came to independence, including Cameroun and the Belgian Congo, "the AEF governments were swept along." "Four Equatorial States," in Gwendolen M. Carter, ed. *National Unity and Regionalism in Eight African States* (Ithaca, 1966), p. 240.

into independent states. Here was where political power rested and here was in principle at least the embryonic paraphernalia needed to maintain a functioning modern society. The problems of nation-building, of establishing or reestablishing a variety of regional organizations, and, for some the most significant aim, the achievement of some form of pan-Africanism—all these could wait until the colonial regimes had been replaced by African rule. The right of the people composing these colonial-states to self-determination, interpreted as independence, was the cardinal tenet of the doctrine, wholly beyond dispute.

The third and last of the propositions, attempting to secure agreement that the existing boundaries were somehow sacred and must be preserved by common consent and action, raises points of evident difficulty. The sword of self-determination is sharp when severing the colony from its metropole; however, its reverse side is blunt and unavailable when minorities within the former colony seek either their own independence or union with more desirable brethren across the frontier. Secession from empire is not only praiseworthy but virtually obligatory, since colonialism has been declared intolerable and illegitimate; secession from a newly established state is banned as a breach of the fundamental proprieties on which the African polities rest. To act otherwise, it is held, would be to destroy nations whose identity and right to survive are, for all practical purposes, established by the fact of their existence. The centrality of this third proposition is evidenced by the provisions of the Charter of the Organization of African Unity which, in the Preamble, the Purposes of Article II, and the Principles of Article III, call for the safeguarding, the defense of, and respect for the sovereignty and territorial integrity of its member states.

I have contended elsewhere,[3] and it deserves prompt and emphatic repetition here, that this approach to self-determination in no significant way distinguishes the African position from that universally adopted by states. It is difficult, and indeed wholly impossible, to conceive any set of circumstances under which states would allow their domains to be fragmented by conceding a general principle that any random segment of their population had an operative right to secede, taking with it any territory it regarded as its homeland. In the shaping of the United Nations Charter, it was specified that the principle of self-determination "conformed to the purposes of the Charter only insofar as it implied the right of self-government of peoples and not the right of secession."[4] Under special conditions a limited and quite precisely defined right of self-determination may be temporarily accepted, as in the present drive to rid the world of colonialism; but even here the continued existence of British, Portuguese, and American colonies, presumably still within the law, makes it more than dubious that any operative right to secede from empire has been entered on the international statute books.

The one element that makes the African position somewhat distinctive is that, to a substantially greater degree than in other major parts of the

[3] See my "Self-Determination Revisited in the Era of Decolonization," Occasional Paper No. 9, Center for International Affairs, Harvard University, December 1964.
[4] *Documents of the United Nations Conference on International Organization*, V, (United Nations Information Office, New York, 1945), 296.

world, its states have not yet achieved an adequate degree of integration and inner coherence. The threat of potential breakup on ethnic lines that would signal a resurgence of tribalism and irrevocably shatter the existing scheme of things is a more real and present danger than is normally the case elsewhere. The issue was succinctly put by President Nyerere of Tanzania in remarking that, despite differences in language, size, and resources, the founding conference of the OAU in 1963 could still agree that "our boundaries are so absurd that they must be regarded as sacrosanct."[5] Boundaries in other continents may be less absurd, but they are no less guarded against the dangers of secession under cover of the symbols of self-determination.

As I have suggested earlier, the only outstanding breaches of the principle that each colony should "nationally" self-determine itself into independent statehood occurred, for reasons that are at least partly obscure, in the case of UN trust territories. Thus British Togoland joined Ghana; the Northern Cameroons joined Northern Nigeria, while the remainder of the British and French Cameroons joined to form the federal state of Cameroun; Rwanda and Burundi, to the dismay of some anticolonialists in the UN, separated from each other to form two independent states; British Somaliland and the trust territory of Somalia joined to form the Somali Republic; and, at a slightly later stage. Zanzibar joined the ex-trust territory of Tanganyika to form Tanzania. In this latter case particularly, the connection with the UN appears quite fortuitous; but the entire array (which might also include the UN decision that Eritrea should join Ethiopia) raises the question of whether, had the UN played a greater role in Africa's decolonization, the outcome might have produced more changes in the political map of the continent than actually took place.

The key issues involved in the translation of the doctrine of self-determination into African political reality find no more dramatic illustration than the tragic decline of Nigeria into, first, political turmoil and military coups, followed by large-scale bloodshed and, finally, a disastrous civil war. It is typical of the structure of the African state system that this most populous African country owes its existence to decisions that were essentially arbitrary. The British authorities might equally have followed quite different courses with very different results. If, for example, they had either drawn Nigeria into much closer association with their other West African holdings or had divided it into three or eight or a dozen separate colonies—as the French did with the considerably smaller populations of West and Equatorial Africa—neither policy would have seemed unusual or in any way outrageous. Indeed, some critics contend that the root cause of Nigeria's troubles today was the misguided British effort to combine markedly disparate peoples within the same political framework; others take the reverse position that Britain encouraged Nigeria's disintegration both by following divergent policies in the North and in the South and by introducing a federal rather than a unitary system of government.

In its later phases, the political evolution of colonial Nigeria centered on the development of self-government in each of the three Regions, with the

---

[5] *The Dag Hammarskjold Memorial Lecture,* January 23, 1964, p. 7.

North lagging behind the East and West, and in 1960 came the grant of independence to the country as a whole. In 1966 the military took over in two successive coups, each of which had strong tribal-political implications. Following the slaughter of thousands of Ibos in the North, the flight of perhaps two million more, and lengthy negotiations that brought no mutually acceptable solution, the Eastern Region, under Ibo leadership, on May 30, 1967, seceded from Nigeria to become the independent state of Biafra and thereby opened the door to civil war.

Whatever one's judgment as to the rights and wrongs of the case and the assignment of responsibility for the breach, one matter which is indisputably clear is that the Ibos, who unquestionably constitute a "people," have by force of arms been denied the right of self-determination which they claimed for themselves.[6] The ability of the OAU to mediate the conflict and help bring it to an end was impaired by its commitment to the territorial status quo. The dragging on of the war and the growing loss of life finally impelled Tanzania and, shortly thereafter, three other African states to break the ban on Biafra by extending recognition to it. In an eloquent statement explaining this action, Nyerere reasserted his country's devotion to African unity but insisted that such unity must rest on freely given consent: if the Zanzibaris were to repudiate their union with Tanganyika, that union would then cease to exist and he could not advocate that the dissidents be bombed into submission. The Biafrans, he held, claimed the right to govern themselves when they were unable to achieve a satisfactory agreement ensuring their personal security:

> The Biafrans are not claiming the right to govern anyone else. They have not said that they must govern the Federation as the only way of protecting themselves. They have simply withdrawn their consent to the system under which they used to be governed.
>
> Biafra is not now operating under the control of a democratic government any more than Nigeria is. But the mass support for the establishment and defense of Biafra is obvious. This is not a case of a few leaders declaring secession for their own glory. . . .
>
> It seemed to us that by refusing to recognize the existence of Biafra we were tacitly supporting a war against the people of Eastern Nigeria—and a war conducted in the name of unity. We could not continue doing this any longer.[7]

Leaving aside the basic political issue raised by Nyerere, a lesser but by no means insignificant point concerns his comment that the Biafrans are not claiming the right to govern anyone else. Here again is one of the central problems of self-determination: Who constitutes the self? It might equally be said that the Nigerians are not claiming to govern anyone but Nigerians; yet who are the Nigerians for this purpose? If they are all the inhabitants of the country, making up a single nation, then Biafrans have

---

[6] After a visit to Biafra, Conor Cruise O'Brien reported in *The Observer* (London) of October 8, 1967: "It is possible that the state of Biafra may be crushed out of existence by the numerically superior and better-armed Federal troops, with their limitless access to outside support . . . What is certain, however, is that a nation has been born and will in some form endure." For an examination of a number of the issues raised by the Nigerian conflict, see S. K. Panter-Brick, "The Right to Self-Determination: Its Application to Nigeria," *International Affairs*, XLIV (April 1968), 254-266.

[7] *The Los Angeles Times*, May 5, 1968.

no right to be heard as Biafrans. Precisely the same proposition applies to Biafra itself, where there are very substantial minority tribes (some five million non-Ibos as against seven million Ibos) whose allegiance to the dominant Ibos certainly cannot be taken for granted—and who, incidentally, inhabit the area where the most valuable oil resources have been found. If the whole former Eastern Region, restyled Biafra by the Ibo secessionists, is the proper unit for self-determination, then the minorities may properly be subordinated to the majority and swept along in its wake. If, on the other hand, these minorities are assumed to constitute "peoples," are their claims to be heard less valid than those of the Ibos? The hope of the minorities for consideration as separate communities was markedly enhanced by the Federal decree of May 27, 1967, that divided the Eastern Region into three states, one for the Ibos and two for the other peoples of the Region[8]—a decree that led immediately to Biafra's declaration of independence. The Federal government asserts that it "has a moral responsibility to the 5,000,000 non-Ibo speaking minorities in the Rivers State and the Calabar-Ogoja State whose areas cannot be handed back to the secessionist leaders. These minorities deserve a place of their own under the Nigerian sun."[9]

Should it be established that minority Efiks, Ibibios, Ijaws, and others have withdrawn (or perhaps never gave) their consent to being part of an Ibo-ruled Biafra, are they then also entitled to secede on the basis of Nyerere's admirable principle of consent freely given, which he applied to Biafra as a single entity? Need it be added that undoubtedly the two new states, subtracted from Biafra in the interest of these minorities, also contain minorities who would be pleased to have autonomous or even independent jurisdiction over their own affairs? It is clear that at some point even the most ardent enthusiast for a permanent and continuing right of self-determination must call a halt to the process of fragmentation.

This general moral, so familiar to African statesmen, was pointed out by Chief Enahoro in his opening address, on behalf of the Federal authorities, to the abortive peace talks held at Kampala in May 1968: "Many African countries which today appear to condone or rejoice at the misfortune of Nigerians may tomorrow find themselves fighting their fellow countrymen and the forces of secession in their midst."[10]

Tribe, State, and African Unity

The existing African states, usually adopting intact the colonially delimited territories and their governmental structures, have been the beneficiaries of self-determination. Moreover, despite some regional and pan-African activity, these states remain the primary locus of political power. The recognition that these states are fragile and rest upon precarious foundations has led to the insistence on preserving them within their inherited boundaries. The result is much the same whether the defense of the status quo is motivated by the desire of the governing elite to cling to power, by

[8] At the same time, the previously dominant Northern Region was divided into six states, making a total of twelve for the whole of Nigeria.

[9] See the two-page advertisement of the Federal government in *The New York Times*, July 8, 1968.

[10] *The New York Times*, July 8, 1968.

the fear that a retrogressive tribalism might take over, or by a more general awareness that each state must have time to consolidate itself and to start on the work of development if the stability of the whole African political system is to be preserved. As President Sylvanus Olympio of Togo put it in referring both to pan-Africanism and to tribalist fragmentation: "In their struggle against the colonial powers, the new African states, arbitrary and unrealistic as their original boundaries may have been, managed at last to mobilize the will of their citizens toward the attainment of national independence. Achieved at great sacrifice, such a reward is not to be cast away lightly; nor should the national will, once unified, be diluted by the formation of nebulous political units."[11]

The assumption is made here that the will of the citizens has been mobilized, but the actual extent of such mobilization remains dubious. To secure an effective and dependable measurement of citizen mobilization is far from easy, and the issue is further complicated by variations in the degree and intensity of national feeling in different situations. To draw upon the most obvious example, it may be possible to count upon the bulk of a colonial population to back its nationalist leaders in the demand for an end to alien rule; but once independence has been achieved the outward show of national unity may give way to internal conflict among the "primordial communities" or other groupings. The two key historical elements are that Africa's natural condition was one of marked fragmentation along tribal lines and that the time available to achieve national integration was exceedingly brief.

On the score of fragmentation, the African inclination is to blame the present state of affairs on the Europeans and to accuse the colonialists of employing the old divide-and-rule principle. The standard term used, with all its pejorative implications, is "balkanization," but Karl W. Deutsch has challenged this usage and proposed instead the term "scandinavianization," which casts a quite different light on the matter. The original fault (if it be a fault and not some form of virtue) surely lies with the Africans, whose precolonial social-political structure was built upon any number of tribes, peoples, and languages. One writer has remarked that, although African aspirations are to the broader unities of nationalism and pan-Africanism, "the instincts of Africa are to fissiparity,"[12] and it is arguable that this trend has continued in the postindependence period, at least in regard to regional or other broader groupings. Frequent threats of the breakup of the existing order, as in the cases of Katanga, Biafra, and the southern Sudan, or the apparently less significant gesture of Buganda toward independence, underscore the divisive tendencies. The story is far too complicated to summarize in a few words, but briefly it may be suggested that, however arbitrarily the colonial boundary lines were drawn in the days of the Scramble, they

---

[11] "African Problems and the Cold War," *Foreign Affairs*, XL (October, 1961), 51. As one of a number of speakers on the same theme at the OAU founding conference in Addis Ababa in 1963, President Modibo Keita of Mali held that those who ardently desire African unity must take Africa as it is: "African unity demands of each one of us complete respect for the legacy that we have received from the colonial system, that is to say: maintenance of the present frontiers of our respective states." *Proceedings of the Summit Conference of Independent African States*, I (Addis Ababa, May 1963), Sec. 2.

[12] John Day, "Democracy in Africa," *Parliamentary Affairs*, XVII (Spring 1964), 168.

probably produced larger political entities than the Africans would have achieved on their own. That these entities often cut across tribal lines was a grave misfortune which might often have been avoided, but in some instances, as in West Africa, the tribal layering from the coast inland made exceedingly difficult any sensible arrangement based on the maintenance of tribal solidarity among disparate peoples. For the period of coming independence, despite the charge that the colonial powers deliberately left discord behind them, the record of the British in Africa appears better than that of their African successors who in West, East, and Central Africa have broken down rather than consolidated regional bonds established under British rule. Belgians certainly played dangerous games with Katanga, but the country most vulnerable to the accusation of balkanization is France which, depending on the view of the observer, either condoned or manipulated the disintegration of the federations of West and Equatorial Africa.[13] That the breaking up of the federations had some strong African supporters— notably Houphouet-Boigny of the Ivory Coast—is clear, but it was also vigorously opposed by many Africans. The French claim that political vitality existed not in the federations but in their component colonial-state units; and it is certainly not inconceivable that an effort to perpetuate the federation might have led to bloody upheavals on the Nigerian model.

The general African charges of balkanization against the colonial powers must derive from some conception of a wider African unity, but the form such unity might take, as well as its political feasibility, remain obscure and highly controversial, though perhaps somewhat less so than when Nkrumah was the most vocal champion of pan-Africanism.

At all events, Africa is left with its present state system. It is generally acknowledged, however, that the achievement of a broadly shared sense of national identity within each of the states is still largely a matter of the future. The bringing together of peoples within a common political framework was frequently arbitrary, and the period during which a sense of national unity might be acquired was shortlived. It obviously could not reach further back than the beginning of the colonial experience, and ordinarily it was considerably shorter, because a period even of decades was often required before the colonial administration could consolidate diverse parts and peoples of the entire colonial territory. In this regard, too, Nigeria serves as a classic example because of the continued separation of the North and the South and the distinctive treatment of the northern Muslim emirates, the effects of which will persist into some remote future. Even if a generally exaggerated figure of eighty years were assigned to the formative colonial period, it would still shrink into insignificance when compared with the centuries that were presumably necessary for the shaping of the European and Asian peoples.

Perhaps the most that can be said is that the colonial experience created the conditions precedent to the emergence of nations. To some degree the nationalist movements began the more positive task of welding ethnic diversity into national unity. Immanuel Wallerstein, acknowledging that most

---

[13] For an account which generally exonerates the French from having acted with evil intent, see James Carl Akins, "French Policy in Afrique Noire, 1955-1960" (unpub. Ph.D. diss., Harvard University, 1966).

African nations do not have long histories as nationalities, asserts that "their nationhood has been created in the crucible of a revolutionary struggle against a colonial power. The unity of the nation was forged in the fight against the external enemy."[14] In this contention there is undoubtedly much truth, but we must also remember that in a good many instances the revolutionary struggle was either limited or even nonexistent: independence was in most cases granted by agreement and was the product less of irresistible nationalist movements than of contemporary events elsewhere, such as the independence of India and other Asian colonies and the impact of the Algerian war, which France and other countries had no desire to repeat. Although the Portuguese were prepared to hold out, denying that their African territories constituted colonies, the British, French, and Belgians accepted the inevitability of the era of decolonization. Nationalist parties, movements, and risings played a role in stimulating a sense of national identity, but in many countries their lifespan was brief and their penetration shallow.

The elements that enter into the shaping and spread of national identity are many, and their bearing on particular countries varies greatly, but the African countries are generally devoid of most of them, although a few nations appear to be consolidating around a dominant or central tribe in a country, as in the case of the Wolof in Senegal or the Fang in Gabon. Where the nation-in-making is composed of discrete and diverse peoples, no common tradition or history prior to the colonial period is possible, and an identity or similarity of cultures is to be sought more in the general African picture than in the local colonial-national setting. Perhaps the most damaging lack of all, however, although Africa is by no means unique in this respect, is the absence of a national language as a key element in communication, identity, and cultural expression. Most African countries have found no other workable solution to the problem posed by their many languages than the adoption of either English or French as the official lingua franca. The hardships, costs, and limitations of this expedient are obvious.

If independence puts an end to the drive to secure national unity against colonialism (although neocolonialism may be conjured up as the new enemy), other nation-building forces are brought into play. Perhaps the most significant force is simply that people continue to live together within the same frontiers and are subject to the same influences, open to the same communication networks, and, at least in some measure, becoming aware of a common destiny. In contrast to the colonial era, all the forces that government and party can muster may now be brought to bear on the problem of nation-building, including the shaping of the educational system to that end. With only rare exceptions Africans look to socialism and planned development, which further emphasize the role of the state as the only available instrument to implement national goals. As Ali A. Mazrui has pointed out, while socialism is assumed to be universalistic in outlook, it "can be inherently *parochial* when it is concerned with national planning. For in the concept of planning the preoccupation of socialism is with the

---

[14] *Africa: The Politics of Independence* (New York, 1961), p. 85.

domestic needs of individual countries and with the control of domestic factors of production."[15]

Nationalist movements rely very heavily on men and women to whom a Western style of education and new types of employment and occupation have opened new horizons. With the coming of independence, the main thrust of development has been within each of the African states, and the expansion and quickening of the processes of modernization have multiplied the number of those who share in the sense of national identity and have achieved some measure of distance from their traditional societies. To a greater degree than was expected, however, the effect of independence and modernization in some cases has not been mobilization into the national community but, rather, a strengthening of the more parochial tribal affiliation. The transition to self-government and independence may well stir up tribal rivalries and animosities when it involves the replacement of the more or less neutral rule of an alien colonial power by the rule of one tribe or coalition of tribes over others—the kind of situation which in India drove the Muslim League to demand independence from Hindu rule. The other major cause of reversion to the tribal attachment is the existence of a substantial differentiation on a tribal basis in the access to means of modernization or in the readiness to make effective use of means that are already available. Thus Crawford Young reports: "The rise of modern nationalism in both Congo and Uganda has been accompanied by an intensified ethnic self-awareness. Imbalances in access to or response toward modernity created fears in the terminal colonial period that groups heavily represented in modern roles would use their political power to consolidate and render permanent their social hegemony."[16]

Development is by no means necessarily a nation-wide phenomenon; indeed, more likely than not it will have a markedly differential impact in different areas and hence on different population groups. Either by inadvertence, deliberate discrimination, or planned economic calculation, one tribe may be much favored over others. Thus it finds good reason to tighten its ranks in order to safeguard its gains while those less favored seek to press their own cause by organizing their community for concerted self-defense. Inevitably, the position of the Ibos in Nigeria and their relationships to the other major peoples of the country are cited as a graphic illustration of these issues.[17] Economic development and modernization cannot be counted on to produce national integration where their impact on the ethnic groups composing the society is significantly differentiated.

In an illuminating article that deals with many of the themes in this arti-

[15] *On Heroes and Uhuru-Worship* (London, 1967), p. 70.

[16] "Congo and Uganda: A Comparative Assessment," *Cahiers économiques et sociaux*, V (October 1967), 381.

"Almost everywhere, the transfer of power from a colonial regime to a locally based regime has intensified the parochial or tribal basis of already existing groups, or has activated latent parochialisms and led to the formation and proliferation of new communalistic political associations." James S. Coleman and Carl G. Rosberg, Jr. *Political Parties and National Integration in Tropical Africa* (Berkeley and Los Angeles, 1964), p. 689.

[17] See Paul Amber, "Modernization and Political Disintegration: Nigeria and the Ibos," *Journal of Modern African Studies*, V, No. 2 (1967), 68-169.

cle, Philip D. Curtin has rightly pointed out that, unless definitions are too tightly drawn, a number of "primordial communities" in Africa must be regarded as nations, since "each had territory, sense of nationality, language, a state up to the recent past, and a consciousness of shared historical experience."[18]

For the most part, however, these precolonial nations have not laid claim to separate statehood in the contemporary world but have, with varying degrees of tension and protest, taken their place in the colonially-determined state-nations that constitute the present political map of Africa. It has cogently been argued that these states are territorial units, each with its own governmental and administrative structure. As the African leaders see it, tribalism is a threat because it introduces a new principle of legitimacy based on precisely the factors cited by Professor Curtin. If legitimacy were accorded to nations on the basis of shared language, culture, and history, the foundations of the present states would be shattered.[19] Although a general return to the tribal divisions on which the colonial boundaries were superimposed is presumably highly unlikely, and despite the eruption of an occasional Biafra, Katanga, or South Sudan, this estimate of future trends should not obscure the fact that for many Africans, tribal membership has a vitality that is missing from their citizenship in a state whose national identity has not yet effectively penetrated to them. For almost any African state in the foreseeable future, the nation will pluralistically embrace the earlier communities that survive within it.

The established ethnic groups and the present states are two of the lines that bound the triangle of African identity. The third line, representing the sense of "Africanness" and African unity, is the most difficult to trace with clarity and precision—no doubt for the simple reason that it is itself neither clear nor precise. In recent years it has been repeatedly established that the concept of Africa as a single entity is not indigenous to Africa[20] but is the product in various fashions of contact with the outside world. One grassroots version of this view is the assertion by Julius Nyerere that "Africans, all over the continent, without a word being spoken from one individual to another or from one African country to another, looked at the European, looked at one another, and knew that in relation to the European they were one."[21]

The slave trade carried off Africans who, as they came to look back on their place of origin, saw an entire continent inhabited by people of their race and who, as they looked at their masters in the new world, found themselves all black in a white society. In the period of the Scramble, it was Africans indiscriminately who were subordinated to colonial rule, and their reactions to colonialism were in great part couched in terms of Africa as a

---

[18] "Nationalism in Africa, 1945-1965," *The Review of Politics*, XXVIII (April 1966), 145. Among others, Professor Curtin lists Ashanti, Mossi, Dahomey, Buganda, Ankole, Bunyoro, Burundi, Rwanda, Bakongo, Barotse, Lunda, Zulu, Sotho, and Swazi nations.

[19] See Panter-Brick, "The Right to Self-Determination," 261.

[20] "The word Africa does not figure in any early Bantu vocabulary; it is perhaps the most important article of export which Europe ever sent south of the Sahara." L. H. Gann and Peter Duignan, *Burden of Empire* (New York, 1966), p. 88.

[21] Cited in Victor C. Ferkiss, *Africa's Search for Identity* (New York, 1966), p. 130. For a skeptical and entertaining examination of questions of African identity, see Ali A. Mazrui, *Towards a Pax Africana* (London, 1967), esp. Chs. 1-3.

whole. In its language, and in some measure in its outlook, African nationalism has been *African;* it has not been Nigerian or Kenyan or Senegalese.
As it was *Africans* and not Nyasalanders or Sierra Leonians who were barred
from clubs and hotels, so it was *Africans* who in due course were admitted
to the civil service and granted increasing representation in the colonial
legislative bodies. In brief, the essence of the confrontation was a racial one:
the black man demanded an end to white superiority and domination, even
though the struggle for recognition and the take-over of power in each instance had to be directed against the particular colonial regime involved. At
least in the first phase of independence, and sometimes on beyond it, the
pressure was to secure a speedy *Africanization* of the public services. In a
different vein, a key issue in East Africa is the question of the treatment of
African, as contrasted with Asian, Tanzanians or Kenyans. Thomas Hodgkin
has commented that the idea of *African* liberation preceded the idea of national liberation;[22] and it remains a distinctive feature of the African political scene that, to a greater extent than in any other major region of the
world, it has been reiterated constantly that no part of Africa can feel itself
wholly free if any part of the continent remains under white domination.
In Asia, aside from general commonplaces of anticolonialism and specific
calculations of political interest, nothing indicated any deep-running concern on the part of any of the colonial or recently freed people about the
continued colonial status of other Asians. The sense of a common African
identity has led to a different conclusion in Africa, with the result that a
constant preoccupation of the OAU and many of its member states has been
the liberation of the black peoples in white-dominated southern Africa. As
a distinguished Ghanaian has put it: "The fact that African nationalism is,
in the first place, a demand for racial equality is its most conspicuous attribute. Africans demand acceptance as equals in the human family. This has
political dimensions, because colonialism in Africa has been marked by the
domination of Africans by Europeans. So the demand for equality finds expression in the demand for the emancipation of all Africa from colonial
rule."[23] This is a cause which none can repudiate and to which many are
passionately devoted, even though the means of action remain scanty and
some of its professed adherents are stouter in words than in fulfillment.

The African problem of identity is a curious one which leaves the states,
despite their political centrality, with what appear to be very meagre resources for their challenging task of nation-building. On one side, with the
exception of pressures brought directly by the states themselves, the forces
that work toward unity in Africa at higher than the tribal level tend to be
Africa-wide in bearing and do not coincide with the states and their nations-
in-making. The principal elements involved here are the obvious ones which
have already been mentioned: race and color; the common humiliation embodied in the white assumption that blacks are primitive and, if not inherently backward, at least retarded; slavery and the slave trade; and the almost complete subjection of the continent to white colonial rule. On the
other side, at the lower level of the "primordial communities," the usual

[22] "The Idea of Freedom in African National Movements," in David Bidney, ed.
The Concept of Freedom in Anthropology (New York, 1963), pp. 183-184.
[23] Kofi A. Busia, *The Challenge of Africa* (London, 1962), p. 139.

nation-building elements of language, culture, religion, tradition, and history are all associated with ethnic groupings that are usually substantially smaller than the states and only rarely and accidentally coincident with them.

When all this has been said, however, the likelihood remains that it is the states which will consolidate their position as the key political actors in Africa, subject to relatively minor adjustments of frontiers and alignments. While it is impossible that the colonially-imposed pattern of states will remain wholly intact, it appears to be a reasonable presumption at the moment —given the folly of undertaking predictions in the midst of Africa's uncertainties—that neither a return to tribalism nor a swing to full-bodied pan-Africanism on the Nkrumah model presently seems likely to occur. Accepting the probability that an occasional defection from the existing state structure may be expected (Nigeria and the Congo?) and that amalgamations, or at least strong regional unions, similarly may appear (among some of the French-speaking states and in East Africa?), the political framework of the continent has acquired a considerable measure of fixity.

If, as I have suggested earlier, it is correct to assume that the bulk of Africans have yet to achieve any positive identification with the states to which they belong, it seems also true that they are relatively abstinent in political action, modest in their political demands, and largely absorbed in their parochial concerns.

The resources available to the states for nation-building *are* slight in many respects, and yet, if they are given time for the gradual mobilization of their citizens, they have impressive potentialities for shaping the sense of identity of their people. If they do not set off in possession of the elements ordinarily associated with a sense of national identity, they do work with a spreading lingua franca which can be propagated through a national school system and by other means. By their continued existence they have an opportunity to create a common history and tradition, to establish the national heroes and symbols, and to start on the road toward a common culture. The greater the degree of national planning, economic and social development, and social welfare activity, the more each local community and individual is likely to be integrated into the larger society. Political participation has for all practical purposes been restricted in a number of African states to response to the propaganda of a plebiscitary one-party system, but even this sort of activity has its integrative value. Where the military have taken over, participation is at a still lower level, if it exists at all.

As things now stand, it seems improbable that either the rural or the urban rank and file will rise up to reassert their tribal identity in any but isolated and sporadic instances, and neither the presently established civilian leadership nor the military is prone to turn in that direction. As for pan-African unity, it is presumably among the elite or some segments thereof that it has its strongest hold, and it has been persuasively argued that the most ardent advocates of unity on a continental basis are the radical "revolutionary core" of the postindependence leadership.[24] For the most part, however, African political leaders are too much preoccupied with the man-

[24] See Immanuel Wallerstein, *Africa: The Politics of Unity* (New York, 1967).

agement of the present states and too much the beneficiaries of the existing order, enjoying the legitimate and illegitimate perquisites of office, to be attracted to anything beyond consultative and cooperative arrangements between the African states. However illusory the substance of sovereignty may be, it is not lightly to be sacrificed even in so desirable a cause as pan-Africanism. Another significant feature is the high degree of representation now accorded each African state in the United Nations and other international agencies, which both gives an opportunity to individual African political figures to shine on the international stage and enables Africa, with its extraordinary voting strength, to make a far more spectacular showing than either its population or its political, economic, or military weight would otherwise allow.

Functional organizations on a regional basis are more likely to flourish than either regional or pan-African organizations that seek to trespass significantly on state sovereignty. No regional organization, however, is likely to capture the allegiance of the individuals who at one remove compose it. The only exception which should perhaps be noted is that some of the francophone states, with a memory of the two French African federations behind them and an awareness of their own grievous shortcomings, might perhaps accept merger in a new federation, although since 1960, when most of them were granted independence, no move nearly so far-reaching as this has been undertaken. Pan-African unity, on the other hand, has an emotional pull that may yet prove of great consequence. It is wholly possible that the strongest driving force for a limitation on state sovereignty and the building up of allegiance to pan-Africanism would be the felt need for common action against the white rulers of southern Africa.

The African Image

No one image of Africa, we may be sure, can possibly embrace all the divergent images which must emerge from differences in geographical setting, life experience, education, occupation, and all the other elements that distinguish one man, one community, or one class from another. Here I attempt only to sketch briefly one image which I believe represents much of contemporary Africa's view of itself, although in any rounded picture this image must be corrected and challenged by many others. It is a highly optimistic and favorable image, as becomes peoples setting out on independent paths after the bitter cruelties and indignities they have suffered in recent centuries.

To lay firm foundations for this image it has been necessary to recompose and reevaluate African history by getting away both from the widely prevalent earlier conception that Africa, a continent of primitive peoples, had no precolonial history worth recording and from a history of the colonial era that inevitably portrayed Africans as inferior to their white rulers. As might be expected, the swing of the pendulum has occasionally gone too far in presenting the African past as something of a golden age: for African countries, like others throughout the world, there is a nationalist temptation to look back to a past that in fact never existed in the kind of terms used about it. If the major aim is to demonstrate that Africans have a history no less worthy and splendid than that of other peoples, a secondary aim has been to read back into this past, as justification for present and future hopes, attributes which are currently regarded as virtues. I have in mind particularly democracy and the kind of "communitarian" society which lends itself to the fruitful development of one or another variant of African socialism. Finding democracy wherever people agree to stick together, Ndabaningi Sithole denied that it was introduced to Africa by the Europeans and, instead, found it to be "as native as the African native himself."[25] In combination, democracy and socialism as the Africans put them forward produce a society which might perhaps be seen as the extended family writ large: classless, collectivist rather than individualist, solicitous of the interests and well-being of all its members, and listening patiently to all as decisions are gradually worked out by common consent.

To these attributes may be added one or two others. The first, as has already been seen in a different context, is that the African society is suffused with a sense of the common African identity, finding its institutional expression in some form of pan-Africanism. As a variant of this, susceptible of turning in quite different directions, is the *négritude* of Senghor and others in the French-speaking African world. Here at least the potentiality of some brand of racism begins to intrude itself—a potentiality that is ordinarily vigorously denied by African spokesmen but that in fact cannot be ignored in the African scene. The blackness of Africa has come to be accepted as an eminent good; but, if so, where do the yellows and browns and whites fit in?

Saving the racist element that crept in at the last moment, this is on the whole an idyllic African image. Happily, it is not my task to square it with an Africa in which one-party authoritarian regimes have taken over, sometimes to be elbowed aside by military coups; in which preventive detention or similar devices have put many outside both the protection of the law and the service of their communities; in which development lags sorely behind the all too evident needs; and in which something on the order of a million refugees testify to the disaffections, feuds, and hostilities which rend the African societies. The image which I have suggested represents much that is admirable and forward-looking in Africa; but image and reality also have sharp divergences that cannot be ignored.

[25] *African Nationalism* (Capetown, 1959), p. 98.

POLITICS AND THE SOCIAL ORDER

Introduction

In analyzing Third World States, it is a basic and obvious point that the pattern of politics and the structure and functioning of society are deeply, if not extricably interwoven. Not surprisingly, the most widely discussed factor of the social order with broad implications for Third World politics is the existence of cultural pluralism, the severe fragmentation of a polity along subnational "identity" lines.

While the fragmentation issue (examined in the preceding section) is a recurrent one throughout this volume and is of unquestionable importance, it is not the only aspect of the interconnection of politics and the social order which need be explored. In short, there remain additional dimensions of the behavioral linkage between politics and the social order in Third World countries which draw our attention.

In part, this linkage can be investigated through the perspective of "political culture." This perspective, closely connected to the "behavioral persuasion" in political science, is based on the observation that "every political system is embedded in a particular pattern of orientation to political actions."[1] A political culture, therefore:

> [I]s the set of attitudes, beliefs, and sentiments which give order and meaning to a political process and which provide the underlying assumptions and rules that govern behavior in the political system . . . . [It is] the manifestation in aggregate form of the psychological and subjective dimension of politics.[2]

Although the political culture approach implies that the realm of the political is to some degree distinguishable from the general culture,[3] it also evokes a series of relationships which move from the psychological basis of a social order to the spillover of that order into the political arena. It is several aspects of this serial relationship, rather than the general and elusive concept of political culture, that provide the focal points for this section.

Our first area of inquiry revolves around the question of clientelism; a question of great consequence for the predominately rural societies of the Third World. Lemarchand and Legg, in the opening article of this section, speak of political clientelism as a "personalized, affective, and reciprocal relationship between actors, or sets of actors, commanding unequal resources and involving mutually beneficial transactions that have political ramifications beyond the immediate sphere of dyadic relationships." Lemarchand and Legg regard clientelism "as a generic trait" of political entities and their typology of client-tage systems, which includes the normative orientations of actors as well as the penetration and scope of political structures, indicates the interactions existent among individual orientations, the ordering of society, and the pattern of politics within a particular reference frame.

Arguing that the study of clientage (or patron-client) relations has tended to ignore political implications, Lemarchand and Legg attempt to articulate the role of clientelism within the context of "political development" and the concern with modernization, political integration, and system equilibrium. Of particular importance, from our perspective, is Lemarchand and Legg's analysis of the impact of clientelism in "patrimonial-modernizing regimes" (viz., the countries of the Third World), including their view that the very successes of a clientelist model in promoting economic and social developments ultimately leads to the disintegration of that model. And though they conclude on a note of pessimism for the future of clientelism in many developing situations Lemarchand and Legg leave open the possibility that clientelism can "contribute to breakthroughs in political modernization . . . by ushering in a breakdown of the preexistent system."

The significance of clientelist politics and micro-level perspectives in societies that are primarily agrarian is also touched upon by the second essay in this section. In "Participation and Efficacy: Aspects of Peasant Involvement in Political Mobilization," Mathiason and Powell explore "one face of the individual consequences of political change" through the use of attitudinal survey data. This study of the peasantry[4] in Colombia and Venezuela focuses on the question "to what extent does participation affect an individual orientation to government?" In other words, the authors ask if *participation* (defined by Huntington and Nelson as "activity by private citizens designed to influence governmental decision-making"[5]) by *peasants* has, as one of its consequences, the development of a sense of national *political efficacy* which "defines an individual's orientation to institutions in the political process."

The analysis of this question by Mathiason and Powell and their conclusions contain a number of valuable insights which range from the recognition of type and subtype distinctions in the nature of efficacy, to the "individual attitudinal consequences of being caught up in a political revolution" and the relationship of ecological/economic factors to politically relevant attitudes. Even without commenting on all of these issues, we can see that Mathiason and Powell's article offers a perceptive exploration of the complex connections existent between the social order as an action system and politics.

At this juncture, two points emerge for our consideration, the first of which is related to our use of the phrase "action system".[6] Leaving aside the numerous Parsonian intricacies of this idea, the action construct implies "the structures and processes by which human beings form meaningful *intentions* and, more or less successfully, *implement* them in concrete situations."[7] Thus the social order as a term is used to signify the broad field of patterned interactions aggregated within the societal unit of the state. In this sense, we can view the "multivariate relationship"[8] existing between the social order and the analytically distinguishable realm of politics in the following way: *SOCIAL ORDER*/ SO_1 (including factors such as personality, values, resources, and social and ecological structure)$\rightarrow$*POLITICS*/P_1 (embracing the structures and processes of decision-making, policy-making, and resource and value distribution)$\rightarrow$*SOCIAL ORDER*/SO_2 (the effects of $SO_1 \longleftrightarrow P_1$) . . .

This leads us to our second point, which is that the SOPSO frame of reference involves a dual directionality in the flow of influence between the social order (including its personality dimension) and politics. While the pattern of politics is affected by the overall social order, that pattern also establishes its own effects on the ordering of society.

Both of the articles discussed provide illustrations of this "multivariate relationship." Lemarchand and Legg, for example, note that "[t]he forms which [clientelism] takes depend to a considerable extent on the structure of the society and on the political system in which it operates"; and Mathiason and Powell point out that "[a]n explanation must be sought for the process by which a person develops an orientation such as efficacy, and of the system of behaviors which maintains, changes, or otherwise influences his belief in his ability to influence his government."

Returning to our earlier consideration of political culture, we can see that while a political culture has importance for political actions, it is no less true that political actions themselves have an impact on the nature of a political culture. The serial relationship that we spoke of is neither unidirectional nor static, but rather is characterized by dynamic and multi-faceted interactions.

The concluding essay in this section, Weiner and Fields's "India's Urban Constituencies" contributes an additional perspective to the examination of the relationship between politics and the social order by exploring behavior in the political realm in terms of an ecological dimension of the social order. Although the Third World remains overwhelmingly rural, it nonetheless contains more than one-third of the urban population of the globe.[9] The urban explosion in *le Tiers Monde* is expected to continue, and with this explosion come the strains of change and transformation.

Like other complex phenomena that we have concerned ourselves with, the exact meaning and significance of urbanization is subject to various interpretations, each containing differing views on the impact of urbanization on people and political actions. Weiner and Field, for example, begin their article by outlining two views of "the political characteristics of cities in low-income countries." The first of these is a model of political uniformity which suggests "a progression from politicization to radicalization to polarization in urban political life, together with a tendency for the city to be a diffusion center shaping the political character of the rural region in which is it located."

The second model, rather than "emphasizing the political imperatives imposed by the attributes . . . of urban life," stresses "the common features of cities" in a given context "with their rural surroundings." This second model implies "urban political diversity" wherein "political culture, political organization, and processes of social change shape the city as they do the rural environment."

With these models in mind, the authors examine the voting behavior of India's large urban constituencies since 1952. The central theme that emerges from their analysis is a bimodal one in which India's large urban constituencies are seen to be "similar to the rural constituencies of the states in which they are located;" while, at the same time, the urban centers are found to have "much in common with one another irrespective of their location" in the country. Therefore, Weiner and Field conclude that the "electoral trends from 1952 to 1972 suggests that the urban constituencies are becoming more distinctive insofar as electoral protest and electoral polarization are concerned, but less distinctive with regard to electoral participation (if only because the rural areas have caught up)." In other words, the appropriateness of either of the models discussed depends on the form of behavior one wishes to examine. Moreover, they hold that: "If the polarization and radicalization trends continue, it seems likely that urban constituencies will command even more of the attention of the resources of party and government leaders than they do at present."

In this case, it may be argued that the 1975 Proclamation of Emergency by the government of Prime Minister Gandhi rendered this analysis meaningless. Such shortsightedness is not warranted on two counts. The first of these, as Weiner and Field point out, is that the developments in 1975 do not stand in contradistinction to the implications underscored by their article, but rather "have tended to confirm the trends described in this study." The second of these is that elections returned to India in 1977, producing the first defeat of the Congress Party and the fall of Prime Minister Gandhi. Thus insights into voting behavior as part of the complex connections between politics and the social order not only help us in explaining the past, but also provide assistance in that continual search for an understanding of the present and the future.

NOTES

1. Gabriel Almond, "Comparative Political Systems," in Almond, *Political Development* (Boston: Little, Brown, 1970), p. 35.

2. Lucian Pye, "Political Culture," *International Encyclopedia of the Social Sciences,* Vol. 12 (New York: Macmillan, 1961), p. 218. Also see Lucian Pye and Sidney Verba (eds.) *Political Culture and Political Development* (Princeton: Princeton University Press, 1963); and Samuel Beer, "Political Culture," in Beer, et. al., *Patterns of Government* (New York: Random House, 1973).

3. Lucian Pye, "Culture and Political Science: Problems in the Evaluation of the Concept of Political Culture," in Louis Schneider and Charles Bonjean (eds.), *The Idea of Culture in the Social Sciences* (Cambridge: Cambridge University Press, 1973), p. 68.

4. On peasants, see Eric Wolf, *Peasant Wars of the Twentieth Century* (New York: Harper and Row, 1969), p. xiv.

5. Samuel Huntington and Joan Nelson, *No Easy Choice: Political Participation in Developing Countries* (Cambridge: Harvard University Press, 1976), p. 4.

6. See Talcott Parsons and Edward Shills (eds.), *Toward a General Theory of Action* (Cambridge: Harvard University Press, 1951).

7. Talcott Parson, *Societies* (Englewood Cliffs: Prentice-Hall, 1966), p. 5.

8. Richard Braungart, "Introduction," in Braungart (ed.), *Society and Politics* (Englewood Cliffs: Prentice-Hall, 1976), p. 8.

9. See Raanan Weitz (ed.), *Urbanization and the Developing Countries* (New York: Praeger, 1973).

Political Clientelism
And Development

A Preliminary Analysis

Rene Lemarchand and Keith Legg *

> *All contacts among men rest on the schema of giving
> and returning the equivalence.* . . . *Social equilibrium and
> cohesion do not exist without the reciprocity of service and
> return service.* . . . *Beyond its first origin, all sociation
> rests on a relationship's effect which survives the emergence
> of this relationship.*

—Georg Simmel, *The Sociology of Georg Simmel*

Long before Simmel, classical historians have drawn our attention to the persistence of "the schema of giving and returning the equivalence" at various levels of human interaction. In one form or another, evidences of personalized reciprocal relationships have been uncovered in a variety of contemporary and historical settings, both Western and non-Western, and in many different guises. Whether termed "patronage," "machine politics," or "political clientelism"—as it is here designated—this type of relationship must indeed be regarded as a generic trait of political systems regardless of their stages of development.

That the phenomenon should rarely, if ever, have been analyzed by political scientists on a cross-national basis is therefore all the more remarkable. Certainly, little systematic effort has been made to establish its relevance to an understanding of the processes of change associated with the growth—and decline—of political institutions.[1] Our purpose

* Part of the information upon which this article is based has been drawn from a series of monographs presented at the Colloquium on Clientelism organized by Professor Georges Balandier under the auspices of the Groupe de Recherches en Anthropologie et Sociologie Politiques (GRASP) in Paris, March 29 and 30, 1968.

[1] Qualified exceptions to this include Sidney Tarrow's discussion of *clientelismo* in the Italian Mezzogiorno in his *Peasant Communism in Southern Italy* (New Haven, 1967), and John D. Powell, "Peasant Society and Clientelist Politics," *American Political Science Review*, LXIV (June 1970), 411–25. The most am-

in this article is to place the concept of political clientelism within the mainstream of the literature on developmental politics. Specifically, an attempt will be made to incorporate the notion of clientelism into current theories of development in the hope that it may provide a useful theoretical connection between micro- and macro-level or state-centered analyses. With this end in view we shall try, first, to provide a conceptual clarification of the notion of political clientelism; second, to distinguish among different types of clientelism; and, third, to discuss their relationship to processes of modernization and integration in both developed and less developed polities.

Whether by default or misappropriation, the field of clientage relations has tended to become the exclusive preserve of sociologists and anthropologists concerned with small communities. In general, however, the approaches and methods of sociologists investigating community power have obscured the political implications, if not the very existence, of clientage phenomena.[2] If such charges can scarcely be leveled against anthropologists, however much they may disagree among themselves over definitions,[3] professional boundaries continue to raise major obstacles in the way of meaningful interdisciplinary dialogue. Between those who insist upon equating clientelism with machine politics and those who use the term to describe a "particular type of relationship . . . not within a formal system of government authority,"[4] there is room for almost endless discussion and disagreement.

Although differences in definition and terminology have undoubtedly obscured the similarity of the phenomenon observed by scholars in the

---

bitious attempt so far to analyze the political implications of clientelism has come from an anthropologist; see Alex Weingrod, "Patrons, Patronage, and Political Parties," *Comparative Studies in Society and History,* X (July 1969), 376–400. For an illuminating discussion of selected aspects of clientelism in the African context, see Elizabeth Colson, "Competence and Incompetence in the Context of Independence," *Current Anthropology,* VIII (February-April 1967), 92–111.

[2] By and large students of community power have focused on policy decisions rather than on routine relationships between individuals and power holders. See Robert Agger, Daniel Goldrich, and Bert Swanson, *The Rulers and the Ruled* (New York, 1964), chap. 2.

[3] Anthropologists have been less than unanimous in their definition of clientelism. Either the very breadth of the definition offered precludes its operationalization— see, for example, Jeremy Boissevain, "Patronage in Sicily," *Man,* I (March 1966), 18, who characterizes patronage as "the complex of relations between those who use their influence, social position, or some other attribute to assist and protect others, and those whom they so help and protect"—or else its restrictiveness tends to distort the nature of the phenomena involved, as in the phrase "contract of pastoral servitude" to describe the clientage institution in prerevolutionary Rwanda. See Jacques J. Maquet, *The Premise of Inequality in Rwanda* (London, 1961).

[4] Weingrod, pp. 378–79.

various disciplines, the uncritical transposition of definitions from one discipline to the other can easily lead to misinterpretations of the locus and ramifications of clientelism in any given political system. In a recent discussion of "models of politics," Samuel Barnes asserts that the "clientelistic model" should be treated as an entity distinct from the "authoritarian, democratic, and totalitarian species"—noting, however, that the paucity of data available would make a general analysis of this fourth type "impossibly difficult and incomplete." [5] There is, in fact, little evidence on which to base this distinction, but if much of the literature on clientelism is admittedly narrow-gauged and anthropologically oriented, the available data is nonetheless sufficiently abundant and diversified to permit an interim assessment of the place and role of clientelism in the context of comparative politics.[6]

What Is Political Clientelism?

Unlike "class" and "ethnicity," both of which are group phenomena, clientelism refers to a personalized and reciprocal relationship between an inferior and a superior, commanding unequal resources; moreover, in contrast with the "ideal type" of bureaucratic relationship, the norms of rationality, anonymity, and universalism are largely absent from the patron-client nexus. Instead, affectivity serves as the primary social adhesive for binding a patron to his client and vice versa. Political clientelism, in short, may be viewed as a more or less personalized, affective, and reciprocal relationship between actors, or sets of actors, commanding unequal resources and involving mutually beneficial transactions that

[5] Samuel H. Barnes, "Mobilization and Political Conflict: A Theoretical Enquiry into the Structural Bases of Consensus and Dissent" (Paper delivered at the Seventh World Congress of the International Political Science Association, Brussels, 1967), p. 7.

[6] In addition to the works mentioned above, passing reference must be made to the following sources: Frederick G. Bailey, *Politics and Social Change in Orissa in 1959* (Berkeley and Los Angeles, 1963); Lloyd Fallers, *Bantu Bureaucracy* (Cambridge, 1958); George M. Foster, "The Dyadic Contract in Tzintzuntzan: Patron Client Relations," *American Anthropologist*, LXV (December 1963), 1280–94; Jean Grossholtz, *Politics in the Philippines* (Boston, 1966); Arnold Hottinger, "Zuama in Historical Perspective," in Leonard Binder, ed. *Politics in Lebanon* (New York, 1966), pp. 85–105; Keith Legg, *Politics in Modern Greece* (Stanford, 1969), chap. 3; Rene Lemarchand, "Les Relations de Clientèle comme moyen de contestation: Le cas du Rwanda," *Civilisations*, XVIII (4/1968), 553–73; Lucy Mair, "Clientship in East Africa," *Cahiers d'Études Africaines*, II (6/1961), 315–26; Lucy Mair, *Primitive Government* (Baltimore, 1965); Edward I. Steinhart, "Vassal and Fief in Three Interlacustrine Kingdoms," *Cahiers d'Études Africaines*, VII (4/1967), 606–24; Eric Wolf, "Kinship, Friendship and Patron-Client Relations," in Michael Banton, ed. *The Social Anthropology of Complex Societies* (New York, 1966).

have political ramifications beyond the immediate sphere of dyadic relationships. However vague, this formulation suggests at least three general criteria for characterizing political clientelism: (1) the variable pattern of asymmetry discernible in the patron-client relationship; (2) the locus, extensiveness, and durability of the relationship; and (3) the character of the transactions attendant upon such relationships.

Although patron-client relationships are by definition invested with a certain quotient of affectivity, clientelism differs from mere instrumental friendship in the conditional character of the personal loyalties involved. This is largely a reflection of the discrepancies in status, power, and influence which serve both to segregate and to unite patrons and clients. The asymmetry inherent in the relationship is neatly expressed in Eric Wolf's phrase, "lopsided friendship." [7] The element of "lopsidedness" is the really crucial element in the clientage relationship, as it expresses the differential control of patrons and clients over resources, and the resultant asymmetry of statuses and obligations between them. Thus, the vassal owes personal service to his lord, but the lord owes protection to his vassal in time of war; the client-chief owes tribute to his ruler, but the ruler owes him political rights and privileges commensurate with his rank; the peasant and his family provide votes for a politician, and he in return must cater to their material needs. Status differences in this sense involve complementary role relationships rooted in expectations of reciprocal rights and obligations. One may further hypothesize that, other things being equal, the greater the status differences, the higher the quotient of affectivity entering into the patron-client relationship. Rather than the "friendship" becoming more precarious as the relationship becomes more lopsided, the reverse is the case. On the other hand, equalization of status diminishes both the degree of asymmetry and the affective component of the relationship.

Pushed to its limit, equalization of status logically spells the dissolution of patron-client ties and their replacement by bargaining among equals, as individuals or as groups. In practice, however, elements of clientelism may persist behind the facade of new social referents or institutions. Notables and influentials commanding unequal or non-additive resources may in fact relate to each other in a manner not unlike that of patrons and clients, and the analytic structure of clientelism may reappear in the guise of concrete institutional structures that have all the outward appurtenances of a legal-rational universe. Ad hoc, transitory relationships may be substituted for the more permanent nexus that normally prevails between patrons and clients; the scope of their relationships may, likewise, become more restricted; and the affective com-

[7] Wolf, p. 16.

ponent may play only a minor role in binding them together. Despite these variations in the contours and permanence of clientage networks, their role structures may nonetheless remain fairly stable.

Although individual status differences may set the tone in specific contexts, the role-sets associated with patrons and clients go beyond the dyadic tandem of individuals as actors to involve formal structures such as corporate groups, parties, and bureaucracies, and informal ones such as cliques and coteries within and outside the more formal structures. A role-set can best be defined in terms of the paired relationships that link a client to his patron and vice versa; a clientage network, on the other hand, involves an aggregate of role-sets, serially linked in such a way that a patron also stands in the position of a client toward his superior.[8] Although the hierarchical element involved in the ordering of role-sets is also a key characteristic of any formal organization, two essential differences should be noted. One is that clientage networks are invested with a higher quotient of affectivity than normally exists in a formal organization, and the criteria which enter into patron-client hier-archies are thus conspicuously unbureaucratic, being neither "rational" nor impersonal. Moreover, and as a consequence of the foregoing, where clientage networks insert themselves into a bureaucratic framework, the chances are that interpersonal relations between patrons and clients will operate at cross purposes with, or at least independently of, the formal role relationships specified in statutory rules and regulations. The main point here, however, is not only that patron-client relations may replicate themselves at the level of intergroup relations and within the framework of formal institutions, but that the simple and straightforward dyadic relationship observable at the level of the individual may be little more than a link in a network of reciprocities extending across a segment or even the whole of a society.

The critical linkage in this case is supplied through intermediaries—"social brokers," "hinge groups," or "middlemen."[9] The significance of their role emerges with special clarity from Jeremy Boissevain's discussion of brokerage in Sicily: "The social broker places persons in touch with each other either directly or indirectly for profit. He bridges gaps in communication between persons, group structures, and even cultures. A broker is then a professional manipulator of people and information

---

[8] See Adrian Mayer, "Quasi-Groups in the Study of Complex Societies," in Michael Banton, ed. *The Social Anthropology of Complex Societies* (New York, 1966), p. 100.

[9] One is also reminded of the concept of "gate-keeping" as the process by which wants are injected into the political system and converted into demands. See David Easton, *A Systems Analysis of Political Life* (New York, 1965), pp. 86 ff.

to bring about communication." [10] Several points need to be emphasized here. One is that the significance of brokerage functions increases in proportion to the expansion of state structures at the center, providing in effect the linkages necessary for bureaucratic action to reach into the periphery and meet the demands of the rural communities. Secondly, as political development proceeds and new institutions are being built, the linkages established through brokers increasingly tend to supersede or complement the channels of influence heretofore provided through kinship and family ties. Still later, as the state structures become more and more differentiated and complex, as individual interests change and are transformed into collective interests, brokerage functions tend to be performed not only by nation-oriented influentials, but by national institutions, parties, and pressure groups.

The variable character of contextual referents, ranging from the purely individual plane to "situations structured by corporate groups, or in situations in which the institutional framework is strong and ramifying," leads one to predict, along with Eric Wolf, that "patron-client relations [are liable to] operate in markedly different ways." [11] Wolf himself, as he contrasts relationships in situations where "the patron is incorporated into the lineage to form solid patron-client blocs" with situations where "the institutional framework is extensive and the ties between multiple sponsors and multiple clients diffuse and cross-cutting," shows the importance of identifying clearly the location and the corporate ramifications of clientelistic ties in the political system. In the one case, the relationship is conspicuously intimate and reasonably stable; in the other, "the patron's hold on the client is weakened, with clients moving from one orbit of influence to another." [12] Durability, as noted earlier, is also contingent upon status differences. The more asymmetrical the relationship, the more severe the deprivations inflicted upon the client by a withdrawal of support from the patron. Similarly, the more extensive the clientage network, that is, the fewer the gaps in the chain of reciprocities that run from the bottom to the top of the political system, the greater the chance of durability of the role-sets operative at the individual level. This is not to suggest, of course, that patrons and clients are locked forever in the same nexus of reciprocities. As Frederik Barth points out, "Each actor in a set of role relationships keeps a kind of mental ledger of value gained and lost in relation to other actors. Each subsequent action changes the balance and influences future behavior.

[10] Jeremy Boissevain, "Patrons as Brokers" (Paper presented to the Conference on Patronage, Dutch Sociological Association, Amersfoort, The Netherlands, June 6 and 7, 1969).

[11] Wolf, p. 18.

[12] Ibid.

The less asymmetrical the relationships, the greater likelihood of the obligations remaining open-ended. Under conditions of near status equality, each transaction may be viewed as complete in itself." [13]

The transactions involved in clientelist relationships also vary. Basically, a transaction involves an exchange of mutually benefitting obligations between the transactor (the patron) and the respondent (the client). The volume of transactions depends upon the context, including both the needs of the client and the influence of the patron. In some situations the transaction is completed at the local level; in other instances the flow of patronage (i.e., the benefits accruing from such transactions) will run through the entire government hierarchy, "[growing] upwards, and through lawyers, other persons of influence, and Members of Parliament," resulting in a situation where "the organization of government and the structure of patronage are parallel hierarchies." [14] In such instances the hierarchies could better be described as "identical" rather than as "parallel." Without in any way denying the selectivity with which government officials and members of parliament act out their roles—moving alternatively from the conventional roles of civil servants or representatives to that of "patron," as the circumstances and settings may require—their relationships with their rural constituents are essentially based on personalized, affective, reciprocal ties. The deputy-constituent relationship in this case is but the extension into the modern parliamentary arena of the patron-client relationships discernible at the local or regional level.

The greater the volume of transactions, the greater the diversity of political resources handled through clientelism. Thus one may distinguish, with Boissevain, between directly and indirectly controlled resources—between resources such as "land, work, scholarship funds, which [a patron] controls directly" (i.e., "first order resources") and "strategic contacts with other people who control such resources directly" (i.e., "second order resources"). Relying on concepts drawn from communication theory, Boissevain makes a strong case for analyzing the relations between strategy, resources, and environment in terms of the distinction between first and second order resources, which he goes on to identify, respectively, with "patronage" and "brokerage." [15]

[13] Fredrik Barth, *Models of Social Organization*, Royal Anthropological Institute, Occasional Paper No. 2 (1966), cited in Burton Benedict, "Family Firms and Economic Development," *Southwestern Journal of Anthropology*, XXIV (Spring 1968), 3.

[14] John K. Campbell, *Honour, Family and Patronage* (Oxford, 1963), p. 260.

[15] Centering his analysis on the notions of "capital" and "credit" (i.e., the actual communication channels [a broker] controls, and what others *think* his capital to be), Boissevain argues that a broker's "ability to bring about communication rapidly and effectively is in large measure determined by credit, and credit is

Suffice it to note here that, regardless of the level at which they occur or the resources they may involve, transactions are likely to cut across different social sectors. As has been shown by John Powell in his discussion of "rural problem-solving systems" in Venezuela and Italy, the economic and social benefits received in the rural environment are usually repaid by voting support in the political environment. A strikingly similar pattern of reciprocity characterizes contemporary Turkey, the Philippines, and pre-1967 Greece.[16] The essence of the phenomenon lies in the reciprocal character of the benefits involved. And because the norm of reciprocity is "by nature malleable and indeterminate" in terms of the obligations it implies, being, in Alvin Gouldner's words, "like a kind of plastic filler, capable of being poured into the shifting crevices of social structure, serving as a kind of all-purpose moral cement," [17] it can be adapted to a variety of contexts.

In short, "clientelism" cannot be meaningfully considered apart from the setting in which it exists. The forms which it takes depend to a considerable extent on the structure of the society and on the political system in which it operates.

The Determinants of Clientelism

For some anthropologists clientelism is the determining factor in the development of centralized state systems—or, as Lucy Mair puts it, "the germ from which state power springs." [18] Inasmuch as it implies the breaking up of kinship ties, their replacement by broader loyalties, and the expansion in scale of the original community, clientelism must indeed be regarded as a necessary, though not sufficient, condition for the emergence of centralized state systems.

---

usually dependent upon ability to bring about communication. It is a cumulative process. . . . It is this flexibility in transaction which gives the broker his high credit: people can be led to think all sorts of things about the nature of his network and his ability to manipulate it. With the patron they come to know his limits more quickly." Boissevain, "Patrons as Brokers," pp. 5–6.

[16] We do not suggest that all clientelistic situations will necessarily lend themselves to this type of "rural problem-solving" device. In tropical Africa the exchange processes described by Powell operate within a much more limiting set of parameters where ethnic, religious, and social factors combine to circumscribe and define patron-client relationships. In these conditions the range of options available to the elites at the center to foment change on the periphery is correspondingly restricted. See Rene Lemarchand, "Political Clientelism and Ethnicity in Tropical Africa: Competing Solidarities in Nation-Building" (Paper presented to the Harvard-MIT Joint Faculty Seminar on Political Development, February 1970).

[17] Alvin Gouldner, "The Norm of Reciprocity: A Preliminary Statement," *American Sociological Review*, XXV (April 1960), 175.

[18] Mair, "Clientship in East Africa," p. 315; see also her *Primitive Government*, p. 166.

At this point two related questions arise. Since clientelism appears to pervade a variety of systems, including those centered on kinship ties, some other intervening variable must logically account for the rise of centralized state structures. Further, assuming that clientelism is the *fons et origo* of the state system, what, then, accounts for the origins of clientelism? To this last question anthropologists offer a two-pronged answer: clientelism originates in part from *environmental conditions*—in essence from conditions of psychic or material insecurity (in this sense a Hobbesian view of the state of nature is a logical if not always authoritative reference for those who see in clientelism an insurance mechanism against "natural" insecurities). To these environmentalist claims, however, another explanatory factor is usually added: clientelism also comes about as a result of specific *situational factors.* For example, the original client is sometimes said to have been a "refugee" or "an essentially kinless man in search of a protector." [19] According to Lucy Mair, "the greater turbulence that one should expect among pastoral people" is the main reason why "clients sought the protection of other men than the territorial representatives of the king." [20]

Whatever the cogency of these arguments, there is another vantage point from which to approach the phenomenon of clientelism—one that emphasizes not its causal but its functional properties and which, in turn, provides us with the key to our first question. Again to quote Mair, the quest for a patron may not be dictated as much by "a necessity for survival" as because of a desire to "advance one's economic and social status." [21] In this case clientelism may be viewed as one of the functions generated by the state to ensure its equilibrium. As a means for achieving social mobility, clientelism provides cohesiveness for the system as a whole; to use the language of structural-functional analysis, it is "functional" in terms of system-maintenance, and this regardless of the structural characteristics of the system itself.

From this angle clientelism may just as legitimately be regarded as the symptom rather than the cause of the social and economic transformations which made possible the emergence of a state system and molded its subsequent evolution. This is roughly the position adopted by J. J. Maquet in his discussion of feudalism in Africa. Although specific situational factors may have been instrumental in creating or activating patron-client relations, clientelism, according to him, could not have developed on a meaningful scale without (1) economic conditions favoring a surplus production of consumer goods (i.e., agricultural pro-

[19] Mair, "Clientship in East Africa," p. 325.
[20] Ibid.
[21] Ibid.

duce), and (2) a means of control by a dominant group or patron over this economic surplus.[22] Although the manner in which such control was established varied, involving conquest, immigration, self-selection to leadership positions, or some combination of these, in the last analysis economic control made possible the creation of a political clientele by the "sovereign." Only then could "prebends" be allocated to a body of loyal followers. Political control through clientelism in this sense is thus intimately related to prior changes in the social and economic spheres.

The essential point here lies in the process of circular causation that links clientelism to the political and socioeconomic environment. Thus, if there is any plausibility to the argument that clientelism develops out of the sense of generalized insecurity that presumably exists in so-called "stateless" or segmentary societies, it is equally reasonable to view both insecurity and clientelism as by-products of the development of state structures. Certainly the penetration of centralized state structures, with concomitant demands for taxes, tribute, and manpower, is more often than not a cause of deep insecurity. It is equally clear that psychic and material insecurities often tend to reflect the perceived inadequacy of the protective or distributive capacity of the state. Clientelism in these conditions operates as a kind of functional alternative to the "social security" functions of the modern welfare state.

Just as the elements which enter into the definition of clientelism are liable to vary at any given stage of political development, the types of relationships involved in clientelism may also condition the speed and direction of political development. Two widely different types of situation suggest themselves. (1) Technological and economic changes may merely serve to reinforce the position of preexistent patrons; their clientele may change but their position *qua* patrons remains fundamentally unaltered. Indeed, even when one set of patrons gives way to another, the displacement of incumbents may not fundamentally alter the role structure associated with patrons and clients. (2) Alternatively, local patrons are converted into "brokers" or "middlemen," thus providing the crucial linkages between the center and the periphery. Along with this change in the extensiveness of clientage networks there occur substantial shifts in the source and type of resources available to these "middlemen." No longer solely dependent upon the resources extracted from their following, they are now in a position where they can use state resources (usually in the form of policy outputs) to exert new forms of control and manipulation over their clients. At this point the forms of control inherent in patron-client ties constitute a new type of

[22] Jacques J. Maquet, "Une hypothèse pour l'étude des féodalités africaines," *Cahiers d'Études Africaines,* II (6/1961), 292–315.

allocative mechanism for inducing further economic and social change. What was previously a rather fragmented, locally centered nexus, limited to traditional exchanges in the form of tributes and prebends, becomes a far more encompassing network of relationships, directly dependent upon the volume and allocation of resources from the center, and more clearly susceptible to the techniques of political bargaining. In short, intervening socioeconomic changes may fundamentally alter the original basis of patronage and yet have relatively little effect on the clientelistic underpinning of the regime.

Before further suggestions can be formulated along these lines, one must examine in somewhat greater detail the characteristics and types of clientage systems which suggest themselves for analysis.

A Typology of Clientage Systems

The substitution of one type of clientelism for another (see Table 1) may be said to reflect a broad historical movement from the small-scale, kin-centered community to the expansion in scale and modernization of both state and society. The effect of this transformation on the characteristics of clientelism may be seen in the light of four interrelated variables suggested by current literature on political development: (1) the rate and extent of social mobilization, (2) the extent of penetration and the scope of formal governmental structures, (3) the degree of differentiation between system boundaries, and (4) the distributive capacity of the political system. The first, based on socio-demographic indices originally suggested by Karl Deutsch, refers to the degree to "which people become available for new patterns of socialization and behavior" in consequence of processes which erode and break down the major clusters of old social, economic, and psychological commitments.[23] The second and third refer to major structural characteristics of modernization, namely, the extent to which the social, economic, and political systems are differentiated and the extent to which the latter penetrate society. The fourth emphasizes a specific aspect of system performance—the capacity of the political system to distribute goods, services, honors, statuses, and opportunities to individuals and groups.[24] Obviously these variables seldom operate independently of each other.

[23] Karl Deutsch, "Social Mobilization and Political Development," *American Political Science Review*, LV (September 1961), 494.

[24] Gabriel Almond and G. Bingham Powell, Jr., *Comparative Politics: A Developmental Approach* (Boston, 1966), p. 198. For a further elaboration of the concept of "distributive performance," see Gabriel Almond, "Political Development: Analytical and Normative Perspectives," *Comparative Political Studies*, I (January 1969), 463.

Table 1 Typology of Clientage Systems

	I. Feudal	II. Patrimonial a. Traditionistic	II. Patrimonial b. Modernizing	III. Industrial
A. System (political) variables				
1. Rate and extent of social mobilization	Slow Minimal	Slow Partial	Rapid Partial	Continuous Extensive
2. Differentiation of system boundaries	Little	Poor	Partial	Complete
3. Penetration and scope of political structures	Limited	Limited	Variable	High
4. Distributive capacity	Limited	Minimal	Variable	Extensive
B. Subsystem (clientage) variables				
1. Configuration of clientage nets	Bilateral or hierarchical Formal permanent	Hierarchical Nonformal Precarious	Segmented Informal Shifting	Segmented Informal Cross-cutting

2. Occupancy of role-sets	Lord-vassal	Ruler-staff (i.e., king-client chiefs)	Political, social, economic elites Masses and subordinates	Officials Group representatives
3. Normative orientations	Deference-affection	Mutual trust and loyalty	Conditional loyalties—"private regardiness"	Pragmatic Empirical "Public regarding"
4. Character of transactions	Protection-service	Offices-administrative and political	Political, social or economic reciprocity, i.e., votes, economic assistance, influence, intercession	Variable political support—policy, personal satisfaction, and commitment. Public and private privilege access, etc.

NOTE: The above typology is intended to suggest a set of concomitant variations between types of political systems and varieties of patron-client relationships. The underlying assumption is that processes of change (referred to above as "system variables") associated with system transformations have a direct bearing upon the character of clientage ties. Though presented in the form of a sequential developmental model, this typology is not intended to suggest that individual political systems must in fact be transformed over time from one category to another; nor is it meant to imply that *all* clientage characteristics must *logically* transform themselves in response to changes in system variables. The model, in other words, does not exclude possibilities of dyssynchronization. Its purpose is merely intended to illustrate a certain range of variations in patron-client relationships in the light of what we consider to be the most appropriate historical stages of development for the analysis of such relationships.

As social mobilization progresses, the quantity and scope of demands upon the political system increase correspondingly. In particular, demands for individual opportunities and benefits—demands that activate others—are raised. But this alone is not a sufficient condition for the flowering of clientage relationships. Whether or not an individual seeks satisfaction through clientage depends very much on the structure of opportunities existent in the social system and on whether the individual has access to them. Social mobilization in a society with little structural differentiation is likely to nurture clientelism; on the other hand, where the political, economic, and social spheres are highly differentiated, individual demands are most likely to be satisfied through channels other than those offered by ties of political clientage. In one case, politics and society so replicate each other as to offer relatively few opportunities for advancement other than those identified with "favors," "pull" or "patronage"; in the other, the social and economic sectors constitute more or less autonomous spheres of activity, and thus offer an alternative range of opportunities to those that might otherwise be derived from political clientelism.

Other environmental factors may intervene. In a situation characterized by constant insecurity, regardless of societal differentiation, demands for general amelioration and for opportunities are likely to gravitate to the visible and autonomous political structures. Moreover, when governmental structures fail to extend beyond the confines of a relatively narrow perimeter, usually the capital city, and where the scope of governmental activity is equally restricted, no amount of structural differentiation at the center can prevent the development of clientelism on the periphery. Under such conditions, the rural patrons are likely to serve as intermediaries between the rural population and governmental officials. Conversely, the more extensive the penetration of government into the periphery and the wider the scope of governmental activities, the lesser the chance for clientelism at the grass roots.

It is at this point that the fourth variable takes on significance. If the distributive capacity of the political and economic systems is high and the beneficiaries are not restricted to special or privileged groups, demands, including those for opportunities, are likely to be satisfied. The other sectors of society will relieve the burdens these demands might otherwise impose upon the political system. In such settings, individuals may not find it necessary to activate potential clientage relationships. Another possibility is that, as the potential sources for needed goods and services become more numerous, the less dependent the client becomes on any particular network. But conversely, if the distributive capacity is low, even if government penetration and activity are high, clientelism may reappear embedded within the bureaucratic structures. Indeed, in a society characterized by scarcity, patron-client ties may well extend throughout the political system.

The typology, suggestive of a process model, notes elements of clientage systems identified with feudal, patrimonial, and industrial polities. These polities and the types of clientage systems found within them are not to be treated as accurate representations of historical situations, but as "ideal" responses to social change, indigenous or exogenous in inspiration. To borrow David Easton's term, social change as measured by social mobilization is responsible for the socioeconomic "inputs" introduced into the political system.[25] The remaining categories (i.e., differentiation of system boundaries, penetration and scope of governmental structures and distributive capacities) can be viewed as measures of modernization. In this context, these measures can be viewed as intervening variables. It is here suggested that the kinds of clientelism associated with each type of political system are to a large extent a reflection of the interaction over time between the input and the intervening variables.

In reality, of course, the distinctions between types of political systems and the different configurations of clientelism are not nearly as clear-cut. Most contemporary political systems are mixed systems; they retain elements common to less "modern" political systems, including differing types of clientage relationships.[26] At times this mixed character is the outcome of uneven social mobilization or incomplete "modernization." [27] In other cases it is the result of specific historical factors, sometimes traceable to events and circumstances occurring outside the boundaries of the system itself.

The Feudal Clientage System

Nowhere is the relationship between clientelism and the political system more evident than in the feudal polity. "Feudalism," as Rushton Coul-

[25] Easton, pp. 27–56. In this discussion the term "input" would include expectations, public opinion, motivations, ideology, interests, and preferences, all of which are excluded by Easton from both "inputs" and "demands."

[26] See Frederick G. Bailey, *Stratagems and Spoils* (New York, 1969), intro.

[27] Italy provides examples of "mixed" clientelistic structure. For an analysis of the socioeconomic roots of the geographical variants of the *padrone-mezzadro* relationship, see Sydel F. Silverman, "Agricultural Organization, Social Structure, and Values in Italy: Amoral Familism Reconsidered," *American Anthropologist,* LXX (February 1968), 120. Silverman's article suggests that the ethos of "amoral familism" is a consequence rather than the basis of the social characteristics. For industrial clientelism see Joseph LaPalombara, *Interest Groups in Italian Politics* (Princeton, 1964).

born points out, "is a method of government in which the essential relationship is not that between ruler and subject, nor state and citizen, but between lord and vassal." [28] Whether this relationship developed out of the enlargement and transformation of a smaller, more "primitive" society or as a result of the disintegration of a larger and more centralized polity is not directly relevant to our argument. The essential point is that some degree of social mobilization must have preceded the establishment of the feudal nexus between lord and vassal. That this process of social mobilization could not have taken place in the absence of some degree of internal differentiation—whether through "the appearance of a professional military class," "the conquest and subjugation of some enemy people," or "land settlement under feudal terms"—emerges with striking clarity from Max Weber's discussion of "seigneurial proprietorship." [29] The end result, then, was the emergence of a contractual, personalized relationship between individuals of unequal wealth and power in which personal and political ties became virtually synonymous. Regardless of whether the state's power was taken over by local men, or whether the kin-centered community was incorporated and expanded, the result was a substitution of one set of personal relationships for another. To cite Coulborn once again: "A society moving in a feudal direction is one in which the personal relations of loyalty between leader and follower, or lord and vassal, come to serve as a political system and to take the place of the political system operating through officials serving the state." [30] Seen in this light, clientelism may be said to serve as a functional alternative to the state, reflecting an institutionalized response to the disruptive influences that either caused the disintegration of the preexistent political system or at least seriously challenged its capacity to cope with demands.

Of the feudal type of dependency relatively little needs to be said. The formulations of historians and anthropologists generally confirm the image of a highly formalized, legally sanctioned, and permanent hierarchical relationship.[31] The value expectations underlying this relationship were those of "unfaltering devotion" and deference to the lord, matched by a commensurate affection of the lord for his vassal. The submission of a vassal to his lord entailed the grant of a "benefit" from one to the other—i.e., of a "fief" in exchange for the vassal's services; the reverse was also conceivable, since a lord might receive a fief from

[28] Rushton Coulborn, ed. *Feudalism in History* (Princeton, 1956), p. 4.

[29] Max Weber, *General Economic History,* trans. Frank H. Knight (Glencoe, 1927), pp. 51–57.

[30] Coulborn, p. 189.

[31] Marc Bloch, *Feudal Society* (London, 1961), vol. 1, *passim.*

a vassal in return for a promise of support and protection. Whatever the case might be, the nature of the exchange process is clear: at the root of the lord-vassal relationship lay an economic transaction ("the wherewithal to eat") that tended to complement and reinforce its affective component. Where this type of relation might differ from the patron-client ties normally encountered in primitive and patrimonial systems is, first, in the degree of professional specialization involved in the services attached to fief-holding, in time leading to a variety of fiefs (villein tenement, stipendiary tenement, etc.). Secondly, the element of "lopsidedness" involved in the lord-vassal relation was far less in evidence than in the usual patron-client relationship.[32]

The really important characteristic of the feudal type of dependency, however, was its institutionalization in the form of fief-holding and vassalage or vassal homage.[33] From these institutions feudal relations derived the contractual basis which distinguished them from those prevailing in both "primitive" and patrimonial polities.

Patrimonial-Clientage Systems

Unlike feudalism, patrimonialism as a political system operates through a specialized administrative officialdom appointed by and responsible to the ruler.[34] There is, nonetheless, an obvious parallel in the nature of the relationships that linked state officials to the patrimonial ruler and the lord-vassal relationship. As Weber's discussion of the rise of patrimonialism makes clear, both types of relationships were clientelistic in character: "The community was transformed into a stratum of aids to the ruler and depended upon him for maintenance through usufructs of land, office fees, income in kind, salaries, and hence through prebends. The staff derived its legitimate power in greatly varying stages of appropriation, infeudation, conferment and appointment. As a rule this

---

[32] Indeed, if one is to subscribe to the argument advanced by Fallers and Lombard, feudal relationships can only obtain among equals (i.e., among nobles). If so, only between serfs and vassals can one discern something approximating the client-patron nexus; but then the question arises as to whether the element of coercion does not tend to overshadow the force of contractual obligations between them. In brief, if the lord-vassal relation might conceivably be regarded as too "equal" to fit the requirements of a patron-client relation, that of vassal-serf would seem far too "unequal" to meet these same requirements. See Fallers, *Bantu Bureaucracy*, and Jacques Lombard, "La vie politique dans une ancienne société de type féodal: Les Bariba du Dahomey," *Cahiers d'Études Africaines* I (5/1960), 5–45.

[33] See, for example, Steinhart, "Vassal and Fief in Three Interlacustrine Kingdoms," and Bloch, vol. 1, *passim*.

[34] On the characteristics of "patrimonialism" as distinct from both "feudalism" and "patriarchalism," see Almond and Powell, p. 44.

meant that princely prerogatives became patrimonial in character. . . ." [35]

A major point of contrast between the patrimonial patron-client relationship and its feudal counterpart is that the former never acquired the same degree of formalization. Particularly instructive in this connection is J. Russel Major's discussion of the "new feudalism" or "bastard feudalism" in Renaissance France: "The new feudalism differed from the old in that the client did not render homage to the patron and the patron did not provide the client with a fief or in most instances with money payments at regular intervals. It was similar to the old feudalism in that it was an honorable relation based on mutual loyalty and interests." [36]

Perhaps an even more meaningful distinction is that which hinges on the relationships between clientelism and political office accompanied by prospects of prebends. In the feudal system the vassal-lord relationship was both the expression and the cause of the political relationship arising therefrom; in the patrimonial system appointment to office becomes the essential precondition of the patron-client relationship. This in turn focuses attention on yet a third distinguishing feature, namely, that the patrimonial relationship is comparatively less personalized and hence more precarious than that arising out of feudal homage.[37] In one case fidelity of the client to his patron is contingent upon conferment of office; in the other it is implicit in the very nature of the clientelistic institution.

Patrimonialism has two possible forms. In one, the traditionalistic variant, the patron-client relationship permeates the entire political system. The infeudation of the staff to the ruler expresses itself in the form of reciprocal loyalties based on expectations of mutual benefit. The differentiation of official roles at the center does not imply differentiation of system boundaries. Nor does the greater penetration and scope of government structures (as compared with the feudal situation) really affect the clientelistic nature of individual relations at the local level. The limited distributive capacity of the system and the fact that resources are distributed or squandered for purposes of political recruitment positively encourage the maintenance of clientelistic relations both at the center and at the periphery of the political system.

In the second, the modernizing patrimonial system, the greater rate

[35] Cited in Hans H. Gerth and C. Wright Mills, eds. and trans., *From Max Weber: Essays in Sociology* (New York, 1958), p. 297.

[36] J. Russel Major, "The Crown and the Aristocracy in Renaissance France," *American Historical Review*, LXIX (April 1964), 635.

[37] The point is undoubtedly overstressed by Maquet in his discussion of the client-chiefs of the Busoga. See Maquet, "Une hypothèse pour l'étude des féodalités africaines," p. 306.

and extent of social mobilization lead to potential discontinuities in the net of patron-client relationships, not only between different levels of governmental authority but between different sectors as well. This situation is typical of that category of systems somewhat inaccurately characterized by Gabriel Almond and G. Bingham Powell, Jr., as "pre-mobilized," in which "large numbers of individuals have been urbanized, have become literate, and have been exposed to differentiated economic enterprises." [38] Precisely because change is restricted to specific sectors, mobilization is uneven and a hiatus tends to develop between the clientel-istic structures inherited from the previous model and incipient "legal-rational" orientations of leading members in the mobilized sector. Despite the growing differentiation of the social, economic, and political spheres, the expansion of bureaucratic structures, the emphasis on welfare values and secularization—all reflective of responses to social mobilization—social change at the mass level tends to lag far behind the structural changes' effect at the center. Thus, in its actual operation, the system constantly tends to swing back into the clientelistic mold of its predecessor. The result is a hybrid situation in which clientelism resuscitates itself in the traditionalistic interstices of the modernizing polity. [39]

Traditionalistic and modernizing types can be distinguished along several dimensions. Where the former tends to embrace the entire political system with a consequent congruence of political relationships and patron-client ties at every level of the government hierarchy, the latter is generally more segmented and shifting. In the traditionalistic type, dependency is likely to radiate from a single point in the political system (i.e., the ruler); in the modernized variant, on the other hand, dependency relationships can originate in a variety of sectors—the party, bureaucracy, trade unions, and even from the more traditional oligarchs. In this case, the shifting character of dependency relationships frequently reflects the existence of competition among various sectors. Where the traditionalistic type involves the allocation of political office in return for political service or allegiance, in the modernizing variant the transactions are by no means confined to the political sector. [40] As the bases of patronage become more diversified, so does the position of the patrons in society. This group comes to include not only government officials but new men of status such as the "professionals" and businessmen. More often than not, elections under these conditions are little

---

[38] Almond and Powell, p. 284.

[39] See Fred Riggs, *Administration in Developing Countries* (Boston, 1964).

[40] The modernizing type of dependency relationship is thus very similar to that which Tarrow associates with *clientelismo* in the Italian Mezzogiorno. See Tarrow, p. 74.

more than devices through which clienteles are given the opportunity to register their loyalty to competing patrons through the vote. The fundamental distinction, however, is between state structures which coincide with, and replicate, the client-patron relationship with the state acting as the major source of "prebends," and state structures which are superimposed upon patronage networks, with the latter acting as intermediary links between rulers and ruled.

The dominant trend in modernizing-patrimonial systems is clearly in the direction of a greater variety of clientage networks, a diversification of transactions, and a greater precariousness in the incumbency of patron-client roles. At the point where demands previously met through personalized clientage networks are met predominantly through the economic system or by universal governmental action, the stage of the industrial polity has been reached.

Industrial Clientage Systems

The line of demarcation between modernizing patrimonial and industrial systems is highly arbitrary: all industrial systems share some aspects of modernization as do most contemporary modernizing societies.[41] Since an industrial polity is presumably characterized by continuous and extensive social mobilization, considerable differentiation of system boundaries, and governmental structures with a relatively high distributive capacity that thoroughly penetrate the society, relationships within this polity can be identified, following Weber, as "legal-rational." Officials, and by implication individuals occupying roles in other subsystems, act as they do because of "impersonal bonds to the generally defined and functional duty of office." [42] There is apparently no place in this political system for personalized, affective bargaining relationships and, therefore, no room for political clientelism. In fact, contemporary industrial polities do not conform very closely to this "ideal" model,[43] in part because modernization is discontinuous. Certainly the United States still has political machines, vestiges of a clientelism characteristic of an earlier stage of political development. Much more important, however, are the personalized, affective bargaining relationships found among the political and economic elites of these systems. The term "establishment" in the United Kingdom defines these relationships in aggregate form and the consequences are well publicized.[44] The importance of family ties and

[41] This seems to be the point of Frederick G. Bailey, *Strategems and Spoils*.

[42] Gerth and Mills, p. 299.

[43] The model is elaborated in Almond and Powell, pp. 258–80.

[44] See, for example, Ian Weinberg, *The English Public Schools* (New York, 1967), chaps. 2 and 6.

affective relationships within the Japanese political and economic elite has also been amply demonstrated.[45] Italian interest-group officials have similar affective ties with high-level state bureaucrats in the appropriate ministries.[46] Even in nondemocratic industrial systems, personal relationships among members of the ruling elite are used to explain policy configurations and political recruitment.[47] Admittedly, the near status equality of the participants may make it difficult to separate the roles of client and patron. However, the character of the transactions—their system-wide ramifications—clearly identifies the relationships as those of political clientelism.

Despite assumptions of widespread political involvement, most individuals in an industrial polity do not require personalized political relationships: affluence and opportunity have diminished insecurity. Moreover, the prevalence of universalistic standards obviates any need for political clientage. As Samuel Hays suggests, "politics is necessary for those below the poverty line and an item of luxury consumption for those above it."[48] Most citizens have crossed that line in industrial polities. Partisanship is now traced to historical party attachments; memberships decline or become involuntary and thus meaningless as interest-group structures remain after the original goals are realized. Political involvement for most individuals is largely an exercise in good citizenship.[49]

For the political elite politics, however, is not a luxury; it is a necessity. Political careers and top-level posts in the economic subsystem are scarce and tenure uncertain.[50] To the specific, affective, personalized bargaining relationships necessary for beginning individual careers will be added new sets of similar relationships at each career level.[51] In such a context, group leaders, high-level bureaucrats, and public officials are likely to have similar requirements.[52] The interest-group official needs to justify his continued existence to the membership; the bureaucrat must do the same thing in a different setting, and the politician may need sup-

---

[45] Chitoshi Yanaga, *Big Business in Japanese Politics* (New Haven, 1968), chap. 1.

[46] See LaPalombara.

[47] See, for example, Sidney Ploss, *Conflict and Decision-Making in Soviet Russia* (Princeton, 1965), esp. appendix.

[48] Quoted by James Scott, "Corruption, Machine Politics, and Political Change," *American Political Science Review*, LXIII (December 1969), 1156.

[49] John P. Nettl, *Political Mobilization* (New York, 1967), p. 139.

[50] See Joseph Schlesinger, *Ambition and Politics* (Chicago, 1966).

[51] William Whyte, *Street Corner Society* (Chicago, 1955), pp. 210–11.

[52] See T. Alexander Smith, "Toward a Comparative Theory of the Policy Process," *Comparative Politics*, I (July 1969), 498–515.

port, both within political structures and at the grass roots.[53] At the highest levels, individuals drawn from different sectors of the elite with control over different types of resources are likely to mesh in the collective pursuit of individual goals.[54]

Noncollective personal interests in the political system are likely to remain important for some individuals in the industrial polity. On the subnational level, some demands will always fall into this category—demands for licenses, contracts, permits, etc. The pressures for political careers or top positions in economic hierarchies, as well as concerns for maintaining attained positions, are likely to remain. Political clientage in some form, perhaps labelled "influence peddling" or "interest conflict," will probably remain an integral part of the industrial polity.

In short, generalizations about the effect of patron-client relationships on the political system must take into consideration: (1) the shape of the stratification system—i.e., the kinds of cleavages, vested interests, and group values that coexist with clientelism; (2) the bases of patronage, here meaning both the social bases of the more influential patron groups and the way in which they exercise control over politically significant resources; and (3) the relationships between clientage networks and the formal institutions of government, in particular the extent to which patrons have access to, and are able to influence, the political process. These factors are not only useful for purposes of classification; they are also directly relevant to an understanding of how clientelism relates to political development.

Clientelism and Political Development

The literature on clientelism invites consideration of three related themes: modernization, political integration, and system equilibrium.

The case for clientelism as an agent of modernization may be argued from two different perspectives, depending on how one conceptualizes the notion of modernization. If the latter is equated with the creation of centralized state structures and the concomitant enlargement of the effective political unit, the argument advanced by anthropologists that clientelism is "the germ from which state power springs" is directly relevant. Inasmuch as clientelism implies the severance of familistic or kinship ties and their replacement by more universalistic loyalties, value orientations ordinarily associated with a modern secular political culture

---

[53] See Frank E. Myers, "Social Class and Political Change in Western Industrial Systems," *Comparative Politics*, II (April 1970), 405–12.

[54] See Donald R. Hall, *Comparative Lobbying: The Power of Pressure* (Tucson, 1969).

can be found in germ, as it were, in traditional clientelistic societies.[55] Thus clientelism, in its patrimonial form, represents a quantum jump in modernization in relation to the preexistent kin-centered community.

On the other hand, if one focuses on the enhancement of the adaptive and innovative *capacity* of the political system as one of the main characteristics of modernization, John Powell's thesis is much more to the point. He maintains that clientelism provides the basis for a network of reciprocities between the center and the periphery through which policy outputs can be mediated and implemented on a regional or nationwide scale. What Powell refers to as the "rural problem-solving system," which he explicitly identifies with clientelistic politics, serves as the mechanism through which rural societies adapt themselves to sociopolitical change. In Powell's terms, it may be that, in this case, "traditional patterns of behavior are not only consistent with the requirements of modern organizational life, but may even enhance the performance of such requirements in a highly competitive environment." [56]

Closely related to the theme of modernization is that of political integration. Just as the rupture of preexistent kinship ties may signal the advent of modern social and political organizations, the latter may serve to incorporate within the system a variety of otherwise unrelated ethnic or regional groupings. The integrative function of clientelism is nowhere more forcefully argued than in Alex Weingrod's analysis of "party-directed patronage"—a phenomenon associated with "the expanding scope and general proliferation of state activities, and also with the growing integration of village, city and state." [57] Although the author carefully distinguishes between this particular form of institutionalized clientelism (i.e., the institutionalization of patron-client ties within the framework of a nationwide party apparatus which also exercises significant control over the institutions of the state) and mere "patron-client ties," in the anthropological sense, and goes on to stress that "the major distinctions [to which they refer] are between segmentation and integration," it is clear that in both cases some degree of integration does occur. Even in the context of "relative segmentation," there are usually "mediators"—"lawyers, merchants, politicians"—"who may act to bridge the different regions or levels." [58] Clientelism, in such instances, is viewed as more or

[55] This, roughly, is the core of Fallers' hypothesis that where patron-client ties exist in conjunction with a hierarchical, centralized political structure, the incorporation of a Western-type civil service structure occurs with less strain and instability than in segmentary ones. Fallers, *Bantu Bureaucracy*, pp. 241–42.

[56] Powell, "Peasant Society and Clientelist Politics," p. 424.

[57] Weingrod, p. 381.

[58] Ibid., p. 382.

less instrumental in fostering national integration, operating in effect as a conduit through which power is funnelled into the system.[59]

A third theme is that of the social and political equilibrium which presumably obtains wherever patron-client ties are to be found. Just as patron-client relationships are presumed to be reciprocal and self-equilibrating, so the functional interrelationships among elements of the political system are sometimes described in terms of complementary values and expectations. In this sense the consensual agreement which exists between patrons and clients is taken as an index of political harmony in the larger system of which they form a part. Nowhere is the point more clearly argued than in Maquet's analysis of the "premise of inequality" in Rwanda: [60] the clientage system provided the social ballast which made it possible for a caste society like Rwanda to maintain a modicum of stability and harmony in the midst of inequality.

None of these hypotheses can be adequately tested without consideration of the types of clientelism as well as of their normative and structural correlates. Equally plain is the fact that certain intervening variables may be of equal or greater value for explaining the consequences of change for the political system.[61] For example, the difference between an environment of plenty and one of scarcity may spell the difference between a stable all-embracing clientelistic polity and one in which the incidence of clientelism is intermittent, with limited scope, with unstable and shifting bases. Indeed, it may even spell the difference between an environment in which modernization takes place in spite of rather than because of clientelism.

Perhaps the critical point to bear in mind in assessing the impact of clientelism on political development is that it cannot be evaluated independently of other variables in the social and political systems. An examination of these variables in each of the four types of clientelism discussed here is beyond the scope of this article. Since the issues raised at the beginning of this section take on a special urgency in the context of developing polities (i.e., of "patrimonial-modernizing regimes"), we shall limit our observations primarily to this type.

[59] The role played by political machines in the United States in facilitating the integration of immigrant populations into the political system is well known. See also Grossholtz, p. 124.

[60] Maquet, *The Premise of Inequality in Rwanda.*

[61] The influence of exogenous factors on the structure of clientelism is well illustrated in the incorporation of immigrant political values into the structure of American local government. See, for example, Richard Hofstader, *The Age of Reform* (New York, 1955), pp. 8–9. See also Edward Banfield and James Q. Wilson, *City Politics* (Cambridge, 1963), p. 46. For a critical appraisal, see Raymond E. Wolfinger and John Osgood Field, "Political Ethos and the Structure of City Government," *American Political Science Review*, LX (June 1966), 306–26.

The impact of the stratification system on modernization depends in part on the character and saliency of the cleavages that permeate and define stratificatory phenomena, and in part on the emphasis one places on any particular aspect of modernization. Cleavages of caste and ethnicity, no matter how sharp they may appear in retrospect, did not prevent the rise of archaic state systems. Clientelism created vertical solidarities which cut across and, for a time, mitigated cleavages of caste and ethnicity. Even though some degree of social mobility does take place through the opportunities created by clientage ties, ethnic or caste divisions nonetheless persist.[62] In conditions of rapid social mobilization the latter are likely to reassert their primacy and supersede the chain of personal loyalties created by clientage networks. Or else the polarization of ethnic or caste interests may lead to a radical shift in the bases of clientelism. Instead of contributing to the maintenance of the status quo, clientelism may thus become the instrument through which polarization is accentuated. Though perhaps an extreme case, Rwanda is indeed illustrative of a situation where social change, once filtered through the prism of clientelism, produces an extreme ethnic polarization, in time ushering in a major revolutionary upheaval.

In brief, if there is enough historical evidence to suggest that clientelism may have been instrumental in the creation of ethnically heterogeneous, stable, archaic polities, the contemporary evidence points in precisely the opposite direction. Countless examples might be cited, both in Asia and in Africa, of unstable modernizing polities wracked by ethnic dissensions. It is clear that, where ethnic or cultural cleavages are not only sharp and persistent but tend to coincide with the geographical spread of clientage networks, the chances of extending the scope of patron-client ties beyond the range of ethnic boundaries are relatively slight. So also are the chances of clientelism promoting an extension of state structures on a nationwide scale. It is not only that the activation of ethnic loyalties threatens the territorial integrity of the state; it also creates major obstacles for operationalizing Powell's "rural problem-solving" formula. It may be that group loyalties become so exacerbated as to make the communities concerned look upon all reformist initiatives as threats to their cultural autonomy.

Another weakness in the "clientelism as a source of modernization" argument is that it concentrates on the specific aspects of the modernization process (i.e., "capacity," on the one hand, and the enlargement of the size of the effective political unit, on the other), and overlooks two

---

[62] "By itself clientage is unlikely to dissolve sectional boundaries wherever differences of culture, religion or race are prominent." Michael G. Smith, "Institutional and Political Conditions of Pluralism," in Leo Kuper and Michael G. Smith, eds. *Pluralism in Africa* (Berkeley and Los Angeles, 1969), p. 56.

other and equally important criteria: (1) *differentiation of authoritative roles and structures,* as "the dominant empirical trend in the historic evolution of human society," and (2) *equality* as "the core ethos and ethical imperative pervading the operative ideals of all aspects of modern life." [63] Clientelism, as noted earlier, involves a set of relationships which operate independently of, and often at cross purposes with, the type of role differentiation associated with bureaucratic rule. Some basic incompatibilities (expressing, in essence, a conflict of norms between "particularism" and "universalism," and eventually leading to conflicting goal orientations within the bureaucracy) may thus arise from the juxtaposition or interpenetration of clientelistic and bureaucratic structures. Similarly, the differences of status which normally enter into the definition of client-patron relationships may seriously hamper the equalization of wealth and opportunities associated with the modernization process. Where clientelism becomes identified with a type of transaction geared to the perpetuation of conspicuous consumption or "display," where economic resources are circulating almost exclusively upwards— from client to patron—and where the channels of personal influence are regarded as the only productive ones for the investment of human efforts and wealth, the prospects for modernization are bound to be extremely dim. Worse still, where ethnic cleavages tend to replicate the patron-client cleavage, and where the group values held by the patrons tend to legitimize the position of collective inferiority of their ethnic clients, the result of rapid social mobilization may be a violent confrontation between patrons and clients.[64]

The bases of patronage represent yet another intervening variable in any systematic discussion of modernization and integration. The basic distinction here is between patronage as "the response of government to the demands of an interest group that desires a particular policy in the distribution of public jobs," [65] and patronage as a mere exchange of favors among individuals enjoying differential social status. The presumption is that, whereas the former serves as an incentive system—"a political currency with which to purchase political activity and political responses" [66]—which ultimately leads to both innovative and integrative transformations, the latter is necessarily too fragmented, personalized, and status-quo oriented to perform any such function. Yet the record

[63] See James S. Coleman, ed. *Education and Political Development* (Princeton, 1968), p. 15.

[64] For a discussion of this phenomenon in the African context, see Rene Lemarchand, *Rwanda and Burundi* (London, 1970).

[65] Frank Sorauf, "The Silent Revolution in Patronage," in Edward Banfield, ed. *Urban Government* (New York, 1961), p. 309.

[66] Ibid.

shows that, even when "party-directed patronage" is the rule rather than the exception, the outcome may still be very problematic.[67]

Before the "party-directed patronage" thesis can be validated, i.e., that a clientelistic party organization can induce changes in society while preventing it from falling apart, a number of preliminary questions must be asked. Who are the patrons who direct patronage? What are the types of transactions involved in party patronage? Can the volume of demands channelled through patronage be sustained by the system without endangering its viability? The answers are likely to vary substantially from one case to the next. Furthermore, the concept of "party-directed patronage" subsumes under the same rubric too many facets of social life. Although this is obviously an empirical question, one can nonetheless conceive of situations where at least some degree of innovation and integration does take place independently of a clientelistic party organization (as in Ethiopia, Rwanda, and Burundi at specific stages of their evolution); conversely, clientelism may occur within the framework of party machines that are so restricted in scope and particularistic in orientation as to positively hamper nationwide integration (as in Nigeria); again, the presence of clientelistic networks within a single party system may lead to bitter factional struggles (cf. the Philippines, India, Senegal, and Turkey).

The coexistence of "primordial" identifications (i.e., caste, ethnic or regional ties) with patron-client loyalties frequently results in a very lopsided distribution of patronage. Where party or government officials use the privileges of office to extend special favors to their own group of origin, region, or relatives, where competence is sacrificed to friendship and efficiency to profit, the result may be, as in India, that "concessions to the traditional order critically undermine the modernizing aims of the national leadership." [68] Moreover, chances are that in these conditions the transactions effected via patronage will seldom lead to the kind of basic structural changes required by modernization. Turkey is a case in point. The strategic "connections" of the Turkish Federation of Farmers' Organizations proved eminently useful in blocking attempts at land reform after the 1960 coup. Or consider the case of India again, where the local elites were attracted to the Congress because it could assure favors and preferential treatment. For their part, party politicians were relatively unconcerned about national development programs.[69]

---

[67] See Francine R. Frankel, "Democracy and Political Development: Perspectives from the Indian Experience," *World Politics*, XXI (April 1969), 448–69. One must note, parenthetically, that the evidence adduced by Weingrod in support of his contention that "party-directed patronage" leads to integration is largely contradicted by the findings of Francine Frankel and others.

[68] Ibid., p. 456.

[69] Ibid., p. 458.

Moreover, modernization may simply fail to occur because of the excessive volume of demands imposed upon the system via party-directed patronage. Commenting on the "sharp increase in centrifugal forces" observable in India even before Nehru's death, Francine R. Frankel states that, "The increased burden on the aggregative capabilities of the Congress party came at a time when the amount of power in the Indian political system (i.e., the expansion of political offices and of functions of state and local government) had reached a plateau, and when earlier concessions to local and sectional elites had already lowered the rate of economic advance that barely kept pace with the population growth." [70] This system is not unlike that which may yet develop in the Philippines. Although there is evidence of institutionalization, particularly on the level of the presidency, quid pro quo relationships still predominate at other levels, and this may well cause system overload. There is evidence that, as transactions come to involve policy as well as more individualized forms of payoffs in exchange for political support, the long-term growth of the system, including its economic and political capacities, may be seriously impaired. [71] In each of these situations the obstacles in the path of modernization imply corresponding threats to national integration and stability as they tend to further intensify regional, ethnic, or religious discontinuities.

Finally, just how far clientelism may assist innovation in the economic and social spheres depends in part on the control of the means of production. Where society is almost wholly dependent on the allocation of resources from the center, or where private enterprise remains firmly under governmental control, clientelism offers unique opportunities for initiating change, whether through quid pro quos, prebends, or "honest graft." Very different is the situation where the government is economically and politically dependent on the willingness of local patrons to deliver the goods, that is, where the hold of the local patrons over their clients permits them to control both economic production and the vote. This, for example, is roughly the situation one finds in Senegal. [72] Just as there are limits to how far traditional patrons can tolerate reformist moves without destroying their own bases of support at the same time, there are obvious limits as well to how far national politicians are willing to forego electoral support for the sake of implementing economic and social reforms.

[70] Ibid., p. 464.

[71] See Jesse F. Marquette, "Peasant Electoral Politics in the Philippines" (Masters thesis, Department of Political Science, University of Florida, Gainesville, 1968), chap. 4.

[72] For a further elaboration on this point, see Donal Cruise O'Brien, "The Murids of Senegal: The Socio-Economic Structure of an Islamic Order" (Ph.D. diss., University of London, 1969).

Thus, just as the access of traditionalist patron groups to the political arena may seriously inhibit developmental goals or focus the government's attention on the preservation of its own special interests, the result is likely to be much the same when development-minded bureaucrats and politicians are confronted with strongly entrenched conservative local elites. Such conditions are in part responsible for the failure of the Greek political system to handle developmental crises successfully. The same also applies to India.[73] Another fact to bear in mind is that, even in the absence of opposition from local elites, the sheer extensiveness of clientage networks and the remoteness of the lower links from the centers of power may create fundamental obstacles to the enhancement of the system's distributive capacities. Commenting on the failures of the clientele pattern in southern Italy, Sidney Tarrow points out that, "when the chain of personal acquaintances . . . reaches up to the state bureaucracy with little adjustment in structure," the clientele chain is likely to "grow too long for effective political allocation." "It is this," he adds, "which has made the South ineffective in the political arena; faced by the well-organized interest groups of Milan, Turin and Genoa, southern clienteles are unable to bargain effectively since they can trade only in personal favors." [74] Tarrow's conclusion that, "the clientele system . . . resists or modifies the forms and techniques of a modern party system" has a wide applicability. Quite aside from the corruption which such phenomena usually entail, the clustering of clienteles around influential patrons imposes upon the party systems of many developing polities the same kinds of structural handicaps that continue to plague the Italian Communist party in the Mezzogiorno. No matter how monolithic in appearance their facade may seem, there is no way of articulating and implementing broad development goals where personal friendships and favors predominate.

Paradoxically, whatever success the clientelistic model may achieve in promoting economic and social development must ultimately lead to its disintegration. The introduction of social and technological changes in a predominantly rural society accelerates the rate of social and political mobilization of the hitherto inert peasant masses and eventually leads to a severance of patron-client ties. As rural elements become conscious of their numerical strength, as they organize themselves politically and articulate their demands through separate institutional channels, gaps are likely to develop in the system. Conflicts of interest and legitimacy may occur between those who still move within the existing circuits of patronage and those who are left out—between mobilized peasants or

[73] See Legg.

[74] Sidney Tarrow, "Political Dualism and Italian Communism," *American Political Science Review*, LXI (March 1967), 44.

"urban villagers" and intellectual elites on the one hand, and the surviving clienteles on the other. Or else competing networks of clientelism may emerge among parochial groups, or between intellectuals and politicians, each vying for a maximum share of available resources. In an environment of scarcity the struggle is likely to become particularly intense. Violence and chronic instability are predictable under these conditions.

However pessimistic, Frankel's concluding assessment of the contemporary Indian scene provides a fairly realistic summary of the future of clientelism in many developing contexts: "The politics of patronage has long ceased to be functional for the Indian political system—if, indeed, it ever was. Its continuation under present circumstances can end only in the complete breakdown of the parliamentary system of government." [75] Whether, by ushering in a breakdown of the preexistent system, clientelism can in any way contribute to breakthroughs in political modernization is an altogether different problem.

[75] Frankel, p. 468.

Participation and Efficacy

Aspects of Peasant Involvement in Political Mobilization

John R. Mathiason and John D. Powell *

The impact of rapid political change on individual peasants has been described more often by novelists than by political scientists. Some of the better political novels written in the twentieth century by authors from developing countries have been concerned with this theme. The tragedy of Akunkwo in Chinua Achebe's *Things Fall Apart* or the romance of Mehmed in Yashar Kemal's *Mehmed My Hawk* come to mind. Among numerous Latin American descriptions of the effects of cataclysmic political events on the individual peasant, Mariano Azuela's tale of the Mexican revolution, *The Underdogs* (*Los de Abajo*), the tragicomic novels of Brazil's cacao country by Jorge Amado, and the portrayals of rural Peru in Ciro Alegria's *El Mundo es Ancho y Ajeno,* and of rural Colombia in Gabriel Garcia Marquez' *La Mala Hora,* are outstanding.

The literature of social science, however, includes few works dealing with political change and the individual peasant. In part this may be because opportunities for systematic empirical research in the midst of great political ferment are limited, in part because many of the cases of rapid political change are now matters of past history. Personal histories of the Mexican revolution have been analyzed [1] and, long after the fact, its individual effects have been studied by survey methods.[2] Some consequences of the Communist revolution in China have been observed indirectly by looking at village social structure [3] or by inter-

---

* This is a revised version of a paper presented to the panel on The Individual and Political and Social Change at the Annual Meeting of the American Political Science Association, New York City, September 4, 1969.

[1] Oscar Lewis, *Pedro Martinez: A Mexican Peasant and His Family* (New York, 1967).

[2] Gabriel A. Almond and Sidney Verba, *The Civic Culture* (Princeton, 1963), esp. pp. 414–28.

[3] C. K. Yang, *A Chinese Village in Early Communist Transition* (Cambridge [Mass.], 1959).

viewing refugees.[4] A rare exception is found in *Fanshen,* William Hinton's first-hand observations of revolution in a Chinese village.

Another reason for the paucity of studies is that until recently the peasantry as a political factor was not considered sufficiently important to merit the large outlays of funds necessary to mount a major research effort. However, the realization that peasants make up more than half of the population of the developing countries, that there is a nascent world crisis in the production of food, and that peasants can furnish the bases for "wars of national liberation," as in Vietnam and China, has in the past few years produced an increasing number of large-scale studies of peasants. Some, such as Everett Rogers' studies of the diffusion of innovations in Colombia, have little political content. Others, like "Plan Simpático" in Colombia, were left unfinished in the wake of the "Project Camelot" fiasco. Still others with political content, for example, the 1962 study of rural Turkey, were carried out after the time of most rapid political change.[5]

In fine, the existing literature contains very little systematic information about how peasants are drawn into political participation and what effect such participation has on the individuals concerned.[6] There is much information, mostly anthropological, about the nature of the traditional peasant. Summarizing this, one might conclude that traditional peasants are conservative, that they are difficult to organize, and that they tend to be passive, feel politically powerless, and lack interest in politics.[7]

[4] Robert B. Lifton, *Thought Reform and the Psychology of Totalism* (New York, 1961); Paul Hiniker, *Chinese Attitudinal Reactions to Forced Compliance: A Cross Cultural Experiment in Cognitive Dissonance* (Cambridge [Mass.], Center for International Studies, Monograph No. C65/18, 1965); Richard Solomon, "Communications Patterns and the Chinese Revolution," *The China Quarterly* XXXII (October/December 1967), 88–110.

[5] The basic outlines of this study are reported in Frederick W. Frey, "Surveying Peasant Attitudes in Turkey," *Public Opinion Quarterly,* XXVII (Fall 1963), 335–55.

[6] The most ambitious attempt to date is by Eric Wolf, *Peasant Wars of the Twentieth Century* (New York, 1969). The data for this study are mostly drawn from anthropological studies.

[7] This characterization of peasants is drawn from the mainstream of literature on the subject. Some of the commentators include Charles Wagley and Marvin Harris, "A Typology of Latin American Subcultures," *American Anthropologist,* LVII (June 1955), 428–51; Charles Wagley, "The Peasant," in John J. Johnson, ed. *Continuity and Change in Latin America* (Stanford, 1964); Eric Wolf, "Types of Latin American Peasantry," *American Anthropologist,* LVII (June 1955), 452–71; Wolf, *Peasants* (Englewood Cliffs, 1966); Everett Rogers, "Motivations, Values and Attitudes of Subsistence Farmers: Toward a Subculture of Peasantry" (Paper delivered at the Agricultural Development Council Seminar on Subsistence and Peasant Economics, Honolulu, March 1, 1965); Edward C. Banfield, *The Moral Basis of a Backward Society* (Glencoe, 1958).

One observer goes so far as to state that, because of peasant values, co-operative effort and hence political activity, are impossible.[8] In other words, much of this literature implies that peasant attitudes inhibit political participation. On the other hand, much of the material on political participation drawn from studies in the United States and Western Europe postulates a sense of political efficacy among other attitudes as a necessary—though not sufficient—prerequisite to active political participation.[9]

Drawing the two strands of literature together, one might conclude that, unless their attitudes were extremely "modern" for some reason, peasants would not participate in politics. This synthesis, of course, sets up a straw man, because peasants do in fact become involved in the political process, often in a manner which is both episodic and extreme, as in the revolutionary situations in Mexico, Bolivia, China, Cuba, and Vietnam. In addition to such dramatic interventions in the national political process, of course, we find that peasants participate in other, more orderly ways. The important questions seem to be how and under what conditions peasants participate significantly in politics, and what difference such participation makes to them.

In terms of the last question, it is clear that there can be many possible consequences of participation. In this article, however, we are concerned basically with only one—national political efficacy. Political efficacy, which goes under a number of different names,[10] is usually defined as "the feeling that an individual political action does have, or can have, an impact upon the political process . . . ." [11] As such it defines an individual's orientation to institutions in the political process. Political efficacy has been termed a key "regime norm" underlying a person's participation in a stable political system,[12] and one which distinguishes between systems in which individuals are mere subjects and those in

[8] George Foster, "Peasant Society and the Image of Limited Good," *American Anthropologist*, LXVII (April 1965), 293–315.

[9] Cf. Lester B. Milbrath, *Political Participation* (Chicago, 1966), and Almond and Verba.

[10] Political efficacy has been variously termed "subjective political competence" (by Almond and Verba); "powerfulness" by Melvin Seeman, "Alienation, Membership, and Political Knowledge: A Comparative Study," *Public Opinion Quarterly*, XXX (Fall 1966), 353–67; and "political effectiveness" by Robert Lane, *Political Life: Why People Get Involved in Politics* (Glencoe, 1959).

[11] Angus Campbell, Gerald Gurin, and Warren Miller, *The Voter Decides* (Evanston, 1954), p. 187.

[12] David Easton and Jack Dennis, "The Child's Acquisition of Regime Norms: Political Efficacy," *American Political Science Review*, LXI (March 1967), esp. 25–27.

which they are participants.[13] Certainly we would expect that an individual, caught up in a momentous change in his participation in the political process, would alter his orientation to that process. By orientation we mean the behavior in which an individual says he would engage in a given situation with reference to a given object. Our measure of national political efficacy specifies an object—national government, and a situation—national government proposing to do something that the individual respondent considers to be harmful and unjust. His orientation would then be his proposed action, ranging from nothing, or inability to express an action, to some influence behavior.[14] We are, therefore, specifically concerned with the question—to what extent does participation affect an individual's orientation to government?

Stimulated by these and other questions, we have collected data which

[13] See Almond and Verba, esp. pp. 3–36.

[14] We use only a few discreet measures of efficacy rather than the indices customarily used by other scholars who have dealt with the attitude. We have what we consider to be compelling reasons for so doing, though we are aware of the measurement problems which our procedure presents. For one thing, there are difficulties in translating scale items across cultures. In the Colombia study we attempted to translate the Campbell et al. efficacy index, but got extremely low inter-item correlations. Similarly in Venezuela we attempted to use a variety of efficacy measures, again with an eye toward index construction. Here, too, inter-item correlations were either extremely low or null, indicating that our measures were not tapping the same attitude dimension.

Of all the measures attempted, that which we call "national efficacy" seemed to be the most successful. First, the form of the measure is, "Suppose that the national government were considering doing something which you considered harmful and unjust, what could you do to impede this?" This is rather unambiguous in that it is almost a direct restatement of what is usually defined as efficacy. Moreover, since the question involves a specific level of the political process, it may eliminate some of the conceptual problems produced by broader definitions of efficacy. Unlike many of the items on political efficacy indices in common use, the national efficacy measure is relatively less intrusive in that it does not specify alternative responses and thus eliminates the difficulty that the question response may not have previously occurred to the respondent. An efficacious response is simply defined as any response which indicates some concrete action. These actions can be easily classified as "direct" or "indirect" depending on the behavior suggested (e.g., writing one's congressman is a direct action, while talking to one's precinct captain is indirect with respect to the object of the problem).

With only very slight variations this specific measure has been used in a number of cultural contexts. Almond and Verba have used it in the United States, United Kingdom, Germany, Italy, and Mexico; Frey has used it in Turkey; and it was included in all of the Venezuelan surveys. There are thus clear grounds for cross-national, as well as over-time comparisons. Finally, of all of the efficacy items in our various surveys, the measure of "national efficacy" has the most consistent correlations with other variables, especially those of the same type of form. These advantages outweigh any disadvantage which might be imputed from the use of a single measure as our dependent variable.

we hope will shed some light on this subject, particularly on the relationship between political participation and political efficacy. Our interests have been focused on Colombia and Venezuela, two countries which have experienced an upsurge in rural political activity since World War II. In Colombia, peasant participation has tended to be either violent and anomic, epitomized in large-scale civil strife,[15] or to take the form of traditional clientelist politics.[16] In Venezuela, on the other hand, the peasant has been the object of a massive, systematic political mobilization by reformist political parties, which began in 1936 but reached its peak between 1958 and 1967. Singly or jointly, we participated in conducting surveys involving national samples of Venezuelan peasants in 1963 and 1967, a national sample of local peasant union leaders in Venezuela in 1966, and a smaller sample of Colombian peasants in 1968.[17]

The data for both countries show that peasant political participation, whether in semipolitical peasant unions or political parties, is of a high

[15] Cf. German Guzman Campos, Orlando Fals Borda, and Eduardo Umaña Luna, *La Violencia en Colombia,* 2 vols. (Bogotá, 1962, 1964); Vernon L. Fluharty, *Dance of the Millions* (Pittsburgh, 1957); Richard S. Weinert, "Violence in Pre-Modern Societies: Rural Colombia," *American Political Science Review,* LX (June 1966), 340–47; and James L. Payne, *Patterns of Conflict in Colombia* (New Haven, 1968).

[16] John Duncan Powell, "Peasant Society and Clientelist Politics," *American Political Science Review,* LXIV (June 1970), 411–29.

[17] The 1963 Venezuelan peasant sample survey was conducted as part of the "Study of Conflicts and Consensus in Venezuela," jointly sponsored by the Centro de Estudios del Desarrollo (CENDES) of the Universidad Central de Venezuela and the Center for International Studies of the Massachusetts Institute of Technology. This study is described in Frank Bonilla and José A. Silva Michelena, *A Strategy for Research on Social Policy: The Politics of Change in Venezuela,* vol. 1 (Cambridge [Mass.], 1967), and in John R. Mathiason, "Political Mobilization of the Venezuelan Campesino," (Ph.D. diss., Department of Political Science, Massachusetts Institute of Technology, 1968). The 1967 Venezuelan peasant sample survey and the 1966 peasant leader survey were conducted as part of a large-scale study of the Venezuelan agrarian reform jointly sponsored by CENDES and the Interamerican Agricultural Development Committee (CIDA) of the Organization of American States. These samples are described in Mathiason. The 1969 Colombian peasant survey was conducted as part of a program to assist the National Agrarian Federation of Colombia (FANAL) in its efforts to organize peasants into unions and was jointly sponsored by FANAL and the Center for Rural Development, of Cambridge, Massachusetts. While the Venezuelan surveys are national samples, for financial reasons the Colombia survey is a sample of peasants in the Department of Cundinamarca living in villages with less than 400 population. This sample is described in John Duncan Powell, "Organizing Colombian Peasants" (Cambridge [Mass.], The Center for Rural Development, 1968), mimeographed.

order, especially in Venezuela.[18] It should also be noted that the surveys uncovered the existence of a rather high level of political efficacy, whether considered in an absolute sense or in comparison with the existence of this attitude in other countries, including highly developed ones. In expounding our thesis, we shall concentrate on the relationship between the political participation indicated in Table 1 and the political efficacy demonstrated in Table 2.

Colombia: Traditional Politics and Modern Influences
Rural Colombia has long been characterized as among the more backward and traditional areas of Latin America. Extreme disparities in socioeconomic status, physical and mental well-being, standard of living, political power and influence have tended to flow from extreme in-

Table 1 Peasant Political Participation in Venezuela and Colombia, in Percentages

Type of Participation	Venezuela (1963) (Agrarian reform beneficiaries) (N=191)	Venezuela (1967) (Agrarian reform beneficiaries) (N=1260)	Colombia (1968) (Village sample of Cundinamarca) (N=168)
	%	%	%
Attended political party meetings..	35.1	55.0	13
Worked for political party..	24.6	Not asked	12
Attended peasant union meetings.	61.3	70.2	No unions

[18] The striking nature of these participation figures may be seen by comparing them with the figures obtained in five countries by Almond and Verba, pp. 302 and 308.

	United States (N=968)	United Kingdom (N=860)	Germany (N=952)	Italy (N=991)	Mexico (N=1007)
	%	%	%	%	%
Member of a civic-political organization	11	3	3	8	3
Member of a union	14	22	15	6	11
Member of an organization with political overtones	24	22	18	6	11

Table 2   Comparative National Political Efficacy in Various Studies

Country and Sample Population	Percent Efficacious	N
United States (national)........................	75	(950)
United Kingdom (national).....................	62	(967)
Venezuela (national peasant agrarian reform beneficiaries 1967)	52	(1,260)
Venezuela (national peasant nonbeneficiaries)......	46	(826)
Germany (national)'	38	(955)
Mexico (national urban)	38	(1,007)
Colombia (peasants in Cundinamarca)............	38	(168)
Italy (national)	28	(995)
Turkey (national peasant).....................	26	(8,443)

NOTE: The figures for Table 2 are drawn from Gabriel A. Almond and Sidney Verba, *The Civic Culture,* and Frederick W. Frey, "Five Nations Plus One: Comparative Survey Research on Political Efficacy" (Paper delivered at the Annual Convention of the American Association for Public Opinion Research, Excelsior Springs, Mo., May 1964). The measure of national political efficacy used in all of the studies cited in tables is the same, deriving from the Almond and Verba study (see footnote 14).

equities in ownership and control of land. This basic context has changed relatively little over the past century. The formal political world of the Colombian peasant has historically been dominated by his relationship with the local large landowner, who was usually a partisan of one of Colombia's two major political parties, the Conservatives or the Liberals. Political ties to these parties tended to be quite strong, tying individuals, families, neighborhoods, villages, and even entire regions to one party or another for generations. Peasant party identification derived from the identification of the local landlord under whose influence he fell. Our field observations suggest that this pattern—derivative political identification—still holds up, and a variety of studies, utilizing voting statistics as well as other data, confirm this for most regions of Colombia.[19]

Relations between the peasantry and the landed elites who have dominated the formal political system of Colombia fall into two broad patterns, one of conflict and one of accommodation. Resistance to the encroachment of large landholdings and the imposition of various obligations on the peasantry by the landed elites has resulted in periodic local turmoil, rural-to-rural migration and, more recently, rural-to-urban migration, as discontented peasants have either fought the local land-

[19] Weinert and Payne.

lord or moved out of his sphere of influence.[20] On the other hand, whether by choice or by circumstance, many peasant families have accommodated themselves to their low status relative to the large landholders. Smallholders in the vicinity of large holdings, tenants, sharecroppers, day laborers, and squatters alike have fashioned a modus vivendi with large landlords based to a greater or lesser degree on a patron-client relationship, or clientelist politics. Within this basic pattern, the local large landowner generally determined which party and candidates would be supported in his zone of influence and, in return, occasional benefits were provided for the peasantry. When the landlord's party was in power, government jobs, road repairs, and perhaps agricultural credits might be obtained. When the landlord's party was out of power, of course, those benefits tended to flow to the loyalists of the other party. The rural violence in Colombia, which was most intense from 1948 to 1958, can be understood in its first stage as an intensification of the historic struggle between landed elites adhering to one party or the other and their "followings" of peasant loyalists.[21] Indeed, writers on this phase of the violence have labeled it "political hatred"[22] or a "defensive feud."[23] Traditional peasant political behavior, then, has tended to take one of two forms: either resistance to large landlords, usually followed by a flight away from the domains where formal politics occurred; or enlistment in formal politics in the service of a large local landlord, who required ritual voting or more violent forms of political behavior as the situation, and his perceived interests, dictated.

The zone in which we conducted our peasant attitude survey is one which we would categorize as an area of accommodation to the presence and influence of large landlords. We would stress that accommodation does not mean approval of, or satisfaction with, the status quo; indeed, there was much criticism and resentment over the inequitable distribution of land in the communities surveyed. But there was also a clear recognition of who held power and of who must be respected as a result.[24]

Seeking now to relate our findings on political participation to our

[20] See T. Lynn Smith, *Colombia: Social Structure and the Process of Development* (Gainesville, 1967), for a detailed presentation of the rural sociology of Colombia, emphasizing the land problem.

[21] For an analysis of the concept of peasant "following," see Benno Galjart, "Class and 'Following' in Rural Brazil," *America Latina,* VII (1964), 3–24.

[22] Guzman Campos et al., *La Violencia,* vol. 2.

[23] Payne, *Patterns of Conflict.*

[24] Not only did our interviews pick up much criticism of the influence of local large landowners, but one can see from Table 3 that, while landlords are recognized as respected and influential, they are not recognized for using this influence to help the peasant community.

Table 3   Person in Colombian Community Seen as Most Respected, Influential, and Helpful, in Percentages

Role Type	Most Respected Person *	Most Influential Person *	Person Who Most Helps Community *
	%	%	%
Local landlord	41.0	42.3	17.9
Priest, school teacher........	13.7	7.7	1.8
Leader of local voluntary organization	4.8	6.5	12.5
Local government official.....	9.5	5.4	5.4
Local peasant	4.8	3.8	4.8
Storekeeper, other local economic influential	4.8	4.2	2.4
"No one"	11.3	12.5	38.7
Don't know	9.0	16.0	18.5

* N=168.

findings on political efficacy, we might formulate the following hypothesis. Those peasant respondents who scored positively on a measurement of political efficacy toward national government (38 percent of the sample) are those who fall into the pattern of traditional political participation, that is, a clientelist pattern. They should be affiliated with the landlord's party, attend party meetings, work for the party's candidates, name the landlord as the most respected, influential, and helpful person in the community, have frequent face-to-face contact with the landlord, and name him as the person to whom they would turn in case of specific daily problems. Each of these items was measured in our instrument— yet none were related in a statistically significant degree (.05 level) to the measurements of political efficacy.

Knowing that rural Colombia has in recent times been deeply penetrated by various modernizing influences, such as roads, newspapers, and radios (in our sample, 40 percent say they read a newspaper at least once a month, one-half of those at least weekly, and 63 percent say they listen to the radio every day), we might formulate another hypothesis, one congruent with much of the literature on political modernization in traditional societies.[25] Those peasant respondents who scored positively on a measurement of political efficacy toward national government are those who "participate" directly in national affairs

[25] See Daniel Lerner, *The Passing of Traditional Society* (Glencoe, 1958), for the most detailed early statement of this hypothesis.

through exposure to the mass media. Once again, however, none of these measurements of exposure to modern influences is related to political efficacy to a statistically significant degree—although level of education and newspaper reading approach the .05 level.

If political efficacy among our peasant respondents is related neither to traditional and obvious forms of political participation nor to exposure to a variety of modernizing influences, what is it related to? Who are our efficacious peasants, and why? In brief, our efficacious peasants are the smallholders in our sample, for land tenure status was the only independent variable related to a sense of political efficacy toward national politics at the .05 level or better.

We lack sufficient data to explain definitively why smallholders should be disproportionately efficacious toward national government in Colombia. What evidence we do have tends to support one of two rather straightforward, common-sense hypotheses. The first might be called the venal landlord hypothesis. Peasants who are smallholders living in communities dominated by large landlords are more efficacious than tenants, sharecroppers, day laborers, and squatters because they are relatively more independent of the landlord and the agricultural resources he controls.[26] They are better able to resist being drawn into the clientele system with its attendant exactions, including involvement in large-scale violence on behalf of landed elites in the name of party competition. Consistent with this hypothesis, but indirect in its impact, is the finding (Table 4) that squatters and day laborers are the least efficacious peasants; these categories of peasants have historically been the most exploited—and the most resistant—in their dealings with the landed elites.[27]

Table 4 Tenure Status and National Efficacy in Colombia, in Percentages

National Efficacy	Owns Land (N=82)	Rents Land (N=52)	Squats on Land * (N=34)
	%	%	%
Yes	48.8	38.5	17.6
No	51.2	61.5	82.4

Chi square=9.79, 2 degrees of freedom p<.01

* Includes day laborers not farming own land.

[26] Concerning the crucial role of smallholders in peasant conflict with landlords, see Arthur Stinchcombe, "Agricultural Enterprise and Rural Class Relations," in Jason L. Finkle and Richard W. Gable, eds. *Political Development and Social Change,* (New York, 1966), p. 491.

[27] Smith, *Colombia,* pp. 83–89.

The second might be called the *kulak* peasant hypothesis. Peasants who are smallholders living in communities dominated by large landlords are more efficacious than other peasants because of their high status and well-being relative to the other members of the peasant community; and because of their higher status, they tend to identify with and emulate the political attitudes of the landlords. Consistent with this hypothesis, but only fragmentary, is the finding that among the efficacious, over 70 percent described some form of direct action—such as talking to a government official or legislator—when asked what they would do in the case of an adverse action by the national government. Direct action, usually face-to-face, is the typical mode of influence behavior followed by landlords within the pattern of clientelist politics; and to this extent it might be said that smallholding peasants emulate their social betters, the large local landlords. (On the other hand, only 25 percent of our entire sample reported that they had ever actually tried to influence the national government at one time, and almost all of these, when asked to specify what they did, said that they had voted in the national elections. To the extent that our peasant efficacy is based on their belief that they could act like a local landlord if they chose to, it is an untested belief).

In conclusion, political efficacy among our sample of Colombian peasants is unrelated to political participation, whether of the traditional, clientelist type, or through exposure to modernizing influences such as the mass media. Instead, political efficacy is a characteristic of the upper strata of the peasantry, the small landowners. While we do not have the data to explain adequately why this should be so, we would argue that the explanation is tied to the smallholders' relationship to the traditional local power holders, the large landlords; the smallholder is somehow insulated from the sense of powerlessness and resignation which infects other strata of the peasantry.

We have presented the Colombian case first, not because our analysis of participation and efficacy there is in any sense definitive, since the limited nature of our data—both in terms of sample size and geographic coverage—precludes this. Rather, the data give us a meaningful contrast to the more precise data on the Venezuelan peasant. The efficacious peasant in Colombia is one who stands apart from the dominant political process by virtue of his status as an independent smallholder. The Venezuelan case is striking in contrast. The erosion of a traditional, landlord-dominated political process in the rural areas left the peasantry open to becoming caught up in what was, in effect, an agrarian revolution. And, we shall argue, the efficacious Venezuelan peasant is not one who stood apart from this process. Instead, he was at the very heart of it.

Venezuela: Agrarian Revolution

Venezuelan politics have been characterized since 1936 by a change from one of the most nearly absolute dictatorships in Latin America to a democratic state with high degrees of citizen participation at all levels. More specifically, this change is the story of the successful attempt by a reformist political party, Democratic Action (AD), to take political power by systematically organizing the previously nonpolitical Venezuelan masses, which in turn meant organizing the peasantry.[28] The growth of the peasant union (*sindicato agrario*) as a mobilizing force can be seen in Tables 5 and 6. Table 5 shows the number of legally operating

Table 5 Number of Legally Operating Peasant Unions in Venezuela, 1958–65

Year	Number of Peasant Unions
1958	130
1959	782
1960	1,813
1961	2,197
1962	2,632
1963	2,936
1964	3,156
1965	3,476

[28] The general outlines are as follows. After an unsuccessful student uprising in 1928 against the dictator, Juan Vicente Gomez, Romulo Betancourt and other revolutionary leaders determined that the most effective way to power was by mobilizing Venezuela's disfranchised masses. In 1936, after Gomez' death, these leaders began organizing both the urban working class and the peasantry. Since political parties per se were still proscribed, this was done through labor and peasant unions under a liberal labor law passed as part of the post-Gomez liberalization. Considerable success was met, especially in the urban areas and in the countryside surrounding Caracas, the national capital. The AD party was formed officially in 1941 and came to power in a joint civil-military coup d'etat in 1945. During 1945–48, AD was in power. Among its first acts was to extend suffrage to all adults, bringing peasant and urban masses directly into politics for the first time. In three successive elections, AD obtained 80 percent of the total vote, which meant that most peasants began their voting with AD. In addition, through its peasant unions, the party began formally organizing peasants. By the time AD was overthrown by another military coup in 1948, much of the peasantry in the states surrounding Caracas and other central highlands cities had been organized and had benefited from a radical land redistribution program. After another coup in January 1958 brought civilian government back, AD recaptured the government in the 1958 elections, largely because of an almost total control of the rural vote. One of the AD's first postelection reforms was a comprehensive agrarian reform law which was used as a further vehicle to organize the remaining peasants into unions. In the 1963 elections, AD once more won the presidency, but with a bare 33 percent of the vote, mostly from the rural areas. For detailed

Table 6 Yearly inscription in Venezuelan Peasant Unions, by Percentages

Year First Joined Peasant Union	Agrarian Reform Samples (1967)	
	Beneficiaries (N=1260)	Nonbeneficiaries (N=826)
	%	%
1936–48...............	14.0	11.1
1949–57...............	9.2	5.3
1958–59...............	17.2	14.5
1960–61...............	17.4	12.1
1962–63...............	13.9	11.7
1964–65...............	5.8	7.6
1966–67...............	4.8	6.9
Percent never joining union	17.7	30.6
Total	100.0	100.0

unions from 1958–65. Table 6, drawn from the 1967 national samples of agrarian reform beneficiaries and nonbeneficiaries, indicates that, depending on the group, between 70 and 80 percent of all peasant heads of household had been organized into unions by 1967.

In contrast to Colombia, the main vehicle of peasant participation in Venezuela has been the peasant union rather than the landlord's political party. This is due in part to the historical fact that in the latter country unions were legal organizations before parties attained legal status. More important, however, the union is established in the agrarian reform process as the unit for distribution of benefits. This has made membership in a peasant union a de facto prerequisite for obtaining agrarian reform benefits.

In theory, peasant unions are apolitical; in practice, however, they are extensions of the various political parties. In 1967, national officials of the Venezuelan Peasant Federation estimated to us that around 65 percent of the local unions were controlled by AD, another 30 percent by the Christian democratic party (COPEI), and the remaining 5 percent by a third party. The relationship of the party to the union is somewhat indirect. Historically, local peasant union leaders were recruited

discussion on this general context of peasant mobilization, see John Duncan Powell, "The Politics of Agrarian Reform in Venezuela" (Ph.D. diss., University of Wisconsin, Madison, 1966); John Martz, *Acción Democratica: Evolution of a Modern Political Party in Venezuela* (Princeton, 1965); Robert J. Alexander, *The Venezuelan Democratic Revolution* (New Brunswick, 1964); and Mathiason, "Political Mobilization."

from party militants. But the party cells were usually located in larger towns to which the local party members would have to travel for meetings. Data from our surveys suggest the indirect role of the party as a mobilization agency. In 1963, there were few participators in party activities in relation to participators in union activities, although by 1967 this was changing (see Table 8). What the data seem to show is that a person's participation in the party is achieved through a mediating institution, the peasant union.

The peasant union serves a number of functions for the individual peasant. It is a broker between him and the plethora of government agencies which, under the agrarian reform, have recently entered his environment. A peasant with a grievance will approach a local union official who will, if the grievance is deemed valid, carry it through official or unofficial (i.e., party) channels. In addition, the union serves as about the only organized social activity that an individual has. On most agrarian reform settlements, the union runs everything. This is apparent from data on peasant perception of the most respected and influential people in their villages. Some 50 percent named local union leaders as the most respected person, and 53 percent named a peasant leader as the most influential.

This is quite a contrast with the Colombian data, in which the landlord occupied the position of the most respected and influential person in the community. Essentially the contrast lies in the social class of local power holders. In most agrarian societies, the landowning class comprises the local elite, enjoying power, privilege, and prestige. In Venezuela, however, the members of this elite have been replaced by elected representatives of the peasant class—a replacement which has been rapid and widespread enough to merit the description of agrarian revolution.[29]

Despite the change in class origin of the incumbents of the local power role, however, the role itself remains remarkably unchanged. In Colombia the local landlord determines who gets access to land and water resources and who does not; in Venezuela the same power accrues to the union leader on an agrarian reform settlement. The Colombian landlord provides the linkage between the peasant and his government; in Venezuela, it is the union leadership. In Colombia the landlord mobilizes the political participation of the peasant; in Venezuela, it is the agrarian union leader who does this. While the local power holders in Venezuela are much more accountable than their counterparts in Colombia (in being effective and honest benefactors to their peasant followers), the similarities between the sources and types of their various powers are striking.

[29] John Duncan Powell, "Venezuela: Agrarian Reform or Agrarian Revolution," in Robert Kaufman and Arpad von Lazar, eds. *Reform or Revolution: Readings in Latin American Politics* (Boston, 1969).

Why Did Venezuelan Peasants Participate Politically?

Several conclusions emerge from our data. First, Venezuelan peasants joined peasant unions and political parties for rather unspecific reasons, most commonly in an expectation of general improvement in conditions, rather than to obtain some specific benefit. Second, they joined en masse in each locality, usually at the initiative of outside organizers. And third, before participating in political organizations, the majority of peasants did not have a sense of political efficacy, which in most studies done in the United States is assumed to be a causal factor in participation.

Concerning the first point, explanation of why peasants join unions is complicated by the fact that, individually, peasants give a wide variety of reasons for so doing. In response to a direct question on a series of pretests for the 1967 survey, several broad but different types of responses can be seen (Table 7). What these reasons seem to have in common is that they reflect, from the point of view of the individual peasant, difficult-to-cope-with problems of daily life. The most general explana-

Table 7 Perceived Reasons for Belonging to Local Unions in Five Venezuelan Villages, by Percentages

Reason for Belonging to Union	Village				
	San Juan (N=32)	San Pablo (N=11)	Las Marias (N=32)	El Chivo (N=24)	El Zamuro (N=21)
	%	%	%	%	%
To obtain specific government service (such as land, water, credit)....	29	54	43	27	28
To obtain some unspecified benefits....	27	..	40	41	22
Personal or social reasons *	44	46	17	32	50

* These include such responses as "I like it," "One ought to belong," or "It is obligatory."

NOTE: The percentages in the table are calculated from data obtained in stratified samples in each village. These were not self-weighted samples and hence a weighting factor had to be introduced. Thus, a respondent in San Juan, for example, could represent 7.5, 6.35, 5.67, 2.3, or 2.0 actual members of the population depending on the stratum from which he was drawn. Thus the cell frequencies in the table are not necessarily whole numbers.

All but San Pablo are villages where the agrarian reform has redistributed land. San Pablo has no union of its own. Instead, the peasants in the community who are union members (less than half of the heads of household in the village) go to a nearby town. This case is discussed in Mathiason, p. 85.

tion of why peasants join unions, then, is for assistance in dealing with a variety of these problems. Indeed, union organizers in Venezuela used the "community problem" focus for their initial recruiting appeals, presenting the collective benefit of union membership as both a means to solve existing problems and as insurance against future disasters.

There is, perhaps, an additional explanatory factor which helps to reinforce this general interpretation. Peasants face similar types of problems in all agrarian societies, but only join unions in some of them. In most agrarian societies, the patron-client system becomes the established, traditional means for coping with environmental stresses. Even when such a system does not function to the satisfaction of most peasants, as in Colombia, there may be no perceptible alternatives. But when this system fails, or disintegrates for any reason, the peasant is faced with the task of finding some new mechanism for coping with the same problems—or coping with them more satisfactorily. The peasant union appeals to him as just such a mechanism. This seems to have been the historic process in the case of Venezuela, and similar findings about the peasant leagues of northeast Brazil lend credence to this interpretation.[30]

Regarding our second conclusion about Venezuelan participation, it happens that local peasant unions were founded either at the initiative of local peasants or at the initiative of outside organizers. The 1967 data on agrarian reform beneficiaries suggest that, in general terms, the two types of initiative were equally common. According to local informants in each case, 48 percent of the local unions on or near agrarian reform settlements were founded at the initiative of local peasants, 46 percent were founded at the initiative of professional Peasant Federation (FCV) organizers, and the remainder by political party leaders. This matter of local initiative is not as voluntaristic as it would seem on the surface, however. We made several intensive case studies of unions in which there had theoretically been local initiative in founding the union. In each case, the founders were local AD party militants who also happened to be peasants who had been ordered to organize unions in their areas. In short, it seems that most peasant unions were not founded as the result of grass-roots pressure, but rather by indirect (via the Peasant Federation's organizers) or direct (through local party leaders) initiative from the political parties.[31]

[30] For the Brazilian case see Galjart, "Class and 'Following'." Detailed evidence for the Venezuelan case is presented by John Duncan Powell, *Political Mobilization of Venezuelan Peasants* (Cambridge [Mass.], 1971).

[31] These two factors combined to produce membership en masse in the local union. An organizer would come and either almost everyone would join or no union would be founded. There was a certain indirect compulsion for this, since agrarian reform benefits are distributed to unions of peasants rather than to individuals making union membership on all-join-or-nothing basis a de facto require-

We consider our third finding regarding political participation by Venezuelan peasants the most interesting. Contrary to the implicit assumption in studies done in the United States that political efficacy is a causal factor in political participation, we found the opposite to be true: that participation seems to be a causal factor in producing efficacy. This is evident from the data in a number of ways. First, over time rates of political participation exceed those of political efficacy. Comparing samples of Venezuelan peasants taken in 1963 and 1967, one finds that levels of participation exceed those of efficacy in both years, but especially in 1963 (see Table 8). This in itself would seem to indicate that participation preceded development of a sense of political efficacy.

Table 8 Comparative Rates of Participation and Efficacy among Venezuelan Peasants, 1963 and 1967, by Percentages

Participation	1963 (CONVEN Samples)*		1967 (Agrarian Reform Samples)	
	Beneficiaries (N=191)	Nonbeneficiaries (N=182)	Beneficiaries (N=1,260)	Nonbeneficiaries (N=826)
	%	%	%	%
Attend political party meetings......	35.1	26.8	55.0	50.0
Worked for party or candidate........	24.6	16.4	not asked	not asked
Attend peasant union meetings	61.3	34.4	70.2	55.3
Efficacy				
Opinion efficacy (believe personal political opinions are important)	17.3	16.4	50.6	49.6
National efficacy (believe could influence national government)	19.9	21.3	52.4	45.8

* NOTE: CONVEN—Conflict and Consensus Study.

ment for peasants to share government-provided benefits. This is reflected in the 1967 data in a high level of correlation between the year a union was founded and the year most of its present members first joined a union.

A comparison of peasants in the 1967 agrarian reform beneficiary sample who had belonged to a union with those who had not revealed that sex, level of education, age, and income—all found to be related both to political efficacy and to political participation in other studies—were unrelated to efficacy in this case. If there had been self-selection based on prior feelings of efficacy, there should have been differences in terms of participation as far as these attributes were concerned between those who joined unions and those who did not.

If our hypothesis is incorrect, and political efficacy *did* precede political participation, it must have come from some change-producing experience other than political participation. The major types of change-producing experience evident in Venezuela on the same scale as political participation are migration to the cities (observable among peasants as urban experience—i.e., having lived in a city) and exposure to the mass media. Each of these is related to political efficacy in the 1967 data. But politically participant peasants are no more likely than nonparticipant peasants to read newspapers, to listen to the radio, or to have lived in a city at some time. Thus, if something produced efficacy which in turn produced participation, that something must be a variable whose identity is not common in the literature and one which is not very evident in Venezuela. Additionally, there is a lack of relationship between source of initiative in founding unions and levels of efficacy (see Table 9). If in fact political efficacy preceded the act of political participation, unions which were founded at some local initiative should have higher levels of efficacy among their membership than those founded at outside initia-

Table 9 Source of Initiative in Founding Union and Political Efficacy in Venezuela, in Percentages

Efficacy Measure		Source of Initiative	
		Campesinos Themselves (N=525)	Outside Organizers (N=595)
		%	%
Believe political opinions are important	Yes	51.0	53.9
	No	49.0	46.1
Believe could influence national government decision	Yes	53.3	55.6
	No.	46.7	44.4

tive, even given the somewhat induced participation where local party militants led the founding of the local union.

Our conclusion is that what occurred among the Venezuelan peasantry was a mobilization for which, according to most of the assumptions common to the literature on political participation, the attitudinal requisites were lacking. Organizers simply walked into areas with apolitical peasants and convinced them to form unions.

Why it was so easy for organizers to convince Venezuelan peasants to form themselves into political peasant unions is not completely clear from the data, especially since evidently there were few of the attitudinal prerequisites usually associated with political activism. There are several possibilities which could be suggested, however. First, the typical Venezuelan peasant has been a member of a rather unstable social structure. In contrast to Colombia, where peasants live for generations in the same villages dominated by a local landowning aristocracy, Venezuelan peasants have characteristically been perpetual migrants. Most Venezuelan peasants were slash-and-burn cultivators (*conuqueros*) whose livelihood was gained from farming small plots of unoccupied land. Living in isolated villages and paying no fees for land use, the *conuqueros* would farm the land until it became exhausted and then move on to a new locality and repeat the process. The dimensions of this pattern can be seen from the 1963 survey data, which revealed that 43 percent of the peasants had lived in three or more different towns in their lives.

At the same time, there was little of the plantation structure which existed in Colombia. Most landlords were absentees, living in larger cities off rents collected by local foremen. Until the agrarian reforms which accompanied the AD accession to power, government was largely absent in the rural areas. Furthermore, under the dictator Gomez, much of the land, especially in the central coastal states of Aragua, Carabobo, and Miranda, in which some social stability existed via the plantation system, was appropriated by the dictator and his lieutenants, driving that group of peasants off the land. Under those conditions, there was little chance for the clientelist structure found in Colombia to develop. In fact, prior to the coming of the union, no local competing sociopolitical structure existed to confront the union organizers. The sole exception to this was the Andean region, bordering on Colombia, where the Catholic church and freehold agriculture had existed as strong forces since the colonial period.[32] It is perhaps significant that this area was the one in which the organization of peasant unions met with least success.

When the agrarian reform, which was based on a combination of idealism and practical politics, was initiated under AD leadership, gov-

[32] Domingo Alberto Rangel, *Los Andinos En El Poder* (Merida, 1964), pp. 7–37.

ernment began to penetrate the rural areas with appurtenances of modern societies such as schools, roads, and government officials, and peasants were confronted for the first time with a need to interact with a previously irrelevant factor in their lives. The spread of the peasant union movement was in effect a solution supplied by the very forces which created the need for it.[33] We will proceed, therefore, on the assumption that, rather than preceding participation, political efficacy was its consequence.

Attitudinal Effects of Political Participation: Political Efficacy

The 1967 data confirm that a sense of national efficacy is strongly related to having belonged to a peasant union (see Table 10). But the data

Table 10   Membership in Rural Unions and Political Efficacy in Venezuela, in Percentages

		Has Belonged to a Rural Union at Some Time	
		Yes (N=986)	No (N=202)
		%	%
National Efficacy *	Yes	55.3	37.6
	No	44.7	62.4
Opinion Efficacy **	Yes	51.8	39.6
	No	48.2	60.4

* chi sq.=21.524; p.001; phi=.14***.
** chi sq.=10.027; p.05; phi=.09*.

reveal more than this about the relationships between participation and efficacy and about those among efficacy and other factors in the peasant's life. In designing the study, we were concerned with the particular aspect of the participation experience which would result in efficacy. The relationship between participation and efficacy (although inverted conceptually) has, after all, been a common finding.

In simple cross tabulations using national efficacy as the dependent variable, a number of aspects of political participation suggested by other studies as being influential were found to be related to national

[33] This interpretation seems to follow also from the fact that the temporal spread of peasant unions was outward from Caracas, with the first unions being founded in the central states of Aragua, Carabobo, and Miranda in the 1940s and in the remote states of Bolivar, Apure, and Barinas only in the late 1950s and early 1960s.

efficacy. These included the overall "effectiveness" of the individual's union (a computed score),[34] frequency of attendance at union meetings, frequency of attendance at party meetings, speaking up or expressing an opinion in union meetings, and service as a union officer.

National efficacy was not related to the length of time an individual had belonged to a union. What this seems to indicate is that it is the quality (in terms of the union itself) and intensity of the participation which is important in producing efficacy, rather than the duration of the experience. As it happens, length of membership in unions is unrelated to the other variables. This would be expected if participation were induced among previously nonefficacious people. A long association with a political organization, if the association were passive, apathetic, or in an ineffective context, would do little to change one's attitudes toward government. But participation is not the only factor related to political efficacy. Urban experience, defined as having lived in a city at some time, frequency of reading newspapers, and level of education are also related to efficacy. Moreover, there are interrelationships among all of the national efficacy-related variables as well, leaving the precise role of political participation somewhat unclear.

To unravel these interrelated variables, we decided to use a multivariate analysis technique for categorical data suggested by James Coleman (1964).[35] This technique has the advantage that it can partial out the relative effects of different independent variables controlled simul-

[34] The effectiveness score for each union in the sample was based generally on the assumption that an "effective" union was one which maintained its internal organizational structure and had a wide range of activities. The score which ranged from 0 to 9 was calculated on the following basis: a union was given one point if it regularly meets at least twice a month; two points if 60 percent or more of its members regularly attend meetings and one point if 40–59 percent regularly attend; one point if the union maintains at least two of the three legally required record books; one point if it undertakes five or more different types of activities in a given year (petitions, social events, e.g.); one point if it sent a delegate to the most recent National Peasant Congress; one point if government or Peasant Federation officials addressed a meeting during the last year; and two points if delegations were sent twelve or more times to one agency and six to eleven times to three more. In the 1967 sample, the 1,260 respondents were distributed among 107 peasant unions. A score of four or less was classified as "low effectiveness" and a score of five to nine as "high effectiveness." Thirty-one percent of the unions with 30 percent of the members had "low effectiveness" scores.

[35] James S. Coleman, *Introduction to Mathematical Sociology* (New York, 1964), chap. 6. The "effect parameter," as Coleman terms the statistic, is the average percentage difference across all cells in a multi-variate contingency table accounted for by a given independent variable with respect to the dependent variable, holding all other independent variables in the table constant. The specific use of this statistic in this research is described in detail in Mathiason, Appendix B. Another application of this technique to similar problems is found in Robert R. Alford and Harry M. Scoble, "Sources of Local Political Involvement," *American Political Science Review*, LXII (December 1968), 1192–1206.

taneously and produce a statistic (a_1), which Coleman calls an "effect parameter" that can be tested for significance. Controlling all possible pairs of the previously determined "significant" independent variables (Table 11), it may be observed that only speaking up in union meetings, frequency of reading newspapers, and urban experience independently affect efficacy in the sense that their relationship to it is not by way of some other intervening variable.

In terms of participation this means that frequency of political party meeting attendance is related to efficacy mostly because political party attenders also tend to speak up in union meetings. Similarly, having been a union officer is related to national efficacy because officers also tend to speak up in union meetings. The two other participation factors, union "effectiveness" and frequency of participation in union meetings, however, have, at the pair level, a significantly independent effect relative to speaking up in union meetings. But simultaneously controlling for frequency of attendance at union meetings, speaking up in union meetings, and frequency of newspaper reading in terms of national efficacy, it was found that the effect of frequency of attendance at union meetings washed out. The independent effect of syndicate "effectiveness," however, remained when it was similarly controlled. This left four independent variables, but in controlling for urban experience, frequency of newspaper reading, and speaking up in union meetings in terms of national efficacy, it was found that the independent effect of urban experience washed out.

A feeling of national efficacy, then, is principally the result of three factors: (1) frequency of reading newspapers; (2) verbal participation in union meetings; and (3) the level of effectiveness of the syndicate. These variables are generally additive in their effect on efficacy. Peasants who speak up in union meetings are proportionately more efficacious than those who do not, but when these intense participators are members of more effective unions, efficacy is proportionately higher. It would appear that the "demonstration effect" of effective unions stimulates efficacy among those peasants inclined to participate more actively.

On the other hand, newspaper reading is an alternative source of national efficacy. Persons who read newspapers tend to choose individual action to influence the government in the hypothetical situation posed by the question measuring national efficacy (Table 12). Persons who do not read newspapers tend to choose indirect action by way of the syndicate. For political participants, the union not only teaches efficacy, but it becomes the main channel for efficacious action. Newspapers, however, teach other channels of influence, perhaps by demonstration in the news of how most people in practice influence government. This type of

Table 11 Average Effect of Paired Independent Variables in Terms of National Efficacy in Venezuela

	Speaks up in Meetings	Was Union Officer	Read Newspapers	Syndicate Attendance	Party Attendance	Urban Experience	Syndicate Effectiveness	Level of Education
Speak	—	.066	.126*	.088	.070	.111†	.100*	.067
Officer	.129†	—	.143*	.105	.087	.096†	.076	.047
Newspapers	.191†	.176†	—	.168*	.117*	.067*	.198†	−.007
Syndicate attendance	.112**	.119*	.140*	—	.082	.140†	.063	.087
Party attendance . .	.169†	.177**	.133*	.123	—	.143†	.115	.081
Urban experience .	.209†	.205†	.139†	.160†	.123†	—	.142†	.056
Syndicate effectiveness . . .	.140†	.110*	.130*	.118†	.112	.151†	—	.059
Education	.200†	.196†	.157*	.157*	.142*	.096*	.149	—

* Significant at .05 level (two tail test).
** Significant at .01 level.
† Significant at .001 level.

Table 12 Efficacious Peasants (as Percent of Peasants in Cell) Categorized by Effectiveness of Syndicate, Speaking up in Union Meetings, and Reading Newspapers

Effectiveness of Syndicate	Speaking up in Union Meetings	Weekly	N*	Read Newspapers Less	N*	No	N*
		%		%		%	
High	Yes	83.3	(12)	87.5	(8)	64.7	(17)
	No	80.0	(10)	50.0	(12)	57.1	(77)
Medium	Yes	85.7	(56)	73.5	(34)	62.5	(72)
	No	75.5	(49)	61.2	(49)	58.6	(220)
Low	Yes	69.6	(23)	46.2	(13)	53.3	(30)
	No	58.8	(27)	56.7	(30)	41.3	(92)
No Union**	Yes	——		——		——	——
	No	30.8	(13)	40.0	(25)	30.8	(65)

a_1 (Average effect of syndicate effectiveness)=.104*.
a_2 (Average effect of speaking up in union meetings)=.097*.
a_3 (Average effect of reading newspapers)=.128**.
* N is the total number of peasants from which each percentage was calculated, e.g., of the 12 peasants in a high effectiveness union who speak up in union meetings and read newspapers weekly, 83.3 percent are efficacious.
** Category does not enter into calculation of a_1.

information would not be obtained merely by living in a city, which would explain the lack of effect on national efficacy of urban experience.

Participation in peasant unions is one of several sources of national efficacy among Venezuelan peasants. *Campesinos* exposed to other change forces in the society, especially the mass media, can and do develop a sense of political efficacy. But for those who have not lived in cities and/or cannot read newspapers, the experience of political participation may be the most important force for altering one's orientation to government in favor of efficacy. This participation is a means of accelerating the process of acquiring a sense of national efficacy in that it does not await the evolution of an "urbanized" or literate peasantry.

There are qualitative differences, however, between efficacy which is the product of experiences other than participation and that which results from participation. Participation in the mass media produces a belief in the individual's capacity to act alone to influence government, while the political participation experience creates the belief in group action. Moreover, peasant unions themselves are the groups through which most *campesinos* would channel their influence. This in itself may explain why efficacy has increased rapidly in rural Venezuela. The syndicate is something concretely visible and understandable to peasants. No ability to imagine oneself individually trying to influence national government is required for a sense of efficacy. A peasant need only learn that the syndicate exists to act as broker between himself and the government—and this lesson is learned by observing and especially by participating in the brokerage activities of the union through verbally joining in its discussions. Consequently, if the union is adept at brokerage (or "effective" as we have operationally used the term), there is a greater likelihood that its members will be taught that they are, in fact, efficacious.

Participation and Efficacy: Some Conclusions
A comparison of Venezuela with Colombia gives some insight into the individual attitudinal consequences of being caught up in a political revolution. Rural Colombia has manifestly not had a revolution; rural Venezuela has. Although the old rural power structure in Colombia and the new union-based structure in Venezuela are superficially similar, it is evident that they are quite different in their effects. Participation in Colombia, at best, ties the individual peasant closer to his traditional liege lord and, at worst, involves him in anomic, fratricidal violence. It certainly does not equip him to deal with national government. Participation in Venezuela involves the peasant in a structure in which he can directly interact with government, change his local leaders if necessary, and which, up to now, has provided an alternative to violence in producing change. This experience of participation has been instrumental in fostering a feeling that the individual can influence the government and thus channel the government's influence upon himself.

In terms of Venezuela, where participation is high, this has meant that most participant peasants are efficacious. In Colombia, efficacy tends to accrue only to higher-status peasants. Table 13 shows, comparing the two countries in terms of the variables most generally related to efficacy in each, that we have a step-wise progression in terms of efficacy. The least efficacious group is made up of low-status Colombian peasants. It is this group in Venezuela which has been most greatly affected by the political participation involved in the peasant union. In short, what most differentiates Colombia and Venezuela in our data is the fact that in Venezuela there has been a revolution which has lifted up the lowest stratum of peasants, and in Colombia there has not.

Between the two countries, however, we have two types of national political efficacy. One, which we could call "direct" efficacy, is the feeling that an individual can influence national government decisions directly, by himself. It is this type of national efficacy which characterizes

able 13 National Efficacy in Venezuela * and Colombia by Major Independent Variable in Each, in Percentages

'ational fficacy	Venezuela Union Members Verbally Participant (N=258)	Venezuela Union Members Not Verbally Participant (N=542)	Colombia Peasant Landowner (N=82)	Colombia Peasant Renter (N=52)	Venezuela Nonmember of Union (N=202)	Colombia Squatter or Day Laborer (N=34)
	%	%	%	%	%	%
'es	69.0	55.4	48.8	38.5	37.6	17.6
'o	31.0	44.6	51.2	61.5	62.4	82.4

* 1967 agrarian reform beneficiary sample.

stable, modern nations such as the United States. This type of efficacy also is present among those Colombian peasants who are efficacious and among the Venezuelan peasants who derive their sense of national efficacy from exposure to the mass media.

The other type of national efficacy might be termed "mediated" political efficacy. By this we mean that a person feels that he can influence government because he enjoys an instrumental relationship with a network of mediators, or brokers, who are in turn influential in the local and national political systems. As such, the sense of efficacy is tied to a personally felt system (in Venezuela, the peasant union) which both creates and sustains the attitude. This qualitative nature of "mediated" national efficacy explains why the attitude spread so rapidly among the Venezuelan peasantry, and why no variables indicating length of time were related to it. Once the mediating structure was created and the individual became involved in it, he acquired a sense of national political efficacy since the attitude is tied more to the mediating structure than to the individual.

But beyond the case of acquisition there is another difference between direct and mediated efficacy. Because the kind of national efficacy acquired by participation is so easily come by, it seems that it exists, as it were, in an attitudinal vacuum in the sense that other attitudes and values which in the United States are frequently found to be associated with national efficacy are lacking. Among Venezuelan peasants, for example, there is no relationship between having a sense of national efficacy and identifying with, or according loyalty to, the nation. In contrast, nationally efficacious Colombian peasants, who seem to have "direct" efficacy, also tend strongly to be those who identify with the nation. In short, there is some doubt as to the persistence and duration of an attitude, like "mediated" national efficacy, which is entirely pegged to a given socio-political matrix rather than internalized individually and applied regardless of which party or group happens to be in power.

Our present data do not allow us to pursue that particular implication of our research. We offer it as a next step for research. The meaning of political efficacy as an orientation requires further refinement and reflection. Researchers must do more than measure the presence or absence of a certain set response to a question in a survey. We must also seek to understand the significance of the response, and its meaning, within its particular sociocultural matrix. *An explanation must be sought for the process by which a person develops an orientation such as efficacy, and of the system of behaviors which maintains, changes, or otherwise influences his belief in his ability to influence his government.* We must be on guard against assuming that the developmental process of efficacious feelings is the same in most cultures and through time. In the United States, for example, a great deal of research has shed light on the process of how efficacy is developed through the process of political socialization of children. This makes a good deal of sense in a political culture with a fairly well defined, stable system of beliefs, political values, and legitimated forms of political behavior, which parents quite naturally and easily pass on to their children. The same type of socialization may make little sense in a society undergoing drastic and perhaps violent change in its forms of government, political doctrines, and acceptable standards of political behavior. In such a society, and the Venezuelan case seems particularly instructive here, *what one encounters is primary socialization of adults, occurring as a direct learning experience, with new phenomena such as collective action in a variety of nonviolent and violent forms.* Only later—and only then if the changes become sufficiently stabilized to be articulated into a coherent set of orientations—can parents transmit the political culture to their children in a process of effective socialization.

Within this context of attempting to add dimension to the meaning of political participation in terms of national political efficacy, we have tried to illuminate one face of the individual consequences of political change. To the degree to which we have succeeded in stimulating discussion and, hopefully, further research on peasants caught up in social change, we hope that we have helped place the political scientist in a more competitive position with the political novelist.

India's Urban Constituencies

Myron Weiner and John Osgood Field*

I. Introduction

There are two widely held views concerning the political characteristics of cities in low-income countries. One school holds that the urban experience in developing countries makes individuals more politically aware, stimulates citizens to expect more of their political system, generates frustrations as governments fail to meet these expectations, and leads urban dwellers to become increasingly radical and their politics to become polarized by ideological cleavages. There is, or so this model suggests, a progression from politicization to radicalization to polarization in urban political life, together with a tendency for the city to be a diffusion center shaping the political character of the rural region in which it is located.[1]

An alternative way of looking at urban areas in low-income parts of the world is to note that they differ significantly from one developing country to another, that they are affected by the rural areas around them in addition to having an effect of their own on those areas, and that, even within a single country, there are likely to be substantial variations from one city to another as to the degree of politicization, radicalization, and polarization of politics. These variations depend upon such factors as city size, migration, levels of development, occupational complexion, and the political character of the surrounding regions. This second model emphasizes interaction with the countryside. It assumes that the city shares many of the political features of the countryside; thus, political culture, political organization, and processes of social change shape the city as they do the rural environment. Therefore, we should not expect the cities of one developing country to resemble those of another politically, nor should we assume that the cities in one region within a developing country are necessarily like those of another.[2]

The first model is essentially attributional, emphasizing the political imperatives imposed by the attributes or characteristics of urban life. The second is more contextual, stressing the common features of cities with their rural surroundings. The first model implies political uniformities; the second suggests urban political diversity.

This study describes how India's urban constituencies have voted since 1952. India is a useful case for exploring these alternative models. It has had more than twenty years of elections, thereby providing uniform data on one type of political activity over an extended period of

Figure 1   Urban India: Cities of 50,000 or More People (1961 Census)

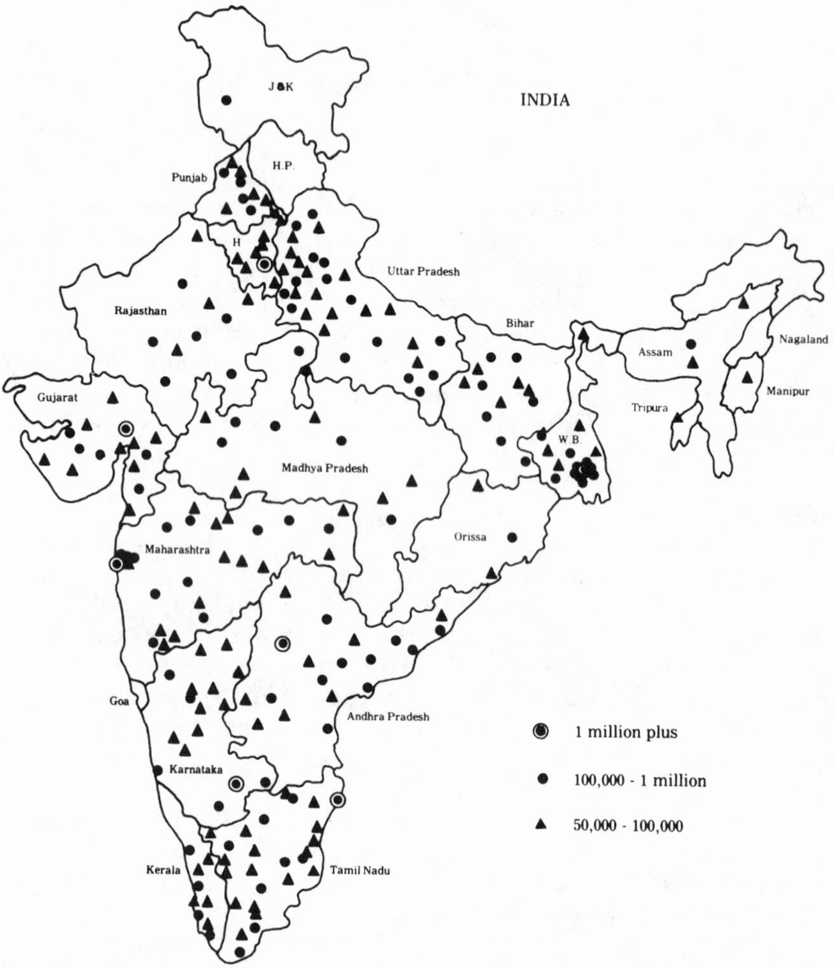

time; it has competitive political parties, thereby making it possible to find out the political preferences of urban dwellers; and, despite being a preponderantly rural country, it has a large number of cities, thereby making intercity comparisons meaningful.

In this study we pose three sets of questions. The first asks how India's urban constituencies compare with rural constituencies regarding (1) politicization, (2) radicalization, and (3) polarization. The aim is to find out whether India's cities are electorally like the rural countryside in which they are located, or are like each other. If there is an urban-rural "gap," where does it exist, and with respect to what political characteristics?

Second, how have India's urban constituencies changed over time? Which parties have gained and which have lost? Have the urban areas become more participant, more radicalized, and more polarized in the past two decades? And have differences between rural and urban areas widened or narrowed?

Third, what are the differences among urban areas from one region of the country to another? And among large, medium, and small cities? Are, for example, smaller cities like the countryside and larger cities more like each other?

These are questions that cannot be answered wholly with the data at our disposal. Since we are working with election results rather than survey interviews, we can report how aggregate electoral units have behaved, not how individuals have voted. But if urban areas in the aggregate do not assume the characteristics which various theories attribute to them, then little is added by examining individual behavior. Moreover, while this study is primarily descriptive rather than explanatory, we can at least examine whether our findings are more consistent with one model than with the other and suggest that some explanations are simply incompatible with the election data.

India's urban constituencies: a profile Slightly less than one-fifth (18 percent) of India's population was classified as urban in the 1961 census—a total of 78,900,000 people dispersed in 2,700 urban settlements. A very substantial portion of this urban population lived in small towns: 19 million alone resided in settlement clusters of less than 20,000 persons. Only 45 million, or slightly over half (58 percent) of the officially classified urban population, lived in towns and cities of 50,000 or more. These 45 million urban inhabitants, living in 245 towns and cities, constitute the focus of this study.

We have focused on these 45 million urban dwellers for three reasons. The first, and most obvious, is that they and their towns are the groups most commonly thought of as "urban." The second is that an increasing proportion of India's urban population is living in these larger settlements—64 percent in 1971 as against 58 percent in 1961. The third reason is a practical one: only in settlements of at least 50,000 do state assembly constituencies match the urban unit. Smaller towns are generally located in constituencies with substantial numbers of rural voters, while only a rare urban area with a population of 50,000 fails to constitute a single constituency.[3] Table 1 shows how these 45 million persons are distributed among the states.

Our analysis covers 239 cities (omitting those in Jammu and Kashmir and the ex-union territories). These 239 cities were divided into 383 constituencies in 1967; and they contained an eligible electorate of

Table 1   Urban Population and the Number of Cities Containing 50,000 or More People* (1961)

States	Population	Number of Cities	Number of Constituencies 1952	1957	1962	1967–72
Andhra Pradesh**	3,076,000	19	23	29	28	30
Assam	242,000	3	2	3	3	4
Bihar	1,676,000	12	11	13	14	15
Gujarat	2,813,000	15	24	21	25	27
Haryana	706,000	9	9	9	9	9
Jammu and Kashmir	388,000	2				
Kerala	1,066,000	9	11	11		11
Madhya Pradesh	1,951,000	12	17	21	21	21
Madras	4,668,000	28	31	37	41	43
Maharashtra	7,775,000	27	49	47	57	61
Mysore	2,676,000	16	21	24	22	25
Orissa	374,000	4	4	4	4†	4
Punjab	1,229,000	10	14	13	15	15
Rajasthan	1,482,000	10	14	14	14	15
Uttar Pradesh	6,010,000	35	39	43	45	49
West Bengal	5,949,000	30	53	53	54	54
Union Territories	2,446,000	4				
Totals	44,527,000	245	322	342	352	383

*Population is from 1961 census. Constituencies are located according to state boundaries as of 1967.
**The number of constituencies indicated for Andhra Pradesh in 1957 includes urban units in the coastal districts which held elections in 1955.
†Orissa, 1961.

approximately 27 million people.

In 1961 slightly under one-third of India's 45 million urban dwellers lived in seven cities with populations exceeding 1 million: Ahmedabad, Bangalore, Bombay, Calcutta, Delhi, Hyderabad, and Madras. Another 35 million lived in thirty-nine cities and town groups whose populations ranged from 200,000 to 1 million, while 7 million lived in sixty-one urban settlements of 100,000 to 200,000. The remaining 9 million lived in 135 cities with populations under 100,000, but greater than 50,000. We have classified these as metropolitan, large, medium-sized, and small cities, respectively.

Throughout this study we have utilized the 1961 census since it was employed by the Election Commission for determining constituency delimitations for elections throughout the sixties and early seventies. The 1971 census revealed that urban India continues to grow, and at an accelerating pace. The latter census reported 70 million persons living in towns larger than 50,000, compared with 45 million in 1961.

In its entirety, India's urban population rose to 109 million, representing a growth rate of 38 percent from 1961 to 1971 as against a rural increase of only 22 percent. Increases were greatest in cities with more than 100,000 persons: 10.4 percent of India's population now live in places of this size or larger, as against 9 percent in 1961 and 6.5 percent in 1951. Settlements with 50,000 or more now contain 64 percent of India's urban population, reflecting both their high growth rates and the lower growth rates of India's smaller towns. This report on India's urban constituencies, therefore, describes and analyzes the voting patterns of the most rapidly growing sector in Indian society, one whose influence may be expected to increase in the decades ahead.

II.   Urban Electoral Participation

Urban-rural comparisons   India's urban constituencies are electorally more politicized than the Indian countryside. Urban residents have a greater tendency to vote in state assembly elections than do rural dwellers. There are, however, substantial variations from one election to another and among the different states which serve to qualify any simple generalizations.

During the First General Elections in 1952, voter participation in urban constituencies was the same as in rural constituencies, with only half of the eligible electorate casting valid ballots in each context.[4] A significant gap appeared in the Second General Elections in 1957, when urban turnout increased noticeably to 55 percent, while that in the countryside actually declined slightly to 46 percent. In the Third General Elections of 1962, the level of voter participation increased throughout the country, from 55 to 61 percent in urban constituencies, 46 to 52 percent in rural; but the gap between them remained much the same.

This gap began to diminish in the Fourth General Elections of 1967. Urban turnout was 63 percent, hardly an increase at all, whereas turnout in the rest of the country continued its upward swing, reaching 58 percent. Elections in several states between 1968 and 1971 indicate that both urban and rural turnout continued to expand slightly, but that the difference between them narrowed further. In 1972, urban turnout actually declined modestly to 60 percent, while rural turnout held at 58 percent, all but eliminating the gap once again.[5] These trends, through 1972, are portrayed in Figure 2.[6]

In any country so large and diverse as India, there are bound to be variations from national patterns and trends. In 1952, for example, when turnout was the same in rural and urban India, the cities of Madhya Pradesh (nineteen constituencies) had an average turnout 12 percent greater than the rest of the state, as presently constituted.[7] The urban take-off that began nationally in 1957 did not appear in the four states of South India until 1962.[8] After unusually high levels of

Figure 2   Turnout in India: Urban and Rural Constituencies Compared (1952-72)

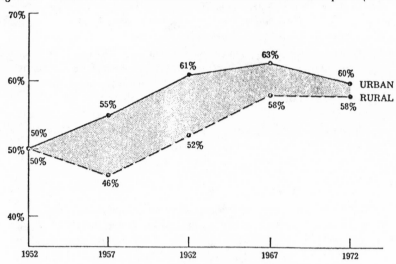

NOTES:

Only elections held in the years shown are included in the calculations. Returns for Rajasthan, 1972, were not available to us at the time of writing and therefore are not included.

Urban-rural differences in turnout were significant at .01 degree of confidence or better in 1957, 1962, and 1967. It was not possible to establish significance for 1972, since the figures that year were hand-tabulated.

The figures for 1952 and 1957 apply to single-member constituencies only.

voter participation in the cities of united Bombay State in 1957, stimulated by urban preoccupation with demands for division of the state, turnout dropped in the cities of both successor states (Maharashtra and Gujarat), even though it increased nationally and in the rural constituencies of each successor state.[9] In 1967, when it became evident that the national trend of expanding urban turnout had begun to level off, voters in Bihar's fifteen urban constituencies went to the polls in record numbers, producing the largest gap between urban and rural voting that state has seen.

Notwithstanding these and other deviations, several patterns and trends are clear at the state level. Although the difference in electoral participation between urban and rural constituencies has all but disappeared, urban turnout remains substantially greater than rural turnout in the least developed regions of India, particularly in the Hindi-speaking states of the north (notably Madhya Pradesh, Bihar, and Uttar Pradesh, along with Orissa), while more developed or more politicized states now reveal very minor urban-rural differences.[10] Madhya Pradesh has consistently shown the largest urban-rural gap over the years. In Andhra, Mysore, and Assam, rural turnout has actually exceeded urban quite regularly (the lone exception being 1962). Kerala is the only state in which urban and rural turnouts have been virtually identical in all elections; the greatest disparity between them was 5 percent in 1970.

In absolute terms, urban turnout between 1952 and 1972 has been highest in the cities of Kerala, Tamil Nadu, Punjab, and Haryana, lowest in Orissa, Assam, and Bihar (1957-67), and average, since 1962, in West Bengal and Maharashtra.[11] For the most part, these distributions mirror those for turnout in rural constituencies as well.

To summarize, India's urban areas became increasingly politicized after the 1952 elections, much more so than the rural areas; but by the 1960s and early 1970s the rural areas had also substantially increased their turnout, thereby narrowing, eliminating, or reversing the gap between the two. As of 1974, urban turnout continues to exceed rural turnout by impressive margins only in Madhya Pradesh, Uttar Pradesh, and Orissa.

Attributional versus contextual explanations   To what extent are urban areas more similar to each other with regard to levels of participation than to the rural constituencies of the state in which they are located? This is part of the larger question concerning the extent to which cities in India possess political qualities that are not shared, or shared to the same degree, by rural India. According to the model that conceptualizes urbanity as an attribute, urban constituencies possess political characteristics, such as levels of voter participation, which resemble those of other urban constituencies rather than those of rural constituencies. The contextual model indicates that the urban constituencies have less in common with urban constituencies elsewhere in the country than they do with the rural constituencies in their own state.

The attributional model is so widely used in analyses of urban politics in developing countries ("The cities of the Third World are . . .") that it warrants explicit testing with the Indian election data. We are able to test this model in three ways. First, we can compare the average turnout of urban constituencies in each state with the national urban average, on the one hand, and with that state's average turnout in rural constituencies, on the other. If a state's urban constituencies resemble those in the country as a whole more than they resemble rural constituencies in the same state, then we can infer that being urban is more important than being in a particular location. If they resemble the rural constituencies more, it would appear that the state context is more relevent for understanding urban turnout than is the fact of urbanity.

Second, we can identify urban constituencies whose level of turnout deviates from the national average in order to learn whether they are

predominantly in states where turnout generally deviates from the
national average, and we can then look within these states to ascertain
whether deviant urban constituencies merely reflect the state norm.
By locating specific urban constituencies that deviate from the national
average, we can thus further explore the possible influence of state
context.

Finally, by examining the relationship between city size and turnout
we have still another measure of whether urbanity makes a difference.
Presumably, if it does, larger cities ("more" urban?) might show different electoral patterns than the smaller towns, while the smaller
towns might more closely resemble rural areas.

Urbanity versus state context   We first sought to determine whether
we could learn more about the level of turnout in the urban constituencies of a state by knowing that they are urban (B as part of C in
Figure 3) as against knowing that they are in that particular state (B as
part of A). If the former is the case, then urbanity is the more meaningful piece of information; if the latter, then state context is.

The state-level data produce such a cacophony of evidence that no
simple generalization will suffice. In each election there are states
where urban turnout resembles the all-India average more than rural
turnout in the same states, leading to the belief that being urban is a
distinctive characteristic insofar as turnout is concerned. However, in
each election there are also states where the urban-rural association is
stronger than that between state-urban and national-urban figures. And
there are several states that cannot be tallied on one side of the ledger
or the other.[12]

In general, urbanity is a dependable guide to turnout in approximately half of the states electing each year, although in many of these
same places the state context is relevant as well. Clearly, the attributional and contextual models are not empirical alternatives between
which it is necessary to choose. Urbanity and state context are equally
valid guides to voter participation overall, and their influence is often
felt simultaneously in the urban constituencies of a given state.[13] Moreover, the fact that neither urbanity nor context identifies levels of turnout in a handful of states only indicates that, singly or together, the
two quite powerfully inform the magnitudes of urban turnout at the
state level.[14]

The only state in which urban turnout has consistently resembled the
national average more than its own rural turnout is Madhya Pradesh,
one of India's most backward regions, which has had the largest urban-
rural gap over the years. It is noteworthy, too, that such typically low-
turnout states as Bihar, Orissa, Uttar Pradesh, and Rajasthan are also
among the states with the largest annual urban-rural cleavage in voter

Figure 3 Urbanity versus State Context

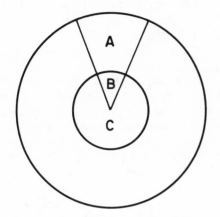

A = a state

B = urban constituencies in that state

C = urban constituencies generally

participation. But the key to urbanity's relevance is not consistently a function of rural backwardness and of low levels of political mobilization. In two instances when urbanity has prevailed over context, the Punjab in 1952 and Andhra Pradesh in 1967, rural turnout actually exceeded urban by significant amounts. The rural-urban electoral gap has also been substantial in Maharashtra and West Bengal, two states that are not generally regarded as economically or politically underdeveloped. On balance, however, it would appear that urbanity is more relevant to backward states and context to advanced. Nevertheless, there are enough exceptions (and overlap) to leave this hypothesis unverified.[15]

The fact that urban turnout at the state and national levels may differ greatly does not exclude the possibility that within a state urbanity functions much as it does in the country at large. Consider the case of Bihar in 1962. Voter participation in Bihar's fourteen urban constituencies was well below the national urban average (national urban: 61 percent; national rural: 52 percent; Bihar urban: 52 percent; and Bihar rural: 44 percent), making the national average a largely irrelevant piece of information for identifying the level of urban turnout in that state. Nevertheless, it is clear that urbanity in Bihar had the same essential effect of increasing turnout over the rural norm as it had for India as a whole in 1962.[16] If urbanity is held to be a distinctive characteristic for turnout in India in 1962 because it significantly exceeded rural turnout, the same must be said for Bihar. The similarity of patterns indicates that a common influence was at work.

When the inquiry is extended to consider whether urbanity has the same *effect* at the state level as it does nationally, the influence of urbanity is even more apparent. Yet so is the influence of state context, usually in depressing the levels of turnout attained in a state's cities (as in the case of Bihar, 1962). Once again, the impact of being urban and of being in a particular state is brought out. The two models co-exist; they do not conflict.

The location of deviant urban constituencies   The importance of state context is confirmed when urban constituencies with significantly high and low turnouts are tested for similar deviance from the mean turnout of their states. Are deviant urban constituencies in deviant states? More specifically, where are urban constituencies with unusually high levels of turnout? And where are urban constituencies with unusually low levels of turnout? Are they in high- and low-turnout states, respectively?

With impressive regularity high-turnout urban constituencies are located in high-turnout states, such as Kerala, Punjab, Madras (except in 1957), and Andhra Pradesh (see Table 2). In these states, rural

Table 2 Distribution of High-Turnout Urban Constituencies

Type of States	1957*		1962		1967	
	N	%	N	%	N	%
High-turnout states	43	81.1	51	87.9	64	91.4
Average states	9	17.0	6	10.3	4	5.7
Low-turnout states	1	1.9	1	1.7	2	2.9
Totals	53	100.0	58	99.9	70	100.0

*Andhra Pradesh is excluded for 1957 because only a portion of the state elected that year. Double-member constituencies are also excluded.

turnout has consistently exceeded the turnout for urban areas in India as a whole. The overwhelming majority of high-turnout urban constituencies are concentrated in states which themselves have levels of voter participation significantly above the national average in each of the three elections examined.[17] Moreover, there is a tendency for the concentration to be more pronounced each year, while the incidence of high-turnout cities in low-turnout states is extraordinarily rare.

The distribution is less clear with regard to the location of low-turnout urban constituencies. A fairly large number are found in states with low levels of turnout each election, such as Bihar, Madhya Pradesh, Orissa, Rajasthan, and Uttar Pradesh (1962 and 1967); but the patterns tend to be weak. In none of the three elections do the low-turnout states have a majority of the low-turnout urban constituencies, although a trend in this direction is apparent. Moreover, each year there has been a sizable minority of low-turnout urban constituencies, ranging between a fifth and a third of the total, in states with levels of turnout significantly *above* the national average.

In sum, high-turnout urban constituencies are found almost invariably in states with significantly high turnouts themselves. Low-turnout urban constituencies are more evenly distributed.[18] High urban turnout is powerfully conditioned by context, low urban turnout very much less so. Knowing in the abstract that an urban constituency has a low level of voter participation is a poor guide to identifying where that constituency is likely to be. Nevertheless, an examination of the turnout in individual urban constituencies as it relates to state turnout when both are compared with national averages suggests that urban turnout in India does reflect, to a considerable degree, the turnout of the rural areas within which the urban constituencies are located.

A further test of the contextual model lies in what happens when deviant urban constituencies are contrasted with other constituencies in the same state. If a high-turnout urban constituency in a high-turnout state is not significantly different from other constituencies in that state, then its classification as a high-turnout constituency is merely a function of state context. The same applies to a low-turnout constituency in a low-turnout state.

Our findings leave little doubt concerning the importance of context. For example, *not one* of the twenty-eight low-turnout urban constituencies located in low-turnout states in 1967 was low in relation to other constituencies in the same state. A more striking confirmation of the relevance of state context would be hard to find. A similar, if less spectacular, attrition took place among the sixty-four high-turnout constituencies in high-turnout states, forty-four of which were average in their states. The prevailing pattern of deviant urban constituencies in similarly deviant states is, therefore, no coincidence; it is causality. These constituencies are where they are because they are creatures of their states, at least with regard to turnout.

Table 3 Distribution of Low-Turnout Urban Constituencies

Type of States	1957*		1962		1967	
	N	%	N	%	N	%
High-turnout states	11	21.6	17	33.3	15	24.2
Average states	25	49.0	15	29.4	19	30.6
Low-turnout states.	15	29.4	19	37.3	28	45.2
Totals	51	100.0	51	100.0	62	100.0

*Andhra Pradesh is excluded for 1957 because only a portion of the state elected that year. Double-member constituencies are also excluded.

City and size turnout   City size is consistently a poor predictor of turnout. Contrary to popular conception, India's metropolitan centers are not more politicized than smaller cities. They cannot even claim a level of turnout above other cities in the same states. Calcutta and Bombay, for example, are no different from most other cities in West Bengal and Maharashtra in their level of turnout for each election. Madras, Hyderabad, and Bangalore have typically been among the lowest turnout cities in their states. Only Ahmedabad among India's largest cities has shown a somewhat higher rate of voter participaticn than other cities in its state; but Ahmedabad's distinctiveness pertains to the first two elections only. For once, a flat statement may be made: India's major cities are not especially politicized electorally. Being "more urban" does not translate into being more participant.

Conversely, small cities are no more likely to resemble rural areas than are medium-sized or large ones. If anything, the constituencies comprising small cities tend to have higher levels of turnout than larger cities, although the differences are never very substantial at the national level.[19] In sum, small cities possess no likeness to rural constituencies that is not generally shared by larger cities as well.

III.   Urban Electoral Protest

Political protest, as measured by electoral preferences, is greater in urban than in rural India. This observation must be qualified by three reservations, however. One is that spatial factors are at work in the distribution of protest among urban constituencies, an observation consistent with our findings concerning the importance of state context in accounting for variations in turnout. The second qualification is that the extent of urban electoral protest is closely related to the competitive

Table 4 Turnout by City Size (1952—72)

City Size	1952*	1957*	1962	1967	1972**
	%	%	%	%	%
Metropolitan (1 million +) 48		52	61	61	
Large (200,000 – 1 million) 50		55	62	62	59†
Medium (100,000 – 200,000) 48		53	61	63	
Small (50,000 – 100,000) 52		56	61	65	61
Rural	50	46	52	58	58

*Single-member constituencies only.
**Finer distinctions for 1972 are not available, since the data were hand-tabulated that year.
†This percentage covers the first three categories.

strategies pursued by "protest" parties. And the third is that electoral protest based on ethnic or regional sentiments is as prominent in rural as in urban constituencies.

For purposes of exploring the nature, depth, and geographical extent of electoral protest in urban constituencies, we can distinguish between two basic types of electoral protest. One is ideological, the other essentially regional. Because the former challenges the state, we call it "radical" protest. Because the latter seeks a redistribution of authority within the existing constitutional framework, we call it regional protest. We shall analyze each in turn.

"Radical" protest voting   With regard to radical protest, we have focused somewhat arbitrarily on two political parties, the Jana Sangh and the Communists, the former representing the most important militant party of the Right, and the latter representing the largest (although not always the most militant) party of the Left. Both parties have taken part in every election. Both are large, and since 1962 one or the other has been India's largest opposition party. Moreover, both present fundamental attacks against the existing political structure, and both supplement their electoral activities with mass protest movements.[20]

Support for the Communists   India currently has three Communist parties: the Communist party of India (CPI), a pro-Soviet group; the more independent-minded and militant Communist party of India (Marxist), conventionally known as the CPM; and the revolutionary Communist party (Marxist-Leninist), or Naxalites. Prior to the 1967 elections (1965 in Kerala), there was only the CPI. Since 1967 both the CPI and CPM have contested.elections, sometimes against each other. The revolutionary Naxalite movement has never openly taken part in an election.

A comparison of voting for the Communist parties in urban as against rural India over the five general elections between 1952 and 1972 reveals that the Communists have consistently won a larger vote in urban constituencies and that Communist support in both urban and rural India has increased quite steadily.

In any analysis of Communist support in India it is necessary to distinguish West Bengal, Kerala, and Andhra Pradesh from the remaining states, for these are the three states in which the Communists have consistently performed best in all elections. Only once have Communist candidates in West Bengal, Kerala, and Andhra Pradesh received less than 10 percent of the popular vote statewide,[21] whereas in no other

Figure 4   The Communist Vote in Urban and Rural Constituencies: All India
(1952-72)

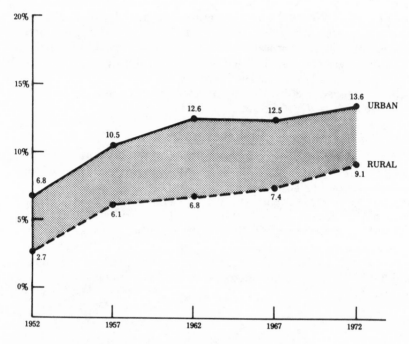

*Denotes significance (difference of means) at .01; # at .05.
NOTES:

For 1952 and 1957, only single-member constituencies are tabulated.

Because the figures for 1972 were hand tabulated, no difference of means test was possible. Figures represent the average of state percentages controlling for the number of constituencies in each state, but not for constituency size. Jammu and Kashmir and Goa are excluded from the calculations; data for Rajasthan were not available to us at the time of writing.

The recent increase in Communist support is somewhat greater when all elections between 1970 and 1972 are taken into account.

state (aside from tiny Tripura in the remote northeast) have they done even this well more than once.[22]

The difference between these states and the rest of India is less clear with respect to urban constituencies because much Communist strength elsewhere is concentrated in the urban areas; and on occasion it is mildly impressive. Nevertheless, the distinction remains valid; and when the urban Communist vote from West Bengal, Kerala, and Andhra Pradesh is compared to the urban Communist vote in other states, we can see that the former is at least three and usually four times as large as the latter (see Table 5). Moreover, a solid majority of Communist victories in urban constituencies each year is in these three states.[23]

Table 5   The Communist Vote: Urban Constituencies in West Bengal, Kerala, and
Andhra Pradesh (Combined) versus the Rest of the Country (1952–72)

	1952*	1957*	1962**	1967	1972†
	%	%	%	%	%
West Bengal, Kerala,	15.3 (70)‡	22.3 (74)	29.0 (81)	28.9 (95)	26.8 (95)
Andhra Pradesh . . .			CPI	10.1	8.2
			CPM	18.8	18.6
Rest of India	4.3 (204)	6.7 (229)	7.5 (264)	7.1 (286)	7.1 (234)
			CPI	4.3	5.4
			CPM	2.8	1.8

*Single-member constituencies only. For 1952, constituencies now in Kerala are omitted;
nine of 11 urban and most rural were in Travancore-Cochin, where CPI candidates ran as independents.

**Kerala, which elected in 1960 and 1965, omitted.

†Kerala, 1970, is included in the absence of elections there in 1972. Orissa 1971, and
Tamil Nadu, 1971, are also included. West Bengal, 1971, is not included to avoid distortion in
the time comparisons, since 1972 is included. Data for Rajasthan were not available to us at the
time of writing. Averages reflect the number of urban constituencies in each state.

‡Figures in parentheses are numbers of urban constituencies in which elections were held.

Indeed, a very substantial proportion of the disparity between the
Communist vote in urban and rural India in each general election simply
reflects the strong urban support given to the Communists in West
Bengal. Of the three states in which the Communists are consequential,
only in West Bengal does the Communist vote in the urban areas exceed
that of the rural areas. In West Bengal the Communists have consistently secured a larger vote in urban constituencies than in the countryside.[24] In Andhra, rural support for the Communists always exceeded
urban support until 1972, when there was little difference. And in
Kerala the Communists did better in the cities than in the countryside
in 1954, but thereafter they have been stronger in rural constituencies.
These distributions are shown in Table 6.

Elsewhere in India the Communists are a negligible force. Nonetheless, it is important to note that, as a matter of political strategy, they
do contest a larger proportion of urban than rural constituencies
throughout the country, and have consistently done so in every election.
This strategy, which reflects the recruitment patterns of the Communist parties in many states as well as their ideological predisposition to
contest industrial working-class constituencies, has reaped limited
rewards for them in either votes or seats. They have won only a handful of urban seats outside of their three "stronghold" states: eight in
1952, eleven in 1957 and again in 1962, eighteen in 1967, and twelve

Table 6 The Communist Vote in Urban and Rural Constituencies: West Bengal, Kerala, and Andhra Pradesh (1952-72)

West Bengal	1952	1957	1962	1967	1969	1971	1972
	%	%	%	%	%	%	%
Urban	14.4	25.5#	35.7*	37.4*	39.5	47.2	36.6
			CPI	10.6	11.1	9.5	8.2
			CPM	26.8	28.4	37.7	28.4
Rural	10.6	13.2	19.6	19.9	22.0	37.6	35.6
			CPI	5.2	5.8	7.8	8.6
			CPM	14.7	16.2	29.8	27.0

Kerala	1952	1954	1957	1960	1965	1967	1970
	%	%	%	%	%	%	%
Urban	x	25.3	32.0	31.3	25.4	28.1	22.4
				CPI	6.8	9.3	4.8
				CPM	18.7	18.8	17.6
Rural	x	16.4	34.5	39.8	28.2	32.7	33.4
				CPI	8.2	8.3	9.4
				CPM	20.0	24.3	23.9

Andhra Pradesh	1952	1955-57	1962	1967	1972
	%	%	%	%	%
Urban	17.5	19.9	16.2	13.9	10.6
			CPI	9.4	9.4
			CPM	4.5	1.2
Rural	22.2	30.4	18.4	15.4	9.0
			CPI	7.7	5.6
			CPM	7.7	3.4

*Denotes significance (difference of means) at .01; # at .05. Statistical testing was applied to every election year in West Bengal; but this could not be done for Kerala in 1954, 1960, 1965, and 1970, nor for Andhra Pradesh in 1952, 1955-57, and 1972.

NOTES:

Figures for Kerala, 1954, pertain to constituencies in areas which became part of Kerala when the state was formed. Figures are not reported for 1952 since the CPI was under ban in Travancore-Cochin, and its candidates ran as independents there. The 1970 figures are derived from newspaper reports of constituency results.

Figures for Andhra Pradesh, 1952, pertain to territories which became part of greater Andhra in 1956. The figures for 1955 and 1957 are combined since the elections were held in different parts of the state. The CPI contested in Hyderabad State in 1952 and in interior Andhra in 1957 as a member of the People's Democratic Front. The Communist vote may therefore be slightly overstated both years.

in 1971-72. And although the Communists do proportionately better in urban than in rural areas in most states, the bulk of their seats and votes are still rural. For example, only 18 percent of the assembly seats won by the Communists in 1967, when they secured their largest number of victories nationally, were in urban constituencies.[25]

Still, this strategy has made it possible for the Communists to win a scattering of seats and a substantial vote in a variety of cities throughout the country, even in states where the Communists hardly count. In Assam, for example, the Communists are insignificant in the state, but they have often won the assembly seat in the city of Gauhati. Similarly, in such cities as Muzzaffarpur and Jamshedpur in Bihar, Bhopal in Madhya Pradesh, Coimbatore in Tamil Nadu, and Mangalore in Mysore, the Communist vote has often exceeded 25 percent. And in Bihar the urban vote for the Communists has been at least double the rural vote over the decade 1962-72.

The Communist vote does not appear to be influenced by city size. In the country as a whole Communist support has shown remarkable uniformity across size levels, a pattern which holds in the states where Communist strength is concentrated.[26] One surprising finding is that Calcutta has consistently yielded a lower vote for the Communists than have other urban constituencies in West Bengal.[27] Thus, while urbanity is a factor in Communist voting vis-à-vis rural India, the "degree of urbanity," as measured by city size, is not.

Even though the Communists have generally done better in urban than in rural areas in most states other than Kerala and Andhra Pradesh, two qualifications must be kept in mind. The first, as we have noted, is that, outside of West Bengal, it would be inappropriate to say that the Communists are a substantial force in urban India; and the second is that there is little evidence (again outside of West Bengal along with Bihar) to suggest that the Communists are becoming stronger in India's cities. In the country as a whole, the urban Communist vote has increased modestly since 1952, but no more so than the rural Communist vote. Moreover, these increases are confined primarily to West Bengal and Bihar, where the growth in Communist support has been dramatic. Between 1952 and 1971 support for the CPI and CPM in West Bengal jumped from 14 to 47 percent in urban constituencies, while in rural constituencies it jumped from 11 to 38 percent. In Bihar, urban Communist support increased from virtually nothing in 1952 to 26 percent in 1969, and in the countryside from 1 to 11 percent.[28] But in Andhra Pradesh the urban Communist vote in 1967 (14 percent) was below the vote in the same cities in 1952 (18 percent), while the rural vote declined even more substantially, with further losses sustained in both contexts in 1972. And in Kerala, the Communist split took its toll in 1965, reversing a marked growth trend up to that point. The combined Communist vote in Kerala's eleven urban constituencies in 1970 was below the level of 1954.

In short, outside of West Bengal and Bihar and the small state of Tripura, left-wing radicalism (as measured by votes for the Communists) has not been on the increase, despite occasional spurts in electoral effort. This observation is further confirmed by an examination of the vote for the two Communist parties in 1967 and thereafter. Were left-wing radicalism growing, we might expect an increase in votes for the more radical CPM rather than for the CPI. The very existence of the CPM reflects discontent within the Indian Communist movement that the CPI was too soft on Congress. Since the split, the CPI has become an ally of Prime Minister Indira Gandhi's Congress, supporting it at the center and in West Bengal, while in turn being supported by it in Kerala. If urban radicalism were moving in a leftward direction, it should favor the CPM over the CPI.

For the most part, this is not the way in which Communist support has been distributed. To be sure, in West Bengal the CPM has been substantially stronger in urban constituencies than the CPI (38 to 9 percent of the vote in 1971, and 28 to 8 percent in 1972), a pattern which holds in rural Bengal as well. Similarly, the CPM has outpolled the CPI in both urban and rural Kerala, with a somewhat better vote in the latter. But elsewhere the urban balance has usually been tipped in the other direction. In Andhra the CPI emerged the stronger in the cities in 1967, whereas the two Communist parties were of equal strength in rural constituencies. This pattern persisted in 1972. (Actually, in both Andhra and Kerala, the CPM has been more successful in the countryside than in the cities.) Elsewhere, the CPI's urban vote in 1967 exceeded the CPM's in five states; there was no real difference in six states (typically featuring a very poor performance by both parties); and the CPM came out on top in only one state, Tamil Nadu. In 1970-72 the CPI vote was greater in nine states; in four states neither party rallied much support; and the CPM's urban vote exceeded the CPI's only in West Bengal, Kerala, and Tripura.

To summarize, West Bengal and Bihar are the only states with extended electoral experience in which the Communist vote has shown marked growth. This is almost as true of the rural constituencies in these states as it is of the urban. All in all, the Communist vote in India's cities is hardly notable, except in West Bengal, Kerala, and to a lesser extent now in Andhra Pradesh and Bihar; and it is not very distinctive vis-à-vis the rural Communist vote either. If in fact the cities are radical, or radical to a substantially greater degree than the countryside, it is radicalism of a different color.

Support for the Jana Sangh   India's largest right-wing party, the Bharatiya Jana Sangh, wins proportionately more of its vote in urban than in rural areas and, like the Communists, has grown quite steadily since 1952. In 1967, for the first time, the Jana Sangh secured a larger vote than the CPI and CPM combined in both urban and rural constituencies, and it won more urban and rural seats than the Communists that year, also for the first time. Although these trends were reversed in 1972, right radicalism is quite possibly a more dynamic force than left radicalism in India.

Just as Communist strength is largely confined to West Bengal, Kerala, and Andhra Pradesh, the appeal of the Jana Sangh has been regionalized to the six states of the Hindi-belt of northern India: Punjab, Haryana, Rajasthan, Uttar Pradesh, Madhya Pradesh, and Bihar. Jana Sangh candidates have been most active in these states over the years; and, with the possible exception of Madhya Pradesh, they have been consistently and markedly more successful in the cities than in the countryside in each of them.[29] In Bihar, for example, the Jana Sangh won only 1.8 percent of the rural vote in 1962, as against 15.8 percent of the urban; ten years later, the figures were 11.0 and 25.6 percent respectively. Similarly, in Haryana the Jana Sangh received almost a third of the urban vote (30.8 percent) in 1972, a somewhat smaller

Figure 5   The Jana Sangh Vote in Urban and Rural Constituencies: All India (1952-72)

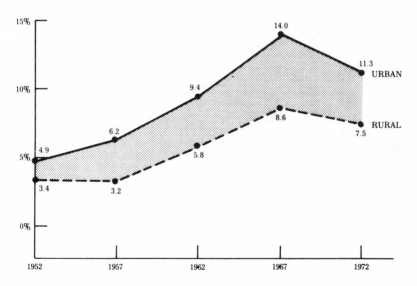

*Denotes significance (difference of means) at .01; # at .05.

NOTES:

For 1952 and 1957, only single-member constituencies are tabulated.

Because the figures for 1972 were hand tabulated, no difference of means test was possible. Figures represent the average of state percentages controlling for the number of constituencies in each state, but not for constituency size. Jammu and Kashmir and Goa are excluded from the calculation; data for Rajasthan were not available to us at the time of writing.

The small decline in support indicated for the Jana Sangh in 1972 would have been somewhat greater if states electing in 1970-71 (Kerala, Tamil Nadu, Orissa, and West Bengal) had been included in the calculations.

Table 7   The Average Jana Sangh Vote in the Six States of the Hindi Region and
the Rest of India, Showing Urban-Rural Differences for Each (1952—72)

Region	1952*	1957*	1962	1967	1968-** 69	1970-† 72
	%	%	%	%	%	%
Urban						
Hindi region . .	10.9	15.1	21.0	29.6	26.5	27.3
Rest of India . .	1.6	1.6	3.5	6.5		5.6
Rural						
Hindi region . .	5.2	6.5	10.8	16.9	15.2	15.7
Rest of India . .	.8	.6	.4	2.7		2.1

*Single-member constituencies only. The elections in Delhi in 1952 are not included.
**Assembly elections in 1968-69 were held in Haryana, Punjab, Uttar Pradesh, and Bihar among the Hindi-region states and only Nagaland, West Bengal, and Pondicherry elsewhere in the country (not shown in table).
†Elections were not held in Uttar Pradesh during this period. Data for Rajasthan, 1972, were not available to us at the time of writing. The 1971 and 1972 elections in West Bengal have been averaged and counted once to avoid distortion. Each of the figures shown represents averaged state percentages with the number of constituencies taken into account.

share than in 1967 and 1969 but still very much greater than the 3.6 percent obtained in rural constituencies that year. In summarizing the Jana Sangh vote, Table 7 brings out both the regional concentration of the party's strength and its primarily urban character.

The Jana Sangh's vote in the six Hindi states has shown impressive growth over the years, notwithstanding a slight downturn in 1969. The Jana Sangh has been in the ascendancy throughout this area but especially in the cities, where its vote has increased so much that it continues to be almost double the party's growing rural vote. The urban right-wing radicalization suggested by these trends is quite spectacular, despite some recent reverses in the Punjab and Haryana (Table 8).

The strong urban position of the Jana Sangh did not show itself in seats held, however, until the 1967 elections, when the party won 48 out of 123 urban constituencies in the Hindi states (compared with 13 of 117 urban constituencies in 1962).[30] In other words, the Jana Sangh won 39 percent of the urban seats in 1967 (as against 17 percent of all the seats in the Hindi states; or 245 seats out of 1,408). In 1962 they won 11 percent of the urban seats (compared with 7.5 percent of the total, or 115 out of 1,352 seats).[31]

Neither the increased vote for the Jana Sangh through 1967 nor the mild decline thereafter is a reflection simply of the number of Jana Sangh candidates contesting. In city after city, Jana Sangh candidates won a larger proportion of the vote in 1967 than in the same constituencies in 1962. Moreover, although the Jana Sangh remained a party of the Hindi region in 1967 (forty-eight of its fifty-four urban victories were

Table 8 The Jana Sangh Vote: Urban Constituencies in the Six Hindi States (1952–72)

Constituency	1952	1957	1962	1967	1969*	1972
	%	%	%	%	%	%
Punjab	11.1 (14)	20.7 (12)	23.4 (15)	31.9 (15)	26.7 (15)	21.4 (15)
Haryana	24.0 (7)	28.0 (7)	29.2 (9)	37.2 (9)	33.3 (9)	30.8 (9)
Rajasthan	11.9 (14)	10.4 (14)	22.5 (14)	30.5 (15)		NA
Uttar Pradesh . . .	11.1 (34)	16.3 (41)	22.3 (45)	27.2 (49)	24.8 (49)	
Madhya Pradesh . .	8.0 (22)	12.1 (18)	16.2 (21)	33.2 (21)		31.3 (21)
Bihar	6.2 (11)	7.7 (12)	15.8 (14)	25.5 (15)	27.9 (15)	25.6 (15)

*Haryana, 1968.
NOTE:
Figures in parentheses are the number of urban constituencies in which contested elections took place. Urban units have been clustered according to the present demarcation of states.

in the Hindi region), it did make some modest inroads into the urban centers of Andhra Pradesh (notably Hyderabad, Guntur, and Nellore) and Maharashtra (Bombay, Poona, Nasik, and Akola). In 1969 and 1972 the Jana Sangh dropped out of very few of the urban constituencies it had contested in 1967; it simply did less well in them, especially outside the Hindi region.

The Jana Sangh has tended to secure a stronger vote in cities of 200,000 to 1 million than in either the great metropolitan centers or smaller cities. The absence of appeal for the Jana Sangh in India's largest cities, however, is nothing more than a reflection of the party's regional concentration of strength. There is only one million-plus city in the Hindi region—Delhi—and it was omitted from our analysis since it does not have a state legislative assembly. However, in parliamentary and municipal elections the Jana Sangh has been a powerful force in Delhi. (In 1967 it swept all but one of Delhi's parliamentary seats.) Similarly, while the Jana Sangh vote has tended to be higher in larger than in smaller cities (those between 50,000 and 200,000),[32] the patterns vary from state to state; within the Hindi states the votes are so consistently small that city size hardly emerges as a significant factor in Jana Sangh performance.

All in all, radical voting in India may be more urban than rural, but neither in the case of the Jana Sangh nor the Communists can urban distinctiveness be further specified according to city size.[33]

Congress and the "radical" protest vote   This survey shows that the Communist parties and the Jana Sangh have consistently won a larger portion of India's urban than its rural vote and that between 1952 and 1967 they grew stronger in the cities. By 1967 the Jana Sangh, CPI, and the CPM together secured more than a quarter of the urban vote nationally (as against a ninth in 1952), and about a sixth of the rural vote. It now remains to determine at whose expense these parties have grown.

Surprisingly, support for the Congress party in both urban and rural India remained remarkably constant in the first three general elections, with no significant disparities between urban and rural voting for Congress.[34] In other words, the virtual doubling of the Jana Sangh and Communist vote prior to 1967 was not accompanied by any comparable decrease in the Congress vote. During this early period the Jana Sangh and the Communist parties grew at the expense of independent candidates and other opposition parties.[35] Thus, between 1952 and 1962, the vote going to "other parties and independents" declined by 10 percent in urban constituencies and by 6.7 percent in rural constituencies. The parties which lost the most, especially in urban India, are the various socialist parties.[36] Their combined nationwide vote in the first three general elections was 9.7 percent, 10.1 percent, and 9.7 percent, respectively; but in the urban areas their decline was dramatic: 13.5, 9.9, and 5.9 percent in cities of 100,000 or more.[37]

From 1957 to 1967 Congress and the radical protest parties won approximately two-thirds of the urban vote nationally. In 1962, for example, Congress and the radical parties together shared 67.3 percent of

Table 9   The Congress Vote in Urban and Rural Constituencies: All India (1952–72)

Constituency	1952 -	1957	1962	1967	1972
	%	%	%	%	%
Urban . . . . 45.6#	46.8	45.3#	38.2*	48.7
Rural 43.2	45.1	43.4	41.6	46.2

*Denotes significance (difference of means) at .01; # at .05.
NOTES:
For 1952 and 1957, only single-member constituencies are tabulated. Figures in 1972 represent the average of state percentages controlling for the number of constituencies in each state, but not for constituency size. Jammu and Kashmir and Goa are excluded from the calculation; data for Rajasthan were not available to us at the time of writing. Because the figures were hand tabulated, no difference of means test was possible.

the urban vote as against 56.0 percent of the rural vote. Urban politics is thus somewhat more polarized between Congress and the radical parties than is the politics of rural India. This has always been the case; and while other parties and independents have generally received a smaller share of the total vote with each election in both rural and urban constituencies, their decline has been more precipitous in urban India.

The expansion of the vote for radical protest parties in urban India in the 1967 elections was, for the first time, at the expense of Congress rather than of independents or other opposition parties. In 1967 the urban vote for Congress was 38.2 percent as against 45.3 percent in 1962, a decline of seven percentage points compared with a decline of less than two percent in rural India. While many parties benefited from the attrition in Congress' urban support in 1967, the most impressive gains were made by the Jana Sangh.

In short, from 1952 through 1967 the cities of India were increasingly polarized between the radical left- and right-wing parties, on the one hand, and Congress, on the other. In the cities of the Hindi region the clash was between Congress and the Jana Sangh, while in many of the cities of West Bengal, Andhra, and Kerala (plus a scattering of cities elsewhere in the country), the polarization was between Congress and

Table 10   Distribution of Vote among the "Radical" Parties, Congress, and Other Parties and Independents in Urban and Rural Constituencies: All India (1952–72)

Parties	1952*	1957*	1962	1967	1972**
	%	%	%	%	%
Urban					
Communists and Jana Sangh	11.7	16.7	22.0	26.5	24.9
Congress	45.6	46.8	45.3	38.2	48.7
Other parties and independents	42.7	36.5	32.7	35.3	26.4
Rural					
Communists and Jana Sangh	6.1	9.3	12.6	16.0	16.6
Congress	43.2	45.1	43.4	41.6	46.2
Other parties and independents	50.7	45.6	44.0	42.4	37.2

*Single-member constituencies only.
**Figures represent the average of state percentages controlling for the number of constituencies in each state, but not for constituency size. Jammu and Kashmir, Goa, and Rajasthan are excluded from the calculation.

the Communists. From 1952 through 1962 Congress and the radical parties appear to have taken their votes from independents and other opposition parties. In 1967, when the smaller parties and independents improved their position in urban India, the struggle was more sharply between Congress and candidates either of the radical Left or Right.

Thus, the elections of 1967 were critical for the Congress party. Its fortunes declined throughout India, but nowhere more than in the urban centers, where the Jana Sangh in particular reaped major gains in both votes and seats. Congress managed to win almost half (49 percent) of the rural state assembly seats, down from 62 percent in 1962; but in the urban areas Congress won only 43 percent of the seats, compared with 67 percent in 1962. Congress was in a beleaguered position everywhere; but now, for the first time since independence, urban India gave Congress a smaller proportion of votes and seats than rural India.[38] Moreover, for the first time the Congress party failed to win a clear majority of assembly seats. Indeed, in half of the states the opposition parties were able to band together to form coalition governments, and in several instances the urban seats provided the non-Congress parties with the margin necessary to form a government.

The urban crisis for Congress was even more dramatic in the national parliament. When the Congress ministers faced the opposition benches in parliament after the 1967 elections, it was apparent that the M.P.'s from the urban areas (parliamentary constituencies in cities with more than a quarter million population) were predominantly with the opposition. Congress had won only eighteen of the fifty-two urban parliamentary constituencies in 1967, even though victorious in a clear majority of the rural constituencies.

Although the decline of Congress in the urban areas in 1967 was an all-India phenomenon, the losses were substantially greater in some states than in others. The decline exceeded the national urban average in Bihar, Uttar Pradesh, Madhya Pradesh, Punjab, and Haryana, states in which the Jana Sangh's urban vote had sharply risen. In city after city it was clear that the decline in support for Congress was accompanied by comparable Jana Sangh gains (rather than gains for the Communist parties). The 1967 elections thus indicated that India's increasingly radicalized urban population was moving quite rapidly to the Right in the Hindi states, while elsewhere the movement toward the radical Left had leveled off (except in Bihar). In West Bengal, for example, which contains India's most leftist urban population, the combined urban Communist vote was 37.4 percent in 1967, not unlike the 35.7 percent which the united CPI had received in 1962.

Although in percentage terms the decline in Congress votes was small in 1967, the margin of victory in previous elections had already become so narrow that a slight shift in votes per constituency was decisive for many Congress candidates. Cities that had consistently elected Congress candidates in previous elections now elected Congress opponents. In the Punjab, Congress lost all four assembly seats in Amritsar, the three seats in Jullundur, and the seats in Patiala, Bhatinda, Hoshiarpur, and Chandigarh. In Madhya Pradesh, Congress lost the three seats of Gwalior and three of the four seats in Indore along with the seats including Burhanpur and Khandwa. In Tamil Nadu, Congress lost all twelve seats in Madras City (as against six in the previous elections), the three seats in Madurai and two in Salem, and fifteen of the seventeen seats for cities with populations between 50,000 and 100,000, which had previously been won. In Uttar Pradesh, the Congress was routed in all four seats of Lucknow, three in Benaras, two in Meerut, and the constituencies in Gorakpur, Mathura, Aligarh, and Dehra Dun, plus every one of the ten smaller cities it had won in 1962. Elsewhere in the country Congress lost two of its three seats in Baroda, two seats in Mysore City, and two in Ajmer.

Perceptions of a changing urban politics   Why did Congress lose so much of the urban vote in 1967, and suffer even more severely in the cities than in rural India? Why did the combined vote for the Jana Sangh and the Communists increase consistently in four consecutive elections? Is urban India leading the way, so that what we see there today we shall see in rural India tomorrow?

To turn to the last question first: there is some evidence that electoral changes in rural areas are often preceded by changes in urban areas. In virtually every state, the rise in turnout in rural constituencies was preceded by substantial increases in urban turnout. Similarly, in almost every state in which the Jana Sangh and the Communist parties are active, a disparity in votes between the urban and rural areas (with the Communists or the Jana Sangh having a higher urban vote) is followed by a rise in rural support in the next election.

But a shift in the same direction, even when one type of constituency changes before the other, may only indicate that similar factors are at work, not that the urban areas are influencing the rural sections. Moreover, there are too many exceptions to this pattern to suggest causal linkages. The urban vote for the various socialist parties, for example, has been declining, while in several states the socialist vote in rural areas has increased. In only eleven out of twenty-three statewide elections (involving eight states with a substantial vote for socialist parties) has a higher or lower socialist vote in urban constituencies in one election been followed by a comparable increase or decrease in the socialists' rural vote in a subsequent election.

Many explanations have been suggested for the growth of radical protest parties in urban India: the discontent of the urban unemployed; the social and economic frustrations of younger voters; the increasing dissatisfaction of the middle class with the slow pace of economic growth (or, an alternative explanation, the too rapid pace of social change!); and, in the case of the growing vote for the Jana Sangh, an increase in anti-Muslim sentiment among Hindus. Our data do not permit us to test any of these hypotheses. Nor, for that matter, have Congress politicians been any more sure of how particular social groups in the cities vote and why the vote for radical protest parties has increased.

After the Congress debacle of 1967, many Congress leaders concluded that the country was moving toward the Right, especially in the urban areas. Many state Congress leaders reasoned that certain measures might meet the political threat from the Right: a more aggressive anti-Pakistani policy; a stronger military (perhaps including nuclear arms); more caution on land reform, cooperative farming, and other possibly threatening agrarian changes; and more attention to party work.

Mrs. Gandhi, however, concluded that the growth in Jana Sangh strength in 1967 was more an expression of radical antiestablishment protest than of right-wing sentiments per se, and that a radicalization of the Congress program (and image) would be a more effective way of attracting votes from the Jana Sangh. The new policies that she pursued after 1967, and especially following her break with the more conservative Congress leadership in 1969, often appeared to be directed at urban constituencies: the nationalization of banks, the proposal for a ceiling on urban property, and even the attack against the privileged princes (which many Congressmen interpreted as a politically counterproductive policy in the rural areas of Rajasthan and Madhya Pradesh, where the princes remained powerful and popular).

It was clear by 1969 that Mrs. Gandhi had begun to capture the protest sentiment of urban Indians. Lower-echelon civil servants, taxi drivers, university faculties and students appeared to be her most enthusiastic supporters. Some of the largest crowds and demonstrations on her behalf were in New Delhi, hitherto a center of Jana Sangh strength.

Mrs. Gandhi's conviction that the drift of voters, both urban and rural, to right-wing parties could be halted most effectively by more, not less, radicalization proved, as we know, to pay dividends. The new, more radical Congress swept the polls in the parliamentary elections of 1971, with substantial victories in the urban constituencies. In 1971 the new Congress won thirty-three of the fifty-two urban parliamentary constituencies (as against eighteen in 1967) and captured all nine of the parliamentary urban constituencies previously won by the Jana Sangh. The trend continued at the state assembly level in 1972, when the Congress secured a larger urban vote (48.7 percent)[39] than in all previous general elections—an increase of more than 10 percent from the 1967 low and larger once again than its revitalized rural vote. Congress won four out of every five urban seats (demolishing the CPM in

Calcutta in the process) compared with less than half of those seats in 1967.

Notwithstanding Congress' comeback, however, the Communist vote in 1972 held in urban constituencies, while urban support for the Jana Sangh declined only marginally (Figures 4 and 5).[40] More than ever before, urban India was polarized in 1972 between Congress and the CPI, the CPM, and the Jana Sangh, with other parties and independent candidates combined obtaining only one-quarter of the total urban vote. India's urban areas thus remain politically volatile in spite of the Congress victories. While Congress was able to recapture some of the radical protest vote from the Jana Sangh and the CPM by co-opting their radical images in the parliamentary elections of 1971, in the state assembly elections of 1972 the improved Congress vote was at the expense of other parties and independents, not the Jana Sangh or the Communists. India's most recent elections, therefore, reveal a growing radicalization in urban electoral behavior, as much reflected in the new radical image asserted by the Congress party as by the per-sistent long-term growth of both the Jana Sangh and Communist parties.

Regional protest   Apart from the enduring left- and right-wing op-position of the Communists and the Jana Sangh, Congress has ex-perienced, from time to time and place to place, severe challenges from regionally based and ethnically defined parties. Examples include: the

Table 11   Regional Protest in Bombay State, 1957

	1952*	1957*	1962 Gujarat	1962 Maharashtra
	%	%	%	%
Congress vote**				
Urban	52.3	50.1	50.9	48.9
Rural	49.9	47.7	52.1	51.7
Seats won by Congress**				
Urban	78.6 (77/98)	54.8 (46/84)	72.0 (18/25)	80.7 (46/57)
Rural	85.6 (309/361)	60.3 (188/312)	73.6 (95/129)	81.6 (169/207)

*In order to make the 1952 and 1957 data comparable, figures for 1952 have been adjusted to include constituencies which in 1952 were not in Bombay State and to exclude those which were in Bombay State in 1952 but not in 1957.

**The vote figures pertain to single-member constituencies only for 1952 and 1957. Those for seats and seats won include all constituencies.

Table 12   Regional Protest in Tamil Nadu (1962-71)

	1962	1967	1971
	%	%	%
DMK vote			
Urban	25.3	41.2	45.7
Rural	27.5	40.7	48.4
Seats won by			
DMK			
Urban	19.5	67.4	74.4
	(8/41)	(29/43)	(32/43)
Rural	25.4	57.1	79.6
	(42/165)	(109/191)	(152/191)

rise of the DMK as the champion of cultural nationalism among the
Tamil population of Tamil Nadu;[41] the agitations of the Sikh-based
Akali Dal over Punjabi Suba in the united Punjab; and the multiparty
coalitions that arose in Bombay State in the latter 1950s aimed at
separate Gujarati- and Marathi-speaking states.[42] In each instance, we
can identify one or more elections in which the regional protest
dominated the partisan scene.

At least two characteristics of these agitations distinguish them from
the radical opposition we have examined thus far: they arose in states
or parts of states where neither left- nor right-wing opposition to Congress had been strong; and they have proved to be much more
successful—either as one-shot campaigns or as sustained movements—
than the Communists and Jana Sanghis. We might well ask whether the
social dynamics of regional protest are not also very different. Is it
possible that the principal source of support for regional protest is not
urban at all, but reflects instead a broad-based cultural and ethnic assertion of identity even more salient to rural populations? Alternatively,
since the leadership of such movements is generally urban-based and
the appeals largely developed by an urbanized intelligentsia, is
regional protest, like radical protest, urban centered?

Our data reveal very little difference between urban and rural constituencies in supporting regional protest. In Bombay State, for example, the Congress vote did not decline substantially in 1957, despite
the Gujarati and Marathi movements for dividing the state. It remained
much the same in urban constituencies overall, significant losses in
some cities (notably Ahmedabad, Thana, and Poona) being offset elsewhere. Congress did, however, lose many urban seats, mainly as a result of the multiparty coalitions facing it that year. But then, Congress
lost many of its rural seats as well. Most of these seats, both rural and
urban, were regained by Congress in the 1962 elections, when the

Table 13   Regional Protest in Modern Punjab: 1962 Compared with Other Election Years

	1952*	1957**	1962*	1967†	1969	1972‡
	%	%	%	%	%	%
Akali vote						
Urban ..	12.0		8.0	11.4	12.6	8.0
Rural ..	25.9		23.4	27.1	32.3	32.0
Seats won by Akali Dal						
Urban ..	20.0		6.7	13.3	26.7	0
	(3/15)		(1/15)	(2/15)	(4/15)	(0/15)
Rural ..	29.4		25.4	27.0	43.8	27.0
	(28/95)		(18/71)	(24/89)	(39/89)	(24/89)

*The figures for 1952 and 1962 have been adjusted to reflect the existing Punjab following states reorganization. The 1952 figures pertain to double-member as well as single-member constituencies.

**In 1957 the Akali Dal was merged with Congress.

†The 1967 figures combine the records of the ADS (Sant Group) and the ADM (Master Group).

‡The 1972 figures combine the records of the Shiromani Akali Dal, the only Akali party to win seats, and the SAG (Gurnam Singh Group) and All-India Shiromani Baba Jiwan Singh Mazabhi Dal.

coalitions broke up following satisfaction of their demand for linguistic states.

Similarly, the rapid expansion of the DMK in Tamil Nadu from 1962 onward, reflecting the politicization of Tamil cultural consciousness, was as substantial in the rural as in the urban areas, both with regard to votes secured and seats won. Nor is city size a factor, although the DMK's initial urban victories were largely confined to Madras City (five of seven seats in 1962).

The agitation for Punjabi Suba is another instance of regional protest. The Akali Dal, a Sikh party, campaigned for the creation of a Sikh-majority state out of the Punjab in the 1962 elections. Surprisingly, the Akalis did not do as well either in votes received or seats won in the regions of the state that were eventually converted (in 1966) into a Punjabi Suba as they had previously (1952) or were to do subsequently (1967 and 1969).[43] Moreover, in none of the five elections contested by the Akalis was their urban support as great as their rural support, obviously because the Sikh population is more heavily rural, while the cities of the Punjab have higher proportions of Hindus than most rural constituencies. The Akali-Jana Sangh alliance in recent elections has, in this sense, been a rural-urban alliance of anti-Congress political forces.[44]

The three regional protest movements reviewed here were among the most active opposition forces in the 1960s; and in two instances the

regional parties continue to have well-established institutionalized roots
in their respective states, Tamil Nadu and the Punjab. As we have seen,
the major regional parties in Bombay (in 1957) and Tamil Nadu (since
1962) won as much electoral support in rural as in urban constituencies;
and in the Punjab the Akali movement is more solidly based in the rural
areas in which the Sikhs reside. In all three instances, therefore, regional protest takes the form of solidarity movements based on linguistic, religious, and cultural affinities that cut across urban-rural differences. Overall, regional protest differs from "radical" protest in not
being distinctively urban.

IV.   Urban Electoral Polarization

There are two dimensions to electoral polarization: the extent to
which the vote is concentrated among a small number of candidates as
against dissipated among many, and the degree of competitiveness indicated by the margin of victory separating a winner from his nearest
competitor. One dimension identifies the distribution of the vote, the
other the closeness of results.

In the previous section we observed that assembly elections in India
are becoming more polarized between Congress and its radical opponents, and more so in urban constituencies (but in the countryside
as well).[45] A concentration of the vote is evident also in the several
states where regional protest has produced durable partisan alternatives
to Congress, although there is no particular distinctiveness to urban
constituencies in these instances.

In this section we shall examine the second dimension of electoral
polarization: the competitiveness of elections in urban India. What
was the margin of victory in urban as compared with rural constituencies
between 1952 and 1967? What is the effect of politicization (turnout)
on polarization (margin of victory)? Is the level of competition influenced by which parties compete?

Elections in both rural and urban areas of India are not as competitive
in outcome as might be expected from the amount of effort and money
that candidates invest in a campaign. For rural India the average margin
of victory between 1952 and 1967 ranged from 17.1 to 22.8 percent,
while in urban India it ranged from 13.9 to 22.4 percent. The urban-
rural differences have never been very large. Nationally there was no
difference in 1952 and 1957. A small difference appeared in 1962,
which increased to only 3.2 percent in 1967.[46] The disparities are
sometimes greater in individual states, but in different directions and
with little consistency over time. Moreover, statistically significant
differences at the state level are rare, which suggests that the competitiveness of urban constituencies in a state is largely influenced by the
competitiveness of elections in the state as a whole.

The lowest average margin of victory for urban constituencies nationwide was 13.9 percent in 1967, a year when the average margin of
victory in rural constituencies was 17.1 percent. The closest vote in
urban constituencies across the four general elections (states with only
one or two urban constituencies omitted) was 9.1 percent in Uttar
Pradesh in 1967.[47]

The trend over time in both rural and urban constituencies is toward
greater competitiveness. The trend is somewhat more pronounced in
urban India (Figure 6). The urban areas were more polarized than
the rural areas in eight of twelve states in 1962 and in nine of fifteen
states in 1967; and the percentage of the gap widened in the 1969
elections.

Figure 6   The Competitiveness of Elections in India: Urban and Rural Constituencies Compared (1952-67)

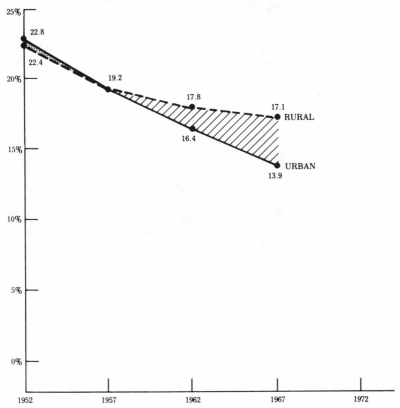

NOTES:

Only elections held in the years shown are included in the calculations. Figures for 1952
and 1957 pertain to single-member constituencies only.

The difference for 1967, although small substantively, is significant at .01. For other
years, the difference is not significant even at .05.

Table 14 The Average Margin of Victory in Constituencies Won by Congress, 1962 and 1967*

	1962		1967	
	%		%	
All constituencies won by Congress nationally . . .	19.5	(1759)	17.5	(1663)
When the nearest competitor was:				
Jana Sangh	20.1	(191)	17.8	(336)
CPI	15.8	(287.)	15.7	(118)
CPM			14.9	(134)

*The percentages shown are for all constituencies, not simply urban. Figures in parentheses refer to the number of constituencies involved.

It is often assumed that an increase in voter participation will be accompanied by more competitive elections, especially when a challenging party succeeds in mobilizing new votes that may enable it to overcome the established strength of a typically dominant party such as the Congress. The reverse, of course, is also thought to be true—that highly competitive elections mobilize nonparticipants to vote.[48] There is, in fact, a tendency in Indian elections for the margin of victory to decrease when turnout increases; that is, politicization and competitiveness are related. But the coefficients are typically small; the amount of variation in competitiveness explained by turnout is typically minuscule; and few values of F are significant below the national level (where the large n makes even a low R^2 significant). The patterns are too weak and inconsistent to conclude that turnout and competitiveness in India are meaningfully related, either in urban or in rural constituencies.

The margin of victory does not seem to be affected by whether or not there is a polarization between Congress and the radical Left or Right, or between Congress and a regional protest party. The radicalness of the principal opposition has little apparent effect on the competitiveness of constituencies won by Congress. As shown in Table 14, the differences are small. Neither the Jana Sangh nor the Communists seem to have polarized the vote to any unusual degree, although the vote does appear to be slightly closer when the polarization is between the Communists and Congress.

Elections seem to be somewhat more competitive in the Punjab and Tamil Nadu, where regional protest parties are in opposition to Congress. In both states the margins of victory for Congress candidates were close, especially in Tamil Nadu in 1967, when Congress candidates won by an average of 5.5 percent in the state, and only 4.3 percent when the DMK was the nearest competitor. In the Punjab, Congress won seats by an average 10.8 percent and against the Akalis by 8.4 percent. But since elections in both states are highly competitive, even in constituencies in which the regional parties are not the principal opponents to Congress, we must be cautious in attributing the competition in these states wholly to the presence of regional protest parties.

V.   Urban Voting Trends

Demographic changes guarantee the urban areas an increasingly important role in India's electoral future. In 1971, 70 million Indians lived in urban settlements over 50,000, a 47 percent increase over 1961. By 1981, if current urban growth rates continue, 103 million people will live in towns and cities of this size, and by 1991 these urban areas will contain 152 million Indians. In the 1961-71 decade, urban India grew at a rate nearly twice that of India as a whole (24.7 percent). By 1971, one out of every eight Indians lived in an urban constituency; and if urban growth continues at twice the rural growth rate over the next decade and a half,[49] one out of every five and a half Indians will live in a town or city larger than 50,000 persons by 1991.[50]

Neither electoral turnout nor party preference adequately captures the importance that these urban areas play in electoral politics. The state capitals and the district and taluka towns invariably are the headquarters of political parties; party workers are often disproportionately recruited in urban settlements; and the urban business community provides a substantial share of the money spent in India's heavily financed elections. Urban-based students (even when they are below voting age) provide much of the energy in election campaigns, and while colleges and universities are typically located in the towns and cities, a large proportion of their students are of rural origin with persistent rural connections. Then, too, urban areas are communication diffusion centers. Not only do newspapers and radio radiate their messages from urban centers, but students, migrant workers, truck and bus drivers, wholesale grain dealers, itinerant merchants, and a variety of other businessmen and government officials link the cities and towns to the countryside. For these reasons party leaders have always given more attention to urban areas, or at least to particular social groups within the urban areas, than a mere counting of urban voters might warrant.

A central theme of our analysis of India's urban constituencies is that they are similar to the rural constituencies of the states in which they are located. At the same time, and without contradicting this statement, we have noted that India's urban centers have much in common with one another irrespective of their location. There are at least three respects in which these contextual and attributional perspectives have been reconciled:

1.   In electoral participation the urban constituencies are closely linked to whatever turnout level is prevalent in the rural constituencies of their state, but the urban turnout has typically been slightly higher.
2.   When radical parties of the Left or Right are active in a state, then the urban areas tend to give these parties more support than do the rural constituencies.
3.   If parties are polarized in the state and elections are close, then the elections are generally even closer in the urban constituencies.

Electoral trends from 1952 to 1972 suggest that the urban constituencies are becoming more distinctive insofar as electoral protest and electoral polarization are concerned, but less distinctive with regard to electoral participation (if only because the rural areas have caught up). To put it another way, the attributional model is more appropriate for understanding radicalization and polarization, while the contextual model is as appropriate for understanding participation.

If the polarization and radicalization trends continue, it seems likely that urban constituencies will command even more of the attention and resources of party and government leaders than they do at present. Let us briefly review, then, these two long-term trends, both so suggestive of future developments.

First, elections are becoming more closely contested all over India. As the margins of victory become small, relatively slight shifts in votes can mean a substantial shift in the number of seats that a party wins or loses. The massive defeat of Congress candidates in the urban constituencies in 1967 involved only a small decline in the Congress vote. To the extent that state assembly or parliamentary elections become more closely contested, the constituencies where victories are by the smallest margins will be given the most attention by political parties— and by the government. In nearly three-fourths of the state elections in 1967 the margins of victory were smaller in the urban than in the rural areas; and in each successive election between 1952 and 1967 the urban constituencies became competitive more rapidly than the rural constituencies. In Maharashtra, nearly one out of four voters lives in an urban constituency; in West Bengal, one out of five; in Gujarat and Tamil Nadu, more than one out of six; in Mysore and the Punjab, one out of seven; and in Andhra, one out of eight. Closely contested elections in these states are likely to make their urban areas the political battlegrounds for competing parties.

Second, between 1952 and 1967, the "radical" vote—i.e., the vote for both the Communist parties and the Jana Sangh—increased more rapidly in the cities than in the countryside. This trend only slowed in the early 1970s, when the governing Congress party itself assumed a more radical posture. The protest vote was particularly acute in the 1967 elections, a time of growing food shortages and rising prices, factors that are again appearing in the mid-1970s as a concomitant of petroleum and fertilizer shortages.

While the lowest-income groups in the countryside suffer the most during periods of food shortages and inflation, the urban middle class and the organized working class have the political resources to harass the government and threaten the regime. Certain urban occupational groups occupy strategic nodal points in the economy, with the capacity to inflict damage far beyond their own local constituencies: the port workers in Calcutta and Bombay, railway workers in Hyderabad and Madras, state government employees in Patna and Lucknow, engineers in electric power stations, and so on. There appears to be a long-term trend toward greater political militancy in India's urban areas, a militancy that can be tapped by parties either of the Left or Right if it is not tapped by the governing Congress party.

Postscript

Recent developments in India have tended to confirm the trends described in this study. Severe inflation in 1974 and 1975 (estimated at 30 percent) was accompanied, to quote from a resolution of the Congress Working Committee, by "organized strikes, go slow movements by government employees, railway employees and industrial employees . . . acts of sabotage paralyzing the railway and communication systems . . . student agitations and indiscipline,"[51] all urban-centered protest movements. Mass campaigns against the government, first in Bihar, then in Gujarat, were followed by a stunning Congress defeat at the hand of a coalition of parties in elections for the Gujarat legislative assembly in mid-June 1975. To a significant degree urban discontent seemed to be striking a responsive chord among rural people as well. When Prime Minister Gandhi's own legal difficulties surfaced a few days later—the Allahabad High Court ruling that she had violated the electoral law and that her election to parliament in 1971 was therefore invalid, a mass public rally, organized by several leading opposition parties, was held in New Delhi on June 25, calling for her resignation and announcing plans for a nationwide protest movement.

On the very next day the Indian Government issued a Proclamation of Emergency under the provisions of the Indian Constitution, arrested more than a thousand members of the opposition (according to official reports), amended the Maintenance of Internal Security Act so that no grounds had to be given for detention, imposed censorship on the press, and banned twenty-six political organizations, including the Rashtriya Swayam Sevak Sangh (a militant group associated with the Jana Sangh), the Naxalites (pro-Peking militant Communists), and a number of other Marxist groups. The government subsequently announced that elections scheduled for the state of Kerala in September would be postponed.

The opposition parties had clearly been able to mount organized urban protest and to influence rural sentiment on a scale that was far more alarming to the central government than any earlier movements. Whether the government's actions to suppress the opposition, combined with new measures announced by the Prime Minister to "revive the health of the economy," will alter the situation or whether urban protest, with or without rural sympathy, will persist in the form of extralegal movements and anti-Congress voting (if free elections are again held) remains to be seen.

NOTES

*This article is a product of the M.I.T. Indian Election Data Project, funded by a grant from the National Science Foundation. The results of the research will appear in a four-volume series, *Studies in Electoral Politics in the Indian States,* edited by Myron Weiner and John Osgood Field (New Delhi: Manohar Book Service; distributed in the United States by South Asia Books, Box 502, Columbia, Mo. 65201). A somewhat longer version of this article, with statistical appendices and the results in each urban constituency between 1952 and 1972, will be published in Volume 3, *Electoral Politics in the Indian States: The Impact of Modernization.* We would like to express our appreciation to Priscilla Battis, our programmer and statistical collaborator in the entire project; to Glynn Wood for his painstaking assistance in confirming the urbanity of ostensibly urban constituencies by assessing the magnitudes of rural population in them; and to Jessie Janjigian for research and editorial assistance.

[1] Many studies have examined urban distinctiveness with reference to such political characteristics as participation, radicalization, and polarization. The principal theoretical base for these studies is the modernization-social mobilization paradigm common to much comparative analysis. See in particular Daniel Lerner, *The Passing of Traditional Society: Modernizing the Middle East* (New York, 1958), and Karl W. Deutsch, "Social Mobilization and Political Development," *American Political Science Review,* LV (September 1961), 493-514. Additional interest has been stimulated by the presumably combustible effects of large-scale rural-to-urban migration. For a critical review, see Joan M. Nelson, "Migrants, Urban Poverty, and Instability in Developing Nations," Monograph # 22 (Cambridge [Mass.], Center for International Affairs, Harvard University, September 1969).

[2] Recent empirical research has questioned the importance of urbanity insofar as popular political dispositions and basic political dynamics are concerned. For example, see Norman H. Nie, G. Bingham Powell, Jr., and Kenneth Prewitt, "Social Structure and Political Participation: Developmental Relationships," *American Political Science Review,* LXIII (June 1969 and September 1969), 361-78 and 808-32; and Alex Inkeles, "Participant Citizenship in Six Developing Countries," ibid., (December 1969), 1120—41. The apparent weakness of urbanity as an explanatory variable has kindled renewed appreciation for contextual explanations of aggregate political behavior. Our analysis treats context as political space, typically the state in which certain urban constituencies are located. For a more varied, social treatment of context as applied to India, see David J. Elkins, "Regional Contexts of Political Participation: Some Illustrations from South India," *Canadian Journal of Political Science,* V (June 1972), 167—89.

[3] Small cities are rarely divided into two or more constituencies, while even a city of 50,000 typically forms the dominant part of an assembly constituency in India. In 1967, when constituencies tended to include more people than in earlier elections, the average number of eligible electors was 69,920 per constituency. Instances where constituency boundaries combined portions of the urban area with a substantial rural area are excluded from our analysis. Delhi is also eliminated because, as a union territory, it has had infrequent state assembly elections. For methodological reasons we are occasionally obliged to omit double-member

constituencies in cities during the 1950s (none appear after 1960); the substantive significance of doing so is typically minuscule.

[4] The figures on turnout presented in this study pertain to the valid vote actually tabulated. In every constituency a number of ballots are disqualified by officials of the Election Commission for one reason or another. Usually the rate of invalidation is around 2-3 percent of the total votes cast, although on occasion it has exceeded 10 percent. Invalidation is not a factor in our findings, but the reader should keep in mind that we are referring to effective electoral participation, not total turnout. All turnout figures have been rounded to the nearest percentage.

[5] The 1972 assembly elections are not exactly comparable to earlier elections, since a number of states (Uttar Pradesh, Orissa, Tamil Nadu, and Kerala) did not go in the polls that year.

[6] Like the tables in this section, the data shown for 1952 and 1957 in Figure 2 pertain to single-member constituencies only. Removing double-member constituencies is a methodological convenience that has the effect of overstating the level of turnout, but never by enough to make a meaningful difference.

[7] Our analysis is based on the state divisions obtaining in 1967. For the sake of continuity and clarity, we shall refer to earlier electoral patterns as if they occurred within the contemporary boundaries.

[8] Kerala did not go to the polls in 1962. The spurt in urban turnout there took place in the special elections of 1960.

[9] Urban turnout in the Maharashtra region dropped from 63 to 60 percent in 1962, while rural turnout increased from 51 to 55 percent. The same pattern occurred in Gujarat: urban turnout declined from 59 to 55 percent, as against rural figures of 52 to 54 percent for each year. The decline in urban turnout in Gujarat is almost entirely a function of downswings in Ahmedabad, the capital city, and Baroda, a major cultural-intellectual center where states' reorganization sentiment had been strong in 1957. In Maharashtra, the urban decline was greatest in Bombay and Poona, also the capital city and major cultural-intellectual center.

[10] The persisting urban-rural gap in such states as Madhya Pradesh, Bihar, and Orissa is partly a function of the large numbers of low-voting tribal peoples in these states, most of whom are located in specially reserved constituencies. However, even when tribal constituencies are removed from the comparison, the urban-rural gap remains large. Low tribal turnout is therefore not the only reason for the gap; it merely accentuates it. For a detailed analysis of electoral politics in tribal India, see Myron Weiner and John Osgood Field, "How Tribal Constituencies in India Vote," in Weiner and Field, eds. *Electoral Politics in the Indian States: Three Disadvantaged Sectors* (New Delhi, 1975), vol. 2.

[11] Urban turnout in Kerala has shown a steady decline since 1960, but it remains well above the national urban average.

[12] Operationally, urbanity is imputed to be a relevant attribute when a difference of means test fails to reveal a significant (.01) difference between the state urban mean and the national urban mean for a given election year. Context is said to be a relevant guide to urban turnout when the same test fails to reveal a significant (.01) difference between urban and rural constituencies in the same state. In each case significance is determined by a two-tailed test of Z scores produced by the conventional part-whole formula

$$Z = \frac{M_1 - M_0}{\sigma_0 \big/ \sqrt{N_1}} \;.$$

[13] Both urbanity and context are said to be dependable guides to turnout when a difference of means test fails to reveal a significant (.01) difference either in the urban-rural comparison or in the state urban-national urban comparison. This occurred in nine states between 1952 and 1967, most commonly in Mysore. The considerable overlap probably has something to do with the generally small differences between urban and rural turnout in India as a whole (a maximum of nine percent) and in many states over the past two decades.

[14] Neither urbanity nor context is deemed an adequate guide to turnout when a significant (.01) difference exists between a state's urban constituencies and the national urban mean, on the one hand, and the state's rural constituencies, on the other. Resembling neither in the

statistical sense, the urban constituencies in question cannot be identified by either urbanity or context. This was the case for urban constituencies in Saurashtra and West Bengal in 1952, Bihar and Madras in 1962, and Uttar Pradesh in 1962 and 1967.

[15] The low turnout of distinctly backward states may be due as much to low population density as to their economic backwardness. R. Chandidas has argued and provided indirect evidence that the distance people must travel in order to vote affects how many actually do vote ("Poll Participation Slump," *Economic and Political Weekly*, 15 July 1972, 1359-68; see Table 9 and the surrounding discussion). Because low rural density and economic backwardness often go together, their effects are difficult to sort out. At the state level the evidence on density is mixed. Some states with a low rural turnout (e.g., Orissa, Madhya Pradesh, and Rajasthan) are below the all-India level in population density. However, Gujarat, another low-density state, has a higher electoral turnout; and Bihar, which has generally had a below-average rural turnout, is one of India's most densely populated states.

[16] Urbanity made a difference for both Bihar and India. Urban-rural differences were significant at a .01 level of confidence or greater, as was the difference between the national urban and Bihar urban figures.

[17] As with urban constituencies, we have performed difference of means tests at the state level for all constituencies.

[18] The same basic patterns emerge when the comparison is made against all urban constituencies in a state. The high-turnout states tend to have the largest proportion of urban constituencies which, by national urban standards, are also characterized by high-turnout, whereas states that have the largest proportion of low-turnout urban constituencies are not consistently low-turnout states. On the contrary, they are almost as likely to be high-turnout states.

[19] Nor are they substantial at the state level. The only instances in which turnout in small cities revealed a distinctive bulge over that in larger cities and rural constituencies generally were in Madras State in 1957 and 1967.

[20] Several readers of our manuscript quite legitimately objected to our use of the word "radical" to characterize the Jana Sangh and Communist parties, preferring instead to describe them as "extremist" or simply "right-wing" and "left-wing." Of course, some people argue that the Jana Sangh is neither radical nor extremist, although one or the other term might be appropriate for the recently banned Rashtriya Swayam Sevak Sangh, a militant youth-oriented affiliate of the Jana Sangh. "Right-wing" is appropriate only insofar as the Jana Sangh has a pro-Hindu orientation, since its economic platform proclaims a socialist program. The Communist parties are equally difficult to characterize, for the pro-Soviet CPI is no longer viewed by most Indians as "radical" or "extremist," and some no longer regard it as a party of the "Left" given its present collaboration with the "bourgeois" government of Prime Minister Gandhi. In short, none of the nomenclature is adequate to describe the two major groups that have for most of the elections analyzed here been the major nationally recognized ideological opponents of the ruling Congress party. Two reasons underlay our selection of these parties for special analysis and our designation of them as "radical": they have an organizational base in many urban constituencies, and they tend (especially in their youth wings) to attract those who are ideologically opposed to the existing political order as well as those who are merely in opposition to the governing party.

[21] In Andhra Pradesh in 1972, when the CPI and CPM combined acquired only 9.2 percent of the total vote.

[22] The CPI received 17.7 percent of the vote in what is now Punjab in the 1957 elections, when it provided the only real opposition to the ruling Congress (the Akali Dal having merged with Congress that year). In 1969 the CPI secured 10.1 percent of the vote in Bihar, the CPM polling another 1.2 percent. Tripura gave the Communists (mostly the CPM) 29 percent of the vote in 1967, and 40.8 percent in 1972. These are the only instances in which the Communists have received as much as 10 percent of the vote in any state other than West Bengal, Kerala, and Andhra Pradesh.

[23] Twelve of twenty in 1952 (seven in West Bengal alone, which has more urban constituencies than Andhra and Kerala combined), twenty-one of thirty-two in 1957 (nineteen in West Bengal), twenty-seven of thirty-eight in 1962 (twenty-three in West Bengal), twenty-eight of forty-six in 1967 (twenty-one in West Bengal), and twelve of twenty-four in 1972 (nine in West Bengal; these figures include Kerala elections in 1970). The 1952 figures are understated because the CPI contested under the banner of the People's Democratic Front in parts of what is now Andhra Pradesh and as independents in Travancore-Cochin. Many of these candidacies

were successful, including in urban constituencies. The 1962 figures do not include Kerala, where assembly elections were not held that year.

[24] Only 1 percent separated the two in 1972, reflecting the serious attrition of support for the CPM in the Calcutta metropolitan area.

[25] Fifteen percent of all constituencies were urban (50,000 +) in 1967.

[26] This finding runs counter to findings from Colombia, where larger cities tend to be more radical. See Lars Schoultz, "Urbanization and Changing Voting Patterns: Colombia, 1946-1970," *Political Science Quarterly*, LXXXVII (December 1972), 40. In our analysis the national urban data were examined in the following size categories: 1 million plus; 200,000 to 1 million; 100,000 to 200,000; and 50,000 to 100,000. At the state level the comparisons are almost always above as against below the 100,000 threshold.

[27] To be sure, most urban constituencies in West Bengal are in the greater Calcutta metropolitan area. However, those that are not tend to be quite similar to those that are.

[28] In 1972 the urban Communist vote declined by 2.3 percent in Bihar and by 10.6 percent in West Bengal.

[29] In Madhya Pradesh the Jana Sangh has tended to do almost as well in the countryside as in the cities.

[30] Elsewhere in the country the Jana Sangh failed to win a single urban seat in 1962. In 1967 it managed to win six out of 258.

[31] The year 1972 witnessed a general downturn in Jana Sangh victories in the face of the "Indira Wave" which swept the country. In the Hindi region the Jana Sangh won seven of sixty urban seats (excluding Rajasthan, for which we were unable to secure returns); elsewhere it won only one urban constituency (in Poona).

[32] For example, in 1967 the Jana Sangh won 20.4 percent of the vote in cities with 200,000 to 1 million people as against 13.9 percent in cities between 50,000 and 200,000. For 1952, the figures are 8.8 and 4.7 percent, respectively.

[33] Difference of means tests yield almost no significant results, and regressions indicate that the value added from introducing size categories is rarely significantly greater than the variation already explained by the urban category alone. We might note that these same tests indicate constituencies encompassing cities of 50,000 to 100,000 to be clearly "urban" in their support for the radical parties. Wherever the urban threshold is politically, it is not above the 50,000 cutoff employed in this analysis.

[34] The differences in 1952 and 1962 are statistically significant at .05, a somewhat loose standard when the number of cases is so great (more than 2,000 constituencies each year). The absence of highly visible disparities during the first decade, true in most states as well as the country at large, means that urban areas were no different from rural in their support for Congress. It is possible that urban centers influenced the rural areas around them (or were influenced by them), but the spatial plotting of deviations from state means reveals such seemingly random distributions that proximity and influence hypotheses appear to be inadequate. It would seem that through the 1962 elections urbanity was neither distinctive nor influential in this regard.

[35] Voting for nonparty independent candidates cannot easily be separated from the vote for smaller political parties not recognized by the Election Commission. Typically, as much as one-fifth of India's voters will support such candidates, although somewhat less in urban than in rural India.

[36] The socialist parties include the Socialist party and the Kisan Mazdoor Praja party in 1952, the Praja Socialist party (PSP) in 1957, the PSP and Socialist party in 1962, the PSP and Samyukta Socialist party in 1967, and the Socialist party in 1972.

[37] The performance of the socialist parties has not been analyzed in the smaller cities of 50,000. We have no reason to believe that their record should be any different there.

[38] Not only was the balance in urban-rural support for Congress reversed in 1967, but for the first time the difference was significant at .01.

[39] This figure excludes Rajasthan, for which returns were not available to us at the time of writing, along with Jammu and Kashmir and Goa.

[40] Both the CPI (in alliance with Congress in a number of states) and the CPM actually improved their urban vote in 1972, although marginally in each case.

[41] See Marguerite Ross Barnett, "Cultural Nationalist Electoral Politics in Tamil Nadu" in Weiner and Field, eds. *Electoral Politics in the Indian States*, vol. 4.

[42] During the 1960s a similar dynamic emerged at the local level, particularly in Bombay, where the Shiv Sena led a nativist reaction to the inmigration of South Indians. For a detailed

analysis, see Mary Fainsod Katzenstein, "Political Nativism: Shiv Sena in Bombay" (Ph.D. diss. in preparation, Department of Political Science, Massachusetts Institute of Technology).

[43] In 1972 the urban Akali vote declined to the 1962 level and no urban seats were won. This comparatively poor performance mirrored a rural decline as well, both in part at least a function of the factionalism gripping the Akali movement, which led three Akali parties to contest in 1972.

[44] For a detailed analysis of the Akali movement and Punjabi politics generally prior to reorganization of the state, see Baldev Raj Nayar, *Minority Politics in the Punjab* (Princeton, 1966). See also Paul R. Brass, "Ethnic Cleavages and the Punjab Party System, 1952-1972," in Weiner and Field, *Electoral Politics in the Indian States*, vol. 4.

[45] Table 10 provides summary data.

[46] We are unable to report data for 1972. The returns that year were hand tabulated, and margins of victory can only be derived from time-consuming calculations which we did not perform.

[47] The vote may have been unusually close in urban Uttar Pradesh, but it was also quite fractionated, as is typical of Uttar Pradesh generally.

[48] For an empirical analysis of the relationship between polarization and participation, see Peter McDonough, "Electoral Competition and Participation in India," *Comparative Politics,* IV (October 1971), 77-87.

[49] This is a reasonable assumption if fertility rates continue to decline while rural-urban migration remains at present levels.

[50] Most (84 percent) of these urban dwellers will live in cities larger than 100,000.

[51] *Overseas Hindustan Times,* 24 July 1975.

THE ORGANIZATION OF POLITICS

Introduction

"Seek ye first the political kingdom and all else shall come unto you. . . ."[1] This simply stated, biblically based aphorism of the late Kwame Nkrumah lies at the center of a storm of controversy: a controversy as old as organized political societies, and one which has not lost its vitality through the passage of time.

For Third World states, this aphorism generates two immediate questions. On the one hand there is the question of face *validity,* since the exposition of a doctrine is not equal to a statement of a truth; while on the other hand there is the question of the *translatability* of what may be an abstract truth into concrete realities within a given time/condition context. In other words, we need ask not only if the proposition is true, but also if it is achievable.

Obviously, such questions are not easily answered; yet, whether or not there exists in Third World states a "primacy of politics,"[2] the ways in which the political realm is organized and the ends toward which the organization of politics is directed are of clear and fundamental importance. While the organization of politics itself does not exist in a vacuum, multi-level inquiries dealing with the construction of a state framework provide a critical orientation in any analysis of *le Tiers Monde.*

To nationalist movements, the attainment of independence was but the first step in the organization of politics. The world of "the morning after" brought with it the crises of organization and management, in which goals needed to be formulated, resources mobilized, and patterns established.[3] The issue, for many observers, was one of institutionalization — "the process by which organizations and procedures acquire value and stability."[4] The primary imperative in the Third World was to construct the framework of the state, to build an institutionalized political order.

According to Samuel Huntington, the major spokesman for the institutionalization perspective, the high level of instability and disorder in many Third World countries was produced by the gap between increasing social mobility and political participation and enfeebled political organization and institutionalization. From this view, it is the strength of political organizations and procedures which provide for the viability of the political community existing within the boundaries of a state. And though simplified institutionalism is **not** without its difficulties (e.g., what are we trying to institutionalize? toward what ends? and at what costs?), it is nonetheless based on the compelling logic that before a state can run, it must stand.

The first essay in this section, Joungwon Alexander Kim's "The Politics of Predevelopment," makes a valuable contribution by emphasizing that the widely used term "political development", in fact, refers to two very different, if interrelated, concepts. In other words, "political development" deals with both the creation and institutionalization of "a viable new political system" and the adaptation of "an existing political system" to the complexities of the modern world.

While Third World states often have to face both challenges simultaneously, Kim suggests that there is utility in distinguishing one from the other. The politics of regime formation need be separated from the politics of regime functioning.[5] Thus "development" politics are viewed in terms of modernization and adaptation and "predevelopment" politics are concerned with the building of a new framework of governance.

According to Kim, the "predevelopment" process revolves around consolidation and institutionalization (wherein "consolidated control becomes routinized" and society resocialized). And it is in a "predevelopment" system that the role of leadership is so important (see Part V).

Holding that institutionalization is not static and "does not imply a freezing of the system," Kim points to that factor as the critical variable in Third World politics. For "once institutionalized the system is no longer within the realm of the politics of predevelopment. It is only then that it may move into the phase where it can begin to develop effectively or to modernize."

Yet, whatever the significance attributed to the establishment of institutionalized patterns, a meaningful discussion of the organization of politics in Third World states must move beyond such imagery. The value of a generalized map of institutional growth lies in its ties with more specific details. Here we can see that interwoven throughout the political consolidation process are questions dealing with intra-elite bonding, elite-mass relationships, and centre-periphery linkages.[6] The situational context of each of these factors provides a critical environment within which the organization of politics takes place.

These factors, in turn, are connected to the cross cutting issues of participation (or departicipation[7]), legitimacy, and ideology in Third World political systems. The complex interactions of all of these variables lead one to a consideration of several very different perspectives on the organization and purpose of politics in *le Tiers Monde*.

To a significant degree, our attention is drawn to the problems of political consolidation in societies that exhibit considerable cultural fragmentation. On the one hand, the consolidation of national institutions, as well as their broad penetration into society, is thought to be necessary to hold the system together in the face of strong centrifugal pulls. Yet, on the other hand, the very efforts to consolidate may well intensify centrifugal forces and thereby prevent achievement of the desired goal.

Even where cultural fragmentation itself is not originally a major factor, the existence of severe political segmentation in many Third World countries places these states in a similarly precarious position. This situation has led to discussions of national governments in terms of political machines and patrimonialism.

Interestingly, arguments over this question have come full circle. We have gone from an emphasis on federal-accommodative policies to an emphasis on unitary-consolidationist policies, and then have begun to work back to the former view.[8] In part, this is related to the reemphasis on micro politics in Third World states. All too often, the symbols and expressions of organized political power at the centre were devoid of substance, while the actual influence of the periphery, of the villages, was ignored.

The examination of a primary organizational mechanism, the political party, and discussions of one-party systems, for example, were very different dependent upon whether one's view was guided by the rhetoric from top or the actual impact as seen from below. Yet, if a more micro-level perspective is needed to counterbalance an unbridled macro-level vision of societies that is not to say that macro-level orientations should be abandoned. The struggle to establish a national political framework implies some degree of shifting in the hierarchical ordering of subunits within a society. As Teune and Ostrowski have noted: "The very idea of a local political system . . . connotes membership in a larger political system, and the importance of that membership must be examined."[9] The emperor may well be wearing scanty and threadbare clothes, but he is not quite naked.[10]

The second essay in this section, "The National Electoral Process and State Building," brings into focus a number of the interactive factors delineated above within the context of Ugandan politics. While recognizing that elections in the Third World are viewed as an "activity which exacerbates, rather than ameliorates system divisiveness," Provizer also notes the argument that elections can serve a positive purpose relative to the mobilization of political consciousness. The political organization and procedures, which produce the strength of the political community, are, after all, themselves dependent not only on their level of institutionalization, but also on the scope of support provided to them.[11]

Integrating a discussion of the clash of sub-central autonomy and nationalist politics with an overview of party development, this essay traces the movement toward a consolidationist system in Uganda and the unfulfilled proposals for a new method of elections in that country. Aspects of inter and intra-party rivalries, the role of ideology, and the impact of organizational change come together in the discussion of this attempt to maintain individual participation while promoting departicipation along sub-national, ethnic lines.

Although these proposals were never translated into action (interrupted by a military coup d'etat), they nonetheless provide us with some interesting perspectives on the organization of politics in a Third World state, including the numerous political dilemmas that cannot be wished away.

This brings us to the final essay in this section, Hudson's most interesting study of "Democracy and Social Mobilization in Lebanese Politics." From Hudson's perspective:

Scholars and policy-makers frequently assume that the new states must develop stability before they can hope to operate the complex and delicate institutions of liberal democracy. But in the case of the Lebanese Republic this relationship is reversed: democratic institutions have brought about and maintained stability in an unfavorable political environment.[12]

Given the events in Lebanon since the open outbreak of "externalized" internal warfare in 1975, Hudson's position that formal institutions can play a role as causal agents in the processes of political modernization and development may appear to be meaningless. Such a judgment, however, is precipitous in that the specific flow and context of events in Lebanon in recent years does not reduce to obsolescence the view that in many Third World states (from Uganda to Malaysia) the organization of politics along the lines of a balance of power system is a viable, if difficult, intermediate developmental model from both the standpoint of pragmatic politics and morality.

The "powder keg" status of Lebanon would have produced uncertainty for any approach to the organization of politics, especially when consideration is extended to the compounding factor of "social mobilization." For not only does social mobilization as an aggregate strain Third World political systems, but the unevenness of social mobilization patterns often reinforces already existent divisions found within the state.

Throughout his analysis and in his postscript, Hudson recognizes the numerous and complex problems which confronted the attempts at organizing politics in Lebanon. Yet, in holding that responses could be made to those problems, Hudson reminds us that the organization of politics is not without its significance and impact. Specific failures do not totally erode either the logic or value of an approach which endeavors to answer that most difficult of questions for political societies — how to organize a viable framework for governance.

NOTES

1. Kwame Nkrumah, quoted in Bob Fitch and Mary Oppenheimer, *Ghana: End of An Illusion* (New York: Monthly Review Press, 1966), p. 25.

2. See Herbert Spiro (ed.), *Africa: The Primacy of Politics* (New York: Random House, 1966) and the discussion in Robert Gamer, *The Developing Nations* (Boston: Allyn and Bacon, 1976), pp. 330–333.

3. See Gerald Heeger, *The Politics of Underdevelopment* (New York: St. Martin's Press, 1974), p. 47.

4. Samuel Huntington, *Political Order in Changing Societies* (New Haven: Yale University Press, 1968), p. 12.

5. Also note Dankwart Rustow's distinction between functional and genetic inquiry in "Transitions to Democracy: Toward a Dynamic Model," *Comparative Politics*, Vol. II, No. 3 (April 1970).

6. These issues overlap with questions of political integration. See, for example, Myron Weiner, "Political Integration and Political Development," *The Annals*

of the American Academy of Political and Social Science, Vol. CCCLVIII (March 1965).

7. Nelson Kasfir, *The Shrinking Political Arena* (Berkeley: University of California Press, 1976), pp. 3–27.

8. See Robert Melson and Howard Wolpe, "Modernization and the Politics of Communalism: A Theoretical Perspective," *The American Political Science Review,* Vol. LXIV, No. 4 (December 1970) and Ali Mazrui, "Pluralism and National Integration," in Leo Kuper and M. G. Smith (eds.), *Pluralism in Africa* (Berkeley: University of California Press, 1969).

9. Henry Teune and Kryzstoff Ostrowski, "Local Political Systems and General Social Processes," mimeo, 1970 (prepared for the VIII World Congress of the International Political Science Association).

10. From Rupert Emerson, "The Prospects for Democracy in Africa," in Michael Lofchie (ed.), *The State of the Nations* (Berkeley: University of California Press, 1971), pp. 249–250.

11. Huntington, *Political Order in Changing Societies,* p. 12.

12. For an overview on democracy, see Giovanni Sartori's, *Democratic Theory* (New York: Praeger, 1965).

The Politics of Predevelopment

Joungwon Alexander Kim *

In recent years studies of political development have dealt with two very different concepts: the problem of creating and institutionalizing a viable new political system, on the one hand, and that of adapting an existing political system to a complex modern world, on the other. Evaluation of these phenomena has been complicated by the fact that both have been termed "political development." It is even more difficult because both tasks have been thrust simultaneously upon many of the so-called "emerging" or "third world" nations. In a practical as well as in a theoretical sense, therefore, it has become almost impossible to separate the two phenomena.

As the third world nations have emerged from colonial rule, many have had to deal with the necessity of creating entirely new political systems, in the absence of existing organizational bases, and turning them into viable political entities. They have also been confronted with the very different task of adaptation to a complex postindustrial international setting in the era of technology, with the perpetual changes and challenges which this world presents to those who were not among the earliest to cross the industrial-technological threshold.

Throughout history, long before the industrial or technological revolutions made the world more complex, nations have faced the task of constructing new political systems. Creating a viable new state has never been a simple task. From the birth of the earliest Greek city-state or the first Chinese state, to the founding of Rome, to the establishment of the American republic, to the independence of the most recently acquired member of the world of nations, societies have been faced with the task of establishing new systems of political organization.

Manfred Halpern has suggested that even the creation of a new system is different in the modern era because one must create an "open" system—i.e., a system which has an intrinsic capacity to generate and absorb further transformation.[1] While it is true that in order to be successful in institutionalizing a new system which will be stable over time,

* The major draft of this article was prepared while the writer was a Senior Research Fellow at Columbia University. I am indebted to Zbigniew Brzezinski, W. Howard Wriggins, and Dankwart A. Rustow for their valuable comments.
[1] Manfred Halpern, "The Revolution of Modernization in International Society," in Carl J. Friedrich, ed. *Revolution* (New York, 1966), p. 180, n. 4.

given the interaction in the international system in the modern world, the system will have to be one which has developmental capacity (i.e., is open to change), the *means* for introducing a new system (as opposed to the type of system desirable) are not significantly different from the means required for introducing new systems in earlier periods. The same generic types of political tools must be utilized, though if the society now contains a much broader politically relevant population, the degree to which political tools must be mobilized to establish a new system successfully will obviously be considerably escalated.

While political societies have faced the problem of creating new systems throughout history, and not simply in the modern era, many nations during the past century have grappled with the dilemma of adapting to the age of perpetual change without having to build new political systems. These nations have sought to expand the capacity of their political systems to adapt to economic advances, industrialization, and the technological revolution, without having at the same time to face the problems which confront a nation whose entire system of political organizātion has vanished overnight, and which must wrestle to fill the vacuum. There have indeed been cases where the inability of the old political system to respond to modern demands has itself led to the collapse of that system and generated the need for introducing a new one. Nonetheless, the two challenges need not come together, and they are not the same.

In order to distinguish between these two very different challenges, it would be useful to give them specific names. Among those suggested for the task of building a new political system are the terms, "nation-building" and "state-building." But these have been used in so many different ways that they could create confusion rather than clarification if we adopted them here. Some have used them interchangeably, while others have given them separate meanings. Gabriel A. Almond and G. Bingham Powell, Jr. use each with a more restrictive meaning than that intended here: *state-building* is the name they give to the problem of penetration and integration of the system into the society, and *nation-building* is used to refer to the problem of creating loyalty and commitment to the system.[2] For the purpose of this article, the term "development" is applied to the process of adapting and increasing structural complexities to meet the changes in the modern industrial and technological world. This process is often referred to also as political modernization. On the other hand, the period during which the nation is undergoing the process of building a new political system is called "predevelopmental." This term is used because it does not seem possible for a

[2] Gabriel A. Almond and G. Bingham Powell, Jr., *Comparative Politics: A Developmental Approach* (Boston, 1966), p. 35.

political system to develop—i.e., to adapt and change to meet complex extrinsic changes—until it has attained a viable pattern of political order.

The Challenge of a Predevelopmental System

Politics in a predevelopmental system cannot be analyzed in terms used by political science to study established political systems. As Raymond Aron has noted, "There is a difference between explaining the *formation of the regime* and the *junctioning of the regime.*" [3] Almost the entire framework of modern political analysis has been developed for the purpose of examining the patterns of order and of interaction in an established political system. Thus, for instance, when Almond speaks of political development, he makes it very clear that he is concerned with a society which already has a legitimate political structure. "There is no such thing as a society which maintains internal and external order, which has no 'political structure'—i.e., legitimate patterns of interaction by means of which this order is maintained," [4] he states. The predevelopmental system is, however, one which does *not* maintain internal and external order. To *establish* such an order is its primary task. Likewise, David Easton's analysis of politics within the framework of a political system begs the question of the predevelopmental system in which the structural framework has disintegrated, or is not yet firmly established. [5] In fact, the whole effort to apply structural-functional analysis, borrowed largely from the sociological studies of Talcott Parsons and Robert K. Merton, has resulted in similar difficulties. [6] Applying structural-functional analysis to political development, Almond and Powell find development to be "the degree of differentiation and secularization." [7] Yet, once again, when a set of institutions does not exist, it is meaningless to speak of its degree of differentiation and secularization. What these theorists have clearly been concerned with is the concept of development which deals with the adaptation of political systems to a more complex and changing world; this assumes the existence of a viable system of political organization and order.

Some current works do deal with the predevelopmental system; notable among them are Samuel P. Huntington's writings concerning the

[3] Raymond Aron, *Main Currents in Sociological Thought,* II, trans. Richard Howard and Helen Weaver (New York, 1970), p. 260.

[4] Gabriel A. Almond and James S. Coleman, *The Politics of the Developing Areas* (Princeton, 1960), p. 11.

[5] For example, see David Easton, *A Framework for Political Analysis* (Englewood Cliffs, 1965), and *The Political System* (New York, 1953).

[6] See Robert K. Merton, *Social Theory and Social Structure,* rev. ed. (Glencoe, 1957), and Talcott Parsons and Edward A. Shils, eds. *Toward a General Theory of Action* (Cambridge, 1951).

[7] Almond and Powell, p. 25.

institutionalization of political systems.[8] In his *A World of Nations,* Dankwart A. Rustow deals with both phenomena which have been termed development; then, in talking of the "founding of a new state," he asserts that the specific problems in founding a state are unique, contrasting with the political tasks in "a well-established commonwealth." [9] It is the task of "founding a state," in Rustow's terms, which faces the predevelopmental system.

Leadership in a Predevelopmental System

One of the basic distinctions between the predevelopmental system and the established system is the creative role played by leaders in formulating and shaping the new political order. As Cyril E. Black has pointed out, "Man is not a captive of history, despite the undeniable persistence of historically evolved traditions, and at many, critical stages individual or group leadership has been dramatic. . . . Leaders are limited by their own origins and by the skills and resources at their command, but within these limits differences of vital significance depend on the particular policies adopted." [10] And Montesquieu noted nearly three centuries ago, "Dans la naissance des sociétés ce sont les chefs des républiques qui font l'institution; et c'est ensuite l'institution qui forme les chefs des républiques." [11] For this reason, leadership in new states has become an important subject of study by such writers as Cyril Black, Lucian W. Pye, W. Howard Wriggins, and Dankwart Rustow, among others.[12]

The undertaking to create a viable new political system is the greatest possible challenge for the practitioner of politics, the era when purposive politics becomes most rewarding, when man's political creativity meets the ultimate test. Glenn D. Paige has pointed out, "Man is a creative being who can envision worlds yet unknown and can strive purposely for their attainment." [13] Because there are no existing "channels" through

[8] See Samuel P. Huntington, "Political Development and Political Decay," *World Politics,* XVII (April 1965), 386–430, and *Political Order in Changing Societies* (New Haven, 1968).

[9] Dankwart A. Rustow, *A World of Nations: Problems of Political Modernization* (Washington, D.C., 1967), p. 153.

[10] Cyril E. Black, *The Dynamics of Modernization: A Study in Comparative History* (New York, 1966), p. 157.

[11] Charles de Secondat, Baron Montesquieu, "Considérations sur les causes de la grandeur des romains et de leur décadence," in *Oeuvres,* I (Paris, 1828), pp. 119–20, as quoted in Huntington, "Political Development," p. 421.

[12] See Lucian W. Pye, *Politics, Personality, and Nation-Building: Burma's Search for Identity* (New Haven, 1962); W. Howard Wriggins, *The Ruler's Imperative: Strategies for Political Survival in Asia and Africa* (New York, 1969); and Rustow, Part II, "Political Leadership in New States."

[13] See "The Rediscovery of Politics," in John D. Montgomery and William J. Siffin, eds. *Approaches to Development: Politics, Administration and Change* (New York, 1966), p. 49.

which to operate, no political tools ready at hand, the leadership must forge them itself from the materials available. It is this leadership which will create the fundamental bases upon which the society will later develop.

Such a task calls for unusual leadership skills, and it is therefore at this stage that the type of leadership Max Weber termed "charismatic" tends to come forward.[14] As Erik H. Erikson has stated, "There are periods in history which are identity-vacua, when a sudden sense of alienation is widespread. . . . It is in such periods that the leaders' deep conflicts and special gifts have found their 'activities on a large scale,' and they have been found and chosen by contemporaries possessed of analogous conflicts and corresponding needs."[15] Such is the time as well for Machiavelli's manipulative prince, for Montesquieu's founder of a nation, for Rousseau's lawgiver.

To create a viable political system, the leadership will make use of four basic instruments of politics—guns, funds, organization, and ideas —first, *to consolidate* political power, and, second, *to institutionalize* the system which has been created. Since the leader in the predevelopmental system must create the tools he is to use, he must employ methods quite dissimilar from the leader who is working within an established system. At the same time, he must create his own source of legitimacy. While the leader in the established system comes to power by institutionalized means and hence becomes legitimate in the very act of achieving power, in the predevelopmental system this leader must create a claim to legitimacy within the national political mythology. In doing so, he may also need to alter and recreate that mythology.

Who the leaders will be is not predetermined, for a predevelopmental system cannot be said to have a single political elite. The existence of "an" elite assumes that there is a means of determining who are the legitimate power holders. Since the question of political legitimacy is unresolved in a predevelopmental system, no single "political elite" exists until one contending leadership group has consolidated power. Contending groups may be drawn from a single social or economic elite,

[14] Max Weber, *Theory of Social and Economic Organization* (New York, 1947), pp. 358–62. Others have commented on the rise of charismatic leaders at this time. See Ann Ruth Willner and Dorothy Willner, "The Rise and Role of Charismatic Leaders," *Annals of the American Academy of Political and Social Science,* 358 (March 1965), p. 80; George McT. Kahin, Guy J. Pauker, and Lucian W. Pye, "Comparative Politics of Non-Western Countries," *American Political Science Review,* XLIX (December 1955); Ann Ruth Willner, *Charismatic Political Leadership: A Theory* (Princeton, 1968); Robert C. Tucker, "The Theory of Charismatic Leadership," *Daedalus,* XCVII (Summer 1968), 731–56; and Carl J. Friedrich, "Political Leadership and Charismatic Power," *The Journal of Politics,* XXIII (Feburary 1961), 3–24.

[15] Erik H. Erikson, *Insight and Responsibility* (New York, 1964), p. 204.

if the social and economic systems have not disintegrated along with the political; however, predevelopmental systems generally face a period of social and economic breakdown. The contest thus becomes wide open, and the society is able to draw forth from various strata the personality types who emerge as leaders in this form of political atmosphere. Black has noted, for example, that, "In periods of rapid change . . . political leaders tend to show a much greater diversity of origin. All societies undergoing change are involved to some extent in the transfer of political power from old hands to new. The source and nature of the new political leadership become a central issue in the study of change." [16] Nonetheless, the leader who is able to claim legitimacy within the framework of the national political mythology has an important advantage in any political contest. Where there is no legitimate institutional system, as in the case of a nation just formulating its political structure, personal legitimacy of a leader often tends to be substituted for the institutional legitimacy of an established system.[17] People tend to turn toward leaders with the greatest claims to legitimacy within the framework of the nation's political mythology. Legitimacy, as Easton has said, is a psychological, not a moral, concept.[18]

If there is some existing means of ascertaining legitimacy within the society—a still-existing monarchy, or a pattern of colonial institutions which has achieved some degree of acceptance by the populace—the individual personality may assume less importance. In Japan and Thailand, for example, the monarchical institution provided the source of legitimacy which charismatic leaders have sought to provide in other nations, while some former colonies, e.g., the Philippines, had accepted the governing process (though not the existence of external controls imposed by colonial rule) as legitimate.

Since the leadership is not predetermined, much of the predevelopmental phase involves a contest between contending leadership groups to determine which will ultimately initiate the new political system and determine its form. This is where the hottest political battles arise, for the future of the entire society hangs upon the outcome of the contest. Ideological battles become extreme, for the shape of the social organization of an entire people for an indefinite future is at stake. Issues are brought to the surface for which men are willing, and historically have been willing, to fight and to die. "Liberty or death" is then a cry which stirs proud resonances in the breasts of men. Death and adventure, terror and honor, are in the winds. It is no time for compromise, for

[16] Black, *Dynamics,* p. 62.
[17] Rustow suggests this, p. 157.
[18] Easton, *Political System,* p. 132.

sweet reason. The very identity of one's nation, of one's family, of one's self hang upon the outcome of the contest. The man who is willing to compromise away his own very basic values and beliefs for the sake of harmony finds no respect in such an atmosphere; rather he is the subject of scorn, of derision, and of suspicion. This mood recedes only after the contest has been won, the power consolidated, the system established.

To succeed in such a milieu, the political leader must be a highly effective political manipulator and consolidator. Yet, in the long run, he must be evaluated not only in this practical dimension, but also in the theoretical dimension—that is, in terms of the validity of the idea systems he espouses and the permanent viability of the political system he is seeking to introduce. In the short run, the more his expectations about the impact of these ideas conform to reality, the more prepared will he be to react to the feedback created by the changes. In the long run, because the leader of a predevelopmental system is introducing an entire form of political system into the society, ultimate evaluation of his ability must be determined by the functional capacity of that system itself. The long-term viability of the system will depend upon whether it is one which, after having been successfully established, is capable of development and adaptability. Too often, however, the leader's view is, and must be, restricted to a short-range span, for his capacity is strained to the utmost with the tasks of consolidating political power. Rare is the leader who can look far beyond these immediate concerns to visualize the construction of a functional and developmental system.

The short-range success of a political leader, therefore, will depend upon two factors: (1) his ability to claim legitimacy, and (2) his capability for handling the tools of politics.

The Tools of Politics
The tools of politics are so obvious that they may be taken for granted by political observers; yet no contestant in the predevelopmental system can ignore them and still survive politically. The success of political leadership will depend upon the ability to use these tools to consolidate a permanent power base in order to support an advocated system, and to institutionalize this system in the society. Only then may the ultimate evaluation of the success of the leadership be made through examining the developmental capacity of the system which has been introduced, after it has become an established system.

Politics involves the use of four basic instruments, which, for the sake of simplicity, we refer to as guns, funds, organization, and ideas. Other political writers have identified similar tools; e.g., Machiavelli emphasized men, money, iron, and bread, and Harold Lasswell stressed symbols, violence, goods, and practices.[19] While these tools are utilized in all political activity, they are most conspicuous in the predevelopmental system because their sources are not yet institutionalized, and leadership groups must create them at great expenditure of effort. Because there is no institutionalized source of these tools in the predevelopmental system, tools provided from external sources—from other nations or from international groups or organizations—may be important in determining the outcome of the political contest for control over the establishment of the system. This is why predevelopmental systems have been viewed historically as "political vacuums," tending to draw in external tools from other nations to assist various contenders in determining the outcome of the contest for control.

The role of guns in politics is often obscured in an established system where an institutionalized "neutrality" of guns between the legitimate internal groups which compete for power permits political contests to operate within the limitations enforced by the system, without concern for guns. Where there is no established system, no means of institutional control over guns can be maintained, and use of violence becomes an essential part of the contest for political control. Thus, Weber said, "Violent communal action is obviously something primordial. Every community, from the household to the political party, has always resorted to physical violence when it had to protect the interests of its members and was capable of doing so." [20]

Guns may come from both internal and external sources. Often a foreign nation may send its military forces in to put down a rebellion, or may provide men or arms and ammunition to support an uprising. Foreign countries may also provide military advisors, bring military groups to their own territory for training, and in other ways assist in bolstering the tool of guns for a particular leadership group.

Because guns are the instruments of force, those who supply them will rarely be motivated by fear of force exerted by the leadership:

> The fact that force must rely on relationships based on something other than force has been pointed out by [Herbert] Goldhamer and [Edward] Shils: the more that force is used in a system, the larger must be the staff needed to apply it—and the greater the dependence of the users on that staff. Although the relationship between those who apply force, on the one hand, and those to whom it is applied, on the other, may be

[19] Niccolò Machiavelli, *The Prince and the Discourses* (New York, 1950), and Harold Lasswell, *Politics: Who Gets What, When, How* (New York, 1958).

[20] Max Rheinstein, ed. *Max Weber on Law in Economy and Society,* trans. Edward Shils and Max Rheinstein (New York, 1954), p. 342.

based entirely on force, there must nevertheless be relationships *within the force-using group* that are based on something else.[21]

The leaders may give their military backers a sense of pride in their role, which calls forth loyalty, or they may promise rewards for support. They may be able to bring in sources of supplies which the force group itself could not obtain, thereby creating a relationship of dependence. Whatever means the leadership group uses to obtain support from its source of guns, it cannot at any cost afford to lose this support. For this reason many other sacrifices costly to the leadership and costly to the society may have to be made.

Funds are another important instrument of political action. Weber made the statements: "It is true . . . that the control over economic goods, i.e., economic power, is a frequent, often purposely willed, consequence of domination as well as one of its most important instruments. Not every position of economic power, however, represents 'domination' in our sense of the word. . . . Nor does 'domination' utilize in every case economic power for its foundation and maintenance. But in the vast majority of cases, and indeed in the most important ones, this is just what happens in one way or another." [22] Funds in this sense encompass not only monetary currency, but any goods, products, or services for which currency might be exchangeable, or to which economics could give a monetary value. Included in the funds of a political group are all of its sources of income. Thus, if a group is funded either secretly or overtly by the government, as where it is an official party in a one-party system, or where the bureaucracy plays a role in funding a political party, the party's ultimate source of funds will be those sources available to the government, including taxation and foreign aid.

In a political system with a high level of individual income, where a large proportion of the population has more than the minimum needed for survival, voluntary contributions to political activities on a broad scale may be a realistic expectation, provided the populace is sufficiently motivated. In an economically underdeveloped country, however, people without enough to eat cannot be expected to deprive their families of food in order to contribute funds voluntarily to political activities, regardless of their high degree of interest in the outcome of a contest.

The source of funds for political activity may be the government itself, which channels in funds from taxes or foreign assistance; or it may be a wealthy landed elite; or it may stem from business profits contributed by entrepreneurs with an immediate stake in the contest. Contributions may be secured from voluntary contributors, by the exertion

[21] Marc J. Swartz, Victor W. Turner, and Arthur Tuden, *Political Anthropology* (Chicago, 1966), pp. 1–41.
[22] Rheinstein, p. 323.

of force through taxation or protection rackets. Some incentive must be present to bring forth political funds, whether it be fear, expectation of reward, or even a disinterested agreement with the idea system provided by the leadership. Disinterested approval, however, will rarely be sufficient incentive to induce persons to dip into sources of funds in such a wildly unstable period as one in which governmental organization has not been stabilized. Thus in predevelopmental systems, either the government must openly fund political activity, which is frequently the case in one-party systems, or the party must extract funds from the population by force (e.g., by protection rackets), or deal with those who hold the financial resources in the system in arrangements which have, in established systems, been termed corruption. Some writers have pointed out that, during a certain phase, corruption may in fact play a functional role in a (predevelopmental) political system.[23] The leadership which is under severe external pressure (perhaps because it depends on external sources of guns) to avoid *any* of these three alternative sources of political funding must rely on external sources of funds, which it must find some means of channeling into political coffers. Thus, the more "clean" the leadership must appear in order to satisfy sources of foreign support, the more it will be led to rely on foreign financial assistance.

Funds are crucial to any political contest. The instruments of force depend upon funds to maintain supplies, and organizations require funds to distribute information and to coordinate activities. Communications are costly whether they employ modern technology or the labor of running messengers; and both military and election campaigns are lost without effective communication.

Though both guns and funds are important political tools, they can neither be controlled nor put to effective use without organization. In nations where the bureaucracy and other formal organs of government have been fairly successfully neutralized in a formalized political contest which follows the established norms and processes of the system, the political role of these organizations which are termed governmental may be obscured. Also, in countries where centuries of efforts have led to a division between church and state, the role of religious organizations in politics has been diminished. In a system where forms of institutional neutrality have not been established, these organizations may well play a far more significant role than those groups which are termed political parties. All politically relevant organizations must be considered as having some function in the political contest.

Weber dealt with the "domination through organization":

[23] Huntington, *Political Order*, p. 64.

Generally speaking, those specific measures of domination which are established by consociation show the following characteristics:

A circle of people who are accustomed to obedience to the orders of *leaders* and who also have a personal interest in the continuance of the domination by virtue of their own participation in, and the benefits derived for them from, the domination, have divided among themselves the exercise of those functions which will serve the continuation of the domination and are holding themselves continuously ready for their exercise.

This entire structure will be called *organization.*[24]

Although guns and funds may come from external sources, organization is difficult to supply externally. Nonetheless, groups may be organized and trained in organizational skills outside the country, or foreign political advisers may assist in setting up an organization within the country. A group may be part of an international or foreign organization, as some local communist parties were at one stage subordinates of the Comintern, and as religious organizations sometimes cross national boundaries.

Persons may be motivated to work within political organizations for various reasons—as a source of employment in a time of turmoil, for prestige or promised rewards, to obtain protection from other groups, out of a sense of sharing a common cause, for fear of retaliation for not joining, out of hero worship for a charismatic leader, or in support of a symbolic or programmatic appeal which the group represents.

Ideas are also used as political instruments. As tools of politics, ideas are measured not by their theoretical validity—i.e., their conformity with truth or with reality—but by their ability to influence the actions of people. Indeed, a set of idea symbols may be used purposely by a leadership group to bring about results contrary to those implied in the ideas themselves. Although the effects of ideas advocated by the leadership group must be measured by their impact on political support to determine how effective they have been as political tools, the validity of the ideas actually espoused by the leadership group (which may or may not be the same as those overtly used as political tools) is important to the extent that these ideas may ultimately shape political activity and have an impact upon the political environment. A distinction must thus be made between the ideas seriously held by a leadership group, and ideas simply used as political tools for the purpose of securing and maintaining political support.

The distinction between ideas seriously held and ideas utilized as

[24] Rheinstein, pp. 334–35.

political tools may be less obvious in a political system with a highly sophisticated populace, for the leaders may be required by their following (which is aware of the ultimate impact of the ideas on political reality) to express valid concepts. Where the audience is poorly educated and politically unsophisticated, however, the winner of a contest of ideas will be the one who uses concepts meaningful to the audience. To a less sophisticated audience, the general appeal of an attractive slogan, such as "a chicken in every pot," may generate more support than the appeals made by leaders who come across as more coldly expert. To the sophisticated audience, the sloganeering politician may seem crude and opportunistic and the "expert" more capable of handling the needs of the system. In the first instance, the leader must divorce his seriously held ideas from those he must use as political tools; in the latter, the politician may be able to utilize his seriously held ideas as tools of politics because they also have audience appeal.

Political ideas may be the invention of the politicians themselves; or they may come from trusted advisors or be borrowed from contemporary or former native thinkers. They may also be taken from foreign thinkers. When ideas are borrowed from abroad, the followers of the line of thought are often sensitive to interpretations of these ideas as they are applied abroad, and thus tend to be receptive to "authoritative" foreigners who criticize or seek to influence their actions, using the framework of the borrowed idea system. For this reason countries which have sought to borrow entire idea systems from abroad have often been subject to extensive external intervention, as foreign analysts have become the best interpreters of what is right within the framework of the borrowed idea system. Thus, for example, Soviet criticism of the "cult of personality" in North Korea led to an effort by two factions of the North Korean party to overthrow Kim Il Sung, using Soviet reprimands as a justification.[25] Similarly, American criticism of the Syngman Rhee government in South Korea as undemocratic, reported widely in the South Korean press, was a factor in the Student Revolution which brought about Rhee's downfall.[26] So long as North Koreans saw Soviet government officials as experts on Marxism, or South Koreans saw American

[25] See Joungwon A. Kim, "Soviet Policy in North Korea," *World Politics,* XXII (January 1970), 237–54. Brezhnev's criticism of the lack of collective leadership in North Korea appears in *Chosŏn Nodong-dang chaesamcha munhŏnjip* [Documents of the Third Congress of the Korean Workers' Party] (Pyongyang, 1956), p. 350.

[26] Kim Sŏng-t'ae, "Sawŏl sipkuilŭi simnihak" [Psychology of April 19], *Sassanggye,* IX (April 1961), 80–81, shows the results of a survey indicating that 45 percent of student participants in the revolution were directly moved to participate by "the agitation of newspapers." For American criticism of the Rhee government as "undemocratic," later republished in the Korean press, see *New York Times,* 17, 18, 21, 25 January, 2 May, and 16 August 1959.

analysts as experts on democracy, criticism by foreigners could seriously affect the government's bases of support.

One fallacy in political analysis has been concentration upon one of the four political tools alone as the primary determinant of the outcome of a political contest. Economic determinists (in the Marxist tradition) would attribute the results of all political activity to the locus of funds and their manipulation. Others concentrate on the role of guns in politics, assuming that the holder of guns will be ultimately responsible for the outcome of any political contest. Organization also has its adherents, while many have seen the battle of ideas as the arbiter of history. Chief Justice Oliver Wendell Holmes referred to the American faith in the power of ideas when he said, "When men have realized that time has upset many fighting faiths, they may come to believe . . . that the ultimate good desired is better reached by free trade in ideas—that the best test of truth is the power of the thought to get itself accepted in the competition of the market. . . . That at any rate is the theory of our Constitution." [27] In fact, all of the political tools interact, so that none alone will determine the outcome of a political contest.

Where one or more of the political tools can be neutralized, so that it will not be available, or be equally available to either side in a political contest, competition with the other tools takes on added significance. Thus, in a political system where the role of guns in the normal political process has been largely neutralized between political contenders, the other political tools have taken on added importance. To read Theodore H. White's *The Making of the President, 1960*, for example, is to witness the operation of a contest of ideas, of organization, and of funds in American politics.[28] In a political system where virtual agreement on ideas is also normal, the contest may be in terms of which side can mobilize the most funds and have the most efficient organization. (Arguably, if one genuinely wanted political contests to become contests of ideas alone, neutralization of the role of funds and organization, as well as of guns, would be necessary.)

The tools of politics are used by the leadership group to consolidate its control, and to institutionalize a new system of political order. The sources of these tools, however, are determined by the three variables described below.

The Internal, External, and Extrinsic Factors
The availability of political tools is subject to three kinds of factors: political factors *internal* to the society; political factors *external* to the

---

[27] Abrams et al. v. United States, 250 U.S. 616 (1919), dissent.
[28] Theodore H. White, *The Making of the President, 1960* (New York, 1961).

society; and nonpolitical factors, i.e., factors *extrinsic* to the political system (though they may be internal to the society).

Internal factors within the society affect the available political tools as well as the general political environment. They include both the "political culture" and the concrete sources of political tools existing in the society. The concept of political culture was first suggested by Gabriel A. Almond and later elaborated by Lucian W. Pye and Sidney Verba.[29] Verba defines political culture as "the system of empirical beliefs, expressive symbols, and values which defines the situation in which political action takes place." [30] We see political culture as encompassing both (1) the political behavior patterns which have developed out of previous political systems, and (2) the national political mythology relating to political values and political legitimacy, on which the leader may draw to reinforce his own legitimacy and to increase support for the new system.

The sources of the tools of politics within the society are those which have developed out of previous political systems—or in opposition to previous political systems—and which have not since disintegrated. The distribution of wealth in the previous system may well determine the locus of funds which will influence the outcome of a political contest; armed groups which either supported or were organized in resistance to the former system may provide the source of guns; organizations previously existing may disintegrate or remain to play a role in the contest; and ideas disseminated previously may continue to shape the outlook of people in the society.

The political behavior patterns which have developed in previous systems have come as a response to the way in which individuals and groups could maximize their interests within that particular system. Although these behavior patterns originated as the result of some functional need, they may persist long after the original cause has ceased to exist. Thus, the behavior patterns may be totally irrelevant to the new system the leadership would seek to introduce, or they may be highly dysfunctional within that system. Nonetheless, they tend to be perpetuated, and will gradually die out only when it becomes clear that they fail to secure, or that they positively deny, the interests of the individual practicing them within the new institutional system.

The national political mythology is the sum of political values and political legends which have developed in the society's political history. A leadership wishing to change the political behavior patterns and es-

[29] Gabriel A. Almond, "Comparative Political Systems," *Journal of Politics,* XVIII (August 1956), 391–409; Lucian W. Pye and Sidney Verba, *Political Culture and Political Development* (Princeton, 1963).

[30] Pye and Verba, p. 513.

tablish a new institutional system may nonetheless successfully draw on the values and legends in the old political mythology to support this change, and indeed may seek to legitimize the change by means of the old myth system. As Machiavelli advised,

> He who desires or attempts to reform the government of a state, and wishes to have it accepted and capable of maintaining itself to the satisfaction of everybody, must at least retain the semblance of the old forms; so that it may seem to the people that there has been no change in the institutions, even though in fact they are entirely different from the old ones. For the great majority of mankind are satisfied with appearances, as though they were realities, and are often even more influenced by the things that seem than by those that are. . . . And this rule should be observed by all who wish to abolish an existing system of government in any state, and introduce a new and more liberal one. For as all novelties excite the minds of men, it is important to retain in such innovations as much as possible the previously existing forms.[31]

In the same way, the leader may draw on the old myth system to support his own individual claim to leadership legitimacy.

In the predevelopmental system, many of the old sources of political tools may have disintegrated or been discredited by the same circumstances which brought the fall of the preexisting political system. In this case, the political tools must be created anew. In such circumstances, external assistance in creating these new tools may be sought by different leadership contenders. And it is because of this that the role of external factors in the predevelopmental system takes on such significance, and has had such a great impact in the contemporary international arena.[32]

Because the sources of the tools of politics are not institutionalized in the predevelopmental system, they may be easily supplied from external sources. The system which has completed the predevelopment phase and has institutionalized internal sources of these tools will be less likely to desire or to tolerate intrusion of these tools from external sources. Because of the temptation in the predevelopmental stage, and, indeed, sometimes the necessity, of securing additional tools from external sources, the "political vacuums" in these areas tend to become the focus of international conflict. As Rustow notes, "During the formation of a new state . . . domestic and foreign affairs are more closely intertwined

---

[31] Machiavelli, *Discourses,* I, chap. 25, p. 183.

[32] The expression "external factors" is used here in the sense employed in R. Barry Farrel, *Approaches to Comparative and International Politics* (Evanston. 1966), not in the sense used by S. N. Eisenstadt, *The Political Systems of Empires* (New York, 1963), pp. 26–28, when he speaks of "external" conditions as "certain developments in the non-political institutions." These are the factors we here term extrinsic, or nonpolitical.

than at any other time; the whole task consists in drawing . . . a boundary between the domestic and foreign spheres." [33]

While the interest of other countries in the outcome of the internal political contest may well affect how the external actors behave, the influence they actually exert upon the power struggle is restricted to the concrete political tools they provide to, or withhold from, the various political contenders.[34] Frequently, external actors may be blinded by their own myth systems to the extent that they are unable to recognize the realities of the internal situation within the predevelopmental system to which they are supplying external inputs. Whatever they may believe about what is happening within the subject system, and however they conceive the results of their assistance, their only effect upon the outcome of the contest is through the political tools they supply. They cannot alter the preexisting political behavior patterns or political mythology of the subject system, nor can they prevent it from exhibiting the characteristics of a predevelopmental system.

Because they are blinded or constricted by their own political myth systems, the external actors frequently take steps which are either irrational or simply not suitable within the framework of the predevelopmental system. For example, an external actor supplying inputs may demand that leaders alter the political behavior patterns of their followers or other members of society, without first supplying sufficient tools to allow the leadership to create a new institutional system which is a precondition for enforcing such an alteration of behavior patterns. The external actors may also supply one tool but withhold another—e.g., supply funds but withhold guns—though both are necessary to the internal leadership group which they are supporting. They may also require irrational concessions, such as renunciation of the use of guns against an armed opponent in exchange for supplying funds. The external supporter, seeing guns neutralized (at least according to its own myths) within its own system, may reach the conclusion that the use of guns is therefore inappropriate political behavior on the part of its protégés in the predevelopmental system. Thus, while external factors may be essential to the success of a group in a political contest, where the internal sources are weak or held by another group, and especially when other contenders are supported by external inputs from other sources, these external factors may also introduce such inappropriate or

[33] Rustow, p. 155.

[34] The promising studies of "intervention" belong under this heading, e.g., "Intervention and World Politics," a special volume of the *Journal of International Affairs*, XXII (2/1968). See also Richard J. Barnet, *Intervention and Revolution* (New York, 1968).

irrational elements as to frustrate totally the leadership group they ostensibly support, and undermine its goals. Frequently, in the emerging nations today, the result is an indefinite prolongation of the conditions of predevelopment. Such unintentional extension of predevelopment as a result of external inputs is what many frustrated leaders in the emerging nations have termed "neocolonialism."

The nonpolitical, or extrinsic, factors include those conditions in the environment which, though extrinsic to politics, nonetheless determine the effectiveness of the political tools.[35] Education, technology, communications facilities, and the like are all extrinsic to politics but will influence the tools of politics available to the contestants.[36]

A nation may emerge from foreign domination, military defeat, or revolution with weak internal resources—no organized army or police, no organized political groups, little concentration of wealth, a fragmented cluster of competing ideological systems—and yet possess nonpolitical factors favorable (or unfavorable) to the quick formation of political tools. An economically developed system is obviously more capable of accumulating funds for political purposes than an economically backward one. A literate populace which possesses various mass media may be more readily indoctrinated with a unifying political ideology or idea system than a populace fragmented by great impediments to communication. An economically and technologically developed system may more readily equip and train an armed force and an effective police force. Because of the relation of these nonpolitical factors to the ability to create effective political tools, these factors have often been used as measures of development. They may well be such in the sense of modernization, but they are not effective measures of the predevelopmental phase, for these nonpolitical factors serve only to provide the raw materials of the tools of politics. The growth of these factors may also, as some writers have pointed out, be disintegrative in the predevelopmental phase, for the existence of too many organizations, too many financially independent groups, and too many competing idea systems, made pos-

---

[35] Paige, p. 54, refers to the extrinsic factors in Korea in the "nonhuman environment." Here we include also those factors in the "human environment" which are measured by demographic studies—e.g., population size, distribution by geographic location and by occupation, literacy and skill levels, and so forth.

[36] See studies of the influence of some of these nonpolitical factors on political development in the Princeton University series on political development, especially Lucian W. Pye, ed. *Communications and Political Development* (Princeton, 1963), and James S. Coleman, ed. *Education and Political Development* (Princeton, 1965). The book, Robert E. Ward and Dankwart Rustow, eds. *Political Modernization in Japan and Turkey* (Princeton, 1964), is concerned with several of these extrinsic factors, including economic development, in Japan and Turkey. Other books in the series are generally concerned with the effects of political factors on development.

sible by the expansion of economic development, communications, and education, may make political consolidation extremely difficult.[37]

The Predevelopment Process: Consolidation

Consolidation, the first predevelopment stage, is the drawing together by a leadership group of sufficient power within a society to oblige the remainder of the society to recognize it as the political elite, and hence to accept its advocated form of political system. Cyril E. Black has pointed out that the first stage in modernization must be the consolidation of a new political leadership which will break with the traditional institutions.[38] Even where such institutions have been largely destroyed by colonial rule or revolution, the new leadership must consolidate political control in order to introduce a new modernizing system (or any form of system). The process of consolidation takes place because, in order to create an effective new system, one basic concept of the form it is to take and its goals must prevail among the political participants. George Kahin, Guy Pauker, and Lucian Pye find one of the basic characteristics of the "non-Western" political process to be "the lack of consensus about the legitimate forms and purposes of political activities. The fundamental cultural conflict between the traditional beliefs and Western influences has gone far toward destroying the earlier basis of political consensus, and the increasing number of participants complicates the conscious attempts at developing a new consensus." [39] The problem of lack of consensus exists in all predevelopmental systems. To create this consensus a group with agreed goals must secure and consolidate power. The result of the consolidation will be determination not only of the leadership in the new system, but, more significantly, of the form the new system will take. It is thus more than a mere power struggle; the contest will decide not simply a temporary leadership for the society but the institutional forms which will shape the political behavior of the society for an indefinite future.

Consolidation by a leadership group which seeks to bring about a particular form of system has occurred in every society in which a political system has been successfully introduced. In nineteenth century Japan, for example, the group was the Meiji samurai; in Russia, the Bolsheviks; in Turkey, the military followers of Attaturk; and in the United States, the "Founding Fathers." In all these countries, the leaders shared a basic consensus on the form of system they sought to introduce, and excluded those who opposed that view, whether their opponents

[37] E.g., Huntington, "Political Development," p. 405.
[38] Black, *Dynamics,* p. 71.
[39] Kahin, Pauker, and Pye, "Comparative Politics," 1022–41.

were labelled "Tories," or "enemies of the people," or some other epithet.

Machiavelli went so far as to suggest that the consolidation of power must be in the hands of one man alone:

> It never or rarely happens that a republic or monarchy is well consti-
> tuted, or its old institutions entirely reformed, unless it is done by only
> one individual; it is even necessary that he whose mind has conceived
> such a constitution should be alone in carrying it into effect. A sagacious
> legislator of a republic, therefore, whose object is to promote the
> public good, and not his private interests, and who prefers his country
> to his own successors, should concentrate all authority in himself;
> and a wise mind will never censure any one for having employed any
> extraordinary means for the purpose of establishing a kingdom or con-
> stituting a republic. . . . The organization of anything cannot be made
> by many, because the divergence of their opinions hinders them from
> agreeing as to what is best.[40]

Weber, however, suggested that it is sufficient that the consolidators be a small number: "The ruling position over the masses of the members of that [ruling] circle . . . rests upon the so-called 'law of the small number.' The ruling minority can quickly reach understanding among its members; it is thus able at any time quickly to initiate that rationally organized action which is necessary to preserve its position of power."[41] Various strategies for political consolidation ("aggregating power") are suggested by W. Howard Wriggins in his *The Ruler's Imperative.*[42]

Consolidation is completed when the leaders have sufficient control over their society so that a group offering an alternative system cannot find means to challenge them successfully. Obviously, if external re-sources of political tools much greater than those available in the society remain accessible to alternative groups, the leaders can remain in con-trol only if (1) they too can secure external resources sufficient to more than offset those available to the alternative group(s), or (2) they can *create* internal tools so strong that the cost to any external power seek-ing to influence the outcome of their struggle will be greater than that power's interest in the contest. For this reason countries that seek inde-pendence from external control feel compelled to expand their internal economic base (to increase internal resources of funds through economic development),[43] to construct large armies (to increase internal sources

[40] Machiavelli, *Discourses,* I, chap. 9, pp. 138–39.
[41] Rheinstein, p. 334.
[42] Wriggins.
[43] The necessity for economic development universally felt by leadership groups has been generally observed, e.g., Rustow, p. 74.

of guns),[44] to create organizations (so powerful as virtually to dominate the society),[45] and to develop idiosyncratic ideological systems (to compete with alternative externally provided idea systems).[46]

This defensive type of development is the compelling force which leads the so-called emerging nations to follow somewhat similar patterns. From the largest Asian nation to the smallest African state, from the Middle East to Latin America, the third world countries have been trying, with or without success, to create their own versions of ideology, to build massive armies, to expand organizational control over their societies, and to promote economic development. Whereas these phenomena have sometimes been viewed as irrational, or as being pursued with an unreasonable degree of zeal, by external observers from established political systems, the phenomena clearly flow out of defensive responses to external factors which otherwise might alter the internal power structure (even irrespective of the conscious intent of the external powers) by the fact that foreign nations have control over sources of political tools within the subject society. Where the political systems are unable to secure enough internal resources to resist the unsettling impact of external factors, consolidation rarely succeeds. Hence, for example, the coup d' etat, a symptom of the failure to consolidate political control, tends to occur in areas most heavily inundated with external influences. It has become virtually synonymous with Latin American— and, increasingly, with Middle Eastern, African, and Asian—politics, largely because those areas of the world are most heavily permeated by external controls over several of the political tools. As previously mentioned, the condition of political inhibition due to the continuing influence (even where unintentional) of conflicting or contradictory external factors is the phenomenon which has frequently been unhappily labelled "neocolonialism" by leaders of political systems suffering from its effects.

The Predevelopmental Process: Institutionalization

Institutionalization, the second predevelopment stage, is the process by which the system introduced by the group which has consolidated control becomes routinized in the society.[47] Talcott Parsons defines in-

[44] See, for example, John J. Johnson, ed. *The Role of the Military in Underdeveloped Countries* (Princeton, 1962).

[45] Almond and Powell, p. 35, speak of this as the need to "penetrate" the society with new structures and organizations. This is often identified as expanding political participation (i.e., political involvement in organizations).

[46] See, for example, a collection of excerpts from numerous "ideologies" in new states in Paul E. Sigmund, Jr., *The Ideologies of the Developing Nations* (New York, 1963).

[47] Huntington, *Political Order,* suggests institutionalization as a measure of

stitutionalization as "the organization of action around sufficiently stable patterns so that they may be treated as structured from the point of view of the system." [48] Huntington says that "Institutions are stable, valued, recurring patterns of behavior," and "Institutionalization is the process by which organizations and procedures acquire value and stability." [49] The idea that what is initially a "charismatic" order will become "routinized" in the society goes back to Weber's concept of this.[50] The sociologist Robert E. Park notes that "collective action . . . may set a social pattern which repetition fixes in habits, and which eventually become institutionalized in the society." [51]

In the author's view, the political system has become institutionalized in the society when it is accepted as both "normal" and "legitimate." It has become "normal" when the behavior patterns within the society have adjusted to the system in such a way that persons behave in a manner which can rationally be expected to maximize their own interests within the particular system. It is accepted as "legitimate" when persons accept this form of behavior as "right"—that is, when there is no longer a conflict between the values of the individual and the way in which he must act to secure what he considers to be at least a minimum of his own interests within the system.

The operation of the system becomes normal when the stability of the system has led to predictability as to what will be the reaction of the system. Marc Swartz, Victor Turner, and Arthur Tuden, anthropologists writing about the political system, consider this to be the measure of legitimacy: "The government of a group will be considered legitimate when the members of the group, its 'public,' believe—on the basis of experience—that the government will produce decisions that are in accord with the public's expectations." [52] Although we would disagree that a people will accept a government as legitimate simply because it is predictable, this is an essential measure of whether or not it will be considered "normal." To be "legitimate," the values as well as the behavior patterns of the populace must be changed.

The idea that value changes will be altered to adapt to behavioral changes has support in psychological theory. Albert Hirschman, the economist, has drawn from work on cognitive dissonance theory to show

---

development. Here, however, we are not concerned with specific autonomous institutions, but rather with the institutionalization of the system as a whole.

[48] Talcott Parsons, "The Position of Sociological Theory," *American Sociological Review,* XIII (April 1948), 156–64.

[49] Huntington, "Political Development," p. 394.

[50] Weber, *Theory,* pp. 363–73.

[51] Robert E. Park, *On Social Control and Collective Behavior* (Chicago, 1967), p. 185.

[52] Swartz, Turner and Tuden, p. 12.

that "when there is an inconsistency between the behavior of men and their values, it is often the values that change." [53] Weber said that, "The mere statistical regularity of an action leads to the emergence of moral and legal convictions with corresponding contents. The threat of physical and psychological coercion, on the other hand, imposes a certain mode of action and thus produces habituation and thereby regularity of action." [54]

According to Robert E. Park, "When the role of the individuals in the action of the group has become fixed in habit, and particularly when the role of different individuals and their special functions have become recognized in custom and tradition, the social organization gains a new stability and permanence which permits it to be transmitted to succeeding generations. In this way the life of the community and of the society may be prolonged beyond the lives of the individuals who compose it." [55]

Cyril Black has noted that the changes in behavior and attitudes needed to support a new leadership ("the informal attributes of tradition and loyalty that hold together the fabric of society") may be achieved only after the leaders have "educated a generation or two of citizens to an acceptance of their policies." [56] Even the most devout advocate of the Marxist view that the politico-economic institutions shape man's vision of reality and hence his behavior may find that "education" of the populace in the required new attitudes must accompany the institutional changes. As Kim Il Sung of North Korea observed: "Remolding the people is much more complicated and difficult than transforming the social system and developing technology. Man's consciousness is determined by the material conditions of society [but] changes in the former are slower than those in the latter. Old ideas and habits are very conservative. Even after the material conditions of social life are changed, old ideas and habits persist for a long time." [57]

In order to institutionalize the system, the leadership group must create regular and dependable sources of the political tools, and then make arrangements which insure that it is in the interests of those who will provide or control these political tools to support the system. Crane Brinton has pointed out that the essential support for a political system

[53] As worded by Myron Weiner in his introduction to Myron Weiner, ed. *Modernization: The Dynamics of Growth* (New York, 1966), p. 11, citing Albert Hirschman, "Obstacles to Development: A Classification and a Quasi-Vanishing Act," *Economic Development and Cultural Change*, XIII (July 1965), 385–93.

[54] Rheinstein, p. 28.

[55] Park, p. 185.

[56] Cyril E. Black, "Revolution, Modernization, and Communism," in Cyril E. Black and Thomas P. Thornton, eds. *Communism and Revolution* (Princeton, 1964), p. 7.

[57] Kim Il Sung, *Kim Il-sŏng sŏnjip* [The Selected Works of Kim Il Sung] (Pyongyang, 1960), VI, p. 289.

comes from certain groups, "normally inclined to support existing institutions." [58] These groups, which are the possessors and wielders of the
political tools, become what has been termed the political "establishment"
in the new "established" system. While insisting that power must be
consolidated and institutions introduced by a single leader, Machiavelli
argued for a transfer of authority from the individual leader to groups
which would support the system:

> The lawgiver should, however, be sufficiently wise and virtuous not to
> leave this authority which he has assumed either to his heirs or to any
> one else; for mankind, being more prone to evil than to good, his suc-
> cessor might employ for evil purposes the power which he had used
> only for good ends. Besides, although one man alone should organize
> a government, yet it will not endure long if the administration of it
> remains on the shoulders of a single individual; it is well, then, to con-
> fide this to the charge of many, for thus it will be sustained by the
> many. Therefore, as the organization of anything cannot be made by
> many, because the divergence of their opinions hinders them from
> agreeing as to what is best, yet when once they do understand it, they
> will not readily agree to abandon it.[59]

Elsewhere he wrote, "The security of a republic or of a kingdom, therefore, does not depend upon its ruler governing it prudently during his
lifetime, but upon his so ordering it that, after his death, it may maintain
itself in being." [60]

Consolidation is an ad hoc establishment of power. To institutionalize,
this must be transformed into a permanent base of support for the system. To achieve this first goal of support for the system, the leadership
will normally direct its primary efforts at securing a permanent source
of instruments of force, for only with the support of guns may the
regime remain in power against armed or potentially armed political
opponents. Only when the regime is securely in power by virtue of the
support of the instruments of force can a permanent source of funds
become dependable, for political stability is essential to eliminate the
psychology of hoarding developed in the era of economic insecurity
which exists in a predevelopmental system. Only when a secure source
of income has become available can organizations take on the nature of
permanent institutions. And finally, only with institutional support may
an idea system be perpetuated in the society.

Once the new system has secured this more permanent basis of support, it may move into broader areas of policy activity. As William J.

[58] Crane Brinton, *The Anatomy of Revolution,* rev. ed. (New York, 1952), p. 34.
[59] Machiavelli, *Discourses,* I, chap. 9, pp. 138–39.
[60] Ibid., chap. 11, p. 148.

Foltz recognized: "The existing regime in most of the newest states must first feel itself secure enough from disruptive internal and external pressures to permit it to accept the necessary loosening of direct political control." Only then will the leaders "Grow out of their initial periods of restrictive consolidation of power and into a more balanced society-wide pattern of national growth." [61]

The second step in institutionalizing the new system involves the resocialization of the society, shaping the behavior patterns and values of the populace in such a way that they will operate within the framework of the new system. Here the leadership must expand the political institutions to penetrate those fundamental areas of society which shape human behavior—e.g., the family and the educational systems—either by reshaping these institutions or by substituting political instrumentalities for some of the functions previously performed by these institutions. The extent to which the new institutions require a change in behavioral patterns will of course determine the extent of resocialization needed. The more heavily traditionalized the society and the less responsive it has been to the challenge of modernization, the more may its modernizing leaders perceive the need for a "cultural revolution" to create a receptiveness to perpetual change—the essence of modernization.

Resocialization is achieved in part through what has been termed "social mobilization," defined by Karl Deutsch as "the process in which major clusters of old social, economic and psychological commitments are eroded or broken and people become available for new patterns of socialization and behavior." [62] There are two stages of this process, he points out: (1) the stage of uprooting or breaking away from old settings, habits, and commitments; and (2) the induction of the mobilized persons into some relatively stable new patterns of group membership, organization, and commitment. Some writers have pointed out, however, that institutionalization may be undermined if the first stage—breaking down the old patterns—is not adequately structured so as to move directly into the second stage, the mobilization into new patterns. Otherwise, the society may move into a condition of anomie, of unpatterned mob or mass behavior, of the kind Park has called the restless behavior of the "herd" which can be easily stampeded.[63] Huntington has referred to this underinstitutionalized system as a "praetorian" society.[64] William J. Foltz points out that, rather than expanding institutional functions, "A state may choose to ride the tiger of exacerbated pluralism and

[61] Karl W. Deutsch and William J. Foltz, *Nation-Building* (New York, 1963), p. 130.
[62] Karl W. Deutsch, "Social Mobilization and Political Development," *American Political Science Review,* LV (September 1961), 493–502.
[63] Park, pp. 212–13.
[64] Huntington, *Political Order,* pp. 192–263.

possible internal strife and disintegration [or] at the other extreme, it may choose to restrain social and economic change to a level that can be handled by the existing political structures." [65] He suggests instead that "a dynamic compromise" is needed whereby social mobilization and the expanding function of political structures may be evenly phased.

The other form of resocialization is indoctrination in the new values and views of the system being introduced. The extent to which these values are acceptable in the absence of the new organizational patterns seeking to support them is questionable; but where they are reinforced by a new pattern of political order, political indoctrination may prove highly effective, as has been demonstrated perhaps most dramatically in the "thought reform" programs in China. [66]

Institutionalization does not imply a freezing of the system. Change can take place in an institutionalized system either in the form of ex-change (e.g., alternation of leadership groups within a regularized process), or development (e.g., available political tools may expand their scope to such an extent that ever greater proportions of the popu-lace become active in wielding political tools). What happens within the system after institutionalization may be development, decay, or disintegration, depending upon the flexibility of the system which has been introduced. As Manfred Halpern has pointed out, the price of maintaining a stable system in modern times may be the intrinsic capacity of the system introduced to "generate and absorb continuing transforma-tion." [67] However, regardless of its developmental capacity, once insti-tutionalized the system is no longer within the realm of the politics of predevelopment. It is only then that it may move into the phase where it can begin to develop effectively or to modernize.

[65] Deutsch and Foltz, p. 128.
[66] See, for example, Robert Jay Lifton, *Thought Reform and the Psychology of Totalism* (New York, 1961).
[67] Halpern, p. 179.

The National Electoral Process and State Building

Proposals for New Methods of Election in Uganda

*Norman W. Provizer**

In mid-January 1971, President A. Milton Obote left Uganda for Singapore and the Commonwealth Heads of State Conference. During his absence, covert maneuverings for positions of political power multiplied and on 25 January, just after the seventh anniversary of the army mutinies in East Africa, the Mechanized Regiment of the Ugandan military carried out a coup d'état.[1] Thus one day before his scheduled arrival home, Obote, the man who had led his country since independence in 1962 and had embarked on a structural transformation of the state in 1966, joined the growing ranks of Africa's politically dispossessed.

The soldiers justified their action with a statement which was read, in Lugbara, over Radio Uganda on the day of the coup. Of the eighteen reasons offered for their intrusion into the political arena, number seven dealt with the electoral process. Specifically, this point emphasized:

> The failure by the political authorities to organize any elections for the last eight years whereby the people's free will could be expressed. It should be noted that the last elections within the ruling party were dominated by big fellows with lots of money which they used to bribe their way into "winning" the elections. This bribery, together with threats against the people, entirely falsified the results of the so-called elections. Proposed new methods of election requiring a candidate to stand in four constituencies will only favour the rich and the well-known.[2]

Like much of the "First Statement by the Soldiers," this position though based in fact, was clearly hyperbolic. Furthermore, the issue of elections was not paramount in the military's decision to act.[3] Yet this discussion does direct us to an extremely important area of comparative political development thought—the relationship of the national electoral process to state building.

In the eyes of many, this relationship is seen as an inverse one in which elections are considered inimical, if not totally antithetical, to the construction of a viable political framework. As one astute observer of inchoate states has written: "In many, if not most, modernizing countries elections serve only to enhance the power of disruptive and often reactionary social forces and to tear down the structure of public authority."[4] From this perspective, in which state building is viewed as the creation of organizations that foster stability, unity, and economic development within an environment of diversity and fragmentation, elections are perceived as an activity which exacerbates, rather than ameliorates system divisiveness. Substantive competition within these societies is severe enough without the multiplier effect produced by legitimized procedural competition.

To a large degree, this position of the inverse relationship between the electoral process and state building was reflected in the thought of the top leadership stratum of Uganda, and thus the Obote regime could increasingly be characterized as a "regime of development."[5] Understood in these terms, it was hardly surprising that " ... Obote failed to resort to the method of legitimization [thought] most natural to the mechanism of democracy— elections."[6]

We would be guilty of unrealistic simplicity if we took this movement to mean that no countertendencies existed within the state. At the same time that national elections were recognized as having a negative impact on state building, the regime also understood that "elections serve a useful purpose in nation-building, in the mobilization of political consciousness and in the control of leaders."[7]

It was the interplay of these contradictory ideas that provided the context from which the proposals for new methods of election in Uganda emerged. These proposals were an attempt to reconcile the electoral process to the perceived imperatives of state building, and thus have been aptly called " ... the most original piece of constitutional theory to have emerged from independent Uganda and one of the most challenging political experiments to have been seriously considered anywhere in Africa."[8]

With the fall of Obote and the rise of military rule in Uganda, the proposals were never implemented, as the very prospect of a national election itself was eliminated. This fact limits our discussion of the new methods of election to what was proposed and what might have been accomplished, but given the important implications of these proposals for comparative political development thought, even such a conjectural analysis is not without merit.

Since the proposals themselves did not emerge from a vacuum, the first part of this study will outline: the national elections of 1961 and 1962; the problems which these elections were thought to create for state building; and the revisions in the electoral process which followed the constitutional crisis of 1966. After establishing this base, we will turn to an examination of the proposals for new methods of election and an evaluation of their meaning for what Sidney Verba has termed ''. . . the most basic questions of politics—the entire set of questions involved in the creation and maintenance of political societies.''[19]

The 1961 and 1962 National Elections

National elections in Uganda, like in much of Africa, have been most conspicuous by their absence. Though two such elections were held in the country's preindependence period, no national elections have been conducted during Uganda's existence as an independent state. In the near decade preceding independence, a number of reports were issued by the British in an attempt to find and implement an organizational framework for a sovereign Uganda.[10] Given the problem areas existing within the country, the establishment of this framework was no simple task, even though the suggestions of the Wallis Report on local government in 1953 were to be rather close to the arrangements provided for in the Independence Constitution of 1962. The Wallis Report argued for a unitary structure based on the British system, except for the Kingdom of Buganda where local government at the *saza* and lower levels would be granted power through the Bugandan, and not the central, administration.[11] It was this problem of constitutional asymmetry and privilege with respect to Buganda which would continue to plague the country.

The Wild Report of 1959 exposed an additional nerve ending when it recommended that direct elections be held in the Uganda Protectorate for a national legislative assembly no later than early 1961, and that there should be no option for indirect selection.[12] This recommendation created a storm of protest in Buganda, for its implementation would undermine the power of the kingdom and the *Kabaka's* (king's) government at a time when such power was needed most. The issue was further complicated by the fact that the British were to send a commission to Uganda in 1961 to investigate the future relationship of the component units of the state to the center; and the results of this commission's investigation would not be made public until after the first national elections were held. Buganda, struggling to maintain its privileged status, hoped that new, more favorable options might emerge from this investigation and thus argued that the elections should not be held until the Munster Commission published its report.

When the kingdom's arguments failed to influence British policy, Buganda declared a boycott of the election and announced its intent to become an independent entity. This unilateral declaration of independence was never actively translated into action, but the influence of the king and traditional nationalism within the kingdom was able to produce a 97 percent effective election boycott in Buganda. This boycott made inoperative the assumption, held by many, ''. . . that the party which won the election and formed the first African government would quite likely win the pre-independence (1962) elections also and thus become the ultimate successor to the British Crown on the attainment of sovereign power."[13]

Before discussing the outcome and implications of this election, it might be useful to offer a brief sketch of the election's main contestants—the Democratic Party (DP) and the Uganda People's Congress (UPC). The DP was established in Buganda during 1954 and within two years this organization, which has been described as " . . . originally more a Catholic pressure group than a party,"[14] spread to the rest of Uganda. Its first president was Matayo Mugwanya, the *Omulamuzi* (chief justice) of Buganda, and its aim, to an extent, was to further Catholic interests and attempt to redress the balance of power that had shifted, in 1900, in favor of the Protestants.[15] The Protestants feared that if the DP was successful in the kingdom, its victory would lead to the emergence of a Catholic *Katikiro* (prime minister) and the decline of Protestant power.

The 1955 selection process for the prime minister exacerbated Protestant fears and indicated the lengths to which the Protestant establishment would go in order to secure its position.[16] Faced with this situation, the DP increasingly looked outside of the kingdom for support and new efforts were made to establish a base in northern Catholic areas such as West Nile. This shift was accentuated in 1958 by the election of B. Kiwanuka, an outward-looking Muganda lawyer, to the presidency of the party.[17]

From the Bugandan perspective this shift was crucial, for there was an important difference between a Catholic faction, however troublesome, competing in the politics of Mengo, and a statewide Catholic party which supported progressive and antiking measures like the direct election of Bugandan MPs to the national legislature.[18] Branded as an organization which worked against the tradition of kingship, the DP found even its base of support in the Catholic population of Buganda eroded.

The other main party involved in the election was the Uganda People's Congress led by a legislative councillor from the northern district of Lango, A. Milton Obote. The UPC had come into existence in March 1960, when Obote joined his primarily non-Bagandan splinter section of the Uganda National Congress with the Uganda People's Union of W. Nadiope from Busoga.[19] As a party, UPC was not strongly centralized, though a loose thread of unity was provided by an absence of pro-Bugandan sentiments.

These were the key rivals in the first countrywide election held in March 1961; an election which would " . . . select the government that would lead Uganda to internal self-government and prepare the way to Independence."[20] The two parties polled between them 92 percent of the vote for the 82 directly elected members of the Legislative Council (or National Assembly after April 1962). The UPC received 49.5 percent of the vote compared to 42.2 percent which went to DP.[21] However, due to the British legacy of the single constituency and the boycott in Buganda, DP captured 44 seats, or 9 more than UPC, and thus formed the first democratic government in Uganda with Benedicto Kiwanuka as its head.

Of the 61 seats contested outside of Buganda, UPC won 35 and DP only 24. The DP's margin of victory clearly came in its capture of 20 of the 21 Bugandan seats; a sweep made possible by the boycott within the kingdom. With only a vote of 17,957 in Buganda, DP gained only 2 fewer seats than it did with a vote of 419,255 outside of the kingdom. In other words, while DP's vote/win ratio outside Buganda was 17,427/1, it was only 898/1 within the kingdom.

By disregarding the Buganda boycott, DP received immediate rewards and remained a channel of gaining redress for the Catholics of the privileged kingdom.[22] Yet by appearing to be above and against Buganda and kingship, the victory of DP was to prove to be a Pyrrhic one. Its triumph in this election set into motion forces which would help insure its defeat the following year.

Within Buganda, the clear implication of the 1961 election was that a need existed for the kingdom to actively strengthen its position in terms of both internal organization and external linkage to the central government; while to UPC the election was evidence of the importance of Buganda's 21 seats for any party which wished to rule the country. In June 1961, the first significant change influenced by the election took place with the formation of the Kabaka Yekka (king only) movement in Buganda. At the outset, this movement was a loose organization whose purpose was to protect the institution of kingship and the traditions of Buganda during a period of political change, but before long an additional variable was introduced which transformed the movement into a political party.[23]

In the latter part of 1961, the Constitutional Conference concurred with the recommendation of the Munster Commission that Uganda would be " . . . a composite state containing a single federal kingdom (Buganda) in association with the rest of the country, which would be governed unilaterally,"[24] and further noted that after direct elections were held to the Lukiiko (parliament), Buganda could opt for the indirect election of the 21 National Assembly members representing the kingdom. The Protestant establishment in Mengo, faced for the first time with the prospect of competitive elections and an organized opposition (the DP), utilized the umbrella of the Kabaka Yekka to rally the support of all factions within the kingdom against the enemy of "Gandaness"—the Democratic Party.[25] Thus KY emerged as a de facto party which could defeat DP within the kingdom and, at the same time, would serve as the instrument through which Buganda could enter national politics, while attempting to preserve its own autonomy and unity.

Due to the option of indirect election for Buganda's MPs, whichever party controlled the Lukiiko would almost certainly be in the position of determining who would govern the country from Kampala. For neither DP nor UPC appeared to be able to gain the 42 seats necessary for the formation of a government in the 61 contests which would take place outside of the kingdom.

The fate of DP was sealed before the Lukiiko elections of February 1961, when an alliance (or perhaps more appropriately a "marriage of convenience") took place between KY and the pragmatic UPC.[26] Registration for the February election was high and not surprisingly KY, under a symbol which greatly resembled the royal throne, decimated DP winning in 65 of the 68 Bugandan constituencies and capturing more than 85 percent of the vote.[27] Two months later the statewide National Assembly elections were held in the remaining areas of Uganda. Both UPC and DP managed to increase their percentage of the vote over their 1961 showing. The DP's vote increased by 4.3 percent, but it won the same total of 24 seats as it had in the 1961 election. UPC's vote increased by only 1.9 percent, but this led to the victory of 37 UPC contestants, or 3 more than in the 1961 election.[28] Despite its alliance with KY, UPC was able to maintain a good deal of its anti-Buganda support throughout the country.

In May 1962, the UPC-KY coalition, which held 58 seats in the National Assembly, formed the government which brought Uganda to independence in October of that year. That government had Obote as prime minister and found KY occupying one-third of the ministerial portfolios. After the selection by the Assembly of the 9 "specially elected members" and counting Attorney-General G. Binaisa (a Muganda UPC backer who held a seat ex officio), the final makeup of the national legislature, resulting from the 1962 election, stood at 68 seats for the governing coalition (44 UPC and 24 KY) and 24 for the DP in opposition.[29]

From Independence to the Constitutional Crisis

From a consolidationist perspective, the 1962 national elections produced several crucial problems for state building. In order to gain power, UPC, the nationalist-progressive party of the country, had to rely on the support of the representatives of parochial nationalism and subcentral autonomy. Just as UPC had supported indirect elections in Buganda so too did it support the selection of the king, Mutesa II, as president of the country in October 1963.[30] The power of Buganda under its federal relationship with the center was reinforced by the imperatives of the national electoral process.

Important shifts were also taking place during the early years of independence, some of which dealt with the relationship of Buganda to the Ugandan state, while others were more directly related to the strength of the parties within the National Assembly. Despite its electoral success, the politics of coalition could not mask the contradictions existing within each group and the society as a whole.

KY's enormous victory in Buganda, for example, did not eliminate the basic divisions found within the party. The party's accomplishment intensified these divisions. Though KY rode to victory on the issue of "Gandaness," it also looked outward from the kingdom's borders. Now the isolationist separatism of Buganda was faced with the reality of nonisolationist participation in the institutions of central government. The divisions expanded and before long the party of Bugandan unity was split. In early 1963, 19 KY members of the Assembly circulated a pamphlet which stated " . . . that it must be understood by those who don't know it, and particularly by those who have forgotten, that Buganda is part of Uganda and so it will remain forever."[31] In June of that year a bloc of 7 KY Assembly members transferred their allegiance to UPC.[32]

The DP, too, was faced with internal difficulties, and like KY, it also began to have its members cross the floor to join UPC. In December 1962, Basil Bataringaya, an MP from Ankole who served as the parliamentary leader of the party since its president, Benedicto Kiwanuka, did not win a seat in the Assembly, had challenged Kiwanuka for that office. Bataringaya's challenge was based on a threefold platform of loyal opposition, a downplay of the party's Catholic background, and a reconciliation policy toward Buganda.[33] Bataringaya was defeated by the Mugandan incumbent, but it became apparent that DP was moving in two different directions.

By June 1964, without benefit of elections, UPC's membership in the Assembly had grown from the original 44 to 60. Obote could now afford to terminate his alliance with KY. In August 1964, the coalition between UPC and KY was dissolved; the final end precipitated by the prime minister's decision to push for the referendum on the "lost counties," a measure considered to be highly anti-Bugandan. The 14 remaining KY Assembly members then crossed over (physically, if not politically) to the DP side. Some four months later, UPC's numerical superiority grew even more when Bataringaya and 5 other DP members of the assembly crossed the floor to join Obote's party. After this move, Alex Latim, from Acholi, became the parliamentary leader of what little remained of the DP.[34]

Both the ally and the opponent of UPC were losing their positions in the power structure of Uganda—positions that the national electoral process had provided. UPC's far from overwhelming success in the 1962 elections had been translated into control of district councils (outside of Buganda) as well as total numerical domination of the single-chambered National Assembly. To some, UPC was emerging as a consolidating entity, as an arena in which Baganda and non-Baganda alike could carry on discussions of the issues facing the country.[35]

The ideological dormancy of UPC had largely resulted from electoral needs, and such dormancy exacerbated problems of organization and mobilization. Now it looked like UPC could transform the government of Uganda into "a regime of development"; but such an ideological awakening would not be without its grave difficulties. To begin with, UPC, like many African political organizations, was both much more and much less than the traditional concept of a political party.[36] Never having had a mass base, even during periods of increased membership, UPC was a superstructure without a solid foundation. The party remained a series of divergent parts congealing on national elections and little else.

The factionalism of the party was apparent during the delegate conference held in Gulu, in April-May 1964, when Grace Ibingira, an MP from Ankole and the purported leader of the pro-Western segment, ousted the incumbent John Kakonge as the party's secretary-general. Kakonge, who was from Bunyoro, was more closely aligned with Obote, thus his defeat not only indicated some of the internal weakness of the party, but also the unsure position of Uganda's leader.[37]

The lack of unity in the leadership of UPC was further intensified by crossovers from DP and KY. Whether or not a conscious policy of infiltration and subversion existed, this large-scale crossing of the floor by non-UPC members of the Assembly was less advantageous to UPC than it might appear.[38] Not only did many of those who crossed over fail to abandon their goals, which were noncongruent with central governmental policy, but the conflicts existing within the party provided an environment for the continuation, rather than eradication, of such goals. In Buganda, to use one important example, the influx of ex-KY members enabled decisive control of the UPC-Buganda to rest with the anti-Obote faction; and in February 1966, the crucial month of the constitutional crisis, E. Lumu (one of the five soon to be arrested central ministers) defeated Obote's attorney-general, G. Binaisa, for the post of district chairman of the Bugandan branch of UPC.[39]

All this points to a situation in which UPC was outwardly ascendant (by January 1966 the party held 75 seats in National Assembly), where the opposition parties were structurally reduced to a shadow of their former selves (by January 1966 both KY and DP each held only 8 seats in the Assembly), yet where the internal conflicts of the governing party were intensified by the inclusion of new members who, nonetheless, remained outsiders. Behind the facade of growing unity, divisions and suspicions existed which would soon explode. Lacking a single, dominant ideological focus, UPC (the "party for everyone") found itself filled with dissent and factions, forces which would move it toward instability.[40]

Before moving to an examination of the explosion which took place in February 1966, there is an additional factor that need be considered—the continued political dilemma which Buganda posed for the central government. As one quasi-governmental study put it:

> So long as the UPC (Uganda People's Congress) was dependent on KY (Kabaka Yekka) support and therefore on Buganda, it was necessary to retain political

support in other Kingdoms and Districts. This could only be done by deferring to some extent to the wishes of politicians in these Districts. Their wishes in some cases were opposed to the best interests of the people and the country as a whole. There was often inefficiency and wasteful expenditures.[41]

Even after the breakup of the UPC-KY coalition in August 1964, Buganda's position remained strong and it was therefore necessary for the center to count on the areas outside of the kingdom for support. Any attempt by the central government to implement stricter control on the local governments of these other units might have created " . . .resentment which would undermine that support."[42] This circumstance provided local governments with a comfortable bargaining position vis-à-vis the center. Despite its numerical superiority in the Assembly, UPC's future national electoral position was uncertain. A study of political parties in Uganda stated it simply: " . . .if the KY continues to command support in Buganda, the position of the UPC in the next election may not be easy."[43] Faced with the fact that the "other" political parties within the country could not yet be discounted, and its own internal weakness, the increasingly impressive UPC superstructure seemed to rest on a foundation of sand.

The Constitutional Crisis and Its Aftermath

During the early months of 1966, the fragile nature of UPC was dramatically exposed. In January, Daudi Ocheng, a KY Assembly member from Acholi, raised the charge that Colonel Amin, along with the prime minister and several other ministers, had profited from gold and ivory received from Congolese rebels.[44] Since it appeared that sufficient business existed on the Assembly's agenda to keep these charges from reaching the floor before the session was scheduled to end, Obote left Kampala for a tour of the Northern region of the country. On 4 February, Ibingira's faction of the cabinet changed the Assembly's agenda and Ocheng's anti-Amin, anti-Obote motion was on the floor. The motion passed with only a single vote, that of John Kakonge, cast against it.

The country was rife with rumors and uneasiness when Obote finally returned to Kampala on 12 February, and in rapid succession advised those ministers who opposed him to resign and announced the establishment of a nonpartisan Commission of Inquiry to investigate Ocheng's charges.[45] At this same time, the previously discussed victory of Ibingira's compatriot E. Lumu (minister of health) over Obote's follower G. Binaisa took place at the delegate conference of the UPC-Buganda.

The prime minister faced a powerful, if poorly coordinated, political challenge, and on 22 February Obote acted. The five ministers, who had been the chief architects of the prime minister's planned downfall, were arrested, and

Obote declared that "In the interest of national stability and public security and tranquility, I have today . . . taken over all powers of the Government of Uganda."[46] Two days later, Obote suspended the 1962 Constitution itself, and within a week he further consolidated his position by integrating the powers of the president and vice-president into his office. The prime minister responded to the constitutional, if provocative, challenge facing him by eliminating the legal framework within which the challenge had developed.

By the end of the first quarter of 1966, there remained little doubt as to who was the victor in this clash over the mantle of political leadership. The challenge to Obote's position failed, and the challenge itself provided the prime minister with an opportunity to transform the rules of the game in Uganda. The compromise Independence Constitution of 1962 had placed real constraints on the central government, especially in terms of its relationship with the Kingdom of Buganda. Such constraints, from a consolidationist perspective, were viewed as being inimical to the state building process: now they would hamper the center no more.

An indication of this direction of change was offered on 15 April 1966, when Obote introduced a new Interim Constitution at an emergency meeting of the National Assembly. Since the 1962 Constitution had been abrogated, the members of the Assembly sat as "citizens of Uganda," and without debate and without actually seeing the new document, these "citizens" (minus the KY and DP members who walked out) voted 55 to 4 to accept the pigeonhole Constitution. Fifty-nine "citizen" MPs then took the prescribed oath and were sworn in as new members of Parliament under the Interim Constitution.[47]

This temporary Constitution largely replicated the 1962 document; however there were several crucial variations. Uganda would now be a unitary state and though the kingdoms remained, there would no longer be any significant intermediary (or federal) institutions of power. Structurally translated this meant a powerful executive president (who would be the leader of the party with the largest numerical strength in the National Assembly) and a Parliament (directly elected except for the specially elected members) which would be the supreme legislative body and thereby not limited by the actions of subcentral legislatures.

Under the terms of the Interim Constitution the Assembly members who took the oath in April 1966 were considered newly elected, and therefore the national elections, which should have taken place in 1967, would not have to be "legally" held until April of 1971.[48] Time for the consolidation of central authority was thus gained by the delay of the electoral process.

Not surprisingly, the new Constitution provoked a negative response from many, especially within Buganda, the area most affected by the changes spelled out in the document. On 20 May 1967 the Lukiiko approved a de facto motion of secession, and within days the central government declared a state of emergency in the kingdom and utilized the military to crush the Mengo government. The Obote regime had triumphed, yet its endeavor to transform Uganda had led to a loss of legitimacy in certain sectors of the country and therefore the regime found itself increasingly dependent on the military forces of the state. A dependency which would not be without serious consequences in the future.

This attempt at reshaping Uganda from a fragmented political system into a concentrated political system was made even more manifest when the Interim Constitution was replaced by the Republican Constitution of 8 September 1967. Unlike its predecessor, the Republican Constitution was the subject of open debate and was discussed for several months by Parliament sitting as a Constituent Assembly. The arguments in the Assembly were heated and before the body voted 62 to 0 to enact the document, one of Obote's ministers, C.J. Obwangor, resigned his position and crossed over to the opposition.[49]

Once the new Constitution was enacted, Uganda became a republican state. The kingdoms no longer existed, even in name, and Buganda was divided into four distinct districts (East Mengo, West Mengo, Mubende, and Masaka). The 1967 document also strengthened, in toto, the unitary system in the country. As J. Ochola, the minister of regional administrations, put it: "Today there is no such thing or creature as local government in Uganda. There is one Government and one Government only and that is the Government of Uganda."[50]

Not only would political roles (i.e., the offices of secretary-general and assistant secretary-general) be provided in the districts so as to ensure the adherence to and implementation of center policy, but the very selection of district council members was now a prerogative of the central government.[51] Returning to the issue of the selection of national leadership, the new legal framework provided that the strong executive president would be indirectly elected. Each future candidate for the National Assembly would be required to state whom he supported for the post of president before the election; and the choice of the majority party, or if there was no majority party, the party with 40 percent of the Assembly seats, would be named president.[52] By this procedure the selection of the president would be directly tied to the support he enjoyed in a political party.

The 40 percent figure is also very important, because when no party had a clear majority, the largest party, if it had 40 percent of the seats, could then select as many specially elected members (SEMs) as necessary to give it a ten-vote majority in the Assembly. The exact number of SEMs selected would thus work on a sliding scale; if the dominant party already had a ten-vote majority there would be no SEMs, while if the dominant party held the minimum 40 percent of the seats, 26 SEMs could be selected.[53]

The basic idea of specially elected members was not new to Uganda, however their role under the Republican Constitution was noticeably different than under the Independence Constitution. In the latter document, SEMs could provide a working margin for the majority party, while in the former, they could transform a minority party into the majority party. The lesson of the 1962 election had not been forgotten. Whereas in 1962 UPC had to join with KY to form a government with a working majority (and select nine SEMs—six UPC and three KY), under the new arrangement the same numerical distribution of seats (45+ percent UPC, 29+ percent DP, 26− percent KY) would have allowed UPC to form a government and choose as many SEMs as needed to provide the party with a ten-vote majority, and thereby avoid coalitions.

The changes instituted by the 1967 Constitution (including: the "legal" delay of elections until April 1971; the 40 percent rule; the increase in the number of SEMs; and the prescription that when two parties each held 40 percent or more of the seats the candidate nominated by the party with the greatest numerical strength in the preceding election, i.e., UPC, would become president) were all intended to control the competitive electoral process and bring that process in line with the Obote regime's consolidationist perspective on state building.

Proposals for New Methods of Election

Uganda's new constitutional order provided a framework for increased center penetration and control. With the structural elimination of local level and individual autonomy, a concentrated political system began to take form; and though the Republican Constitution did not create a de jure one-party state, the forces and attitudes at work within the country made the road of opposition parties a difficult one to travel and their future dim.

The increased identification of party and state created problems both for segments of UPC and for members of the opposition. The UPC had never been a monolithic organization and that fact was not changed by the new Constitution. Thus UPC district council members who spoke against government policy also found themselves removed from office. The imperatives of a concentrated system knew no party boundaries. Opposition was anathema whether it came from without or from within the party.[54]

The Republican Constitution was a large step in the restructuring of the Ugandan state and was an important expression of the Vicoist faith in the efficacy of active conscious will over passive acquiescense to "natural courses," but before long the political, economic, and social thought of dominant national leadership would go beyond the document. From the party government viewpoint, the new Constitution had moved Uganda closer to the goal of Uhuru but not to the goal itself. Further unity and central consolidation were thought to be necessary.

In order to achieve this new political culture of social unity and political consolidation, President Obote declared that Uganda would have " . . . to move ideologically and practically to the Left."[55] The changes demanded by this "move to the Left" were set forth in five key documents that appeared from the latter part of 1969 through mid-1970.

The central building block for Uganda's new political culture was "The Common Man's Charter," which was adopted during the Annual Delegates' Conference of UPC in December 1969. The conference also resolved that the Republican Constitution be amended so that the country would officially be a one-party state. That resolution became academic on 19 December, when at the close of the meetings Obote was shot. Though the president was not seriously injured, the following day the National Assembly extended the state of emergency, still in effect in the Bugandan region, to cover the whole of Uganda, and banned all political parties except for UPC.[56] The Ugandan Parliament had now discarded its inheritance of a house divided along party lines.

Each of the remaining documents in the "move to the Left" expanded the basic philosophy stated in "The Common Man's Charter," and developed specific dimensions of change to be implemented by the state. The last of these documents was the "Proposals for New Methods of Election of Representatives of the People to Parliament."[57]

With the abrogation of the Independence Constitution and the institution of the Interim and then the Republican Constitutions, certain palliative measures were established to lessen the difficulties raised by the election of national leadership. Though Uganda had witnessed movements toward increased central consolidation and changes in the procedure for exercising control within the National Assembly, the basic structure of elections remained substantially unchanged. In form, if not in function, Uganda continued within the tradition of European parliamentary systems.

The "Proposals . . .," produced under Obote's name and dated 17 July attempted to shift away from palliative adjustments and to introduce fundamental changes in the structure of the national electoral process. Changes which would work " . . .to reduce the influence of tribal loyalty on the relationship between members of Parliament and their constituents, to promote participation in elections based on the nation as a whole, and to require a politician to seek support from different corners of the country".[58]

According to the "Proposals . . .," a single presidential candidate would be 1970, was divided into three sections. The first or introductory section offered a discussion of the need for elections, as well as for unity and one-partyism in Uganda. The crucial problem for the country was seen as the parochialism in both the election and the functioning of National Assembly members. What was needed was a new method of election which would establish the National Assembly and members of that Assembly as representatives of the nation as a whole. The second and third sections of the document presented the specifics of the restructuring of the electoral process, with regard to the president and MPs, in order to accomplish this stated goal.

According to the "Proposals...," a single presidential candidate would be slated by the party (i.e., UPC) and would be directly elected by universal adult suffrage.[59] During national elections, the voters in each Parliamentary constituency within the state would cast their ballots either for or against the candidate. The votes would then be translated into electoral votes and if the candidate received more positive electoral votes than negative ones he would be declared president of the country.[60] This electoral vote system would prevent a possible overwhelming negative vote in "certain" constituencies from determining the outcome of the election. Once again, the lessons of the past had not been forgotten.

It was in the method of electing MPs that this document made its most striking contribution to the development of a new political culture in Uganda. In an attempt to make the members of the National Assembly truly national, the single constituency method of election, which was believed to reinforce and promote fragmentation and parochialism within the state, was eliminated. Now, under the "Proposals . . .," the two or three candidates running in each of the 96 parliamentary constituencies would have to stand for election not only in that specific or "basic" constituency, but also in three other "national" constituencies. In other words, the 96 constituencies in Uganda were divided into four electoral regions (Northern, Eastern, Western, and Southern or Bugandan), and a candidate would have to run for election in a constituency in each of these four regions.[61]

The simplified Diagram 1 (based on the existence of only four constituencies) indicates how this "basic" plus "national" (or 1 + 3) system would work. Here we see that candidates A, B, and C are running for the Assembly seat representing constituency 1 in the Northern electoral region. This "basic" constituency is linked to three "national" constituencies (2, 3, and 4), and thus our candidates are standing for election in all the regions of the country. The same holds true for the other three sets of candidates; the only difference being, in each case, which constituency is designated as "basic" and which ones are labeled "national."

On election day, the voters in each constituency would cast five votes: "one for the Basic candidate of his choice, three for the National candidates of his choice, one from each of the three Regions outside the Region of the Basic constituency, and the fifth vote for the election of the President."[62] Using the example of our diagram again, a voter in constituency 1, in addition to his vote on the president, might cast his ballot for candidate A in the "basic" constituency race and for candidates D, G, and J in the "national" races, while a voter in constituency 4 might vote for candidates J, B, E, and H respectively. The popular vote for every candidate would then be translated into electoral votes in

Diagram 1

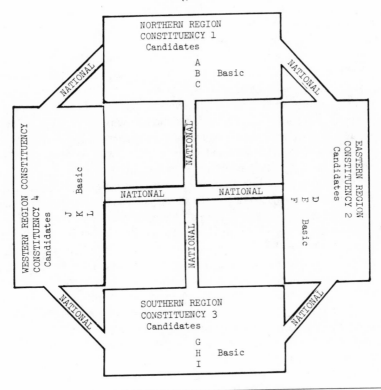

each constituency, and the "basic" candidate who received the largest combined electoral vote (i.e., from the "basic" and "national" constituencies) would be the victor in his "basic" constituency. In this way, a candidate who did extremely well in only one constituency and poorly in the others would have a difficult time in being elected. The system forced all candidates for the National Assembly to look beyond their own parochial borders for victory, even though they remained attached to one of the 96 constituencies in the country.

This plan for " ... a unique and complex experiment in multiple constituency elections"[63] was presented by Obote to the National Council of UPC in mid-August 1970. During this meeting in Kampala, it became apparent that, despite Uganda's movement toward a consolidationist, de facto one-party system, the ruling UPC remained far from a monolithic entity. The National Council accepted the new method of election suggested for National Assembly members, but rejected paragraphs 26-34 of the "Proposals ... " which dealt with the selection of the republic's president. In taking exception to these paragraphs, the National Council stated that from its perspective the president of the party must automatically be the president of the state, and that the changes put forward in the "Proposals... " could only be adopted by the Annual Delegates' Conference of UPC.[64]

Thus Obote's desire, as president of the country and of UPC, to have, for both philosophical and pragmatic political reasons, the aura of popular legitimacy surrounding the office of the president was thwarted by the Council.[65] To some observers this meeting was a subcutaneous maneuver executed by people like Felix Onama (the minister of defense and secretary-general of UPC) and intended to undermine Obote's position within the party.[66] The president may have been the only leader that an independent Uganda had known, but his role within the state and party was not beyond challenge.

Two weeks after the National Council meeting, the Delegates' Conference of UPC assembled in Mbale to reach a "final" decision on the proposed method of election of the republic's president. In a "Memorandum" dated only four days before the conference, Obote discussed the position taken by the National Council and reiterated his own views on the importance of electoral legitimacy for the presidential candidate so as not to "... alienate the Party from people."[67] Obote expressed willingness to amend some paragraphs of the "Proposals... " and accepted the idea that the party president should also be the republic's president, but on the necessity of a popular vote he remained firm.[68]

The Delegates' Conference supported the National Council's nonelectoral position on the presidency, and despite the "Memorandum," Obote's arguments were not heeded.[69] Discussions of this crucial issue, however, had not yet ended, and a compromise arrangement was accepted by the National Council and the Delegates' Conference held during December 1970 in Mbale.[70] The compromise arrangement shifted responsibility for the nomination of presidential candidates from the single Delegates' Conference to the 96 Parliamentary Constituency Conferences. Thus any party candidate for the presidency of the republic who received the support of 32 (i.e., one-third) of these Parliamentary Constituency Conferences would become an official party nominee for president of the country. If two or three candidates were nominated in this manner, a popular vote would determine the winner.[71] In this way the compromise did allow for the option of popular participation in the selection of the state's president, although the delineation of such specific circumstances under which citizen participation would take place constituted a significant variance from the intent of the original position set out in the "Proposals...."

By the end of 1970 the new system of elections was ready to be put into practice. Lots had been drawn to link "national" constituencies to each "basic" constituency, and the Electoral Commission, chaired by Ateker Ejalu, had filed its report on the makeup of the 96 parliamentary constituencies. A Presidential Electoral Commission (whose members were nominated by the president) was set up to provide the mechanism through which the slate of candidates for each constituency would be prepared for the voting public of Uganda; but the elections scheduled under this system for April 1971 were not to be.[72]

Conclusion

The "Proposals..." developed within the context of the national election/state-building controversy and utilized "... the written word for the purposes of formulating new social directions and new political goals."[73] Since the procedural competition of elections was viewed as an accelerator of the substantive competition which fragmented the state, it was considered necessary to alter the form of elections in order to further the process of state building.

To some, such an alteration could only be meaningful if it resulted in a total abjuration of procedural competition; while others held the position that the system of national elections could be transformed so as to eliminate the problems created for state building without extracting all aspects of popular legitimacy. The plan proposed by Obote followed this latter manipulative course, and offered a method of reconciling the imperatives of state building with the perceived need for elections.

With the overthrow of the Obote regime, the words of document five in the "move to the Left" were never translated into action. Even before the military coup d'état occurred, there was some question as to whether the first national election since independence would actually be held. Given the volatile nature of African politics, no certain answer can be provided for this question; but it does not seem unreasonable, in light of the branch and constituency elections of 1970 and the large-scale debate over the "Proposals...," to assume that the elections for the National Assembly would have taken place.[74]

Though the new method of elections obviously reflected an increasingly consolidationist perspective and furnished numerous safeguards for the Obote regime, it is not so clear that this plan completely "preordained" the election and was merely a "trick... to keep [Obote's] henchmen in power."[75] In short, it appears that the national elections were intended to cohere national leadership, revitalize the organization of UPC, offer limited accommodation to Buganda, and legitimize the move toward a one-party state.[76] Under the 1 + 3 system, all of this was to be accomplished while the actual parameters of procedural competition were narrowed.

Needless to say, the change in procedural competition spelled out by the new electoral system was not without its critics. To many, the new method of elections meant an overwhelming advantage to those candidates with wealth and exposure; a dilution of the quality of representation due to the lack of contact with a specific constituency; and an unhealthy increase in the formation of pragmatic alliances among candidates.[77] In questioning whether the social gains produced by the "Proposals . . ." compensated for the problems created by the document, commentators also pointed to the language difficulties built into the system and the "error" of not weighting the vote in the basic constituency over votes in the national constituencies.[78]

Beyond these real but not insurmountable problems, there remained even more fundamental difficulties. Difficulties which were primarily related to the persistent pattern of substantive competition which continued both between identity groups and within the ruling party itself. Although the "Proposals . . ." presented a method of election which would have centralized and "nationalized," to a degree, the selection process for members of the National Assembly, it was unlikely that the implementation of the "Proposals . . ." would have been able, in itself, to eliminate either parochial tendencies within the state or intraparty fractionalization. The very attempt to eradicate the ethnic-tribal factor may itself have led to the resurgence of other parochial predispositions (viz., religion).[79] The translation of the rhetoric of unity into reality would not be so easily achieved, especially since the institutional power of the center exhibited far from total dominance over the system as a whole.

Despite the existence of such problem areas the "Proposals . . .," in its recognition of the positive as well as the negative dimensions of the electoral process, deserves to be described as an "original piece of constitutional theory." This is not to say that the structure of the single party, upon which the "Proposals . . ." was built, is the " . . . only viable alternative to multi-party anarchy or government by brute force,"[80] or that the mechanism of the one-party state is not perverted to support the practical goal of the retention of power within a political society.[81] What it is meant to imply is simply that the "Proposals . . .," both as a symbolic expression and as a pragmatic policy, offered a viable approach to the continual search for that illusive balance point which lies between freedom and order.

NOTES

*The author would like to express his appreciation to the Anspach Institute at the University of Pennsylvania, the Makerere University Library, and the Makerere Institute of Social Research. He is also grateful to Mr. James Ellis and Dr. Lucy C. Behrman for their assistance.

1. Michael Twaddle, "The Amin Coup," *Journal of Commonwealth Political Studies*, X (July 1972), 99-112; and David Martin, *General Amin* (London, 1975), pp. 44-45, 158-61. Also see Cynthia Enloe, "Ethnicity and the Myth of the Military in African Development," *Ufahamu*, IV (Summer 1973), 35-36; and Ali Mazrui, "The Lumpen Proletariat and the Lumpen Militariat," *Political Studies*, XXI (March 1973), 1-4.

2. The Government of Uganda, *The Birth of the Second Republic*, (Entebbe, n.d.), p. 27.

3. See Padma Spinivasan, "Uganda's Malaise: An Attempt at Coup Analysis," *Africa Quarterly*, XIII (July-September 1973), 86-104; Michael Martin, "The Ugandan Military Coup of 1971: A Study of Protest," *Ufahamu*, III (Winter 1972), 81-121; and Michael Lofchie, "The Political Origins of the Uganda Coup," *Journal of African Studies*, I (Winter 1974), 464-96.

4. Samuel Huntington, *Political Order in Changing Societies* (New Haven, 1968), p. 7. "The problem," in Huntington's words, "is not to hold elections but to create organizations."

5. Richard Lowenthal, "Government in the Developing Countries," in Henry Ehrmann, ed. *Democracy in a Changing Society* (New York, 1965), pp. 195, 204, 206, 208.

6. Spinivasan, 97.

7. From a statement made by Basil Bataringaya in November 1970, quoted in Colin Legum, ed. *Africa Contemporary Record 1970-71* (London, 1971), p. B191.

8. Mazrui, *Cultural Engineering and Nation-Building in East Africa* (Evanston, 1972), p. 70.

9. Sidney Verba quoted by B. Schaffer in "The Concept of Preparation: Some Questions about the Transfer of Systems of Government," *World Politics*, XVIII (October 1965), 42.

10. See Norman Provizer, *Politics and the Political Economy of Penetration in Uganda* (Ph.D. diss., 1974), pp. 70-88.

11. *Report of an Inquiry into African Local Government in the Protectorate of Uganda* (Entebbe, 1953), pp. 14-15.

12. *Report of the Constitutional Committee, 1959* (Entebbe, 1959), p. 46.

13. G.S.K. Ibingira, *The Forging of an African Nation* (New York, 1973), p. 186.

14. Joseph Nye, Jr., *Pan-Africanism and East African Integration* (Cambridge, 1965), p. 107.

15. See D.A. Low, *Political Parties in Uganda, 1949-1962* (London, 1962), p. 24; A. Hughes, *East Africa: The Search for Unity* (Baltimore, 1963), p. 176; and Terrance Hopkins, "Politics in Uganda: The Buganda Question," in Jeffrey Butler and A. Castagno, eds. *Boston University Papers on Africa* (New York, 1967), p. 256.

16. David Apter, *The Political Kingdom in Uganda* (Princeton, 1967) p. 374-75.

17. Donald Rothchild and Michael Rogin, "Uganda," in Gwendolen Carter, ed. *National Unity and Regionalism in Eight African States* (Ithaca, 1966), pp. 353, 380.

18. Ibid., p. 353; and Audrey Richards, "Epilogue," in Fallers, ed. *The King's Men: Leadership and Status in Buganda on the Eve of Independence* (London, 1964), p. 381.

19. See Martin Lowenkopf, "Uganda's Prime Minister Obote," *Africa Report*, VII (May 1962), II; Low, *Political Parties*, pp. 30-31; Apter, *Political Kingdom*, pp. 347-48; and F. Welbourn, *Religion and Politics in Uganda, 1952-1962* (Nairobi, 1965), p. 21.

20. Robert Byrd, "Characteristics of Candidates for Election in a Country Approaching Independence: The Case of Uganda," *Midwest Journal of Political Science*, VII (February 1963), 4.

21. Ibid., p. 27. Outside of Buganda, the figures were 50.3 percent and 41.3 percent, respectively.

22. Low, p. 47.

23. C.J. Gertzel, "How the Kabaka Yekka Came to Be," *Africa Report*, IX (October 1964), 9-10.

24. *Report of the Uganda Relationships Committee, 1961* (Entebbe, n.d.), p. 55.

25. Nye, *Pan-Africanism*, pp. 107, 109; Welbourn, *Religion and Politics*, p. 27; and Fred Burke, *Local Government in Uganda* (Syracuse, 1964), p. 19.

26. The UPC supported the idea of indirect elections in Buganda for this election. See "Policy Statement of the UPC," mimeo (1962), p. 2. Consult Byrd, 23-24, on the terms of the alliance between UPC and KY.

27. R.C. Peagram, *A Report on the General Elections to the National Assembly of Uganda Held on the 25th April, 1962* (Entebbe, n.d.), pp. 23-28.

28. Ibid., pp. 29-33; and Byrd, 27. The elections in two of the Toro constituencies took place a week after the general election due to protests over federal status for the Kingdom of Toro.

29. Of the nine specially elected seats, three went to KY and six to UPC.

30. See the background provided in the Institute of Public Administration, "Evolution of Local Administrations and District Councils," mimeo (Kampala, 1967), pp. 9-10.

31. Quoted in Low, "Buganda and Uganda," in Low, *Buganda in Modern History* (London, 1971), p. 240.

32. Gertzel, "Kabaka Yekka," 12-13; and Mazrui and G.F. Engholm, "The Tensions of Crossing the Floor in East Africa," in Mazrui, *Violence and Thought* (New York, 1969), p. 126.

33. Rothchild and Rogin, "Uganda," pp. 389-91; and Gertzel, "Report from Kampala," *Africa Report*, IX (October 1964), 5-6.

34. Colin Leys, *Politicians and Policies: An Essay on Politics in Acholi, Uganda, 1962-65* (Nairobi, 1967), p. 18.

35. Hopkins, "Politics," pp. 263, 279; and George Shepherd, Jr., "Modernization in Uganda: The Struggle for Unity," in Stanley Diamond and Burke, eds. *The Transformation of East Africa* (New York, 1966), pp. 330-33.

36. Martin Staniland, "Single-Party Regimes and Political Changes," in Leys, ed. *Politics and Change in Developing Countries* (Cambridge, 1969), pp. 137-38.

37. See Emory Bundy, "Uganda's New Constitution," *East Africa Journal*, III, (June-July 1966), 26.

38. See A. Milton Obote, "The Footsteps of the Ugandan Revolution," *East Africa Journal*, V, (October 1968), 12; and Mazrui and Engholm, "Tensions," pp. 122-46.

39. According to the UPC-KY alliance, UPC was not to actively organize in Buganda, but by early 1963 UPC was opening branches in the Kingdom. Ibid., 127. On previous splits within the internal structure of UPC-Buganda, see Apolo Nsibambi, "Political Integration in Uganda: Problems and Prospects," *East Africa Journal*, VI, (February 1969), 38.

40. W. Arthur Lewis, *Politics in West Africa* (New York, 1965), p. 60, argues that "Singlepartyism is logically attainable if the party has a single ideology to which all of its members adhere."

41. Institute of Public Administration, "Evolution of Local Administrations," p. 11.

42. M. Davies, "Central/Local Government Relations," Institute of Public Administration, mimeo (Kampala, 1966), p. 2.

43. "The Development of Political Parties in Uganda," mimeo (Kampala 1966), p. 13.

44. For a brief review of this crisis, see M. Crawford Young, "The Obote Revolution," *Africa Report*, XI (June 1966), 8-14. An interesting, though far less objective, portrait of the crisis is painted by Akena Adoko, *Uganda Crisis* (Kampala, n.d.), pp. 23-112. Also useful is The Government of Uganda, *The Birth*, pp. 6-15.

45. The commission consisted of: Sir Clement deLestang of the East Africa Court of Appeals; Justice E. Miller from Kenya; and Justice A. Saidi from Tanzania. The report was not made public for several years. Before the 1971 coup, Obote had finally decided to publish it and Amin allowed publication to take place after he took power. See Martin, *Amin*, p. 89.

46. The five ministers arrested were G. Ibingira, E. Lumu, G. Mugezi, B. Kirya, and M. Ngubi. Obote's statement can be found in The Government of Uganda, *The Birth*, p. 7.

47. The KY members, led by A. Sempa, who refused to take the oath had their seats declared vacant. The DP members, who had walked out, later took the oath and were seated.

48. See *The Constitution of Uganda*, 15 April 1966 (Entebbe, n.d.), Chapter V, Part III, 73. (5).

49. *Uganda Parliamentary Debates* (Hansard), 2nd ser., LXXVII (September 1967) (Entebbe, n.d.), p. 1631; and The Government of Uganda, *The Birth*, p. 17.

50. J. Ochola, "Consultations between the Government and Local Authorities," mimeo (July 1970), p. 6.

51. O.G. Ivorian Jones, "The Legal Framework of the District Administration in Uganda," The Institute of Public Administration, mimeo (Kampala, June 1970), p. 2.

52. See *The Constitution of the Republic of Uganda* (Entebbe, n.d.), chap. 4, pt. 1, 26. (1) (a)-(e).

53. Ibid., chap. 5, pt.1, 40. (1) (b), (2), (3). The original proposals for the Republican Constitution offered a somewhat different system in which the nominated members would be selected by the president and could number one-third of the total of elected members.

54. In Acholi, for example, in March 1968 the UPC secretary-general suspended several party officials for making statements against the government. A few days later, the minister of regional administrations dismissed them from their positions on the District Council.

55. Obote, *The Common Man's Charter* (Entebbe, n.d.), Forward.

56. See the *Uganda Parliamentary Debates* (Hansard), 2d ser., XCVIII (December 1969) (Entebbe, n.d.), esp. pp. 101-7; the vote was 60 to 0 in favor of the extension of the state of

emergency. However, this did not mean that all DP members joined the UPC; see the comments of Latim and Okelo in the *Uganda Argus*, 17 July 1970, p. 1.

57. Documents two ("Proposals for National Service"), three ("Communication from the Chair of the National Assembly"), and four ("Labour Day Speech") can be found as appendices to Obote, *Common Man's Charter*, pp. 12-43. For document five, see Obote, *Proposals for New Methods of Election of Representatives of the People to Parliament* (Kampala, n.d.).

58. Mazrui, *Cultural Engineering*, p. 70.

59. Obote, *Proposals*, p. 14, par. 28. The presidential candidate would either be the party's president at that time, or a person selected by the Delegates' Conference of the party.

60. If the candidate was not elected, the National Assembly would select one of its members to be an interim president for up to one year. See ibid., p. 18, par. 34 b.

61. The National Assembly (Prescription of Elected Members) Act, 1970, set the number of elected MPs at 96, an increase of 14 over the then current number. The delineation of the 96 constituencies is presented in The Government of Uganda, *Report of the Electoral Commission* (Entebbe, n.d.). The electoral regions basically followed the already established regional division within the state. However, in August 1970, Teso North-West, East Mengo North, and Bunyoro North were placed in the Northern region to give all four regions 24 constituencies. See the *Uganda Argus*, 14 Aug. 1970, p. 1.

62. Obote, *Proposals*, p. 22, par. 40. See also Peter Willetts, "The Mathematics of Document No. 5," *Uganda Argus*, 12 Aug. 1970, pp. 5-6.

63. Special correspondent, "Uganda Under Military Rule," *Africa Today*, XX (September 1973), 12.

64. See Obote, "Memorandum," in his *Proposals*, pp. ii-iii, pars. 3-4; D. Cohen ana J. Parsons, "The Uganda Peoples Congress Branch and Constituency Elections of 1970," *Journal of Commonwealth Political Studies*, XI (March 1973), 52; and *Uganda Argus*, 14 Aug. 1970, p. 1.

65. Ibid.; and Garth Glentworth and Ian Hancock, "Obote and Amin: Change and Continuity in Modern Ugandan Politics," *African Affairs*, LXXII (July 1973), 245-46. For a brief discussion of the act of voting as an integrating device, see A.J. Milnor, *Elections and Political Stability* (Boston, 1969), p. 99.

66. Legum, *Africa 1970/1971*, p. B187; and Legum, ed. *Africa Contemporary Record 1971/72* (London, 1972), p. B227.

67. Obote, "Memorandum," p. xiii, par. 18. See also comments on the "Memorandum" in the *Uganda Argus*, 22 Aug. 1970.

68. Obote, "Memorandum," pp. vii-ix, par. 12.

69. Cohen and Parsons, 53, and the *Uganda Argus*, 29 Aug. 1970.

70. Both of these bodies had been "reconstituted" following the party elections of October-November 1970; see Cohen and Parsons, 53. Also see the *Uganda Argus*, 17 and 21 Dec. 1970.

71. Kampala Domestic Service, 15 December 1970, reported in Foreign Broadcast Information Service, *Daily Report: Middle East and Africa*, 16 December 1970, p. U4.

72. See Obote, *Proposals*, p. 20, par. 37c; Cohen and Parsons, "Uganda Peoples," 49; and Legum, *Africa 1970/1971*, p. B191.

73. Mazrui, *Cultural Engineering*, p. 67.

74. This is also the opinion expressed by Cohen and Parsons, 54. An example of the contrary view can be found in a press statement issued on 27 January 1971 by Idi Amin Dada, the head of Uganda's military government, and reprinted in Martin Minogue and Judith Molloy, eds. *African Aims and Attitudes* (Cambridge, 1974), p. 363.

75. On the election as a "shame" see Peter Gukiina, *Uganda: A Case Study in African Political Development* (Notre Dame, 1972), pp. 170-72.

76. Legum, *Africa 1970/71*, p. B187, points to the election as a means for Obote to rid himself of many of his comrades and potential rivals. Lofchie, "The Uganda Coup: Class Action by the Military," *Journal of Modern African Studies*, X (May 1972), 31, writes of the election in terms of legitimizing the one-party system. And Legum, *Africa 1971/1972*, p. B226, discusses Bugandan participation in the party elections of 1970.

77. See Cohen and Parsons 50-51 (and 52, where they note the negative aspects of exposure).

78. See the comments of Makerere professors Ryan and Gomboy in the *Uganda Argus*, 12 Aug.

1970, pp. 1, 4. According to Donald Morrison et al., *Black Africa: A Comparative Handbook* (New York, 1972), p. 27, Uganda ranks 27th out of 32 countries in terms of the "percentage of its population speaking the dominant vernacular language" (which is Luganda). Unlike its neighbors Kenya and Tanzania, Swahili as a lingua franca is not widespread in Uganda.

79. Mazrui, "Piety and Puritanism under a Military Theocracy: Uganda Soldiers as Apostolic Successors," in Catherine McArdle Kelleher, ed. *Political Military Systems: Comparative Perspectives*, Sage Research Series on War, Revolution, and Peacekeeping, IV (Beverly Hills, 1974), p. 114.

80. See Benjamin Neuberger, "Has the Single-Party State Failed in Africa?" *African Studies Review*, XVII (April 1974), 178. For a critical analysis of the one-party system, see S.E. Finer, *Comparative Government* (Harmondsworth, 1970), pp. 506-73.

81. Ibid., p. 528.

Democracy
and Social Mobilization in
Lebanese Politics

Michael C. Hudson*

Scholars and policy-makers frequently assume that the new states must develop stability before they can hope to operate the complex and delicate institutions of liberal democracy. But in the case of the Lebanese Republic this relationship is reversed: democratic institutions have brought about and maintained stability in an unfavorable political environment. The Lebanese case suggests that formal institutions, although neglected in behavioral political science, deserve renewed attention as causal agents in the process of political modernization.[1] At the same time, it raises the question of whether such institutions can supply enough systematic flexibility to meet the social mobilization demands of a rapidly changing society.

Lebanon's fragmented body politic—its traditional pluralism—has necessitated a political system based upon the balance of power, in the absence of positive legitimacy for the institutions of the state. In turn, the balance of power has required institutions that promote democratic values. Without the democratic institutions the balance of power would cease to be stable, and without stability the state would cease to exist. Lebanon's representative institutions are an essential condition of its stability, not a lucky by-product. This relationship, of course, has not gone unnoticed by Lebanon's politicians. In his inaugural address of September 23, 1964, President Charles Helou said: "I believe that the democratic system is an intrinsic necessity for our country. . . . It assures a balance between powers and makes possible a fruitful meeting among the Lebanese spiritual families. Thus their energies are activated within the democratic foundations, and their needs are met within a framework of brotherly cooperation. Rule is consultative, and the consultative system in Lebanon is one of the conditions of cooperative and stable life."[2]

This situation, however, is no cause for unrestrained optimism on the part of advocates of moderate democracy. First, the Lebanese system is democratic only in a limited sense. Second, modernization creates a dilemma for this balance-of-power system because it burdens a weak governmental

* I gratefully acknowledge the support of the Harvard Center for International Affairs, the Brooklyn College Research Center in Comparative Politics and Administration, the Yale World Data Analysis Program, the American Philosophical Society, and the comments of Ahmad Haffar, Joseph S. Nye, Leonard Binder, Manfred Halpern, and Samuel P. Huntington, none of whom necessarily agrees with the views expressed.

[1] Samuel P. Huntington, "Political Development and Political Decay," *World Politics*, XVII (April 1965), 386-430.
[2] *al-Anwar* (Beirut), September 24, 1964, p. 4.

apparatus with additional social demands. If the political system becomes capable of handling these demands and more responsible to the people in general, then it will threaten the existing democratic values that are a product of the balance of power among autonomous traditional groups. Yet attempts to maintain the status quo may run afoul of rising popular demands and the demonstration effect of efficient administration in other countries.

I. The Bases of Stability

A basic question in Western political science has been about the conditions of democracy, and the orthodox answer has been that democracy is the product, first, of a civil order in which tolerant and rational politics may occur. This civil order depends on an integrated political culture and political legitimacy. Second, democracy is the product of a pluralistic political culture in which competing groups constitute the matrix for democratic politics. Students of American society in particular, especially those writing in relatively tranquil periods, such as Tocqueville and David Truman, have found the question relevant and the answer plausible: democracy to them is an unusual phenomenon that calls for explanation, and in their perspectives consensus and pluralism loom as the primary explanatory factors.[3]

Today political scientists might express reservations about both the relevance and the completeness of this theory of democracy. In an era in which many polities, the United States included, are experiencing domestic turmoil, the increasingly relevant question is not the conditions of democracy but the conditions of civil order. The orthodox answer—that democracy is a fragile end-product of increasingly rare conditions—obscures the possibility that democratic practices may contribute to rather than result from civil order. Lebanon is a country in which pluralism and democracy exist without a prior legitimacy or an integrated political culture.[4] Yet independent Lebanon has not experienced the domestic strife that might have been expected. The case of Lebanon suggests not only that democracy may survive without legitimacy, but also that democracy may function in place of some prior legitimacy to promote domestic tranquillity. Although, as will be argued shortly, Lebanon has not solved its integration problems through its peculiar

[3] Tocqueville, *Democracy in America*, 2 vols. (New York, 1958), I, 433-436, and Chs. 16 and 17; David Truman, *The Governmental Process* (New York, 1951), Ch. 3 and pp. 519-524.

[4] The question arises of whether or not it is Lebanon's high living standard that supports its democracy. There is little doubt that there is a rough association between wealth and stable democracy in the world. See, e.g., S. M. Lipset's correlations of wealth and stable democracy for fifty countries in *Political Man: The Social Bases of Politics* (New York, 1960), pp. 51-54. I would argue that although the correlation holds for Lebanon— Lebanon scores relatively high on the economic indices and can also be classified as democratic—the correlation is not a causal relation. If there is a causal relation in Lebanon it would—once again—seem to be the other way around. Wealth has not made Lebanon any more pluralistic than it would otherwise be, nor has it invested the organs of the state with legitimacy. Neither has it affected the balance of power, which in Lebanon would not become much more or much less democratic than it now is if the per capita income were either half or twice its present level of around $400 annually. For a contrary argument, see Charles Issawi, "The Economic and Social Foundations of Democracy in the Middle East," in Walter Z. Laqueur, ed. *The Middle East in Transition* (New York, 1958), esp. pp. 48-49.

democratic institutions (and indeed may be losing the battle), its semisuccess in a generation of independent existence may yield an important lesson: democratic procedures can be instrumental in developing a just and stable political life under conditions of political disintegration. If valid, it is a lesson that might be applicable not only in the new states but also in some of the troubled older ones.

In Lebanon, pluralism is rich: every individual has strong regional, client, and family-group affiliations, and many have a number of voluntary or interest-oriented ties as well. How does Lebanon perform with respect to civil order? Instead of a culture in which security is the product of widespread regard for the legitimacy of the state and its institutions, we find a situation in which security is the product of a complex balance of power among the several traditional groups. Thus, even though the Lebanese state is relatively weak, the security requirement is met because the individual finds safety in his immediate groups, and the groups find it in their own relations with other groups rather than beneath an umbrella of national sovereignty.[5]

This balance is effected through certain democratic procedures. In Lebanon, pluralism plus democratic practices (the mechanism for the balance of power) makes public security possible. In the Western states, democratic values may wither because the "consensus" is too strong, but in Lebanon there must be a certain degree of liberal democracy (neither too little nor too much) to avoid civil strife. Liberal democracy in the settled states may be an alternative to other possibly more efficient forms of government, but it is nothing less than a deterent to anarchy in states where assimilation has not occurred. And in the complicated game of Lebanese politics most of the players seem to hold this proposition as axiomatic.

Lebanon's political environment   The key to understanding the connection between traditional pluralism, the balance of power, democratic values, and stability lies in the environment of the Lebanese political system. Let us quickly review its basic characteristics: (1) a particularistic "mosaic" society;[6] (2) an authoritarian and hierarchical family structure;[7] (3) religious institutions that are politically influential;[8] (4) power dispersed in religious sects, regional groupings, economic pressure groups, and ideologically

[5] Confining himself to traditional group orientations, John Gulick, in a study of al-Munsif, a Greek Orthodox village north of Beirut, suggests that the individual is involved in six concentric spheres of association: the family, the lineage, the village, the nation, the sect, and the linguistic group. *Social Structure and Cultural Change in a Lebanese Village* (New York, 1955), p. 163. Note that the nation ranks only fourth. For similar findings, based upon a sample of undergraduates at the American University of Beirut (not all of whom were Lebanese), see Levon Melikian and Lutfy N. Diab, "Group Affiliations of University Students in the Arab Middle East," *Journal of Social Psychology*, XLIX (1959), 145-159. In general, the students ranked the family first, the ethnic group second, the religion third, citizenship fourth, and the political party fifth.

[6] Carleton Coon, *Caravan* (New York, 1951), pp. 1-9 et passim; Albert H. Hourani, *Syria and Lebanon* (London, 1946), p. 127.

[7] See, e.g., Afif I. Tannous, "The Village in the National Life of Lebanon," *Middle East Journal*, III (April 1949), 151-164; Raphael Patai, "The Middle East as a Cultural Area," *Middle East Journal*, VI, No. 1 (1952), 1-21.

[8] Gabriel Puaux, *Deux Années au Levant: 1939-1940* (Paris, 1952), Ch. 7, "Le panthéon syrien." Puaux was High Commissioner of Lebanon and Syria at the time.

oriented political movements;[9] (5) foreign influence in politics;[10] (6) a distinct entrepreneurial habit that has produced both a small class of "merchant princes" and a large, stable, petty bourgeoisie;[11] (7) a cult of leadership, historically the result of feudalism, which has produced factions of notables, each with a local clientele;[12] and finally, (8) a territory that is about three-quarters the size of Connecticut, with five geographically well-defined regions, and a population about one-quarter the size of New York City's.

This environment has formed and maintained autonomous power centers and has imposed enough interdependence among them to necessitate balance-of-power politics. Boundaries imposed from outside and tensions generated within have given the balancing mechanisms a remarkably democratic cast: the state must permit every important traditional group a carefully-defined share in governing within a carefully defined area. Without imparting any significant legitimacy to the state itself, the traditional groups utilize it warily to preserve their own security. Attempts to arouse a national consciousness have not yet succeeded in overcoming particularistic suspicions, and those affirmations of Lebanese nationalism that can be heard are greatly qualified. For example, the Armenian parliamentary deputy declares that his primary loyalty is to the Lebanese state because the Armenian minority is particularly vulnerable to any alternative to it. The Najjadeh party official, who believes in the redevelopment of an Islamic civilization, supports the state because it is a reasonably acceptable compromise with an entrenched Westernized enclave. The Maronite cleric speaks fervently of preserving the Lebanese entity, but his idea of that entity conforms more closely to the boundaries of old Mount Lebanon than to the existing republic with its Muslim Arab "face."[13]

In short, the state is accepted for certain limited purposes by most of the important groups most of the time, but it commands little inherent respect, and the idea of a public interest is but poorly developed. The Lebanese system is stable, as the indicators of institutionalized political behavior will show, but it is also weak and probably will always be so since it is vulnerable to elements beyond its control. Here, therefore, is the most interesting and perplexing question about Lebanese politics: considering all the factors

[9] A thorough description of the power configuration before and during the 1958 crisis will be found in Fahim I. Qubain, *Crisis in Lebanon* (Washington, 1961), esp. pp. 28-69. In the summer of 1958, widespread disorders broke out, stemming (1) from President Chamoun's attempt to wrest powers from certain traditional notables and to renew his term of office and (2) from his relatively pro-Western and anti-Nasser position.

[10] For historical examples, see Kamal Salibi, *The Modern History of Lebanon* (London, 1965), Chs. 5, 8, and Part II. Also Puaux, Ch. 10, and Charles W. Thayer, *Diplomat* (New York, 1959), pp. 1-37.

[11] Doxiadis Associates of Athens, *Economic Data for the Ekistic Programme of Lebanon* (LGHP-1, R-LA-42/19-10-57), prepared for the U S Operations Mission in Lebanon (Beirut, 1957), p. 32. The Doxiadis investigators estimated that about 27,500 (or two-thirds) of the 41,570 "Businessmen and Self-employed" were in the middle-income groups (i.e., with annual incomes from $500 to $3,000). Of the total work force, 46 percent was in the middle-income group and 3 percent was in the $3,000 and over category.

[12] Arnold Hottinger has described this phenomenon in two papers, "Zu'amā' and Parties in the Lebanese Crisis of 1958," *Middle East Journal*, XV (Spring 1961), 127-140; and "Zu'amā'" in Historical Perspective," a paper delivered at the University of Chicago Conference on Democracy in Lebanon, May 28-31, 1963, published in Leonard Binder, ed. *Politics in Lebanon* (New York, 1966), pp. 85-105.

[13] These sentiments were expressed by representatives of the various political tendencies in interviews I conducted in Lebanon in the period 1962-1965.

weighing against it—a divided citizenry, low national feeling, the pressures of Arab politics, the strains of modernization—how can it perform so successfully?

Lebanon's balance of power   Lebanon's traditional pluralism has given rise to a political process analogous to the classic international balance-of-power system. In each case the possibility of any of the actors being eliminated is remote; in each case this fact is perceived by the actors. It follows that intergroup strife on a large scale is the most likely alternative to cooperation. Lebanese politicians therefore have exhibited an unusually high degree of responsibility in the absence of a controlling authority. In fact, they have on the whole been more responsible than their international counterparts.

The effects of the balance of power on Lebanese politics fall into institutional and behavioral categories. In the first category are three important manifestations: an unwritten constitution, a presidential system of government, and pluralistic representation.

Limited government   The first institutional manifestation is the National Pact (*al-mīthāq al-watani*), an informal agreement between President Bechara al-Khoury (a Maronite Christian) and Prime Minister Riad Sulh (a Sunnite Muslim), concluded in November 1943 during the birth of Lebanon's independence from France. At that moment Khoury and Sulh enjoyed a degree of support unequalled by any Lebanese politicians before or since, and the agreement therefore is thought by some to have received the tacit approval of all the people.[14] The Pact (which supplemented but did not replace the official constitution written in 1926 and amended in 1943) prescribes the policy goals of the state, foreign and domestic, and draws the limits beyond which it cannot reach. Lebanon must be completely independent of any state, Western or Arab. Lebanon should have an Arab "face" while remaining culturally distinct. Lebanon should cooperate with all the Arab states, providing that they recognize her boundaries. The National Pact in effect articulates the balance of power. Should Lebanon lean too far West, its Arab Muslim elements will resist; should it lean too far toward the Arab East, the Christians of the Mountain will fight. A domestic policy that brings Lebanon into excessively close relations with any country upsets the balance. The crises of the middle 1950's showed that the formula was not universally accepted: the Moslem communities became increasingly restive about the inaccessibility of the presidency and other positions of power; and the growing nontraditional interest groups chafed at their exclusion from public affairs. Nevertheless, the system has worked tolerably well for two decades. Without investing the state with innate worth or trust, the Lebanese (with the assistance of both the British and the French) have been able to engineer a stability formula based on democratic institutions and the principle of the concurrent majority.

---

[14] Bechara al-Khoury, *Hagā'iq lubnāniyyah [Lebanese Truths]*, the memoirs of the former President, 3 vols. (Beirut, 1961), II, 289-300. See also the memoirs of President Camille Chamoun, *Crise au Moyen-Orient* (Paris, 1963), pp. 118-119.

Presidential system   The second institutional manifestation of the balance of power is a presidential system tempered by sectarian and regional checks. The term "presidential system" may seem inappropriate; in theory, the Lebanese state has a parliamentary system loosely based on the French Basic Laws of 1875. But in practice an unwritten set of arrangements makes the president more powerful than the prime minister in regulating traditional group conflicts.

Under the 1926 Constitution the popularly elected parliament elects the president of the republic, who names a prime minister who in turn must form a cabinet that will hold the confidence of the parliament. Members of the cabinet are responsible collectively and individually for all the acts of the government. In theory, both president and cabinet are responsible to the parliament. In practice, however, the president had developed independence by making use of certain powers granted him through the French (who, not unreasonably, assumed that they could always control his election). These powers include the right to promulgate "urgent" legislation by decree,[15] to veto bills,[16] to dissolve the parliament,[17] and to appoint and dismiss the prime minister and the cabinet.[18] As a result, it has always been the president, not the parliament, that brought down governments. Prime ministers and cabinets have never been able to initiate legislative programs without presidential backing. The president has even been able to persuade the parliament to amend the constitution to permit him a second term, and the parliament has been too divided and dependent to resist effectively. This is one of the reasons that the opposition has occasionally taken to the streets. Instead of being a figurehead, the president is a participating umpire; instead of being a government, the cabinet is the battleground of notables; and instead of being a legislative body, the parliament is a sounding board for local leaders. Nevertheless, because he is the most powerful element, the President helps the system ride out crises resulting from fights among traditional leaders. He can adjust Lebanon's internal and foreign policies to prevent serious troubles, and he can pacify unhappy groups with patronage and office. Thus the president acts as the balancer in the balance of power.

The president, too, has group affiliations. He must be a Maronite. Thus he is not only the balancer but a representative of the most influential traditional group in the country. There is therefore a danger that a president will act as if he were the Maronite patriarch. President Chamoun played such a role in 1958. The danger is somewhat offset, however, by the actual existence of a Maronite patriarch. Traditionally the patriarch has looked after the political as well as the spiritual interests of the Maronites, and traditionally he has fallen into rivalry with the president. The result has been functional for the system: it has kept the Maronites from exercising too much direct control.

Not only is the president a Maronite, but also he is the head of family, client, regional, and interest groups. Since he cannot divorce himself from

15 *The Lebanese Constitution: A Reference Edition in English Translation*, prepared by the Department of Political Studies and Public Administration, American University of Beirut (Beirut, 1960), Article 58.
16 Ibid., Article 57.
17 Ibid., Article 55.
18 Ibid., Article 53.

these associations, it is very difficult for him to maintain a reputation for impartiality. This difficulty has led to instability in the balance, and all four of independent Lebanon's presidents have been attacked for favoring such special groups. President Khoury was accused of permitting his relatives to use the state for private purposes; President Chehab, a former general, elevated a few army officers into positions of great influence. Some observers complain that the president is too powerful, but if he were any less so the balance might break down altogether. On the contrary, the country's increasing administrative demands seem to require an even stronger, if less partial, president. This would seem to be the main lesson of the regimes of President Chehab and, to date, of President Helou.

Representation   Representing institutions in Lebanon have developed as a response to anarchy. Following the religious and social turmoil of 1840-1860 and until the beginning of World War I, Lebanon was ruled by a *mutasarrif* (a Christian, appointed by Constantinople with the approval of the Great Powers) who was advised by a representative council, the precursor of the modern parliament.[19] When the French replaced the Turks, they too established a representative council to advise the High Commissioner, and after the Constitution of 1926, they established a representative Chamber of Deputies and a short-lived appointive Senate. These early representative institutions were based upon sect, region, and family because the French thought that these categories had to be represented if stability were to be maintained. (Deputies also had to be cooperative with the Mandate.) Under the Mandate, for example, one would usually find a member of the Muqaddam family, Muslims of Tripoli, in the Chamber. Tripoli was generally hostile to the French but had to be controlled; the Muslims of the North were also hostile but had to be given at least token representation; and it was important that some of the leading notables be represented. The Muqaddams satisfied all these requirements. The motives for this representation were not liberal-democratic: both under the *mutasarrifiyyah* and the Mandate representation was a means to avert civil strife. Similarly, the systemic function of the modern Lebanese parliament is not to promote democratic values (although it does so to a significant extent) but to keep autonomous elements satisfied.

The most unusual characteristic of representation in Lebanon is confessionalism. Confessionalism is institutionalized separatism on a sectarian basis in the parliament, the cabinet, and the administration. Written into the 1926 Constitution,[20] confessionalism was condemned in the National Pact and yet has not been seriously challenged. Seats in the ninety-nine-member Parliament of 1968, for example, were not allocated simply by district, as in most countries, but also by sect: the Maronites were guaranteed thirty seats; the Sunnites, twenty; the Shiites, nineteen; the Greek Orthodox, eleven; the Greek Catholics and Druzes, six each; the Armenian Orthodox, four; the Armenian Catholics, one; the minorities, one; and the Protestants, one. The Constitution also called for an equitable distribution of admin-

[19] For two descriptions see Salibi, *Modern History*, Part II, and Pierre Rondot, *Les Institutions politiques du Liban* (Paris, 1947).
[20] Article 95. The Constitution stipulates that this is only a provisional measure.

istrative posts, not just by ability but also by sect. Every cabinet still is a carefully designed mosaic of the regional and sectarian forces of the *pays réel.*[21]

An important supporting institution for confessionalism in the parliamentary elections is the list system. Voters in each district are obliged to elect several deputies, usually including some of a confession different from their own. This requirement has led to the formation of powerful lists under the patronage of the most powerful notables of the district. Aspirants for the minority seats will often pay handsomely to join the list—and therefore ride the coattails—of a major notable from the majority sect. In districts in which the sects are closely matched in size, the process of making a strong ticket requires recruiting the most popular members of each sect. In all cases, confessionalism requires that a candidate be popular among his co-religionists and that he have the underlying interests of the sect at heart.

The list system has had two important effects on the balance of power. Within the election district, it has strengthened the position of the two or three leading notables of the majority sect—thus reducing and consolidating the number of important power groups in the state—without sacrificing the interests or jeopardizing the security of the minority sects. Voters can usually make a choice between lists of candidates according to criteria important to them. We may regret that sect should be one of these criteria, but we cannot therefore call the method undemocratic—indeed, quite the opposite conclusion is suggested. Second, within the country as a whole, the list system has retarded the development of programmatic politics and parties. A deputy is the representative of his district, his sect, and his group before he is the representative of socialism or administrative reform. Liberal democracy is sought through particularistic rather than universalistic channels.

The behavioral manifestations of the balance of power reveal a pattern of regularized instability. This is a systemic response to Lebanon's fragmented political culture and weak legitimacy. Its hallmarks are a frequent alternation in the holders of public office, temporary coalitions, and chronic minor crises. The object of every player is to make small gains without upsetting the structural balance. As a result, the political situation seems to be changing constantly, yet very little really happens.

A few quantitative indicators will show the regularity of institutionalized instability.[22] Lebanon experienced thirty-seven significant changes of government in its first two decades of independence; a government survives, on the average, for 6.8 months. But such instability is more apparent than real, and Lebanon, the 1958 crisis notwithstanding, is the only developed Arab state not to have experienced a revolution since World War II. We have to look behind the statistics. It appears, for example, that cabinet life-spans are lengthening: the seventeen cabinets under President Khoury (1943-1952) averaged 6.35 months, but the seven cabinets under General Chehab (1958-1964) averaged 9.3 months, and one of them lasted longer

---

21 Clyde G. Hess, Jr., and H. L. Bodman, Jr. "Confessionalism and Feudality in Lebanese Politics," *Middle East Journal,* VIII, No. 1 (1954), 10-26.

22 See also Malcolm H. Kerr, "Political Decision-making in a Confessional Democracy," a paper delivered at the University of Chicago Conference on Lebanese Democracy, May 28-31, 1963, and published in Binder, *Politics in Lebanon.*

than any in history—two years, three months, and nineteen days. Even so, these figures would be alarming if Lebanese politics were programmatic or ideologically oriented. Cabinet changes, however, are simply indicative of the balance of power in operation, routinized expressions of endlessly shifting coalitions of the same elite. Another indicator of stability is the recruitment process. The mean age of cabinet entrants consistently hovers around forty-seven years. The sectarian composition of every cabinet adheres rigidly to the unwritten constitutional prescriptions, with half the seats going to Christians and half to non-Christians. Moreover, certain portfolios are normally alloted to particular sects: the minister of defense is usually Druze; the foreign minister, Maronite. The regional balance in every cabinet is scrupulously calculated; there has rarely been a cabinet of any duration without representation from each of the five regions.[23] The rate of entry of newcomers into cabinets not only has remained below fifty percent during the two decades, but has actually declined consistently. This indicates that the proportion of veterans is going up and that the political process displays continuity as well as change.

II. Social Mobilization and Political Modernization

In speaking of the limited successes of the Lebanese system in achieving democratic values and stability, it has been necessary to assume other things equal. But in order to consider the question raised earlier as to whether the Lebanese system can cope with massive social change, it is necessary to scrap that assumption. It is also necessary to describe as clearly as possible the environmental trends and their political relevance. Finally, the capacity of the political system for meeting these presumably increasing environmental loads must be charted over time in order to draw sound conclusions. Actually, neither current theory nor data will adequately support any scheme for showing numerically to what extent Lebanese environmental loads exceed or fall below Lebanese political capabilities. The more modest objective is to provide evidence for intuitively comparing loads and capabilities, and the result will be judgment, not proof.

Social mobilization   Deutsch's concept of social mobilization is perhaps the most elaborate indicator of the strength of social change.[24] Comparisons with Deutsch's hypothetical model of a country undergoing rapid social mobilization suggest that Lebanon's population is shifting rapidly into the category of socially mobilized. Lebanon scores within the ranges Deutsch postulates on all indicators of changes (for which data are available) that make increased demands on the political system: shifts into mass-media audience, increase in voting participation, increase in literacy, and population growth.[25] As for that set of changes "related to the capabilities of the government for coping with these burdens," Lebanon again falls within the hypothesized ranges: the occupational shift out of agriculture, the change

---

[23] Hess and Bodman, 23.
[24] Karl W. Deutsch, "Social Mobilization and Political Development," *American Political Science Review*, LV (September 1961), 493-514.
[25] Ibid., 503, Table 1.

from rural to urban residence, and the income-growth and per capita income-growth indicators leave no doubt that social mobilization is occurring.

Table 1 summarizes certain trends indicative of social mobilization in Lebanon in the period of its independence. Even casual inspection of the figures shows clearly that Lebanon is a society in the process of rapid modernization. Taken together or separately, the data indicate the development of a typically complex urban society: the trends are toward urban

Table 1. Summary of Social Mobilization Trends in Lebanon

	Year	Data	Year	Data
Demographic trends:				
Population (millions)	1943	1.02	1963	2.00
Population per sq. km.	1943	101	1963	193
Percentage of population in cities				
of 20,000 and over	1943	28.7	1963	37.4
Economic trends:				
Energy consumption per capita (metric tons				
of coal equivalent)	1960	520	1964	689
Electricity (millions of kwh)	1959	267	1962	551
Per capita income	1959	$362	1963	$449
Number of banks	1951	5	1966	93
Exposure trends:				
Telephones (per 1,000 population)	1948	10.8	1963	47.3
Passenger vehicles (per 1,000 population) ...	1948	6.7	1963	36.4
Radio audience (thousands)	1948	200	1963	2,000
Newsprint consumption (kgs. per capita) ...	1951	0.9	1964	3.9
Primary school students				
(per 1,000 population)	1950	115	1963	160
Secondary school students				
(per 1,000 population)	1950	20	1963	31
University students				
(per 1,000 population)	1950	2.4	1963	8.2

Sources: IRFED Report, cited in text, fn. 28; Doxiadis, *Economic Data*; Republic of Lebanon, Ministry of Labor and Social Affairs, Ministry of National Education, documents and reports; United Nations, *Statistical Yearbook*; UNESCO, *World Communications* (Paris, 1964).

density, a certain material advancement, and an increasingly politically aware population. But what do these numbers signify about political loads?[26]

The answers are not as obvious as the popularized analyses of modernization suggest. It would, for example, be difficult to identify among the Lebanese a tide of rising expectations leading to political chaos. Indeed, if material demands were the primary load produced by social mobilization, we could—as many Lebanese do—point to the country's affluence relative both to earlier periods and to neighboring states. Nor would it seem plau-

[26] For a complete discussion of Lebanese modernization, see my study *The Precarious Republic: Political Modernization in Lebanon* (New York, 1968), Chs. 2 and 3.

sible to argue that because Lebanon is shifting, in a linear manner, from traditional to modern society its people are psychologically distressed and therefore politically volatile. On the contrary, the Lebanese display a capacity—astonishing to the student of political development—for embracing tradition and modernity with only minimal politically relevant psychological effects. In Lebanon, modernization does not mean destroying the old but simply adding the new.

Modernization in Lebanon, however, does pose political loads of another and more mundane sort. It complicates enormously the ordinary problems of administration and exposes the rather limited capacities of a government whose primary function, as I have suggested, is maintaining an internal balance through democratic procedures. The population rate takes on political significance when the public authorities ignore what promises to become a critical unemployment problem. The social security plan is hampered by the inability of the government to take a census. High urbanization becomes politically relevant when the government has no effective housing policy. Other public services in the urban core seem unable to keep pace with its burgeoning needs:

> Il est impossible de dire qui est chargé de surveiller la nourriture presentée dans un grand hotel de la montagne: le municipalité locale? le Commissariat du Tourisme? le Service de la Répression des Fraudes? ou le Ministère de la Santé? Quand on ouvre une nouvelle artère dans la capitale, on n'a pas fini de l'asphalter que le Service des Eaux, ceux des égouts, de l'électricité, et du téléphone viennent chacun à son tour éventrer la chausée pour y installer leurs cables ou leurs tuyaux. . . .[27]

In addition to the routine administrative problems, two kinds of unevenness in Lebanese social mobilization add to the loads upon the political system. The trends reveal what might be called a structural unevenness in the modernization process. Certain indicators of material prosperity, such as energy consumption per capita and income per capita, show an impressive rise. The distribution of this new prosperity, however, has hardly conformed to the criteria of social justice which ciritics of the present situation —moderate as well as extremist—hold. A 1960 study showed that 35 to 40 percent of the population in certain Western countries earned more than the mean annual income, but that in Lebanon the percentage was only 18.[28] The same study calculated that while the agricultural sector constituted nearly half the work force, it received less than 16 percent of the national income.[29] While the number of banks showed an explosive rate of increase, indicative of the overdevelopment of high finance, the share of GNP from the industrial sector remained at a relatively constant 12 percent over time. The collapse of Beirut's huge Intra Bank in October 1966 is an instructive example of the country's fragile prosperity: a confluence of factional rivalries within the Lebanese elite and in the Arab world, together with an international tightening of money, produced a crisis that severely eroded the

[27] *L'Orient* (Beirut), October 22, 1958.
[28] République Libanaise, Ministère du Plan, *Besoins et possibilités de développement du Liban*, a report made by the Institut pour Recherche et de Formation en Vue de Développement (IRFED), 2 vols. (Beirut, 1960-1961), I, 93.
[29] I, 81, Table 26.

attractiveness of Beirut for investment. While the need to industrialize has long been recognized, every effort to shift the basis of the Lebanese economy in this direction has been feeble. A similar imbalance is apparent within the exposure trends of social mobilization. Literacy and school attendance have unquestionably increased since independence, but they have not increased as fast as access to the radio. There can be little doubt that the Lebanese population is saturated with information and propaganda from many different sources. At the same time, demands for more, better, and cheaper educational facilities become increasingly intense. Yet even meeting these demands raises an additional political problem: Will the numerous secondary school graduates be able to find satisfying or useful occupations?

Table 2. Social Mobilization by Region

Indicator	Beirut	and the Mountain	North	South	Biqa
Population per sq. km.	23,034	340	191	137	47
IRFED development scores		2.22	1.70	1.75	1.92
Per capita income, 1957*	$803	$205	$200	$151	$206
Television owners (percentage of population)	39	35	27	28	18
Radio owners (percentage of population)	85	85	85	78	91
Newspaper consumption (percentage of total circulation)		70		30	
Percentage of newspaper readers interested in internal politics**	68	63	53	45	49
Percentage of students in population	18.8	17.4	16.3	13.5	13.2

* Doxiadis, *Economic Data*, pp. 23–27.
** Association Libanaise des Sciences Politiques, "Presse, radio, télévision et opinion publique" (Beirut, May 1963), mimeographed, p. 13.

The second type of unevenness in the Lebanese social mobilization pattern is regional. It is scarcely an exaggeration to speak of two Lebanons, in terms of within-country variations in levels of social mobilization. Table 2 provides a crude picture of the magnitude of this variation. On every indicator of social mobilization with the exception of radios, the Beirut area stands far ahead of the peripheral regions. Lebanon's other city, Tripoli, is a very distant second. Great Beirut (which now includes the major surrounding towns of Mount Lebanon province) has generated and absorbed the prosperity of the independence era, while outlying regions in the southern and northern provinces show little material change. These regional imbalances are a formidable obstacle to developing a positive national consensus, particularly since the outlying regions are predominantly Muslim and only recently (1920) have become Lebanese. Social mobilization, writes

Deutsch, "may tend to strain or destroy the unity of states whose population is already divided into several groups with different languages or cultures or basic ways of life."[30]

Problems of modernization   If the political issues posed by social mobilization are serious, Lebanon's capacity for dealing with them appears
meager indeed by all the usual standards of political modernization. Lebanon
ranks well up among the upper half of all the countries in the world on
selected indicators of social mobilization, yet it falls into the lower half on
"political development" indicators such as political deaths per million,
political party representation, government expenditures as a percentage of
GNP, voting participation, and executive stability.[31] Specific countries that
rank near Lebanon on social mobilization rank generally above it on the
political indicators, while its political "neighbors" exhibit generally lower
levels of social mobilization.

Observers and practitioners of Lebanese politics alike condemn the corruption and inefficiency of political life, although it is by no means clear
that Lebanese are any more "developed" in these qualities than, say, Italians
or Americans. However, two weaknesses in Lebanon's performance as a
political system are particularly notable: the country has hardly been able
to develop and integrate nontraditional interest groups and parties; and its
vulnerability to sudden crises remains extremely high. The system has succeeded in integrating, in a functional sense, only those groups and organizations compatible with the requirements of the balance of power. These
include the pressure groups representing Lebanon's overdeveloped financial
sector, which influence tariff policies, public works programs, and general
domestic policy, and the so-called parties, such as the Destour and the
National Bloc, which are in reality only the followings of certain traditional
figures. The new interests generated by economic growth have been accommodated within the traditional framework through an interlocking directo-
rate of notables.

Centralized parties too must conform to the traditional requirements. For
example, the Kataeb (Phalanges Libanaises), established during the late
1930's and the only significant nonclandestine party in operation today, is
a vehicle for maintaining Maronite interests in an independent Lebanon.[32]
Yet even the Kataeb, in its most successful year (1960), placed only six men
in a parliament of ninety-nine members; and in 1964 it placed only four.
It is only occasionally represented in the cabinet. But perhaps the classic
case is Kamal Jumblat's Progressive Socialist party. It is distinctly unsuccessful as a party, as Jumblat himself has admitted, but it is effective as a
regional-sectarian grouping. The PSP is an ideological cover for Jumblat's
personal following as the dominant leader of the Chouf district and the
hereditary chief of one of the two Druze factions. This party currently commands one of the largest followings in parliament—ten deputies. But its

30 "Social Mobilization," 501.
31 Michael C. Hudson, "A Case of Political Underdevelopment," *Journal of Politics*,
XXIX (November 1967), 821-837.
32 Kataeb Party, *Declaration* (Beirut, n.d.), issued (in 1956?) in English, French, and
Arabic, containing *inter alia* a speech by Pierre Gemayel setting forth the party's beliefs.

programs[33] are too radical—at least in the Lebanese context—to command serious attention from the establishment. The Lebanese are unlikely to permit the government to nationalize industries, curtail freedom of trade, institute effective progressive taxation, and "reorganize society on the basis of the family."

Parties of a more radical cast have appeared, but have never attained legitimacy because they deny the traditional requirements. The Social Nationalist party (formerly the Syrian National party) demanded a revolutionary adaption to modernization: secularism, social reform, a "greater Syrian" nationalism, and income redistribution. It drew membership from various minority sects, organized itself along paramilitary lines in the fashion of the Fascist and Nazi parties, and was guided by intellectuals— university professors, students, and lawyers. This party was never able to operate within the traditional limits of the system. Only once did it place a man in parliament, and never were its policy recommendations seriously considered. The party was felt to be so dangerous to the political structure that President Khoury's regime dissolved it in 1949 and executed its leader, and the Chehab regime tried to destroy it again in 1962 when it attempted a coup d'état. The other nontraditional parties, the Communists and the Baathists, are also beyond the pale and function as semiclandestine organizations. In this category also fall the Arab nationalist clubs and societies, although Nasserist sentiment is sufficiently widespread to assure them of a broader measure of tolerance. Again, the membership appears to come from the young, socially mobilized, discontented intellectuals of Beirut, Tripoli, and the Mountain.

The second problem in Lebanon's political modernization is also a product of the growing politicization of its inhabitants. It is sometimes said, with some justification, that Lebanon is like a powder keg: a sharp disturbance may make it explode. While this quality undoubtedly deters some of those who desire to tamper with the political system, it obviously cannot guarantee complete deterrence, particularly in the turbulent Arab world. A rock thrown at a curé, or an inflammatory radio speech, can and does shock the system to its foundations. The Lebanese public is highly exposed to various transnational ideologies that unavoidably compete with allegiance to the Lebanese state. Public demonstrations, general strikes, and attempted coups d'état weaken the balance and those democratic values that flow from it. Political assassinations, while infrequent, present a severe threat to the delicate balance when they do occur. Labor unions are becoming politically significant as they develop their organizational power.

Twice during the 1950's, institutional devices proved unable to resolve a major crisis and the "solution" was spurred by a general strike. In 1952 the Khoury regime found that it had alienated a strong coalition of notables, and President Khoury was unable to find a prime minister: none of the eligible Sunnites would serve. The threat of a general strike and disorders persuaded the President to resign. In the impasse Khoury naturally called upon the army to maintain order, but the commander, General Chehab, would not commit his forces to a "political" struggle. As a result the regime

[33] See *Mīthāq al-hizb al-taqaddumi al-ishtirākī* [*Covenant of the Progressive Socialist Party*] (Beirut, 1961).

fell. Owing to the deterrent built into the traditional system, civil and confessional disorder was avoided and the old institutions were preserved. But the 1958 crisis was more serious. Pan-Arabism was stronger than it had ever been. The Chamoun regime seemed to be violating the neutrality principle of the National Pact, denying the traditional representation of notables, and trying to amend the constitution to permit Chamoun's reelection. Chamoun became the ruler of a country polarized by the pro-Western, Christian faction, which controlled the disintegrating coercive instruments of the state, and the pro-Nasser insurgents, consisting of many of the leading notables. Once again General Chehab refused to use the army to save the regime. American intervention helped bring to an end a summer of violence.

It would be naïve to underestimate the gravity of these problems, yet it is an oversimplification to suppose that the Lebanese system is incapable of responding to them. The fact that the state has weathered the crises of its first two decades, showing remarkable persistence and durability, is surely significant in itself and can hardly be attributed to the United States Sixth Fleet. Why, if the political system is as anachronistic in its environment as theory and data indicate, does it survive as well as it does? The political scientist pondering this question is inevitably reminded of the visiting economist who, when asked for advice, replied, "I don't know what you are doing, but whatever it is, keep it up." No simple answers seem adequate, and any analysis that takes account of the subtleties of the Lebanese situation is likely to appear unduly hedged to some readers.

Despite its serious problems, the Lebanese system has two important characteristics that mitigate to some extent its weaknesses. Both provide limited political means for coping with a dynamic situation; but, as we shall see, neither can be expected to resolve the fundamental dilemma of political modernization in Lebanon. Although ideal political modernization is virtually impossible under present conditions, these two positive factors supply a certain capacity for muddling through. One of these factors may be described as increasing institutional strength; the other is a degree of democratic procedure.

The most important sign of growing institutionalization in Lebanon has been the growth in power and capability of the executive branch. As we have seen, the president of the Lebanese republic has considerable formal power. During the brief period since independence this power has steadily increased; yet, with the exception of the 1958 crisis, it has not increased dramatically enough to set the traditional notables into open revolt. Bechara al-Khoury, the father of Lebanese independence, succeeded in welding most elements of the elite together with all the skills of Lincoln and Boss Tweed. Despite his inglorious retirement in 1952, his was a considerable accomplishment. Camille Chamoun, who had the misfortune to rule during the turbulent period 1952-1958, was if anything too aggressive; and his bid to reform the "feudal" system was singularly tactless. During the postcrisis regime of General Fuad Chehab, Lebanon experienced its first taste of planning for national development and a degree of military interference in politics and administration. Expenditures of the Public Works Ministry nearly tripled between 1961 and 1964, and the state began to engage in deficit spending.[34] The number of civil servants rose from around 18,000 in 1957 to 26,000 at the end of his regime. *"Chéhabisme"* became synonymous with national development and represented perhaps the least controversial position between the advocates of the "free economy" and the advocates of "Arab socialism." Chehab's successor, Charles Helou, a compromise candidate in the tense succession struggle, although less dynamic than his predecessors, still managed to guide Lebanon through the Intra Bank collapse of 1966 and the Arab-Israeli war of 1967—crises of the first magnitude. That a relatively weak leader could weather such storms is due in part to the growth in the effectiveness of the presidential office and the resilience of the system as a whole.

Institutionalized representative processes have also shown a notable expansive capacity, though perhaps a less spectacular one than the growth of the executive branch. Lebanon's growing politically conscious population is reflected in the increase in voting participation. The ratio of voters to total adult population has risen markedly since 1943, the most spectacular increase occurring in 1953 after the granting of suffrage to women. In the 1960 parliamentary elections, some 522,000 people voted, and by 1964 the number had increased by around 14 percent to 595,000.[35]

The composition of the Chamber of Deputies is also changing. Especially notable is the declining percentage of great landowners. In the first representative council under the Mandate (1922-1925), landowners accounted for two-thirds of the membership; in the 1943 parliament the percentage was 44; in the 1960 parliament it was 22; and in the 1964 parliament it was down to 15. While the lawyers maintained a fairly constant level of representation (around 30 percent), the big businessmen—financiers and the professionals (including teachers, engineers, former judges, and civil servants) increased their representation.[36] The change is also reflected in the differing political atmospheres of the 1940's and the 1950's. During the earlier period politics was a game played by traditional notables; during the latter the game was opened up to some new players from the upper middle class and the non-Christian sector, and several of the notables, especially those of Beirut, adopted ideological means to consolidate and increase their popular following. Although the new complexities added strains to the system, the institutions proved capable of operating under them. Admittedly, these trends are far less impressive than many observers might wish; everybody has his anecdotes about corruption, and nobody, including the major participants, has any illusions that the system works well. These qualifications, however, do not obscure the evidence that the system is far from static: even if traditional pluralism retards institutions such as a party system and perhaps checks presidential power too much, it has not robbed executive and legislature of limited capacities to develop.

[34] See Sleiman M. Gemayel, *Evolution de budget libanais* (Paris, 1962), p. 70; and *Le Commerce du Levant* (Beirut), March 3, 1965.

[35] Voting statistics published in *L'Orient* (Beirut), April 7, 15, and 28 and May 3, 1964. See also Michael C. Hudson, "The Electoral Process and Political Development in Lebanon," *Middle East Journal*, XX (Spring 1966), 173-186.

[36] These data are from the Library of Parliament and the newspaper *L'Orient*. Cf. the generally similar findings, but different conclusions, reported by Jacob Landau, "Elections in Lebanon," *Western Political Quarterly*, XIV (March 1961), 130. Classification is difficult since many deputies can reasonably fit in more than one category.

The second factor ameliorating Lebanon's theoretically underdeveloped political condition is the same one discussed earlier as functional for maintaining the internal balance of power. But it is easier to argue that democratic procedures permit a stable balancing process than it is to contend that they contribute to the development of the political capabilities that social mobilization requires. Indeed, it can be argued that the kind of democratic procedures found in Lebanon are actually dysfunctional in this respect, in that they tend to paralyze the policy process.[37] The issue boils down to the question of whether Lebanon's limited democratic procedures serve only to lubricate the balance among sects and traditional factions.

During the Mandate and in the early years of independence Lebanese democracy could generally be described in those limited terms. But 1952 —the year of the Egyptian revolution and the deposition of President Khoury —marked a turning point for Lebanon. From that time on the Lebanese people and elite alike seem to have become conscious of the imperatives of development, social justice, and national dignity which social mobilization has precipitated. What was hitherto primarily sectarian democracy has begun to acquire elements of populist democracy.

In domestic affairs these concerns are reflected in the persistent efforts at administrative reform and, especially during the Chehab regime, in government-directed development policies such as the social security program, the Central Bank, the Social Development Office, and the agricultural development program ("The Green Plan"). In foreign affairs they may be seen in the abandonment of the traditionally close Western relationship so carefully nurtured by the Maronites, as well as in the acceptance of Lebanon as an Arab state whose destinies, for better or worse, are inextricably tied to the Arab world. These policies are evidence that the political system has become responsive to newly crystallized populist demands that transcend the primordial, sectarian perspective of the early democracy. The attempts to promote development, social justice, and closer Arab solidarity have not arisen primarily out of sectarian pressures; they have come out of peculiarly modern political conditions and they have been transmitted, albeit imperfectly, into public policy through democratic procedures. The events of the last decade suggest that while sectarianism at the popular level shows no signs of disappearing, the political system can to some extent transcend the confessional, corporate democracy.

That this "remedy" should have emerged may be explained by precisely the same condition which gave rise to the old, sectarian democracy. This condition is insecurity. Today, however, in the modernized and turbulent Arab world, insecurity for the inhabitants of Lebanon is not confined to historical sectarian and parochial fears. Modernization generates new and broader insecurities: fears of the violence that can arise out of ignoring the modern ideas now prevalent throughout the Arab world, in "progressive" and "conservative" states alike. However imperfect Lebanon's institutions may be, its politicians cannot ignore new demands. For Lebanon more than most states, survival today requires political responsiveness to broadly populist demands, and this fact is recognized by Lebanese politicians. Lebanon does not need a party system to make these realities apparent and a

[37] See, e.g., Kerr, "Political Decision-making."

determinant in policymaking. Indeed, the very vulnerability of the system increases its responsiveness.

This is not to say, however, that Lebanon will overcome the persistent challenges of modernization in the long run. Institutional growth and democratic procedures are palliatives, not cures. In order to explain Lebanon's surprising durability it is necessary to point out these little-noticed capacities for adaptation in a dynamic situation. But a question remains: Are these capacities likely to be sufficient to respond to the persistent and increasing challenges posed by social mobilization in Lebanon and the Arab world? The further relevant questions are now whether a Lebanese government can actually implement its social security scheme or save the country from financial disasters; whether it can be sufficiently Arab in its foreign policy without awakening sectarian fears; whether it can integrate the modernizing radicals as it once integrated sectarian radicals; whether, in short, it can innovate as well as adapt.

To those who value the present system the outlook cannot be encouraging. Many Lebanese feel discontented, disenfranchised from active political participation, perhaps by their sect or lack of money, with no means of legitimate political expression. They see the country ruled by a clique of wealthy landlords, bankers, and lawyers. In their view, parliament is an obstacle on the road to effective power, and reform within the present system is ephemeral. Here lies a dilemma. If democracy is Lebanon's guarantor of stability and if stability is threatened by these increasing pressures, then the obvious need is more democracy. More democracy for Lebanon means a government more successfully responsive to popular demands, a political arena in which more people can be influential, and a system in which popular majorities rule. If these were the only consequences then there would be reason for optimism. But "more democracy" also will create new power centers, which might displace, by one means or another, the incumbent elite. If more democracy would assuage the discontent of those whom the present system excludes and would produce effective administration it would also challenge the traditional powers. The 1958 crisis amply demonstrated that such a confrontation can completely disrupt civil order. On the other hand, if modernization were in fact eradicating the old group structure as fast as it molded "participant personalities," then the players in the old balance-of-power game might just fade away peacefully, a modern democratic state might appear, and Lebanese nationalism might arise to invest the state with enough legitimacy to enable it to tackle the new social problems effectively. But this idea, held by some critics of confessionalism and the status quo, is unrealistic too: it is utopian to imagine that the traditional power-holders will disappear quickly or that individuals in the "modernized" state will forsake their traditional ties for a "rational" social contract that denies such ties. Hence the dilemma: too little democracy may lead to social disorder and revolution; too much may bring down upon the state the wrath of the traditional leaders.

This dilemma is reflected in discussions that took place in the summer of 1968 regarding the next presidential election, scheduled for 1970. The political modernizers who are identified with former President Chehab, in a candid assessment of developments during the Helou regime, arrived at some pessimistic conclusions. Despite a decade of struggle since the 1958 crisis, they feel that *"Chéhabisme"* has not gained general acceptance; indeed, the 1968 parliamentary elections appeared to repudiate the Chehabists in favor of former President Chamoun and his supporters, representatives of the traditional, conservative politics. Neither the 1958 events nor six years of Chehabist rule succeeded in supplanting the old notables and cliques or reducing sectarian tension. The long-term effects of the Intra Bank crash and the 1967 war, in their opinion, continue to exacerbate the unresolved domestic tensions in the country and pose certain dangers. Among these dangers are a possible duality of power between the army and the regime, a paralysis of democratic procedures owing to a resurgence of uncontrolled clique politics, and a further diminution of political and social reform which could crystallize tendencies toward revolution, civil disorder, or military dictatorship. Some seasoned observers of the Lebanese scene see the present situation as potentially more dangerous than that of 1956-1957 because the army is now regarded as partisan (pro-Chehab) rather than impartial; because the threat of new Israeli aggressive in the area (Lebanon included) is real, greatly complicating the delicate foreign-policy compromise embodied in the National Pact; and because the younger generation is dissatisfied with the traditional politics of compromise.

"Like the states of seventeenth-century Europe," Samuel P. Huntington has written, "the non-Western countries of today can have political modernization or they can have democratic pluralism, but they cannot normally have both."[38] Lebanon, however, has been showing signs of abnormality for over two decades; the balance-of-power situation has forced it to enjoy a little of each. Lebanon's skillful politicians, undaunted by grim logic, have thus far avoided the dilemma by maintaining "just enough" democracy. In the absence of positively legitimized central control, a kind of democratic pluralism has been a necessity rather than a luxury. Similarly, under the increasing pressures of modernization, the balance has been altered to accommodate the moderate development of rationalized authority, differentiated political structures, and mass participation. How much future alteration will such a delicately balanced system sustain without collapsing? How strong are the disintegrative tensions inherent in such a fragmented political culture, shaken as it is by conflicting external and domestic demands? These questions must be analyzed, as I have suggested, in a setting of interrelated demands. Failure to handle the higher-order problems of national development and social justice will have adverse repercussions for the basic problem of stability, and by the same token, too much success in those areas may be equally disastrous.

[38] "Political Modernization: America vs. Europe," *World Politics*, XVIII (April 1966), 412.

Postscript

Since the original publication of this paper, the worst forebodings expressed in it unfortunately have come to pass, and with a degree of violence that has shocked even the most pessimistic analysts of Lebanon's future. An unbearable convergence of domestic and external loads, coupled with a relapse of the political system itself into a particularly atavistic traditionalism, set the stage for one of the bloodiest civil wars the world has known in the twentieth century.

Lebanon's political deterioration during these years began with the Arab defeat by Israel in 1967 and the subsequent meteoric rise of the Palestinian resistance movement. This movement took root wherever there were Palestinians, but especially in Lebanon where the concentration of Palestinians—Lebanon had the biggest refugee camps—and the relative freedom of political action led to active Palestinian forays into Israel from bases in south Lebanon. Israel retaliated massively with air, artillery and ground attacks which destroyed villages and crops. The Israeli actions caused a substantial depopulation of south Lebanon and created enormous political problems for the Lebanese state. Inasmuch as most of the Muslim, Arab-oriented Lebanese strongly supported the Palestinians while the conservative Maronite Christian elite opposed them, government fell into a condition of quasi-paralysis.

In 1970 Suleiman Frangieh, a parochial mountain *za'im* from north Lebanon, was elected president by a one vote margin, thus bringing the modernizing reformist impulse of Chehabism (flawed as it was) to a definitive end. What followed was a return to traditional neo-feudal politics: virtually no new social welfare programs were undertaken, and such reform efforts as were tried (for example, in the education ministry), soon collapsed in failure. The army (as forecast in the paper) did in fact become polarized—not in a Chehabist direction, however, but rather in the direction of the most conservative Maronite tendencies. Against a background of increasingly serious conflicts between the Palestinian organizations and the army in collusion with the Maronite militias, the Lebanese Muslims began to demand once again structural reforms giving them greater influence in political life. They demanded in particular a greater representation in the key commands of the army. But these demands went unheeded, and Lebanon continued with its unchecked social mobilization and corruption.

Many Lebanese thought that the 1973 Arab-Israeli war, which Israel failed to win, would set in motion a general settlement process for the entire Middle East conflict, one in which the Palestinians would find a degree of redress and Lebanon a degree of respite. But this did not happen, and Secretary of State Henry Kissinger's "step-by-step" diplomacy pointedly sidestepped the Palestinian question. Thus Lebanon was left in turmoil as conservative and militant forces among the Lebanese, each aided by outside Arab and non-Arab regimes, continued to vie for position. The point of no return may have been reached in April 1973 after an Israeli raid on Beirut in which three Palestinian leaders were murdered and a violent but inconclusive clash between Palestinian guerrillas and Lebanese army units, in which the army failed to dislodge the Palestinians from certain refugee camps near the Beirut airport. From then on it appears that the conservative Maronite leaders, led by former president Camille Chamoun, began preparing for all-out war with the Palestinians and their many Lebanese leftist and Arab nationalist sympathizers. The two precipitating events of the civil war took place in February and March of 1975. One was the ambushing of a bus carrying Palestinians by Lebanese Phalangists; the other was a violent clash at Saida between Lebanese and Palestinian fishermen, on the one hand, and Lebanese army units, on the other. Nineteen months later, in November 1976, the savage fighting and enormous destruction appeared to have ended when a largely Syrian-manned Arab peacekeeping force moved into Lebanon to restore order. Between 40 and 60 thousand Lebanese and Palestinians, nearly all of them innocent civilians, were dead; Beirut's port, commercial center, and several suburbs were in ruins; and the economic and political future of the country was at best problematical. While nearly all prominent leaders on both sides publicly proclaimed their insistence on a reunified Lebanon, some (especially conservative Maronites) spoke privately of the desirability of partitioning the country on grounds that the hostility between the two sides was now too deep for reconciliation.

The dilemma of the post civil war period lay in the fact that while the old system of confessional democracy had proven itself to be totally and disastrously inadequate, the only viable long-term alternative for Lebanon's political development—gradual secularization—seemed virtually impossible to achieve in light of the effects of the civil war itself.

POLITICS AND THE MEN ON HORSEBACK

Introduction

Writing in the early 1960s, Lucian Pye noted that:

> Only a few years ago it was generally assumed that the future of the newly emergent states would be determined largely by the activities of their Westernized intellectuals, their socialistically inclined bureaucrats, their nationalist ruling parties, and possibly their menacing Communist parties. It occurred to few students of the underdeveloped regions that the military might become the critical group in shaping the course of nation-building.[1]

But the unexpected has become the rule, and throughout the Third World military involvement in politics has emerged as standard operating procedure. Now, in few states of *le Tiers Monde* do the men on horseback[2] sit as silent observers of the process of governance; and increasingly they have ridden at full stride into the political arena to capture unmediated control of the reins of state.

To students of Latin America, military involvement in politics is neither a unique nor a new experience, yet even in these Western Hemisphere states of the Third World "[t]he recent decades of rapid change and social crisis . . . [have] brought the armed forces back into a position of political prominence they had not held since the nineteenth century."[3]

Although the number of military coups in the world of the South has been enormous, the forms and functions of military interventions remain varied and the theoretical explanation for their occurrence stands subject to debate. While it can be argued that "[n]o generalizations are likely to reach a useful level of specificity and at the same time embrace all relevant material,"[4] there nonetheless are several general lines of inquiry into the nature of military coups and regimes within the context of development in the Third World which should be understood. Such inquiries focus on the reason, the value, and the results of military intervention in politics.

Political activity by the men on horseback (or, to borrow Samuel Decalo's phrase, the colonels in the command car) within the Third World is often explained in terms of the societal crises of legitimacy and stability. From this broad perspective, it is both the fundamental weakness of the civilian institutions of state and their inability to legitimize their rule which provoke political action on the part of the military. Given the failure or, if one prefers, the instability of civilian regimes, the men on horseback act to fill the void.[5] Underlying this position is the view that ". . . the most important causes of military intervention in politics are not military but political, and reflect not the social and organizational characteristics of the military establishment but the political and institutional structure of the society."[6] In effect, Third World countries are often seen as praetorian states (an idea rooted in the historical role of the Roman Praetorian Guard) wherein "private ambitions are rarely restrained by a sense of public authority; [and] the role of power (i.e., wealth and force) is maximized."[7]

The first essay in this section, Perlmutter's "The Praetorian State and the Praetorian Army," is a basic statement of this perspective. To Perlmutter, "a modern praetorian government may develop when civilian institutions lack legitimacy or are in a position to be dominated by the military." Thus, a modern praetorian state is a state in which the political processes at work (including the civilian government's inability to successfully pursue "nationalist-modernist goals") favor the emergence of the military as the "core group" in the political arena.

While Perlmutter concentrates on the Middle East and North Africa, his discussion of praetorianism as representative of "certain stages of development" and his analysis of the social and political conditions contributing to a praetorian state clearly have wide applicability throughout the Third World.

However, despite both the utility and seductiveness of the position which finds the reason for military intervention in the pull effect of systemic weakness and the interrelated push effect of military organization (i.e., the "characteristics of professionalism, nationalism, cohesion, and austerity" that impel the armed forces "to move into the political arena and to rescue the state . . ."[8]), the logic of that position is not without its difficulties and its critics. Samuel Decalo, for example, writing on the African experience has argued that: "It is both simplistic and empirically erroneous to relegate coups in Africa to the status of a dependent variable, a function of the political weakness and structural fragility of African states and the failings of African civilian elites."[9]

Without overemphasizing the "personal" element as the source of military intervention, as does Decalo, Bienen's essay in this section, "Military and Society in East Africa," raises several questions about the overall validity of the praetorian mode of analysis for our understanding of the action of Third World armed forces in the arena of politics. Primarily, Bienen expresses the view that we must be extremely careful not to "overhomogenize" Third World states and neglect what can be termed idiosyncratic factors.

In short, then, the praetorian and idiosyncratic perspectives on the reasons for military intervention in politics need not be viewed dichotomously. While the focal point of each perspective is different, the two views can be combined to complement one another. For example, S. E. Finer, in a volume from which part of our section title is borrowed, notes that the reasons for military intervention are found in two sets of forces: "The capacity and propensity [or disposition] of the military to intervene, and the conditions in the society in which it [the military] operates."[10] In line with the former set of forces, Finer further states that the military's disposition to intervene can be explored in terms of five, mutually non-exclusive motivations which range from the defense of the *national interest* and *class interests*, to the pursuit or maintenance of *corporate/military self-interests, particularistic/ethno-regional interests,* and *personal/individualistic interests.*[11]

to intervene based on the military's brokerage involvement in politics, for our purposes two major propositions stand out. The first is that within the Third World there exists a variety of reasons for military intervention in politics, with certain reasons being paramount in specific cases. The second is that in all cases it is of the greatest importance to examine the position and motivation of the armed forces, the nature of the total societal context, and the linkages that exist between society and the men on horseback.

No less complex a situation surrounds our second line of inquiry into the value of military activity in politics. The analysis of the military as leaders in the Third World has been influenced by two conflicting images.[12] The first image, largely derived from the historical experience of Latin America, is a negative one in which the military is viewed as a retrogressive force in society. The second image, rooted in the optimism of the early 1960s, has a positive orientation wherein the men on horseback are seen as a progressive force for modernization and development. This latter image looks to the military as a modern organization (and its officers as modern men) to act as an agency of progressive change in the Third World.

From such a viewpoint, the military is considered to be the last chance for the continuance of the processes of state and nation building within a context of instability and fragmentation. The men on horseback not only bring order, but they bring an order which pays homage to the gods of development. Strongly influenced by the role of Kemal Ataturk in post World War I Turkey, this image holds up the men on horseback not as intruders into politics, but rather as the saviors of politics in the Third World.

But if the 1960s witnessed a shift from the negative to the positive image of the value of military intervention, the 1970s have seen the pendulum swing back. It is true, as one of the essays in this section points out, that a military government "... may lead a successful modernization effort," but it is equally true to note that more often than not military regimes have failed in this effort. The "Kemalist achievement" has not been approximated elsewhere; promise and performance have remained on two separate planes.

Inquiries into the value of military intervention clearly link up with inquiries into the results of military rule; for it is the empirical study of results which reinforces, or erodes our assumptions of value. While all of the essays in this section address themselves somewhat to the issue of the results of the military's role and rule in Third World societies, it is the article by McKinlay and Cohan, "A Comparative Analysis of the Political and Economic Performance of Military and Civilian Regimes," which most clearly focuses on this question. Their cross-national aggregate study, which includes the more developed as well as the less developed countries, indicates "that the nature of military regimes cannot be adequately understood in terms of assisting or inhibiting modernization or in terms of a typology based on a simple distinction between military and civilian regimes."

Just as we have come to realize that despite their surface hierarchies, individual military organizations are not monoliths, so too have we increasingly recognized that as an aggregate, military regimes are marked more by diversity than homogeneity. The military, acting either as an arbiter or ruler, has no greater immunity to societal conditions and cleavages than does a civilian regime. And often military intervention, rather than establishing a firm foothold on the difficult path of socio-economic and political transformation, leads to the further corrosion of already fragile institutions and ideas.[13]

Yet whether we approach the political activity of the military from a position of admonishment or approbation, such activity will continue to be of great importance. Whatever its ideological cloak, military involvement in politics will remain a critical factor in the politics of the Third World for some time to come. For even if the military "shares" the reins of power with civilians, the men on horseback will not soon retreat to the barracks. The military coup may be "a method of change that changes little," [14] but it is not a method of change whose end is in sight.

NOTES

1. Lucian Pye, "Armies in the Process of Political Modernization," in John Johnson (ed.), *The Role of the Military in Underdeveloped Countries* (Princeton: Princeton University Press, 1962), p. 69.

2. This phrase is borrowed from S. E. Finer, *The Man on Horseback*, Second Edition (Harmondsworth, England: Penguin Books, 1976).

3. Edwin Lieuwen, "Militarism and Politics in Latin America," in Johnson (ed.), *The Role of the Military*, p. 131.

4. Robert Dowse, "The Military and Political Development," in Colin Leys (ed.), *Politics and Change in Developing Countries* (Cambridge: Cambridge University Press, 1969), p. 217.

5. See Claude Welch, Jr., "The Roots and Implications of Military Intervention," in Welch (ed.), *Soldier and State in Africa* (Evanston: Northwestern University Press, 1970); Claude Welch, Jr. and Arthur Smith (eds.), *Military Role and Rule* (North Scituate, Massachusetts: Duxbury Press, 1974); Morris Janowitz, *The Military in the Political Development of New Nations* (Chicago: The University of Chicago Press, 1964), pp. 75–106; and Gavin Kennedy, *The Military in the Third World* (New York: Charles Scribner's Sons, 1974), pp. 1–154.

6. Samuel Huntington, *Political Order in Changing Societies* (New Haven: Yale University Press, 1968), p. 194.

7. David Rapoport, "A Comparative Theory of Military and Political Types,"

in Samuel Huntington (ed.) *Changing Patterns of Military Politics* (New York: The Free Press, 1962), p. 72.

8. Samuel Decalo, *Coups and Army Rule in Africa* (New Haven: Yale University Press, 1976), p. 12.

9. *Ibid*, p. 13.

10. Finer, *The Man on Horseback*, p. 224.

11. *Ibid*, pp. 229–231.

12. This analysis draws on the work of: Kenneth Grundy, *Conflicting Images of the Military in Africa* (Nairobi: East Africa Publishing House, 1968); Finer, *The Man on Horseback*; Pye "Armies and the Process of Political Modernization;" Henry Bienen, "The Background to Contemporary Study of Militaries and Modernization," in Bienen (ed.), *The Military and Modernization* (Chicago: Aldine-Atherton, 1971); and Decalo, *Coups and Army Rule*.

13. See Eric Nordlinger, "Soldiers in Mufti," *The American Political Science Review*, Vol. LXIV, No. 4 (December 1970); Nordlinger, *Soldiers and Politics* (Englewood Cliffs: Prentice-Hall, 1977); and Henry Bienen (ed.), *The Military Intervenes* (New York: Russell Sage, 1968).

14. Ruth First, *Power in Africa* (Harmondsworth, England: Penguin Books, 1972), p. 22.

The Praetorian State and the Praetorian Army

Toward a Taxonomy of Civil-Military Relations in Developing Polities

Amos Perlmutter*

What was considered an unnatural and deviant phenomenon before 1945 has now become widespread: the active and increasing role of the army in politics. A government dominated by an army was considered "unnatural" not because it was a new phenomenon—it had been recognized by political philosophers from Machiavelli to Mosca—but because some social scientists refused to accept military rule as being as natural as civilian rule. This hesitation of social scientists to study the military has had a variety of causes, ranging from ignorance of historical and political facts to antagonism toward war and the military profession. As recently as the 1930's, military government was identified as the ultimate type of totalitarianism.[1]

Military political interventionism has recurred in the form of coups and countercoups, both successful and unsuccessful, in most Latin American republics, in five independent Arab states, in fourteen new African states, in several Southeast Asian polities, and in Pakistan. These events confirm the historical and political fact that when civilian government is ineffective, the executive is unable to control the military. Many civil-military combinations are possible: the army can take over the government with or without the consent of civilian politicians, on their behalf or against them, in order to eliminate one civilian group and establish another, or to eliminate rivals in the military.

This article is an attempt to classify and explain types of civil-military relations in developing polities. We will examine, analyze, and compare various sets of propositions. Since the Middle East and North Africa is the immediate area of our interest, it will naturally receive a large share of our attention. Several of the propositions emerge from a close study of civil-military relations in the Middle East over a period of several years.

Extending our study beyond the Middle East, we have examined our propositions as they relate to Latin America, Africa, and Southeast Asia. The scope of this article cannot include a comprehensive examination of all the propositions.[2]

* The list of colleagues who have read various versions of this article is too long to include here. I am especially grateful to Professors S. M. Lipset, S. P. Huntington, J. C. Harsanyi, E. Nordlinger, and E. Rosenstein, and to M. D. Feld, L. North, and G. Orren for their great help in clarifying the concepts of this article.

[1] Harold D. Lasswell, "The Garrison State," *American Journal of Sociology*, XLVI (January 1941), 455-468.

[2] I am now engaged in relating the propositions to the cases of twelve states in depth

Toward a Definition of a Modern Praetorian State

In order to establish an analytical model, we must distinguish clearly between historical and modern praetorianism. An example of historical praetorianism would be the action of a small military contingent in the Imperial capital of Rome, who moved to preserve the legitimacy of the empire by defending the Senate against the encroachment of triumphant or rebellious military garrisons marching on the capital.

The influence of the Roman Praetorian Guard was based on three factors: the Guard's monopoly on local military power, the absence of definitive rules of succession, and the prestige of the Roman Senate. In other words, though there was no hard and fast rule as to how the *princeps* was to be chosen, the Senate's decree made him a legitimate ruler. The provincial armies would accept that decision. As the sole resident military force, the Praetorian Guards were able to impose their candidate upon the Senate. They were thus able to manipulate a widely subscribed *concept of legitimacy* and to attain a degree of political influence and power far beyond their actual numerical and military resources. When, however, the provincial armies stumbled upon the secret that emperors need not be made in Rome, the legitimizing powers of the Senate disappeared, and with them the strength of the Praetorians.[3]

Here is the link between historical and modern praetorianism. A modern praetorian state is one in which the military tends to intervene and *potentially* could dominate the political system. The political processes of this state *favor* the development of the military as the core group and the growth of its expectations as a ruling class; its political leadership (as distinguished from bureaucratic, administrative, and managerial leadership) is chiefly recruited from the military, or from groups sympathetic, or at least not antagonistic, to the military. Constitutional changes are effected and sustained by the military, and the army frequently intervenes in the government. In a praetorian state, therefore, the military plays a dominant role in political structures and institutions.

Broadly speaking, a modern praetorian government may develop when civilian institutions lack legitimacy or are in a position to be dominated by the military.

Praetorianism has existed in all historical periods. In view of the general trend toward modernization, it may be said that various types of praetorian-

---

(in four areas), comparing the states along the continuum of praetorianism. (The countries are Mexico, Argentina, Brazil, Turkey, Egypt, Syria, India, Burma, Indonesia, Tunisia, Ghana, and Nigeria.) The propositions are divided into five clusters: (1) the military and society—particularly the transformation from oligarchical to radical praetorianism; (2) military intervention—coups and patterns of military intervention; (3) types of military roles, particularly along the continuum of arbitrator-ruler; (4) the military and modernization-development—whether military rule has brought about *more* or *less* stability than nonmilitary rule; (5) the relationship between military organization and political skill. I have also begun quantitative analyses of qualitative data on military and modernization in five Middle Eastern countries. These analyses will be based on cross-national data (1950-1962) and on quantitative correlations between social, political, and economic indicators and the level and pace of military, economic, and political performances.

[3] I am grateful to my friend M. D. Feld of Harvard University for this analysis, which he has written especially for the benefit of this article.

ism probably represent certain stages of development.[4] At present, praetorianism often appears in states which are in the early and middle stages
of modernization and political mobilization.[5] In underdeveloped states, the
army is propelled into political action when civilian groups fail to legitimize
themselves. The army's presence in civilian affairs indicates the existence
of corruption that is not expected to disappear in the near future;[6] that
material improvements and ideological perspectives do not match; that
traditional institutions are unable to bring about material improvement;
and that modernized elites are incapable of establishing political institutions and structures which will sustain the momentum of social mobilization
and modernization. Moreover, modern institutions which could direct these
changes are difficult to organize because of the traditional orientation of
the people. In the ensuing disorganization, both economy and ideology
suffer setbacks.[7]

The salient characteristic of modern military organizations in developing
policies is their professionalism. The professionalism and institutionalization of the military entails the establishment of military colleges, specialized
training, the formation of a unified professional group and of a national
army. Praetorian conditions are connected with professional military estab-
lishments and structures, some of which are institutionalized ahead of
concomitant political and socioeconomic structures—political parties, par-
liaments, a centralized administrative bureaucracy, national authority, middle classes, and a national ideology. Therefore, corporate professionalism is
not a guarantee against praetorianism. In fact, in praetorian polities the
military interventionists are the professional soldiers, the graduates of the
military academies, whose life career is the army.

[4] David C. Rapoport, "Praetorianism: Government Without Consensus" (unpub. Ph.D.
diss., University of California, Berkeley, 1960), pp. 14-15, defines praetorianism as a
constitutional form of "government without consent." Rapoport's thesis provides an
outstanding theoretical discussion of praetorianism. Although the present essay closely
follows Rapoport's definition of praetorianism, it emphasizes the descriptive aspects
of the subject and foregoes discussions of constitutionalism, consensus, and authority,
which are discussed at length in Rapoport's work.

[5] This essay has been directly influenced by the works of Professor Samuel P. Huntington, especially his seminal essay, "Political Development and Political Decay,"
World Politics, XVIII (April 1965), 386-430. For some time, we have carried on an intellectual dialogue which, I hope, has resulted in a more positive approach to a theory
of civil-military relations in developing polities. Especially excellent is Huntington's
most persuasive chapter, "Praetorianism and Political Decay," in *Political Order in
Changing Societies* (New Haven, 1968), pp. 192-263. He argues there that the concept of
praetorianism becomes a useful operational tool to explain the relationship between
political development and modernization. In our view Huntington's analysis of the role
of political decay in modernizing polities becomes most crucial in the case of
praetorianism.

[6] Huntington's central thesis (the Gap hypothesis) is that political modernization
breeds both political instability and praetorian political order. *Political Order*, pp. 32-39,
53-56. See Gino Germani and Kalman H. Silvert, "Politics, Social Structure and Military
Intervention in Latin America," *Archives européennes de sociologie*, II, No. 1 (1961),
62-81.

[7] The most impressive analysis of breakdown in modernization is found in S. N.
Eisenstadt's extensive studies (by the author's admission, mostly of a preliminary nature)
of the relationship between traditionalism, modernization, and change. See especially
his "Breakdowns of Modernization," *Economic Development and Cultural Change*, XII
(July 1964), 345-367; "Political Modernization: Some Comparative Notes," *International
Journal of Comparative Sociology*, V (March 1964), 3-24; *Modernization and Change*
(Englewood Cliffs, 1966); and "Some Observations on the Dynamics of Tradition,"
Working Paper, Ballagio, July 1968.

Praetorianism occurs when the civilian government comes to a standstill in its pursuit of nationalist and modernist goals (modernization, urbanization, order, unification, and so forth).

Thus, praetorianism is generally associated with the disintegration of an old order and the rise of a decapitated new one. Another distinction between modern and historical (i.e., patriarchal, patrimonial, and *caudillismo* types[8]) praetorianism is that, in the latter, the authority relationship between the military establishment and political order was based on a traditional orientation. In modern praetorianism, authority relationships are based on a legal-rational orientation.

Conditions conducive to a praetorian state may exist even before the army has intervened in politics. However, as these conditions generate other, supporting conditions, which we will discuss later, the chances for military intervention increase.

Social Conditions Contributing to Praetorianism

Low degree of social cohesion In a state with low social cohesion, personal desires and group aims frequently diverge; the formal structure of the state is not buttressed by an informal one; institutions do not develop readily or operate effectively; social control is ineffective; and channels for communication are few. These conditions indicate the lack of meaningful universal symbols that can bind the society together. The syndrome of disintegration of which these conditions are a part is typical in a state in which the traditional patterns of social cohesion have broken down and have not yet been replaced by new ones.[9]

A break in the syndrome of social and economic disorganization is made possible only by the action of a group separated from the society—a revolutionary group, a party, a bureaucracy, or the army. If the ruling civilian leaders lack political experience and symbols of authority, military personnel may be able to manipulate the symbols of their institution to rule and introduce some coherence by force. Although the level of articulateness and sophistication in most cases tends to be lower in military than in civilian leaders, attributes such as impartiality and courage that may accrue to the military may also make the military leaders effective. They may be more able to communicate with the people at large because they

[8] It is most interesting to observe that some of the historical types of praetorianism were also associated with the disintegration of legitimate authority. After patriarchal power had declined, patriarchal praetorianism no longer exercised authority without restraint. The military took over, but only for a short period. In patrimonial (prebureaucratic) political systems, the military became a permanent establishment. Since the military was the most powerful and rational structure after the patrimonial system, it took over when patrimonial legitimacy disintegrated. In the *caudillismo* case, the union of personalism and violence seized the disintegrating patrimonial state apparatus. Under the guise of Republicanism (in Latin America) and Liberalism (in nineteenth-century Spain), the *caudillismo* became the driving force of the new nation. On personal patriarchal and patrimonial types of domination, see Max Weber, *Economy and Society*, III, ed. G. Roth and K. C. Wittich (New York, 1968).

[9] See Nadav Safran, *Egypt in Search of Political Community* (Cambridge, Mass., 1961), p. 2, for an analysis of the consequences of this lack of parallelism in the development of Egypt.

can elicit a psychological response on the symbolic level. And they may be able to overcome the praetorian syndrome to the extent that they maintain some isolation from the divisions of the politically active population and blur the existing lines of cleavage.

The existence of fratricidal classes   In addition to the polarization between the wealthy few and the many poor in underdeveloped countries, a praetorian state may exhibit gradation and variation within these two groups as well as in the middle class (if it exists). The different and unequal groups within all three major social layers—the bottom, the middle, and the top— will therefore tend to conflict. The result is a lack of class consciousness.

The top group is usually divided between traditionalists and modernists. The latter includes landowners who have adopted modern technology. The top-layer division between traditionalists and modernists is paralleled by a bottom-layer division. For example, large foreign-owned industrial enter- prises may employ an urban worker elite. Because of the benefits this elite receives from the system, it is little inclined to suffer the deprivations that political action designed to benefit its less privileged brethren may entail. Yet, it is precisely these elite workers, concentrated in large enterprises, rather than the hundreds of thousands of domestics, shopkeepers' ap- prentices, and others, who technically could be organized.[10]

Such "buying off" of the urban workers who have the greatest potential for being organized for revolutionary action was characteristic of pre- revolutionary China. The phenomenon appears throughout the under- developed world. The urban workers in the large enterprises may be quite well off, but the masses of unemployed, semiemployed, and agricultural workers may live in near subhuman conditions. With reference to the urban workers of Cuba, MacGaffey and Barnett write: "Permanently employed skilled and semi-skilled workers tended to develop a stake in the existing political and economic order. Even those not organized into unions had their interests carefully protected by labor laws. Although they themselves might be denied opportunities for upward social mobility, skilled workers and those at the foreman level were in a position to provide their sons with an education that would enable them to move ahead."[11]

Thus, not only does the underdeveloped society as a whole lack unifying orientations, but its various sectors tend to be further fragmented and incapable of mounting unified action even for the narrower benefits of a particular sector. This is not to argue that similar differences within classes were absent during the developmental process in Western Europe or North America. It merely emphasizes that such divisions are particularly acute in the underdeveloped countries, where social and economic development have been rapid and where many stages of development have occurred simultaneously.

Social polarity and nonconsolidated middle class   The absence of a strong, cohesive, and articulate middle class is another condition for the establish-

[10] See Jean and Simmone Lacouture, *Egypt in Transition* (New York, 1958), pp. 367- 387, for a discussion of divisions of this type in the Egyptian working class.
[11] Wyatt MacGaffey and Clifford R. Barnett, *Cuba* (New Haven, 1962), p. 144.

ment of a praetorian government. This absence is manifested in the polarization of the class structure—the gap between the few rich and the many poor.

Cohesiveness is necessary for the development of political and ideological articulateness. Such articulateness, when combined with socioeconomic power, constitutes the foundation for the political influence of any class. A struggle for power among the different strata of the middle class—the class which historically has acted as the stabilizer of civilian government during modernization—creates conditions beneficial to praetorianism.

The middle classes in most praetorian states are small, weak, ineffective, divided, and politically impotent. In the Middle East, for example, according to Morroe Berger, the middle class in most states amounts to no more than 6 percent of the population, and at the most 10 percent. Berger emphasizes that the composition of this middle class differs from that of the West during its industrialization process. The Middle Easterners of this class are either bureaucrats or small self-employed businessmen. They are rarely employers.[12] Not only is this middle class small, but, since it occupies different types of economic positions, the economic interests of its members diverge. Furthermore, their political interests diverge. Middle-class parties in underdeveloped countries are thus extremely fragmented.

In Latin America (Argentina and Brazil, for instance) we see a large, growing, and more cohesive middle class (10 to 19 percent, 20 percent and more), yet these middle classes are precipitators of military intervention and praetorianism. There is no common denominator between the fratricidal middle classes of the Middle East and the large middle class in Argentina-Brazil except that in Latin America military interventionism assures the middle class of power if and when they fail to come to power by electoral means. In the Middle East the military does not intervene as a class or even as surrogate for the middle class. Preconditions for praetorianism obtain when social classes are *politically* impotent, or when one social class is at least potentially more powerful than the rest.

One could look at the political expectations of middle classes in order to explain military intervention, but praetorianism does not depend solely on the structural weaknesses, fratricide, and political impotence of the middle class. When the middle class looks for political allies, the military class could become its most useful instrument. The chances for the opposite, however, are better.

Recruitment and mobilization of resources Low levels of recruitment for group social action and for mobilization of material resources are further conditions of praetorianism. A state in the transitional stage not only lacks commonly valued patterns of action but also lacks common symbols that contribute to mobilization for social and political action. The most encompassing organization in theory—the government—is supported by only a few divided groups of the inchoate larger social groups. The government thus has difficulty in obtaining support for its activities. Its programs are subverted, and development projects fail. This failure in human mobiliza-

[12] Morroe Berger, "The Middle Class in the Arab World," in Walter Lacqueur, ed. *The Middle East in Transition* (New York, 1958), pp. 63-65.

tion results from the disparate value orientations of groups and members of society.

Material resources, needed by the government as much as human resources, are also withheld from it. Industrialists disguise their profits to cheat on taxation, bureaucrats take bribes, peasants hoard. The withholding of resources may take many forms but the result is always the same—the developmental activities of the government are subverted.[13]

Political Conditions Contributing to Praetorianism

Center and periphery[14]   On the whole, the roles of intellectuals, scholars, bureaucrats, merchants, colonial administrators, and modernizing elites have been centralized in developing polities. An affirmative attitude toward establishing authority "imposes the central value system of that society."[15] The whole movement of modernization has revolved around the authority of the center. The conflict between the center and the periphery has been overlooked by nationalist leaders and their modernizing elites, as it has been by colonial administrators. Modernizing groups have invested greater intellectual efforts, administrative craftsmanship, and wealth into the center. In the end, the neglected periphery retaliates. Several African military coups have occurred when the periphery has struck back against the center, while the center, subject to the onslaught of modernization, is itself torn asunder. The backlash is not wholly traditionalist; the clash is not necessarily between the center and the periphery, but between coalitions of traditionalists and modernizing elites, associated with the center and the periphery, who are manifestly exposed to one another.[16] Here the military organization becomes instrumental—and its characteristic as a mobilizing force is exposed. In cases where the military sides with the periphery (the Alawi-Druze in Syria and the minorities in Nigeria since 1966), the center of authority is challenged by the periphery, which claims that the military is the center. The confrontation is even more bitter when the military organization really represents the center. The military then operates as a mobilizing force in the "gap" (Huntington) between social mobilization and political institutionalization—processes which, again, are attracted toward the center.

Low level of political institutionalization and lack of sustained support for political structures   According to Samuel P. Huntington, "the strength of

[13] For a discussion of the importance of resource accumulation and use by the political institutions, see S. N. Eisenstadt, *The Political Systems of Empires* (London, 1963), esp. Chs. 6, 7. For Eisenstadt, the promotion of ". . . free resources and . . . [the] freeing [of] resources from commitments to particularistic-ascriptive groups . . ." is one of the conditions for the creation and maintenance of autonomous political institutions. P. 119.

[14] These ideas are borrowed from Edward Shils' seminal studies on ideology and civility. See "Primordial, Personal, Sacred and Civil Ties," *British Journal of Sociology,* VIII (June 1957) 130-146; "Ideology, Center and Periphery," in *The Logic of Personal Knowledge* (Glencoe, 1961), pp. 117-130. A parallel interpretation of the role of primordial forces in the process of political integration is given by Clifford Geertz, "The Integrative Revolution," in Clifford Geertz, ed. *Old Societies and New States* (Glencoe, 1963).

[15] Shils, "Ideology, Center and Periphery," p. 117.

[16] See Aristide R. Zolberg, *Creating Political Order* (Chicago, 1966).

political organizations and procedures varies with their *scope of support* and their *level of institutionalization*."[17] In praetorian states the level of support for political organizations—that is, the number and diversity of the members of such organizations—is low. Thus, the political parties tend to be fragmented, each supported by different social groups which in themselves are not cohesive. The labor movement is similarly fragmented: each category of worker belongs to a different union, and the unions are distrustful of one another. This phenomenon is a political manifestation of the lack of social cohesion discussed above.

The level of institutionalization—that is, the degree to which political organizations develop their own traditions and the extent to which these organizations act autonomously—is also low in praetorian states. Traditional political institutions, incapable of dealing with social and economic changes, have been eliminated and new institutions are not yet accepted as legitimate. Their legitimacy is often hampered by the degree to which they represent particular interests, because their values belong to a small group and are not the autonomous values of the institutions. Huntington notes also the frequency of military intervention in states in which institutionalization has not taken place.[18]

Although a state may exhibit most social characteristics of praetorianism, its political institutions and procedures may have a relatively high degree of stability. If so, the political institutions themselves will be able to act upon the society, and army intervention in constitutional changes will be rare. Such a state is not praetorian, but it may become so. India is a nonpraetorian nation that fits this description. Again it must be emphasized that the presence of some praetorian conditions does not necessarily lead to army intervention. Conversely, army intervention may occur even though some praetorian conditions are missing.

Weak and ineffective political parties Weak and ineffective political parties manifest a low level of political institutionalization. This condition deserves special mention because strong parties have been the most successful agents of comprehensive modernization and industrialization and of the resulting elimination of conditions that lead to praetorianism. Strong parties need not be totalitarian; they can include pluralistic groups, as do the *Partido Revolucionario Institucional* (PRI) of Mexico and India's Congress Party.

Few underdeveloped countries have strong parties of the pluralistic type. In Egypt, the Wafd party was captured by land-owning interests and lost the support of other politically articulate and more progressive forces. Similarly, in Peru, *Alianza Popular Revolucionaria de América* (Apra) has tended to lose its acceptance among the masses because it has increasingly represented the interests of the newly-arrived middle class. When such politically ineffective parties more and more represent particular interests, their leaders become less capable of promoting projects necessary for the economic growth and integration of their countries. Many underdeveloped countries do not have parties even of the low degree of effectiveness and strength of the Wafd and Apra.

17 Huntington, "Political Development," 394.
18 Ibid.

Frequent civilian intervention in the military   Military intervention into civilian affairs is usually not precipitated by military groups. In most cases, civilians turn to the military for political support when civilian political structures and institutions fail, when factionalism develops, and when constitutional means for the conduct of political action are lacking. The civilians therefore begin to indoctrinate the military with their political ideologies. Several examples of this process can be found in the Middle East and Latin America.

In Turkey, the Committee for Union and Progress, founded by the Young Turks, brought about the revolution in 1908 which helped the Young Turk movement to power. More recently, the People's party, or at least affiliations among the officers, intervened indirectly in the Turkish coups of 1960-1961. Prime Minister Menderes, head of the Justice party, interfered in military affairs and meddled with military appointments. Elsewhere in the Middle East the politicization of the military was begun by extremist nationalist politicians. The Iraqi nationalists, led by the socialist Ahali group, perpetrated a series of coups and countercoups in Iraq between 1936 and 1940. Since its initial participation, the army has not withdrawn from the political scene: between 1940 and 1958 it contributed to the establishment and maintenance of a relatively stable government under the oppressive measures of Nuri al-Sa'id.

The Muslim Brotherhood and Young Egypt (Misr al Fatat)—nationalist and fascist movements—have collaborated with Egyptian army officers since the late 1930's.[19] The Ba'th party and the Arab Socialist party, led by the latter's founder, the Syrian nationalist Akram Haurani, changed the Syrian army from an obscure colonial force into the most militant nationalist force in the country. Since that time, only two Syrian coups in more than twenty (successful and unsuccessful) were neither initiated nor sponsored by the new Arab Ba'th Socialist party that emerged from the union of the two original parties.

A similar pattern of politicization of military officers by civilian groups emerged in Latin America.[20] The politicization of the military in twentieth-century Latin America has been precipitated by middle-class parties. According to José Nun, a divided middle class has provoked military intervention (the military being the best organized institution of middle-class origin) to protect class interests when they have been threatened by a ruling oligarchy or by working-class organizations.

[19] On Muslim Brotherhood-army relationships, see Richard P. Mitchell, "The Society of the Muslim Brothers" (unpub. Ph.D. diss., Princeton University, 1960), pp. 61-250; Ishak Musa Husaini, *The Moslem Brethren* (Beirut, 1956), pp. 125-130; Eleizer Beeri, "On the History of the Free Officers," *The New East (Hamizrah Hehadash)*, XIII, No. 51 (1963), 247-268; Kamil Isma'il al-Sharif, *al-Ikhwan al-Muslimin Fi Harb-Filastin (The Muslim Brotherhood in the Palestine War)* (Cairo, 1951); J. and S. Lacouture, *Egypt*, pp. 131 ff. On relationships between Free Officers, Egypt, and the Axis, see Lukasz Hirszowicz, *The Third Reich and the Arab East* (London, 1966), pp. 229-249.

[20] José Nun, "A Latin American Phenomenon: The Middle Class Military Coup," in *Trends in Social Science Research in Latin American Studies: A Conference Report* (Berkeley, 1965); and Liisa North, *Civil-Military Relations in Argentina, Chile, and Peru* (Berkeley, 1966). For a related argument concerning the military and the "new" middle class in the Middle East, see Manfred Halpern, "Middle Eastern Armies and the New Middle Class," in John J. Johnson, ed. *The Role of the Military in Underdeveloped Countries* (Princeton, 1962), pp. 277-315.

The factors mentioned in connection with civilian politicization of the military are general conditions for praetorianism. Other factors—defeat in war,[21] death of a powerful army leader, foreign intervention, and conflicts among senior and junior officers—are secondary causes. If the primary conditions are absent, these secondary causes alone cannot bring about a praetorian state.

The Praetorian Army

The code of the professional army dictates that promotions be determined by ability, expertise, and education. In reality, such principles of professionalization are not well inculcated or observed. Character (i.e., class) or political leanings often overrule expertise in the selection and promotion of officers. In some cases, professional standards do not exist, either because the praetorian army does not have a professional tradition or because the tradition has deteriorated. For example, in Argentina at the end of the nineteenth century, "institutional formal norms were never sufficiently enforced for the maintenance of discipline. Personal relationships and political affiliations remained major factors in the preservation of cohesion within the army and its control by civilian governments."[22] In the Imperial German army, the emphasis on aristocracy and the distrust of the bourgeoisie made character take precedence over intellect as a criterion for officer selection.[23]

Today, army affairs have become intertwined with politics. In Argentina, for example, appointments and promotions still are made on the basis of the political affiliations of the officer rather than on his professional qualifications. The officer's career is insecure, and in order to advance in the military hierarchy, he must establish political alliances with key superiors.

Political activity is contrary to the professional ethics and standards of the modern military, and yet, even in praetorian states, the remnants of professionalism may survive to the extent that conflicts arise between political activity and formally adopted professional norms. Often, however, these conflicts merely deepen the political involvements of the officers by drawing a widening circle of political activists from the officer corps. The officer corps, therefore, tends to break into factions and cliques.

Army coups in Iraqi politics between 1936 and 1941 illustrate this tendency. They eliminated moderate political leadership and transformed the government into a military dictatorship although, by itself, no single group in the army was capable of sustaining army rule. The army's inability to sustain its rule resulted in the assassination of such key military leaders as Bakr Sidqi and Ja'far al-'Askari. The military coups in Iraq left the army divided. Although the army became the single deciding factor in the political life of Iraq between 1936 and 1941, it could not serve as an effective and stabilizing alternative to the regimes and cabinets that it had toppled.

[21] See Edward A. Shils and Morris Janowitz, "Cohesion and Disintegration in the Wehrmacht in World War II," *Public Opinion Quarterly,* XII (Summer 1948), 288-292. Shils and Janowitz demonstrated that the defeat and disintegration of the Wehrmacht were due to the collapse of primary-group cohesion.

[22] North, p. 17.

[23] R. Kitchen, *The German Officer Corps, 1890-1914* (Oxford, 1968), pp. 28-32.

In fact, the army turned into a source of political instability as it sought to replace cabinets that were "corrupt" or "collaborating" with the British. Iraq inaugurated the first praetorian army in the Middle East since the Young Turk army intervention in 1908, and Iraq was looked upon by many Arab ideological groupings as the future Arab Prussia.[24] Curiously enough, the political failures of the Iraqi army did not discourage Middle Eastern praetorian armies, including the Iraqi army itself. Since the 1958 coup the Iraqi army has returned to its former practices, eliminating civilian politicians from left to right as well as decimating its own ranks. Since 1958, the Iraqi army has propelled Iraq into a praetorian syndrome from which there seems to be little chance for return to civilian rule or stability.[25]

A decade after the army's political debacles in Iraq, the Syrian army chose a similar pattern, and it became notorious for mixing internal army rivalries with politics. There are many examples of ambitious Syrian army officers, especially the Ba'thist (steadily growing in strength among senior officers), who have eliminated their army rivals by allying with a Ba'th faction that these rivals oppose, or, especially since the left Ba'th party's rise to power in 1966, who have created a wedge between rival Ba'th factions to advance personal causes and have finally achieved a complete takeover of the Ba'th by the army, which represents the extreme wing of the Ba'th. This wing was overthrown in the 1969 coup, and the army, run by Alawi officers, has finally destroyed the Ba'th left wing. This, of course, does not preclude the reemergence of the left under the aegis of another officer.

Finally, the divisiveness and political involvement of the officers may be abetted by foreign intervention—such as the counterinsurgency training and military aid of the United States in Latin America[26] and Egypt's intervention in the internal rivalries of the Syrian, Iraqi, Yemeni, and Jordanian armies.

Two Types of Praetorian Armies

The two basic types of praetorian armies are the arbitrator-type and the ruler-type. The former tends to be more professionally oriented (with a greater emphasis on expertise) and has no independent political organization and little interest in manufacturing a political ideology. The latter has an independent political organization (an instrument for maintaining order) and, in most cases, a fairly coherent and elaborate political ideology.

The arbitrator-type army imposes a time limit on army rule and arranges to hand the government over to an "acceptable" civilian regime. The arbitrator-type army does not necessarily relinquish its political influence when it returns to the barracks; in fact, in many cases, it acts as guardian of civilian authority and political stability. Such is the essence of the Kemalist legacy in Turkey: the army serves as the guardian of the constitution.[27]

[24] Majid Khadduri, *Independent Iraq: A Study in Iraqi Politics from 1932-1958*, 2d ed. (London, 1960), pp. 124-125.

[25] Uriel Dann, *Iraq Under Qassem* (Jerusalem, 1969).

[26] See Irving Louis Horowitz, "The Military in Latin America," in Seymour Martin Lipset and Aldo Solari, eds. *Elites in Latin America* (London, 1966).

[27] The transformation of army rebels of 1960-1961 into permanent senators only reiterates the persistence of the Kemalist legacy in Turkey, at least as of 1967.

The army of Brazil similarly defends the constitution.[28] A time limit was imposed by Generals Nagib of Egypt (1952-1954) and Abboud of the Sudan (1958-1963); it may yet be imposed by General Ayub Khan of Pakistan (since 1958) and possibly by the Burmese military group. It is essential that the arbitrator rule in cooperation with civilians ("non-corrupt") and that his source of political power not be in the barracks.

An arbitrator army may eventually become a ruler army, if the conditions for the return of a civilian regime are not fulfilled. It is even possible for a ruler army eventually to turn the reins of power over to a civilian regime, if the conditions for the return of civilian rule are fulfilled. Although the arbitrator army is committed to a time limit, the ruler army is not. The arbitrator army expects an eventual return to the barracks; the ruler army makes no such provision and, in most cases, does not even consider it.

When civilian political viewpoints are first diffused within an officer corps, ideological divisions tend to develop. Later, one political orientation may succeed in becoming dominant. This orientation may or may not parallel that of some civilian group. Thus, given extreme conditions for praetorianism, the arbitrator will become the ruler.

The arbitrator-type tends to preserve military expertise; it is conservative and, on the whole, tends to maximize civilian power.[29] The ruler-type, although it does not abandon expertise, sometimes subordinates it to political considerations and may even support an already existing political ideology. It sacrifices professionalism to political expediency. In general, the ruler-type prefers to maximize an army ruler. It is imperative that he rule with the help of the army. A radical ruler dominates only with the help of the army and always at the expense of civilian rule and politicians.

Both types are ideologically committed, and here, too, the differences between them depend on their attitudes toward their role in politics and on the state of praetorian conditions in the respective polity. Since the ruler army usually has an independent political organization, it tends to manufacture an ideology to legitimize its rule. It identifies with a popular ideology manufactured elsewhere, or with symbols such as "nation," "progress," "modernization," and so forth.

Although the arbitrator army tends to be more conservative than the ruler army, we find ideologically motivated radicals and conservatives in each. Thus, the two types can be placed on a left-right continuum. The actions of either type are conditioned by three factors: (1) the internal structure of the army and the extent to which it has developed an identifiable political consciousness, organization, and autonomy; (2) interaction with civilian politicians and structures; and (3) the type of political order that the army desires to eliminate and the type of political order that it wishes to establish (or reject, if it has no alternative regime in mind).

Although the present analysis treats the civilian and military spheres of action analytically as independent variables in conflict and interaction, the military organization cannot be fully divorced from the civilian social con-

[28] Charles Simmons, "The Rise of the Brazilian Military Class, 1840-1890," *Mid-America*, XXXIX (October 1957), 227-238.
[29] Samuel P. Huntington, *The Soldier and the State: The Theory and Politics of Civil-Military Relations* (New York, 1964), pp. 80-81, 93-94.

text that determines civilian politics. Initially, the political commitments and ideological positions of the military in the praetorian state are sustained either by the civilian politicians who encourage the army to enter politics, or by the general, sociopolitical, civilian context. After a certain level of political involvement has been attained, officers can then influence positions taken by civilian politicians. This development has been true of the Ba'th party in Syria, which originally infiltrated the army to avoid losing its support and which now shares the same goals as the army. The more fully the army is immersed in politics, and the greater is its desire to change the sociopolitical context, the greater are the chances for political instability.

An army may display most characteristics of the ruler-type army—including a well-articulated ideology to which the officer corps adheres—*without* actually ruling. An example of this situation is the Peruvian army.[30] In such a case, the army presents a unified point of view and acts as the stabilizer of civilian governments that hold views similar to its own.

The arbitrator-type of praetorian army   The arbitrator-type army has several distinguishing characteristics which we will now describe.

Acceptance of existing social order   In an underdeveloped country, acceptance of the existing order often implies antirevolutionary ideology. Thus, the arbitrator-type army may be the instrument of conservative and antiliberal forces as, for example, were the Ottoman army before the 1908 coups and the Iraqi army in the 1920's.[31] The Argentine military establishment has displayed an arbitrating orientation since the fall of Juan Perón in 1955; it has been anti-leftist and, especially, anti-Castro.[32] Traditional Latin American *caudillismo* may also serve as an example because the *caudillos* usually do not attempt to change the social order.[33] On the other hand, the arbitrator-type army may ally itself with labor, as Perón did in Argentina. Huntington demonstrates patterns of civil-military alliances where the military allies with nonconservative forces.[34] On the basis of military interventionism in the Middle East, we propose that the radicalization of the society and the army eliminates the chances for an arbitrator-type and that a radical-army coalition brings a ruler-type to power (Egypt, 1952-1954). On the whole, a ruler-type implies structural reforms in society and formation of a new bureaucracy; in the case of arbitrators, there is little fundamental change in regime and society.

Willingness to return to the barracks after civilian disputes are settled   The officers of the arbitrator-type army are civilian-oriented. Even where the civilian groups are not organized enough to set up a government, and where officers occupy positions in the government, the officers obey the instructions of civilian political groups. They do not inject their own viewpoint. They desire to return to normality, which means that they accept the status

[30] North, pp. 52-57.
[31] Khadduri, pp. 78-80.
[32] Kalman H. Silvert, "The Costs of Anti-Nationalism: Argentina," in Kalman H. Silvert, ed. *Expectant Peoples* (New York, 1963), pp. 366-369.
[33] North, pp. 1-10.
[34] Huntington, *Political Order*, pp. 219-237.

quo. The arbitrator-type army returns to the barracks because its officers are aware that they lack the skills to govern and are content to avoid further political involvement.

An example of a return-to-the-barracks army is the Chilean military from 1924 to 1933. When officers participated in politics because civilian political groups had become disorganized, the participation was limited, and the professional norms of the military establishment were largely retained even during periods of fairly deep involvement.[35]

No independent political organization and no attempt to maximize army rule This point can be illustrated by examples from Egypt, Iraq, and elsewhere.

General Nagib of Egypt (1952-1954), who was recruited by Nasser and the Society of Free Officers as early as 1951 to head the list of Free Officers in the elections for the administrative committee of the Officers' Club, had no political organization of his own.[36] He was not a charter member of the Free Officers, but he was chosen from among three candidates to become the titular head of the 1952 coup.[37] Lacking the support of a political organization of his own, Nagib was finally ousted in 1954 by the Free Officers' political organization, the Revolutionary Command Council (RCC), which was the executive committee of the Free Officers' first political party, the Liberation Rally.[38] Nagib had made efforts to maximize civilian participation in the RCC cabinet and had opposed the policy of Nasser and the RCC to legitimize the military dictatorship.

In Iraq, the officers responsible for the first coup d'état of October 29, 1936, led by General Bakr Sidqi, had no political organization of their own. After Bakr Sidqi's assassination they were left leaderless and divided. The coup was followed by a countercoup, and that one by several military coups, until a civilian government was finally established in 1941.[39]

Time limit for the rule of the army until an alternative and "acceptable" regime is established The arbitrator-type army will return to the barracks if it is assured that corruption and other evils of the former regime have been eliminated. This type views prolonged army rule as detrimental to the professional integrity of the army. The arbitrator army encourages political groups which it considers capable of establishing order, preserving stability, and guaranteeing that the new government will not return to the practice of the old.

The existence of organized civilian groups has a bearing on the army's decision to surrender its rule. Where no such groups exist—that is, in a state of near anarchy—the arbitrator-type army may continue to govern despite its civilian orientation and its desire to return to its own affairs. In such a situation the arbitrator army continues to govern by default, because it is the only organized group in the state. Where organized civilian

[35] North, pp. 34-37.

[36] Lacouture, pp. 144-145.

[37] Eleizer Beeri, *The Officer Class in Politics and Society of the Arab East (Ha-Ktzuna ve-hashilton Ba-Olam ha-Aravi)* (Israel, 1966), pp. 78-80.

[38] Shimon Shamir, "Five Years of the Liberation Rally," *The New East (Hamizrah Hedadash)*, VIII, No. 4 (1957), 274.

[39] Khadduri, pp. 76-80, 126 ff.

groups do exist, the military as a whole withdraws from the government, although at times a key military figure will continue as chief of state. Thus, in Chile, Ibañez, an officer, was chief of state in the late 1920's and early 1930's, but the military institution as a whole was not politically involved.[40]

Concern with professionalism   In an arbitrator-type army, the officer corps, or important sectors of it, is strongly opposed to political involvement because involvement may destroy the professional norms of the military institution. Professional norms are valued because they provide security and predictability for the officer's career. When we speak of professionalism here, we mean corporateness. We do not refer to the collective sense that arises from organic, professional unity and consciousness,[41] but rather to the "military mind" and Huntington's definition of the military ethic.[42] Professionalism here is related to the *political* attitude of the military. Unlike lawyers and physicians, soldiers depend upon the state for security. Because a change of regime may threaten its position, the military is usually extremely sensitive to political change. The civil service, likewise dependent on the state, is also politically sensitive; but it has little physical power—the element which places soldiers in office. The arbitrator-type tends to defend the existing regime, lest its professional integrity be violated. In fact, this type may intervene to protect the military against the threat posed by a disintegrating or unstable regime.

Tendency to operate from behind the scenes as a pressure group   Because of its fear of open involvement in politics, the arbitrator-type army tends to influence civilian governments to respond to popular demands, thereby making it unnecessary for the military to intervene openly. However, the refusal by the military to take open responsibility for its actions may increase instability. The arbitrator army constitutes "power divorced from responsibility";[43] moreover, since the arbitrator-type officer corps lacks cohesion, factionalism may result or existing factionalism may be aggravated. This factionalization may then lead to a pattern of coup and countercoup which makes little sense to an outside observer, because the frequent changes in government are not accompanied by changes in policies but reflect instead personal rivalries in the officer corps. Most of the unsuccessful coups in Syria have been of this type, and the number of opportunistic officers has increased since the collapse of the United Arab Republic in 1961. The Ba'th party, since coming to power in 1963, has become an avenue of advancement for ambitious officers.

Civilians usually are also involved in these personalistic cliques and attempt to use them for their own ends. Such entanglements may result in a vicious circle: civilian action tends to deepen military cliquishness, and vice versa, because the mixing of army and civilian motives blurs the separation of the army from the civilian sociopolitical context and results in the army's inability to change the political situation. This pattern has ap-

[40] North, pp. 34-37.
[41] Huntington, *The Soldier,* pp. 10-11.
[42] Ibid., Ch. 3, pp. 59-79.
[43] Dankwart A. Rustow, "The Military in Middle Eastern Society and Politics," in Sydney Nettleton Fisher, ed. *The Military in the Middle East* (Columbus, 1963), pp. 34-37.

peared in the Latin American sequences of coups d'état *(cuartelazos)*.[44] More recently, it has manifested itself in Syria under the rule of the leftist Ba'th officers who have governed there since the coup of February 26, 1966.[45]

Low level of national consciousness On the whole, this type of military has a low level of national consciousness and identification. The absence of such attitudes characterized Arab officers in the Ottoman army before the turn of the century, Circassian and Turkish officers in Muhammad 'Ali's army, the nineteenth-century Latin American *caudillo* type, Kurdish and Assyrian officers in the Iraqi army before 1936, Druze, 'Alawi, and Ismai'li officers in the Syrian army before independence in 1945, Bedouin officers in the Jordanian Arab Legion until 1956, and Druze officers in the Israeli army.

Fear of civilian retribution Such a fear was apparent in General Gürsel's attitude during the 1960-1961 coup in Turkey.[46] The presence of organized civilian groups may produce fears in the military concerning the actions that civilian politicians might later take—such as the dismissal of officers, demotions, unprestigious appointments and assignments. Moreover, if an army has become unpopular because of repressive measures, and especially if the soldiers have been recruited from the native population, doubts about the civilian population's willingness to follow its orders may cause the army to withdraw, fearing violent mass action as well as civilian political retribution.

The ruler-type of praetorian army The ruler-type of praetorian army has characteristics that oppose those of the arbitrator-type.

The officer corps rejects the existing order and challenges its legitimacy. Throughout developing countries, traditional parliamentary politics and liberalism have become identified with status quo politics. The ruler type of praetorian army increasingly tends to abandon or convert existing institutions, ideologies, and procedures in favor of the newer institutions for modernization, industrialization, and political mobilization that are proposed by theories of rapid growth. To nonconservative praetorians, these new theories are more suitable for altering traditional institutions than are the old and "corrupt" ideologies of traditional liberalism and parliamentarianism. But they also reject as corrupt those radical-revolutionary civilian regimes which favor rapid modernization under a one-party system. Thus, the ruler-type officers oppose both the political corruption of the traditional parliamentary liberal regimes and some of the modernizing authoritarian one-party systems. Their opposition does not mean that the officers are revolutionaries; rather, they tend to be reformers, and their

[44] See George Blanksten, *Ecuador: Constitutions and Caudillos* (Berkeley and Los Angeles, 1951), pp. 51-54, for a discussion of this phenomenon. For Latin American cases of this type, see L. N. McAlister, "Civil-Military Relations in Latin America," *Journal of Inter-American Studies* (July 3, 1961), pp. 342-343.

[45] Amos Perlmutter, "From Opposition to Rule: The Syrian Army and the Ba'th Party," *Western Political Quarterly*, forthcoming.

[46] See Walter F. Weiker, *The Turkish Revolution 1960-1961* (Washington, 1963), for a complete discussion of this event.

sometimes self-proclaimed conversion to revolutionary causes is likely to be much more superficial than their conversion to anticonservatism.[47] Of all reformist groups in the state, the army tends to be least reformist. As a reformer it may be adamantly opposed to Communism or, as in contemporary Latin America, to Castro. In Peru, the military in general has opposed the local revolutionary party (Apra), but this has not prevented reform orientation in the army.[48]

Thus, we can distinguish at least three subtypes of the ruler army that reject the existing order and challenge its legitimacy: (1) *the antitraditionalist radical reformer army*, represented by the regimes of 'Abd al-Karim Qasim in Iraq (1958-1963) and Juan Perón in Argentina (1945-1955); (2) *the antitraditionalist antiradical reformer army*, represented by the military regimes of Gamal Abdel Nasser in Egypt (since 1952), Houari Boumedienne in Algeria (since 1965), General Suharto in Indonesia (since 1965), the army junta in Ghana (since 1966), and the anti-Castro, anti-Communist military rulers in Latin America; and (3) *the antitraditionalist republican reformer army*, represented by Mustafa Kemal (Ataturk) of Turkey (1919-1923) and Ayub Khan of Pakistan (since 1958).

With these subtypes in mind, we can place the praetorian type on a left-right continuum linked to political order. The ruler army chooses the new political order as a reaction to that order which it has replaced. Therefore, the ideology of the praetorian army depends on the nature of the ideology it has rejected. Choice here is rather limited; it will depend on what means the army takes to transform society into "something else," most often into something initially unknown to the army. It took Nasser a decade to opt for Arab Socialism; in that period it was clearer to him what political system to destroy than what political system he ought to create.

Thus, Nasser is more leftist than the Wafd, just as Ayub Khan is more radical than the old Muslim League party. Boumedienne is to the right of Ben Bella, and Suharto is to the right of Sukarno. "Basic democracy" in Pakistan grew as an alternative to the regime it replaced. Although the Pakistani army, as an offshoot of the British Indian army, had kept aloof from politics, the need for reform and modernization enhanced its propensity for institutional autonomy and made a temporary ruler of a professional and antitraditionalist reformer like Ayub Khan, who had been dedicated to military professionalism and maximizing civilian rule.[49] Ayub Khan, imbued with the British Civil Service tradition, chose to blend a very modified version of British democracy with the "military mind" and the political reality of Pakistan. The resulting mixture of traditional values and professionalism brought forth the concept of "basic democracy"—the ideology of the Pakistani army since 1958.[50]

[47] Huntington, *The Soldier*, pp. 93-94, discusses briefly the conservatism of the professional officer, albeit in nonpraetorian states.

[48] See Richard Patch, "The Peruvian Elections of 1962 and Their Annulment," *American Universities Field Staff Reports* (West Coast South America Series), IX (September 1962), 6.

[49] Huntington, *The Soldier*, pp. 83-85.

[50] For an analysis on parallel lines, emphasizing the role of the army as the bearer of explicit political norms and images, see Moshe Lissak, "Modernization and Role-Expansion of the Military in Developing Countries: A Comparative Analysis," *Comparative Studies in Society and History*, IX (April 1967), 249-255.

Houari Boumedienne rejected the radicalism of Ben Bella's regime. However, he has not abandoned Arab Socialism, but has merely reduced its ideological intensity and commitments. In this process he has become an antiradical type of ruler. Although he has so far adopted no ideology of his own, by eliminating the Ben Bella legacy he has moved toward the modernization of Algeria without Ben-Bellist radicalism.

In Indonesia, the army since the 1965 Communist coup has been liquidating the old regime, whereas Sukarno's "guided democracy" had radicalized it. The political evolution of the Indonesian army[51] indicates that, even if it does not offer an alternative ideology, it may proceed along the lines of a modified guided democracy without the vehemence, the radicalism, and the messianism that marked the reign of President Sukarno.

The Ghanaian military junta has been acting as a temporary ruler since 1966. It has presided over the dissolution of Nkrumah's radical-socialist and mobilization system. It also has decided in favor of modernization without radicalism and eventual return to the barracks.

No confidence in civilian rule and no expectation of returning to the barracks This attitude may be a consequence of the development by an important sector of the officer corps of an independent political orientation opposed to the ruling civilian groups. Alternatively, civilian disorganization may have reached the point where progressive elements are unable to put their programs into effect. Ruler-type officers distrust politicians to the extent that they themselves feel it necessary to occupy formal positions in the governmental structure. Thus, by the time the ruler army intervenes, the civilians have already manifested their inability to control the situation. In Egypt, for example, officers blamed civilians for the Palestinian crisis and for the Cairo riots of January 1952, and they did not even trust those civilians—such as the more radical members of the Wafd or the Muslim Brotherhood—who held political philosophies similar to their own.

In the early 1950's, after a number of years of civil war, the Colombian army led by Rojas Pinilla lost confidence in civilian rule, took control of the government, and implemented a Perón-type developmental program. When this occurred, only part of the army shared Rojas Pinilla's orientations. Since that time, the army has shown an inclination to adopt developmental ideologies based on technological and evolutionary change. The army may again take over the government of Colombia; as yet it has no confidence in civilian rule.

Political organization and tendency to legitimize and maximize army rule. The ruler-type army considers itself the one elite group capable of governing; therefore, it usually tries to assure the indefinite continuation of army rule by capitalizing on the uncertainty of politics. Taking advantage of the lack of political and social cohesion, the ruler-type army establishes an independent organization and strengthens its rule in order to manipulate unruly, disorganized forces. In order to achieve stability, it must legitimize itself through the creation of its own political party or some type of corporate group and create an ideology to support its political organization.

51 Daniel S. Lev, "The Political Role of the Army in Indonesia," *Pacific Affairs*, XXVI (Winter 1963-1964), 349-364.

In Egypt, the Society of Free Officers, led by Nasser, was officially established in 1949. Its origins date back to 1938-1939. After 1945, the group became active, especially in recruiting allies in the army. Nasser's was not the only political organization in the Egyptian army: the Muslim Brotherhood had organized an army cell led by Mahmud Labib and later by 'Abd al-Mun'im 'Abd al-Ra'uf, and Anwar al-Sadat, who joined Nasser in 1949, had previously headed an army political club of his own.[52]

As far back as the 1930's, Egyptian officers, imbued with the radical nationalist atmosphere of Egypt and inspired and guided by civilians, helped to establish independent political organizations, cells, and secret societies in the army. Most of these organizations were intended to maximize the political consciousness of the officers (this was especially true of Nasser's group, 1949-1952) and, especially, to recruit officers for nationalist political parties and movements. Once in office after the coup, they established a Revolutionary Command Council (RCC) which acted as the executive committee of the Free Officers but was actually the executive arm of the new government run by the army. Almost immediately, the Liberation Rally, the army-dominated party, was established.[53] These organizations illustrate Nasser's attempts to legitimize army rule and its nationalist ideology and to *eliminate* all civilian opposition to the army.

In Syria, Adib Shishakly founded the Arab Liberation Movement in 1952 in order to legitimize the military dictatorship he had established in 1951.[54] Since the coups by Shishakly and Nasser, military coups in the Middle East have followed the precedent of establishing a Revolutionary Command Council to legitimize army rule and eliminate civilian and army opposition. The formation of an RCC does not guarantee the success of this type of army political organization, nor does it guarantee the legitimacy of army rule. However, it gives the army independence in political action and maneuverability where strong civilian organizations exist. Where they do not exist, the army's political party serves to preserve the military dictatorship.

Legitimization of the army as the guarantor of stability and progress does not necessarily imply permanent army rule. In Turkey, the Kemalist legacy serves as a watchdog to prevent the civilian regime from returning to corrupt practices. By civilianizing his regime through the army, Ataturk also legitimized the army's role in politics as the defender and protector of the constitution and of republican and honest civilian rule; in effect, he maximized civilian rule by legitimizing the army as its sole protector. On the other hand, Nasser gave a civilian role to army-created political parties and bureaucracies; this practice has maximized Egypt's modernization and army domination but does not guarantee civilian rule.

An army need not have an ideology or a political organization of its own in order to favor a ruler-type of praetorianism. In Iraq, when the army came to power after the 1958 revolution, like all other national organizations it participated in the struggle between the oligarchs and the new gen-

---

[52] For the most detailed description of Egypt's officer-politicians, see Lacouture, *Egypt*, pp. 125-129, and Beeri, *The Officer Class*, pp. 67-73; also, Anwar al-Sadat, *Revolt on the Nile* (London, 1957), p. 74. See also fn. 19.

[53] Shamir, "Five Years," 261-278.

[54] Patrick Seale, *The Struggle for Syria* (London, 1965), pp. 124-131.

eration, and many military leaders were closely associated with ideological groups. Nevertheless, the army as a separate group never formulated its own set of ideals but merely carried out the programs of other civilian groups under army rule.[55]

It is interesting that, although the army and the Ba'th party in Syria share a common political ideology, they do not hold the same view of army rule. Whereas the Ba'th advocates parliamentary rule, the army prefers a ruler-type of praetorianism. The Febuary 1966 coup indicates the trend toward such army rule: an army faction took over Ba'th's left wing, signifying further attrition of Ba'thist and civilian groups in Syria. In this case, the ideology of a civilian party served to legitimize the rule of the army.

The political consolidation of the Indonesian army occurred when many officers were absorbed into the national elite. They supported Sukarno's "guided democracy" to keep political parties out of power and to weaken the Indonesian Communist party. The army, then, participated in civic action and boosted economic development to compete with the Indonesian Communist party at the grass-roots level. The evolution of the army as a political organization in Indonesia strengthened its ruler-type position. When the Indonesian Communist party struck the army, the army struck back, and since 1965 it has been engaged in dissolving the old order and establishing the new order under army rule.[56]

Conviction that army rule is the only alternative to political disorder This point, a corollary to the preceding three points, is seen clearly in Nasser's political philosophy. In his book *Philosophy of the Revolution*, Nasser argues that "only the army" can meet and solve the praetorian conditions of Egypt and that the army plays the "role of vanguard" in the Egyptian revolution.[57]

This was also the attitude of some of the extreme radical nationalists in the Iraqi army during the late 1930's, among them Salah al-Din al-Sabbagh.[58] His antiforeign and anti-imperialist convictions led him to believe that the army was destined to relieve Iraq and Islam of the yoke of external and internal oppressors.

In 1951, two years after his coup d'état, Adib Shishakly of Syria (1949-1954), after meddling unsuccessfully with bitterly divided civilians, established a military dictatorship. Most army leaders in the Middle East now tend to espouse Shishakly's and Nasser's enterprises. If many still act as arbitrators, especially in Syria, it is more because of the effective opposition of civilian groups and army rivalry than because the army favors civilian rule.

The politicization of professionalism Where the army has—or dominates

55 Khadduri, "The Role of the Military in Iraqi Society," in Fisher, ed. *The Military*, p. 47.

56 I am indebted to Daniel S. Lev for his help in my understanding of the Indonesian army. For most of the points made here on the Indonesian army, see Lev, "The Political Role," 360-364. For the interpretation of Lev's analysis, only I am responsible.

57 Gamal Abdel Nasser, *Egypt's Liberation: The Philosophy of the Revolution* (Washington, 1955), pp. 32-33, 42-45.

58 Khadduri, *Independent Iraq*, pp. 200-206. See Col. Salah al-Din al-Sabbagh, *Fursan al Uruba fi al Iraq (The Knights of Arabhood in Iraq)* (Damascus, 1956), pp. 29-30.

—an independent political organization, however minimal, the ruler-type is common. We have seen that this pattern is widespread in the Middle East. In Latin America, the military neither acts as an autonomous group nor possesses an independent political organization; it acts, rather, as an agent of more powerful social classes or political groups, and here an arbitrator-type is more likely. Thus, in oligarchical praetorianism we often find the ruler-type, whereas in radical praetorianism the arbitrator-type prevails.[59] In the latter case, the military must act in alliance with stronger and better-deployed political groups. In the Middle East, fragmented and impotent social forces are challenged by military organizations, which seem to provide the elements for maintaining order. Thus the military organization becomes a surrogate political structure, at least for the purposes of maintaining an *ad hoc* order and suppressing violence.

When the ruler-type army is committed to political action, it is forced to break with traditional concepts of the professional soldier. Political considerations take precedence over internal organization and career security. When political objectives become paramount, career stability suffers. Politicization will, to some extent, destroy professional status and rank. A low-ranking military officer may, in certain political situations, be superior to an officer of higher rank who is not politically inclined. Such has been the case in the Syrian army since 1966. The politically-involved officer corps must have a set of norms different from those of the nonpolitical officer corps.

The Thai army, which is rooted in the traditional bureaucracy, challenges the thesis that army rulers' political involvement diminishes the professional integrity of the army. Since 1932, "army officers have led the ruling group, dominated the institutions of government, and set the style of Thai politics."[60] But the "style of Thai politics" is bureaucratic. Thus Thailand, whose politics and social structure are bureaucratic[61] and patterned on subordinate-superordinate lines,[62] mixes well with the professional norms of the officer class.

Operation in the open   The ruler-type army operates in the open because it wants to use the symbols attached to the military institutions to gain support for its programs and activities. As Lucian W. Pye points out, the military has both traditional and modern components, and organizationally it is a peculiar combination of the two.[63] The army, therefore, may be quite acceptable to a population for whom it represents a technologically advanced organization. For the traditionalists, the army symbolizes heroic leadership and honor, even though the officers in fact may be technologists and managers. Since the military operates in the open, it can use these symbolic representations, as well as other types of ideological appeals, to obtain popular support. In Pye's words, "The great stress placed on profes-

[59] Huntington, *Political Order*, pp. 208-219.
[60] David A. Wilson, "The Military in Thai Politics," in Johnson, ed. *The Role*, p. 253.
[61] Fred W. Riggs, *Thailand: The Modernization of a Bureaucratic Polity* (Honolulu, 1966).
[62] Wilson, pp. 266-268.
[63] Lucian W. Pye, "Armies in the Process of Political Modernization," in Johnson, ed. *The Role*, p. 75.

sionalism and the extremely explicit standards for individual behavior make the military appear to be a more sacred than secular institution."⁶⁴

High level of national consciousness   In a praetorian country, the commitment to nationalism is more intense in the ruler-type army than in any other section of the population. Ideologically, nationalism is the most popular and most successful common denominator of praetorianism. It can be a rallying point for all civilians and militarists, a point of least rivalry, and a common factor for ideological consolidation. The praetorian ideology is not, however, limited to nationalism. In contrast to the arbitrator-type, whose ideological commitments are lower, the whole spectrum of radical political ideologies has at one time or another been supported by praetorians.

Little fear of civilian retribution   By the time ruler-type praetorianism develops, the army tends to exercise so much power that it does not need to fear civilians. In Egypt the emergence of the army as ruler took place after an extended period of disorganization, growing violence (especially in urban areas), and the manifest failure of civilians to maintain order—not to mention the failure of civilian leadership in constructive development programs. Furthermore, the civilians were incapable of defending Egypt against imperialist powers.

The Praetorian Army as Modernizer and Leader of Political Development
The military has failed in many efforts to establish effective and longlasting political parties or other sustaining political institutions and procedures. Despite his attempts to do so on three separate occasions, Nasser has yet to establish a lasting and viable party. In the states discussed here, we doubt the durability of army-created tutelary political structures—"basic democracy" and, especially, Arab Socialism—beyond the period of army domination and rule.

Tutelary political structures are no guarantee for relieving the praetorian syndrome, although they are established in the hope that political stability and progress may be achieved, at least in the long run. The praetorian armies lack confidence that civilian rule can achieve these goals. Therefore, some tutelary political structures established under military rule have weaknesses similar to those of the political structures they replace, and others are no more than a shadow of the military-dominated state. When a military dictatorship uses the army to determine the dictatorial apparatus, praetorianism merely entrenches itself further.

A military dictatorship may lead a successful modernization effort. In such cases the army, adopting technocratic and scientific orientations, may withdraw from attempts at leading political development. Concentration on technology and science lessens the threat to military dictatorship that might result from the formation of civilian organizations. It is for this reason, perhaps, that Nasser has not abandoned the "philosophy of the revolution" that provides a praetorian political philosophy in which army

⁶⁴ Ibid.

rule converges ideologically with economic and scientific modernization.[65]

The ruler-type army tends to prefer organizational models to political institutions as a system of control. Whereas civilian ideologists search for political utopias, officers seek managerial models to conduct social reform and modernization. The politicized army acts as a bureaucracy. Modernization is clothed in organization. Nasserism, Arab Socialism, and the emerging ideological consolidation of the Peruvian army[66] are thus the ideologies of scientific and organizational models.

The only successful case of a militarily-established political party remains that of Ataturk, who did it by dissolving the military dictatorship and making the civilian cause primary. Turkey may be described as the country which most closely fits the model of a praetorian army that has altered the sociopolitical context and created civilian political organizations. The steps taken by the Turkish officers were inspired initially by civilian actions, but the officers soon became independent of civilian groups. In the Kemalist transformation, the Turkish officers (1) took the primary role in selecting a system of government for the country; (2) chose their allies from among civilian politicians and from the civil services; (3) became the source of revolutionary change, making an effort to transfer the state from praetorian to nonpraetorian rule; (4) formed their own "civilian" political party; and (5) institutionalized the Kemalist tradition that the army in the barracks must serve as the protector of civilian rule.[67]

In the future, the example of Turkey must be more carefully examined. Most praetorian ruler-types have fulfilled the first three goals of the Kemalist transformation. But because of failures to satisfy the latter two, no praetorian ruler as yet has approximated the Kemalist achievement—stable, sustaining, and progressive civilian political order.

In the absence of evidence to the contrary, dedication to modernization and social change does not necessarily alter the political conditions of praetorianism. In fact, once civilian political groups and organizations have been eliminated, modernization could enhance the military domination over political institutions and procedures.

[65] No penetrating and objective study yet exists concerning the army's role in the economic modernization of Egypt, where the army has demonstrated limitations in the management of large-scale economic and industrial enterprises. One article on that subject is James Heaphey's "Organization of Egypt: Inadequacies of a Non-political Model for Nation-building," *World Politics*, XVIII (January 1966), 177-193.

[66] Ibid.; see also Patch, "Peruvian Elections," 6.

[67] On Ataturk's political program and accomplishments, see (in addition to Rustow, fn. 43, and Weiker, fn. 46) George Antonius, *The Arab Awakening* (New York, 1965); Rustow, "The Turkish Army and the Founding of the Republic," *World Politics*, XI (October 1958), 513-552; Kemal Karpat, *Turkey's Politics* (Princeton, 1959); and Daniel Lerner and Richard D. Robinson, "Swords and Ploughshares: The Turkish Army as a Modernizing Force," *World Politics*, XIII (October 1960), 19-44.

Military and Society
In East Africa

Thinking Again about Praetorianism

Henry Bienen*

I. The Problem

The army seized power in Uganda in January 1971.[1] It had revolted in 1964, along with the armies of Kenya and Tanzania, but civilian regimes were restored and maintained in all three East African countries until the Uganda coup.[2] In the latter country, however, there was considerably more friction between civilian leaders and armed forces and much more instability within the army from 1964–71 than in Kenya and Tanzania. This article will consider whether the concept of praetorianism, as developed in the works of Samuel Huntington, helps explain the differences in the evolution of relationships between armed forces and society in these three East African countries.

Huntington's fundamental proposition about military intervention states that "... the most important causes of military intervention in politics are not military but political, and reflect not the social and organizational characteristics of the military establishment but the

*This article was written under the auspices of the Center of International Studies, Princeton University.

[1] Reports of the Uganda coup may be found in: *Foreign Broadcast Information Service*, Daily Report, Middle East and Africa, 25 January 1971 –1 February 1971; *New York Times*, 25 January–1 February 1971; *Economist*, 6 February 1971, p. 27, 30 January 1971, pp. 14–15; *East African Standard* (Nairobi), 25 January 1971 ff., and *Uganda Argus* (Kampala), 25 January 1971 ff.

A recent analysis of the 1971 Uganda coup is in Michael F. Lofchie, "The Uganda Coup: Class Action by the Military," *Journal of Modern African Studies*, X (May 1972), 19–36. Two replies critical of Lofchie's arguments are: John D. Chick, "Class Conflict and Military Intervention in Uganda," *Journal of Modern African Studies*, X (December 1972), 634–37; and Irving Gershenberg, "A Further Comment on the 1971 Uganda Coup," in ibid., 638–40. Another major analysis of the Uganda coup is Michael Twaddle, "The Amin Coup," *Journal of Commonwealth Political Studies*, X (July 1972), pp. 112–28.

[2] For a discussion of the revolts in 1964, see Henry Bienen, "Public Order and the Military in Africa: Mutinies in Kenya, Uganda, and Tanganyika," in Bienen, ed. *The Military Intervenes: Case Studies in Political Development* (New York, 1968), pp. 35–70.

political and institutional structure of the society.''[3] The author will argue here that variations in the social and organizational character-istics of armed forces *do* make a difference with regard to the propensity of the military to intervene. Moreover, while there is always *some* relationship between the social/organizational charac-teristics of the military and the political/institutional structure of the society, ways in which the evolution of the social and organizational characteristics of the military can to some extent be cut away from happenings in the wider society will be shown. In other words, at a certain level of generality changes within the military do not depend very closely upon changes within the larger society. Comparisons will be made of both the political/institutional structures and the armed forces of East Africa in order to defend this point of view.

It must be acknowledged in advance, however, that there is insuf-ficient information about the various East African military. Indeed, until we have more detailed empirical studies of the African military, we cannot deal with major questions concerning their modernity or how these military regimes make decisions, who makes them, and what political goals govern their decision making. So far, the argu-ment that the military are the relatively modern groups in society rests solely on assertions. No one has shown how the military become rational, cohesive, universalistic, disciplined, and industry oriented.[4]

The point is not that all military regimes have failed to be mod-ernizers. But there is a risk in inferring qualities about armed force organizations because they have chains of command, tables of orga-nization, uniforms, and weapons. This warning should have partic-ular force in respect to African armed forces, for many of these are still extremely small-scale organizations with only a few battalions and some thousands of men in large countries with populations in the millions. They are usually predominantly infantry battalions with little firepower or mechanization.

In addition, information is inadequate as to how officer corps are recruited, what norms govern officer behavior, how officers, non-commissioned officers, and enlisted men relate to one another, and how the latter categories operate.[5]

---

[3] Samuel Huntington, *Political Order in Changing Societies* (New Haven, 1968), p. 194.

[4] For a discussion of the modernizing capabilities of the military in developing countries, see Bienen, ed. *The Military and Modernization* (New York, 1971).

[5] Some interesting work has been done recently on compositions of officer corps in Africa. For a general study, see J. M. Lee, *African Armies and Civil Order* (London, 1969). On Nigeria, see John Colas, "Social and Career Correlates of Military Intervention in Nigeria: A Background Study of the January 15th Coup Group" (Paper delivered at Annual Meeting,

II. The Concept of Praetorianism

The idea of praetorian societies has made an impact on recent studies
of the military in developing countries for two reasons: (1) because
its proponents have often been critical of the idea that the military are
best suited to modernize their societies; and (2) because the analysis
moves away from a discussion of the actual organization of armed
forces and focuses instead on society at large and, more specifically,
on patterns of political participation and institutionalization.[6]

Huntington defines a praetorian society as one in which there is a
general politicization of social forces and institutions. "Countries
which have political armies also have political clergies, political
universities, political bureaucracies . . . ,"[7] he declares. These
institutions involve themselves in politics not only over issues that
concern them but also over issues that affect society as a whole. The
praetorian society has neither specialized political institutions to mediate conflict nor accepted rules of the game for resolving conflict.[8]
Another important feature that Huntington attributes to such a society
is the fragmented nature of political power: "It [power] comes in
many forms and in small quantities. Authority over the system as a
whole is transitory . . . ."[9]

Huntington distinguishes between types of praetorian society according to levels of participation. Societies with weak political institutionalization can be oligarchical praetorian, radical praetorian, and
mass praetorian, depending on the breadth of the participation. Conflict becomes more intense as participation increases: "In a praetorian
oligarchy politics is a struggle among personal and family cliques; in
a radical praetorian society the struggle among institutional and occupational groups supplements that among cliques; in mass praetorianism, social classes and social movements dominate the scene."[10]

Inter-University Seminar on Armed Forces and Society, Chicago, October 9–11, 1969). Also
on Nigeria, see Robin Luckham, "Authority and Conflict in the Nigerian Army, 1966: A Case
Study in the Transfer of Military Institutions" (Paper presented to Seventh World Congress of
Sociology, Varna, Bulgaria, September 1970).

[6] The ideas of the praetorian state and praetorian society have been developed in Huntington's *Political Order* and in Amos Perlmutter, "The Praetorian State and the Praetorian
Army," *Comparative Politics* (April 1969), 382–404, and Perlmutter, "The Arab Military
Elite," *World Politics*, XXII (January 1970), 269–300. Also see David Rapoport, "A
Comparative Theory of Military and Political Types," in Huntington, ed. *Changing Patterns
of Military Politics* (New York, 1962), pp. 71–101, especially pp. 71–74. This essay was
based on Rapoport's "Praetorianism: Government without Consensus" (Ph.D. diss., University of California, Berkeley, 1960). Huntington's arguments will be used for discussion
here.

[7] Huntington, *Political Order*, p. 194.

[8] Ibid., p. 196.

[9] Ibid., pp. 196–97.

[10] Ibid., pp. 197–98.

While Huntington does not deal with tropical African cases in much detail, he classifies the African pattern as one of radical praetorianism in which political participation is brought about first by a civilian nationalist intelligentsia. This is then dislodged by middle-class officers because the civilians lack the ability to mobilize political support continuously and because they cannot organize political strength "to fill the vacuum of authority and legitimacy left by the departing colonial rulers."[11] In radical praetorian systems, according to Huntington, military intervention is usually a response to political action by others, and especially to the escalation of social conflict by such groups as students or labor organizations. In this context, military intervention serves to halt the rapid mobilization of social forces into politics. It defuses the explosive situation and often marks the end of a sequence of violence in politics.[12]

Huntington has much more to say about praetorian societies in Latin America, the Middle East, and Asia than in Africa. He compares Africa in the 1960s to Latin America in the 1820s, finding a decay of political authority and institutions in both. He argues that African elites failed to impose mass institutions; and he cites the single parties as inappropriate for their societies, declaring that "The African one-party state became a no-party state."[13] Since Africa was less stratified than Latin America and the middle class broke into politics at a later historical period, radical rather than oligarchical praetorianism came about.[14] Presumably Huntington considers the African armies a progressive force, since he states that, "Thus, paradoxically but understandably, the more backward a society is, the more progressive the role of its military; the more advanced a society becomes, the more conservative and reactionary becomes the role of the military."[15]

The discussion of praetorian systems by Huntington is not an ideal-type analysis. While the different types of praetorian society are described in terms of clusters of characteristics having to do with levels of participation, the analysis is not really typological. Real societies in time and place are put into a particular category. Indeed, the discussion proceeds without reference to "pure forms" or caveats about classifying real systems in terms of typological constructs. Yet the concept of a praetorian society is broad and Huntington's own

---

[11] Ibid., p. 200.
[12] Ibid., p. 212 and pp. 216–17.
[13] Ibid., p. 200.
[14] Ibid.
[15] Ibid., p. 221.

discussion proceeds with fairly large brush strokes, although much historical detail is provided in addition. While there are many insights and useful contributions in Huntington's treatment of military intervention, this author has many doubts about the applicability of the praetorian analysis to tropical Africa.

The military and society in Uganda, Tanzania, and Kenya will be examined here with a view to evaluating the usefulness and pointing out the limitations of the idea of praetorianism and specifically to making comparisons of the roles of the military in East Africa.[16] The discussion will first focus on the societal context, as Huntington properly directs, and then examine military characteristics and interventions.

III. East Africa: Praetorian Societies?

In trying to assess the applicability of the praetorian concept to East African societies, a few basic points can be made.[17] First, Kenya, Uganda, and Tanzania have significant differences in degree of industrial development, scope and modernity of communications systems, and levels of urbanization. Kenya stands highest on the indices in all these areas. Second, there are major differences in ethnic composition; ethnic politics are less salient in Tanzania than in either Uganda or Kenya. Ethnic conflict has been extremely complex in Uganda, which has undergone north–south cleavages, Bantu–non-Bantu divisions, Baganda–anti-Baganda axes, religious splits, clan and regional conflicts in the north, and separatist movements in various parts of the country.[18] Kenya has had major tribal and regional conflicts, too, and an increasing Luo-Kikuyu polariza-

---

[16] In the discussion which follows, my aim is to consider Huntington's idea of praetorianism for the light it may throw on civil-military relations in East Africa. I am not here interested in reviewing *Political Order in Changing Societies*.

[17] For political analyses of East African countries, the following may be consulted: Stanley Diamond and Fred G. Burke, eds. *The Transformation of East Africa* (New York, 1966); Bienen, *Tanzania: Party Transformation and Economic Development* (Princeton, 1970); William Tordoff, *Government and Politics in Tanzania* (Nairobi, 1967); G. Andrew Maguire, *Toward "Uhuru" in Tanzania* (New York, 1969); Goran Hyden, *Tanu Yajenga Nchi: Political Development in Rural Tanzania* (Lund, 1968); Burke, *Local Government and Politics in Uganda* (Syracuse, 1964); David Apter, *The Political Kingdom in Uganda* (Princeton, 1962); Julius Nyerere, *Freedom and Socialism* (Dar es Salaam, 1968); Nyerere, *Freedom and Unity* (Dar es Salaam, 1967); M. P. K. Sorrenson, *Land Reform in the Kikuyu Country* (Nairobi, 1967); John Nottingham and Carl Rosberg, Jr., *The Myth of Mau Mau* (New York, 1966); Oginga Odinga, *Not Yet Uhuru* (New York, 1967); Cherry Gertzel, *The Politics of Independent Kenya* (Nairobi, 1969); Gertzel, Mauré Goldschmidt, and Don Rothchild, *Government and Politics in Kenya* (Nairobi, 1969),

[18] See M. Crawford Young, "The Obote Revolution," *Africa Report*, XI (June 1966), 8–15.

tion. While all three countries have had one-party systems at various times, they have arrived at this state by quite different routes and the end condition has had different meanings in Uganda, Kenya, and Tanzania.

Despite the differences noted in the preceding paragraph, plus their many social, economic, political, constitutional, and cultural distinctions, all three East African countries share one feature common to tropical African polities: power is fragmented. Here Huntington's characterization holds, at least if it is roughly drawn. This author has argued elsewhere that central or national authorities in Africa are unable to exert authority over the whole territorial entity they rule because a great deal of political life goes on outside the reach of the central rulers. Values are not being allocated for society as a whole by central authorities, whatever the rhetoric of mobilization for development through centralized political structures. Nationwide political structures are too weak to enforce the will of ruling national elites, whether these elites are traditional lineage groups, a party elite, civilian bureaucracies, or the military.[19]

After admitting a fragmentation of power and a weakness of central institutions common to all three countries, however, it does not follow that the level of effectiveness of political institutions is the same in Kenya, Uganda, or Tanzania, or that the presence or absence of legitimate intermediaries does not vary significantly in East Africa. The fact that power is fragmented reveals a lot, but by no means everything, about the nature of power and authority in a system. Central institutions may be weak, but there can still be authority as well as accepted "rules of the game."

It is important not to overhomogenize our treatment of political societies in Africa. Indeed, much of the writing on African parties has done just this. After observing the weakness of parties in terms of the goals set by party leaders and the needs of society, and after comparing the rhetoric of rule with the performance of political structures, many observers have dismissed African parties out of hand. The fact remains, however, that not all African parties have become defunct; and not all one-party systems have become no-party systems.[20]

TANU (Tanganyika African National Union) cannot mobilize the

[19] These remarks are taken from Bienen, "What Does Political Development Mean in Africa?", *World Politics*, XX (October 1967), 128–41.

[20] For a discussion of one-party systems in Africa, see Bienen, "The Ruling Party in the African One-Party State: TANU in Tanzania," *Journal of Commonwealth Political Studies*, V (November 1967), 214–30 and "One-Party Systems in Africa," in Huntington and Clement H. Moore, eds. *Authoritarian Politics in Modern Society* (New York, 1970), pp. 99–127.

population of Tanzania for economic development tasks in the way that the Communist party functioned in the Soviet Union in the 1930s.[21] TANU was unable to avoid a military revolt in 1964 or to mobilize the civilian population against the rebellious soldiers in Dar es Salaam or up-country towns. It was no more effective in obviating a revolt or ending it in 1964 than civilian institutions in Kenya and Uganda that same year.[22] Nonetheless, TANU provides legitimacy to leaders at low, middle, and high levels in a way that the Uganda Peoples Congress and KANU (Kenya African National Union) do not. The Uganda People's Congress which incorporated elements of two former opposition groups—the Democratic party and the Kabaka Yekka party—had always been faction-ridden. President Jomo Kenyatta and the civil service invest KANU with authority. Only at very local levels do party leaders *qua* party leaders make decisions in Kenya and even here civil servants play a major policy as well as executive role. In Kenya, too, the ruling party incorporated former members of opposition parties—the Kenya African Democratic Union, the African Peoples Party, and the Kenya Peoples Union. KANU has been essentially a party of fragmented district organizations.[23] But Kenyatta's role has been such that he could prevail in KANU and the Cabinet with less challenge than President Obote was subject to in Uganda. Furthermore, when the late Tom Mboya was secretary general of KANU, some attempt was made, albeit rather unsuccessful, to create a national KANU headquarters staff and a meaningful KANU center.

The argument here is that all East African parties have been weak, but that there have been major differences in the role and functioning of TANU as compared to the UPC and KANU. And even as between the Kenyan and Ugandan parties, there were significant differences. While the KANU government was challenged by KANU back-benchers in 1965–66 and while the breakaway KPU had a bastion in the Luo areas of south and central Nyanza, KANU was never on the verge of coming apart as the UPC was in early 1966.[24]

Huntington's framework allows for political development in poor countries; he singles out the Congress party in India and TANU in Tanzania as vital parties which provided an institutional base to the political system.

[21] Bienen, *Tanzania*.

[22] See Bienen, "Public Order and the Military in Africa: Mutinies in Kenya, Uganda, and Tanzania," in Bienen, ed. *The Military Intervenes*, pp. 35–70.

[23] For the district base of KANU politics, see John Okumu, "Charisma and Politics in Kenya," *East Africa Journal*, V (February 1968), 9–16.

[24] There are certainly many "almost"parallels one could draw between KANU and the UPC. Ugandan cabinet ministers were arrested under Obote, while in Kenya Odinga and other

The institutional differences can be pushed with regard to nonparty organizations, also. Tanzania has perhaps had the weakest civil service of the three countries, Kenya the strongest; but Tanzania has had TANU as compensation. In Uganda the civil service has been relatively competent for a tropical African country, but southerners, and particularly Bagandans, have dominated that service. Ethnic tensions in Uganda have given rise to more sustained and sharper outbreaks of violence than have taken place in Kenya since independence.[25] There has been less mobility of civil servants in this context and less consensus among civilian elites, with the result that creation of a national civil service has not proceeded in Uganda to the extent that it has in Kenya.

So far the argument has been that Uganda has the least effective civilian institutions and the most severe ethnic tensions in East Africa. Tanzania has the most institutionalized political system in that it has the strongest, best articulated party, with a set of professional political leaders who are legitimate intermediaries able to moderate group conflict. Civil servants in Kenya carry out many of the political functions that the TANU officials do in Tanzania. Current party strength in Tanzania and civil service strength in Kenya depend on the authority of Julius Nyerere and Jomo Kenyatta, respectively.

It is difficult to say with any certainty which of these two institutions will survive better the passing of the "Founding Father." Kenya's civilian institutions seem under greater pressure now because Kenyatta is an old man and the succession struggle is already underway. But the Kenya civil service delivers more goods efficiently than TANU does and it provides the Kenya government with a stronger grid for influencing behavior through its administrative services. Kenya's civil service, acting in conjunction with police and armed forces, or threatening to invoke these actors, is probably a stronger coercive force than TANU. TANU, on the other hand, seems more effective in working for longer term value change and even short-

---

Luo M.P.'s were incarcerated in late 1969 after they had left the government and were already in opposition. Bildad Kaggia, a former assistant minister, had earlier been put in detention after he also had left the government.

[25] For a discussion of violence and ethnicity in Uganda, see Martin R. Doornboos, "Kumanyana and Rwenzururu: Two Responses to Ethnic Inequality," in Robert Rotberg and Ali A. Mazrui, eds. *Protest and Power in Black Africa* (New York, 1970), pp. 1088–1138. Also see G. S. Engholm and Mazrui, "Violent Constitutionalism in Uganda," *Government and Opposition*, II (July–October 1967), 585–99; Colin Leys, "Violence in Africa," *Transition*, V (March–April 1965), 17–20; Young, "The Obote"; A Special Correspondent, "The Uganda Army: Nexus of Power," *Africa Report*, XI (December 1966), 37–39.

term exhortation. Any judgment about institutionalization must there-fore be made in terms of different kinds of functions performed. It would be rash to conclude, given the general situation of power fragmentation and transient authority, that either TANU or the Ken-yan civil service will prove durable vehicles for rule in their present forms.

Before turning directly to the East African military, it may be useful briefly to examine Tanzania, Kenya, and Uganda in the light of some of Huntington's other characterizations of radical praetorian societies. One of the major facets of these societies in his view is that they provide a setting in which social forces confront each other nakedly.[26] What is striking about many African societies, however, is the low degree of politicization of social forces in national politics. First, social classes themselves are rather weakly formed. Although Tanzanian leaders may fear the formation of an urban and working-class aristocracy, urbanization in Tanzania is very low and the indus-trial labor force very small.[27] In Uganda there is a growing number of cash crop farmers with significant differences in income. There are, in addition, more stratified land relationships in Buganda than have existed elsewhere in most of East Africa.[28] But Uganda is not a country where one can see social forces organized in class terms (if by class we still mean economic-occupational divisions). There are, of course, elite-nonelite distinctions in both Uganda and Tanzania, as well as levels of power, wealth, and status within the elites. The Tanzanians have moved, in the Arusha formulations, to try to mini-mize these distinctions.[29] But in both Uganda and Tanzania the African middle class consists almost entirely of government (both civil and party) servants, a very few military officers, some more prosperous farmers and traders, and a few professionals—mostly teachers.

The government elites participate in *national* issues and are located at the national arena much more than others in middle-class roles. In Uganda and Tanzania, however, the elite has been a narrow one and a "rules of the game" has operated, at least outside of the realm of

---

[26] Huntington, *Political Order*, p. 196.

[27] While Dar es Salaam has recently been growing by about 10 percent annually, the urban population as a whole grows at about 6 percent in Tanzania. In 1970, the urban population was around 5 percent of the total; there were 10 towns of 15,000 or more people. See *Tanzania Second Five-Year Plan for Economic and Social Development, 1st July 1969–30th June 1974*, I (Dar es Salaam, 1969), pp. 176–82.

[28] Tanzania's northwestern region has also had a stratified land system, called the *nyarubanja*, in the Eastern Buhaya area, which was not so different from Buganda. See Hyden, p. 79.

[29] Bienen, "An Ideology for Africa," *Foreign Affairs*, XLVII (April 1969), 545–59.

overt ethnic conflict. In Kenya, on the other hand, much more social division has taken place in class terms: the industrial working force is bigger, and there are more gradations among African urban and rural dwellers. Kenya has a landless proletariat and a more severe "land hunger" problem than Uganda or Tanzania. Moreover, class divisions have proceeded furthest among the government's own ethnic base—the Kikuyus. And since the commercial and industrial sector was more developed in Kenya than elsewhere in East Africa and government has been rapidly Africanizing the commercial sector and pressuring for Africanization of small businesses and managerial position in larger enterprises, a Kenyan African business class is growing up. Individuals in this group have interlocking relationships with political elites. Yet, in Kenya, too, there is low participation in national politics by economically defined social forces.

Social forces face each other "nakedly" in East Africa, as elsewhere in Africa, in the realm of ethnic politics. In Uganda, ethnic groups have vied for control of the central institutions of authority and power; but many ethnic conflicts are fairly localized as, for example, the hostilities in western Uganda. These localized conflicts have national ramifications when the national balances of power are disturbed or when the local conflict is carried to the national level through central institutions—either party, civil service, or army. Since the army is recruited mostly from northerners in Uganda and since there are many ethnic conflicts in the north, the stability of the national political arena is called into question. Where class and ethnic relationships intersect as, for example, when cocoa farmers in Ghana are mainly Ashanti or when cotton and coffee farmers in Uganda are heavily Baganda, then the chances that social forces will confront each other at the national level increase. But even in Uganda and in Kenya, where class and ethnicity are heavily intertwined, it is difficult to see large-scale group involvement in national politics.

Nor has East Africa been characterized by urban instability up to now. Violence, which has been more pronounced since the end of colonial rule in Uganda and in northern Kenya than elsewhere in East Africa, has been essentially a rural phenomenom. Neither the city mob, nor the students in the national universities in capital cities, nor even the capital garrisons have been determining factors in politics or created much violence. If, as Huntington says, the distinctive character of radical praetorianism is urban instability, East African is notably free of this. Only in Kenya is there a sense that the government is looking to a rural middle class and trying to maintain Kikuyu peasant support as its major base of strength against other ethnic communities. The regime is aware also of the potential of the cities for future instability. In Tanzania, the TANU government has consistently tried to mobilze the rural areas. But this is less a reaction to challenge from urban elements than an attempt to create development in an overwhelming rural society and to build political support somewhere in the system so that rural goals can be carried out.

One of the major difficulties in judging the praetorian character of a society is the problem of measuring political participation. Elections alone do not give much indication of the involvement of people in politics. An analysis of the strength and direction of interest group demands would be essential. How does one weigh persistent demands against ad hoc participation on certain salient issues? Levels of interest in national politics rise in Kenya every time a rumor about President Kenyatta's health spreads. The army is not a day to day actor in Kenyan internal affairs but at times of crises—when Tom Mboya was assassinated, when Oginga Odinga was arrested, when riots occurred in Kisumu in Central Nyanza, i.e., whenever tensions rise and the fear of increased mass participation in politics takes place—the armed forces become more salient. A massive increase in participation could trigger military intervention in Kenya. But this kind of participation would itself be a response to political crisis, not the result of long-term trends.

In both Kenya and Tanzania it is difficult to measure the ratio between institutionalization and participation. In part, the measures for each are not precise. Furthermore, scholars may not even be looking in the right places to understand participation. If the military were suddenly to intervene again in Tanzania or Kenya, one could not attribute the specific intervention to the society's becoming "more praetorian," unless it were possible to show an increase in participation or a weakening of institutionalization.

In Huntington's analysis, the condition of the society as one with weak institutions is of course important. Under these conditions, military intervention is a possibility and the focus is not on the specific timing of the intervention or the relationship of the intervention to an ad hoc set of political events. Still, one wants to know why a condition—in this case nonintervention by the military—may persist for some time and then suddenly change. If the importance of participation and institutionalization and the relationship that obtains between them are singled out as the critical variables, one would look for some change in those variables if intervention occurs. Thus, even if one avoids making ex post facto judgments about the nature of the praetorian society after a coup, it is still necessary to take into account factors specific to individual armed forces in order to have complete explanations about military interventions and military regime performance. Can anything be learned in this respect which can be applied to the Uganda coup?

IV. East African Armed Forces

Huntington suggests that at one phase of a society's development, instability and coups are to be explained in terms of changes in the nature of the military. This is when instability and coups are associated with the emergence of the middle class. Instability and coups associated with the emergence of lower classes are, however, due to changes in the nature of society itself.[30] It is probably more profitable to look at relationships between the military and society as interacting processes. Even in societies where there is rapid expansion of lower-class participation, differences in the armed forces may well be significant for short-run outcomes in politics. Where the military is the carrier par excellence of middle-class interests and values, differences in the military's recruitment, organization, career experiences, size, and the like may also be crucial for politics. Indeed, it is necessary to distinguish between armed forces organizations in societies that may roughly look alike precisely because it is impossible to attribute to the military the qualities of modernity that Huntington ascribes to them in praetorian societies.

The levels of discipline and organization of armies vary enormously in tropical African countries. Many of these armed forces have been neither melting pots nor well-assimilated groups forged into a cohesive entity. Relative to other groups in a society, the military may or may not be a modern institution. It may or may not be honest and efficient compared to other national institutions such as ruling parties and civil services. It may or may not monopolize the individuals in a society who have technical skills or entrepreneurial talents. As more information about the recruitment and operations of the individual military becomes available, it will be possible to judge the accuracy of the general statements about armed forces both for the military themselves and as compared to other groups in African societies. This author predicts that the new data on African armies will significantly modify the generalizations on armed forces organizations.

There are some notable differences among the armed forces of Uganda, Kenya, and Tanzania in their relationships with civilian

---

[30] Huntington, *Political Order*, p. 222.

Table 1 Armed Forces and National Statistics in Three East African Countries, 1968–70*

Factor	Country		
	Uganda	Tanzania	Kenya
Population	9,675,000	13,000,000	11,075,000
Gross National Product**	$785 million	$900 million	$1,230 million
Total armed forces	6,700	7,900†	5,400
Estimated defense expenditures, 1968 . . .	$20,030,000	$10,900,000	$17,900,000
Total national budget, 1968–69 . . .	$183,050,000	$255,000,000	$248,000,000

*All figures are from Richard Booth, "The Armed Forces of African States, 1970," *Adelphi Papers*, No. 67 (May 1970); The Institute for Strategic Studies, London, pp. 18–19, 22.

**All monetary figures are quoted in $ United States.

†Plus 4,000 voluntary reserves.

institutions and with each society as a whole. Variations in the politics of the three countries are apparently related to differences in the military as well as in the institutionalization of the political systems. Moreover, at least some major variations among the armed forces do not depend on the wider societal development. They are differences intrinsic to the evolution of the armed forces that can be explained by both indigeneous and exogenous factors in the development of the respective military and their narrowly conceived experiences.[31] The differences in the East African armed forces thus become independent variables which must be evaluated.

The three East African armed forces differ little in terms of size or force components. Table 1 reproduces the vital statistics of the

[31] I argued in *The Military Intervenes*, pp. 45–46, that the decisive factor in the army mutinies of 1964 was the fragility of East African institutions *per se*. I am now arguing that we must explain the role of the armed forces in East Africa since 1964 in terms of the interaction of *specific* armed forces with their environments. While the emphasis here is on domestic environments—that is, the societies of each East African state—a full consideration would include the interactions of the East African armies with the international environments. The 1964 mutinies, for example, must be related to the Zanzibar Revolution. (See Bienen, "National Security in Tanzania after the Mutiny," *Transition*, V [April 1965], 39–46.) Explanations of subsequent civil-military relations must take into account the liberation movements in southern Africa and Tanzania's army, the Kenya–Somali conflict, the Congo upheavals, and also refugee problems in southern and northern Uganda and the reaction of the Uganda army to the refugees.

Ugandan, Kenyan, and Tanzanian armed forces in societal perspective.

The statistics for size of armed force and for defense expenditures usually vary from source to source. There is fairly close agreement, however, on the figures given in the table.[32] Kenya's army is put at a total strength of 4,700 by the Institute of Strategic Studies. It is comprised of one brigade of four infantry battalions and a support battalion, including a paratroop company. Uganda had two brigades in 1970, each consisting of two infantry battalions, and an independent infantry battalion. Tanzania has four infantry battalions, plus tanks and some artillery.

All three armies have grown in firepower in the last few years; the Tanzanian army has doubled in size and the other two have grown by almost 1,000 men each. The Tanzanian armed forces started from a smaller base in the mid-1960s; they were more thoroughly dismantled and reorganized after the mutinies of 1964. The Kenyan army had already been built up by 1964 to confront the Somali *shifta* in northern Kenya.[33] Uganda's defense budget was over seventeen million dollars per year by 1967. Thus, it had risen less rapidly than Tanzania's, which was up more than 50 percent, and Kenya's, which had grown by almost 75 percent. Uganda's early high cost of defense probably represents buildup of air force. Presently, Uganda has an air force of 450 men and 19 combat aircraft, including MIG 15s and 17s and 12 Magister armed trainers. Tanzania has an air force of 300 men and no planes; but it is the first to expect combat aircraft from the Soviet Union.[34] Kenya also has no combat aircraft, although it has 450 men in the air force. In addition, Kenya has 250 men in the naval forces and Tanzania has 100.

In discussing African armed forces it is impossible to ignore police and gendarme units, particularly because "military" regimes have more often than not consisted of coalitions of army and police. (This was clearly the case in Ghana.) African police forces have sometimes performed security and paramilitary functions and have been motorized and had significant firepower in comparison to the army

[32] Colonel T. N. Dupey, ed., *The Almanac of World Military Power* (Harrisburg, 1970) gives armed forces figures very close to Richard Booth, "The Armed Forces of African States, 1970" (See Table 1) for Uganda, a smaller armed force number for Tanzania, and considerably larger figures for Kenya because internal security forces are included in the latter. See pp. 208–9, 246–47, 252–53.

[33] In 1967, armed forces were put at 3,000 for Tanzania, 4,775 for Kenya, and 5,960 for Uganda. See Charles Stevenson, "African Armed Forces," *Military Review*, XLVII (March 1967), 18–24, and David Wood, "The Armed Forces of African States," *Adelphi Papers*, No. 27 (April 1966).

[34] Dupey, p. 248, puts the size of the Tanzanian air force at 400 men.

proper.[35] In Kenya, in particular, the police force is large—11,500 men—and well equipped. The civil police operate a light plane wing and include general service units. Each GSU is a paramilitary force for riot control. These units were used by the government to clear the University College of students in 1969.[36] Police units were used in the north (in addition to army units) to provide security against Somali *shifta* raiders. Tanzania has a police force of 7,500, which includes a marine unit. Uganda's police force of about 7,000 has an air wing and an 800-man general service unit. The Ugandan army, or at least elements within it, have feared at times that the GSU was becoming a personal arm of Obote under the direction of his security chief and cousin, Akena Adoko.

While there are surface similarities in terms of size, size as a percentage of total population, firepower and defense expenditures, the three East African armed forces are different in several important respects, such as discipline, professionalism, the nature of the officer corps, and military-civilian relationships.

Since 1964 the Ugandan army has been the most salient in the politics of East Africa. It has been relatively the least disciplined armed force; it has been called upon to play the most active internal role; and it seems the most riven by internal factionalism. There is of course an interaction between the weakness of the civilian institutions and the degree of discipline and factionalism inside the armed forces. But it can be shown that certain patterns within the armed forces and the specific tasks that the Ugandan army was called on to perform accentuated the prominence of the army in politics and at the same time weakened its internal cohesion.

At the beginning of 1964, all the East African armies were in the process of trying to build an African officer corps. (Africanization of the officer corps took place later in East Africa than in those West African states that became independent sooner.) Kenya was newly independent in 1964; Tanganyika had become independent only at the end of 1961, and Uganda in 1962. At the time they attained independence, Tanganyika, Uganda, and Kenya had six, fourteen, and eighty African commissioned officers respectively.[37] This repre-

---

[35] For a discussion of African police forces, see Christian Potholm, "The Multiple Roles of the Police as Seen in the African Context," *Journal of Developing Areas*, III (January 1969), 139–58.

[36] See Bienen, "When Does Dissent Become Sedition?", *Africa Report*, XIV (March/April 1969), 10–14. Also see his "Foreign Policy, the Military, and Development: Military Assistance and Political Change in Africa," in Richard Butwell, ed. *Foreign Policy and the Developing Nation* (Lexington, 1969).

[37] From Lee, p. 44.

sented 9.4 percent, 21.9 percent, and 48.5 percent of the commissioned officer corps of the three countries.[38] By the summer of 1963, 40 percent of Tanganyika's sixty-three commissioned officers above the rank of Warrant Officer were Tanganyikans (one was an Asian).[39] The figure was 58 percent if twenty-eight Warrant Officers are included.[40] As Harvey Glickman has pointed out, it was not until 1957 that East Africans were accepted at Sandhurst.[41]

In the rapid Africanization programs, roughly three streams of officers came into being: (1) former noncommissioned officers, often with World War II experience, who were promoted to officer rank; (2) British-trained officers who had attended overseas schools, some of whom could be broken into a subgroup of those who had had short-service training (For example, in 1963 Tanganyika had eight lieutenants on short-service commission who had trained at Mons Officer Training School in Britain.[42]); and (3) political protégés who went for military training to new military assistance donors—not to England. Michael Lee reports that a Ugandan Minister sent some of his protégés for military training to Israel, without informing or consulting commanding British officers.[43] Kenyans were sent to the Soviet Union under the sponsorship of Oginga Odinga. Tanzania proliferated the number of military aid donors so that at one time her armed forces were receiving assistance from Great Britain, Canada, Israel, China, and West Germany. Not all officers who went to non-British training programs were "politicals," however, and thus there could be movement from one category to another. Brigadier General Opolot, commander of the Ugandan army from 1964–66, was a long-time professional who had served as an NCO in the colonial army, but who also received Sandhurst training later in his career.[44]

The conflict between these officer streams was most pronounced in Uganda, which experienced the most rapid military growth in tropical Africa outside of Nigeria. The former expanded its army by over 40

[38] Ibid. At the time of independence, Kenya had 13.9 percent Africans in its gazetted police officers; Uganda had 42.9 percent, and Tanganyika 10.4 percent. Since police played a large internal security role in Kenya after Mau Mau, the relatively high percentage of Kenyan African officers in the army may have been the other side of the coin of low percentage of Kenyan Africans in the police officer corps.

[39] Harvey Glickman, *Some Observations on the Army and Political Unrest in Tanganyika*, Duquesne University, Institute of African Affairs, Paper No. 16 (Pittsburgh, 1964), p. 4.

[40] Ibid.

[41] Ibid.

[42] Ibid.

[43] Lee, pp. 75–76.

[44] A Special Correspondent, p. 38.

percent a year without a large reserve of trained manpower to call back into service.[45] Uganda had good reason to expand its army, since civil war in the Congo spilled over creating refugee problems and instability in western Uganda. Similar situations existed in the north as refugees from the southern Sudan moved in and out of Uganda,[46] and in the south, when Tutsi refugees from Rwanda came into the country. In addition, there has been a long-standing problem of intratribal cattle raids between Turkana and Karamojong in the north,[47] which has necessitated sending in the army from time to time to keep the peace in that huge and sparsely settled area.

In western Uganda, an even more serious problem confronted the army. Two tribes, the Bwamba and the Bankonjo, were trying to free themselves from domination by the Batoro in what came to be known as the Rwenzururu separatist movement. Because this movement was in the Ruwenzori Mountain area bordering on the Congo, it was difficult for the Uganda army to operate there.[48] Indeed, the army itself was a disruptive force in the area, foraging and sometimes using roadblocks to extort money. Eventually, the army moved out to the plains area and essentially gave up the mountains to the movement.[49] On the Congo border also the army did not seem to function as a disciplined body. Arbitrary arrests of individuals took place,[50] and the then Deputy Commander of the Army and Army Chief of Staff, subsequently Commander of the Army, Idi Amin, was accused by opposition members of Parliament of looting from the Congolese.[51] In both the Congo area and the Ruwenzori region, the army failed in its mission to provide public order, experiences that were demoralizing for the army. In the Congo operations, in addition, factionalism developed within the army over differences in policy toward the Congo rebels.

The army was more successful when it confronted Buganda, parts of which rose in arms against the central government in May 1966. The army defeated the force of the Kabaka (King) of Buganda,

[45] Lee, p. 105.

[46] From time to time the Government of the Sudan threatened to pursue Sudanese rebels into Uganda.

[47] Leys, "Violence in Africa," *Transition*, V (April 1965), 18–19. Leys reports that in only nine months of 1961, 253 people were killed in Karamoja.

[48] For a discussion of the separatist movements in western Uganda, see Doornbos, esp. pp. 1088–1136.

[49] A Special Correspondent, p. 39.

[50] Ibid.

[51] A motion by an opposition M.P. to suspend Colonel Amin was passed in the National Assembly with only one dissenting vote. (See *Africa Report*, XI [March 1966], 22.) Colonel Amin was later cleared by a commission of inquiry and became head of the army as Obote consolidated his power with Amin's support. Also see Young, p. 12.

consisting of Buganda police and exservicemen, in a battle at the Kabaka's palace.[52] It then had to occupy Buganda. Again, charges of brutality and arbitrary behavior were made, and the occupation was a continuing source of tension between civilians and military. Since the army was heavily northern or "Nilotic," its role in Buganda was perceived in ethnic terms. When the Kenyan army was involved against Somali *shifta* in northern Kenya, it could by contrast project an image in the country of a national unifier. But northern Kenya is a sparsely settled area, removed from major concentrations of people, and the Somalis were a small minority of Kenya's total population. Buganda, on the other hand, has been the heartland of Uganda. It is the wealthiest part of the country, its people are the best educated, and it is the geographic center. Destruction of the Buganda regime by a northern army raised fears among Bantu peoples at large. Thus, the Buganda occupation did not project the army as a national unifier, at least not in the short run.

The increase in the size of Uganda's army and the defense costs incurred could be explained by border problems and internal security needs. But the pressures for increase came also from the army itself, and these were weakly resisted by the civilian leadership. In the mutinies of 1964, Uganda's civilian leadership responded far more weakly than either Kenya's or Tanzania's. Jomo Kenyatta told his people: "During the colonial days men of the King's African Rifles served the British Government loyally. Now that we have our own African Government, the world and our own people are justified in expecting even greater loyalty from the Kenya army."[53] Under his leadership Kenya disciplined mutineers and intensified efforts to train a professional army. Tanzania, too, moved decisively against a mutinous force, court-martialing leaders and trying to build a new army tied to TANU politically. In Uganda, Prime Minister Obote, like his fellow East African leaders, called in British troops, but he justified his appeal for the troops on the grounds that security forces were stretched thin across Uganda and that "unruly elements," which existed in all countries, might try to take advantage of this situation.[54] At the same time that he called in British troops, Prime

---

[52] There were more than 18,000 Baganda exservicemen in the 1950s who were veterans of World Wars I and II. See Eugene Schleh, "Post-Service Careers of World War Two Veterans: The Cases of Gold Coast and Uganda" (Paper delivered at 1967 Annual Meeting, African Studies Association, New York City, November 1–4), p. 9.

[53] *East African Standard*, 27 January 1964, quoted in Mazrui and Rothchild, "The Soldier and the State in East Africa: Some Theoretical Conclusions on the Army Mutinies of 1964," *Western Political Quarterly*, XX (March 1967), 83.

[54] Bienen, "Public Order and the Military in Africa," p. 50.

Minister Obote said they would not be long needed; he promised an upward revision of pay, and he called the mutiny a "sit-down strike." Indeed, Mr. Obote denied that a real mutiny had occurred and he affirmed the loyalty of the troops.[55] His sentiments were strikingly different from those expressed by Kenyatta and Nyerere. The Uganda civilian authorities did not deal harshly with the mutineers. While the Tanzanian army was totally reconstructed, the Ugandan army was granted its major demands: pay increases[56] and immediate Africanization of the officer corps. A new infantry battalion was formed with officers promoted from the ranks.[57]

The assertion has been made that Uganda's officer corps is strikingly different from Kenya's.[58] While no direct surveys of Kenyan or Ugandan officers' attitudes have been undertaken, it appears that Kenya's promotion of African officers came later than Uganda's. Thus, Uganda had a greater share of promoted NCO's compared to foreign-trained officers. As late as the end of 1966, Uganda had only twelve officers in training abroad compared to four times that many Kenyans.[59] But at the senior levels, more than 60 percent of those holding the rank of major or above in Kenya had been *effendis,* a position in the colonial armies halfway between officers and enlisted men—i.e., a warrant officer position.[60]

The difficulties between younger and better educated officers and former NCO's who had been promoted was greater in Uganda than in Kenya. Lee states that by 1964 the Uganda army had reached a delicate state, and he relates the mutiny to the return from Britain of cadets who had trained at Mons. The direct entry officers now outnumbered the former NCO's by twenty-one to sixteen.[61] General Opolot, who himself bridged the gap between the two categories, was replaced in October 1966 and arrested under emergency regulations operating in Buganda.[62] Indeed, Uganda's rapid expansion of the army was marked all along by a very high rate of officer dismissal.[63] A number of captains and junior officers were brought

---

[55] Ibid. Although the mutineers held the Minister for Defense captive, they did not move out from Jinja, where they were barracked, to the main centers at Kampala and Entebbe.

[56] As of 1967, the annual starting salaries of nonofficers were considerably higher in Uganda than in Kenya. A Kenyan sergeant received about $1,000 a year compared to a Ugandan's $1,500. A private received about $350 in Kenya, $600 in Uganda. Officers had more nearly comparable salaries from Second Lieutenant up. Lee, p. 94.

[57] A Special Correspondent, p. 38.

[58] Ibid.

[59] Ibid.

[60] Lee, pp. 42, 108–9.

[61] Ibid., p. 108.

[62] A Special Correspondent, p. 39.

[63] Lee, p. 105, says that it may be the highest on the continent.

up for court-martial on charges related to an alleged aborted coup in 1965. When Obote purged his cabinet in 1966, a number of younger, better educated Bantu officers were implicated with the dismissed ministers in a plot against the prime minister.[64]

J. M. Lee has described the breakdown in discipline and the factionalism within African armies in general in terms Huntington might well have used:

> The conventions of colonial days which separated the army from the rest of the community were broken down, precisely because the officer corps tended to be subject to the same tensions as civilian elites. . . . the regime in power was not obliged to take measures which would give it control over the army; the political community recolonized it. The army became the battleground for warring factions if large sections of the community found it impossible to identify with the regime. In these conditions it is not surprising that the army's sense of professionalism is significantly lowered. . . .[65]

The fact remains that Kenya's army did not break down in the way that Uganda's did. Although Kenya had a mutiny, the army was stabilized once civilian authority was reasserted. This may be in part because Kenyatta had more personal authority than Obote. Furthermore, Kenya's ethnic splits had not reached the point that Uganda's had in 1964. Kenya was not without ethnic struggle, however, especially Luo-Kikuyu conflict, which became more intense later on.

Kenya had an advantage in that its army recruitment worked to insulate the army from the major ethnic conflict. The Kamba had provided a disproportionate number of recruits to the colonial King's African Rifles and they maintained this position. They were still the largest single tribe represented in the officer corps in 1966, with 28 percent of the total compared to their population share of 11 percent. The Kikuyu had 22.7 percent of the officers and 19.2 percent of the population, and the Luo officer component was 10.3 percent although Luos made up 13.9 percent of the total population. The Luyha were the most underrepresented large tribe, with only .4 percent of the officers whereas they comprised 12.9 percent of the people.[66] Thus the Kamba, who were outside the main ethnic conflict, were the most important group in the army.[67]

[64] A Special Correspondent.

[65] Lee, p. 106.

[66] Ibid., p. 110. The Luyha had 16.5 percent of the police, while the Kikuyu had 11.2 percent, Luo 8.5 percent, and Kamba 9.8 percent. Lee's figures for officers are for 1966, but the population shares are based on the 1962 census. The police figures are also for 1962.

[67] The Kamba areas also had given support to a Kamba leader's own party—the African People's Party, in the 1963 elections, rather than to either KANU or KADU, the major parties. In the 1966 Little General Election, Kamba areas gave some support also to the opposition Kenya Peoples Union. The Kamba, then, have been an important "swing" tribe in Kenya.

Kenya was not without its own tribal competition for positions of authority in military and police forces, however. Indeed, Kenya's political leadership tried early on to master its own armed forces in a self-conscious way. But the importance of the Kamba in the Kenyan army may have insulated that army from Kikuyu-Luo tensions at a critical period. There has, however, been a progressive Kikuyuization of the officer corps in the last few years as there has of the civil service. The Kikuyu are the best educated Africans in Kenya, and political sponsorship of Kikuyus in the government service is a clear feature of Kenyan political life.

Lee reports that the Kikuyu had as many officers as the Kamba by 1967. He sees the growth of Kikuyu officers and the relative diminution of officers from small tribes such as the Nandi and Kipsigis, who had played some role in the colonial army, as an attempt to make the army more broadly representative.[68] Yet the fact that the general service unit has increasing numbers of Kikuyu officers, and that the army proper has been commissioning more Kikuyus than any other tribe[69] has led many to feel that the Kikuyus are becoming overrepresented.

The issue of Kikuyuization is a sensitive one in Kenya; the insulation of the army from ethnic struggle cannot be taken for granted in the future. But there are factors which may continue to work for armed forces in Kenya more disciplined and freer of ethnic conflict than those in Uganda. Uganda and Tanzania moved in 1964 to end a British presence in their armed forces. But in Kenya, British training missions continued; British officers remained seconded to the Kenya armed forces; British units trained in Kenya, and had contact with the Kenya armed forces even when the British base system in Kenya was ended and facilities were turned over.[70] Kenya continues to send most of her naval cadets to the Royal Naval College at Dartmouth; her airmen and signalmen learn their duties in England, and army personnel train at Sandhurst, Mons, and the Imperial Defense College. The British impact remains great and works in the direction of making the Kenyan armed forces relatively well trained and effective.

---

[68] Lee.

[69] The social pages of the *East African Standard* frequently announce the marriages of young Kikuyu officers to daughters of prominent Kikuyus. A study of marriage and political/economic relationships would be most interesting in this area.

[70] A 1968 issue of *Majeshi Yetu* (Armed Forces journal) makes interesting reading. It is published with English and Swahili pages, is well written and professional. By-lined articles can be found by C. L. Galloway, Commander A. A. Pearse, and Major A. M. Tippett, among others.

The very factor of past success is important in the future evolution of. the armed forces. It has been suggested earlier in this article that Uganda's army was not up to the military tasks it was given. Kenya's army, on the other hand, has acquitted itself well. This keeps rather narrowly defined professional norms viable as action within the scope of the norms is perceived to be feasible. If the Kenyan army were called on continuously to put down overt ethnic strife, as appeared possible after Tom Mboya's assassination, it would be increasingly difficult to keep the army insulated from tribal conflict. The Kenyan army, like the Ugandan, might well be unsuccessful in such endeavors. Furthermore, it cannot be assumed that Kenya will avoid indefinitely the factional alliances between civilian and military groups that have occupied Uganda's army. Up to now, however, a balancing of battalion commands and even an increasing Kikuyuization of the officers corps have not led Kenyan civilian politicians to use the army or parts of it as a political base for their own personal power.

Kenya does have nonmilitary bases for political power. The present Kikuyu ruling group can rely on its civil service, on a growing commercial and small business group, and on a more prosperous farming class. It can appeal at large to Kikuyu sentiment. Unlike President Obote in Uganda, the Kenyan political leadership is not forced to politicize the army. In Kenya, then, factors intrinsic to the armed forces have interacted with wider societal factors to create a military less engaged in politics in a day-to-day way and not the sole arbiter of the regime. A particular crisis around the succession to Kenyatta could conceivably trigger military intervention; but it does not appear that the basic problems in Kenya attendant on phenomena of social change will in the short run lead to military intervention on the praetorian model. In other words, Kenya's class evolution, the conjunction of tribe and class, regionalism, and Kikuyuization do not seem to be leading to military intervention along the lines set forth in Huntington's concept of praetorian society.

The argument here has been that we can compare Uganda's and Kenya's societies, their armies, and the interaction of army and society. But there are fundamental differences between the Ugandan and Kenyan armies that are not entirely dependent on societal factors but themselves operate as independent factors. It may be useful to look briefly at the way Tanzania as well went about reconstructing its army in order to see if any factors unique to the Tanzanian military can be isolated.

It was stated earlier that the then Prime Minister Obote in effect denied that a mutiny had taken place in Uganda in 1964. In Kenya, Kenyatta noted the gravity of the army action that year, but he did not condemn the entire armed forces as such. Kenya reconstructed its army by continuing with a process of professional training which utilized British officers.[71] In Tanzania, on the other hand, Nyerere condemned the army as a whole,[72] disbanded it, and set about creating new armed forces.[73] The aim was to construct an army that would be politically loyal. Of course, that was the aim in Kenya, too, but in Tanzania the pool for recruitment of the army was to be TANU and TANU-affiliated organizations and commitment to party norms was to be the basis for the initial formation of the new armed forces.[74]

Immediately after the landing of British troops in Tanzania on January 25, 1964, Nyerere called for a new army to be built around the TANU Youth League (TYL). By February 12, however, Second Vice-President Rashidi Kawawa said that, although the Youth League was "another nation-building group," it lacked leadership. A new group—National Servicemen—would be instituted to provide the necessary leadership, and TYL members would be recruited into special village schemes, each headed by National Servicemen.[75] The result was that Youth League members flocked to be recruited into the National Service. Local TANU secretaries used the promise of an army job to get people to take out TANU cards or to pay back dues, though some of the people promised army positions by local secretaries were patently physically unfit. Recruitment was carried out by traveling teams, which moved from place to place reviewing men assembled by the regional police officers and the regional commissioners. Parliamentary secretaries (junior ministers) along with loyal noncommissioned officers also helped recruit.

Although many TYL members were eventually recruited into the army, the idea of using them to form a new army was not sustained. It soon gave way to the more encompassing concept of the National Servicemen, whose recruits had to have exhibited political loyalty, to

[71] See the statement by then Prime Minister Kenyatta of 25 January 1964, reprinted in Gertzel, Goldschmidt, and Rothchild, eds. *Government and Politics in Kenya* (Nairobi, 1969), p. 562.

[72] Kenneth Grundy, *Conflicting Images of the Military in Africa* (Nairobi, 1968), p. 29.

[73] The bulk of the two battalions in Tabora and Dar es Salaam were dismissed and mutineers were sent back to their home areas. They had to report periodically to area commissioners. Internal security was provided first by British and then by Nigerian troops.

[74] The following discussion is taken from Bienen, *Tanzania: Party Transformation and Economic Development* (Princeton, 1970), pp. 374–80. I have also commented on the formation of new Tanzanian armed forces in the previously cited "National Security in Tanzania after the Mutiny," and "Public Order and the Military in Africa: Mutinies in Kenya, Uganda, and Tanganyika."

[75] *Tanganyika Standard*, 12 February 1964, p. 5.

be citizens aged eighteen to twenty-five, and to be able to read and write Swahili. Infantry officers were required to have completed Standard XII.

In May 1964, defense became the responsibility of Second Vice-President Kawawa; both the National Service and youth sections and the headquarters of the Tanzanian People's Defense Forces are now part of his portfolio. A regular army composed of four infantry battalions, one artillery battalion, and one tank company was formed by 1970. An air wing was also created.

Initially, it was stated that all young men would be liable for national service duty, but limited funds have restricted the number of national servicemen. Recruitment begins with three months of national service training, which includes taking part in such nation-building activities as, for example, bush-clearing or road construction. Following this, recruits may join the army, the police, or a specialist unit for six months of paramilitary training. Those who do not enter the armed forces are to establish new village settlements where they may settle if they like; but they are recallable for military duty.

It has been estimated that about 2,000 of the 5,000 who had passed through national service by the end of 1967 were absorbed into the security forces as regular soldiers or policemen.[76] The national service provided a reserve which could be called up as well as a sizable number of recruits to the regular army. It is important to note that the army's recruitment was selective, and it became standarized. Not all army recruits were from national service.[77] Moreover, those who entered the army became full-time soldiers.

The government adopted a number of measures aimed at ensuring political loyalty and integration of the armed forces with TANU, among which was to invite all members of the military and the police to join TANU. On June 24, 1964, Second Vice-President Kawawa told recruits that they were citizens of the country and could participate fully in the politics of the United Republic. The former practice of refusing soldiers the right to political participation had been instituted by the colonialists, according to Mr. Kawawa.[78] (The independent Tanganyika government took three years to change this rule.)

Police and soldiers have responded en masse to TANU's invitation. In fact, they enroll as whole units, and company commanders become heads of the TANU committee, elected by the company.

---

[76] Lee, p. 150. I estimate that somewhat fewer than 5,000 men actually passed through the national service by 1967.

[77] Ibid.

[78] *Nationalist*, 25 June 1964, p. 2.

Officers are expected to do party liaison work and to explain to the troops their role in Tanzania's development. President Nyerere granted an honorary commission in the People's Defense Forces, with rank of colonel, to S. J. Kitundu, the Coast Regional Commissioner and a resident of Dar es Salaam. The President also appointed Mr. Kitundu Political Commissar of the Tanzania Defense Forces effective November 6, 1964. This post is not listed with the Ministry of Defense; it is designed to give a TANU official a high army position. Mr. Kitundu has, however, had no open operational direction of the armed forces.

Before the mutiny, TYL members were often assigned to police duties at meetings or formal roadblocks; they were instructed to prevent smuggling and sometimes even to collect taxes. In certain places, TANU members did constabulary work. But these informal and irregular procedures have now been formalized.[79] To prepare them to defend Tanzania in the event of an attack, members of the nation's police force, prisons service, national service, and TANU Youth League were supposed to undergo full military training with modern weapons. Yet Nyerere later (1968) promised a mass rally in Dar es Salaam that trusted youths who proved to be hard working would be given weapons training. Apparently, the original intentions of 1964 had not been implemented.[80]

Another intention was to expand the defense force beyond the limited number of national servicemen and army by creating a national reserve. A field force of militarized police was to be formed in each region, and special village police, consisting of volunteers working under two regular policemen, were to be posted to villages —particularly border areas and other places where there has been occasional trouble.[81] The people have been told that they are obliged to help these policemen.

There is no information as to whether this national reserve has become an effective force. Villages are, in fact, sparsely settled areas spread out for miles and hard to police. And Tanzania has had one of the smallest salaried police forces in the world in relation to the population and size of the country.[82] In response to this situation, a special constabulary of volunteers has been established to train for police work; its members are recruited from the TYL. Although most regions have such a force, it is best organized in Dar es Salaam.

[79] The Reserve Forces Bill legalizes paramilitary training and functions of the TYL.

[80] *Africa Report*, XIII (April 1968), 23–24.

[81] *Reporter* (Nairobi), 12 February 1965; *Nationalist*, 2 February 1965, p. 1.

[82] The police force grew by 11 percent per annum between 1961–67 (Lee, p. 105). This was the highest rate of growth in East and Central Africa.

None of these measures guarantees a loyal and pliable security force, however. For one thing, an army with a large element of politically aware TYL youth may be difficult for the leadership to digest, for the TYL has caused trouble in the past. Despite sporadic attempts to governmentalize it by incorporating it into a Ministry of Culture and Youth, the TYL has managed to retain its identity. Difficulties not related to the new recruits have also sprung up in the army since 1964. When the Congo border became very unstable, the government decided to allow some of the disgraced mutineers back into the army as a stop-gap measure; shortly thereafter, unexplained trouble broke out in the army.[83] There have also been rumors to the effect that a Zanzibari unit posted near Mozambique was very undisciplined and had to be shipped back. In 1969–70 other army officers were arrested and accused of plotting to overthrow Nyerere.

Conclusions

Certain inferences may be drawn about the three countries under discussion. It does not appear that the Tanzanian People's Defense Force has been completely free of internal conflicts or that relations between the military and civilian leaders have been without any tension, although the army has posed no threat to the TANU government since 1964. Both the Kenyan and the Tanzanian governments seem to have insulated their respective armies from major political and ethnic issues during the last ten years. In both cases, the personal position of the leader was stronger than in Uganda. In addition, the Kenyan civil service and TANU provide institutional bases of support not available in Uganda. At the same time, the Kenyans were able to build on a military much less internally split and with better trained men than the Ugandan army. The Tanzanians started afresh in 1964 with a much more thorough housecleaning than the Ugandans undertook. In a more consensual society, the Tanzanians appear to have had some success in welding the army to the TANU government, although it is not clear that specific TANU institutions have played a major role in this process. The Tanzanian army is itself occupied with conflict on the southern border with Mozambique; and

---

[83] The 12 September 1964 headline of the *Nationalist* read: "U. R. [United Republic] Army Arrests." The text of a government announcement was printed: "In active pursuance of its duty to maintain the integrity and safety of the United Republic the government yesterday found it necessary to arrest and detain a small number of servants of the Republic. This number included Officers and other ranks of the United Republic Army, who were of doubtful loyalty and guilty of insubordination by default." It was on this occasion that Elisha Kavonna, who had been nominated by the 1964 mutineers, was arrested.

such a preoccupation with external rather than internal conflicts acts to keep an army out of constant intervention in domestic affairs. If the army handles the external conflict creditably, it works to increase the possibilities of building a disciplined force in the future.

It cannot be assumed that the Kenyan or Tanzanian armed forces will not become increasingly active in domestic politics or that their military will never make coups. But this article has tried to suggest that there is a much greater probability of military intervention in Uganda because of the nature of the society. Indeed, as General Amin was reported to have said after the 1964 coup, the Uganda army had been rather openly keeping the regime in power. The Uganda coup may not have been well planned;[84] it may have been triggered by Amin's own perception that he would be removed soon and his awareness of the growing power of nonregular army forces.[85] But these were mere precipitants of the coup;[86] basically, it was caused by underlying conditions in Uganda that differed from those in Tanzania and Kenya in important respects.

We can perhaps draw some conclusions about the prospects for military rule from certain features shown by the intervention itself. The reason why a military intervenes is important. Armed forces can make coups for rather narrow professional and interest group reasons: they can claim that the army is not being paid enough, that its honor is being sullied, or that it is being destroyed by the politicians; or they can have personal fears of particular officers. Alternatively, the military may intervene for broad political goals.

In Uganda, the military seems to have reacted to personal fears of the officers, to growing discontent with the way the regular army was being treated, and to unhappiness about the political situation, especially its ethnic components. An important factor is that the military was internally split before and during the coup. In effect, one part of the military fought against another part that was more closely allied

---

[84] The *Economist* made this assertion in its issue of 6 February 1971, p. 27.

[85] General Amin reportedly said that a secret meeting was held on January 11 at which a decision was taken to murder him and others. Amin was said to have claimed that the president, then in Singapore, was kept abreast of the plot throughout by communications with the Minister of International Affairs. *Foreign Broadcast Information Service*, Middle East and Africa, January 1971, p. U–6.

[86] Twaddle also uses the language of "precipitants" and "preconditions" following the terms in Harry Eckstein, "Introduction. Toward the Theoretical Study of Internal War," in Eckstein, ed. *Internal War* (Glencoe, 1964), pp. 1–32. Twaddle sees the Uganda coup not so much as an army mutiny as part of an internal war situation. Lofchie (p. 19) argues that the Uganda army "can best be understood as a kind of economic class, an elite stratum with a set of economic interests to protect." Chick (p. 634) takes Lofchie to task over the notion of stratum and class as applied to the Uganda army, and both he and Gershenberg doubt whether the Obote government threatened the military's interests.

with Obote. Yet General Amin and his colleagues moved slowly and cautiously after the coup. They do not appear to have had clearly drawn political goals. The new cabinet that Amin announced was composed largely of civil service personnel—it had two soldiers, three politicians, and seventeen civil servants. Only three Baganda were in the cabinet although the coup was at first enthusiastically received in Baganda. If the military remains internally split and if the officers in Uganda are not political animals, then the prospects for either successful or long-term military rule are diminished.

This article has tried to show that we should not overhomogenize African societies or their armed forces. We shall have to continue to explore the interrelationships between armed forces and societies and our comparisons are going to have to deal with interactions.

All three East African countries discussed in this article have problems of political participation and political order. However, the army's intervention in politics cannot be deduced from a ratio of participation to institutionalization. We must agree that military explanations do not explain military interventions and that the general politicization of social forces and institutions must be examined.[87] At the same time, knowing about rates of mobilization, degrees of social cohesion, and levels of political institutionalization will not tell us all we want to know about the potentialities of military intervention in a given society.

The discussion of East African armies and societies suggests that institutionalization and performance of the armed forces are critical factors.[88] But analysis of the armed forces—the special conditions which pertain to each individual military—must be linked to wider societal factors.[89] This means we should be studying the *connections* among variables.

We examine the recruitment procedures of armed forces within the context of analysis of class, ethnicity, and factional cleavages in society at large. We examine attitudes of soldiers not in isolation, but by looking at the various groups and social formations that espouse ideologies and programs. Thus we look at the nature of the participation of armed forces in politics by analyzing patterns of political participation throughout a society.

[87] Huntington, *Political Order*, p. 194.

[88] I have greatly benefited from reading Abraham Lowenthal's "Armies and Politics in Latin America: A Review of the Recent Literature," *World Politics*, forthcoming. Lowenthal emphasizes the need to examine institutionalization within armies and to analyze the comparative strength of civilian and military organizations in specific countries.

[89] Perlmutter, "The Arab Military Elite," p. 276.

At the same time, in order to understand political participation in society at large, we must examine the internal workings of armed forces organizations.

A Comparative Analysis of the Political and Economic Performance of Military and Civilian Regimes

A Cross-National Aggregate Study

R. D. McKinlay and A. S. Cohan*

The analysis of military intervention in the form of coups has achieved the status of an institutionalized topic in comparative politics. In marked contrast, the examination of the performance of military regimes established as a consequence of coups has attracted little attention.[1] This is particularly unfortunate since it is the performance of a regime rather than its origin (i.e., whether it emerged as a consequence of an election or a coup), which is of greater significance when assessing the regime's effect on the processes of economic and social change.

This article is the second of a series of reports on a cross-national aggregate project designed explicitly to examine the performance of military regimes. The main purpose of the piece is to evaluate the performance of military and civilian regimes along a range of political, economic, and military variables.

Research Design

It is clearly impossible to assess adequately the performance of military regimes without comparing their performance to that of civilian regimes. This requirement has led to the definition of four populations of regimes. The first consists of military regimes (MR). A military regime is one in which the armed forces have made a coup, established a government in which the main executive post is held by a military person, and have stayed in power for at least the major part of one year. If a country has experienced several periods of military rule, these have been aggregated. The second population consists of the periods of civilian rule in countries that have experienced a military regime (CRM). The third population consists of all other low-income countries which have experienced only civilian rule (CR 900–). The fourth population is that of the high-income systems (CR 900+) and is included primarily for reference purposes.[2] This article deals mainly with the MR, the CRM, and the CR (900–).

The total population, constituted by the four subpopulations cited, consists of all independent countries in the world with a population greater than one million. The Communist countries were excluded due to data shortage and data incomparability. The time span over which performance is examined is the period 1951–70.

The comparison of the three main regime types attempts to look for differences and similarities among the populations. In the exercise not only can we use a variety of standard tests; but we can also rely on the designs of the populations. The strongest part of the design relates to the comparison between the MR and the CRM. Although the populations of the MR and the CRM cannot be regarded as matched pairs, they are as close to matched pairs as one is likely to find in macro cross-national aggregate research, and, as such, control for a large number of intervening variables. Even this form of comparison, however, is inadequate without an additional reference point; hence, the inclusion of the CR (900–).

The advantages of this type of design may be seen from a brief survey of the types of outcome that can be anticipated when these three populations are compared on any variable. Four main types of outcome may be defined; these can be summarized conveniently by an adaptation of simple set theory.[3] If we let X, Y, Z represent three sets, each of which corresponds to the mean score of the distribution of the three populations MR, CRM, and CR (900–) on a particular variable, then the four main types of outcome can be defined as:

$$1. \ (X \sim Y) \sim Z \equiv X \cap Y = \phi, \ X \cap Z = \phi, \ Y \cap Z = \phi$$
$$2. \ (X \not\sim Y) \not\sim Z \equiv X \cap Y \neq \phi, \ X \cap Z \neq \phi, \ Y \cap Z \neq \phi$$
$$3. \ (X \not\sim Y) \sim Z \equiv X \cap Y \neq \phi, \ X \cap Z = \phi, \ Y \cap Z = \phi$$
$$4. \ (X \sim Y) \not\sim Z \equiv X \cap Y = \phi, \ X \cap Z \neq \phi, \ Y \cap Z \neq \phi.$$

The first outcome implies that all three sets are disjoint. The second outcome implies no sets are disjoint, i.e., all intersect. The third implies that one set is disjoint, but that the other two sets intersect. (In the example given above, Z is disjoint.) The fourth outcome implies that two sets are disjoint, but that both intersect with the third (in the example given above, X and Y are disjoint). In outcomes 1 and 2 there is only one possible combination, whereas in outcomes 3 and 4 there are three possible combinations dependent on which set or sets are disjoint. Each of these outcomes will, of course, yield quite different interpretation.[4]

The data set and the variables along which performance of the different types of regime are compared can now be examined. Performance is compared across twenty-one variables, categorized into five main groupings. These variables were collected on an annual basis and, where appropriate, means or percentages or growth rates have been calculated. Annual data collection is essential, because the variables generally show marked fluctuations which cannot be accommodated by one-year observations. The standard political science compilations could not be used since many of the variables used in this study are not included in these works or are included only for a single observation point.[5]

The first category consists of six political variables.[6] Four of these tap levels of political activity which are measured by the following: (1) the percentage of years that the constitution is not observed; (2) the percentage of years that the legislature is banned; (3) the percentage of years that parties are banned; and (4) the mean percentage of cabinet posts held by military personnel. Each of these four variables measures a particular aspect of institutionalized political activity. The constitution is the most formal statement of political norms and structure; the legislature represents one of the primary central locations of political activity; political parties constitute the main mass form of political organization; and the number of cabinet posts held by military personnel gives some indication of the extent of formal control that the military exercises over the main executive body. As the score of each of these variables increases, some decrease in certain formal manifestations of civilian political activity is represented. A fifth, related indicator is the percentage of years that the Communist party is banned. This is included to give some information on the popular concept of the antipathy of the military to communism. The sixth indicator is the average tenure of the main executive, measured in months. This is included because executive change is a standard indicator that represents circulation, and, on occasion, high levels of change are taken to be synonymous with instability.

The second category consists of two military variables—the mean size of the armed forces per 10,000 population, and the mean military expenditure as a percentage of GNP.[7] The rationale for the inclusion of a category of military variables should be clear, given the importance of military affairs to most political systems.

The remaining three categories of variables are economic.[8] The first of these consists of three background variables: (1) the constant per capita gross national product (GNP); (2) the budget as a percentage of GNP; and (3) primary production as a percentage of gross domestic product. These are considered background variables because, although they do change over time, they are not as dynamic in the short term as the other economic variables. Collectively, they provide both a good basic composite picture of any economy and the reference points against which other economic variables may be evaluated. GNP, despite its well-known limitations, is the most general measure of the economy; the relative size of the budget gives some indication of the role of the central government in the economy; and primary production gives some measure of the sophistication and complexity of an economy.

The second of the economic categories consists of five international trade variables: (1) exports and (2) imports taken as percentages of GNP; (3) international liquidity as a percentage of imports; (4) goods and services balance; and (5) direct and other private investment balance (the last two measured as a percentage of GNP). Export and import levels give some indication of a commitment to international trade, which, in general, is extremely important for low-income systems, given that much of their growth is export-led. International liquidity holdings, which include official gold holdings, foreign exchange, and reserve positions in the International Monetary Fund, are particularly important for overcoming short-term economic difficulties. These difficulties are more acute for the low-income systems, which tend to have unstable exports. International liquidity is measured as a percentage of imports, thus giving some indication of the capacity to finance imports in the event of short-term difficulties. Balance of payments accounts provide a summary picture of a country's external account with the rest of the world. The first variable covers the balance on goods, services, and private unrequited transfers, thereby giving an aggregate picture of the basic trading position. The second variable covers direct and other forms of private investment, reflecting a country's position on the private market.[9]

The final category of variables measures economic performance. Five variables are employed: the rates of growth of (1) constant per capita GNP; (2) cost of living; (3) exports; (4) the food index; and (5) primary education. The rate of growth of GNP provides the most generalized aggregate indicator of the dynamics of economic development. The rate of growth of cost of living is partially incorporated in GNP growth rates, since the latter are measured in constant terms. It is, however, included because, even in situations of constant growth, a high rate of growth of the cost of living can be destabilizing when the payoffs from economic development are not evenly distributed to all consumers. The export growth rate is included on account of the importance of exports to the economic development of low-income systems. The rates of growth of food and primary education give more precise information on two aspects of socioeconomic change.

The primary objective of this article is to determine whether the performance of military regimes is such as to differentiate them from civilian regimes. This is attempted primarily by examining the differences between MR and CRM, and by comparing both of these with the CR (900–). The consequence of each of these comparisons gives one of the outcomes outlined earlier. The next section describes a cluster analysis of the total population of regimes, which provides a generalized picture of the relation between the populations of MR, CRM, and all CR. The remainder is divided into five sections corresponding to the five categories of variables. Each section includes an aggregate comparison among MR, CRM, CR (900–), and CR (900+). The aggregate comparison is then extended by comparing MR, CRM, and CR (900–), using the controls of GNP and area.

Cluster Analysis

Before the different types of regime are compared in detail across the range of political, military, and economic variables, it is useful, given the large number of cases and the large array of variables, to construct a summary picture of the population. The most appropriate multivariate technique for this purpose is cluster analysis. As a method of empirical typology formation, cluster analysis permits the construction of profiles, thus providing an excellent way of simplifying and categorizing the population. Specifically, cluster analysis enables us to find out which regimes group together, and which variables provide the defining characteristics of any such groupings. Thus, in addition to providing an empirical clustering of cases, and an empirical profile of each cluster in terms of the political, military, and economic variables, it is possible to examine in general terms whether the MR cluster separately from the CRM, and whether the CRM cluster separately from the CR, and which variables, if any, make the MR distinctive.

The cluster analysis was run on 115 cases, with 23 variables. An interactive method—relocation—was used. This is superior to a number of other hierarchical methods in that it permits relocation of cases once fusion has begun. The similarity coefficient used was the error sum, which basically seeks to minimize variance within clusters. One main problem of cluster analysis is that clustering takes place even in the absence of empirical justification for clustering. However, there are two ways in which the accuracy of the clusters may be checked. First, the dendrogram gives a measure of the error scores at which fusion takes place, and, second, examination of the F ratio and T

Table 1   Distribution of Types of Regime, by Clusters

Regime Type	Clusters						
	1	2	3	4	5	6	Total
MR.	0	0	5	6	15	6	32
CRM	1	2	4	19	0	6	32
CR.	18	1	14	13	1	4	51
Total	19	3	23	38	16	16	115

tests gives a measure of the degree of homogeneity of each of the clusters. Using these criteria, the cluster level chosen for the extraction of clusters was level six.[10]

With reference to the distribution of cases between the various clusters, two questions are of interest. The first is whether the distribution of each of the three subpopulations is randomly placed within the clusters, or whether there is evidence of clustering of cases. The second question is more specifically concerned with the distribution of matching MR and CRM. It examines whether the pairs are located in the same cluster.

As seen in Table 1, the three subpopulations are not randomly distributed within clusters. The expected ratio of MR:CRM:CR is 1:1:1.6.[11] Although the presence of zeros inhibits the calculation of actual ratios, no single cluster manifests the expected ratio. Forty-seven percent of MR are contained in a cluster in which the MR represent 94 percent of cases; 59 percent of the CRM are contained in a cluster in which they constitute 50 percent of the cases; 35 percent of the CR fall in one cluster in which they constitute 95 percent of cases. A summary indication of the skewness of the distribution is that, in five of the clusters, one subpopulation represents 50 percent or more of the cases.

The distribution of CRM compared with MR, where individual CRM and MR are matched by country, is shown in Table 2. Reading across from the vertical axis reveals the cluster in which a civilian regime is located. Reading upwards to the horizontal axis indicates the cluster in which the counterpart military regime of that country is found. The bracketed figures show the number of pairs of MR and CRM contained in the same cluster.

Three interesting features are indicated in Table 2. First, 34 percent of the coup countries have the military and civilian periods (i.e., MR and CRM) contained in the same cluster. Thus, in just over one-third of the coup country cases, the similarities between the military and civilian periods of rule are sufficient to hold both types

Table 2   Matched Distribution of MR and CRM, by Clusters

CRM by Cluster Number	MR by Cluster Number						
	1	2	3	4	5	6	Total
1	(0)	0	1	0	0	0	1
2	0	(0)	0	0	0	1	1
3	0	0	(1)	1	2	0	4
4	0	0	2	(4)	11	0	17
5	0	0	0	0	(0)	0	0
6	0	0	0	0	1	(5)	6
Total	0	0	4	5	14	6	29

of regime in the same cluster. Second, the four clusters containing MR show marked differences in the propensity for holding matching CRM. In cluster six, 83 percent remain in the same cluster; in cluster four, 80 percent remain. However, in cluster three, only 25 percent remain; and in cluster five, none remains in the same cluster. Thus, while the defining characteristics of clusters six and four identify sufficiently powerful common denominators to retain MR and their counterpart CRM in the same cluster, clusters three and five do not. Finally, there is a particularly strong relationship between two clusters concerning the pairs which do not remain in the same cluster. Of the nineteen MR which do not have their counterpart CRM in the same cluster, thirteen have their CRM in cluster four, and eleven of these thirteen move from cluster five. In sum, the individual clusters show very different propensities to contain pairs of MR/CRM. Thirty-four percent of pairs are located in the same cluster; 57 percent of MR have their counterpart CRM in cluster four; and 38 percent of all pairs have the military period located in cluster five and the civilian period in cluster four.

We may now relate the distribution of each of the subpopulations to the cluster characteristics. The first point concerns the location of the subpopulations. The major grouping of MR falls in the cluster characterized by high political restrictions, small military, low background economic factors, low international economic commitment but average balances, and the poorest economic performance. The other cases of MR are fairly evenly distributed among three other clusters. Only one of these clusters has low political restrictions and, in aggregate, no MR fall into either of the two clusters which have low restrictions. Only six MR fall into the cluster which has the very high military expenditure and size, however. Indeed, the majority of MR fall into the clusters characterized by the lowest military expenditure and size. The majority of cases of MR fall into clusters having the lowest economic background characteristics. The state of the MR on international economic variables is rather varied. The majority of cases fall into clusters having low export and import levels, but average balances. However, the remaining cases fall into the two clusters having the poorest trade balances; but in the case of one of these clusters it is offset to some extent by a very high investment balance. Finally, MR are characterized either by average or below-average economic performance.

The CRM are located primarily in the cluster characterized by mixed political restrictions, small military, the lowest background economic factors, low international trade but average balances, and low economic performance rates. Of the remaining CRM, half are located in clusters with low political restrictions and half in one cluster with high restrictions. The same pattern is repeated for military size and expenditure, with half located in clusters with low scores and half in those with high scores. As for background economic variables, the majority of the remaining cases are located in clusters with above average scores. However, the opposite is the case for international trade, with the majority of CRM located in clusters with poor trade balances. The pattern is again reversed with reference to economic performance; the majority of remaining cases are located in clusters with higher than average performance.

The CR do not show the same concentration as the MR and CRM; i.e., clearer subpopulations within the CR population can be identified. The most distinctive subpopulation is contained in the first cluster. This cluster is characterized by minimal political restrictions, large military size and expenditure, exceedingly high scores on background economic factors, sound international trading position, and good economic performance. The second main concentration of CR is located in the cluster characterized by low political restrictions, small military scores, below-average background economic scores, very low trade balance but high investment balance, and close to average economic performance. The third concentration falls in the cluster dominated by the CRM, already described.

The second general point concerning the relationship of the distribution of cases to the cluster characteristics relates to the nature of the clusters which contain both the MR and the CRM counterparts. Clusters four and six achieve this, but these two clusters are quite different across each of the five categories of variables. Presumably, the factors responsible for holding MR/CRM counterparts in cluster six are the exceedingly high military scores and the high political restrictions. The capacity of cluster four to retain MR/CRM counterparts can best be illustrated by comparing cluster four to cluster five.

Table 3   Executive Change and Restriction on Political Activity, by Regime Types

Political Variables	Regime Types			
	MR	CRM	CR (900–)	CR (900+)
Mean tenure main executive	40.8	54.5	101.7	55.7
Percent years constitution not full	62.7	13.2	13.4	0.0
Percent years assembly banned	73.4	7.8	5.1	0.0
Percent years parties banned	53.5	9.3	12.1	0.0
Percent years Communist party banned	90.5	58.7	65.1	3.3
Percent military personnel in cabinet	44.2	8.3	3.6	0.2

As suggested, cluster five contains the largest concentration of MR but no CRM, and the most popular relocation of these MR is in cluster four. Actually, cluster four closely resembles cluster five in all respects but one—levels of restriction on political activity. It would seem, therefore, that the absence of a high level of restrictions on political activity in some MR keeps them in the same cluster as their CRM counterparts. Further, a decline in the level of political restrictions in the CRM, whose counterpart MR lie in cluster five, seems to be responsible for their relocation in cluster four.

Political Performance
The analysis of variance on each of the political indicators shows highly significant variation (at .01 level) among the regime types. Difference testing for each variable produces two main patterns. One indicates executive change where the CR (900–) appear to be the deviant population; the other represents all remaining political variables where MR have much higher scores than both CRM and CR (900–)—which, in turn, have slightly higher scores than the CR (900+).

The average tenure of the main executive is significantly shorter in the MR than in the CRM (at the .10 level). The average tenure in the CR (900–), however, is approximately twice that of the CRM (with differences between the CR [900–], with both the MR and the CRM significant at the .01 level.) Two explanations are suggested for the difference. The greater circulation of the main executive in the CRM may be responsible for encouraging military coups, although this explanation does not seem to be satisfactory since the average tenure of the main executive in the CRM closely correlates with that in the CR (900+). The more likely explanation is that military coups terminate civilian (CRM) regimes, and the shorter tenure is more a consequence than a cause of coups.

The restrictions on the constitution, assemblies, and political parties demonstrate a consistent and expected pattern. The MR are clearly differentiated from the very similar CRM and CR (900–), both of which have higher scores than the CR (900+).[12] Using the CR (900–) as a reference point, this general finding suggests two conclusions. First, CRM do not maintain the types of restrictions imposed during the period of military rule. Second, military regimes are not likely to occur in systems where levels of political activity are generally low.

The restrictions on political activity under the MR are much higher than in any of the other regime types, but they are not total. Assemblies are banned for approximately 75 percent of the regime, but parties are banned for only half the period of military rule. It is, however, obvious that one function of political parties is terminated if assemblies are banned. This lower priority on the part of military regimes to ban parties may be explained by several factors: (1) any ban on assemblies must entail some restriction on parties; (2) the practicalities of curtailing party activities are likely to be greater than imposing and maintaining bans on the constitution or assemblies; and (3) the military may find it advantageous to rely on an existing party or parties either to recruit civilians with governmental expertise or to provide some means for political mobilization through a party led by the military.

The view that military regimes are hostile toward communism is convincingly supported by the fact that Communist parties are scarcely tolerated at all.[13] The scores for both the CRM and the CR (900–) indicate that they also discriminate against the Communist party.

Political restrictions, measured by the percentage of cabinet posts held by the military, again show the MR with a significantly higher score than either the CRM or CR (900–), which in turn have significantly higher scores than CR (900+).[14] For the first time, however, there appears to be a significant difference between the CRM and the CR (900–). These results are of interest because it is clear that, while military regimes place little reliance on assemblies, much more extensive use is made of civilians in terms of composition of the main executive body. In addition, the absence of significant differences between CRM and CR (900–) on the other political variables indicates the lack of any continuity between military and civilian periods of rule, at least in terms of political restrictions. The appearance of a significant difference on this variable would seem to indicate some continuity, but any continuity between military and civilian periods of rule can be easily explained. Thus, a greater percentage of cabinet posts held by military personnel in a civilian regime may predispose the military to initiate a coup. On the other hand, with the termination of a military regime, the military may wish to retain some degree of formal control through the retention of certain cabinet posts. While the significant difference between the CRM and the CR (900–) cannot be denied, it should be noted that the scores for neither regime are very high, nor is the absolute difference between them substantial. Therefore, it is suggested that the general finding on the absence of continuity between MR and CRM in terms of political restrictions is not weakened.[15]

A two-way analysis of variance of GNP and regime type on the political variables shows, with few exceptions, the persistence of differences among regime types and the absence of differences among GNP levels.[16] In other words, the patterns of restriction apparent in the aggregate findings are attributable to regime type rather than to GNP. The first slight deviation relates to executive tenure. While there is still the significant variation between regime types, there is also an interaction effect (both at the .01 level). Closer examination shows this to be due to GNP level three, where the score for the MR is almost twice that for the MR in the two other levels; where the CRM actually have a lower score than the MR; and where the CR have the lowest score.[17] If there were any relation between civilian institutionalization and GNP, it might have been expected that as GNP increased, the military regimes would become more unstable. This is not the case, however; and, in terms of tenure, military regimes are more stable at a higher GNP level.

A second exception relates to the ban on the constitution—the only factor which varies significantly with GNP. This variation is largely attributable to the very low score of the military regimes in GNP level three. Since these military regimes ban assemblies and parties to a degree similar to other levels, however, little importance can be attached to this deviation.

A final point is that, although there is little variation and interaction effect among GNP levels, the civilian regimes in GNP level three consistently have the least restrictions. Since the scores of both the MR and CRM in this level are no lower than the same type of regime in the other levels, the disparity between countries that have experienced military regimes and those which have not is most acute in the low-income systems with the highest level of economic development.

The introduction of area controls does not lead to any important changes in the aggregate findings.[18] Irrespective of area, levels of

Table 4   Military Size and Expenditure, by Regime Type

Military Variables	Regime Type			
	MR	CRM	CR (900–)	CR (900+)
Size per 10^4 population	51	49	38	89
Expenditure percent GNP	3.4	4.0	2.6	4.0

political restrictions are highest in military regimes, whereas little difference appears between the two types of civilian regimes.

Perhaps the most interesting variable is the percentage of cabinet posts held by the military. There is a significant difference in every area between the MR and the CRM, and between the MR and CR. This variable is the best differentiator of military and civilian regimes. While political restrictions generally are a function of military regimes, there are a number of high scores by CRM and CR although the higher scores in the percentage of military personnel in the cabinet are typically a feature of military regimes. Even in the Middle East, where both the CRM and CR restrictions on parties, assemblies, and constitutions are high, there is a low percentage of military in the executive.[19] Also of interest is the fact that Central and South America have markedly higher CRM scores than the Middle East, and the latter reporting a significant difference between the CRM and the CR (at the .05 level) which would suggest some continuity between the MR and CRM in Latin America.[20] This may mean that the longer exposure to military regimes has given rise to a greater continuing prominence of the military even during periods of civilian rule.

Military Performance
When all four populations are compared by analysis of variance, significant variation at the .05 level appears on military size, but not on expenditure. Closer examination, by difference of means tests, shows that, with reference to size, the deviant category is the CR (900+). No significant differences appear among the other three populations, but all have military forces significantly smaller than the CR (900+) at the .01 level. While no significant variations appear for military expenditure, the absence of difference is undoubtedly due to the substantially higher GNP of the CR (900+). The CR (900+) would again have been deviant if military expenditure had been measured on a per capita basis.

From these findings four main conclusions may be drawn. First, the absence of any significant differences between MR and CRM seems to indicate that military rule does not lead to an increase in military expenditure or in the size of the armed forces. If military rule periods precede civilian rule periods and if there is the usual steady rate of growth over time in military size and expenditure, then time may obscure an actual expenditure increase by military regimes. (The distribution of military regimes, however, is such that the majority are of more recent origin.) Considering positive rates of growth, it is surprising that size and expenditure under military regimes are not higher. No evidence is given to support the popular concept that military regimes show a special predisposition to the armed forces in terms of increased size and expenditure.[21] Second, it may be argued that military regimes occur in systems presently demonstrating large military size or high expenditure, thereby obviating the need for military regimes to increase size or expenditure; but the absence of any significant differences among MR, CRM, and CR (900–) indicates that this is not the case. Inversely, we may further conclude that noncoup systems avoid coups by catering to the military; but again, the absence of any significant differences between MR and CRM and CR (900–) seems to disprove this. A final conclusion concerns the position of CRM vis-à-vis CR (900–) and MR. Unlike the political variables, where significant differences between MR and CRM appeared, with CRM lying closer to CR (900–) than to the MR counterparts, there is no evidence that the type of regime is an adequate predictor of military size and expenditure.

Controls for GNP fail to produce any significant differences, thereby reinforcing the main finding that there are no differences in military size and expenditure between the MR, CRM, and CR (900–). Two-way analysis of variance of regime type by GNP on size shows no significant variation between regime types controlling for GNP and no significant interaction effect, while controlling for regime type shows significant variation among GNP levels.[22]

Two-way analysis of variance on expenditure shows similar results. There is no significant difference between types of regime controlling for GNP, but there is a significant variation between

Table 5   Military Size, by Regime Type and GNP Level

GNP Level	Regime Type		
	MR	CRM	CR
1	36	35	9
2	59	61	74
3	80	64	32

Table 6   Military Expenditure, by Regime Type and GNP Level

GNP Level	Regime Type		
	MR	CRM	CR
1	3.1	3.6	1.5
2	3.8	3.3	3.9
3	1.9	2.2	1.8

GNP levels.[23] Size and expenditure seem to bear rather different relationships to GNP levels. Size doubles from GNP level one to GNP level two and remains high, while expenditure increases by some 30 percent from level one to level two, but then decreases by some 50 percent. Another difference between size and expenditure is found when one-way analyses of variance are run on size and expenditure for each of the different GNP levels. A significant difference (at the .05 level) appears between the expenditure of the three regime types at GNP level one. While this single finding can hardly disturb the observation that GNP controls do not provide major differences, it does indicate that, in low-level GNP systems, the countries with high military expenditure have military regimes. Since there is no significant difference between MR and CRM, however, there is no evidence that military regimes in low-level GNP systems take advantage of military rule to increase expenditure. It is more likely that any armed force must reach a certain level of development before it is capable of establishing a regime.

Two-way analysis of variance shows no significant variation between regime types controlling for area, and no significant interaction effect; but it does show significant variation (at the .01 level) in both military size and expenditure among areas. This latter finding is attributable to the enormous range in military size and expenditure from Africa to the Middle East and Asia.[24] As with GNP controls, adjustment by area does not conflict with the main finding of the absence of significant variation between different regime types. However, when area controls are employed by holding area constant rather than adjusting for area, a number of significant differences among regime types emerge. The MR and CRM of Central America both have size and expenditure scores significantly higher than the CR (at the .10 level); the MR and CRM of Africa have significantly higher expenditures than the CR (at the .01 level); and the CRM, but not the MR, of Asia have higher expenditure than the CR (at the .05 level). The only time a CR score greatly exceeds those of MR and CRM is in South America, where the size of the armed forces in the CR is significantly higher (at the .01 level).

In general, there are no significant differences among the three types of regime in terms of military size and expenditure. While substantial variations occur among different GNP levels and different areas, no significant variations emerge among regime types controlling for area and GNP. Examination of within-category differences in both area and GNP shows that differences never appear between MR and CRM, but only between these two types of regime and CR, and, with one exception, the CR scores are lower. Therefore, there is no evidence to indicate either that military regimes use periods of military rule to increase military size and expenditure or that CR avoid coups by catering to the military. There is, however, some indication that in a number of instances the systems that experience military rule have higher military size and expenditure.

Economic Background Performance

One-way analysis of variance shows highly significant differences among the four regime types on each of the three background economic variables. The obvious location for this variation lies in the CR (900+) category.[25] While difference of means testing shows no significant differences among MR, CRM, and CR (900–) in terms of GNP and primary production, both the MR and CRM have significantly lower budgets than the CR (900–)—at the .10 and .05 levels.

Three observations may be drawn from these results. First, there are no significant differences between MR and CRM, though this absence of differences is considerably less interesting and important than in the case of the military variables. Since background variables do not change substantially in the short run, major differences between MR and CRM could not be expected. The slightly higher scores of the MR are due to the more recent occurrence of a majority of MR compared to the CRM counterparts. Second, when the high-income systems are removed, there is little evidence that military regime systems have weaker background economic characteristics

Table 7   Background Economic Variables, by Regime Type

Background Variables	Regime Type			
	MR	CRM	CR (900–)	CR (900+)
Constant GNP per capita $	228	213	257	1528
Primary production,				
percent GNP	32.8	34.3	31.4	11.1
Budget percent GNP	16.0	15.7	17.9	20.8

than nonmilitary regime systems. The one caveat that must be made is that the role of government in the economy, as measured by the budget, seems to be greater in noncoup systems. Finally, on the one indicator where differences among MR, CRM, and CR (900–) appear, the CRM are closer to the MR than to the CR (900–).

When GNP is controlled, the only meaningful comparison is with reference to the budget. Two-way analysis does not show any significant variation among MR, CRM, and CR when GNP is controlled, nor is there any significant variation among GNP levels. This suggests that the significantly higher budget of CR (900–) over MR and CRM derived from the aggregate comparison is misleading, since once GNP is adjusted, the higher budget of the CR (900–) is no longer significant.

Although the aggregate picture shows little variation among MR, CRM, and CR (900–), the introduction of area controls shows some substantial variation. Two-way analysis of variance of regime type and area on GNP and primary production manifests significant variation among regime controlling for area and areas controlling for regime.[26] Two-way analysis of variance on budget shows significant variation only among areas.[27] The more important results for our purpose are the significant variations in GNP and primary production among regimes.

Only in the Middle East and North Africa do no significant differences among regimes appear.[28] In all other areas, both the MR and CRM have significantly lower GNP than the CR. While it may seem strange that the aggregate analysis of variance should not have detected these differences, there is a greater observed ratio of MR and CRM to CR in the higher-income areas, i.e., Latin America, than would be expected from the total ratios of MR and CRM to CR, and a lower ratio in the low-income areas, especially Africa. Although MR and CRM generally have lower GNP than the CR within areas, the overrepresentation of MR and CRM in higher-income areas could account for the absence of any significant variation in the aggregate analysis of variance. The results of the difference testing, therefore, provide an important qualification to the general finding previously outlined, i.e., that MR and CRM are not located in weaker economic systems. The indication is that, if adjustments are made for area, then MR and CRM have significantly lower GNP than CR.

With reference to primary production in three areas (Central and South America, the Middle East, and North Africa), MR and CRM have significantly higher levels of primary production.[29] Again, the overrepresentation of MR and CRM in Latin America accounts for the absence of significant variation in the aggregate picture. The general absence of significant variation among regimes vis-à-vis level of primary production is quite correct; but it must be qualified to the extent that, once adjustments for area are made, then significant variations among regimes appear, with MR and CRM having higher levels of primary production.

The findings on the budget work in the opposite direction from those of GNP and primary production. While the aggregate picture shows significant variation, two-way analysis of variance manifests no significant variation among regimes controlling for area. Difference testing indicates that only in South America do MR and CRM have lower budgets than the CR (at the .05 level). In contrast to the cases of GNP and primary production, Latin America does not have the highest budgets; therefore, the overrepresentation of MR and CRM in these areas does not inhibit the emergence of significant variation in the aggregate analysis of variance. The aggregate finding indicating that MR and CRM have significantly lower budgets than CR is correct. Once area is adjusted, however, the role of the government in the economy in MR and CRM would appear to be equivalent to its role in CR.

Thus, no significant variations occur between MR and CRM either in aggregate terms or when area and GNP controls are introduced. While MR and CRM have lower budgets in aggregate terms than CR (900–), GNP and area adjustments cause the significant variations to disappear. In contrast to this, aggregate comparisons among the three types of regime show no significant variation in terms of GNP and primary production, but the introduction of area controls does appear to place MR and CRM in a weaker economic position.

International Trade Performance
One-way analysis of variance and difference testing on the international trade variables provide three main conclusions. First, MR do not differ significantly from CRM on any of the variables. In aggregate this suggests that in systems that have experienced military rule, it is of little importance whether the government is controlled by civilians or by military personnel. This finding seems to destroy both the image of the military as a conservative, pragmatic organization sensitive to deficits as well as the image of the military as totally incompetent in all affairs outside those of organized force. Of further interest in this context is the fact that private direct investment does not seem to vary with periods of military rule. Second, both MR and CRM have significantly lower export and import levels than CR (900–), but there are no differences in terms of trade and investment balances or in international liquidity holdings.[30] Therefore, while

Table 8   International Trade, by Regime Type

International Trade Variables	Regime Type			
	MR	CRM	CR (900–)	CR (900+)
Exports percent GNP	19.1	20.3	27.5	23.7
Imports percent GNP	21.3	21.6	27.4	24.3
Trade balance percent GNP	–3.0	–4.0	–3.2	–0.5
Investment balance percent GNP	1.3	1.2	1.8	0.5
International liquidity percent imports	36.9	38.1	36.1	41.5

export and import levels are lower in MR and CRM, and may possibly have deleterious ramifications for certain aspects of economic growth, these lower levels do not have any adverse effects on balance of payments. This finding on the investment balance is of interest. It is often asserted that private capital avoids situations of political instability and the absence of any significant difference on investment balance indicates that the occurrence of a military regime is not seen as an indicator of political instability by private investors. As in the case of the background economic variables, whenever a difference appears among MR, CRM, and CR (900–), the CRM are closer to the MR than to the CR (900–).

The third conclusion relates to the position of the CR (900+). Although these countries do not have export and import levels which differ substantially from the other three populations, they are distinctive in terms of a significantly better trade balance and lower investment balance. The trade balance is attributable simply to the stronger trading position of the high-income systems largely by virtue of the preponderance of the export of manufactured goods. The lower investment balance is due to the large export of capital contingent on the high-income levels of these countries.[31]

Controls for GNP, while not substantially altering the aggregate picture, introduce one qualification on the lower commitment to international trade on the part of MR and CRM. In general, import levels are lower only in the low and middle GNP levels, while exports are lower only in the low level.

The controls for area are rather more complicated, with a greater number of differences.[32] The main findings are that in Africa and Asia in general the MR-CRM have a weaker commitment to international trade than the CR; the MR have better trade balances than the CRM, but are similar to the CR; and the CR have equally good or

Table 9   Economic Performance, by Regime Type

Economic Performance Variables	Regime Type			
	MR	CRM	CR (900–)	CR (900+)
Rate of growth constant GNP per capita	3.2	2.1	2.6	5.3
Rate of growth exports	5.8	4.8	7.7	8.5
Rate of growth cost of living	8.6	8.5	4.9	3.8
Rate of growth food index	2.8	2.2	2.3	2.4
Rate of growth primary education	2.8	4.5	4.3	0.2

better direct investment balances than the MR or the CRM. In some instances differences could be accounted for by known variations in GNP, but in an approximately equal number of cases, this phenomenon could not be explained by such differences.

Economic Performance
One-way analysis of variance for each of the five performance variables shows significant relationship only among the variables of the rate of growth of GNP and of primary education, and regime types. Closer examination by difference testing shows that, in the case of rate of growth of GNP, the MR, CRM, and CR (900–) have significantly lower growth rates than the CR (900+), with each difference significant at the .01 level. In the case of primary education, the CR (900+) have a significantly lower rate of growth than each of the other populations (at the .01 level). The low score for the CR (900+) is accounted for by the existence of universal primary education for the entire period. However, MR have a significantly lower rate of growth than either the CRM or the CR (900–), at the .05 and .10 levels, respectively.

Two conclusions stem from these findings. The first concerns the relationship between the MR and the CRM. As with other economic variables, the differences between the MR and the CRM in general are not very pronounced, although a significant difference between the two appears for the first time in the rate of growth of primary education. It is impossible to make any major inferences from this finding, to the extent that increases in education levels are frequently used as an indicator of modernization; yet this result would not support the concept of the military as a major modernizing force. Again, the fact that most MR follow CRM rather than preceding them may explain this finding, since the work of establishing and building up the educational system may have occurred prior to the advent of the MR. It should also be noted, however, that the MR have higher rates of growth of exports and GNP. Although none of the differences is significant, the rate of growth of GNP under MR is substantially higher than that under CRM. In general, the major finding is that there is little evidence to differentiate MR from CRM. One possible interpretation of the absence of any major difference between the MR and CRM is that the control of government has little influence on economic development; and it is of little importance whether the government is military or civilian. This interpretation, however, hardly fits with the literature on economic development which generally shows the substantial role of the central government in influencing the economy. The most likely explanation, therefore, would be either that military governments basically pursue the same types of policy as their civilian counterparts, or that military governments entrust control of the economy to civilian groups—with the sole difference that the military government pursues the policies slightly more successfully or that the civilian groups selected by the military are slightly more skilled in economic planning.

A second conclusion concerns the relationships of MR and CRM to CR (900–). While CR (900–) have a higher export growth rate and a lower cost-of-living growth rate than either MR or CRM, neither of these differences is significant. With the exception of the lower primary education growth rate in MR, there is no evidence to differentiate the economic performance of three main populations. It would appear, therefore, (1) that the occurrence of a military regime does not have a pronounced effect on economic performance when MR are compared with CRM, and (2) that there is no pronounced effect on economic performance produced by military regimes when both MR and CRM are compared with CR (900–).[33] Thus, the only deviant population appears to be the CR (900+), which are characterized by a very high GNP growth rate and a very low primary education growth rate.

The introduction of GNP controls provides results that are generally consistent with the aggregate comparisons. Two-way analysis of variance controlling for GNP levels and regime types shows no significant variation among regimes, but does show significant variation among GNP levels for the rates of growth of exports, food index, and primary education (at the .05, .10, and .01 levels, respectively). When exports are increased by GNP, the food index increases up to the middle GNP level and then falls below the low

GNP category, and primary education decreases with GNP.[34] The cost-of-living growth rate shows no variation either among regimes or among GNP levels. The most interesting two-way analysis is for the rate of growth of GNP. There is no variation among regime types, confirming the aggregate comparison; but there are both significant variation among GNP levels, and a significant interaction effect. The variation among GNP levels indicates an expected progressive rise (1.71 to 2.93 to 5.30). The interesting finding is the interaction effect. This means, basically, that regime types and GNP levels interact in such a way that the different combinations produce different rates of growth. Closer examination of Table 10 reveals that MR have the highest rate for low GNP, the lowest rate for middle GNP, and an intermediate growth rate for high GNP; CRM have the highest rate for the high GNP level; and the CR (900–) have the highest rate for the middle GNP level. These findings can be extended by examining difference testing within GNP levels. The only significant result appears in the low GNP category, where the MR has a growth rate significantly higher than either the CRM or the CR (at .01 and .05 levels). Thus, while there are no significant variations among regime types in the middle and high GNP levels, the MR of the low GNP level perform significantly better than either of the other two regime types. It appears, therefore, that, in the low GNP level, military regimes are the most successful type in terms of economic development, while at other levels there is not much difference among regime types.

Three main findings contingent on the introduction of area controls may be noted. First, only five significant differences appear between MR and CRM; and three of these would be expected from the GNP comparison.[35] Second, in both Central and South America, MR have better aggregate performance rates than the CR. In Central America, the MR have much higher GNP and primary education growth rates (at .10 and .05 levels) and a significantly lower cost-of-living growth rate (at .10 level). In South America, both MR and CRM have a lower cost-of-living growth rate than the CR (at .01 level), and a

Table 10   Rate of Growth of GNP, by Regime Type and GNP Level

GNP Level	Regime Type		
	MR	CRM	CR
1	3.2	0.4	1.5
2	2.3	2.7	3.8
3	5.7	6.5	3.9

higher rate of food index increase (at .01 level). Additionally, MR have rates of growth of GNP and exports which are significantly higher than the CR (both at .10 level). Third, in five cases—three in Africa, two in Asia—the CR have better scores than either the MR or CRM.[36] Although area tabulations of regimes show that both the MR and CRM have generally weaker background positions than the CR, both the MR and CRM perform comparably to the CR, and there is some evidence to indicate that Latin American MR perform somewhat better than the CR.

Conclusion

It is useful to compare our summary picture of military regimes with the current literature in which three quite different views of military regimes are represented. The first of these, most prevalent in the early sixties, proposes that the military are agents of development and modernization.[37] The second view, generally accepted from the mid-sixties onward, sees the military as antithetical to development.[38] A major problem arises in our attempt to set our findings in perspective with other studies if we support the view that the concepts of development and modernization have little utility. Indeed, given the criticisms that have been levelled against the concepts of development and modernization from the mid-sixties, it is rather curious that writers still persist in their endeavors to "explain" certain facets of military regimes by reference to these concepts.[39] Thus, there is no agreed set of criteria for either development or modernization through which the performance of military regimes can be evaluated.

If we examine the two opposing views of the military, some of the differences are easily explained. One source of difference lies in the fact that these studies often look at quite different phenomena. In this respect, it is not surprising that their general pictures differ. This perfectly legitimate divergence only becomes anomalous when findings are processed through the concept of modernization. A second source of difference arises because many studies are either lacking in empirical data or tend to draw overgeneralized conclusions on the basis of their data. There is an interesting similarity, however, between the two opposing views in that both sides tend to see military regimes as an homogeneous group clearly differentiated from the group of civilian regimes. On this basis we would diverge most strongly from many studies of military regimes.

This point of divergence has given rise to the third view of military regimes. Our study supports the more recent studies of the case or area variety, strongly emphasizing the diversity of military regimes.[40] At the most general level, our findings suggest three main points: (1)

military regimes do not in aggregate form a distinctive regime type in terms of performance; (2) there is a degree of diversity within military regimes, which is not dissimilar to the diversity found within civilian regimes; and (3) the general degree of similarity or dissimilarity between military and civilian regimes varies from one variable or one category of variables to another.

In this respect, we have found the type of picture generated by the cluster analysis the most useful general overview of military regimes. This has shown that, while some military regimes are quite clearly distinct, as indeed are some civilian regimes, a sizable proportion of military and civilian regimes are indistinguishable in terms of performance. We would argue, therefore, that the nature of military regimes cannot be adequately understood either in terms of assisting or inhibiting modernization or in terms of a typology based on a simple distinction between military and civilian regimes. Rather, it is the overview generated by the cluster analysis and complemented by the array of difference tests which more accurately and profitably describes the diversity of military regimes.

NOTES

*This article is the second report on a project funded by the Social Science Research Council (U.K.). The authors would like to thank Anthony Mughan, who was the research assistant.

[1] For a review of the literature and a bibliography, see Henry Bienen, "The Background to Contemporary Study of Militaries and Modernization," in Bienen, ed. *The Military and Modernization* (Chicago, 1971), pp. 1–39. Most of the work on military regimes is of a case or area study nature, but there is one cross-national aggregate study to which we would call attention, Eric A. Nordlinger, "Soldiers in Mufti," *American Political Science Review*, LXIV (December 1970), 1131–48. This study is the one most analogous to ours, but it differs in that some of Nordlinger's findings do not tally with ours and the general tenor of Nordlinger's paper is dissimilar. There are valid reasons why our study differs from Nordlinger's and why we consider our study a more accurate representation of the performance of military regimes. (1) We have a different range of variables—Nordlinger uses seven, while we have used twenty-one; and only two of ours are directly comparable to Nordlinger's. (2) We use a different time period. Our data have been collected annually over the period 1951–70, whereas Nordlinger uses data from the study by Irma Adelmann and Cynthia T. Morris, *Society, Politics, and Economic Development* (Baltimore, 1967), which generally covers the period 1957–61 and in some cases, 1950–63. (3) We use a slightly different independent variable. Nordlinger uses a threefold categorization of the political strength of the military (measured over 1957–62, even though this does not correspond with those dependent variables measured over 1950–63), whereas we have focused explicitly on regimes. (4) We use a rather different design which permits us to isolate the effects of military regimes more systematically and rigorously. Since we have collected data annually, means or rates of growth can be measured independently over periods of military or civilian rule. Thus, we have specifically compared military rule against civilian rule in countries that have experienced military rule and again compared both of these with civilian regimes in countries which have not experienced military rule. (5) We have used a more comprehensive population than Nordlinger. (6) We consider that Nordlinger rather overstates his use on the basis of the data he presents. The controls could have been better handled and some of the variables are very loosely defined and operationalized.

[2] The GNP division of the CR is made because the higher income category differs markedly in economic terms from the rest of the world. The empirical justification for this will be seen in

the next section, which deals with a cluster analysis. Further, no country with a mean per capita GNP greater than $900 (1951–70) experienced a military regime.

[3]Set theory notation fits very well with difference testing. The null hypothesis and the alternative hypothesis for a two-tailed test may be written as $X \cap Y \neq \phi$ and $X \cap Y = \phi$. If two population means do not differ significantly, their distributions would overlap in a way in which two sets may intersect in a Venn diagram. The principle of significance can also be applied to the definition of a set when a set is conventionally defined as consisting of a well-defined set of elements. If the mean score of a variable set X differs from that of set Y, then we can argue that we have two sets, which are well defined in the sense of being significantly different.

[4]For example, if we let X, Y, and Z represent the population CRM, CR (900–), and MR, other things being equal, outcome type 1 would tell us that each of the populations is distinct. If the scores were arranged $Y < X < Z$, then we would have to inquire whether it is the deviation of X from Y which gives rise to Z, or whether it is the occurrence of Z which gives rise to the deviation of X from Y. To illustrate again, outcome type 3 (as written $[X \neq Y] \sim Z$) would provide strong evidence to indicate that military regimes differ substantially from civilian ones. Had the outcome been written $(Y \neq Z) \sim X$, then we would know that countries which experience military regimes are somehow different from those which do not. We would then be obliged to investigate the case of whether the difference between Y and X gives rise to Z and Z proves unable to redress the balance, or whether it is the occurrence of Z which leads to the difference between Y and X. Had the outcome been $(X \neq Z) \sim Y$, then we would have some evidence indicating that, although military regimes are not distinct, the military regimes in countries which experience military rule rather than the civilian regimes of these countries put them on a par with other civilian regimes.

[5]Some of the more recent standard data compilations such as Charles L. Taylor and Michael C. Hudson, *World Handbook of Political and Social Indicators* (New Haven, 1972), and Arthur S. Banks, *Cross-Polity Time Series Data* (Cambridge, [Mass.], 1971) mark significant advances on earlier collections from the standpoint of the time span covered. But even these proved to be of limited value in view of the scope of the variables utilized.

[6]The main data sources were: *Europa Yearbook* (London, 1958–70); *Statesman's Yearbook* (London, 1951–70); *Political Handbook and Atlas of the World*, ed. Richard P. Stebbins and Alma Amoia (New York, 1970); *Whitaker's Almanac* (London, 1951–70); and *Keesing's Contemporary Archives* (London, 1950–70).

[7]The main data sources were: The Institute for Strategic Studies, *The Military Balance* (London, 1960–72); Stockholm International Peace Research Institute, *Yearbook of World Armaments and Disarmament* (Stockholm, 1968–72); Richard Booth, "The Armed Forces of African States," *Adelphi Papers*, no. 67 (London, 1970).

[8]The main data sources were: United Nations, *Statistical Yearbook* (New York, 1951–72); United Nations, *Yearbook of International Trade Statistics* (New York, 1950–72); United Nations, *Yearbook of National Account Statistics* (New York, 1964–72); International Monetary Fund, *International Financial Statistics* (Washington, 1964–72).

[9]The main areas not covered are central government capital, and monetary transfers involving transactions of deposit money banks and central banks.

[10]The scores for each of the clusters are contained in Appendix 1.

[11]Of the thirty-two cases of MR and CRM, there are twenty-nine pairs (Table 2). Three MR have no CRM and three CRM have no MR. The absence of a counterpart may be attributable either to lack of data or to the fact that a MR has occupied the whole period. Spain, Thailand, and Algeria have no CRM; Libya, Cambodia, and Paraguay have no MR. Since none of the difference tests treat the MR and CRM as matched pairs, these cases are retained for the majority of comparisons.

[12]Analysis of variance across the variables of constitution, assembly and party are significant at the .01 level. Means testing shows significant differences between MR and CRM/CR (900–) on each variable at the .01 level. Tests for the CR (900+) are null and void on account of their zero variance.

[13]Analysis of variance is significant at the .01 level. Means testing shows that the MR have significantly higher scores than the CRM and CR (900–) and CR (900+) at the .01 level; and the CRM and CR (900–) have higher scores than the CR (900+) again at the .01 level.

[14]Analysis of variance is significant at the .01 level. The MR have a substantially higher score than the CRM, the CR (900–) and the CR (900+) at the .01 level: the CRM and CR

(900–) have significantly higher scores than the CR (900+) at the .01 level; and the CRM have a much higher score than the CR (900–) at the .05 level.

[15]This finding can be used to test the hypothesis that civilian regimes may provide greater capacity for the military in the main executive to avoid a coup. If this were the case, it would be expected that the CR (900–) would have a high score. Since this is not the case, there is no evidence to indicate that civilian regimes may avoid a coup by catering to the military in giving the military greater powers in the main executive body.

[16]Per capita GNP is divided into the following categories: $1–150, $151–400, $401–900, and $901+.

[17]One-way analysis of variance for levels 1 and 2 shows significant variation at the .01 level, but means testing shows no difference between the MR and CRM. Analysis of variance in level 3 shows no significant variation:

Executive Tenure by Regime Type and GNP Levels

	MR	CRM	CR
GNP level 1	36.5	52.5	104.8
GNP level 2	34.3	44.6	118.9
GNP level 3	77.6	66.2	48.7

[18]The areas are: Central America, South America, the Middle East and North Africa, Sub-Saharan Africa, and Central and Southeast Asia.

[19]Scores for the CRM and CR on constitution restrictions are 20, 48; for assembly restrictions, 26, 29; for party restrictions, 39, 35. For military posts in the executive, however, the scores are 3.8 and 0.3.

[20]The scores for the CRM of Central and South America are 11 and 19, compared to 1, 3, 4 in Africa, Asia, and the Middle East.

[21]These data conflict with those presented by Nordlinger, p. 1135. However, in footnote 1 of this article we have outlined some reasons that may account for this. Like Nordlinger, however, we find that countries that have had military regimes have higher levels of expenditure and larger armies than countries which have not had military regimes, even though the differences are slight. It could be argued that we place excessive faith in difference testing but, on the other hand, if we remove the difference tests, we could only substitute quite arbitrary judgments. Furthermore, if we examine growth rates of size and expenditure in countries that have and have not had military regimes, we find for size they are 8.1 percent and 7.9 percent, and for expenditure, 8.8 percent and 11.7 percent. Thus, while growth rates for size are similar, growth rates for expenditure are actually higher in countries that have not had military regimes (difference is significant at .10 level), Thus, the lower level of expenditure in countries that have not had military regimes seems to be countered by a higher rate of growth.

[22]The variation is significant at the .05 level, and the mean scores for levels 1, 2, and 3 are 27, 65, and 58, respectively.

[23]The variation is significant at the .05 level, and the mean scores for levels 1, 2, and 3 are 2.70, 3.67, 1.96, respectively.

[24]The scores for Central America, South America, Middle East, Sub-Saharan Africa, and Central and Southeast Asia on size are 23, 40, 86, 10, 90; on expenditure they are 1.17, 2.24, 5.83, 1.71, 4.92.

[25]The one-way analyses of variance on each of the variables show significant variation at the .01 level.

[26]The GNP variations among regimes and among areas are significant at the .01 level; and for primary product at the .05 and .01 levels.

[27]The variation between areas is significant at the .01 level.

[28]The variation is significant in Asia at the .01 level; in Africa, at the .10 level; in South America, at the .05 level; and in Central America, at the .10 and .05 levels, for MR and CRM, respectively.

[29]In Central America and the Middle East variation is significant at the .10 level; and in South America at the .05 and .01 levels, for MR and CRM, respectively.

[30]For both exports and imports, MR and CRM have significantly lower scores than the CR (900–) at the .01 and .05 levels, respectively. On trade balance, the MR, CRM, and CR (900–) have lower scores than the CR (900+) at the .01 level, and higher scores on the

investment balance for MR and CRM at the .05 level, and for CR (900-) at the .10 level. There are no differences on international liquidity.

[31]The return on this capital is included in the exports of the trade balance and is one reason for the stronger trade balance position of the high income systems.

[32]An important problem is that area differences may simply reflect GNP differences. Unfortunately, the number of cases is too small to combine regimes, GNP, and area into contingency tables, and there would be too many dummy variables to use multiple regression. However, since we know the scores on the international trade variables of regimes by GNP, and since we know the GNP location of regimes by area, we also know what score would be predicted for regimes by area using scores taken from GNP tabulations. The problem can be partially overcome, therefore, by comparing actual scores of regimes in areas to those that would have been expected from GNP.

[33]Our findings for rate of growth of GNP do not seem to differ markedly from Nordlinger's; he finds a correlation of .13 between political strength of the military and rate of growth of GNP. We differ in the inferences drawn in that we would argue that military regimes certainly perform no worse than civilian regimes and, if anything, slightly better. Nordlinger seems to turn the absence of a high correlation into an assertion that military regimes do not promote— and even retard—change. Of course, Nordlinger would have needed a significant negative correlation to support this claim.

[34]The mean scores for GNP levels 1, 2, and 3 for exports are 3.37, 7.26, 8.79; for the food index, 2.29, 3.00, 1.29; and for primary education, 4.19, 3.52, 1.24.

[35]These differences are: (1) in Africa the MR have higher rates of growth of GNP and (2) lower primary education growth (at .10 levels) than the CRM; (3) the MR in Asia have lower primary education growth than the CRM (at .10 level); (4) the MR in Central America have higher primary education growth than the CRM (at .05 level); and (5) the MR of South America have a higher export growth rate (at .05 level).

[36]In Africa the CR have a significantly higher GNP and a lower cost-of-living growth than the CRM (at .05 levels) and a higher primary education growth rate than the MR (at the .10 level). These are consistent with the GNP tabulations.

[37]For examples of this view, see: Lucian W. Pye, "Armies in the Process of Political Modernization," and Edward A. Shils, "The Military in the Political Development of New States," in John H. Johnson, ed. *The Role of the Military in Underdeveloped Countries* (Princeton, 1962); Manfred Halpern, *The Politics of Social Change in the Middle East and North Africa* (Princeton, 1962); Guy J. Pauker, "South East Asia as a Problem Area in the Next Decade," *World Politics*, XI (April 1959); Hans Daalder, *The Role of the Military in the Emerging Countries* (The Hague, 1962); Marion J. Levy, *Modernization and the Structure of Societies* (Princeton, 1966), pp. 571–605.

[38]For examples of this view, see: Bienen, ed. *The Military Intervenes* (New York, 1968); and Bienen, ed. *The Military and Modernization*; Nordlinger, "Soldiers in Mufti"; and Edwin Lieuwen, *Generals v. Presidents* (London, 1964).

[39]See, for example, M. R. Doornbas, "Political Development: Search for Criteria," *Development and Change*, I (January 1969); Chong-Do Hah and Jeanne Schneider, "A Critique of Current Studies of Political Development and Modernization," *Social Research*, XXXV (Spring 1968); Samuel P. Huntington, "Political Development and Political Decay," *World Politics*, XVII (April 1965); J. P. Nettl and Roland Robertson, "Industrialization, Modernization and Development," *British Journal of Sociology*, XVII (March 1966); Karl de Schweinitz, "Growth, Development and Political Modernization," *World Politics*, XXII (July 1970).

[40]Manfred Kossok, "Changes in the Political and Social Functions of the Armed Forces in the Developing Countries: The Case of Latin America," and Philippe C. Schmitter, "Military Intervention, Political Competitiveness and Public Policy in Latin America: 1950–1967," in Morris Janowitz and Jacques van Doorn, eds. *On Military Intervention* (Rotterdam, 1971); E. Be'eri, *The Army Officers in Arab Politics and Society* (London, 1970); Jacob C. Hurewitz, *Middle East Politics: The Military Dimension* (London, 1969); Robert Pinkney, "The Theory and Practice of Military Government," *Political Studies*, XXI (February 1973); James A. Bill, "The Military and Modernization in the Middle East," *Comparative Politics*, II (October 1969); Edward Feit, "Pen, Sword, and People," *World Politics*, XXV (January 1973).

Appendix 1:   The Cluster Analysis

List of Variables

1. Average tenure of main executive
2. Percent of time Constitution is banned
3. Percent of time legislative houses are banned
4. Percent of time political parties are banned
5. Percent of time Communist party is banned
6. Percent of Cabinet composed of military personnel
7. Size of military per 10^4 population
8. Expenditure on the military as percent of GNP
9. Type of service in military forces*
10. Duration of service in military forces
11. Per capita Gross National Product (GNP)
12. Budget as percent of GNP
13. Primary production as percent of GNP
14. Exports as percent of GNP
15. Imports as percent of GNP
16. Trade balance as percent of GNP
17. Direct investment balance as percent of GNP
18. International liquidity as percent of imports
19. Rate of growth of GNP
20. Rate of growth of cost-of-living index
21. Rate of growth of exports
22. Rate of growth of food index
23. Rate of growth of children in primary school

(*voluntary service = 1, selective service = 2, compulsory service = 3)

Mean Scores of Clusters

| | Clusters | | | | | | Population |
Variable	1	2	3	4	5	6	Mean*
1.	52.8	99.3	61.0	76.5	30.6	65.2	62.1
2.	0	0	5.91	17.1	79.1	36.1	22.8
3.	0	0	21.2	4.52	88.7	33.9	22.8
4.	0	1.03	5.17	7.74	81.4	24.9	19.8
5.	6.42	66.0	58.1	59.4	99.0	77.9	58.6
6.	0.78	2.66	6.48	13.0	51.8	20.2	15.8
7.	80.63	39.6	23.9	27.7	30.6	160.6	54.8
8.	3.51	2.83	1.62	2.4	2.35	7.53	3.14
9.	2.15	2.33	1.22	1.97	2.06	2.93	2.0
10.	9.84	20.0	3.65	9.78	11.4	32.63	12.2
11.	1477.3	390.0	356.8	182.9	200.8	285.3	453.6
12.	20.21	26.3	19.3	13.45	14.31	21.43	17.3
13.	11.2	15.3	24.9	38.2	36.38	29.6	29.0
14.	23.8	59.6	32.2	16.21	18.75	17.93	22.4
15.	23.1	42.3	33.5	17.76	20.63	24.19	23.7
16.	−0.06	3.93	−4.71	−2.98	−2.77	−4.93	−2.91
17.	0.36	0.53	3.18	1.02	1.21	0.70	1.31
18.	45.8	82.67	35.3	32.4	39.0	51.1	40.0
19.	4.77	13.6	2.79	2.13	1.68	3.79	3.16
20.	14.7	4.10	3.24	12.12	5.51	6.01	7.15
21.	7.37	19.4	6.93	5.06	3.68	7.60	6.35
22.	2.29	−4.80	1.97	2.80	3.34	2.88	2.44
23.	0.35	9.33	2.98	3.95	1.86	2.84	2.85

*The overall population mean is included in order to present the general picture compared with the individual clusters.

List of Regime-Countries, by Cluster

Cluster	1	2	3
CRM:	Venezuela	CRM: Iraq	MR: Algeria
CR:	Australia	Libya	El Salvador
	Austria	CR: Zambia	Panama
	Belgium		Venezuela
	Canada		Zaire
	Denmark		CRM: Dominican Republic
	Finland		Ghana
	France		Panama
	Italy		Sierra Leone
	Japan		CR: Ceylon
	Netherlands		Costa Rica
	New Zealand		Ireland
	Norway		Jamaica
	Sweden		Kenya
	Switzerland		Lebanon
	United Kingdom		Liberia
	United States		Malawi
	Uruguay		Malaysia
	West Germany		Nicaragua
			Singapore
			South Africa
			Trinidad and Tobago
			Tunisia

	4		5		6
MR:	Bolivia	MR:	Argentina	MR:	Greece
	Brazil		Burma		Iraq
	Dominican Republic		Colombia		South Korea
	Indonesia		Dahomey		South Vietnam
	Pakistan		Ecuador		Syria
	Spain		Ghana		United Arab Republic
CRM:	Argentina		Guatemala	CRM:	Greece
	Bolivia		Honduras		South Korea
	Brazil		Nigeria		South Vietnam
	Burma		Peru		Syria
	Cambodia		Sierra Leone		Turkey
	Colombia		Sudan		United Arab Republic
	Dahomey		Thailand	CR:	Israel
	Ecuador		Togo		Jordan
	El Salvador		Turkey		Portugal
	Guatemala	CR:	Morocco		Taiwan
	Honduras				
	Indonesia				
	Nigeria				
	Pakistan				
	Paraguay				
	Peru				
	Sudan				
	Togo				
	Zaire				
CR:	Cameroun				
	Chad				
	Chile				
	Ethiopia				
	India				
	Iran				
	Ivory Coast				
	Malagasy Republic				
	Mexico				
	Niger				
	Philippines				
	Tanzania				
	Uganda				

LEADERSHIP AND PUBLIC POLICY

Introduction

To many analysts of the Third World, leadership is conceived in terms of the consequence of events, rather than their cause. From this perspective, "the possible leadership forms and styles of any given time and place are believed to be *dependent* on social, economic, and cultural conditions."[1] Societal constraints, in short, have such salience so as to relegate politics and political leadership to the world of shadows. The actions taken by national leaders are determined by primary societal factors and the idea of political choice is an illusion.

It would serve no useful purpose to attempt to deny that this perspective, so closely linked with the "post legal/formal scholarship" of much of the 1960s, has value for our analysis of politics in the Third World. Clearly, the vitality of socio-cultural forces and the reality of economic conditions in *le Tiers Monde* act to constrict the parameters within which choice can be exercised. Yet even constricted choice remains choice nonetheless; and increasingly the recognition of this position has turned political leadership into a focal point of concern. For if politics in the states of the Third World is not merely a reflection of other societal sources (i.e., if politics can act, at the very least, as a quasi-independent variable), then is not the role of national political leadership critical? Given the political ecology of Third World countries (an ecology marked by weak institutionalization) does not the source of political "will and capacity" flow in large part from the reservoir of leadership?

It vas Montesquieu who wrote: "At the birth of societies, it is the leaders of the commonwealth who create the institutions; afterwards it is the institutions that shape the leaders."[2] Thus for political societies undergoing the trauma of birth connected with independence and/or the difficulties of rebirth associated with modernization and development, the role of leadership is of no small significance. However, it is important to recognize that this viewpoint does not hold leadership to be a completely independent and isolated variable; Third World societies are not pliant clay to be molded into any form by a master sculptor. Limits exist. "Folkways" are not chimerical within the Third World context; yet "stateways" are not without their impact. History remains shaped by people who say yes or no.

Leadership is thus seen as a nexus point wherein limitations are reflected, ideologies are activated, and public policies are actualized. To use the words of Dankwart Rustow:

> The leader as a figure omnipresent in any political process, as the maker of decisions, originator and recipient of messages, performer of functions, wielder of power, and creator or operator of institutions can bring . . . disparate elements into a single, visible focus. The study of leadership, moreover, can readily be supplemented with an examination of the social and political organizations that he founds and transforms, with an analysis of the psychological appeals and political sanctions that give leader and organization a hold on their mass following.[3]

In a sense, leaderhsip is like the "O" (organism) in behavioral psychology; the variable that changes mechanistic "S" (stimulus) → "R" (response) relationships into dynamic S ⟷ O ⟷ R systems. Along this line, the second essay in this section, Dettman's "Leaders and Structures in 'Third World'. Politics," argues that "explanations of 'Third World' politics cannot be limited to structural analysis but must give due consideration to the impact of the leadership variable." Here Dettman examines the approaches to legitimacy taken by six Third World leaders (Nehru, Nyerere, Kenyatta, Sukarno, UNu, and Nkrumah) and the interaction of those approaches with the structures of each leader's society "in order to ascertain whether or not there is a relationship between this interaction and [the leaders'] success or failure in maintaining authority."

Not surprisingly, Dettman, in his analysis, makes use of Weber's enduring ideal type classification of charismatic, traditional, and rational-legel patterns of authority.[4] Traditional authority, from this Weberian perspective, refers to obedience based on habit, while rational-legal authority connotes obedience based on interest and charismatic authority is associated with obedience based on the extraordinary quality of the leaders themselves. Given the context of transition and transformation that characterizes the Third World, enormous emphasis has been placed on charismatic rule; for rule by charisma ". . . is not managed according to general norms, either traditional or rational, but in principle, according to concrete revelations and inspirations . . . [it] is 'revolutionary' in the sense of not being bound to the existing order."[5] Although change and charisma are often discussed in tandem, with the latter viewed as both the product and progenitor of the former, charismatic authority is not without its pitfalls. Under certain circumstances charisma may well be "the one great revolutionary force in epochs bound to tradition,"[6] but primary reliance by leadership on charismatic norms can also produce "expectancy gaps" which can undermine leadership legitimacy and success.

Despite the use (and often misuse) of this Weberian typology, Edinger's opening essay in this section correctly notes that the study of political leadership has only recently emerged in the United States as a field of political science "after a long period of neglect." In "The Comparative Analysis of Political Leadership," Edinger provides a basic overview of leadership analysis and a strategy for comparative inquiry which focuses on "the acquisition, performance, and consequences of leadership."

While Edinger's essay is multi-faceted, two aspects of his work stand out for our discussion at this point. The first of these is his examination of the quality of leadership, wherein he distinguishes analytically intrinsic from extrinsic criteria for evaluating leadership. By intrinsic criteria, Edinger refers to "objective" judgments of leadership performance and goals in terms of the actual degree of attainment or instrumental efficiency of leadership. In other words, if leader A sets out to achieve X, the question is how close he or she comes to reaching that goal and at what benefit/cost ratio. Extrinsic criteria, on the other hand, most often are "based on explicit or implicit preferences rooted in an investigator's philosophical beliefs and values." Here judgments are based on leadership's proximity to the means and ends "valued by the observer."

The utility of this distinction can be seen clearly in the reevaluation of the Third World leadership that has taken place in recent years. It had been argued that the leaders of the Third World countries ". . . must be given carte blanche to modernize their lands without overlordship of the West, and we must understand the methods that they will feel compelled to use."[7] The necessities of hastening the processes of "social evolution" and establishing order and freedom within the context of "predevelopment" might well impel these leaders toward authoritarian means, but we should, neither be shocked nor dismayed at such occurrences. Since it is the leaders who ". . . stand between their countries and the twin evils of chaos and tyranny,"[8] we must grant them wide latitude in their behavior. We must accept the necessity of their actions for they are the saviours of their nations.

Although this position was not without a base in reason, increasingly it has been questioned by a view of leaders not as saviours, but as sharks of freedom.[9] This judgment is based on both intrinsic and extrinsic criteria. From the extrinsic perspective, Third World leaders are viewed to have generally failed to meet " . . . the challenge of human rights and the dignity of man, held to be especially dear to them after the experience of colonialism;"[10] while from the intrinsic perspective, leaders are seen to have had but limited success in meeting the challenge of governance and the establishment of a meaningful and cumulative political order.

In short, with the images of Field Marshall Amin and Emperor Bokassa in mind, the meliorative force of leadership is thought to be problematic, at best. Third World leadership undeniably faces real dilemmas in the policies and politics of its rule, but the recognition of such dilemmas does not eliminate the moral and political weaknesses of systems based on self-justification and faith, nor does it extirpate the responsibility of leaders who stand neither between their countries and tyranny, nor their countries and chaos.

This leads us to the second aspect of Edinger's essay which is most relevant for our discussion, that is, the connection of leadership with public policy. Edinger notes that whatever exact definitions are given for leadership, wide acceptance is granted to the view that political leadership focuses " . . . directly on governmental control over *public policy* decisions at the intra, and interstate level, and indirectly on control over the sources and consequences of such decisions." Obviously, this does not mean that a simple 1:1 correlation exists between the leader's wishes and the output of public policy in a system; numerous intervening variables play too great a role in the complex exchanges found in the decision-making and decision-implementation processes of all political societies for such an unsophisticated perspective to be of consistent and general value. What is implied, however, is the idea that political entrepreneurship by leaders can and often does matter in the formulation and effectuation of policy in the Third World.[11]

The third essay in this section, Kautsky's "Revolutionary and Managerial Elites in Modernizing Regimes," explores the connection of leadership (the allocaters of scarce resources) and policy ("a pattern of allocating scarce resources") in terms of the hypothesis that in "underdeveloped" countries there is some link between industrialization . . . and . . . the replacement of the leadership of revolutionary modernizers by that of managerial modernizers." This link can be seen, according to Kautsky, either to suggest "that if industrialization modernization is to proceed, the replacement of elites [revolutionary by managerial] must take place or that if industrialization does proceed, the replacement of elites will take place."

Using the examples of more than thirty leaders, Kaustky discusses the position "that revolutionary modernizers are distinguishable from managerial ones with respect to [1] their background, experience, and training, [2] their attitudes, and [3] their policies." While his conclusions are tentative and, in fact, raise more questions than they answer, Kautsky argues "that we cannot distinguish sharply between revolutionary and managerial modernizers" relative to the categories examined and ends with the viewpoint that: "It may be merely the times and the types of societies that create the distinctions between the two kinds of modernizers, and it may therefore be hopeless to look for distions between them apart from the times and societies in which they live"

Our final selection, Baldev Raj Nayar's "Political Mainsprings of Economic Planning in the New Nations: The Modernization Imperative versus Social Mobilization," examines the broad issue of the public policy pursuit of economic development. Nayar offers a brief historical perspective on industrialization in the North Atlantic region, Japan, China and Russia, and then utilizes the example of India as an "illustration of the various crosspressures, both national and international, involved in the industrialization effort." For to Nayar, it is only effectiveness in the pursuit of industrialization that gives meaning to the controversial terms "political development" and "political modernization."

Furthermore, Nayar adds that "since political development . . . refers to the pursuit of what has already been achieved elsewhere, it is valid to speak of the division between 'advanced' or 'reference' societies and 'follower,' Third World ones." Within the "modernization imperative," national independence as well as mass welfare plays an important role; and under that imperative national leadership "may at times be persuaded . . . to undertake measures which may result in strain on, or erosion of, political institutions, thus creating political decay."

Nayar's view is certainly one that is subject to debate, but in a real sense it brings us full circle in our analysis of the Third World. We have returned to our point of departure in the Introduction of this book. Many unanswered questions remain, but they have not gone unasked or ignored.

Before ending, we should note that this discussion of leadership and public policy has taken place within certain limiting parameters. We have not, for example, dealt extensively with the role of intellectuals *per se*, or with the impact of non-political leadership, or for that matter, with the significance of subnational political leaders. Clearly, none of these factors are without import. Yet, within the context of the Third World, the concentration on national leadership has a definite logic. More than anyone else, national leaders are linked to the interrelated processes of choice, politics, and policies: an interrelationship aptly expressed by the words:

> Politics is always a matter of making choices from the possibilities offered by a given historical situation and cultural context. From this vantage point, the institutions and procedures of government and the legitimate powers of state to shape the course of economy and society become the equipment provided by a society to its leaders for the solution of public problems.[12]

In thinking about the interaction of choice and constraints, it is worthwhile to remember the statement by deTocqueville in *Democracy in America*:

> Providence has not created mankind entirely independent or entirely free. It is true that around every man a fatal circle is traced, beyond which he cannot pass; but within the wide verge of that circle he is powerful and free; as it is with man, so with communities.

Given our penchant for certainties, such a response, to the human condition, based on an archetypical but indefinite mixture of *fortuna* and *virtù*, leaves us with an undeniable uneasiness. The search for verities is continual in the examination of the problems and prospects of the Third World; yet the result of that search is often ambiguity. Thus the gap persists between knowledge and true understanding. But through analysis the gap narrows. The quest continues, uncertainty remains: "That is our fate."[13]

NOTES

1. F. LaMond Tullis, *Politics and Social Change in the Third World* (New York: John Wiley, 1973), p. 79. Emphasis added.

2. Cited by Dankwart Rustow, *A World of Nations* (Washington: The Brookings Institution, 1967), p. 135.

3. Dankwart Rustow, "Introduction to 'Philosophers and Kings: Studies in Leadership,'" *Daedalus*, Vol. XVCII, No. 3 (Summer 1968), 689.

4. See the discussion in H. H. Gerth and C. Wright Mills (eds.), *From Max Weber: Essays in Sociology* (New York: Oxford University Press, 1968), pp. 245–264, 295–299. Also note Peter Blau's "Critical Remarks on Weber's Theory of Authority" and Reinhard Bendix's "Reflections on Charismatic Leadership" both reprinted in Denis Wrong (ed.), *Max Weber* (Englewood Cliffs: Prentice-Hall, 1970).

5. Gerth and Mills (eds.), *From Max Weber*, p. 296.

6. Weber cited by Rustow, *A World of Nations*, p. 150.

7. Richard Wright, *White Man Listen!* (Garden City: Doubleday, 1964), p. 65.

8. W. Howard Wriggins, *The Ruler's Imperative* (New York: Columbia University Press, 1969), p. 6.

9. See Okot p'Bitek, "Song of Prisoner," in p'Bitek, *Two Songs* (Nairobi: East Africa Publishing House, 1971) and Norman Provizer, "The Other Face of Protest: The Prisoner and the Politician in Contemporary Africa," *Journal of African Studies*, Vol. II, No. 3 (Fall 1975). Compare with Ann Ruth Willner and Dorothy Willner, "The Rise and Role of Charismatic Leaders," *The Annals of the American Academy of Political and Social Science*, Vol. CCCLVM (March 1965).

10. Rupert Emerson, "The Fate of Human Rights in the Third World," *World Politics*, Vol. XXVII, No. 2 (January 1975), 203.

11. See the section on "Development Strategy and Leaders," in Norman Uphoff and Warren Ilchman (eds.), *The Political Economy of Development* (Berkeley: University of California Press, 1972 and Uphoff and Ilchman's *The Political Economy of Change* (Berkeley: University of California Press, 1969).

12. Charles Anderson, "Comparative Policy Analysis: The Design of Measures," *Comparative Politics*, Vol. IV, No. 1 (October 1971), p. 121.

13. These are the concluding words of Otto Neurath's, *Foundations of the Social Sciences*, Vol. II, No. 1 of *Foundations of the Unity of Science: Toward an International Encyclopedia of Unified Science* (Chicago: The University of Chicago Press, 1944).

The Comparative Analysis
Of Political Leadership

Lewis J. Edinger*

The study of political leadership appears to be "an emerging field" of political science in the United States after a long period of neglect.[1] Only a decade or so ago, comparative studies of the subject by American authors could be served up on a half shelf in most college libraries, and undergraduate courses and texts gave it relatively scant attention. Today, in contrast, the interested student is confronted by a virtual embarrassment of riches; elite studies, psycho-biographies, and what have you provide a rich and variegated fare. The problem for the potential consumer is no longer product scarcity, but choice among an abundance of products bearing the same or similar labels.[2] Whether such growth is all to the good and indicative of real progress in the field, or whether it represents, at best, no more than pouring various mixtures of old wine into new bottles with fancy designations is a matter of some dispute.

*This article owes a great deal to stimulating discussions with the author's students at Michigan State, Washington, and Columbia Universities. The author is indebted for financial assistance in support of research to the John Simon Guggenheim Foundation, the National Science Foundation (Grant NSF-GS-28086), and the Ford Foundation (through funds granted to the Institute on Western Europe at Columbia University).

[1] See Glenn Paige, ed. *Political Leadership: Readings for an Emerging Field* (New York, 1972).

[2] This surge of interest in leadership analysis seems to reflect to some degree the overcoming of a cultural lag as American political science has become increasingly internationalized, intellectually as well as substantively. To some extent, too, it appears to be a response to contemporary developments that have posed new normative issues about the ability of liberal democratic systems to produce political leadership "adequate" to the needs of advanced industrial societies. Previously, American scholars, nurtured on writings that put little emphasis on political leadership—such as the works of John Locke and the Federalist Papers—tended to slight its analysis in favor of the exploration of collective patterns of mass attitudes and behavior. But of late the realization that not just the recruitment, but the actions of governmental decision-makers can be critical determinants of political developments, has evidently led participant observers in the social sciences to concern themselves more extensively with all the ramifications of leadership patterns.

The More the Better?

Variety may add spice to scholarly production, but it can also give the indiscriminate consumer intellectual indigestion. An enormous variety of new conceptual definitions, contending theories, and incongruent standards of measurement appear to have complicated rather than simplified the comparative analysis of political leadership. Profusion seems merely to have compounded confusion about the reasons for different forms and degrees of political leadership. Consequently, some scholars conclude that we are no closer now than we were a decade ago to answering such standard questions as why one rather than another person is or was a leader, and, if there, why not here, and, if then, why not now? Political leadership, in their view, remains an enigma that eludes systematic, comparative analysis.[3]

Perhaps so. But even if one were to grant that the quantitative increase in leadership studies has done little or nothing to enhance the quality of our understanding of the phenomenon, this does not seem to warrant throwing out the baby of comparative analysis with the baths various analysts have placed it in. A number of developments suggest that the proliferation of studies should not be taken to reflect nothing more than all too many exercises in futility. For one, critical analysis has demonstrated the shortcomings of once popular approaches, such as those associating leadership with inherent "traits" of particular individuals. For another, students of political leadership have become more disciplined in their analytic methods, more comparative in their focus, and more sensitive to their normative biases. If nothing else, they have learned to put their questions more systematically as a first but critical step in the search for persuasive answers.

The purpose of this article is two-fold. In the first place, it will extract from the current literature basic themes and questions that delineate different aspects of leadership analysis. Secondly, it will examine these with reference to the comparative analysis of political leadership across time and space.[4]

[3]In 1960 Eugene Jennings observed that "the attempt to study leadership scientifically has not provided a widely accepted body of knowledge of what leadership is and does" (*An Anatomy of Leadership* [New York, 1960], p. 1ff). Twelve years later, the eminent editors of a popular comparative text wrote: "When does leadership emerge? How, and under what conditions, can it manage to restructure opinions? What techniques does it use to gain support without strongly antagonizing or alienating powerful interests? Frankly we do not know." Roy C. Macridis and Robert E. Ward, "Introduction," *Comparative Political Systems* (Englewood Cliffs, 1972), p. 24.

[4]The very large number of studies on which this essay is based makes it inadvisable to include extensive footnote citations. The interested reader is referred to the following bibliographies: Lewis J. Edinger and Donald D. Searing, "Leadership: An Interdisciplinary Biblio-

What is Leadership?

A fundamental source of confusion for comparative analysis is the many definitions of leadership. This is certainly not a new problem; but it has been compounded as political scientists have sought to broaden the conceptual scope by utilizing definitions employed in other social sciences. "There are almost as many definitions of leadership as there are leadership theories" in psychology;[5] and in other social sciences implicit and explicit definitions are perhaps even more numerous than theories. The current literature is replete with definitions that variously associate leadership with the exercise of power, influence, command, authority, and control in ways that may suit the purposes of some scholars, but not of others.[6]

Furthermore, whether and how such definitions can be applied to comparative studies of leadership is a matter of widespread argument. Apparently identical or similar conceptualizations are often translated into very different operational criteria for empirical research; and seemingly different ones are operationalized in much the same way.[7] Then, again, political leadership will be defined at a level of abstraction that may suit formal deductive theories, but defies empirical analysis.

Still and all, there is a certain degree of coherence to this seeming anarchy which allows us to delineate two major definitions—the positional and the behavioral. For the purposes of comparative inquiry both of these meet three conceptual requirements:

1.   Leadership is defined in noncontradictory, inclusive as well as exclusive terms.
2.   Leadership is defined at a level of generality that permits broad, if not universal, application.
3.   Leadership is defined at a level of specificity that allows empirical examination of specific propositions and hypotheses.

When leadership is positionally defined, it is associated first and foremost with the rights and duties of an office or status in a hierarchical structure, whether a formal organization or an informally stratified collectivity. For example, it may be attributed to someone in a "position" of authority or command. In this sense, leadership is identified with the properties of a superior position, and followership

graphy," in Lewis J. Edinger, ed. *Political Leadership in Industrial Societies* (New York, 1967), pp. 348–66; George T. Force and Jack R. Van Der Silk, eds. *Theory and Research in the Study of Political Leadership: An Annotated Bibliography* (Carbondale, 1969).

[5]Fred Edward Fiedler, *Leadership* (New York, 1971), p. 1.

[6]Cf. Edinger, *Political Leadership,* pp. 6–8.

[7]Cf. Edinger, ed. *Theory and Method in Comparative Elite Analysis* (New York, 1969).

with those of related subordinate ones. Accordingly, such asymmetrical relationships are established and terminated by structural changes in the collectivity, rather than by the entry and exit of particular positional incumbents.[8] Thus, particular heads of government may come and go in an institutionalized political system, but the leadership position of prime minister or president will transcend their tenure in office. On the other hand, structural changes may "revolutionize" the constitutional order and establish entirely new positions of leadership.

When leadership is behaviorally defined it is identified with persons who shape the actions of other persons. In that sense, it is associated primarily with followership and processes of interpersonal relations, rather than with interrelated positions in a hierarchial structure.[9] According to this transitive definition, the occupant of an executive office in a political organization does not exercise leadership if his formal subordinates do not execute his commands. "Poor Ike," as Harry Truman is supposed to have said about his presidential successor, "[he] will say do this and do that and nothing will happen." On the other hand, leadership may rest with formal subordinates as expressed in the statement, "I am their leader and therefore must follow them." Or it may manifest itself in an informal group of ostensible peers when one member gets the others to do what he wants them to do.

The narrower concept of political leadership is also defined in a number of ways, depending on what is taken to be the nature and realm of politics. Certain explicit or implicit definitions identify politics with manifest or latent conflicts within and between states, for example; and by this token they exclude administrative leadership. Some definitions are derived from analytical parameters that

[8]John Kenneth Galbraith writes, for instance, "On any form of organized activity—a church, platoon, government bureau, congressional committee, house of casual pleasure—our first instinct is to inquire *who is in charge*. Then the inquiry is to the qualifications or credentials which accord such command. Organizations almost invariably invite two questions: Who is the head? How did he get there?" (*The New Industrial State* [London, 1967], p. 47). By way of contrast, consider the proclamation of a short-lived, acephalous organization by students at Columbia University in 1968. "Those who approach such organizations with the request, 'Take me to your leader,' are likely to be met with the response.... 'We're all leader.'" ("What Leader?", *Student Voice* [1 October 1967], p. 7.)

[9]For some recent examples of this approach, see James MacGregor Burns, "Toward the Conceptualization of Political Leadership" (Paper presented at 69th Annual Meeting, American Political Science Association, New Orleans, September 1973); Léon Dion, "The Concept of Political Leadership," *Canadian Journal of Political Science,* I (March 1968), 1–17: Fiedler, *Leadership* (New York, 1971); Cecil A. Gibb, "Leadership," in Gardner Lindzey and Elliot Aronson, eds. *Handbook of Social Psychology,* 2nd ed. (Cambridge [Mass.], 1969), vol. 4, pp. 206–81; Andrew S. McFarland, *Power and Leadership in Pluralist Systems* (Stanford, 1969), pp. 153–76.

restrict the concept to matters that clearly pertain to governmental activities, others from parameters that encompass all sorts of social relations, such as "office politics."

Whatever the definitions—and regardless of whether they are linked to positions, processes, or both—on the whole all of them conceive political leadership in terms of some form of control over the authoritiative assignment of benefits and obligations among the inhabitants of a geographic entity organized as a state. Generally, political leadership is seen as focusing directly on governmental control over public policy decisions at the intra- and interstate level, and indirectly on control over the sources and consequences of such decisions. In this respect, one or more of the following three analytical assumptions runs through the literature:

1. Political authority in a state rests on legally sanctioned or legitimated control over the making and implementation of public policy.
2. What should be done, and how, involves control over the choice between alternative goals, courses, and modes of policy action.
3. Who should do it and when involves control over the agents and timing of policy implementation.

By and large, then, in most studies of political leadership the adjective establishes the general organizational context. Explicitly or implicitly, political is taken to refer to the state and to governmental processes. The acquisition and exercise of political leadership by various actors is, in the last analysis, related to a disproportionate measure of direct or indirect control over public offices and policies. This is most obvious in political biographies and studies of governmental and party leadership, less so in studies where political leadership is associated with underlying socioeconomic phenomena. As noted, some scholars proceed from the assumption that all conflict is political, or that all interpersonal relationships that even remotely involve states and governments are political. The problem with such broad perspectives is that they tend to obscure operational parameters and, therefore, may make it all but impossible to isolate and compare the empirical components of political leadership in different structures.

Who Are the Leaders?

If political leaders are to be compared, they must obviously first of all be identified. This is a relatively simple matter when leadership is considered the inherent attribute of predetermined political positions, such as public offices. It may then involve nothing more than identifying the incumbents of formal offices or the members of assumed ruling groups or decision-making bodies. In any event, an asymmetrical relationship between leaders and followers is taken as given, and therefore need not be established.

This is not so when leadership is made to depend on evidence of followership. In that case, the identification of leaders calls for proof of a cause-effect association. Individuals are said to be the leaders in an interpersonal relationship when it can be shown that the behavior of the other participants is a response to their stimuli, and not random, routine, accidental, or attributable to other factors.

For most analysts who demand such existential proof of leadership identity, it is not sufficient to establish a deterministic relationship between causative leadership and dependent followership variables. Beyond that, the test is whether, and to what extent, the hypothesized leaders can be shown to make the hypothesized followers do what they want them to do, whether this be to take or to refrain from a particular course of action, to change or to maintain a pattern of behavior.[10] In short, there must be intent on the one side, and opportunity for choice on the other.

These restrictive conditions rule out unintended consequences, such as negative responses on the part of the objects of control. They also rule out undirected adaptive and imitative behavior, as when people copy the dress or mannerisms of someone they admire. And they rule out situations where circumstances allow one or both of the parties in the relationship no freedom of choice between alternative courses of action. An individual who merely transmits the orders of others is, in this sense, not a leader; and persons who are allowed no choice are not followers.[11]

The causal approach to the identification of political leaders thus rests on three analytical assumptions. First, hypothesized leaders are assumed to be independent agents; secondly, they are assumed to seek control over the behavior of other actors; and, thirdly, the hypothesized followers are assumed to have a choice. For the pur-

[10]Leadership is usually associated with changes in followership behavior. But logically it can just as well apply to successful efforts to prevent such changes in the presence of countervailing pressures.

[11]Leadership strategy may be directed toward limiting the alternatives open to the objects of control and toward making it appear that the benefits of compliance are greater than the costs. But when a person is given no choice whatever, say over whether he wants to live or die, control over his actions by another cannot be demonstrated. In this respect, variance and nonvariance in the behavior of the targets of leadership control operate along a continuum between the poles of unlimited choice and absolutely no choice.

poses of analysis, other factors are considered to be constant or equal; that is, the proposition that the behavior of one or more actors is a function of directive cues provided by other actors is examined "as if" other variables that might bear on the relationship did not exist.

The basic theoretical question for an empirical investigation is, therefore, whether it can be demonstrated that what happened did happen because supposed "leaders" made it happen. Strictly speaking, the above criteria allow one to designate and compare leadership actions only when it can be shown that those said to be followers would otherwise have behaved differently.

The purpose of such a model is, of course, to delineate the focus of inquiry and to isolate the relevant variables. A more holistic approach can lead to an infinite regression of causal variables and introduce an unmanageable combination of intervening ones. In that case, the more one knows, the less likely one is to know whether or not leadership is indeed analytically the "ultimate" cause of behavior. In short, the theoretical framework limits and delimits the way one examines observed phenomena in an empirical study of leadership.

When, however, it comes to translating theoretical propositions into testable hypotheses, the operationalization of models usually raises two major problems. On the one hand, the closer one gets to the "real world" in an empirical investigation, the more new factors appear that seemingly should be taken into consideration. As intervening variables are introduced to shore up the model in the light of observed phenomena, this process may lead to its transformation into a multivariate model, or even frustrate any sort of analysis. On the other hand, if one chooses to overlook observed phenomena that do not "fit" into the model, the "as if" *ceterus paribus* clause may serve to conceal more than the test of the model reveals.

It is, therefore, not surprising that studies of political leadership based on theoretical foundations tend to employ these more as guidelines than as rigorous paradigmatic rules. To arrive at any findings, it is usually necessary to relax the methodological requirements of a causal model. Except perhaps in carefully controlled laboratory experiments and computer simulations, these are otherwise likely to push the investigator toward a level of theoretical abstraction that fails to account adequately for "real life" leadership phenomena. Imperfect data and inadequate units and tools of measurement have usually compelled analysts to combine evidence with logical inference in order to fill in the missing pieces.

To be sure, there may be instances where a particular event can be convincingly attributed to the actions of a single individual. For example, the extermination of some six million European Jews at a particular time and place can rather conclusively be related to Adolf Hitler's control over those who obeyed his commands.[12] However, the proffered "explanations" usually remain at best inconclusive, probabilistic answers. In the last analysis, investigators are left to speculate about determining causes, about the relative significance of personal and situational factors, and about the "might-have-beens."[13]

The Sources of Leadership

Control over others becomes the dependent variable when the focus of comparative inquiry is the analysis of variations in the acquisition and exercise of political leadership. The object is to explain why some persons become leaders and others do not, or why the same individual demonstrates leadership in some instances and not in others. Answers are sought and provided in terms of a "because" statement that relates variance in successful and unsuccessful leadership efforts to variance in what it takes to be a leader.

Such a deterministic relationship is stated or implied in almost every study that goes beyond description to inquire into the bases of leadership recruitment and control. Apart from this common denominator, the relevant literature offers a large variety of causative factors that extend from very general explanations to highly specific reasons. Some authors relate the rise and fall of leaders to different structural patterns in interpersonal relations or to environmental conditions beyond their control. Others again single out ostensibly unique properties of particular actors or situations. Some proceed from theoretical assumptions that stress underlying socioeconomic or cultural variables, while others emphasize the personal attributes of leaders and would-be leaders. Thus, one finds, for example, that one scholar will "explain" the accession of Lenin primarily in terms of the properties of the man, while another will associate it with a particular, but not necessarily exceptional, constellation of contextual factors.

[12] Other factors may serve to explain how Hitler came to achieve control over the victims and their immediate executioners. But when we ask whether these people would have died there and then had he not ordered "The Final Solution," the answer appears pretty conclusive in the light of the evidence.

[13] Cf. McFarland, pp. 153–76, for the argument that in leadership analysis speculating about the "ifs" of past events is the methodological equivalent of conducting controlled laboratory experiments on leadership patterns in small groups. Note, however, Arend Lijphart's persuasive caveat that "the comparative method is not the equivalent of the experimental method but only a very imperfect substitute," in "Comparative Politics and the Comparative Method," *American Political Science Review*, LXV (September 1971), 685.

On balance, the prevailing approaches to this apsect of comparative leadership analysis rest for the most part on three controlling assumptions. First, the acquisition and exercise of control over others involve the possession of resources valued by the objects of leadership efforts, that is, the personal resources of individuals, the resources associated with their positions, or both. Second, the nature of these valued resources is contextually determined and therefore more or less varies in time and place. Third, their use and efficacy is subject to a benefit/cost calculus—what is to be gained and what is to be lost—on the part of the involved actors.

Proceeding from these shared assumptions, different "schools" diverge in their explanations of observed variance in the leadership phenomenon. Essentially, its presence or absence tends to be associated with determining factors that are accounted for by one or more of the following propositions:

1. Leadership is a function of the context of choice for the involved actors (e.g., organizational rules and norms, exigencies of the situations).
2. Leadership is a function of disequilibrium in the access to, and the distribution of, valued resources (e.g., status, votes, wealth, arms).
3. Leadership is a function of the attitudinal dispositions of the followers (e.g., value preferences, cognitive expectations, sense of solidarity).
4. Leadership is a function of the motivation, orientation, and style of behavior of the controlling agent (e.g., ambition, dedication, skills).

Here, again, a strictly positional approach is relatively uncomplicated, especially when the comparative analysis is confined to organizational structures and leadership offices. However, it also has proven to have rather limited explanatory power when it comes to interpreting particular rather than general variations. If leadership is identified with the formal-legal properties of institutional positions, such as the constitutional powers of heads of government, a comparative analysis is likely to leave many of the observed differences between different occupants of the same offices unexplained. At times positional explanations turn out to be either circular or tautological, as when the fact of election to a leadership office—rather than its reasons—is made to stand for an explanation. And if the sources of leadership are exclusively associated with ascriptive or achievement social background factors—such as age, sex, religion, income, and level of education—the positional approach is prone to yield at best only some very rough discriminating variables.

The trend in the comparative analyses of the sources of political leadership is to transcend the organizational-positional approach.

This apparently reflects a growing awareness that its stress on institutionalized patterns and structural factors may fail to capture contextual and personality dynamics that loom particularly large in relatively unstructured informal relationships and "crisis situations." On the other hand, it has also come to be recognized that situational and psychological variables can be overemphasized and that, particularly with reference to relatively stable political systems, more constant organizational factors should be taken into account. The theoretical and methodological controversies on this score revolve largely around ways to improve the scope of explanations without becoming overly eclectic.

The Magnitude of Leadership

The actions of political leaders are most frequently compared in terms of the extent of their control over the behavior of those led. Different forms of leadership are identified with different degrees of control. The more far-reaching their political impact is thought to be, the greater the usual concern with the efficacy of control actions. The basis for a prescriptive comparative inquiry might be a political ideology that associates the realization of valued ends with the extent of leadership autonomy. The achievement of social justice or national unity, for example, may be said to call for a high degree of leadership control, the realization of maximal individual liberty, for a low degree. Again, the point of departure might be a theory of politics that calls for a comparative analysis of control actions that promote or inhibit the accomplishment of leadership objectives.

In any event, whether it is a question of comparing the degree of control that goes with different political structures and positions, or whether it is a matter of comparing various control efforts by the same or different individuals, leadership is taken to have some directive and intended impact on the led. The focus of empirical inquiry, then, is to identify and explain variance in the magnitude of such impact.

This means that variance must first of all be established for the leader-follower relationships that are being compared. In other words, how much of the change or lack of change in the behavior of the led is a product of leadership efforts to determine such behavior? How well does the observed response of the followers correspond to the assumed intentions of the leaders?

Most often the extent of induced behavioral change—rather than the lack of change—is taken to indicate the efficacy of leadership.

Here the differences can range from relatively small changes of degree to radical changes in kind. For example, in one case leadership may be found to have produced an increase in the rate of active participation among the members of a political organization. In another instance, it may be seen as the cause of a qualitative shift from legal to conspiratorial activities on the part of the led, or from peaceful to violent actions against third parties.

Leadership can then be differentiated descriptively in terms of the magnitude of changes from antecedent patterns of behavior. In this sense innovative leadership produces new forms of behavior, sometimes instantaneously and radically, more often incrementally and gradually. Catalytic leadership accelerates behavioral changes that are already under way.[14] Confirming leadership solidifies new directions in behavior due to other factors.[15]

These may be fairly straightforward classificatory criteria and, on the face of it, they will accommodate most descriptions of leadership efficacy. It is all too evident from the current literature, however, that the ordering of control phenomena under these or any other descriptive labels involves a good deal of arbitrary judgment. Even in the rare instances where intercoder subjectivity tests are employed, the interpretation of raw data is to some degree biased by the preconceived code.

Furthermore, the scales and standards used for measuring the magnitude of behavioral responses to leadership acts vary a good deal between different studies. The more closely the methods and techniques of inquiry are dictated either by a particular theoretical approach or by a particular subject, the more difficult it is to draw upon various studies for a more general comparative analysis. Even such commonplace measures as election returns can be, and frequently are, variously interpreted. When it comes to so-called "softer" data, such as the quality of followership behavior, one scholar's evaluation of a change in kind is often considered merely a change in degree by

[14]In this case leadership serves as a positive catalyst. Contrariwise, if it decelerates behavioral changes induced by other factors, it can be said to have the effect of a negative catalyst or preservative.

[15]Confirming leadership may, for instance, take the form of instrumental actions that facilitate established procedures, or it may legitimate and sanction old or new behavioral norms by symbolic actions. The more closely it comes to approximate the performance of purely routine measures, or what has been called "automatic leadership," the more difficult it will be to differentiate confirming leadership from actions that do not involve control over others. Here one might note the gradual transformation of royal assent to legislative decisions from a means of control to a symbolic gesture of legitimation, or the executive acts of the American president in what Richard E. Neustadt describes as his role of a clerk. Cf. Neustadt, *Presidential Power* (New York, 1969), p. 19.

others, on the basis of the same evidence. For example, at one level of analysis the ability of a leader to produce a major increase in political mobilization may be judged to signify a "revolutionary" development; at another level, and from a different analytical perspective, it may signify very little "real" structural change in more basic political behavior patterns.

But let us say that variance in the magnitude of control has been established in one form or another. How, then, can one explain the variance of variance? What accounts for the observation that different incumbents of identical leadership positions are more effective in exercising control over their subordinates than others, or that a particular leader demonstrates sometimes less, and sometimes more, control over his followers?

The search for explanations, or examination of the validity of proffered answers, involves once again the analysis of causal relationships. The focus of comparative inquiry is closely related to, but not the same as, the identification of leaders and the sources of their control. The problem here is not to account for leadership as such, but to account for the determinants of variance in its efficacy. Accordingly, differences in the extent of change in the behavior of assumed followers represent in this instance the dependent variable, and alleged or possible reasons constitute the causative variables.

This sort of causal inquiry takes us to the very heart of the comparative analysis of political leadership. In one way or another it enters into the study of comparative government, of policy and decision-making processes, and of the careers of various leaders. It is also, however, a particularly complex subject and a good deal of the work of recent years has been directed toward refining earlier modes of analysis and attaining a greater degree of methodological sophistication. Two trends are particularly worth noting in this regard. On the one hand, there has been a pronounced shift from unicausal to multivariate explanations. On the other hand, numerous efforts have been devoted to the development of theoretical frameworks that sharply limit comparative analysis to a few key variables. Insofar as these approaches proceed from entirely different assumptions about human and, particularly, political behavior, they are in effect irreconcilable. On balance there is, however, a good deal of overlap between current attempts to deal with the variance of variance.

Differences in leadership efficacy are generally accounted for in terms of variance in the properties of actors or context. For heuristic purposes, most such explanations can be grouped into a few basic interrelated propositions.

1.   Variance in the magnitude of control is a function of variance in environmental conditions (e.g., "natural" causes, external factors).

2.   Variance in the magnitude of control is a function of variance in orientations of followers (e.g., their definitions of situations and relationships, their evaluation of expected benefits or losses).

3.   Variance in the magnitude of control is a function of variance in leaders' abilities:

     a. to correctly anticipate followers' reactions to their directive cues (e.g., predicted fit between intended and likely behavior);

     b. to maximize their control resources (e.g., positional authority, personal authority, means of communication, persuasion, coercion);

     c. to control factors intervening between their directive cues and follower responses (e.g., time and space, third parties, environmental dynamics).

In contrast to the broader propositions listed under the sources of leadership, the propositions here are more closely directed toward the comparison of specific leadership acts. In other words, the units of analysis are control actions rather than successful and unsuccessful leadership. In aggregate, such actions chart the ups and the downs, the more and the less, in the magnitude of control exercised by a particular leader or various leaders. Explanatory generalizations regarding the variance of variance are then based on the reading and interpretation of such charts in terms of factors found to enhance or inhibit the exercise of political control.

The Quality of Leadership

Statements about good or bad, great or mediocre leaders are based on qualitative standards of comparison. They proceed from some notion of right and wrong about the ends or means of control. Such statements may represent summary judgments about various groups of leaders—say legislative or governmental elites—or about the career of a single individual. Then, again, they may concern specific leadership episodes, such as the formulation of winning coalitions, electoral defeats, and efforts to implement particular objectives.

In general, the assessment of variance in the quality of political leaders is informed by the foci of observation and the nature of the evaluative criteria (see Figure 1). The focus of observation may be primarily the ends or the means of control. The quality of leadership behavior will then be correspondingly interpreted, principally in terms of the goals or the modes of observed activities. The evaluative criteria may be analytically intrinsic or extrinsic, depending on whether or not they are logically inherent in the approach employed.

Figure 1 The Interrelationship between Foci of Observation and Interpretive Criteria

Interpretive Criteria	Focus of Observation	
	Leadership Objective	Leadership Activity
Analytically intrinsic	Degree of attainment (e.g., effective group performance, personal gains)	Degree of instrumental efficiency (e.g., benefit/cost ratio)
Analytically extrinsic	Proximity to ends valued by observer (e.g., peace, social equity)	Proximity to means valued by observer (e.g., "autocratic" or "democratic" style of performance)

Analytically intrinsic criteria are in this sense dictated by explicit theories and methods that allow for replication and falsification of qualitative interpretations. That is to say, within the terms stipulated by a model or analytical framework, they may be confirmed or disconfirmed. Most often they are closely tied to the focus of observation. For example, the subjects for comparison may be particular leaders, or would-be leaders, and their behavior may be evaluated in terms of its functionality for personal motives, intentions, and needs. The comparative quality of their performance may be measured by a benefit/cost ratio. How much of their limited resources did they have to invest in order to attain their objectives? A high rate of expenditure may have won them immediate goals in a political battle but lost them a war for larger objectives over the long run. Or the subject may be informal groups or formal organizations, where the quality of leadership behavior is usually compared in terms of its functionality for other members, or for the collectivity as a whole.[16]

Analytically extrinsic criteria, on the other hand, are independent of the specific mode of comparative inquiry. Qualitative assessments can in this case not be falsified in terms of an inherent logic of inquiry unless they are derived from a more general theory. Most frequently they are based on explicit or implicit normative prefer-

---

[16]The latter approach characterizes most current investigations of leadership in formal organizations and small groups. Thus, social-psychological studies of such collectivities usually evaluate and compare the quality of leaders in terms of their ability to promote group harmony and effective task performance. See, for example, Daniel Katz and Robert L. Kahn, *The Social Psychology of Organizations* (New York, 1967).

ences rooted in an investigator's philosophical beliefs and values; when ideological dogmas or doctrines call for qualitative judgments, they can only be accepted or rejected on their own terms. The question, then, is ultimately whether or not one shares the analytically intrinsic norms of the evaluator. And so leaders who are perceived as heroes by some will be considered mediocrities by others; one man's saint will be another's devil; and leadership means and ends that are fully acceptable to some scholars will be entirely unacceptable to others.[17]

This distinction between analytically intrinsic and extrinsic qualitative comparisons of course represents an oversimplified dichotomy for heuristic purposes. It is intended to orient the reader of leadership studies toward different sorts of biases on the part of their authors, as well as to help him identify those he brings to them himself.

The much debated interrelationship between the analysis of evidential facts and their valued-informed interpretations is as pertinent here as in other areas of comparative political inquiry. When it comes to evaluating means and ends, very few, if any, leadership studies are entirely "objective" in the sense of arriving at some absolute Platonic "truth." And where authors and, perhaps, readers are in fact involved participant observers, their "subjective" value preferences are all the more likely to intrude. To judge by the current literature, it is more difficult "to do justice" to those close at hand than to those observed from a distance. But just in this regard, a consciously employed, analytically intrinsic approach to the comparative assessment of political leaders appears to have much to recommend it. Properly designed, it can minimize normative biases and, accordingly, enhance the persuasive power of evaluative conclusions.

Themes and Variations

In sum, then, comparative study essentially involves three interrelated, but analytically distinct, aspects of political leadership. One is variance in efforts to obtain control; a second is variance in the exercise of control; and a third is variance in the impact of control. To put it another way, comparative inquiry focuses on differences as well as on similarities in the acquisition, performance, and consequences of leadership. Each of these, and all of these, may be the foci of investigations, and the emphasis may be on interconnected positions, interpersonal relationships, or both.

[17]Cf. Edinger, "Where are the Political Superstars?", *Political Science Quarterly*, LXXXIX (June 1974), 249–68.

Furthermore, the conclusions drawn from such comparative leadership inquiries can take the form of one or more of the following types
of statements: (1) Descriptive "is/was" statements designate differences and similarities, either in the form of assumptions or on the
basis of observations. In the latter case, a scholar may simply summarize the findings of an empirical investigation and leave it to others
to draw their own conclusions. (2) Explanatory "because" statements are either deduced from a theoretical model or arrived at
inductively from the evidence at hand. Either way they can lead to
"if-then" deterministic or probabilistic, conditional or unconditional,
propositions and hypotheses. (3) Prescriptive "should" statements
proceed from such causal associations to posit what leaders or followers ought to do to satisfy given criteria of performance or to achieve
stipulated goals.

The accent in current American political leadership research is on
explanatory statements based on systematic comparative analysis. In
this regard, descriptive and prescriptive statements by political scientists have come to be more closely informed by causal models and
analytical frameworks derived principally from either economics or
social psychology. Economic man has entered into political leadership analysis in the form of rational behavior models of exchange
transactions between leaders and led; psychological man in the form
of personality and learning models. In both cases, the effect has been
a shift in emphasis from the positional to the behavioral approach to
leadership, and from the comparison of institutional structures to the
comparison of interpersonal dynamics.

These efforts to bring a greater degree of theoretical sophistication
to the comparative analysis of a universal phenomenon seem, however, a long way from producing a persuasive general theory of
political leadership. Inevitably, the more elegant and logically coherent attempts in this direction have been, the higher the level of
abstraction. Even more modest so-called "partial" or
"middle-range" theories have tended to incorporate too many un-
proved assumptions and epistemological hedges to permit tests of
their validity in concrete leadership situations. Here, too, more questions are likely to be begged than answered when it comes to providing explanations and predictions. The same, however, may be said
about assertions that hold, to the contrary, that the uniqueness of
particular leaders and settings makes them too different to permit any
sort of meaningful comparisons. To assert differences is to make a
comparative statement subject to verification and falsification; an

emphasis on idiosyncratic *sui generis* factors again begs the question of comparability.

As of now the most promising approach to comparative leadership analysis appears to be deductive-inductive analysis directed toward ever broader empirical generalizations. On the one hand, this calls for bringing theoretical abstractions down to the level of "the real world" of concrete human relationships. On the other hand, it means raising particularistic phenomena to a level of generality where patterns of variance may be identified, compared, and, to some degree at least, explained. In conclusion, I shall touch upon some of the key operational issues that seem to be involved here.

The first is the problem of isolation. What are the factors that enter into the causal relationships to be analyzed? What needs to be known in terms of theoretical criteria of significance and relevance in order to examine and compare variance in such relationships?

A second problem is that of information. Here the question is whether what needs to be known can be ascertained, whether reliable data can be obtained through research and observation, and how much missing information has to be extrapolated and inferred.

A third problem is measurement. How much of the variance in the dependent variable can be convincingly related to variance in stipulated causative variables? Do the measures used capture what they are supposed to? In other words, are they valid? And are they reliable measures for examining the particular cause and effect relationships under consideration?

Finally, there is the difficult problem of interpretation. Here one finds in the leadership literature that the greater the gap between theory and data, the greater the degree of reliance on inferential analysis, on empathy and imaginative constructions (or reconstructions), and on reasoning by analogy. But it does not necessarily follow that, because something held true in one historical situation, it also holds true in another, or that what is taken for evidence of leadership in some cases will also indicate leadership in others.

Such considerations apply to all forms of empirical inquiry in comparative leadership analysis, regardless of whether they employ mathematical methods or not. In one way or another, the problems of isolation, information, measurement, and interpretation need to be confronted and resolved in every kind of investigation of the who, the why, the how, and the wherefore.

Leaders and Structures In 'Third World' Politics

Contrasting Approaches to Legitimacy

Paul R. Dettman

Introduction

The tendency of contemporary political scientists to neglect the significant role which leadership plays in political life because of their
preoccupation with political structure has been deplored by
Dankwart A. Rustow.[1] Structurally oriented political analysis either
ignores the leadership variable or treats it as a variable that sets the
limits within which political events can be explained in terms of
political structures. In political contexts in which structural variables
are overwhelmingly salient, the "error" introduced by the leadership
variable is certainly not large. There are, however, political contexts
in which structural analysis tells only part of the story and the
variable of leadership can be omitted only at the cost of a significant
gap in explanation. Such contexts are often those where political
structures are undergoing rapid and substantial change with particular
leaders playing a significant role in bringing this about. The politics
of the "Third World" has been characterized by this type of
political context. Consequently, explanations of "Third World" politics cannot be limited to structural analyses but must give due consideration to the impact of the leadership variable.

The student of Third World politics is faced, then, with the
problem of bringing the leadership variable into the picture. He can,
of course, treat it as a variable unrelated to structural variables—the
method followed by W. Howard Wriggins.[2] The latter analyzes
Third World political leadership in terms of the strategies used to
aggregate power and to build supporting coalitions, e.g., projecting

[1]Dankwart A. Rustow, "The Study of Leadership," in Rustow, ed. *Philosophers and Kings*
(New York, 1970).

[2]W. Howard Wriggins, *The Ruler's Imperative: Strategies for Survival in Asia and Africa*
(New York, 1970).

personality, building an organization, formulating an ideology, providing patronage, suppressing opponents, fostering economic development, encouraging or discouraging popular participation, and pursuing an active foreign policy. In the end, however, Wriggins' analysis tells nothing significant about the role of leadership in Third World politics because the strategies he delineates are the same as those used by politicians throughout the world. The reason for Wriggins' failure to discover anything peculiar in Third World political leadership is clearly that he consciously deprecates the importance of the structural context in which Third World political leaders function. "Politics," he asserts, "is not a matter of structure and process, neatly defined, but rather a drama of human beings, responding to and attempting to affect the behavior of one another."[3] Viewing politics as essentially a human drama abstracted from the structural context in which it takes place, Wriggins inevitably arrives at a universal picture of political strategies which fails to specify the peculiarities of political leadership in the "Third" part of the world.

The meager theoretical results of Wriggins' study make it clear that any attempt to delineate the peculiar role that leadership plays in Third World politics must give due weight to its structural dimensions. Such an attempt cannot focus, as Wriggins does, on leadership variables alone; it must relate these to structural variables. It is easy to say this but extremely difficult to accomplish it. One way to begin would be to examine the relationship between political leadership and socioeconomic and political structures in several Third World countries in order to ascertain what, if any, cross-cultural continuities emerge. The study which follows takes such a comparative approach. This imposes certain limitations upon its scope, however. In order to compensate for the difficulties involved in considering several Third World countries within a single article, one must limit oneself to a single aspect of leadership instead of taking up Wriggins' complete catalog. The single aspect that seems to be most important, legitimacy, has been chosen on the understanding that, even if legitimacy stands preeminent, Wriggins' study has made clear that it is only one aspect of leadership and that much more needs to be said on the subject before the relationship between leadership and structures in Third World politics is fully understood. In other words, what follows is only the beginning of a long theoretical discussion.

The comparative approach calls for a common theoretical framework by means of which the relationship between the legitimacy aspect of leadership and the socioeconomic and political structures of

[3]Ibid., p. 11.

several Third World countries may be analyzed. So far as legitimacy is concerned, it would appear that one can do no better than to follow Max Weber's typological distinctions between "charismatic," "traditional," and "legal-rational" norms.[4] The best analytical framework for the socioeconomic and political structures seems to be Fred Riggs' "model of the prismatic society,"[5] although this model does not perfectly fit the structures of any of the Third World countries which will be studied. Rather, his model will serve as a yardstick to measure the degree to which these structures conform to or deviate from those which he regards as characteristic of Third World nations.

By combining the theoretical frameworks of Weber and Riggs, then, one can attempt to relate comparatively the legitimacy aspect of leadership with structural variables in several Third World political communities. These communities can be chosen on the basis of variations in leadership performance, including some in which civilian leadership has been perpetuated and some in which civilian leadership has given way to military rule. India, Tanzania, and Kenya are examples of the former, Indonesia, Burma, and Ghana of the latter. Moreover, each of these political communities began as an independent nation under a preeminent nationalist leader: Nehru in India, Nyerere in Tanzania, Kenyatta in Kenya, Sukarno in Indonesia, U Nu in Burma, and Nkrumah in Ghana. The interaction between the approaches to legitimacy of these leaders and the structures within which they led can be studied comparatively in order to ascertain whether or not there is a relationship between this interaction and their success or failure in maintaining authority.

India and Nehru

Indian social, political, economic, and normative structures correspond, on the whole, to those of Riggs' "prismatic" society.[6] So far

[4]Talcott Parsons, "Introduction," in Max Weber, *The Theory of Social and Economic Organization*, trans. Parsons and A. M. Henderson (New York, 1947).

[5]Fred W. Riggs, *Administration in Developing Countries: The Model of the Prismatic Society* (Boston, 1964). Riggs' "model" is worked out in considerable detail and is replete with esoteric vocabulary. It is founded, however, on the argument that the "prismatic" society is characterized by several structures, each of which performs several functions. In this respect it is distinct from a "fused" society in which one structure performs all functions and, at the opposite extreme, the "diffracted" society in which there are many structures but each structure performs only one function. He agrees with Lloyd I. and Suzanne H. Rudolph that the relationship between traditional and modern in Third World countries is dialectical rather than dichotomous. See their, *The Modernity of Tradition* (Chicago, 1967), pp. 3-14.

[6]The most useful secondary sources on Nehru's leadership in India are: Michael Brecher, *Nehru: A Political Biography* (London, 1957); W. R. Crocker, *Nehru: A Contemporary's Estimate* (New York, 1966); Donald E. Smith, *India as a Secular State* (Princeton, 1965); and Hugh Tinker, *India and Pakistan* (New York, 1967).

as social and political structure are concerned, however, there are several significant deviations in the "diffracted" direction. In the first place, the "elite-eminent" struggle is not severe. The wealthy and socially preeminent certainly aspire to secure power, but not through displacement of the political "elite." Second, the bureaucracy is not the principal channel of "elite" recruitment; those who aspire for political power do so through political parties, especially the Congress party. Third, bureaucratic political institutions do not dominate nonbureaucratic political institutions. The most potent political institution is the Congress party, which not only constitutes in itself a countervailing political force to the bureaucracy but also provides the continuing support necessary for the government's executive to exercise a significant degree of control over the bureaucracy. On the other hand, the political influence of the Congress party is not sufficiently great to enable the party or the executive to dominate the bureaucracy. Rather, a kind of "stand-off" relationship exists, with neither side able to control the other and, consequently, both obliged to make concessions. The result is that the mutual interference between bureaucrats and politicians characteristic of the prismatic society prevails despite the political preeminence of the Congress party.

There are two respects in which India deviates from the prismatic model of economic structures. In the first place, because the elite-eminent power struggle is not severe, entrepreneurs are not subjected to domination by the bureaucracy. While they do have to face controls and competition from the public sector and to pay for bureaucratic favors, nevertheless entrepreneurs retain a significant degree of influence vis-à-vis the bureaucracy. Second, the absence of bureaucratic domination in political and economic matters makes it possible for nonbureaucratic political and economic institutions to exercise a significant degree of control over public policy in the economic sphere. Although, as in other Third World countries, economic development has been limited by prismatic forces in the society, it has been possible for India to achieve a certain degree of economic progress for both these reasons.

Attention must now be focused upon the manner in which Jawaharlal Nehru achieved legitimacy within these structures. In his political leadership role, Nehru derived his legitimacy from a mixture of Weber's "charismatic," "traditional," and "legal-rational" norms. The Indian populace undoubtedly looked upon him as a charismatic figure, for he had played a major role in leading India to independence and had suffered long years of imprisonment as a result of his opposition to British rule. Nevertheless, his charismatic appeal was limited. His indifference to religion generally, and, in particular, his refusal to follow the precepts and practices of Hinduism prevented him from exercising the supernatural powers that the Indian people believed to emanate from this source. Here he stood in striking contrast to Mahatma Gandhi, a political leader who was considered to exercise these powers to a significant degree. Indians came to Nehru for instruction, but they did not come to him, as they did to Gandhi, for blessing. Although he was a skillful orator, Nehru did not engage in demagoguery or in the coining of slogans. Nor did he make grandiose promises of a good life to be attained in the twinkling of an eye. Rather, he attempted to impress upon his followers that the achievement of progress in an independent but poverty stricken country was a long, uphill struggle. The result was that they were taught rather than inspired, and Nehru became their "Pandit," or teacher, not their "Mahatma," the great soul and dispenser of supernatural merit.

Nehru also derived legitimacy as a political leader from traditional norms. As a member of the Brahmin aristocracy, it was in keeping with Indian tradition that he should be a leader. Moreover, he recognized and used traditional group norms to build up political support. As castes were politicized, they were incorporated into the party and governmental machinery. The factionalism that resulted was prevented from getting out of hand by the mediating role that Nehru played, again in accordance with Indian tradition. Despite the political conflicts which inevitably ensued, he agreed to the redrawing of state boundaries in order to bring these into conformity with the geographical distribution of linguistic groups, thus honoring the traditional norm of linguistic group integrity. On the other hand, he violated certain traditional norms in favor of legal-rational ones. He struggled to make India a unified nation-state rather than a collection of mutually antagonistic language and caste groups. Further, he insisted that India should be a secular rather than a Hindu state. Nehru thus became the legitimate leader both of ardent nationalists and of members of minority communal groups who would have become second class citizens without his support.

Nehru also gained legitimacy from legal-rational norms in the great reliance that he placed upon the Congress party and upon the bureaucracy and through the efforts he made to make both of these strong and durable political institutions. In his view, the Congress party was neither his personal following nor a mere tool of government; rather, it had led India to independence, and the well-being of the Indian nation depended upon his working strenuously to promote party unity and vigor. He did not allow party concerns to monopolize his attention, however. On the contrary, he devoted a substantial amount of time to efforts to ensure the smooth running of the bureaucratic apparatus. Like other anticolonial nationalist politicians, Nehru had a suspicion of the civil bureaucracy because, in his eyes, it was identified to a certain extent with the colonial regime. Nevertheless, he did not allow this suspicion to induce him to dismantle or to politicize the bureaucracy. He not only kept it intact in much the same way that it had functioned under the British; but he also attempted to preserve for it a significant degree of freedom from political pressures. As a result, both Congress party leaders and bureaucrats, who constituted much of the core of the Indian elite committed to legal-rational norms, were willing to accept the authority of a leader who shared their commitment.

On balance, then, Nehru gained legitimacy as a political leader mainly from legal-rational norms, secondarily from traditional norms, and only to a minor degree from charismatic norms. He did so within a set of structures that were predominantly prismatic in the sense that they represented a combination of traditional and modern forces, but deviated from the prismatic model in the direction of the "diffracted" or modern mode, particularly in so far as political structures were concerned. Thus, the norms upon which he relied for legitimacy were congruent with the structures within which he exercised leadership. So far as Nehru's charismatic appeal was concerned, it was validated by the results that he achieved for his followers. He neither claimed to be a miracle worker, nor did he achieve miracles. But he did bring about discernible improvement in the living conditions of the Indian people, and he gave them a respected place among the peoples of the world. These were limited benefits, no doubt, but they corresponded with the limited degree to which his authority depended upon charismatic norms.

Kenya and Kenyatta

Unlike those of India, Kenyan structures correspond very closely to the prismatic model.[7] Jomo Kenyatta functions within these structures as a leader who derives his legitimacy from a combination of charismatic, traditional, and legal-rational norms. He is regarded as a charismatic figure not only because he led Kenya to independence but also because he suffered detention in the process. In addition, his

---

[7] For Kenyatta's leadership in Kenya, see: N. S. Carey Jones, *The Anatomy of Uhuru* (Manchester, 1966); George Bennett and Carl Rosberg, *The Kenyatta Election* (London, 1961); Cherry Gertzel, *The Politics of Independent Kenya* (London, 1970); and Carl Rosberg and John Nottingham, *The Myth of Mau Mau: Nationalism in Kenya* (New York, 1966).

charismatic appeal is derived from the honor he allocates to animist religious beliefs and practices and the oratorical style he uses when he addresses his followers. He resorts to demagoguery and slogans and speaks in language his people can understand. Thus, he is an inspirer rather than a teacher. He is regarded by the populace as the tribal chief, the "wise elder," of the Kenyan nation. Nevertheless, Kenyatta does not capitalize upon his charismatic appeal by claiming that he can work economic and social miracles. Rather, he goes out of his way to emphasize that prosperity cannot be achieved overnight and that progress will come only through the sustained effort of the Kenyan people. His slogan is *"Harambee"* ("Let us all work to-gether"), and he sharply rebuffs those who look to him to accomplish on his own the task of national development.

Kenyatta gains legitimacy also from the traditional tribal norms that dominate Kenyan society. He began his political career and still pursues it as the political leader of the dominant and aggressive Kikuyu tribe. In fact, his position as the Kikuyu's political leader is one of the main foundations of his political strength. Kenyatta's recognition of traditional norms is also reflected in his economic policy. While this policy has sought little alteration in the industrial and commercial sectors of the economy, it has brought about substantial changes in the agricultural sector. Not only has agriculture been emphasized in Kenya's development program, but large tracts of land, formerly reserved for white settlers, have been transferred to African ownership. In terms of traditional norms, Kenyatta's Africanization of land ownership is of paramount importance because a tribe's status depends basically upon the land that it holds. In addition, Kenyatta identifies himself personally as well as politically with traditional norms by the honor he accords to Kikuyu religious beliefs and rites in particular, and to animism in general. During his youth he was baptized a Christian and given the name Joniston Kamau. Later, however, when he began to emerge as Kenya's leading nationalist, he abandoned his Christianity in favor of animism and his Christian name in favor of Kenyatta, the word for a traditional Kikuyu charm belt which he habitually wears.

While Kenyatta's legitimacy is largely based on charismatic and traditional norms, it is derived to some extent from legal-rational ones. So far as political institutions are concerned, he has emphasized the bureaucracy rather than the political party. Although he is the leader of the dominant party, he devotes little attention to party affairs, nor does he rely upon the party to maintain his legitimacy. Rather, the bureaucracy provides his principal legal-rational normative support. Not only has he resisted attempts to politicize the bureaucracy, but he has taken steps to bring it under his direct presidential control, particularly in the police and military areas. In short, so far as legal-rational political institutions are concerned, Kenyatta functions primarily as head of the governmental apparatus and only to a minor degree as head of a political party. He does so because his aim is to maintain the government as the dominant political institution, with the party playing a subservient role in organizing popular support for governmental programs.

As noted earlier, except for significant changes in land ownership and the implementation of agricultural development programs, only limited reforms have been undertaken in the economic realm. The basic reason why Kenya's economy still functions much the same as it did before independence is that Kenyatta recognizes the legal-rational norm of economic efficiency and believes that drastic changes in Kenya's economic structure aimed at meeting the traditional norm of Africanization will in fact work against the realization of this goal. By recognizing the legal-rational norm of economic efficiency, he has gained legitimacy in the eyes of Asian and white Kenyans, who not only share a commitment to this norm, but who stand to gain through the maintenance of the status quo in commercial and industrial sectors of the economy. At the same time, Africanization of substantial tracts of land has pleased the African members of the population. Thus, Kenyatta's economic policy has helped substantially to legitimize his leadership among all three racial groups in Kenyan society.

In summary, it is fair to say that, on the whole, Kenyatta has perpetuated the system of "indirect rule" that the British used in governing Kenya during its colonial history. Kenyatta now occupies the political pinnacle on which the British governor formerly stood and rules through an Africanized civil service rather than through British Colonial Service officers. But, so far as its mode of operation is concerned, Kenya under Kenyatta is as much a bureaucratically dominated administrative state as it was in colonial days. As the legitimacy of indirect rule under the British rested mainly upon a combination of traditional and legal-rational norms, so, too, does the legitimacy of indirect rule under Kenyatta. The only additional element of legitimacy that Kenyatta has added is a charismatic appeal which the British governor never enjoyed. Yet, important as this charismatic appeal is, it is outweighed in the balance by the legitimacy he derives from traditional and legal-rational norms. Thus, he is able to maintain legitimacy within a set of structures which are typically prismatic, a fusion of traditional and modern elements. To the limited degree that Kenyatta's legitimacy is based upon charismatic norms, it has been matched by the limited benefits he has managed to procure for his followers. Although he has not significantly enhanced their economic well-being, he has provided more African Kenyans with land, and he has raised their social status vis-à-vis their white and Asian fellow citizens. At the same time he has seen to it that white and Asian Kenyans have not been overwhelmed by a policy of Africanization of Kenyan society. These are hardly spectacular achievements, but Kenyatta has never promised his followers spectacular results. Consequently, the slow economic and social progress which Kenya has made under Kenyatta's leadership has not weakened the legitimacy he derives from charismatic norms.

Tanzania and Nyerere

The social, political, economic, and normative structures of Tanzania correspond to those of the "prismatic society" except in two important areas,[8] where they depart from the prismatic model in a diffracted direction. So far as social structures are concerned, while "polycommunalism" on tribal and racial lines exists to a significant degree, it is not a decisive factor in Tanzanian life. Political structures are characterized by a fusion of bureaucratic and nonbureaucratic political institutions; the former are not dominant. Since Tanzania is a one-party state, the president is head of the party as well as head of the government. Moreover, both civil and military bureaucracy have been incorporated into the party. Local government officials are party officials as well, and civil servants are party members. The end result is that Tanzania's one-party state is not an administrative state dominated by the bureaucracy; rather it is a state in which the bureaucracy has been merged with the party, each reinforcing the other.

Within these structures, Julius Nyerere has exercised leadership by basing his legitimacy on a mixture of charismatic, traditional, and legal-rational norms. The "father of the nation," who led Tanzania to independence in a remarkably rapid and smooth manner, he is venerated by the masses as a man who has accomplished great things in the past and who can accomplish great things in the future. Nevertheless, his charismatic appeal is limited. He did not suffer for the cause of independence; the only legal penalty imposed upon him was a fine for writing seditious material. His oratorical style is that of

[8] Nyerere's leadership in Tanzania is best evaluated in: Harvey Glickman "One Party System in Tanganyika," *Annals of the American Academy of Political and Social Science*, 358 (March 1965); J. Clagett Taylor, *The Political Development of Tanganyika* (Stanford, 1963); Henry Bienen, *Tanzania: Party Transformation and Economic Development* (Princeton, 1967); and William Tordoff, *Government and Politics in Tanzania* (Nairobi, 1967).

the teacher he was before he became a nationalist leader, rather than that of the demagogue—a fact that can be seen in the honorific title of "teacher" which his followers have given him. He speaks in terms of an African Socialist ideology which the Tanzanian common man cannot understand, not in terms of symbols and slogans which he can. Nor does he promise followers quick and easy progress toward prosperity and high status. He emphasizes instead the need for hard work and perseverance in a steady but slow upward climb. His national slogan is "Freedom and Work." Finally, his personality and life style are almost completely lacking in awe-inspiring qualities.

Nyerere's legitimacy is derived also from traditional African and tribal norms, but, here again, only to a limited degree. His ideology is based upon the African traditions of the extended family and the communal life of the tribe, but while this ideology has been adopted by the educated elite, it has not filtered down to the masses. He has taken steps to Africanize political institutions to a considerable degree and economic institutions to a limited degree, but only under pressure from his lieutenants and followers. Nyerere himself has stood against Africanization on the ground that Tanzanians should be recruited to political and economic roles on the basis of merit rather than race. After vacating the presidential office for two years in order to strengthen the party organization, he succeeded in converting the nation to his policy of racial equality.

Nyerere has made no attempt to gain legitimacy by honoring the tradition of chieftaincy. Although he is the son of a tribal chief, he does not attempt to play the role of the chief of a "national" tribe. To do so would conflict with his role as a leader who transcends tribal divisions. Nor has Nyerere displayed respect for chiefs as such. Chiefs who occupied positions as local administrators under the British have been replaced by party officials. On the other hand, chiefs have not been disqualified from holding administrative positions by virtue of being chiefs. Those who had the competence to administer local areas and who allied themselves with the party have been given appointments.

While he has identified himself with African social traditions, Nyerere has not personally identified himself with African religious traditions. He was baptized a Christian and given a Christian name. Unlike Kenyatta, he changed neither his name nor his religious affiliation when he became a nationalist leader. Moreover, when he became head of the Tanzanian state, he made no bones of the fact that his Christian commitment had an important influence in determining the policies he pursued. So far as his personal religion and morality are concerned, then, Nyerere stands in opposition to the traditions of the vast majority of his followers.

While Nyerere's legitimacy rests upon charismatic and traditional norms only to a limited extent, it is based to a considerable degree upon legal-rational norms. He exercises leadership largely through a fusion of bureaucratic and nonbureaucratic political institutions, each reinforcing the other. He devotes equal attention to government and party and uses each to strengthen his authority—the government to provide stable and efficient administration and the party to enlist popular support. He appeals to the legal-rational norms of efficiency and the secular equality of tribal and racial groups to justify his stand that recruitment to political and economic roles should be based on merit rather than ethnicity.

Nyerere's economic policy also reflects the predominant influence of legal-rational norms. He, again unlike Kenyatta, has not followed traditional norms by concentrating his attention upon agriculture and satisfying himself with institutional changes that involve only land ownership. Instead, he has fostered, under government auspices, an industrial and commercial, as well as an agricultural, development program. The result has been a significant change in the structure of Tanzania's economic system, not only in the direction of Africanization and diversification, but in the expansion of the public sector. At the same time, Nyerere has not suppressed the private sector and has allowed private entrepreneurs to continue to function. Nor has he followed traditional norms by ousting white and Asian businessmen and turning their holdings over to Africans. Africanization of the economy has been furthered, but within the limitation that it should interfere neither with efficient functioning nor with the rights of non-African Tanzanians. In short, Nyerere's economic policy has sought to produce, not only a new system, but one which would run smoothly because it was linked to ability and fair play. The result of this policy, which is based on legal-rational norms, has been to enhance his legitimacy in the eyes of all sectors, tribal and racial, of Tanzanian society.

The constraints imposed by a predominantly prismatic society have naturally prevented this policy from producing a significant degree of economic development. Nevertheless, there has been improvement in the economic situation from which Nyerere's followers have benefited. They have gained even more socially and politically from the higher level of their involvement in public activity stemming from Nyerere's efforts at social and political mobilization. Moreover, the Africans who constitute the overwhelming majority have been brought closer to a position of racial equality with their white and

Asian fellow citizens. These economic, political, and social gains, while limited, have fulfilled the promises Nyerere has made to his followers. Therefore, to the limited extent that Nyerere's legitimacy is based on charismatic norms, it has been validated by the benefits he has provided for his followers.

In summary, it may be said that Nyerere's legitimacy rests upon a mixture of norms in which the traditional and charismatic play minor roles and the legal-rational a major role. Such a mixture of legitimizing norms is congruent with Tanzania's social, political, economic, and normative structures. For, while Tanzanian society on the whole reflects prismatic characteristics, it departs significantly from this model in a diffracted direction in both its social and political structures. In so far as it is prismatic, legitimacy can rest upon charismatic and traditional as well as legal-rational norms. In so far as it is diffracted, greater weight can be placed upon the legal-rational than upon the charismatic and traditional.

Ghana and Nkrumah

Ghanaian society, like that of Kenya, is typically prismatic.[9] During the days of the Nkrumah regime, surface appearances indicated that Ghana's political structure deviated from this model in a diffracted direction because of the role played by the Convention People's party. As events transpired, however, it became clear that, although the party did enjoy a measure of influence in administrative and patronage matters, it did not function as an independent nonbureaucratic political institution exercising control over the bureaucracy. It was in fact Nkrumah's organized political following, depending for its vigor on his control of the governmental apparatus and the spoils derived therefrom. In terms of American urban politics, it was a political machine more than a political party. That is, it drew its strength not from its independent organization but from its "boss" and the spoils of office which he controlled. When the boss lost control of the spoils of office, the party collapsed.

Another misleading surface appearance was that Nkrumah based his authority upon force to a significant degree and that, as the years went by, he relied more on force and less on legitimacy to keep himself in office. Whether Nkrumah's use of force is seen as an

[9]David E. Apter has specialized in studies of Nkrumah's leadership. See his *Ghana in Transition* (New York, 1963), and "Nkrumah, Charisma and the Coup," *Daedalus*, 97 (Summer 1968). Henry Bretton, *The Rise and Fall of Kwame Nkrumah* (New York, 1966), constitutes a rebuttal of Apter at several points. Valuable historical background is provided in Dennis Austin, *Politics in Ghana: 1946-1960* (London, 1964), and "Opposition in Ghana," *Government and Opposition*, II (July-October 1967).

appearance or a reality depends upon the definition of force employed. He jailed and exiled many of his political opponents in order to counter the threat of a political coup, and he organized a special Presidential Security Force, separate from the regular armed forces and under his direct command. Yet those who went into exile or jail did so under laws passed legitimately by Parliament. Moreover, the Presidential Security Force offered no effective resistance to the police-military coup which overthrew him. In fact, therefore, despite appearances to the contrary, Nkrumah's authority was not actually based upon force. Rather, like the other political leaders included in this study, he depended essentially upon legitimacy to keep himself in office. He tried to use force legally, and he succeeded in doing so as long as he maintained his position of legitimacy. When legitimacy was lost, his power to use force went with it, and he was deposed.

Substantial grounds exist, therefore, for arguing that Nkrumah is no exception to the rule that the six political leaders included in this study depended primarily upon legitimacy to keep themselves in office. He was not consistent in the norms to which he appealed for legitimacy, however. During the earlier part of his regime (until he became president under the Constitution of 1960), he based his claim to legitimacy on a mixture of charismatic and legal-rational norms. Of the two, the charismatic was the more important. His charismatic appeal was substantial because he had worked a political "miracle" by making Ghana the first African colony to achieve independence, suffering imprisonment in the process, and by giving Ghana a prominent place in African and even world politics through his personal influence. Touring the country indefatigably, he roused numerous audiences through his demagogic oratory, his use of symbols and slogans, and his promises of a glorious future. He spoke to the masses in a language they could understand and in a manner that incited their support. They responded by conferring upon him the image of the "redeemer" who was destined to restore Ghana to her ancient glory.

Nkrumah's legitimacy at this early stage in his leadership career did not depend entirely upon charismatic norms, however. He gained support also from legal-rational ones. In the first place, he organized his followers into the aforementioned Convention People's party. Because its leader was a charismatic figure, a charismatic norm was "routinized," to use Weber's term, into a legal-rational norm that provided the party organization with legitimacy. It was further "routinized" into a legal-rational norm that undergirded the British Parliamentary structure of government which Nkrumah headed when he became Ghana's first prime minister in 1957. Thus, both party organization and a parliamentary structure of government provided legal-rational norms supporting Nkrumah's claim to legitimacy.

At this early stage in his leadership career, Nkrumah did not appeal to traditional norms for legitimizing support; rather, he attacked them. He castigated tribalism as the principal obstacle to progress, and, practicing what he preached, refrained from building his political following around his own Nzima tribe or any other tribe or coalition of tribes. He removed the tribal chiefs from the positions of authority which they had formerly held in local government. He refused to Africanize the bureaucracy and kept Britishers as heads of the civil service, police, and armed forces, as well as the nucleus of his personal staff. He did not attack traditional animist beliefs and practices, but refrained from commending them as a religious foundation for Ghanaian society. Nor did he repudiate his early education in a Roman Catholic mission school nor his Bachelor of Divinity degree from Lincoln University in the United States. In Nkrumah's view, Ghanaians should "seek first the political kingdom" and let religion take care of itself.

After Nkrumah assumed office as Ghana's first president, however, the norms upon which he based his legitimacy underwent a drastic change. In the first place, his charismatic appeal evaporated. No longer did he tour the countryside arousing his followers and building up support. He shut himself away from public view instead, first to secure his person and, second, to devote his energy and time to directing the apparatus of government. To make matters worse, his charismatic leadership was no longer producing benefits for his followers. After securing independence and an honored place in African and world politics for his people, the "redeemer" stopped delivering. His performance no longer validated his charismatic image, and that image disappeared. Moreover, since Nkrumah had promised much and delivered little, the adoration which he had formerly enjoyed turned into its opposite—disillusionment. When his regime was overthrown in 1966, the people of Ghana danced in the streets to celebrate his downfall.

Nkrumah's loss of legitimacy from charismatic norms was paralleled by loss of legitimacy from legal-rational ones. He ceased to concern himself with strengthening the Convention People's party; instead he weakened it by purging those members he regarded as "disloyal." Nor did he preserve the legitimizing support of Ghanaians committed to the norms of Parliamentary democracy. Following the promulgation of the Presidential Constitution of 1960, he repudiated these norms in favor of an authoritarian rule by one man, President Nkrumah. As he confined himself more to the role of an authoritarian head of government, he increasingly turned his attention to bringing the bureaucracy which constituted its apparatus under his control. In making this effort he concentrated his attention upon its police and military components since they alone could carry out a military coup to depose him. He purged their high commands of officers considered disloyal and replaced them with officers whom he regarded, mistakenly as it turned out, as his supporters. He disarmed the police and reduced the budgetary allocation for the armed forces, with the result that their level of pay fell far behind the rising costs of living and the standards of their equipment deteriorated rapidly. This policy of downgrading the police and armed forces in an effort to make them subservient to his rule inevitably resulted in a refusal by police and military officers to continue to recognize the legitimacy of his authority and, in the end, in a head-on collision with Nkrumah. The result was the coup, led by the very officers whom Nkrumah considered loyal, which ended his regime.

At the same time that support for his legitimacy from charismatic and legal-rational norms was evaporating Nkrumah began to appeal to the traditional norms which he had formerly attacked. Publicly, he started to play the role of the national chief, assuming the titles and trappings of the Ashanti chiefs who had traditionally dominated the military and political life of the Gold Coast. Privately, he replaced his British "inner circle" with a personal entourage of members of the Nzima tribe to which he belonged. Unfortunately for Nkrumah, these efforts to find a new base for legitimacy through a return to traditional norms failed to fill the legitimacy gap that had resulted from his loss of support from charismatic and legal-rational norms. However much the Ghanaian masses warmed to the traditional pomp and circumstance of his occasional public appearances, members of the elite did not take Nkrumah's posings as a national chief seriously. To leaders of the dominant Ashanti tribe, these posings were downright galling, for here was a man who did not belong to their tribe, had never been a warrior, and yet laid claim to the honored titles and symbols of their warrior chiefs. To make matters worse, the leaders of all tribes except the Nzimas began to fear subjugation under a Nzima regime.

In summary, a distinction must be made between the earlier and later phases of Nkrumah's leadership career. In the beginning, his legitimacy was derived mainly from charismatic norms and secondarily from legal-rational ones. In the second phase, charismatic and legal-rational support disappeared, and his attempt to compensate for this loss by returning to the traditional norms which he had earlier repudiated proved fruitless. In considering Nkrumah's leadership career in its entirety, the conclusion must be drawn that his legitimacy was based mainly on charismatic norms, secondarily on legal-rational norms, and only to a minor degree on traditional norms. This emphasis on the legal-rational and neglect of the traditional was incongruent with the prismatic character of Ghana's social, political, economic, and normative structures, in which traditional as well as modern elements play a vitally important part. The predominant weight placed upon charismatic normative support made Nkrumah's legitimacy extremely vulnerable. In order to maintain his charismatic relationship with his followers, he had to remain in constant personal contact with them. Moreover, he had to deliver the benefits which he promised them. When he did neither, it was inevitable that charismatic support for his legitimacy would disappear and that his overthrow would be applauded rather than deplored by the Ghanaian masses.

Burma and U Nu

Burmese structures deviate from the prismatic model in only one respect, but that deviation is in a "fused" rather than a diffracted direction.[10] The social structure is polycommunal, with a dominant Burman majority. The non-Burmese minority is fragmented into a number of small tribal and ethnic groups that are in conflict with each other as well as with the Burman majority. The result of Burman domination is that society and community correspond more closely than is typical of the prismatic case. It is important to note, however, that this deviation is in the "fused" rather than the diffracted direction because it results from the domination of a single communal group rather than from the unification of a number of different communal groups characteristic of the diffracted society.

U Nu exercised leadership within structures that are prismatic, except for this one fused element. His legitimacy was based upon a mixture of charismatic, traditional, and legal-rational norms, in that order. The Burmese people looked upon him as the one man whom they could trust and under whom they could unite. His personal integrity and selflessness were conspicuous, as was his "other-worldliness." He was a devout Buddhist, who not only lived by the moral precepts of his religion but spent long hours in prayer and meditation. His followers even considered that he was on his way to

[10]Richard Butwell has written an excellent biography, *U Nu of Burma* (Stanford, 1963). Valuable additional interpretations are: Donald E. Smith, *Religion and Politics in Burma* (Princeton, 1965); Joseph Silverstein, "Burma," in George H. Kahim, ed. *Governments and Politics in Southeast Asia* (Ithaca, 1964); and Hugh Tinker, *The Union of Burma* (London, 1967).

becoming an "enlightened one," a Buddha. As such he exercised supernatural power in their eyes.

His charismatic appeal was based upon his qualities as a man of religion more than upon his qualities as a politician. It was not he but Aung Saw who had led Burma to independence; the latter was assassinated shortly after independence was achieved. Nor had U Nu, like Aung Saw, suffered so that the nation might be free. He was chosen to succeed Aung Saw as head of the newly independent Burma mainly because his personal integrity and selflessness were such that all the surviving nationalist leaders could agree to serve under him. Nevertheless, U Nu's legitimacy did derive significant charismatic support from his role as a politician, particularly because of his oratorical style and skill. He spoke to the people in their own language and gave voice not only to their aspirations but also to their grievances. He promised them a life of prosperity in which every Burman would have a house, an automobile, and a monthly income of two hundred dollars. He castigated the corruption of Burmese life and called for a return to Buddhist purity. Finally, although U Nu had not worked a political miracle in leading Burma to independence, he had achieved a miracle by preserving Burmese unity when it appeared that independence would be followed by the nation's disintegration under the pressure of tribal and Communist insurrections.

Traditional norms were next in importance as a legitimizing force for U Nu's authority. Because of the dominant position of the Burman majority, the Buddhist religion and culture provided the lifeblood of Burmese society. For this reason, Burmese nationalism had a religious as well as a political dimension. Its political side provided the impetus for pushing toward the conversion of Burma into a modern nation state. Its religious aspect, however, pushed in the opposite or traditional direction—namely, recreating the past glories of Buddhist society. U Nu's personal predilections as a devout Buddhist and his political position both led him to emphasize the traditional religious rather than the modern political dimension. In the hearts of the Burmese people, Aung Saw was the political "father of the nation." If U Nu aspired also to be a "father of the nation," he must be a religious father. Consequently, while he sought to achieve the political goal of making Burma a prosperous modern nation, he tried to attain this goal mainly by traditional religious means, especially by making Buddhism the state religion in order to bring the nation back to the Buddhist ideals of purity and selflessness.

Legal-rational norms were of only minor importance as a source of legitimacy for U Nu's authority. He did not play a major role in the organization of the Anti-Fascist People's Freedom League (A.F.P.F.L.), the vanguard of Burma's independence movement. And his insistence that the disunity that plagued the League after independence was the result of personal corruption among its members led him to undertake a party "purge" which split the League into two factions.

Just as U Nu failed to capitalize on the legitimizing support of party norms, so, too, he failed to capitalize on the legitimizing support of bureaucracy. He politicized the civil bureaucracy by appointing only those considered politically reliable and by making administrators subservient to politicians. The result was to carry over into the civil bureaucracy the factionalism and corruption which characterized the A.F.P.F.L. U Nu attempted to cope with this development in a characteristic manner—by purging the civil bureaucracy of corruption. Once again the result was negative, for this anticorruption campaign only served to undermine further the morale and efficiency of the civil bureaucracy and to diminish U Nu's legitimacy in the eyes of an important element of Burma's political elite.

The Burmese leader's dealings with the military bureaucracy were at best ambivalent, at worst antagonistic. His personal predilection as a Buddhist naturally placed him in opposition to the violence and authoritarianism which provided the rationale of the military system. On the other hand, Burma's most serious problem was the threat to national unity posed by tribal and Communist insurrections. An increase in the military bureaucracy was absolutely essential if this threat were to be met. Consequently, during the first years of his regime, U Nu was forced to support the military bureaucracy. As a result of this joint political-military effort, the government established its control over most of Burma, and the immediate threat to the nation's territorial unity was successfully countered. Following the improvement in the internal security situation, however, U Nu's policy vis-à-vis the military became one of reluctant toleration coupled with outright mistrust. Instead of relying upon military force to keep the insurrectionists under control, he sought to win them over by conciliation and compromise.

After two years of a military caretaker regime, U Nu returned to power in 1960 with a strong popular mandate, which gave him the courage to put the army in a subservient place. He took over the defense portfolio, ousted army officers from their acquired positions of political and economic power, and removed the police from army jurisdiction. These actions convinced the army leaders that U Nu had embarked upon a program which threatened not only the interests of the military bureaucracy but of the nation at large; consequently, they could no longer regard him as Burma's legitimate political leader. Their reaction was a military coup which not only deposed U Nu, but placed him under detention so that he would be unable to carry on further political activity.

Since he failed to capitalize upon the legal-rational norms that provided the rationale of both party and bureaucracy, it is not surprising that U Nu's legitimacy was challenged by opposition from within the ranks of both organizations. It is surprising, however, that this challenge met with such easy success. Having recently won an overwhelming victory at the polls, U Nu could theoretically have anticipated popular support against the military, especially when the leaders of the coup went so far as to place him under house arrest. This did not happen primarily because by 1960 U Nu's legitimacy had also lost the support of charismatic norms. Earlier he had validated the faith of his followers by successfully countering the threat of national disintegration. Unfortunately, as the decade of the 1950s drew to a close his performance deteriorated; and, as the 1960s dawned, Burma stood on the brink of economic and political chaos. Not only was the internal security problem still serious, but the economy had reached a point of almost complete stagnation. As a result, U Nu's followers suffered both political and economic deprivation from his leadership. They had looked upon him as a leader who could bring about the economic and political miracles he had promised them. When he did not fulfill his promises, his followers lost faith in him, and his charismatic appeal evaporated.

On balance, U Nu's legitimacy was based primarily on charismatic norms, secondarily on traditional norms, and only slightly on legal-rational norms. The relative degree of legitimacy derived from these three categories of normative values was not congruent with the social, political, economic, and normative structures within which he attempted to exercise authority. To the extent that those structures contained traditional elements, they sustained the legitimacy he derived from tradition. On the other hand, to the extent that they contained modern elements, they undermined the legitimacy based upon traditional norms. Nor was this undermining effect offset by the slight degree to which U Nu's legitimacy gained strength from the legal-rational norms of Burmese society. In short, given the traditional-modern mix of Burma's prismatic society, it is quite clear that his legitimacy was based too strongly on traditional, and not enough on legal-rational norms.

To make matters worse for U Nu's legitimacy, his primary reliance on charismatic norms was not validated by the limited benefits conferred on his followers. While he succeeded in averting national disintegration, he did not achieve national unity. On the economic front, the results of his leadership were negative. Having benefited to only a limited degree politically and suffered economically, U Nu's followers lost their initial faith in him as a leader gifted with supernatural powers. Thus, his legitimacy lost the support of charismatic norms. The army easily removed him from office, and the Burmese people turned a deaf ear to his protests that he was still Burma's prime minister even though under house arrest.

Indonesia and Sukarno

During the decade and a half in which Sukarno exercised leadership in Indonesia, the structures within which he operated were generally characterized by prismatic qualities.[11] The only exception was the role of the Communist party in the political structure. This party, which was Indonesia's largest and best organized, was neither official nor combative. It functioned independently of the bureaucracy, but it did not seek to overthrow the bureaucracy until the gestapo coup of 1965. When the Communists did assume a combative stance at the time of that coup, a head-on clash with the military component of the bureaucracy ensued. As a result of the victory of the military, the Communist party was destroyed.

Sukarno's legitimacy was based on a mixture of charismatic, legal-rational, and traditional norms, in that order. His principal appeal to the Indonesian people was his image as a political miracle worker. He had led Indonesia to independence, suffering imprisonment and detention in the process. He preserved Indonesian unity in the face of the threats posed by insurrection and political factionalism. And he made Indonesia a power to be reckoned with in Southeast Asia, forcing the Dutch to surrender West Irian and "confronting" Malaysia on the irredentist issue of North Borneo. As an orator, he was a demagogue par excellence, rousing the audiences to a fever pitch by speaking to them in their own language and by translating national goals into symbols and slogans with which they could identify. His top priority was maintaining contact with the masses and rallying them to hear his speeches. In the process, he made the extravagant promise that under his leadership Indonesia would become a rich and powerful nation, a force to be reckoned with not

[11]Sukarno's leadership is best analyzed in Peter Leyon, *War and Peace in Southeast Asia* (London, 1969); Herbert Feith, *The Decline of Constitutional Democracy in Indonesia* (Ithaca, 1962); J. D. Legge, *Indonesia* (Englewood Cliffs, 1964); and Bernard Dahm, *Sukarno and the Struggle for Indonesian Independence* (Ithaca, 1969).

only in Southeast Asia, but in the entire world. His initial nationalist successes validated this claim, with the result that the Indonesian people became his followers in a characteristically charismatic way; that is, they looked upon following Sukarno as a duty to be performed whatever the cost. In their eyes, he was the personification of the Indonesian nation, to whom they could refer personally and affectionately as "Bung," or brother.

While Sukarno's charismatic support was derived largely from his political image, it also drew strength from his religious beliefs. This was true despite the fact that, although Sukarno called himself a Moslem, he did not follow the traditional precepts and practices of Islam. In charismatic style, he challenged the Islamic tradition and reformulated its teachings by making them consistent with the needs of modernization, reducing them to the slogan, "Islam is progress." As the proponent and head of a secular state, Sukarno could hardly appear to his followers as a charismatic figure in the Islamic tradition, but he could and did appear charismatic in the Javanese tradition. Java had a special syncretist religious tradition, one of the myths of which forecast the coming of a "redeemer" who would lead Java to independence and glory. Sukarno was Javanese, and the Javanese, as well as many other Indonesians, saw him as the fulfillment of this prophecy—but in the larger role of the redeemer of the whole of Indonesia.

Sukarno's legitimacy was based also on legal-rational norms, but only to a limited degree. The legal-rational norms to which he appealed were largely those of nationalism. While he sought to make Indonesia a modern and prosperous nation, he aimed above all to make her powerful. He viewed economic and social reform not as ends in themselves but as means of increasing national power. He saw himself primarily as a nationalist and only secondarily as a Marxist devoted to economic development and a reformed Moslem committed to modernizing society. Accordingly, Sukarno did not concern himself with enhancing his legitimacy through the support of political parties or the bureaucracy. He made no effort to strengthen the organization of the National Front which he headed after his elevation to the presidency in 1958. On the contrary, he purposely kept it weak so that it would not interfere with his personal rule. In general, since Sukarno saw political parties as a threat to his dominant position, he sought to rule in spite of them instead of seeking to rule through them.

The one political force that he could not ignore, however, was the Communist party, which by the early 1960s had reached a position almost equal in political strength to the armed forces. Given his

Marxist predilections, Sukarno might have been expected to identify himself with the Communist party and to use it as an institutional base for his regime. Instead, he kept himself separate from the party, although wooing its support against the armed forces. In doing so, he displayed his characteristic style of political manipulator rather than organizer.

He displayed this same characteristic manipulatory political style in his relationships with the bureaucracy. He sought to gain the support of its civil component through a policy of appointing to office only those who were loyal to him and amply rewarding those so appointed. At the same time, he did not attempt to maintain standards of administrative efficiency through the exercise of control and supervision over his bureaucratic stooges. As long as the bureaucrats remained loyal to him, he cared little how they operated. The result was that the legal-rational norms of honest and efficient administration went by the board, and the civil bureaucracy became a law unto itself, degenerating in the process into a self-seeking and corrupt body of mutually antagonistic officeholders. Such a bureaucracy could have only one effect upon Sukarno's legitimacy—that of undermining it.

Sukarno's failure to enlist the legitimizing support of bureaucratic norms by organizing an efficient and honest civil bureaucracy was not, however, as serious as his failure to enlist the legitimizing support of the military bureaucracy, a far more potent political force than its civil counterpart. Indonesia's armed forces had become militarily and politically strong through an unending series of military conflicts. Consequently, they had become an honored institution in Indonesian society and a political force with which Sukarno had to contend if he hoped to maintain his dominant position. Once again, however, he did so not by identifying his regime with the military, but by wooing the latter's support against the Communist party. In short, Sukarno kept himself in power not by securing a bureaucratic or party base of support, but by playing the bureaucracy and party off against each other. He identified himself with neither institution because he saw both as threats to his personal power. By remaining separate from bureaucracy and party, and by making them rivals for his favor, he could secure their support without paying the price of becoming the captive of either. At the same time, Sukarno's manipulative policy had the negative result of creating a situation in which the armed forces and the Communist party inevitably became rivals to succeed him when his regime ended. In the struggle that resulted, the armed forces emerged victorious, and the Communist party was destroyed, as noted earlier. The military bureaucracy thus became the dominant political power; and, since Sukarno had failed to identify himself with it and was no longer a necessary ally, the leaders of the armed forces removed him from office. In the end, then, Sukarno became the victim of his own manipulative policy.

If Sukarno's legitimacy was based only slightly on legal-rational norms, it depended even less on the support of tradition. In fact, he opposed tradition more than he supported it. As already pointed out, although Sukarno remained a Moslem, his version of Islam bore little resemblance to tradition. He stoutly opposed making Islam the state religion, even though 95 percent of the Indonesians were Moslems. Nor did he attempt to build his political following on a Javanese base, although he was Javanese and the Javanese are Indonesia's politically dominant ethnic group. To take a political stand either as a Moslem or as a Javanese was impossible for Sukarno because such a stand would have denied him the position nearest and dearest to him—that of a national leader transcending religious and ethnic divisions. The only point at which he consistently followed traditional norms was in his life style as the traditional "Oriental potentate." This is undoubtedly what the masses expected of their president, but it was not a significant factor in enhancing his legitimacy.

In summary, Sukarno's mixture of legitimizing norms consisted of a large measure of the charismatic, a small amount of the legal-rational, and even less of the traditional. This combination of legitimizing norms was not congruent with the prismatic structures within which he led because it drew support neither from the traditional nor from the modern elements in those structures. Moreover, his primary reliance on charismatic norms made his legitimacy vulnerable. During his early years, his successes validated those norms in the eyes of his followers. When he failed to make good his promise that he would humble Malaysia, however, and when his economic program did not achieve the prosperity he had led his followers to expect, the charismatic faith which the Indonesian people had placed in his leadership vanished.

Conclusions

A division of the six Third World political leaders discussed in this article according to their abilities to maintain their regimes reveals that those who fall into the successful category—Nehru, Kenyatta, and Nyerere—founded their legitimacy upon a mixture of norms congruent with the structures within which they led. None of these successful leaders placed primary reliance upon charismatic norms. As a result, the limited benefits which they were able to confer upon their followers measured up to the limited extent to which their legitimacy depended upon their charismatic appeal. On the other hand, the unsuccessful leaders—Nkrumah, U Nu, and Sukarno—based their legitimacy upon a mixture of legitimizing norms incongruent with their leadership structures. The legitimacy of each of these unsuccessful leaders was based mainly on charismatic norms. When the benefits they conferred upon their followers did not come up to the charismatic promises they had made, the people's faith in their "miraculous" powers disappeared, and, along with it, the principal foundations of their legitimacy.

It is not surpising that these opposite results should have obtained. Since the end of the era in which kings ruled by "divine right," the legitimacy of a political leader has not resided in his person, nor even in his office. Whereas a political office carries with it a corresponding authority, the incumbent must be regarded by those over whom he is set as a legitimate holder of that office, or he cannot effectively exercise that authority. The paradox that the political leader is both the master and slave of his people must not be ignored. He is their slave in the sense that gaining a position of legitimacy among them is a prerequisite for his functioning as their master. Whether or not the people of a Third World country confer legitimacy upon their political leader depends in part upon their personal attitude toward him; that is, upon whether or not he enjoys the support of charismatic norms.[12] This depends also upon the degree to which he conforms to the norms of the structures that make up the society, for these structural norms provide both guidance and standards of judgment for the conduct of its members. If the political leader acts in a way which honors these structural norms, he is legitimate in the eyes of his people. If he does not, he becomes an illegitimate officeholder and rightly subject to deposition.

Max Weber was careful to emphasize the instability of the charismatic norm that derives from a personal rather than a structural source.[13] This must be constantly renewed through personal contact and validated by the benefits that the leader confers upon his followers. The accomplishment of this two-fold task is particularly difficult for a Third World political leader. During the struggle for independence from colonial rule he can tour the country to rally his

[12]For a useful study of the particular importance of charismatic norms in legitimizing Third World political leaders, see Ann Ruth and Dorothy Willner, "The Rise and Rule of Charismatic Leaders," *Annals of the American Academy of Political and Social Sciences,* 358 (March 1965).

[13]Weber, "The Sociology of Charismatic Authority," in H. H. Gerth and C. Wright Mills, eds. *From Max Weber: Essays in Sociology* (New York, 1946).

people to the cause; in the hectic days that follow independence, he can make promises of a glorious future for the newly independent nation. But when it becomes necessary at a later stage for him to head a governmental apparatus and to spur that apparatus to implement programs of social and economic development which will benefit his people, he is forced to neglect the charismatic task of maintaining personal contact with them. Moreover, the slowness which plagues progress toward social and economic development in a Third World country—if indeed there is progress at all—makes it virtually impossible for a leader to satisfy the high expectations of those who followed him because he gave them a grandiose vision of their nation's future.

The six-nation comparative study described in this article provides no settled conclusions on the theoretical question of the relationship between legitimacy of political leadership and the societal structures of Third World countries. It does, however, supply a measure of empirical evidence from the Third World to support Rustow's contentions (1) that politics in any of the three worlds cannot be understood unless the relationship between leadership and structures is taken into account and (2) that the past tendency of theoreticians in the field of comparative politics to neglect this relationship has hindered progress in arriving at such an understanding.

Revolutionary and Managerial Elites in Modernizing Regimes

John H. Kautsky*

I. Introduction

Among the underdeveloped countries that have experienced a modernizing revolution, the Soviet Union and Mexico are the most outstanding cases of successful economic development. The political concomitants of that development have differed widely in the two countries; but in each, the revolutionary leadership that had overthrown the old regime and established a new, modernizing one has in turn, as industrialization has proceeded, been replaced by a new elite of bureaucrats and technocrats. It is not surprising, therefore, that the hypothesis has been more or less explicitly advanced that in underdeveloped countries generally there is some link between industrialization, on the one hand, and, on the other hand, the replacement of the leadership of revolutionary modernizers by that of managerial modernizers.[1] Depending on which of the two variables one regards as the independent and which the dependent one, one may suggest either that if industrialization is to proceed, the replacement of elites must take place or that if and when industrialization does proceed, the replacement of elites will take place.

In favor of the first suggestion one can argue that it is possible, after all, that, apart from the obvious economic and cultural obstacles to successful, rapid industrialization, the leadership of revolutionary modernizers, committed though they are to the goal of industrialization, may itself stand in the way of reaching that goal. Lacking the requisite skills and attitudes, the revolutionary modernizers may have to be replaced if the goal is to be attained. And since they resist being replaced, they adopt attitudes and pursue policies which in fact serve the function of justifying their continuance in power and which may slow or prevent industrialization. In favor of the second suggestion, one can argue that an industrial economy not only requires leadership by people with administrative, managerial, and technical skills but also itself produces such leadership.

The hypothesis that the industrialization of underdeveloped countries

* This article is based on a paper presented to the Symposium on the Evolution of Established One-Party Systems, sponsored by the Center for International Affairs of Harvard University and the Institute of International Studies of the University of California at Berkeley and held at Timber Cove, Jenner, California, April 5-7, 1968. I am indebted to the discussants at this symposium for valuable suggestions and to my colleague Robert H. Salisbury for a critical reading of an earlier draft.

[1] The present article grew out of an attempt to test this hypothesis. I am grateful to some of my graduate students who, by trying to do the same thing with reference to a number of particular countries, have not only provided me with a few of the data I utilize here but have given me a greater awareness of the conceptual and practical difficulties involved in such an attempt.

and the replacement of their revolutionary modernizing leadership by managerial modernizers are linked seems to be in accord with common sense,[2] but sufficient evidence is not yet available to test this hypothesis, let alone to confirm it. In only four major countries—Mexico, China, Russia, and Turkey—did revolutionary modernizers come to power as much as a generation ago. One can hardly expect that many of the other countries that have experienced such a revolution much more recently would by now have progressed very far on the road to industrialization and, hence, to managerial and administrative rule. It is certainly striking that, in the only two of the four countries mentioned that have in fact undergone substantial industrialization, managerial modernizers have come to constitute a powerful—perhaps even the most powerful—elite group. Brezhnev and Kosygin in the Soviet Union and the successors to Mexico's last revolutionary leader, Cárdenas, particularly Avila Camacho, Alemán, and Ruiz Cortines, may be regarded as representing managerial modernizers.

In China, too, industrialization has been progressing, and there, too, managerial modernizers seem to be rising and competing for power. We may also add that in Israel and in the Eastern European countries the transition from revolutionary to managerial modernizers seems to have been in progress for the past few years. In these countries, revolutionary modernizers came to power only about two decades ago, but much of the population and of the economy were, at the time of the revolution, no longer caught up in the traditional order, as they are in most underdeveloped countries.

The general hypothesis that, concomitant with industrialization, an elite of managerial modernizers rises to power does find support, then, in the experience of the few countries that have made substantial progress toward industrialization following a revolution of revolutionary modernizers. (This process of political change is quite different from that which accompanied the industrialization of Western countries and of Japan, with which we are not concerned here). However, evidence derived from the experience of these countries is too limited to be conclusive, and the hypothesis must remain tentative for the present. At best, it will be possible to establish its validity only if and when, perhaps in a few decades, some of the many underdeveloped countries that have in the past few years come under the control of revolutionary modernizers make substantial progress toward industrialization.

In the meantime, it is possible, of course, to look for bits and pieces of relevant evidence to see to what extent processes that occurred in various ways in the Soviet Union and Eastern Europe, in Mexico and Israel, may be repeated in other underdeveloped countries. We furnish some such evidence in the following pages, though our purpose here is not to present newly discovered data but merely to organize some scattered well-known

[2] James S. Coleman also distinguishes between, on the one hand, "the first wave of modern educated elites," or "the politically dominant leaders who carried out the revolution (nationalism or Communist)" and, on the other hand, "the second post-revolutionary generation of technicians and managers." But he and some of the literature he cites cast doubt on the hypothesis that the latter will replace the former. "Introduction to Part III," James S. Coleman, ed. *Education and Political Development* (Princeton, 1965), pp. 358-362.

ones so that they might provide us with some insights into, though not with predictions of, the evolution of postrevolutionary societies in underdeveloped countries. However, even such inconclusive attempts to test the hypothesis of the replacement of revolutionary by managerial modernizers are premature. For, clearly, before we can hope to test it, we must be able to distinguish between the two types of elites. To try to do so is the principal task of this article.

It is commonly and reasonably assumed that revolutionary modernizers are distinguishable from managerial ones with respect to (1) their background, experience, and training, (2) their attitudes, and (3) their policies. In order to test that assumption, we shall attempt to distinguish between them in terms of these three categories. Under each, we shall try to draw the picture of an ideal type of revolutionary modernizer and an ideal type of managerial modernizer. Though we shall illustrate them with selective evidence drawn from the real world, these ideal types as such cannot be expected to be found in pure form in the real world. Rather, they are meant merely to provide us with the analytical categories of revolutionary and managerial modernizers that can help us organize the data of the real world and determine to what extent real leaders fit into one category or the other.

Without anticipating too much of what follows, it may be stated here that the most significant result of our efforts lies not in their success but in calling attention to the difficulties they encounter. Difficulties in "operationalizing" the distinction between the two types of modernizers, i.e., in finding data which will permit us to place real leaders into one or the other of the two categories, cast doubt on the validity of the distinction itself. And this, in turn, renders questionable the possibility of testing—and hence of ever confirming—a hypothesis which at the outset seems quite persuasive.

II. Differences Between Revolutionary and Managerial Modernizers

Background, experience, and training In underdeveloped countries, the leadership of movements pledged to rapid and thoroughgoing modernization can only come from individuals who have broken out of the framework of the traditional society and have adopted values that are appropriate to an industrial society and that are hence revolutionary in the traditional environment. Typical of these values is a belief in the possibility and the desirability of material progress and of a far higher degree of social and economic equality and political participation for the great mass of the population than is characteristic of traditional societies. Contacts between such societies and advanced industrial ones, as they develop under colonialism or under the sponsorship of the native aristocracy or under both provide the opportunity for some natives to acquire these alien values. They may do so in institutions imported or imitated from industrial countries, like modern armies and bureaucracies, industrial and commercial enterprises, or trade unions. Most often, however, modern values are transmitted to members of the traditional society either in their own countries or, even more effectively, in an advanced country, through the process of higher education. We designate the natives who are distinguished from all others by their modern values as "modernizers."

In a traditional society, especially before there has been much modernization, most people who receive a higher education are likely to be drawn from the aristocracy. In any case, responding to the prevailing aristocratic attitudes which regard work and money-making as contemptible, and responding as well to the lack of industry in their societies, most students choose to be educated not in such fields as the natural sciences, engineering, agronomy, or business administration, but rather in law and medicine, in the humanities and the more speculative and value-oriented of the social sciences, in journalism and teaching. Such choices are reinforced where the system of higher education in the advanced country, under whose influence the modernizer has come, is itself strongly shaped by aristocratic attitudes, as has been notably the case in Britain.

If modernizers want to put into effect in their own underdeveloped countries their newly acquired values of material progress and abundance, equality and participation, they must desire rapid industrialization and also, in many cases, land reform. To carry these out, they must control the government and must, therefore, wrest control from the traditional aristocracy or from the colonial power or from both. In the minds of the revolutionary modernizers, defeat of the aristocracy and colonialism may also appear as the end toward which they work, and industrialization and land reform as the means to that end; but in any case demands for industrialization, independence, and control of the government are inextricably intertwined in a program that implies the need for social, economic, and political revolution.

Because they are determined to carry out this program and because they are ideologically committed to a goal of popular participation in government and need to believe that they represent "the masses," the modernizers are likely to try to mobilize some mass support. This they can generally do among workers, who have lately been torn out of their traditional, and usually rural, environment and have thus become physically, psychologically, and intellectually accessible to the modernizers. They can do it less easily, and usually less successfully, among the peasants and among the old middle class, who remain physically and ideologically more caught up in the traditional order.

By our definition, then, at least the first generation of modernizers are revolutionaries vis-à-vis the traditional-colonial society. Some of them may merely think revolutionary thoughts, but many will also come to express these thoughts, especially since the training and professions they chose tend to encourage the development of oratorical, polemical, and writing skills. These skills are employed in attacks on the old order, in argumentation and conflict among the revolutionaries themselves and, wherever possible, in their attempts to gain a mass following. The last task, however, also requires some development of organizational skills. Thus, the process of dreaming and talking about revolution, and then of preparing and finally making a revolution, selects out from among the modernizers those who come to lead the revolutionary movement. From this process there emerges, as the ideal type of revolutionary modernizing leader, a man who combines the qualities of a good thinker, writer, speaker, and mass organizer.

Different circumstances, no doubt, require these skills in different degrees. Thus, it may be hypothesized that, among revolutionaries functioning abroad, as students or as exiles, the most effective thinkers and writers, and perhaps speakers, would emerge as leaders. Among revolutionaries remaining at home, on the other hand, particularly if they must operate illegally, those adept at organizing conspiracies and recruiting mass support may become leaders. Whether at home or abroad, the life of the revolutionary is often a hard one, and those with certain personality traits and attitudes are most likely to survive it and to reach the top of their movements. To the values, the training, and the skills that we have ascribed to the revolutionary modernizers, we might then add such personal qualities as persistence, dedication, fanaticism, and dogmatism.

In order to determine to what extent the experience and training of real revolutionary leaders conform to those of the ideal type of revolutionary modernizer drawn here, some biographical data were obtained about the man who occupied the top position of governmental power immediately after the revolution (and, in Russia and China, also the man who led the second revolution, i.e., Lenin and Mao) in each of thirty societies that have pretty clearly passed through a revolution from a traditional or colonial regime to one pledged to rapid modernization. Only that one man, rather than also those surrounding him, was studied in order to avoid the question of who was, indeed, a revolutionary "leader." Also, data on top leaders are, in any case, more easily available than data on their subordinates. (These data on the top leaders are briefly presented in the Appendix.)

This quick survey reveals that of thirty-two revolutionary leaders:

> 8 (25%) received university or advanced professional training wholly or in part in an industrialized country (Ayub Khan, Banda, Bourguiba, Kenyatta, Madero, Nehru, Nkrumah, and Nyerere);
>
> 17 (53%) received such modern advanced training entirely in their own or some other underdeveloped country (Abboud, Arévalo, Ben Gurion, Betancourt, Castro, Kassem, Kemal, Kerensky, Lenin, Mao, Nasser, Obote, Paz Estenssoro, Sallal, Sukarno, Sun, and U Nu);
>
> 4 (13%) received no higher education, but spent considerable periods living or traveling in industrialized countries (Ben Bella, Ho Chi-Minh, Tito, and Touré);
>
> 2 (6%) received no higher education and did not live or travel extensively abroad, but spent considerable time in a modern institution at home, i.e., the schools (Kaunda), or the colonial bureaucracy (Lumumba);
>
> 1 (3%) fits into none of the above categories, but even he traveled abroad extensively as a seaman (Karume).

In addition to the twenty-five (78 percent) of the thirty-two revolutionary leaders who received a higher education at home or abroad, three (9 percent) attended Western-type secondary schools in their own country (Kaunda, Lumumba, Touré). Thus, a total of twenty-eight (88 percent) received an education appropriate to an industrialized country. Of all the thirty-two revolutionary leaders, eighteen (56 percent) lived or traveled extensively in industrialized countries, for purposes other than their educa-

tion, before coming to power. Including stays abroad for educational purposes, nineteen (59 percent) lived or traveled in industrialized countries.

Our data also disclose that, of all the thirty-two revolutionary leaders,
16 (50%) served in modern institutions, as follows:

> 7 (22%) in the army (Abboud, Ayub Khan, Ben Bella, Kassem, Kemal,
> Nasser, Sallal);
> 7 (22%) in schools or universities (Arévalo, Kaunda, Kenyatta, Mao,
> Nyerere, Paz Estenssoro, U Nu);
> 1 (3%) in trade unions (Touré);
> 1 (3%) in the bureaucracy (Lumumba).

11 (34%) served in modern professions, as follows:

> 4 (13%) as lawyers (Bourguiba, Kerensky, Lenin, Nehru);
> 2 (6%) as physicians (Banda and Sun);
> 2 (6%) as journalists (Betancourt and Ho Chi-Minh);
> 2 (6%) in modern agriculture (Ben Gurion and Madero);
> 1 (3%) in commerce and industry (Obote).
> (Some of the above were chiefly professional politicians and revolu-
> tionaries. This is even more true of the following three leaders.)

3 (9%) were trained in modern professions, but evidently did not practice
them, as follows:

> 1 (3%) as a lawyer (Castro);
> 1 (3%) as an engineer (Sukarno);
> 1 (3%) in philosophy and education (Nkrumah).

2 (6%) were manual workers (Karume and Tito).
None was a peasant or craftsman.

It may therefore be claimed that, while only a very small fraction of the
total population of underdeveloped countries has received a higher education, has lived or traveled extensively abroad, or has served in a modern
institution or profession, all or virtually all of the top revolutionary leaders
in such countries have done one or more of these things. There is thus
ample evidence to show that actual revolutionary leaders are quite close
to our ideal type of such a leader with respect to their experience and
training.

Before we turn to a discussion of the origins and backgrounds of managerial modernizers, we must point, at least parenthetically, to the possibility of a succession of regimes of revolutionary modernizers. Otherwise,
we might give the mistaken impression that the replacement of revolutionary modernizers by managerial ones is inevitable after one generation
of revolutionaries or, for that matter, at some later point in time.

Revolutionary modernizers, especially since they tend to be highly doc-
trinaire, are likely to come into conflict with each other even before the
revolution over questions involving its goals, strategies, and tactics. Once
their common enemies, whose opposition held them together to some extent, have been defeated in the revolution, conflicts among the revolutionary modernizers become even more prevalent. There is a good deal of
evidence, drawn from all parts of the underdeveloped world and from the
experience of several decades, to support the generalization that moderniz-

ing revolutions are followed by such conflicts. One may predict that this will commonly be true of future modernizing revolutions as well. One can also conceive of conflicts among revolutionary modernizers going on well beyond the passing of the first generation of revolutionaries, especially if industrialization does not proceed successfully. Disappointment with the failure of industrialization may then give rise to further generations of revolutionary modernizers fed by growing communication with the industrial world and by an expanded system of education that produces growing numbers of non-technically trained people.

In this context, we need not discuss the conflict among revolutionary modernizers any further,[3] though this conflict may constitute much of the politics of the postrevolutionary era for quite some time. Eventually, however, a new factor may enter the political arena in the form of the managerial modernizers. How do they develop?

Colonialism or a modernizing native aristocracy both generally (by opening up communications between the traditional society and an advanced industrial one) and specifically (by providing education and training to some natives of the traditional society) produce revolutionary modernizers who eventually turn against both the aristocracy and colonialism. Similarly, regimes of revolutionary modernizers, both generally (by popularizing the ideas of rapid industrialization) and specifically (by providing technical training to some individuals) produce managerial modernizers who may eventually turn against the revolutionary ones. One is almost tempted to describe these tendencies in the Hegelian terms of theses giving rise to their own antitheses or in Marxian ones of some elements in society sowing the seeds of their own destruction or producing their own gravediggers.

The victory of revolutionary modernizers arouses vast hopes and aspirations for rapid economic development. These may help overcome the widespread and deep-seated prejudices that prevail in the traditional society against technical and scientific work. Responding to the rhetoric—and to the convictions—of revolutionary modernizers, some students may then be inspired to enter the fields of science, technology, and administration in the hope of being able to contribute to the industrialization of their backward societies.

Committed as they are to the objective of industrialization, the revolutionary modernizers also frequently take more direct steps to create managerial modernizers. Indeed, the creation of such modernizers may be regarded as part of their commitment to create a modern society. Thus, students going abroad for their advanced education may be encouraged to study certain technical fields by the award of government scholarships (a policy practiced even by governments of countries such as Guinea, where very little industrialization has in fact taken place), and they may be prevented by government controls from studying any other subjects.

Similarly, the curricula of schools and universities at home may be changed so that, as Ayub Khan's regime in Pakistan reported: "Our educational system instead of producing clerks and 'babus' for Government offices turns out scientists, engineers, chemists, physicists, plant managers,

[3] I did this briefly in "Patterns of Elite Succession in the Process of Development," *The Journal of Politics,* XXXI (May 1969).

Foreign Service personnel, and other professional people to shoulder the responsibilities of a modern, forward-looking society."[4] It may well be that such attempts to promote the development of managerial modernizers are not simply the outcome of the revolutionary modernizers' ideological commitments to modernization; they may also be more or less deliberate efforts to prevent the growth of a new generation of revolutionaries that might challenge the incumbents for power.

Where revolutionary modernizers take measures to advance industrialization, they must at first rely for the execution of these measures on technical experts who are either foreigners, quite often from the former colonial power, or persons closely linked to the prerevolutionary ruling groups. Since the revolutionaries see both of these groups as politically unreliable, they will wish to replace them as quickly as possible with newly trained managerial modernizers, who will be obligated to the revolutionaries and hence, they hope, controlled by them. Where industrialization is to proceed rapidly and on a large scale, as under Stalin's and Mao's first five-year plans, great numbers of administrators, managers, and engineers need to be quickly recruited and trained. They must, therefore, necessarily be drawn from the lower strata of the population, especially from the industrial working class. This situation accords nicely with the ideology of the revolutionary modernizers, which promises equal opportunities for the formerly disadvantaged. Where the process of early industrialization is accompanied by conflicts among the revolutionary modernizers, as it was under Stalin, purges create openings for managerial modernizers in the bureaucracy, too, and thus enhance the opportunities for the growth of this new group.

It is easy to differentiate between the ideal types of revolutionary and managerial modernizers by their background, training, and experience. To put real leaders into one category or the other is not always equally simple. There is usually not much difficulty in obtaining biographical data on leading figures, and those who were educated to be poets, philosophers, journalists, teachers, or physicians can be distinguished from those who were trained as scientists, engineers, economists, or administrators. However, some practical problems arise. For example, two of the most common professions held by the leaders of underdeveloped countries, the legal and the military, cannot easily be classified as "revolutionary" or "managerial"; lawyers may be akin to philosophers or to administrators, officers to agitators or engineers. Another problem may be the lack of biographical data on decision-makers at the middle level of governmental and economic hierarchies. Yet it is precisely there that managerial modernizers are likely to appear first as industrialization proceeds. Only in countries where this process has gone on for some time can they be expected to reach the top level. Therefore, an analysis of the top leadership, on which biographical information is most easily available, will not reveal the presence of managerial modernizers who may be rising in the system. These, however, are problems that can be overcome by access to needed data. In principle, revolutionary modernizers can be clearly distinguished from managerial

4 *Pakistan News Digest* (Karachi), July 1, 1965.

ones by their training and experience. But we cannot assume that a certain kind of training and experience necessarily leads to a certain kind of behavior; in short, we cannot define the two types of modernizers in terms of their training and experience. Clearly, we would not wish to classify Sukarno as a managerial modernizer because he was trained as an engineer. We turn, therefore, to the next indicator of our distinction, that of attitudes.

Attitudes We have already met the ideal type of revolutionary modernizer —a man fanatically dedicated to the cause of revolution against traditionalism or colonialism or both. To say, however, that he is more idealistic and less pragmatic or realistic than the managerial modernizer is not quite correct. It is not the impractical dreamer who becomes a successful revolutionary but, rather, the highly realistic organizer and agitator.

The distinction between revolutionary and managerial modernizers is not one between idealism and realism but one between the ideals that are being realistically pursued. To the revolutionary modernizer, the revolution itself—that is, primarily, the seizure of political power by modernizers— is the ideal to be obtained. To the managerial modernizer, that revolution lies in the past; his operative ideal becomes the realization of industrialization, which he regards as the prime goal of the revolution. When the job of the modernizers is to stir up and organize masses of people to march and even to die, the manipulation of revolutionary symbols is by no means impractical. It only becomes so after the revolution, and it is only then that the revolutionary modernizer who, for reasons to be noted, continues to engage in this manipulation, appears impractical. By the same token, the managerial modernizer, if he existed in a revolutionary situation, would seem, with his insistence on building factories, a hopelessly unrealistic idealist. After the revolution, however, he emerges as the realist who prefers the computer to the "Thoughts of Chairman Mao Tse-tung" or its local equivalent.

Once the traditional or colonial regime has been replaced by one of modernizers, it turns out that "the" revolution really has two separable aspects. These are, on the one hand, the seizure of power and the destruction of the old regime and its supporters and, on the other hand, industrialization. The managerial modernizers, having been produced by the hopes of the revolutionary modernizers for rapid industrialization, become more and more impatient as these hopes are not realized. To them, the promise of the revolution remains unfulfilled as long as industrialization is not being carried out. That very attitude, however, constitutes a threat to the revolutionary modernizers in power, especially if what hold they had on the lower classes through the use of their revolutionary symbols has begun to weaken in the face of continued misery and rising expectations.

Revolutionary modernizers, lacking the necessary expertise, cannot themselves carry through the complex technical and scientific tasks of planning, organizing, and building industry. If these tasks are to be undertaken, they must turn over some power to managerial modernizers. Most regimes of revolutionary modernizers have in fact done so in order to take some steps toward economic development. However, whether or not they sense that thoroughgoing, effective industrialization would require the complete displacement of revolutionary by managerial modernizers and, indeed, whether or not this is true, the revolutionary modernizers act to maintain a maximum of power. To justify their retention of power, they naturally claim, and feel, that their particular expertise—that in revolution-making—is still needed. Hence the almost universal assertion by revolutionary modernizers that the revolution is not yet complete, that it must go on.[5] To be sure, the managerial modernizers may also hold that the revolution must yet be completed, but to them the completion demands industrialization, while to the revolutionary modernizers it means that the revolution is still threatened by domestic and foreign enemies. Just as, in their conflicts with each other, revolutionary modernizers feel that there is "Not Yet Uhuru"[6] (the title of a recent book by one such modernizer engaged in a conflict of that kind), so in self-defense against managerial modernizers they may see their revolution menaced by betrayal, perversion, or at least stagnation if they do not remain in power or return to power to push it.

Revolutionary modernizers are always inclined to see threats and plots against their regimes by traditional and "neo-colonial" forces at home, in exile, or in foreign governments. These threats may be real or imaginary— or imaginary ones may become real through the mechanism of the self-ful-filling prophecy—but, in any case, they serve to justify the continued role of revolutionary modernizers as defenders of the revolution.

Even where those against whom the revolution was directed have been completely routed, the revolutionary modernizers often perceive the threat of "reaction" when, with a sense of shock, they become aware that the generation growing up under their rule is no longer inspired by what they regard as the values and spirit of the revolution. To men who dedicated their lives to the cause of revolution, the revolution that brings them to power is necessarily the high point of their lives. What follows it is almost inevitably anticlimactic, disappointing, and frustrating. As they grow older, they watch with horror how the younger generation that did not participate in the revolutionary struggles fails to realize their own high ideals. They are seized by feelings of nostalgia for the "good old days" of the revolutionary past, which they now recall in some idealized form. The fears and uncertainties, the doubts and bickering, are forgotten, and the revolution is remembered as a time of selfless idealism and discipline, of courage, simplicity, and camaraderie, and of ennobling suffering. The further the revolution recedes into the past, the more desperately and urgently do the revolutionary modernizers seek to inspire the younger generation with their brand of revolutionary romanticism and puritanism.

The most striking example of what we have described is no doubt the

---

[5] "We may conclude then that the government's intensive concern wtih symbolic activity is a reflection of intra-elite politics as well as of power maintenance. . . . All such activity which underscores the doctrine of the unfinished Revolution justifies the retention of power by a larger group of politician-administrators (including some prominent army officers), who have political qualifications for the positions they hold but no technical ones." Herbert Feith, "Indonesia's Political Symbols and Their Wielders," *World Politics*, XVI (October 1963), 95. Ben Gurion concluded a recent interview, "No, the state of Israel of which we dreamed has not yet come into being." *Le Monde*, Weekly Selection, April 23, 1969.

[6] Oginga A. Odinga, *Not Yet Uhuru* (London, 1967).

movement that Mao significantly designated "the Great Proletarian Cultural 'Revolution' ". It was a wholesale attempt to revive the spirit of Yenan.[7] Mao took his famous swim in the Yang-tse in July 1966 in order to symbolize revolutionary willingness to brave dangers and surmount difficulties. But Mao is not unique. His plain, austere uniform finds its counterpart in the open collar of Ben Gurion who, living in a desert settlement, yearns for the hard days of the courageous and idealistic Zionist pioneers, and for the glories of the struggles against the British and the Arabs that secured Israel's statehood. The parallel is even closer, and the terms "romantic" and "puritan" apply even better, to Castro, who wears a fatigue uniform to recall the excitement and hardships of his "Yenan" in the Sierra Maestra. And, while Sukarno's uniform was anything but plain, his pleas to return to the "spirit of 1945"[8] and to " live dangerously"[9] fit into the same tradition of revolutionary romanticism. Had Lenin lived longer, he might well have displayed symptoms of a similar attitude, as did Trotsky in exile and as Boumedienne may well do if he remains in power long enough. Even revolutionary modernizers who, unlike all the above-mentioned leaders, came to power relatively easily—either in a quick coup d'état or when they were put into office by a departing colonial power—now like to recall the days of "struggle" as both glorious and dangerous.

It appears, then, that attempts to maintain or revive the revolutionary spirit to which they are themselves wedded are common among revolutionary modernizers. (One striking exception is Tito, who seems to be reconciled to its decay.) Consequently, they want to continue the revolution. A continuing revolution, however, requires the continued existence of enemies. Revolutionary modernizers, therefore, tend to see their prerevolutionary and their postrevolutionary enemies in the same light. In fact, their enemies may be genuine counterrevolutionaries, i.e., people who wish to return to the *status quo ante;* they may be rival revolutionary modernizers of the sort we mentioned earlier; they may simply be persons who have lost interest in, or who never shared, the values of the revolutionaries. But they may also be managerial modernizers.

While, in our view, the emergence of managerial modernizers constitutes a step beyond the rule of revolutionary modernizers, to the latter it seems a backward step. Thus, their revolutionary exhortations against "reaction" may well be attempts to defend themselves against the managerial competitors they fear. This appears particularly evident in the case of the present turmoil in China. Mao Tse-tung identifies "revisionism," that is, the rise of managerial modernizers, both in Yugoslavia and the Soviet Union and in China, with the restoration of "capitalism," that is, the prerevolu-

[7] On the Great Proletarian Cultural Revolution, see A. Doak Barnett, *China After Mao* (Princeton, 1967); Roderick MacFarquhar, ed. *China under Mao: Politics Takes Command* (Cambridge, Mass., 1966); and, for background, James R. Townsend, *Political Participation in Communist China* (Berkeley and Los Angeles, 1967). On the conflict in Israel, see Dan Avni-Segre, "Israel, A Society in Transition," *World Politics*, XXI (April 1969), 343-365.

[8] Feith, 81.

[9] Sukarno introduced Mussolini's "vivere pericoloso" as a national slogan in his Independence Day address of August 17, 1964. Willard A. Hanna, "The Indonesia Crisis—Mid-1964 Phase," *American Universities Field Staff Report Service*, Southeast Asia Series, XII, No. 7 (Indonesia), 1.

tionary regime, and insists that the proletarian class struggle and revolution will have to be fought for many decades to come lest future generations in China make their peace with imperialism and join the counter-revolution.[10]

An obvious way for revolutionaries already in power to support their conviction that the revolution is not yet complete and must go on is for them to assert that it must spread beyond the borders of the country. The belief in an international and even a world revolution is generally identified with Communism. In this, as in other respects, however, Lenin and the Bolsheviks of his generation are merely prototypes of the revolutionary modernizers, and the idea of world revolution is not peculiar to them. In the first place, though they saw and formulated it, like all their ideas, in terms of Marxian concepts, world revolution is not a Marxian idea. Marx, after all, was largely unconcerned with the underdeveloped world, and he linked revolution to a high level of industrialization. His advocacy of international solidarity, therefore, could extend only to the relatively few countries where there were industrial workers.

In the second place, the years since the Russian Revolution have seen numerous other revolutions that were led by modernizers who regarded them as international phenomena. Some of these, to be sure, were Communist from the start or became Communist later on. Mao's and Castro's, for example, were seen by their leaders as merely the beginnings of continent-wide or even world-wide struggles against imperialism. However, non-Communist revolutionary modernizers also think of themselves as leaders of international movements and come to sound much like their Communist counterparts—especially since the latter have in recent decades exchanged the Marxian symbolism of proletarian anticapitalism for the anti-imperialism of the revolutionary modernizers of underdeveloped countries. Thus, Nkrumah, writing shortly after his ouster (which he blames on the "neo-colonialists"), not only describes the "African revolution" as "incomplete" but speaks also of "the world-wide struggle . . . between . . . the independent developing states and . . . the neo-colonialist, imperialist countries . . ." and, more simply, of "the struggle taking place in Africa and the world between the forces of progress and those of reaction."[11] Quite similarly, Sukarno considered it his task not only first to liberate Western New Guinea and then to "crush Malaysia," those nearest outposts of neo-colonialism, but also to lead all the "new emerging forces" throughout the world against the foe of "necolim" (neo-colonialism, colonialism, and imperialism.)[12]

The vociferous identification of Ben Bella and Boumedienne with "liberation movements" everywhere; the pan-Arabism of Nasser and of other military and revolutionary modernizers in Iraq and Syria; the pan-African-

---

[10] Edgar Snow, "Interview with Mao," *The New Republic*, February 27, 1965, p. 23.

[11] Kwame Nkrumah, *Challenge of the Congo* (London, 1967), pp. ix, xi.

[12] One observer of Indonesian politics describes some of the "themes recurrent in the rhetoric of guided democracy" as follows: "The nation's aims cannot be achieved by compromise and calculation, but only by enthusiasm and faith; the goals themselves expand, become millenial: the revolution will not be completed until imperialism has been crushed and the just and prosperous society established over the entire world." Ruth McVey, "Indonesia," *Survey*, No. 54 (January 1965), 115.

ism of Touré and other African revolutionary modernizers; perhaps even the anticolonial posture of Nehru—all imply that the revolutions which brought these leaders to power are not yet really complete or secure. And all of these positions may thus serve to justify the continuance of revolutionary modernizers in power.

Revolutionary leaders commonly think of their own revolutions as the proper model for the revolutions they advocate elsewhere, thus again suggesting that their particular experience and skills in revolution-making remain relevant for the future. Lenin insisted that all Communist parties throughout the world, regardless of their environment, be organized in the image of the Bolshevik party, which was preparing for urban-centered coups; Mao thinks of the world revolution as a process of rural guerrilla warfaıe surrounding the cities; Castro, too, conceives of revolution as spreading out from the backward rural areas by means of guerrilla warfare, and Boumedienne now advocates such warfare in Israel.

Evidence concerning the attitudes of managerial modernizers is far less obvious than that concerning the attitudes of revolutionary modernizers, no doubt because fewer of the former have reached positions of top leadership, and perhaps also because they are less vociferous. Nevertheless, the difference between the two types of modernizers appears to be clear. The managerial modernizers impatiently demand effective steps for industrialization, whereas the revolutionary modernizers feel that the revolution must go on. However, analyses of the writings and speeches of both types, and even interviews with them, may well fail to reveal this difference, for each type of leader speaks, and probably thinks, in terms of the symbols both of revolution and of industrialization.

Thus, both the 1961 Program of the Communist Party of the Soviet Union and the Bolshevik Program of 1919 speak of the international revolutionary movement;[13] a Khrushchev and even a Brezhnev, as well as a Lenin, have advocated world revolution; and all of Lenin's successors have stressed that they are merely disciples of the great revolutionary modernizer. They have been able to do so, however, because Lenin stood not only for revolution, but also for industrialization. In his last article, "Better Fewer, But Better" (1923), he proposed that industrialization get under way and added: "In this, and in this alone, lies our hope."[14] And the Bolshevik Program of 1919 had called for "all possible increase of the productive forces" as "the fundamental and principal point" of Soviet economic policy.[15]

That revolutionary modernizers demand industrialization is not surprising. As we saw earlier, that demand is, from the very beginning, closely tied in their minds to their anticolonial and antitraditional demands for independence and revolution. In a sense, it is industrialization, with its promise of future abundance and of greater equality and popular participation in government, that serves as the justification for the revolution. Before revolutionary modernizers make revolutions, while they are making them, and even after they have achieved them, they must keep talking in-

[13] Both programs are reprinted in Jan F. Triska, ed. *Soviet Communism: Programs and Rules* (San Francisco, 1962), pp. 23-153.
[14] V. I. Lenin, "Better Fewer, But Better," *Selected Works*, IX (New York, 1937), 401.
[15] Triska, p. 143.

dustrialization, as well as revolution, to reassure themselves and their followers that the promises of the revolution will be kept.

Since the symbols of industrialization have from the very beginning been closely associated with the revolution, the managerial modernizers, too, can regard themselves as being part of the revolutionary tradition. When they demand that industrialization be undertaken or speeded up, they see themselves as merely asking for the fulfillment of the promises of the revolution. Hence, though we distinguish them from revolutionary modernizers, managerial modernizers also employ both sets of symbols— those of revolution and those of industrialization. Moreover, as the children and, in their own minds, the executors of the revolution, they derive their legitimacy from it. While calling for industrialization, they must invoke the revolution to reassure both themselves and the mass support which their revolutionary predecessors mobilized that, in the process of industrialization, the ideals of the revolution will not be abandoned.

To be sure, although they employ similar symbols, revolutionary and managerial modernizers still can express their different attitudes by using these symbols with different degrees of emphasis and interest. The Brezhnevs and Kosygins speak and write at greater length, and with far greater expertise, on industrialization than on revolution. To Lenin, on the other hand, industrialization was an afterthought, however important, to the subject of revolution. His definition of Communism as "Soviet power plus electrification of the entire country" shows both his commitment to rapid industrialization as a goal and his vague and naive conception of the process.

Similarly, the two Soviet Communist party programs referred to above differ widely in their emphases. The Program of 1919 stresses, and rests upon, the assumption that in 1917 "there had begun the era of a worldwide proletarian communist revolution,"[16] but its section on "Economics" is relatively brief, vague, and visionary, and it contains nothing very specific on industrialization.[17] The 1961 Program, on the other hand, devotes many pages to "the Creation and Development of the Material and Technical Basis of Communism,"[18] employing terms like kilowatt-hours and tons of steel, machine tools and spare parts, chemical industry and telemechanic and electronic devices, which were hardly part of the vocabulary of Lenin and his revolutionary colleagues. On "the international revolutionary movement of the working class," however, the 1961 Program is vague and quite unrealistic, combining some now very threadbare myths about militant proletarian class struggles in capitalist countries with references to quite non-proletarian "anti-imperialist national-liberation revolutions, people's democratic revolutions, broad peasant movements, popular struggles to overthrow fascist and other despotic regimes, and general democratic movements against national oppression."[19]

Our examples of the use of both revolutionary and managerial symbols by both revolutionary and managerial modernizers have been taken from

16 Ibid., p. 130.
17 Ibid., pp. 143-146.
18 Ibid., pp. 71-89.
19 Ibid., p. 50.

the Soviet Union, because there the change from the one type of elite to the other is the clearest and probably the most complete. But the advocacy of rapid industrialization is, as we stressed earlier, virtually universal among revolutionary modernizers, and the employment of revolutionary symbolism seems to be equally common among managerial modernizers no matter where they have come to the fore. Thus, in Mexico and in Yugoslavia, in Israel and in India, not only are the glories of past revolutionary or independence struggles constantly invoked, but even the current modernizing and industrializing efforts are somehow regarded as "revolutionary."

The word "socialism" may well be so popular with modernizers in underdeveloped countries in part because it has both "revolutionary" and "managerial-industrial" implications that blur the differences between the two types of modernizers. "Socialism" has revolutionary connotations from its history both in Western and Eastern Europe; and it acquired "industrial" connotations in the Russian Revolution, where it first became the label of a modernizing movement rather than of Western intellectual or labor movements. Since then, some very different types of existing and hoped-for regimes in underdeveloped countries have been described as "socialist," not only in Communist-ruled countries from Yugoslavia and Poland through Mongolia and China, to Cuba, but also in Africa ("African Socialism"), the Near East ("Arab Socialism"), Pakistan ("Islamic Socialism"), and Burma ("the Burmese Road to Socialism")—not to mention such local varieties as the Mexican, the Algerian, the Israeli, the Indian, and the Indonesian. Soviet, Yugoslav, Mexican, Israeli, and perhaps Indian managerial modernizers can be as "socialist" both as their own revolutionary predecessors and as the revolutionary leaders of China and Cuba, Algeria and Egypt, Ghana and Indonesia. Thus, managerial modernizers can imply that they are revolutionary, and revolutionaries can indicate their commitment to industrialization, by using a single term.

The blurring of the differences between the attitudes of revolutionary and managerial modernizers in their own words and their own thoughts appears, then, to be a common phenomenon. If we assume that the differences in attitudes are nevertheless real, we shall have to look for proof, not in the words, but in the deeds of the two types of modernizing leaders. We turn next, therefore, to a consideration of some of the differences between the policies of revolutionary and the policies of managerial leaders.

Policies No sharp line can be drawn between attitudes, as we have now discussed them, and policies. For our purposes here, however, we mean by a policy a pattern of allocating scarce resources. The different attitudes we have described should give rise to alternative patterns of resource allocation.

Thus, if revolutionary modernizers seek to perpetuate the spirit of the revolution and to restore in the present and the future the momentum of a revolution already in the past, their efforts will necessarily be reflected in educational policy. Policy conflicts between revolutionary and managerial modernizers should emerge over such questions as the allocation of financial resources, of teaching personnel and of the students' time and effort, over emphasis on revolutionary doctrine and values as opposed to administrative, scientific, and engineering techniques—in short, to use Chinese terminology, over whether to train "reds" or "experts."[20]

In China, children receive military training less to produce military expertise (which can hardly be done at an early age) than to indoctrinate them with a spirit of sacrifice and a willingness to face dangers. Urban youngsters are sent to live among peasants not only to teach the peasants but to absorb what is held to be the revolutionary spirit of the rural poor. During the Great Proletarian Cultural Revolution, admission to college on the basis of competitive examinations or scholarly merit was replaced by admission on the basis of social origin and ideological purity. The college curriculum was cut from five years to two, with students spending three years doing manual labor with workers, peasants, or soldiers.[21] The goal of such reforms is said to be the obliteration of the distinction between intellectuals and manual laborers. Although one may doubt that the revolutionary spirit can be rekindled and maintained by measures such as these, it is clear that, whatever young students may learn from illiterate peasants and workers, it will not be managerial and technical expertise. Even if some scientists and engineers continue, as is probable, to receive adequate training in China, there can be no question that the general educational reforms are anti-managerial in their intent and in their effect.

These changes in the field of education are themselves but a reflection of the Chinese revolutionary leaders' growing fear of the experts—the managerial modernizers—whose growth they had themselves fostered in the early 1950's, when they sought to follow the Stalinist model in their first Five Year Plan. During the late 1950's, in the period of the Great Leap Forward and the Commune movement, ideological purity was put ahead of expertise; the generalist, or the "red"—the revolutionary modernizer— was favored over the "expert." Thus, in his report to the Second Session of the Eighth Congress of the Chinese Communist Party, held in 1958, Liu Shao-chi (then still regarded as a good Maoist) demanded that the entire population take a hand in building up industry in order to "refute the mysticism of this supposedly being the monopoly of a few," and in order to "necessarily campaign firmly and steadfastly against the tendency of the one-sided bias towards the latest technology" and "against the tendency of the one-sided overemphasis on the role of the specialists."[22]

Representing the managerial response to such views, a Soviet pamphlet characterized them as showing a "snobbish-leftist attitude to technology and specialists."[23] It similarly commented on the statement in the article "Long Live Leninism!", which constituted the Chinese opening salvo in the Sino-Soviet conflict, that "Marxist-Leninists have always maintained that

---

20 On the conflict between the two, which seems to be at the heart of present-day politics in China, see Franz Schurmann, *Ideology and Organization in Communist China* (Berkeley and Los Angeles, 1966).

21 Chu-yuan Cheng, "Power Struggle in Red China," *Asian Survey*, VI (September 1966), 482. More recently, it has been reported that, in line with Mao's statement that "the lowly are the most intelligent, the elite are the most ignorant," hundreds of thousands of high school and university students are being sent to do manual labor in factories and, especially, in the countryside and frontier regions, not for a few years but presumably for life. Peggy Durdin, "The Bitter Tea of Mao's Red Guards," *The New York Times Magazine*, January 19, 1969, pp. 28-35.

22 Quoted in (no author), *Certain Aspects of the Inner Life of the Communist Party of China* (Moscow, n.d.), p. 15.

23 Ibid.

in world history it is not technique but man, the masses of people, that determine the fate of mankind."[24]

In the present Cultural Revolution, the revolutionary modernizers in China are once again placing the greatest emphasis on the power of sheer will and on the mass mobilization of labor to obtain their goals of industrialization. They evidently hope to achieve industrialization without, in the process, creating a powerful group of managerial modernizers, whom they regard as counterrevolutionaries, and, indeed, by weakening the managers they have already created. Putting "politics in command" of production, they hope that the zeal of revolutionary modernizers can be a substitute for the expertise of managerial modernizers.

The faith of the Chinese revolutionary leaders that will power and manpower can, as they say, perform miracles, if they are guided by the proper doctrine, has been applied not only in the area of production but also in military affairs. It has evidently led to policy conflicts here as well. Military officers who seek to keep the armed forces professional and demand advanced weapons have been opposed with the view, derived from the experience of revolutionary guerrilla warfare, that in war it is man who counts, not weapons and machines. As "Long Live Leninism!" stated, "an awakened people will always find new ways to counteract a reactionary superiority in arms and win victory for themselves."[25] The revolutionary modernizers seem to be inclined to do away with a specialized army, demanding, on the one hand, that military units be employed in agriculture, industry, and public works and, on the other, that civilians be turned into soldiers and that factories, rural communes, and government and party organizations all be turned into "revolutionary schools" like the army.[26]

The contrast between managerial attitudes and policies and the revolutionary downgrading of expertise and faith in will and, especially, in ideology is well illustrated by some informal remarks which Khrushchev made at a conference on productivity, in response to a question as to why machines, rather than party work, had been emphasized. Khrushchev said:

> My dear comrade, if at the factory where you are a party functionary, a defective article is put out while you are giving a lecture on the upbuilding of Communism in our country . . . wouldn't it be more useful if you organized the people for work on a scientific basis and higher qualitative standard? This is precisely what party work is, when everyone does his job, when everyone knows his trade, produces good parts and assembles good machines. What you propose is to give primacy to the reading of lectures

[24] Translated from *Red Flag* (No. 8, 1960) in G. F. Hudson, Richard Lowenthal, and Roderick MacFarquhar, *The Sino-Soviet Dispute* (New York, 1961), p. 92.

[25] Ibid., p. 93.

[26] A similar reliance on will power and manpower, as opposed to planning and expertise, and on the military and guerrilla warfare as "schools" for economic development is to be found in Castro's thought: "The school of war taught us how men can do many things, how they can accomplish many tasks when they apply themselves in a practical way. This was the school of war, where a small nucleus of combatants developed into an army without bureaucracy. Without bureaucracy! It went to war, waged war, and won the war without bureaucracy. . . . And war taught us what man can do when he dedicates himself to working with enthusiasm, interest, and common sense." Quoted from Castro's speech of February 20, 1967, to farm-machine workers in Irving Louis Horowitz, "Cuban Communism," *Trans-action*, IV (October 1967), 9. See also Joseph A. Kahl, "The Moral Economy of a Revolutionary Society," *Trans-action*, VI (April 1969), 30-37.

about how people will think a hundred years after the triumph of Communism. True, this is a wonderful subject for a lecture and don't you take it that I am against good lectures, but we can wait with such reports and lectures for some 50 or 80 years. But if we turn out defective machines and poor quality articles, we shall not go very far.[27]

At the present time, policy conflicts between revolutionary and managerial modernizers are being fought out most openly and, indeed, even violently, on the national level in China and, on the international level, in the Sino-Soviet dispute. It is, therefore, from China and the Soviet Union that we have drawn our illustrations. However, while the views of Chinese revolutionary modernizers may be extreme—and are certainly expressed in extreme language—they are probably not atypical. Lenin, who is virtually our model of the revolutionary modernizer, expressed views not dissimilar to Mao's. In his *State and Revolution* (which was, to be sure, written shortly before, rather than years after, his revolution), he displayed his faith in the ability of the masses, "all under the control and leadership of the armed proletariat,"[28] to organize and run the process of production. Mao's opposition to "material incentives" is paralleled by Lenin's insistence on the payment of "workmen's wages"[29] to administrators. The abolition of ranks in the Chinese People's Liberation Army is reminiscent of a similar measure in the Red Army. One may also note that a similar emphasis on equality prevailed during the early years of statehood in Israel, when the idealism of the pioneers was still dominant.[30]

Like Mao, Lenin showed his failure to appreciate the importance of technical expertise in the process of industrialization when he said (in *State and Revolution*) that the key "functions of control and accounting—becoming more and more simple—will be performed by each in turn, will then become a habit and will finally die out as the special functions of a special stratum of the population."[31] He also described these functions as "already fully within the capacity of the average city dweller"[32] and as "the extraordinarily simple operations of checking, recording and issuing receipts, which anyone who can read and write and who knows the first four rules of arithmetic can perform."[33]

Present-day Chinese statements to the effect that "we will learn to swim by swimming"[34] are strikingly reminiscent of Trotsky's statement in 1920 of the Bolshevik view "that one learns to ride on horse-back only when sitting on the horse."[35] A parallel to Mao's impatience, which led to the Great Leap Forward, may be found in Lenin's 1923 article, "Our Revolution." There he exclaims: "Infinitely commonplace . . . is the argument . . .

27 Reported in *The New York Times*, September 14, 1960, p. 3.
28 V. I. Lenin, "The State and Revolution," *Selected Works*, VII, 48.
29 Ibid., 41-42.
30 In the early 1950's, the ratio between the net incomes of the senior civil servants and those in the lowest grades was 1.3 to 1 (as compared to 12 to 1 in the United States). Edwin Samuel, *Problems of Government in the State of Israel* (Jerusalem, 1956), pp. 63-64. I owe this reference and the one cited in fn. 37 to Yael Ishai, "Transformation from Revolutionary to Managerial Leadership—Israel: A Case Study" (unpublished, 1967).
31 Lenin, *Selected Works*, VII, 48.
32 Ibid., 47.
33 Ibid., 92-93.
34 Quoted from *Jenmin Jih Pao* in *The New York Times*, February 8, 1967, p. 5.
35 Leon Trotsky, *Terrorism and Communism: A Reply to Karl Kautsky* (Ann Arbor, 1961), p. 101.

that . . . the objective economic premises for socialism do not exist in our country. . . . What if the complete hopelessness of the situation, by intensifying tenfold the energies of the workers and peasants, offered us the possibility of proceeding to create the fundamental requisites of civilization in a way different from that of West European countries?"[36] Though directed against the Marxist-Menshevik argument that the "material conditions" in Russia were not ripe for the socialist revolution, does this not reflect, by implication, the anti-managerial, Maoist conviction that the "energies of the workers and peasants," properly led and indoctrinated, can bring about the industrialization, or the "fundamental requisites of civilization"—which, according to orthodox Marxian doctrine, were a prerequisite of the socialist revolution?

Trust in the power of a strong will to overcome obstacles is not confined to Communist revolutionaries. Ben Gurion, faithful to Herzl's motto, "if you will it, it is no legend," furnishes another good example of the belief that strong determination can transcend all difficulties and that such determination is superior to expertise.[37] Indeed, one might suggest that all revolutionary modernizers must share this faith to some degree, for without it they could hardly be revolutionaries; they could not hope to turn their backward countries into advanced ones in the course of a generation.

The romantic puritanism we discussed earlier as being characteristic of revolutionary modernizers idealizes a life of hardship, austerity, equality, and dedication to work; it denounces the display of material wealth, luxury, waste, and corruption. This attitude is opposed to what is now decried in China as the "concept of self" and "material incentives." It thus runs counter to such demands of managerial modernizers as those denounced as "careerism" and those represented by the Soviet economist Liberman's proposals for profit incentives.

Although the views of Chinese managerial modernizers do not reach us, they are probably similar to Soviet views that oppose the Maoist identification of revolutionary purity with poverty. Thus, Professor G. Glezerman replied as follows to the "ultra-revolutionary" Chinese leaders (claiming to be revolutionaries themselves, managerial modernizers see revolutionary ones as "ultra-revolutionary") and their "slanderous accusations" of Soviet "bourgeoisification": ". . . They see the mark of 'bourgeoisification' simply in the growth of the working people's personal earnings and well-being, leading allegedly to loss of revolutionary spirit. To counterpose the growth of material welfare to the preservation of revolutionary purity, however, actually means branding as meaningless the working people's struggle for socialism and communism, the struggle they are waging to insure all the conditions for a prosperous and cultural existence for all, and by no means to perpetuate their poverty."[38]

That such differences in attitudes have policy consequences need hardly

---

[36] V. I. Lenin, "Our Revolution," *Selected Works*, VI, 510-511.

[37] Among Zionists in the pre-State period, "there was a general belief that the strong determination of pioneers could overcome all difficulties predicted by experts and could build a country despite the warnings of scientific and professional knowledge." Benjamin Akzin and Yehezkel Dror, *Israel: High Pressure Planning* (Syracuse, N. Y., 1966), p. 12.

[38] G. Glezerman, "Questions of Theory: Society, the Collective and the Individual," *Pravda*, October 21, 1966, in *Current Digest of the Soviet Press*, XVIII (November 23, 1966), 15.

be repeated. While managerial modernizers are being denounced in China, in the Soviet Union industrial managers, who often still are opposed by bureaucratic managers (but not by revolutionary modernizers), are proposing and obtaining reforms whose main theme seems to be the increase of economic efficiency through the use of modern managerial techniques and through greater autonomy for the local managers.

In international affairs, too, the different attitudes of revolutionary and managerial modernizers lead to different policies or different patterns of allocating scarce resources. We noted earlier the very common tendency of revolutionary modernizers to think of their revolution as being incomplete and, consequently, international in nature. This attitude serves to justify their own retention of power and, furthermore, to inspire the postrevolutionary generation with revolutionary ideals.

Revolutionary modernizers, then, tend to look abroad for revolutions and revolutionary movements that they can consider allied to their own and for foreign forces that they can regard as their enemies. They usually find both, either because such movements and forces already exist, or because they develop in response to the revolutionary modernizers' self-fulfilling prophecy. The two possibilities are often so intertwined that they are difficult to distinguish. Moreover, it is often pointless to ask whether an enemy exists in reality or only in the minds of the revolutionary modernizers. In a sense, he who is regarded as an enemy *is* an enemy, and in any case the enemy existing in the revolutionary's mind will condition his behavior in directions that will probably make the enemy very real indeed. Similarly, though no doubt more rarely, a revolutionary movement abroad that is weak or only potential in character could, if revolutionary modernizers believe in its existence, be activated by their propaganda and material support.

We can cite many examples of foreign enemies who have served to prove that the revolution was threatened and that revolutionary modernizers were still needed at the helm. When the Bolsheviks came to power in Russia, both they and conservative forces in the West were so thoroughly caught up in the myth of the proletarian, anticapitalist nature of the Bolshevik revolution that there was no question on either side that "capitalist" regimes were the natural enemy of the Soviet regime. Both sides acted on that assumption, and thus, through a process of the mutually self-fulfilling prophecy, the myth of inevitable Soviet-Western conflict came true.[39] While the Russian Revolution could hardly be described objectively as chiefly a proletarian, anticapitalist movement, the Chinese Revolution contained from its beginnings strong anti-foreign, anti-imperialist elements. The foreign enemies of the Chinese Communists, first Japan and then the United States, were thus, in effect, given for the revolutionaries, and again their existence was confirmed by the reactions of each side to the other.

Although Castro's revolution was less anti-American in the beginning, here, too, the self-fulfilling prophecy produced the necessary foreign imperialist enemy. Sukarno's revolution was chiefly anticolonial, and specif-

---

[39] I dealt with this process at some length in "Myth, Self-Fulfilling Prophecy, and Symbolic Reassurance in the East-West Conflict," *Journal of Conflict Resolution*, IX (March 1965), 1-17.

ically anti-Dutch, from its inception, and the presence of the Dutch in Western New Guinea constituted rather naturally the neo-colonialist threat he needed. Only after Dutch withdrawal from New Guinea did Sukarno discover that a similar threat emanated from the British in Northern Borneo; each side, then, in the usual fashion, reinforced the enmity of the other.

To Ben Gurion, the hostility of the surrounding Arab states provided a ready-made enemy to perpetuate the spirit of national mobilization in which revolutionary leaders thrive, and, into the early years of Israeli statehood, the Zionists could regard the hostility embodied in the Arab League as a creature of British imperialism. And to Nasser and the other revolutionary Arab leaders in Syria, Iraq, and even in far-away Algeria, Israel could be pictured as an outpost of Western imperialism, a prophecy that became self-fulfilling in the joint British-French-Israeli Suez venture in 1956 and in Israel's reliance on the United States in the 1967 war and thereafter. Thus, in the Arab-Israeli conflict, regimes of revolutionary modernizers on each side have provided the enemy needed by the other side.

But to support the claim and the belief that their revolution is an ongoing and an international phenomenon, revolutionary modernizers need not only foreign enemies but also revolutionary allies. They must, therefore, support revolutionary movements abroad. The Bolsheviks did so, first in Hungary and Germany and later, through the Comintern, in other countries, notably China. In turn, the Chinese Communists have supported a number of foreign revolutionary movements, not only Communist-led ones like the Vietminh but also non-Communist ones like the FLN (National Liberation Front) in Algeria and the UPC (Union of the Peoples of Cameroun) in the Cameroons. Touré and Nkrumah also supported the UPC, and Nkrumah gave aid to rebels in the Congo. Both Ben Bella and Nasser sent arms and money to the Congo rebels; Ben Bella also supported revolutionaries in Angola, while Nasser sent 50,000 troops to help maintain the republican revolution in Yemen. And Castro has been aiding and even stimulating guerrilla warfare in Venezuela and Bolivia.

It goes without saying that attempts by revolutionary modernizers already in power to identify themselves with revolutions still in progress require the allocation of resources that might otherwise be spent on industrialization at home. The same is true of other activities that occupy revolutionary modernizers in pursuit of an internationalist role. Most, like Sukarno and Nasser, spent huge amounts on their armed forces to fight their real or imaginary enemies, to support their revolutionary allies and, more generally, to gain international prestige. To further their prestige abroad, they have also typically spent scarce reserves of foreign currency on national airlines and on elaborate embassy buildings.[40]

In their attempts to appear as leaders of international revolutionary movements, revolutionary modernizers are under some compulsion to demonstrate the unity of the movements they lead. Where several governments of revolutionary modernizers are involved, the result may be

[40] For a listing of numerous other expensive prestige projects initiated by Sukarno, see Feith, "Indonesia's Political Symbols," 83.

"unions" of their countries, even if they are not geographically adjacent. The Ghana-Guinea and later Ghana-Guinea-Mali union, and the various schemes that have united, at one time or another, Egypt, Syria, Iraq, and Yemen, were attempts at such unions. All of them are likely to fail, however, since subordination of the revolutionary modernizing leaders of one country to those of another hardly serves the purposes of the former.

More common than governmental unions as demonstrations of international revolutionary unity and solidarity are congresses that represent governments, parties, trade unions, and even isolated revolutionary groups and individuals from various countries. They involve no loss of power for any participants, but, on the contrary, give the revolutionary leaders of each country an opportunity to present themselves, in their own eyes and in the eyes of their countrymen, as international revolutionary leaders. Here again the activities of the Bolsheviks, with their congresses of the Communist International, the Red Trade Union International, the Toilers of the East, and other "front" organizations, were but forerunners of similar ventures undertaken by later revolutionary modernizers. Into this category fall Nkrumah's and Touré's pan-African and Nasser's pan-Arab meetings; Sukarno's Afro-Asian Conference at Bandung, as well as the Conference of New Emerging Forces that he had planned before his downfall; a second Afro-Asian Conference prepared by Ben Bella before he was deposed; and the Tri-Continental and Latin American Solidarity Congresses held by Castro.

Such congresses also may involve the expenditure of scarce investment capital and may therefore be opposed by managerial modernizers. Indeed, the vast sums allocated to build assembly halls and luxury accommodations for foreign delegates seem to have figured in the downfall of both Sukarno and Ben Bella—though this is not to imply that they (especially the latter) were overthrown by managerial modernizers.

Although the international involvements sought by revolutionary modernizers are probably not intentionally designed to inhibit industrialization at home, in effect they serve that function, and hence also the function of preventing the revolutionary modernizers from being replaced by managerial ones. International commitments do serve explicitly as an excuse for the failure of revolutionary modernizers to produce industrialization and, more generally, the material abundance they have promised. The argument, as familiar in modern Indonesia and Algeria as it was in Leninist Russia, is that these goals cannot be achieved until the revolution is safe, that is, until its foreign enemies have been defeated and it has triumphed internationally. To managerial modernizers growing up under the rule of revolutionary ones, however, expensive international involvements may well seem at least a contributory cause of that failure, and they may well blame their revolutionary leaders for it.

How such different attitudes can produce different policies, though they are expressed by similar symbols, is illustrated by the priorities Lenin and Stalin assigned to the building of industry and the spreading of revolution. Lenin could not envision the success of "socialism" (industrialization) in Soviet Russia until the revolution had been carried abroad, especially to Germany. Stalin, under whom managerial modernizers began their rise to power, reversed this order. He stood for "socialism in one country"—the industrialization of Russia—which only then could serve as the center of world revolution.

To argue that there may be a policy conflict between revolutionary and managerial modernizers over international involvements is not to imply that the latter will necessarily pursue more peaceful policies if and when they come to power. After all, the causes of international conflict are manifold, and many kinds of regimes may be involved in them. It is merely suggested that managerial modernizers are less likely to support revolutionary movements abroad than are revolutionary modernizers. Certainly as the Soviet government has come under the control of managerial modernizers, it has shifted its policy (and that of the Communist parties it can influence) from one of supporting revolutionary movements to one of supporting governments in power, so that it is now in sharp conflict with the revolutionary policies of Mao and especially Castro.[41]

Like their revolutionary predecessors, managerial modernizers are likely to favor governmental control and sponsorship of industry. For one thing, they often exercise their own power through the channels of the governmental bureaucracy and they will not want to yield it either to foreign or to native owners of private capital—which may well not be available in any case. For another, the managerial modernizers probably are themselves caught up in the same ideology and symbolism that motivates the revolutionaries. Even if they are not, they are anxious to establish their own "socialist" and "anti-imperialist" legitimacy, especially as long as they are still competing for power with revolutionary modernizers. To the latter, after all, a relatively friendly attitude toward foreign capital and native private enterprise constitutes a betrayal of the revolution. They are quick to levy such charges against their managerial rivals who may be quite vulnerable to them, particularly where, as is likely, they enjoy less mass support than the revolutionary modernizers.

Nevertheless, being more interested than the revolutionary modernizers in taking practical steps toward industrialization, managerial modernizers may be more willing to attract foreign capital to their countries and, also, to encourage industrialization under the auspices of native private businessmen. A change in policy toward foreign capital and private business has certainly taken place in Mexico between the regime of Cárdenas, the last of the revolutionary leaders, and those of his more managerial successors. There are indications of a similar change in India from Nehru's government to the governments of Shastri and Mrs. Gandhi. And a growing deemphasis on collectivism may also be noted in Israel with the replacement of the revolutionary Ben Gurion by the more managerially-inclined Eshkol and Dayan.[42]

However, similar policy changes had also occurred after the initial revolutionary regimes in Mexico and Turkey had been replaced respectively by those of Calles and his immediate successors and that of Menderes. All of

---

[41] See my *Communism and the Politics of Development: Persistent Myths and Changing Behavior* (New York, 1968).

[42] Ishai, "Transformation." Dayan illustrates the point that managerial leaders are not necessarily more peaceable than revolutionary ones.

these governments were more responsive to foreign and traditional pressures, but they could hardly be characterized as those of managerial modernizers. Greater friendliness to foreign investments and private business
also came after the overthrow of the civilian revolutionary regimes of Paz
Estenssoro, Nkrumah, and Sukarno by their respective military leaders,
Barrientos, Ankrah, and Suharto. There may be some reasons—for example, Suharto's liquidation of Sukarno's "Crush Malaysia" campaign and
the replacement by economists of a number of military men in the cabinet
—to regard the Indonesian military regime, and perhaps those of Bolivia
and Ghana as well, as somewhat more managerially inclined than those of
their revolutionary predecessors, but they cannot, at least not yet, be adequately described as regimes of managerial modernizers. Rather, the civil-
ian-military conflicts in these three countries, like the one in Algeria, can
be treated as the kind of conflict among revolutionary modernizers that
was mentioned earlier.

The difficulty we encounter in using policy differences toward foreign
capital and native private business as a criterion to distinguish between
the revolutionary and managerial modernizers is matched by many other
such difficulties. Thus, it is not necessarily clear that policies of austerity
and belt-tightening are an indication of Maoist revolutionary puritanism
and attempts to revive the spirit of sacrifice; they may also be realistic,
practical measures taken by managerial modernizers in order to fit goals
to available means or, in Stalinist fashion, to squeeze as much capital and
labor as possible out of the population for the purpose of rapid industrialization. On the other hand, one cannot simply assume that the building of a
steel mill or an atomic reactor constitutes a triumph of managerial modernizers; such projects may be merely the revolutionary modernizers' symbols
of their commitment to industrialization and national greatness. Similarly,
increased budgetary allocations for the armed forces may be a demonstration that control is in the hands of revolutionary modernizers, who feel the
need to fight enemies of their revolution at home or abroad, or perhaps that
the military leaders who are thereby strengthened are themselves managerial modernizers, using the armed forces to engage in tasks of economic
development. Clearly, distinctions between alternative policies will have
to be more finely drawn than those we have suggested above, if they are
to serve as indicators of the predominance of revolutionary or managerial
modernizers in a political system.

One might think that the ultimate distinction between the two types of
modernizers, should simply be: Do they or do they not in fact industrialize
their country? But, unfortunately, the matter cannot be that simple. We do
not have sufficient historical evidence to say with certainty that revolutionary modernizers cannot industrialize. Indeed, the Soviet Union and
Yugoslavia became industrialized under the top leadership of the revolutionary modernizers, Stalin and Tito. And China, like many other underdeveloped countries, has moved in some degree toward industrialization
under similar leadership. All we can say is that no society can move very
far in this direction without developing some managerial modernizers in
some positions of power; but they do not by any means have to hold all the
top positions. To be able to claim that necessity, one would have to define

as managerial modernizers all modernizers under whose leadership industrialization takes place. Definition, rather than empirical evidence, would then validate the hypothesis that industrialization and the rise of managerial modernizers are concomitant processes.

Thus, just as successful industrialization does not prove that managerial modernizers are in power, so failure to industrialize a country does not prove that managerial modernizers are not in power. There are obviously many factors besides the absence of managers in power or the prevalence of revolutionary policies and attitudes that can effectively prevent successful industrialization. Surely, even regimes of managerial modernizers could be stymied by lack of capital or resources, lack of needed skills and attitudes in the population, or apathy and resistance on the part of various groups—unless, of course, we once again commit the tempting mistake of simply defining as managerial modernizers only those who do succeed in industrializing.

III. Conclusion

It would appear, then, that we cannot distinguish sharply between revolutionary and managerial modernizers in terms of their experience and training, their attitudes, or even their policies. This is true because there are not, or not yet, enough regimes that could reasonably be regarded as being controlled by managerial modernizers to provide us with sufficient data to support some distinguishing criteria. It may also be the case, however, that our two concepts, and particularly that of the managerial modernizer, are not very useful. We have, of course, regarded them all along only as representing ideal types, and we have assumed that, in the real world, modernizers are ranged along some kind of continuum between the pure revolutionary and pure managerial types. It may turn out, however, that, especially after revolutionary modernizers have come to power in underdeveloped countries, different kinds of leaders will evolve who are not just more or less revolutionary and more or less managerial, but who simply cannot be classified along these lines.

Thus, it appears that in some countries, such as India, where politicians have to compete with each other for popular support, some of the emerging leadership, particularly at the local level, is closer to the traditional culture and hence perhaps less modernizing than the revolutionary leadership it succeeds. This, of course, need not prevent the concurrent emergence of managerial modernizers, particularly in those sections of government and society that are directly concerned with the development of the economy, but also in any others, such as health care and the military, that make extensive use of modern techniques. Quite possibly, the expectation that managerial modernizers will succeed the revolutionary ones in the course of economic development will turn out to be too simple, and what will in fact occur will be a diversification of elites. Managerial modernizers will be but one of the successor elites to the revolutionary modernizers, and managerial modernizers themselves will be subdivided from the beginning —and will later become more so—among various types of administrative, scientific, technical, and engineering personnel.

458   *Elites in Modernizing Regimes*

As we stated at the outset, we cannot test, much less validate, the hypothesis that industrialization and the replacement of revolutionary by managerial modernizers accompany each other if we cannot clearly distinguish between the two types of modernizers. Since this is precisely our position now, the hypothesis will have to remain no more than a hypothesis for some time to come.

It is also possible, however, that a hypothesis relating industrialization to the replacement of revolutionary by managerial modernizers cannot be tested at all, because the two variables—industrialization and elite replacement—are not clearly distinguishable. Whether there really are or are not two distinct sets of attitudes that characterize revolutionary modernizers and managerial modernizers is, as we have noted, difficult to determine and by no means clear. It may or may not be true that it takes one type of man to build a political movement and another to build a factory. But there is, in any case, reason to believe that it is not so much attitudes and values that shape policies (as was assumed above for the sake of argument) as it is the prevailing system characteristics and, especially, the availability of wealth.

Whether revolutionary and managerial modernizers are, or are not, different types of men we do not, and perhaps cannot, know. But we do know that there are different types of societies, especially more or less industrialized ones. Perhaps all we can put forth with certainty is the commonplace that in industrial societies there are managers—since some people must manage industry—and that in societies with little or no industry modernizers cannot be managers. It may be merely the times and the types of societies that create the distinctions between the two kinds of modernizers, and it may therefore be hopeless to look for distinctions between them apart from the times and societies in which they live.

Appendix

Biographical Information on Revolutionary Leaders

Country	Revolutionary Leader	University or Professional Education in Industrialized Country	Other Travel or Stay in Underdev. Country	Experience at Home in Modern Institution or Profession
Algeria	Ben Bella	—	—	France	French army
Bolivia	Paz Estenssoro	—	Bolivia	—	Professor
Burma	U Nu	—	Burma	—	Teacher
China	Sun	(Hawaii school)	Hong Kong	US, England, Japan	Physician
	Mao	—	China	—	Teacher, Librarian
Congo	Lumumba	—	(Mission school)	—	Bureaucracy

Biographical Information on Revolutionary Leaders (Continued)

Country	Revolutionary Leader	University or Professional Education in Industrialized Country	Professional Education in Underdev. Country	Other Travel or Stay in Indus. Country	Experience at Home in Modern Institution or Profession
Cuba	Castro	—	Cuba	—	—
Egypt	Nasser	—	Egypt	—	Army
Ghana	Nkrumah	US	Gold Coast	England	—
Guatemala	Arévalo	—	Argentina	Europe	Professor
Guinea	Touré	—	(French-type secondary school)	France	Trade unions
India	Nehru	England	—	England	Lawyer
Indonesia	Sukarno	—	Indonesia	Japan	—
Iraq	Kassem	—	Iraq	—	Army
Israel	Ben Gurion	—	Turkey	US	Kibbutz
Kenya	Kenyatta	England, USSR	—	England	School Principal
Malawi	Banda	US, England	—	England, US	Physician
Mexico	Madero	France, US	—	US	Modern Landowner
Pakistan	Ayub Khan	England	India	—	British-Indian army
Russia	Kerensky	—	Russia	—	Lawyer
	Lenin	—	Russia	Europe	Lawyer
Sudan	Abboud	—	Sudan	—	British-Sudanese army
Tanganyika	Nyerere	England	Uganda	Europe	Teacher
Tunisia	Bourguiba	France	Tunisia	Europe, US	Lawyer
Turkey	Kemal	—	Turkey	—	Army
Uganda	Obote	—	Uganda	—	Business
Venezuela	Betancourt	—	Venezuela	US	Journalist
Vietnam	Ho Chi-Minh	—	—	France	Journalist
Yemen	Sallal	—	Iraq	?	Army
Yugoslavia	Tito	—	—	USSR	—
Zambia	Kaunda	—	(English-type secondary school)	England, US	Teacher
Zanzibar	Karume	—	—	(Sailor)	—

Political Mainsprings of Economic Planning in the New Nations

The Modernization Imperative versus Social Mobilization

Baldev Raj Nayar*

The quest for the appropriate model or strategy for economic development in the new nations has created serious disagreements among economists. The disputed alternatives have included: a gradualist or Big Push approach; balanced or imbalanced growth; capital accumulation or institutional change; industry or agriculture; centralized planning or laissez-faire; and import substitution or export promotion. Notwithstanding the differences in the debate over the preferred strategy, there is the common although often unstated assumption that the objective of economic development programs is the improvement of living standards for the masses. This assumption has been at times explicitly stated not only as a description of reality, but also as an exclusive normative goal for the new nations. In the course of a critical examination of various growth models, economist Hans Singer states that "this raising of the level of people's life is both the objective of development, and also its instrument," and recommends that "the key concept must be the improved quality of people's life."[1]

W. B. Reddaway, another economist, comments, "Long-range strategy must have one overriding objective: to secure a progressive rise in the level of consumption per head, by methods which will make possible an indefinite continuance of the process and which also satisfy certain social and political ideals (e.g., of liberty and

*I would like to express my sincere appreciation to Professors Henry W. Ehrmann, Department of Political Science, and Jagdish Handa, Department of Economics, both of McGill University, for their comments on an earlier version of this article.

[1] Hans W. Singer, "Social Development: Key Growth Sector," *International Development Review*, VII (March 1965), 3–5.

reduced inequality). Other economic objectives—such as increased capital-formation and industrialization or a viable balance of payments—are essentially dealing with means and not ends.''[2] Similarly, John Kenneth Galbraith speaks favorably of the Popular Consumption Criterion as the planning goal which "anchors economic development to the consumption requirements, present and prospective, of the typical citizen—to the consumption, statistically speaking, of the modal consumer.'' He further states that "the planning goal of the less developed country . . . is the improvement of the well-being of the modal person. This goal is the counterpart of the poverty of the poor and it is not only central but total.''[3] The same concern for improved standards of living as the goal for economic planning serves as the main theme of the three-volume survey by Gunnar Myrdal, demonstrating the utter failure of Asian governments to assure their populations a better life.[4]

Some economists realize that the reality does not always coincide with this desired emphasis on mass welfare due to the existence of the forces of "economic nationalism.'' These forces lead to a stress on economic autarchy, industrialization, economic planning, concern with the public sector, and hostility to foreign enterprise. Such policies of "economic nationalism" are negatively evaluated, however; they are considered irrational, proceeding essentially from the psychic need of national elites to imitate the West.[5] Supposedly such policies do not serve the cause of mass welfare; rather they promote the interests of specific classes. According to these economists, mass welfare would be best served by following the law of comparative advantage, entailing a concentration on the production of primary products by underdeveloped countries.

For the most part, political scientists have not paid much attention to questions of economic development. They have concentrated on political structure and process, deterred by Max Weber's advice not to examine state behavior from the viewpoint of goals or purposes. Where attention has been focused on economic development, political scientists have also operated primarily from the perspective of mass welfare as well as from the viewpoint of the desirability of a democratic regime and of political stability. Accordingly, in discussions of the economic problems of the underdeveloped countries,

---

[2] W. B. Reddaway, *The Development of the Indian Economy* (London, 1962), p. 48.

[3] John Kenneth Galbraith, *Economic Development* (Cambridge [Mass.], 1964), pp. 10–11, 62.

[4] Gunnar Myrdal, *Asian Drama: An Inquiry into the Poverty of Nations* (New York, 1968).

[5] Harry G. Johnson, ed. *Economic Nationalism in Old and New States* (Chicago, 1967), chaps. 1 and 8.

political scientists have emphasized improvements in agriculture, expansion of consumer goods industry, and encouragement of free enterprise. David Apter and Charles Andrain underline Max Millikan's belief that, for the advancement of mass welfare and democracy, "raising agricultural productivity should take precedence over rapid industrialization." They further state:

> Those working on the Committee on Comparative Politics of the Social Science Research Council take a similar position about the need to decentralize the economy and political institutions. For example, according to Joseph LaPalombara, the role of government in furthering economic development should be to create a framework for private enterprise, that is, provide law, order, and security for private entrepreneurs and engage in limited economic planning. . . . Myron Weiner also comes out for decentralized government and private entrepreneurship. To alleviate the economic gap between the rich and poor nations, Lucian Pye supports population control and concentration on agriculture, rather than industrialization.[6]

In a more recent volume on political development, published under the sponsorship of the same Committee on Comparative Politics, Joseph LaPalombara forcefully argues against industrialization, holding it counterproductive for mass welfare. He refers to "the often *unfortunate* notion that 'modernity' means industrialization" and blames "the ubiquitous urge to industrialization" on a tendency in the new nations to ape the West.[7] Similarly, political sociologist Seymour Martin Lipset believes that "to a considerable degree the leaders seek development as part of their more general effort to overcome *feelings* of national inferiority, particularly vis-à-vis the former metropolitan ruler."[8]

The impulse for making the improvement of standards of living for people in underdeveloped countries the central goal of economic development comes not only as a result of an awareness of the depths of poverty prevailing there—which pains the sensitive conscience of the liberal in the affluent West—but also from an acute consciousness of the social and political implications of what Karl Deutsch has called the process of "social mobilization."[9] The expressive term "social mobilization" refers to the transformation of men's percep-

---

[6] David E. Apter and Charles Andrain, "Comparative Government: Developing New Nations," *The Journal of Politics*, XXX (May 1968), 409–10.

[7] Leonard Binder et al., *Crises and Sequences in Political Development* (Princeton, 1971), pp. 241–73 (emphasis added).

[8] Seymour Martin Lipset, *The First New Nation: The United States in Historical and Comparative Perspective* (New York, 1963), p. 46 (emphasis added).

[9] Karl W. Deutsch, "Social Mobilization and Political Development," in Harry Eckstein and David E. Apter, eds. *Comparative Politics: A Reader* (New York, 1963), pp. 582–603.

tion of the world under the impact of a variety of modern social forces, such as the mass media, literacy, urbanization, and commercialization. Through this transformation, social mobilization increases the range and scope of demands on government for greater material welfare, more popularly stated as "the revolution of rising expectations." The governments of these countries, so the assumption runs, ought to undertake the satisfaction of this urge for the better life through programs of economic development. If they fail to do so, one can predict government instability, political chaos or, worse, communism. In the absence of improvement in living standards among a socially mobilized population, governments will be continuously confronted by "the crises of development." Consequently, for peace and stability as well as humanitarian reasons, the new nations must strive to maximize mass welfare through development programs. For these same reasons, it is in the enlightened interest of the Western world to assist these nations through foreign aid programs. This would seem to be the rationale behind apotheosizing the improvement of living standards as a primary goal of economic development.

The Modernization Imperative
The process of economic development—the modernization of traditional economies and the growth of an industrial system—has resulted in a tremendous and revolutionary advance in living standards in the West. But this advance was not necessarily the purpose of economic development. In England—the country that pioneered in economic development—the higher standards of living were the unintended long-run consequence of the activities of a small group of entrepreneurs who undertook the establishment of large-scale industry for private profit. Indeed, the process of economic development has historically been accompanied by such vast exploitation, suffering, instability, and violence that it may well be questioned why any government interested in domestic peace, political stability, and mass welfare would want to initiate it.

It would seem to be a serious misrepresentation both of the historical experience and existential social reality, however, to single out the attainment of higher standards of living from among the several "ultimate" or "long-term" fruits of the process of economic development in the West and afterwards to regard this attainment either as the real purpose or as a desirable goal for economic development in developing countries. Most importantly and obviously, economic development had a drastic impact on the national power and international status of Western nations. Amazingly, however, in their concern with questions of contemporary economic development, North American social scientists remain characteristically silent concerning this aspect of economic development. The neglect of the power consequences of economic development among these social scientists, their refusal to recognize the equal legitimacy of the goal of national power, and their disinclination to realize that the achievement of mass welfare may itself depend on an earlier acquisition of national power, may have many roots. This orientation to the power aspirations of developing states may well be related to the Cold War ethos held by the American academic world.

More immediately, it would seem that the explanation for such an orientation in matters relating to economic development lies in regarding nation-states as closed, autonomous systems rather than as politically embedded members of an international system. This tendency is characteristic of much of the political development literature since World War II. Most of the models, frameworks, and typologies of political systems—from Gabriel Almond and Apter through Samuel Huntington and others to Edward Shils and Aristide Zolberg—exclude the international system from consideration. In a recent article by Huntington, which makes a comprehensive review of the development and modernization literature of the postwar period, there is no reference at all to the external environment.[10] On occasion, political scientists have tangentially recognized the international system as a source of inputs and recipient of outputs,[11] but this recognition remains largely in the abstract and seems to have left unaffected the analysis of the political problems of the new nations. The latest volume on "crises in development" sponsored by the Committee on Comparative Politics is supposedly the theoretical culmination of the Committee's concern with political development.[12] From this book, it is clear that the prevailing model in the mainstream political development literature is still that of the autonomous, closed political system; the international system seems to have no relevance to the "crises in development."

Contrary to the prevailing orthodoxy in the political development literature, it is a fundamental assumption of the argument presented here that an explicit union of development analysis with international

---

[10] Samuel P. Huntington, "The Change to Change: Modernization, Development, and Politics," *Comparative Politics*, III (April 1971), 283–322.

[11] Gabriel Almond, "A Developmental Approach to Political Systems," *World Politics*, XVII (January 1965), 183–214.

[12] Binder, *Crises*.

politics is essential to an adequate understanding of concrete economic and political phenomena in the new nations. Without this union, our understanding of the developmental process and developmental goals will remain fragmentary and truncated. More specifically, if one were to examine economic development from the perspective of political systems within an international system, whose chief characteristic is the struggle for power, one would arrive at a different set of conclusions regarding not only the historical bases of economic development, but also the legitimacy of the aims of economic planning in the new nations.

It is a truism that the struggle for power has been a universal feature in the relations among states, in time as well as in space, and also that war has been the *ultima ratio* in that struggle—and a frequent one at that. In the final analysis, the ability to defend itself militarily defines the very nature of the independence of a given state. In military contests victory has depended in part on the size and population of the country and of the armed forces, as well as on national character and morale. However, victory has depended also on economic power and military technology. Although the economic power of a nation and its weapons technology have always been crucial elements in determining the fortunes of war, their importance was raised to monumental proportions as a result of the industrial revolution. Such was the transformation that the industrial revolution wrought in national power and weapons technology that, wherever an industrialized nation confronted a nonindustrialized one, it also laid down the terms of the confrontation: "Become like us or go under." This is the imperative of modernization: "Modernize or be subjugated." This subjugation need not only take the form of physical occupation, but perhaps also of political penetration and economic control.

As John Kautsky explains, "For over a century now, industrial superiority has been a key element of military superiority, and no regime wanting to avoid military defeats, and perhaps to make conquests of its own, has been able to afford resistance to the introduction of modern techniques of mass production and means of transportation."[13] For the nonindustrialized country, there is no escape from the modernization imperative; there is no other alternative, no other choice. The impulse for modernization thus emerges not *internally* from the demands of a socially mobilized population, nor from the humanitarian instincts of the political leadership, but

[13] John H. Kautsky, *Political Change in Underdeveloped Countries: Nationalism and Communism* (New York, 1962), p. 98.

externally from the security threat presented by the industrialized countries. Confronted by an industrialized nation, a nonindustrialized one was, has been, and still is militarily vulnerable and therefore politically penetrable. Of course, demands for mass welfare are also built into the dynamics of the modernization process but one should not lose sight of the basic or primal factor causing modernization. It is military security in its literal sense that propels nations to modernize and industrialize. Far from spurring modernization, social mobilization and demands for mass welfare—unless controlled and regulated by the government—are often considered obstacles to the kind of modernization that would bolster military security.

In short, it is the built-in compulsions of the situation of military confrontation, actual or potential, that force nations to modernize. The radical difference that modernization and industrialization make to power capabilities dictates their necessity to new nations, regardless of whether the latter are attracted or repelled by other aspects of modernization, or by the social and political implications of the modernization process. These latter implications of modernization are extremely far-reaching, leading to a fundamental and revolutionary transformation of all social systems. Ultimately, different societies are forced to conform to a similar economic mold and, by implication, to similar social and political values. They have to discard their traditional—and perhaps their sacred—ways since there is no escape from doing so. Modernization is not launched because it is pleasurable or exciting, but because it is imperative. This is the reason modernization is undertaken despite its prospect of rootlessness and alienation and why Gandhian schemes of village self-sufficiency are unacceptable to national statesmen.

A nonindustrialized nation confronted by an industrialized one could conceivably buy military weapons from another industrialized country. In order to do this, however, it must create an economic surplus with which to purchase these weapons. This surplus necessitates considerable modernization of the economy, society, and government administration.[14] However, reliance on industrialized countries for military armaments is not without its risks. Military weapons may be provided for a political price, and deliveries may be suspended at the discretion of the supplier. In any case, dependence upon other countries for military supplies is inconsistent with the aspiration for national independence. A country may choose instead to manufacture weaponry itself; but this is not entirely a matter of

---

[14] Fred W. Riggs, *Administration in Developing Countries: The Theory of Prismatic Society* (Boston, 1964), pp. 42–49.

choice. In large part, it depends on the size of the country and the nature of its resources. Where countries choose to manufacture military weaponry themselves, modernization must be more thoroughgoing than for the purchase of weapons from abroad, since such manufacture involves industrialization. And heavy industries play a key role in plans for industrialization. Kautsky comments: "Industrialization, if it is to be rapid and if it is to ensure independence from already industrialized countries and eventually a position of power in international affairs, requires first the buildup of heavy industry and consequently the postponement of the fulfillment of consumer demands."[15]

Thus, the aim of national power, which is directly linked with national independence, lies at the heart of economic development. It is precisely the neglect of the power element that makes it so easy for many economists to dismiss the objective of industrialization along with the Big Push economic models,[16] to advocate the virtues of comparative advantage, and to assert that heavy industries "have no intrinsic virtue in and of themselves."[17] National decision makers are not persuaded by these arguments. Industrialization for them is not a matter of merely imitating the West, of overcoming personal feelings of inferiority, or of pursuing symbolic goals; it is directly tied to life-and-death issues pertaining to national survival. Industrialization is considered imperative for the development of economic power in general, and for military power, in particular. No nation can accomplish these ends by relying on agriculture alone. And there is no first-rate, nor even second-rate, military or economic power in the world today with agriculture rather than industry as its economic base.

Since agricultural growth is often counterposed against industry, it should be emphasized that nothing in the focus on industry automatically precludes stress on agriculture; agriculture is understandably essential for industrial development. But there is an essential difference between a stress on agriculture as an economic end in itself and on its growth as a means toward industrial development. In this context, the crucial test for agricultural performance is the ability "to free investment and growth in industry from restraints by agricul-

---

[15] Kautsky, *Communism and the Politics of Development: Persistent Myths and Changing Behavior* (New York, 1968), p. 174.

[16] See, for example, the contributions in S. Tangri and H. Gray, eds. *Capital Accumulation and Economic Development* (Boston, 1967), pp. 75–86, 86–94.

[17] George Rosen, *Democracy and Economic Change in India* (Berkeley and Los Angeles, 1966), p. 250.

ture."[18] Advocates of industrialization in the new nations have not been ignorant of the importance of agriculture in terms of its functional relationship to industry. Any cursory perusal of Chinese or Indian planning documents—even those of the early 1950s—will bear out this conclusion. However, a real breakthrough can only come from concentration on one sector rather than dissipating energy and effort on a whole variety of operations. The modernization imperative dictates priority be given to industry and particularly, wherever feasible, to heavy industry.

Industrialization: A Historical Perspective

The North Atlantic arena   As the first industrialized nation, England posed a serious threat to the security and independence of other European countries, which subsequently pushed forward with their own industrial development. If the historical record has any relevance for the new nations, it is significant that the national power adjustments among European nations were neither incidental nor unintended side effects of industrialization, but were precisely the fundamental purposes for which industrialization was vigorously undertaken. Historian David Landes points out that, "industrialization was, from the start, a political imperative," and Walt W. Rostow has demonstrated that in the cases of France and Germany security considerations were preeminent in economic modernization. Economic thought in the less industrialized countries also reflected national power needs and aspirations. In Germany, Friedrich List and others of the German Historical School rejected laissez-faire and advocated rapid industrialization through state protection—not for mass welfare, but for the promotion of the economic and political independence of the state. Interestingly, List's own economic philosophy seems to have been derived from Alexander Hamilton's ideas. It is significant that, like the political elites of the new nations today, Hamilton himself viewed economic development in terms larger than welfare: "Not only the wealth but the independence and security of a country appear to be materially connected with the prosperity of manufactures." Before long, even Thomas Jefferson converted to this doctrine, exclaiming "experience has taught me that manufactures are now as necessary to our independence as to our comfort."[19]

[18] Alexander Eckstein, Walter Galenson, and Ta-Chung Liu, eds. *Economic Trends in Communist China* (Chicago, 1968), p. 468.

[19] Walt W. Rostow, *Politics and the Stages of Growth* (Cambridge [Mass.], 1971), pp. 65–69, 189, 195.

As the economic historian, Samuel Rezneck, has noted, "Manufactures, like the Constitution, were expected to strengthen the country and help it achieve true independence."[20]

As the pioneer industrial country, England had an obvious initial advantage. However, European countries had a common cultural heritage and somewhat similar levels of economic welfare. Industrial development was not without its pains for these nations, but they were soon able to diminish England's relative advantage and even to challenge the international position she had achieved by her industrialization. In contrast, the challenge from the European industrialized countries appeared in much starker terms for the countries of Asia and Africa.

Industrial development in Europe had two major consequences for the rest of the world. In the first place, through their new capabilities the industrial powers of Europe created a global international system out of the various largely autonomous regional systems that had formerly prevailed. Secondly, they posed the inescapable modernization imperative to peoples with entirely different cultures and civilizations: "Industrialize or be colonized." Since most nations in Asia and Africa failed to modernize, it was inevitable that they became the pawns for European empires. The pioneer industrial nation established an empire where for many years the sun never set. Karl Marx saw these results of European industrialization though characteristically he viewed them in economic terms alone.

Japan: "A rich country, a strong army" Of the many countries in Asia, Japan was the only one to succeed in launching a self-sustained program of modernization in the nineteenth century. Thus, she developed into an industrial power and, consequently, became a major military power as well. It should be emphasized here that it was neither social mobilization nor demands for mass welfare that brought about Japanese modernization. Nor was it that the Japanese found Western civilization inherently attractive in contrast to their own way of life. Instead, Japan was motivated by the necessity to preserve her sovereign independence in the face of the direct intrusion of American naval power and also by the fate of China and the rest of Asia. Japan's successful modernization may be related to many factors but, indeed, the absence of social mobilization—and its subsequent suppression or control—may account for this success in no small measure. The higher standards of living later attained in

[20] Lipset, p. 47.

Japan were not the motive but the consequence of the modernization program.

The military danger persuaded Japanese leaders to undertake partial modernization even before the end of the Tokugawa rule; but full-scale modernization actually began with the Meiji Restoration of 1868. Contrary to the common impression, Japan did not attempt a replication of the pattern of industrial development in England, with consumer goods industries preceding heavy industries, but reversed the process by establishing the latter first. This pattern of development was dictated by the military situation; and, once initiated, it continued to influence subsequent industrialization. The Japanese summed up their goal in the highly significant slogan *fukoku kyohei*—"a rich country, a strong army." With empathy, E. Herbert Norman explains the rationale behind the Japanese strategy: "To put the sequence of emphasis in logical order, the Meiji leaders thought somewhat as follows: 'What do we most need to save us from the fate of China? A modern army and navy. On what does the creation and maintenance of modern armed forces depend? Chiefly on heavy industries, engineering, mining, shipbuilding, in a word strategic industries.'"[21]

China: From "self-strengthening" to nuclear status   China also perceived the Western impact as a military threat. Shortly after the Opium War, in 1842, Commissioner Lin Tse-hsu recommended that China build her own military arsenal to defend herself against the new "barbarians." Another Chinese official, Wei Yuan, was similarly concerned, and urged the adoption of the superior military techniques of the West. Two decades later, Chinese statesmen Tseng Kuo-fan and Li Hung-chang sought to push forward a program of industrialization as part of the "self-strengthening" movement. As a result, ironworks, shipyards, and arsenals were built. Small as the total industrial effort was under this program, there is no denying the powerful impulse provided by the external threat in bringing about whatever modernization did occur. From the vantage point of military threat, a whole series of activities integral to modernization was launched. As Alexander Eckstein explains:

> The different projects in combination do represent a more or less rational economic design, even if that design was not blueprinted in advance. The

[21] E. Herbert Norman, *Japan's Emergence as a Modern State: Political and Economic Problems of the Meiji Period* (New York, 1940), pp. 125–26, 118.

initial stimulus for the whole undertaking came from the urge to produce weapons and strengthen the defense establishment—thus the arsenals and the Foochow shipyard. It was soon realized that modern transport and communications are essential ingredients of defense, and this led to the organization of the China Merchants' Steam Navigation Company and, somewhat later, the Imperial Telegraph Administration. Then a coal mine was opened to supply fuel for the arsenals and the steamships. This, in turn, made it necessary to provide transportation from the pithead to a suitable port, and so the first railroad line was built. Military requirements also induced the construction of several textile mills to manufacture cloth for the army. Iron and steel works were established to provide the necessary raw materials for the arsenals and to manufacture rails for the new railroads.[22]

In terms of China's needs, however, this self-strengthening movement was a failure; the Chinese effort proved inadequate against the Western challenge. This very failure led to deeper penetration into China by foreign powers, and eventually resulted in a more radical attempt at transformation of China into a modern industrial power under the auspices of a Communist regime. It is important to recognize that the Communists achieved power in China as a nationalist movement, fired by the determination to remove from Chinese soil the military, political, and economic domination of foreign powers. The subsequent political policy and economic strategy of that Communist regime has also been dictated by the objective of securing political and economic independence, and also of claiming a rightful share of political and economic influence in world affairs. The economic strategy of emphasis on heavy industry to the relative neglect of the consumer goods industry and agriculture in the 1950s is also explained in terms of the necessity of adopting the shortest route to an industrial base which would make possible self-defense and the attainment of political aims. The simplistic notion that such an economic strategy provides better prospects of long-term growth will not do. It would be naive to expect otherwise from a country whose leader is the author of the oft-quoted statement that "power flows out of the barrel of a gun."

China's first Five-Year Plan cites Mao Tse-tung in justification for this heavy industry strategy: "Without industry, there can be no solid national defense, no people's welfare and no national prosperity and power." The same plan subsequently elaborates: "The purpose of adopting a positive policy of industrialization, that is, a policy which gives priority to the growth of heavy industry, is to provide a material basis on which to strengthen our national defense, meet the needs of

[22] See Eckstein, *Economic Trends,* pp. 50–51.

the people, and bring about the socialist transformation of our national economy."[23] The proposals for China's second Plan continued to give priority to heavy industry, "because heavy industry provides the basis for a strong economy and national defense, as well as the basis for the technical reconstruction of our national economy."

The Chinese have been insistent in their aim of building an autarkic, self-sufficient, and self-reliant economy: "The socialist industrialization of our country entails building an independent, comprehensive and modern industrial system."[24] Indeed, their ambition for this type of economy was an important factor in the Sino-Soviet rift, which in turn reinforced and fortified China's attempt to build an economy of this nature. Of course, problems have resulted from concentration on industry, especially heavy industry, and these have made necessary subsequent attention to agriculture; but it would be incorrect to conclude that this entails rejection of heavy industry. Dwight Perkins, a careful scholar of the Chinese economy, points out that, "although the economic content of Chinese Communist goals has changed somewhat over time, the emphasis on autarky and military strength has insured that a large portion of state-controlled investment has gone to heavy industry."[25] The basic motivation for economic development should be obvious from the fact that the Chinese have made a spectacular entry into the age of nuclear weapons and space rockets, without a similar dramatic advance in living standards.

Russia: "We do not want to be beaten"   In an original and profound essay, John Kautsky demonstrated that not only in China is communism actually another form of nationalism of the intelligentsia of an underdeveloped country, but also in the Soviet Union.[26] Since the heavy industry strategy as a highly articulated doctrine had its origins in the Soviet Union, it is important to note that defense needs were paramount in its adoption. As Oscar Lange pointed out in 1943, "The Soviet economy was planned not for the harmony of the different branches, but for one single purpose, namely the most rapid industrialization and preparation of effective national defense." He further underlined the fact that "Soviet economic planning did not

---

[23] People's Republic of China, *First Five-Year Plan for Development of the National Economy of the People's Republic of China in 1953–57*, p. 16.
[24] Po I-po, cited in Dwight H. Perkins, "Industrial Planning and Management," in Eckstein, Galenson, and Liu, p. 598.
[25] Perkins, p. 600.
[26] Kautsky, *Political Change*, pp. 3–119.

serve the objectives of a harmonious socialist welfare economy, but served political and military objectives to which all other aspects of economic planning were sacrificed."[27] Stalin himself provides vivid testimony to the fundamental goal of national security in plans for economic development. In 1931, during the course of the first Soviet Plan, he declared:

> It is sometimes asked whether it is not possible to slow down a bit in tempo, to retard the movement. No. This is impossible. It is impossible to reduce the tempo! On the contrary, it is necessary as far as possible to accelerate it. To slacken the tempo means to fall behind. And the backward are always beaten. But we do not want to be beaten. No, we do not want this! The history of old Russia is the history of defeats due to backwardness. She was beaten by the Turkish beys. She was beaten by the Swedish feudal barons. She was beaten by the Polish-Lithuanian squires. She was beaten by the Anglo-French capitalists. She was beaten by the Japanese barons. All beat her for her backwardness—for military backwardness, for industrial backwardness, for agricultural backwardness. She was beaten because to beat her was profitable and could be done with impunity. . . .That is why we must no longer be backward. . . .we are fifty to a hundred years behind the advanced countries. We must cover this in *ten* years. Either we do this or they will crush us.[28]

The Communists seized power in Russia because of their ability to lead a socially mobilized population. However, in order to push through a program of industrialization, supposedly for the achievement of welfare goals, the Soviet Government proceeded to suppress such social mobilization except where it was under governmental direction and control. The subsequent advance in mass welfare was a by-product of a program in which the main purpose was national power. The Soviet Union has not been unique in this regard, but only reflects, somewhat starkly, a universal phenomenon.

It can, of course, be suggested that the eventual or long-run goal, even during Stalin's tenure, was perhaps mass welfare and that national power was only a necessary prerequisite for its attainment. A nation could not make great advances in welfare or even determine its own goals in this regard while a victim of aggression, of foreign occupation, or of alien political control. But such an interpretation of the long-run situation adds little by way of discriminating analysis. Characterization of aims of economic planning can only have meaning in reference to a relevant period of planning. It is precisely in this

[27] Cited in Oleg Hoeffding, "State Planning and Forced Industrialization," *Problems of Communism,* VIII (November–December 1959), 39.

[28] Cited in Irving Louis Horowitz, *Three Worlds of Development: The Theory and Practice of International Stratification* (New York, 1966), pp. 13–14.

sense that one can say that Soviet plans during the Stalin era were oriented toward national and military power, or as Abram Bergson put it, "steel was a final good to Stalin, and bread an intermediate one."[29]

The case of the Soviet Union has great relevance to the understanding of the aspirations of developing countries. For these countries, the appeal of Marxism lies less in the utopian goal of a communist society than in the concrete example of the Soviet Union's elevation to a first-rate industrial and military power. It is not the bifurcation of domestic society in underdeveloped countries that makes Marxism meaningful to the intelligentsia, as Robert Tucker mistakenly believes,[30] but rather the bifurcation of the international stratification system into the industrialized, economically advanced, and powerful nations, on the one hand, and the nonindustrialized, backward, and powerless nations, on the other.

Third World Dilemma: Security versus Welfare
In the nineteenth and early twentieth centuries, while China was being carved up into spheres of influence by the industrial powers, much of the rest of Asia and Africa came under direct colonial rule. The economies of the colonies were integrated as agricultural appendages within the various empires. In the process, some lopsided, "unbalanced modernization" also took place in the colonies. The controlling principle in such modernization was whether it served the interests of the imperial power. Where it did not, or where the undertaking of a modernization program would hurt its interests, the imperial power checked modernization. Thus, modernization remained partial, whether it was in the economic, political, or social sphere. As this modernization occurred, wider and wider strata of the population became "socially mobilized" and, under the leadership of the modern intellectuals, were drawn into a nationalist movement designed to overthrow the colonial rule of alien imperialists.

The adherence to the nationalist movement by large segments of the population resulted from dissatisfaction and frustration with colonial rule. The nationalist leaders also held out the promise of a better life once independence was achieved and a nationalist government in power. These nationalist governments were thus committed to promote the welfare of their peoples. But it would certainly be naive to expect that the quest for national independence should suddenly cease

[29] Cited in Eckstein, *Economic Trends*, p. 460.
[30] Robert C. Tucker, *The Marxian Revolutionary Idea* (New York, 1969), pp. 126–29.

with the formal departure of the colonial rulers. Plans for economic modernization and industrialization are undertaken, indeed, to provide the economic and technological foundation for real political independence and equality among nations. Nationalism provides the major thrust for industrialization; some scholars have even defined nationalism as "the drive of intellectuals for industrialization," and have characterized the motivation for industrialization as "nationalist; that is, anti-colonialist."[31]

Such pursuit of military security and national independence by the new nations cannot be attributed simply to the paranoia of the political elites on the grounds that the international strategic environment has so changed since World War II as to make international violence less possible and military capabilities less relevant. In the first place, those who admonish the new nations to concentrate on agriculture instead of industry do so not mainly on the basis of any change in the strategic environment, bur rather on the exclusion of this environment from consideration altogether. Furthermore, whatever the change in the strategic environment in the postwar period between the nuclear-equipped superpowers and their military blocs in affluent Europe, war has been not merely a continuous potential but a daily presence within the Third World: in East Asia, South and Southeast Asia, or the Middle East and Africa.

One major source of international violence in the Third World has been the direct intervention of the superpowers and the former colonial powers, e.g., in Vietnam since World War II, and in Egypt in 1956. For the Third World countries, such intervention is always possible, as is obvious from the sending of the nuclear-powered *U.S.S. Enterprise* into the Bay of Bengal in 1971. The other source of international violence among Third World countries has been local and regional conflicts, which often give rise to intervention by the superpowers. In the presence of such conflicts, it would be unrealistic to expect economic planning to be pursued solely for mass welfare. In the Arab-Israeli conflict, it is significant that the Israeli Finance Minister, Pinhas Sapir, pointed out: "Our economic struggle is part of our struggle for survival, security, and peace."[32] Concurrently, James Reston reported after a meeting with President Nasser: "His major theme was that he had come to power to bring about the social reconstruction of his country, but that he had been diverted from this to the defense of Egypt through the aggressive ambitions of Israel, the faithlessness of the United States and Britain, and the determina-

---

[31] Kautsky, *Political Change*, pp. 56–57.
[32] *New York Times*, 17 February 1970.

tion of the Jews to poison relations between Cairo and Washington.''[33] What holds true for Israel and Egypt applies to many other countries as well.

The pursuit of national power through industrialization goes beyond the question of actual or potential international violence, however. In the international system there is a hierarchy, with military and economic power concentrated in the hands of a few states. Because of that power concentration, these few states dominate the international system and determine, through cooperation or competition, not only the economic and political fate of the world today— and thereby the national destiny of other countries—but also the evolution of that system in the future. Several Third World countries find the present world domination by a few powerful states unacceptable, not simply because it contradicts the doctrine of equality among nation-states, but also since these countries find it intolerable that their national destiny should be determined by foreign powers. Although the aspiration to equality with the dominant states—to be achieved through the enhancement of national power—may initially characterize only a few countries on the basis of their size, resource endowment, and past histories, such aspirations set up a chain reaction for industrial development among many other underdeveloped countries because of the resulting disruption of regional power balances. Thus, China found it unacceptable to be excluded from the dominant power group and to remain a subordinate member of the Soviet bloc. The very act of assertion of independence and claim to a great power role created problems of national security. At the same time, China's march toward greater national power puts pressure on India and, in turn, Pakistan and Indonesia are forced to reduce the subsequent power imbalance. Again, it is obvious that there is no escape from modernization directed specifically toward national power and national security.

Crucial as national security is for the new nations, the social mobilization of large segments of the population is also an existential fact of life, and governments must, in order to retain political support, provide some satisfaction to the economic aspirations and expectations of the population. Most social scientists and economists in the West have chosen to concentrate exclusively on this aspect as if it alone should be the objective of the new nations, while neglecting or denigrating the goal of national independence anchored in their plans for economic development. As one scholar pointedly remarks,

---

[33] *Montreal Star,* 17 February 1970.

"the ethnocentricity of economists is reflected in the implicit assumption that diverse social goals can be subsumed under the objective of economic growth, which is almost universally defined as increasing per capita real income."[34] On the contrary, Irving Louis Horowitz shrewdly notes, "the paradox is that the simple quantitative growth in national productivity and styles of life is hardly an assurance of international security."[35] Provision has to be made directly and specifically for both short-term and long-term national security, involving a reduction in investment for mass welfare improvement.

As part and parcel of the goal of preservation of the territorial integrity and political independence of a country, military security has a major place in long-term plans for economic development, above and beyond the annual budgetary allocations for defense expenditures. In the inevitable conflict between the goals of mass welfare and national security, nationalist governments are apt to seek a compromise in their plans for development. This compromise need not necessarily take the form of partial incorporation of both these goals simultaneously. Instead, concentrated attention might be alternated over a considerable period of time. Emphasis may be placed on heavy industry during several five-year plans as a necessary means for providing the essential foundations of national security, while demands for mass welfare are ignored or suppressed. Once these foundations are provided, subsequent plans may shift the emphasis to mass welfare. In the ultimate analysis, mass welfare is essential for national security as well, for a deprived population is not a national security asset. But, given the nature of the international system, mass welfare cannot be the sole purpose of economic development.

In the pursuit of independence within an international system characterized by a struggle for power, many nations go beyond the enhancement of national power related directly to security. They work to achieve "economic independence," on the grounds that to be dependent economically is to be vulnerable politically. The concept of "economic independence" is an ambiguous one and varies among countries; but it is an undeniable part of the political ideology of the new nations. In some cases it means autarky; in others, diversification of the economy, exports, and trade partners; and in still others, self-reliance rather than dependence on foreign aid or foreign enterprise. The path to "economic independence" is again through industrialization. Although many of the policies pursued in

---

[34] Frank H. Golay et al., *Underdevelopment and Economic Nationalism in Southeast Asia* (Ithaca, 1969), p. 10.
[35] Horowitz, p. 351.

the name of economic independence may seem prima facie irrational, a different picture emerges from a broader perspective. The protectionist tariff and nontariff barriers placed by the advanced industrial powers, the latters' nonapplication of GATT's principle of nondiscrimination to agricultural products, the secular decline in terms of trade of primary goods of the developing countries, the use of foreign aid (read "loans repayable with interest") often as a political instrument—all these suggest that the policies aimed at the vague goal of economic independence in the new nations are not without a rational basis. Social scientists must utilize a less restrictive frame of reference in the evaluation of economic policies of the new nations.

Although all nations aspire to national independence, obviously the size of the country and the economy, and the nature of available resources are important variables in its achievement. One could argue that the modernization imperative thesis is applicable to very large countries, and that the generalization is based on only a few "special cases."[36] Thus, Hla Myint points out that, of ninety underdeveloped countries, seventy-two have a population of less than 15 million. This point is well taken, but it tends to submerge the importance of the large political units from the viewpoint of the extent of humanity covered. Of the world's total population of 3.6 billion in 1970, 74.1 percent was within twenty-one units containing some 30 million people (2.7 billion), 67.0 percent within fourteen units of more than 50 million (2.4 billion), and 53.7 percent within six units of over 100 million (1.9 billion); China and India constitute more than 63.1 percent of Asia's population (2.0 billion) and, along with Indonesia and Japan, 74.0 percent.[37] Brazil, by itself, accounts for almost half of the South American population.

From the perspective of the vast bulk of mankind involved, the larger states must compel attention. At the same time, their very size makes industrialization an imperative due to the status inconsistency between their power position and size, and the fact that they will be regarded as potential threats by the other powers. For many of the smaller countries the quest for independence may seem so hopeless as to be surrendered in favor of protection by a superpower. Even in this case, however, modernization and industrialization will be pushed to the farthest extent possible, since national pride does not allow the acceptance of complete dependence. Futhermore, the reference point for national independence and power is not necessarily limited to

[36] Hla Myint, *Economic Theory and the Underdeveloped Countries* (New York, 1971), pp. 21–23, 32, 178.
[37] Data from United Nations, *Statistical Yearbook 1971* (New York, 1972).

the superpowers, but encompasses also neighbors and regional powers closer to home. National independence is invariably a fundamental
concern of all states; only the relevant strategic environment varies.
For the large states, it is basically the global strategic environment
that is of importance, while for the small states it is the local or
regional one.

The aspiration for independence and the subsequent modernization
effort do not provide a guarantee of success, however. Success
depends on the political and moral qualities of the population, on the
nature of the political leadership, and on its class interests and
linkages with the industrial powers, as well as on contingent historical circumstance. All these factors are of crucial importance even
though they cannot be treated in detail here. The pursuit of the
legitimate aim of national independence—rooted in the very nature of
the international system—is not without its costs either. Many of the
mounting economic problems of the developing countries are related
to attempts to achieve it. But, whatever the difficulties and the
prospects of success, industrialization continues to cast a magic spell
on the new nations, not merely for the sake of prestige, as is often
alleged, but for the substance of power. History has powerfully
etched the lesson that those who are independent and have political
influence in world affairs are also militarily superior and, by no
accident, industrially powerful.

The aspirations of the developing countries, however, are not the
only operative elements in the international situation. The changes
that would result in the international system from the successful
industrialization of these countries would not be entirely welcomed
by the big powers except insofar as these changes might coincide
with the national interests of the latter. The ranking industrial and
military powers are not anxious to see the development of rival
centers of power. More likely, they will try to see that the economies
of the underdeveloped countries are so managed as to remain, or to
become, subordinate, to that of one or the other chief industrial
powers. The new nations can proceed with their ambitious plans for
industrial development only in the interstices of the rivalries among
the industrial powers; their ability to do so will depend on the
particular configurations of power in the international arena, as well
as on the nature of the domestic regime.

India: The Price of Dependence
India provides an excellent illustration of the various cross-pressures,
both national and international, involved in the industrialization ef-

fort. The country's first Five-Year Plan (1951–56) was rather modest, addressed more to the rehabilitation of an economy exhausted by the impact of World War II and by partition of the subcontinent. With the second Five-Year Plan (1956–61), India pushed forward with an ambitious program of rapid industrialization patterned after the Soviet model, emphasizing heavy industry. The third Five-Year Plan (1961–66) persisted in this program with greater intensification. Considerable progress was made in the industrial sector, but many strains and imbalances developed in the economy, so that in the second half of the 1960s, the government was compelled to jettison its earlier economic strategy in favor of agricultural development.

Economists have characterized Indian economic planning in terms of welfare goals, in accordance with their general understanding of the aims of economic development programs. To refute this orthodox perspective, compelling evidence has been provided elsewhere in support of the revisionist viewpoint that the basic considerations underlying the economic strategy of the second and third Five-Year Plans have been to ensure increasing national power in general, and military strength in particular.[38] These considerations weighed heavily for the important and legitimate reason that national power and military strength are essential to independence of a nation with over half a billion people—more than the combined populations of the two superpowers. The Gandhian myth dies hard, but it is one thing to mount a nonviolent nationalist movement within the constraints of a powerful alien regime, and quite another to operate a polity in the context of an international system whose chief characteristic is the struggle for power.

Although the aim of Indian economic strategy has been national independence, the instrument for its achievement has not been complete self-reliance. While India's political leadership did make a considerable effort at domestic resource mobilization, the very nature of the country's political system—a federal democracy—placed serious limitations on the extent to which material sacrifices could be imposed on the population. Besides, the essentially reformist leadership was unwilling to make any drastic changes in the economic or social structure. This led to a considerable dependence on foreign aid for development programs.

This dependence was less politically inhibiting in the 1950s because of superpower competition and Nehru's political capabilities. In the Cold War era, the Soviet Union assisted in the establishment

[38] See Baldev Raj Nayar, *The Modernization Imperative and Indian Planning* (Delhi, 1972).

of a heavy industry base, while the West provided aid for the development of the economic infrastructure as well as supplying food and raw materials. The détente between the superpowers, along with hostile relationships with China and Pakistan, reduced India's maneuverability in the 1960s, both internally and externally. Indian economic policies as well as its foreign policy were forced to consider the wishes and interests of the donors. Whatever the economic justification, the Western powers coerced India into a devaluation of the rupee in 1966. Her foreign policy became muted, almost acquiescent. Finally, the superpowers' disdain for new autonomous centers of world power forced India to abstain from joining the ranks of nuclear powers.

The India of the 1960s provided a fascinating illustration, on the one hand, of the great emotional pull toward national independence, resulting in the ambitious attempt at the establishment of a gigantic and complex industrial base, and, on the other hand, of the restraints imposed on this independence as a result of reliance on foreign aid for development. In 1971 India did act in defiance of the United States, but only when she became convinced that Indian national survival was at stake.[39] The American suspension of foreign aid was regarded as a necessary price for national survival. The India-Pakistan war of 1971 once again underscored the importance of self-reliance within the economic and military spheres.

Increasing unrest among the populace in the last half of the 1960s justifiably led to a greater emphasis on mass welfare. Indira Gandhi won a landslide victory in 1971 with the slogan, "Remove Poverty." After the elections, economic planners began to lay greater stress on employment and social justice in the formulation of the country's fifth Five-Year Plan. National security and political independence could not be ignored in economic planning, however. Prime Minister Gandhi warned her fellow party leaders to that effect: "Eradication of poverty was an important ideal, but even more important was the preservation of India's freedom—the development of a defense capability against external threats, the building up of infrastructures to strengthen the economy and achieve self-reliance and protect the nation's honor and self-respect. If these aims were neglected in favor of concentrated attention only on aiding the poor, the country's freedom itself would be at stake." The new Planning Minister, D. P. Dhar, announced that in the fifth Plan India would revert to the earlier strategy of emphasis on heavy industry.[40]

[39] On this, see Nayar, "U. S. Policy," *Seminar* (New Delhi), No. 161 (January 1973), 46–55.
[40] *The Statesman Weekly* (14 October 1972), pp. 7, 14.

Conclusions

Studies in economic and political development have for the most part either assumed or advocated mass welfare as the appropriate objective of economic planning. The goal of national independence as a crucial factor in plans for economic development has been treated with studied neglect vis-à-vis today's developing countries. Part of the explanation for this neglect lies in the tendency among economists to concentrate exclusively on wealth maximization, while students of comparative politics rigidly bifurcate national and international affairs and study underdeveloped countries as closed, self-contained systems, unrelated to an international structure of power.

An examination of the historical experiences of Japan, the Soviet Union, China, and India, as well as other major countries in Europe, demonstrates clearly that the goal of national independence has served as a powerful impulse—indeed, as an imperative force—in the modernization and industrialization of these countries, and equally in the form such modernization and industrialization have taken. It is the same goal that often imparts a compulsive, frenetic, and at times desperate, character to the struggle for modernity.

A more adequate understanding of the political development process requires the incorporation of the international system and the activities of foreign powers in the study of the concrete problems of the underdeveloped countries rather than merely including it in abstract political system models. For the present, the notion of the "modernization imperative" suggests reconsideration of several aspects of political development theory.

In recent years specialists in political development theory have pointed out the importance of such "crises of development" in the developing nations as authority, legitimacy, and integration. These are largely seen as emanating from internal forces, which in shorthand language are covered by the term "social mobilization."[41] Insofar as modernization was introduced under colonial rule, this is a correct interpretation. But it is only a partial interpretation, for the same crises are precipitated in the developing countries by the more serious problem of national security. Authority has to be rationalized, society and polity have to be penetrated and integrated, and legitimacy has to be engendered in order to cope with the defense challenge presented by the industrial world. State activity in these direc-

[41] Deutsch, "Social Mobilization"; Lucian W. Pye, *Aspects of Political Development* (Boston, 1966), pp. 62–67; Gabriel A. Almond and G. Bingham Powell, Jr., *Comparative Politics: A Developmental Approach* (Boston, 1966), pp. 35–37; and Joseph LaPalombara and Myron Weiner, eds. *Political Parties and Political Development* (Princeton, 1966), p. 14.

tions is likely to bring on crises in authority, integration, and participation. Thus, it is misleading to look at "crises of development" as something generated internally by self-contained political systems.

Similarly, the notion of the modernization imperative leads us to weigh more critically the usual traditional-modern dichotomies in social science scholarship. Such societal classifications—Henry Maine's status versus contract, Ferdinand Toennies' *Gemeinschaft* versus *Gesellschaft,* Emile Durkheim's mechanical solidarity versus organic solidarity, Max Weber's traditional, charismatic, and legal-rational forms of domination, Talcott Parsons' pattern variables, or Fred Riggs' fused, prismatic, and diffracted types of society[42]—are obviously helpful in understanding some aspects of social behavior; but these do not aid us in understanding the national goals of the Third World nations. The only dichotomy that is meaningful for the underdeveloped countries is the economic one that differentiates agricultural from industrial societies, or one that distinguishes among societies on the basis of animate or inanimate energy utilization in the productive process.[43] To modernize, societies consciously seek the industrial wherewithal and not the characteristics associated with the modern component of the other classifications.

It becomes obvious also that the only meaningful interpretation of the much disputed term "political development" or "political modernity"[44] is effectiveness in the pursuit of industrialization, irrespective of the nature of the political regime and processes involved and regardless of the use of traditional structures and values to subserve that purpose. In this light, the definition of political development as simply enhanced capacity or differentiation only obfuscates matters, for it does not clarify what the capacity or differentiation is for. Strictly speaking, there is no such thing as "political development" that is concretely specifiable and isolatable in political terms; there is only the "politics of development" within the context of a variety of political regimes, and the crucial question becomes how successful it is in achieving developmental goals.

Again, since political development here refers to the pursuit of what has already been achieved elsewhere, it is valid to speak of the division between "advanced" or "reference" societies and "follow-

---

[42] Pye, pp. 58–62; Riggs, pp. 19–31.

[43] Gideon Sjoberg, *The Preindustrial City: Past and Present* (New York, 1960), pp. 7–18; and Marion J. Levy, Jr., *Modernization and the Structure of Societies: A Setting for International Affairs,* vol. 1 (Princeton, 1966), pp. 9–15.

[44] LaPalombara ed., *Bureaucracy and Political Devlopment* (Princeton, 1963), pp. 35–39; and Pye, pp. 31–48.

er" ones.[45] The goals of the follower societies—say, as included in Dankwart Rustow's classification, those of authority, identity, and equality but, equally important, those of security and industry—have already been determined by history insofar as modernization is an accomplished fact in the advanced societies. The creative task for the leadership in the new states is, indeed, not the determination of national goals—which are dictated by the international system—but the forging of novel strategies that enable these states to achieve these goals as rapidly as possible.

Emerging from the compulsion for national independence and political autonomy, the modernization imperative also dictates that governments cannot indefinitely abdicate from intervention in the process of economic development. Oblivious of this, some authors recommend that economic development should be allowed to take its own autonomous, evolutionary course.[46] Nor, for that matter, can the aim of political or institutional stability make any special *a priori* claim for precedence, as others have suggested.[47] National leaders may at times be persuaded, under the compulsions of the modernization imperative, to undertake measures which may result in strain on, or erosion of, political institutions, thus creating political decay.

It is not the intention of the author to suggest that national independence replace mass welfare as the sole causal factor in explaining the nature of economic development programs in the new nations. Rather, the purpose of this article has been to provide a more balanced perspective by redressing the neglect accorded to the goal of national power in studies of economic and political development. This redress does not provide any definitive answers concerning economic or political development, but raises further questions for research. Among these questions are: the different ways nations resolve the tension between the goals of mass welfare and national power in their economic development programs; the conflict between class interests of political elites and the aim of national independence; the relationship of system types to success in the pursuit of economic development and national power; the implications of the problem of national integration for the goal of national power; the impact of failure in

---

[45] Reinhard Bendix, "What Is Modernization?" in Willard A. Beling and George O. Totten, eds. *Developing Nations: Quest for a Model* (New York, 1970), pp. 3–20; and Fred W. Riggs, "Modernization and Political Problems: Some Developmental Prerequisites," ibid., pp. 60–82.

[46] Robert T. Holt and John E. Turner, *The Political Basis of Economic Development: An Exploration in Comparative Political Analysis* (Princeton, 1966), chap. 7.

[47] See Samuel P. Huntington, *Political Order in Changing Societies* (New Haven, 1968), chap. 1.

economic development upon the national independence ideology; the variations among nations in their perception of the goal of national independence; the effect of population size and resource endowment on such perception; the strategies that elites of small countries perceive as available—regional integration, isolation, dependence; the impact of political and economic penetration or domination by the industrial powers on the pursuit and achievement of national goals in the realm of mass welfare and national power. Hopefully, future studies of developing nations will focus on these questions.

APPENDIX

MAP AND DATA
FROM THE WORLD BANK ATLAS (1976)

Population, GNP Per Capita, and Total GNP — by Major Regions (1974)

The area of the top of each region is proportional to population. The height of each region is proportional to per capita GNP. Total GNP is represented by the volume of each region.

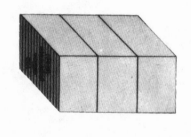

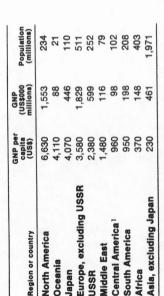

Region or country	GNP per capita (US$)	GNP (US$000 millions)	Population (millions)
North America	6,630	1,553	234
Oceania	4,110	88	21
Japan	4,070	446	110
Europe, excluding USSR	3,580	1,829	511
USSR	2,380	599	252
Middle East	1,480	116	79
Central America[1]	960	98	102
South America	950	198	208
Africa	370	148	403
Asia, excluding Japan	230	461	1,971

NOTE: Agricultural output and services, in particular, are generally priced lower in relation to industrial output in developing than in industrialized countries, and agriculture often accounts for the largest share of total product in developing countries. The currency conversion method used here to obtain GNP per capita, therefore, tends to exaggerate real income differences between less developed and more developed countries.

[1] Including Mexico.

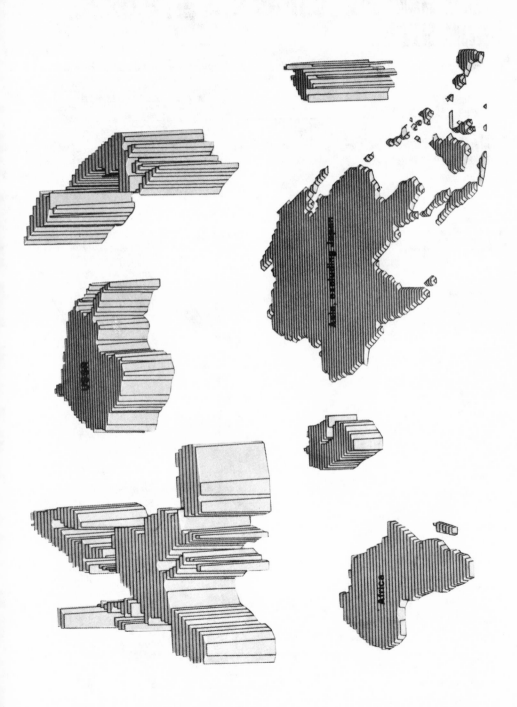

Population, GNP at Market Prices, and GNP Per Capita for 1973, 1974, and 1975

Bank member countries and countries with mid-1974 populations of one million or more.

Region Country	Population (000)	1973 GNP at market prices Amount (US$ millions)	1973 GNP at market prices Per capita (US$)
AFRICA			
Nigeria	71,262	16,680	230
Egypt, Arab Republic of	35,619	8,970	250
Ethiopia	26,550	2,360	90
South Africa	24,310	25,710	1,060
Zaire	23,438	3,050	130
Morocco	15,903	5,790	360
Sudan[2]	14,957	3,000	200
Algeria	14,700	9,750	660
Tanzania[3]	13,974	2,100	150
Kenya	12,480	2,240	180
Uganda	10,829	2,500	230
Ghana	9,360	3,620	390
Mozambique[2]	8,820	3,020	340
Madagascar	8,300	1,400	170
Cameroon	6,980	1,620	230
Ivory Coast	6,118	2,570	420
Rhodesia	5,900	2,670	450
Angola	5,900	3,480	590
Upper Volta	5,610	440	80
Mali	5,380	400	70
Tunisia	5,340	2,940	550
Guinea	5,243	540	100
Malawi	4,833	570	120
Senegal	4,741	1,360	290
Zambia	4,646	2,100	450
Niger	4,304	450	100
Rwanda[2]	3,980	320	80
Chad	3,873	360	90
Burundi[2]	3,580	290	80
Somalia[2]	3,042	280	90
Benin, People's Republic of[2]	2,947	330	110
Sierra Leone	2,841	480	170
Libyan Arab Republic	2,258	8,100	3,590
Togo	2,119	460	220
Central African Empire	1,710	340	200
Liberia	1,452	520	360
Congo, People's Republic of the	1,272	510	400
Mauritania	1,257	280	220
Lesotho[2]	1,165	130	110
Mauritius	860	430	500
Botswana[2]	641	160	250
Gabon	520	860	1,650
Gambia, The	493	70	140
Swaziland[2]	463	150	320
Equatorial Guinea	313	90	280
Comoros[2]	260	50	190

NOTE: Data for GNP at market prices and GNP per capita are rounded to US$ tens of millions and US$10, respectively, and are expressed in current US$ (see Technical Note, pages 21 and 22.)

	1974			1975[1]		
		GNP at market prices			GNP at market prices	
Population (000)	Amount (US$ millions)	Per capita (US$)	Population (000)	Amount (US$ millions)	Per capita (US$)	
73,044	20,810	280	75,023	23,080	310
36,350	10,210	280	37,096	11,550	310
27,240	2,660	100	27,921	2,860	100
24,940	30,180	1,210	25,470	33,540	1,320
24,071	3,530	150	24,721	3,740	150
16,291	7,070	430	16,680	7,890	470
15,227	3,460	230	15,550	4,510	290
15,215	11,100	730	15,747	12,290	780
14,351	2,320	160	14,738	2,560	170
12,910	2,610	200	13,349	2,900	220
11,186	2,700	240	11,556	2,880	250
9,610	4,130	430	9,869	4,580	460
9,030	3,030	340	9,240	2,850	310
8,560	1,570	180	8,835	1,730	200
7,120	1,760	250	7,260	1,940	270
6,387	2,930	460	6,700	3,350	500
6,100	3,200	520	6,310	3,430	540
6,050	4,290	710	5,470	3,710	680
5,760	520	90	5,900	560	90
5,560	450	80	5,677	540	90
5,460	3,560	650	5,590	4,230	760
5,390	630	120	5,540	710	130
4,958	660	130	5,087	760	150
4,869	1,590	330	5,000	1,850	370
4,781	2,470	520	4,920	2,650	540
4,480	540	120	4,562	600	130
4,058	310	80	4,137	360	90
3,952	410	100	4,035	490	120
3,655	330	90	3,732	370	100
3,100	290	90	3,180	320	100
3,027	370	120	3,108	420	140
2,911	540	190	2,982	590	200
2,352	10,430	4,440	2,442	12,400	5,080
2,176	550	250	2,235	590	270
1,748	370	210	1,787	410	230
1,500	580	390	1,549	630	410
1,300	610	470	1,329	660	500
1,290	380	290	1,322	410	310
1,191	170	140	1,217	210	180
871	510	580	883	510	580
654	190	290	666	220	330
528	1,030	1,960	536	1,200	2,240
506	90	170	519	100	190
478	190	390	494	230	470
318	90	290	322	100	320
265	60	230	270	70	260

Population, GNP at Market Prices, and GNP Per Capita for 1973, 1974, and 1975 (continued)

Bank member countries and countries with mid-1974 populations of one million or more.

Region Country	Population (000)	1973 GNP at market prices Amount (US$ millions)	1973 GNP at market prices Per capita (US$)
ASIA			
China, People's Republic of[2]	795,920	216,750	270
India	581,911	73,020	130
Japan	108,350	411,260	3,800
Bangladesh	74,000	6,490	90
Pakistan	65,255	7,690	120
Viet Nam, Socialist Republic of[2]	43,040	5,743	130
Philippines	40,219	11,750	290
Thailand	39,690	11,010	280
Korea, Republic of	32,905	13,410	410
Iran	32,136	32,940	1,020
Burma	28,889	2,520	90
Afghanistan	15,960	1,630	100
China, Republic of	15,430	11,520	750
Korea, Democratic People's Republic of[2]	15,040	5,190	350
Sri Lanka	13,180	1,600	120
Nepal	12,020	1,070	90
Malaysia	11,306	6,630	590
Iraq	10,410	9,120	880
Saudi Arabia	7,745	16,000	2,070
Cambodia[2,5]	7,566	550	70
Syrian Arab Republic	6,948	3,070	440
Yemen Arab Republic[2]	6,217	960	150
Hong Kong	4,160	6,220	1,490
Israel	3,251	10,000	3,080
Lao People's Democratic Republic[2,5]	3,180	200	60
Lebanon[5]	2,977	2,800	940
Jordan	2,540	970	380
Singapore	2,185	4,240	1,940
Yemen, People's Democratic Republic of[2]	1,560	300	190
Mongolia[2]	1,357	740	550
Bhutan[2]	1,124	70	60
Kuwait	880	8,250	9,380
Oman	720	810	1,130
United Arab Emirates	457	4,990	10,910
Bahrain	232	220	950
Qatar	180	1,150	6,360

	1974			1975 [1]		
	GNP at market prices				**GNP at market prices**	
Population (000)	**Amount (US$ millions)**	**Per capita (US$)**	**Population (000)**	**Amount (US$ millions)**	**Per capita (US$)**
809,251	244,640	300	822,800	285,960	350
595,586	80,410	140	609,582	91,810	150
109,670	446,030	4,070	110,950	495,180	4,460
76,200	7,910	100	78,600	8,820	110
67,213	8,760	130	69,229	9,830	140
44,155	6,510	150	45,297	7,100	160
41,433	13,650	330	42,500	15,730	370
40,780	12,670	310	41,870	14,540	350
33,459	15,980	480	34,018	18,650	550
33,100	41,440	1,250	33,996	48,820	1,440
29,521	2,910	100	30,170	3,270	110
16,311	1,880	110	16,670	2,160	130
15,710	12,710	810	16,000	14,210	890
15,443	5,980	390	15,853	6,790	430
13,393	1,760	130	13,600	1,980	150
12,320	1,250	100	12,590	1,390	110
11,702	7,910	680	12,030	8,690	720
10,770	12,000	1,110	11,120	14,260	1,280
8,008	22,670	2,830	8,296	24,960	3,010
7,725	570	70	7,965	n.a.	n.a.
7,177	3,990	560	7,409	4,870	660
6,379	1,160	180	6,471	1,380	210
4,249	6,850	1,610	4,367	7,520	1,720
3,359	11,630	3,460	3,469	12,400	3,580
3,260	220	70	3,345	n.a.	n.a.
3,065	3,290	1,070	3,164	n.a.	n.a.
2,620	1,120	430	2,709	1,240	460
2,220	4,970	2,240	2,250	5,640	2,510
1,632	360	220	1,677	410	240
1,396	860	610	1,436	1,000	700
1,150	80	70	1,176	90	70
930	9,330	10,030	980	11,280	11,510
750	1,250	1,660	773	1,600	2,070
548	6,060	11,060	656	6,870	10,480
245	580	2,350	260	630	2,440
190	1,380	7,240	202	1,680	8,320

Population, GNP at Market Prices, and GNP Per Capita for 1973, 1974, and 1975 (continued)

Bank member countries and countries with mid-1974 populations of one million or more.

| Region
Country | 1973 | | |
| | Population
(000) | GNP at market prices | |
		Amount (US$ millions)	Per capita (US$)
EUROPE			
USSR[2]	249,750	526,170	2,110
Germany, Federal Republic of	61,970	352,680	5,690
United Kingdom	55,930	182,620	3,270
Italy	54,910	138,470	2,520
France	52,130	250,660	4,810
Turkey	38,236	25,010	650
Spain	34,740	75,530	2,170
Poland[2]	33,360	72,080	2,160
Yugoslavia	20,956	23,260	1,110
Romania	20,828	18,680	900
German Democratic Republic[2]	16,980	54,430	3,210
Czechoslovakia[2]	14,572	43,440	2,980
Netherlands, The	13,440	62,780	4,670
Hungary[2]	10,430	19,760	1,890
Belgium	9,740	48,630	4,990
Greece	8,972	17,740	1,980
Portugal	8,994	12,990	1,440
Bulgaria[2]	8,622	13,800	1,600
Sweden	8,140	51,760	6,360
Austria	7,530	29,340	3,900
Switzerland	6,430	45,380	7,060
Denmark	5,020	29,490	5,870
Finland	4,670	19,250	4,120
Norway	3,960	20,560	5,190
Ireland	3,030	6,520	2,150
Albania[2]	2,295	1,060	460
Cyprus	635	940	1,480
Luxembourg	350	1,910	5,460
Iceland	210	1,060	5,030

| 1974 | | | 1975 [1] | | |
| GNP at market prices | | | GNP at market prices | | |
Population (000)	Amount (US$ millions)	Per capita (US$)	Population (000)	Amount (US$ millions)	Per capita (US$)
252,060	598,640	2,380	254,380	665,910	2,620
62,040	388,670	6,260	61,830	408,750	6,610
55,970	200,830	3,590	55,960	214,940	3,840
55,410	156,510	2,820	55,810	164,110	2,940
52,510	285,780	5,440	52,910	304,600	5,760
39,167	29,460	750	40,098	34,590	860
35,109	87,250	2,490	35,358	95,630	2,700
33,690	84,660	2,510	34,020	98,970	2,910
21,155	27,820	1,310	21,330	31,640	1,480
21,029	23,080	1,100	21,245	27,650	1,300
16,920	62,710	3,710	16,850	71,250	4,230
14,690	48,860	3,330	14,820	55,040	3,710
13,540	71,120	5,250	13,650	76,340	5,590
10,460	22,810	2,180	10,495	26,070	2,480
9,770	55,430	5,670	9,800	59,440	6,070
9,020	18,830	2,090	9,101	21,500	2,360
9,014	14,650	1,630	9,357	15,040	1,610
8,676	15,420	1,780	8,731	17,770	2,040
8,160	59,100	7,240	8,200	64,580	7,880
7,550	33,310	4,410	7,520	35,520	4,720
6,440	50,680	7,870	6,400	51,510	8,050
5,050	32,470	6,430	5,060	35,030	6,920
4,690	22,030	4,700	4,710	24,000	5,100
3,990	23,360	5,860	4,010	26,240	6,540
3,090	7,170	2,320	3,127	7,560	2,420
2,350	1,250	530	2,405	1,450	600
645	850	1,320	625	740	1,180
360	2,180	6,050	363	2,200	6,050
220	1,200	5,430	223	1,250	5,620

Population, GNP at Market Prices, and GNP Per Capita for 1973, 1974, and 1975 (continued)

Bank member countries and countries with mid-1974 populations of one million or more.

Region Country	Population (000)	1973 GNP at market prices Amount (US$ millions)	1973 GNP at market prices Per capita (US$)
NORTH and CENTRAL AMERICA			
United States	210,400	1,311,770	6,230
Mexico[6]	55,931	54,540	980
Canada	22,130	123,470	5,580
Cuba[2]	8,920	5,600	630
Guatemala	5,175	2,640	510
Dominican Republic	4,432	2,470	560
Haiti	4,440	610	140
El Salvador	3,771	1,370	360
Puerto Rico	2,950	6,160	2,090
Honduras	2,733	840	310
Nicaragua	1,990	1,090	550
Jamaica	1,972	2,080	1,050
Costa Rica	1,872	1,380	740
Panama	1,570	1,480	940
Trinidad and Tobago	1,059	1,580	1,490
Barbados	240	260	1,090
Bahamas[2]	190	440	2,330
Grenada	106	40	370
SOUTH AMERICA			
Brazil	101,051	79,630	790
Argentina	24,282	31,830	1,310
Colombia	22,500	9,960	440
Peru	14,532	9,470	650
Venezuela	11,280	19,500	1,730
Chile	10,239	7,590	740
Ecuador	6,786	2,710	400
Bolivia	5,331	1,340	250
Uruguay	2,744	2,930	1,070
Paraguay	2,416	1,070	440
Guyana	772	340	440
OCEANIA and INDONESIA			
Indonesia	125,268	18,800	150
Australia	13,130	61,110	4,650
New Zealand	2,960	11,790	3,980
Papua New Guinea	2,596	1,150	440
Fiji[2]	551	420	750
Western Samoa[2]	153	40	270

NOTE: Data for GNP at market prices and GNP per capita are rounded to US$ tens of millions and US$10, respectively, and are expressed in current US$

[1] Preliminary.
[2] Estimates of GNP per capita are tentative.

	1974			1975[1]		
	GNP at market prices				GNP at market prices	
Population (000)	Amount (US$ millions)	Per capita (US$)	Population (000)	Amount (US$ millions)	Per capita (US$)	
211,890	1,413,530	6,670	213,610	1,508,680	7,060	
57,899	63,050	1,090	59,928	71,170	1,190	
22,480	139,260	6,190	22,830	151,730	6,650	
9,090	6,480	710	9,270	7,430	800	
5,284	3,060	580	5,395	3,530	650	
4,562	2,960	650	4,695	3,380	720	
4,514	750	170	4,584	810	180	
3,887	1,590	410	4,006	1,820	450	
3,030	6,770	2,230	3,090	7,100	2,300	
2,806	950	340	2,890	1,010	350	
2,041	1,360	670	2,094	1,510	720	
2,008	2,390	1,190	2,042	2,630	1,290	
1,921	1,610	840	1,971	1,790	910	
1,618	1,610	1,000	,668	1,770	1,060	
1,070	1,810	1,700	1,080	2,050	1,900	
241	290	1,200	243	310	1,260	
199	490	2,460	205	530	2,600	
108	40	330	110	40	370	
103,981	95,920	920	106,996	107,870	1,010	
24,646	37,360	1,520	25,016	39,810	1,590	
23,125	11,640	500	23,767	13,170	550	
14,953	11,110	740	15,387	12,520	810	
11,632	22,780	1,960	11,993	26,670	2,220	
10,408	8,680	830	10,585	8,050	760	
6,952	3,310	480	7,121	3,890	550	
5,470	1,550	280	5,613	1,770	320	
2,754	3,290	1,190	2,764	3,670	1,330	
2,484	1,270	510	2,553	1,460	570	
791	390	500	810	450	560	
128,400	21,780	170	131,610	24,180	180	
13,340	71,080	5,330	13,500	76,190	5,640	
3,030	13,070	4,310	3,090	14,460	4,680	
2,650	1,250	470	2,719	1,220	450	
564	470	840	569	520	920	
157	50	300	160	50	320	

[3] Mainland Tanzania.
[5] GNP per capita estimated on the 1972-74 base period.
[6] GNP per capita estimates do not reflect the significant devaluation of the peso in August 1976.